Martin Bond,
Dan Haywood,
Debbie Law,
Andy Longshaw
and Peter Roxburgh

SAMS Teach Yourself

J2EE

in 21 Days

SECOND EDITION

SAMS 800 East 96th St., Indianapolis, Indiana, 46240 USA

Sams Teach Yourself J2EE in 21 Days, Second Edition

Copyright © 2004 by Sams Publishing

International Standard Book Number: 0-672-32558-6

Library of Congress Catalog Card Number: 2003092625

Printed in the United States of America

First Printing: April 2004

07 06 05 04   4 3 2 1

Trademarks

All terms mentioned in this book that are known to be trademarks or service marks have been appropriately capitalized. Sams Publishing cannot attest to the accuracy of this information. Use of a term in this book should not be regarded as affecting the validity of any trademark or service mark.

Warning and Disclaimer

Every effort has been made to make this book as complete and as accurate as possible, but no warranty or fitness is implied. The information provided is on an "as is" basis.

Bulk Sales

Sams Publishing offers excellent discounts on this book when ordered in quantity for bulk purchases or special sales. For more information, please contact

U.S. Corporate and Government Sales

1-800-382-3419

corpsales@pearsontechgroup.com

For sales outside of the U.S., please contact

International Sales

1-317-428-3341

international@pearsontechgroup.com

ASSOCIATE PUBLISHER
Michael Stephens

ACQUISITIONS EDITOR
Todd Green

DEVELOPMENT EDITOR
Sean Dixon

MANAGING EDITOR
Charlotte Clapp

PROJECT EDITOR
George E. Nedeff

INDEXER
Chris Barrick

PROOFREADER
Tracy Donhardt

EXPERT REVIEWER
Lance Anderson

TECHNICAL EDITOR
Steve Heckler
Kunal Mittal
Christian Kenyeres
Steven Haines

TEAM COORDINATOR
Cynthia Teeters

MULTIMEDIA DEVELOPER
Dan Scherf

INTERIOR DESIGNER
Gary Adair

COVER DESIGNER
Gary Adair

Contents at a Glance

Appendixes 889

Contents

Day 6 Entity EJBs

About the Authors

The authors of this book work for Content Master Ltd., a technical authoring company in the United Kingdom specializing in the production of training and educational materials. For more information on Content Master, please see its Web site at www.contentmaster.com.

MARTIN BOND, B.Sc. M.Sc. C.Eng, M.B.C.S., was born in Blackburn, England and went to University at Aberystwyth, Wales to study Pure Maths and Physics. Discovering Computer Science and programming was a lot easier than mathematics, Martin switched to a Computer Science degree. After graduating Martin did research into large scale software systems until the thought of earning money lured him into the commercial world. Martin was soon managing an R&D team developing parallel processing compilers for the occam language, but preferred to retain his hands-on technical skills and moved in open systems software design and consultancy. Since 1995 Martin has worked primarily as an independent trainer, course writer and technical author specializing in Unix, C, C++, Java and software design. Martin has written training courses on Unix, XML, Java and Solaris Security and co-authored *Tomcat Kick Start* (Sams Publishing, 2002). Martin currently lives on a smallholding in Cornwall, England.

DAN HAYWOOD has been working on large and small software development projects for more than 12 years. These days, he fills his days with consulting, training and technical writing, specializing in OO design, Java and J2EE, Sybase technical consulting, and data modeling. Previously, Dan worked at Sybase Professional Services, performing a variety of roles, mostly in the financial industry, including architect, performance specialist, and project manager. Dan started his IT career at (what was then) Andersen Consulting, working as a developer on large-scale projects in government and in utilities. Dan is married and has a baby daughter.

DEBBIE LAW B.Sc., was born in Romsey, England in 1959. Debbie started on compiler development for parallel processing systems, later working on the design and development of client server applications. Debbie now pays the bills writing technical books and training material as well as doing consultancy work for UK clients. Debbie has an honors degree in computer science from Southampton, England and currently works as an IT consultant based in Cornwall, England.

ANDY LONGSHAW is a consultant, writer, and educator specializing in enterprise platforms, Web-based systems and Web services, particularly the design and architecture decisions required to use these technologies successfully. Andy has been explaining technology for most of the last decade as a consultant, mentor, trainer and conference speaker. A wild rumor suggests that some people have managed to stay awake in these sessions. Despite being well educated and otherwise fairly normal, Andy still subjects himself and his family to "trial by unpredictability" by watching Manchester City FC far more often than is healthy.

PETER ROXBURGH graduated with a first class degree with honors in business, and has since followed a diverse career path. From his home in the medieval walled town of Conwy, North Wales, he authors a wide-variety of training courses, and books including *Building .NET Applications for Mobile Devices* (Microsoft Press, 2002). He has also written and contributed to a number of journals and Web sites on cutting-edge technologies.

Peter spends his spare time playing the guitar and bouldering on nearby sea cliffs and mountain crags. When he is not strumming or risking life and limb, he enjoys spending relaxing and quality time with his daughter, Chloe.

Dedication

To Sarah, for encouragement, advice, and regular supplies of flapjacks; and to Adam and Josh, for providing me with a life that doesn't revolve around computers. —AL

To Sue: Thank you for all these happy years. —Love, Dan.

Acknowledgments

The authors would like to thank the various project managers and editors involved in this book, without whom it would never have seen the light of day. Special thanks go to Beverly Mullock and Lynne Perry at Content Master, and Todd Green, Sean Dixon, and the editing team at Sams. We would also like to acknowledge the work of Alex Ferris and John Sharp in the initial phases of this project.

Martin, Debbie and Andy undertook the work for the second edition of this book upgrading text and examples from J2EE 1.3 to J2EE 1.4.

Tell Us What You Think!

As the reader of this book, *you* are our most important critic and commentator. We value your opinion and want to know what we're doing right, what we could do better, what areas you'd like to see us publish in, and any other words of wisdom you're willing to pass our way.

As an associate publisher for Sams Publishing, I welcome your comments. You can email or write me directly to let me know what you did or didn't like about this book—as well as what we can do to make our books better.

Please note that I cannot help you with technical problems related to the topic of this book. We do have a User Services group, however, where I will forward specific technical questions related to the book.

When you write, please be sure to include this book's title and author as well as your name, email address, and phone number. I will carefully review your comments and share them with the author and editors who worked on the book.

Email: feedback@samspublishing.com

Mail: Michael Stephens
Associate Publisher
Sams Publishing
800 East 96th Street
Indianapolis, IN 46240 USA

For more information about this book or another Sams Publishing title, visit our Web site at www.samspublishing.com. Type the ISBN (excluding hyphens) or the title of a book in the Search field to find the page you're looking for.

Introduction

The world has come a long way since Duke first started tumbling in early versions of Netscape Navigator. Java has outgrown its humble origins as a cool way of providing interactivity on Web pages and has found a new role as a major, server-side development platform. The actual Java language has changed little in the intervening years, but an enterprise-quality infrastructure has risen up around it. This infrastructure, Java 2 Enterprise Edition or J2EE for short, allows Java developers the ability to create sophisticated and powerful enterprise applications that provide mission-critical functionality for many thousands of users.

Unlike competing platforms, such as Microsoft .NET, J2EE is a specification rather than a product. The capabilities and functionality of each release of J2EE is agreed on through the Java Community Process (JCP). The platform is then implemented by application server vendors and producers, such as Sun Microsystems, BEA, IBM, ATG, Macromedia, JBOSS and OpenEJB. This means that J2EE developers have a choice of product vendors from whom to select, based on quality, support, or ease of use. The ability to submit technologies through the JCP, and the two-way flow that exists between the main Java vendors and the open-source community, ensures that a constant stream of new ideas helps move J2EE forward.

This book will take you on a journey through the J2EE landscape, from the simplest components through design considerations and on to the latest Web Services. There is a lot to learn in three weeks—but this book should provide the essential grounding you need to use the J2EE platform effectively. If you need to create robust enterprise applications and Java is your tool of choice, read on.

How This Book Is Organized

Sams Teach Yourself J2EE in 21 Days covers version 1.4 of the J2EE platform. It is organized as three separate weeks that guide you through the different functionality provided by J2EE.

The first week gives you a broad grounding in J2EE before moving on to investigate Enterprise JavaBeans (EJBs) in detail:

- Day 1, "The Challenge of N-Tier Development," defines the landscape in which J2EE applications operate and provides the architectural concepts with which you need to become familiar to create J2EE applications.

- Day 2, "The J2EE Platform and Roles," takes you on a whistle-stop tour of the J2EE platform, the major technologies, the types of components from which J2EE applications are assembled, and the container with which they interact. You also install the J2EE platform and start to look at the case study used throughout the book.
- On Day 3, "Naming and Directory Services," you start using your first J2EE API, the Java Naming and Directory Interface (JNDI), to store, retrieve, and manipulate information that can be accessed by all J2EE components.
- Day 4, "Introduction to Enterprise JavaBeans," introduces Enterprise JavaBeans (EJB)—the core technology of the J2EE platform. You will examine the role of EJBs and how they work. You will then deploy a sample EJB and create a simple client application for it.
- On Day 5, "Session EJBs," you will explore Session EJBs in more depth. This includes the creation of both stateful and stateless Session EJBs.
- Day 6, "Entity EJBs," moves on to Entity EJBs and examines their role and lifecycle. Particular attention is paid to how state is stored and retrieved using Bean-Managed Persistence (BMP).
- On Day 7, "Container-Managed Persistence, Container-Managed Relationships, and EJB Query Language," the discussion of Entity EJBs expands to cover entities that use Container-Managed Persistence (CMP) to store and retrieve their state. This includes an exploration of the EJB Query Language and Container-Managed Relationships (CMR).

The second week moves beyond EJBs to look at asynchronous interaction and the development of Web-based components:

- On Day 8, "Transactions and Persistence," you will delve deeper into the use of transactions in the J2EE platform—what they can achieve and how your components can take advantage of them. Some alternative persistence mechanisms are also explored.
- Day 9, "Java Messaging Service," looks at asynchronous messaging with the Java Message Service (JMS) using message queues and topics. You will apply JMS to implement a producer and consumer of asynchronous messages.
- Day 10, "Message-Driven Beans," builds on the coverage of JMS to associate message queues with Message-driven EJBs. You will create an EJB whose functionality is triggered on receipt of an asynchronous message.
- On Day 11, "JavaMail," another asynchronous communication mechanism is examined—namely email. You will learn how to send and retrieve email under J2EE and how this can be applied to transport data in a J2EE application.

- Day 12, "Servlets," is the first of three Web-oriented days that explore the creation of Web-oriented J2EE applications. This day starts by creating servlets to take advantage of the EJB-based services you built earlier. You will look at the servlet lifecycle and central issues, such as session tracking and state management.

- Day 13, "JavaServer Pages," looks at how JavaServer Pages (JSP) can help to integrate Java and J2EE functionality with HTML content. It examines the role of JSPs and how JavaBeans and the Expression Language (EL) can be used to encapsulate Java functionality in JSPs.

- On Day 14, "JSP Tag Libraries," you will explore the features of the JavaServer Pages Standard Tag Library (JSTL) and then develop custom JSP tag libraries to encapsulate Java functionality to improve the maintainability of the JSP pages.

The third week explores essential aspects of enterprise applications, such as security and integration, before moving on to application design and ending with a look at the Web Service functionality that will form the future of J2EE:

- Day 15, "Security," begins week 3 by applying security to your J2EE application. You will weigh the benefits of declarative and programmatic security and determine how they can be applied within your application.

- On Day 16, "Integrating XML with J2EE," you will examine the role of XML in J2EE applications. You will create J2EE components that produce and consume XML documents and process data using the Java APIs for XML Processing (JAXP).

- Day 17, "Transforming XML Documents," focuses on the transformation of XML documents into other formats, including other dialects of XML, primarily using the XSLT transformation language. Again, JAXP allows you to do this programmatically from within J2EE components.

- On Day 18, "Patterns," you will take some time to consider the bigger picture and examine design issues for J2EE applications. The specific focus will be on common patterns that have been found as people have applied J2EE technologies in live applications. You will use this knowledge to improve parts of the case study design.

- Day 19, "Integrating with External Resources," explores the various technologies that can be used to integrate J2EE applications with non-J2EE components and services. These mechanisms include the Java Connector Architecture, CORBA, RMI-IIOP, and the Java Native Interface.

- Day 20, "Using RPC-Style Web Services with J2EE," looks at how to expose J2EE components as Web Services. You will use the Java API for XML-based RPC (JAX-RPC) to create Web Services based on servlets and EJBs.

- Day 21, "Message-Style Web Services and Web Service Registries," concludes the tour of J2EE-based Web Services. You will create a message-oriented Web Service using the SOAP with Attachments API for Java (SAAJ) and the Java API for XML Messaging (JAXM). You will also examine the role of XML-based registries and how the Java API for XML Registries (JAXR) enables access to this information.

About This Book

This book is a practical, down-to-earth guide for intermediate Java developers. It is not intended to be a reference book, with lists of API calls or extensive discussion of the inner workings of the technologies. Rather, it provides you with a grounding in applying the essential J2EE technologies and leads you through the essential steps required to get a program or component written, packaged, and deployed on the J2EE platform. By the time you finish Sams Teach Yourself J2EE in 21 Days, you should have the confidence to create or maintain code that uses any of the major J2EE APIs.

What's New in This Edition?

This is the second edition of Teach Yourself J2EE in 21 Days. The first edition was targeted at J2EE 1.3 and this edition has been enhanced to include the new J2EE 1.4 features.

The main changes introduced for J2EE 1.4 are:

- JSP 2.0 Expression Language (EL)—covered on Day 13
- JavaServer Pages Standard Tag Library—covered on Day 14
- Web Services—covered on Day 20 and Day 21

Smaller changes were made to incorporate the:

- EJB Timer service—covered on Day 5
- EJB QL enhancements—covered on Day 6
- Enhanced JMS API—covered on Day 9 and Day 10

The code in this edition was developed and validated against the Sun Microsytems' J2EE 1.4 SDK (available from http://java.sun.com/j2ee/1.4/download-dr.html).

This edition also includes:

- Full instructions for developing and deploying J2EE components using the J2EE SDK 1.4.
- Revised and updated JavaMail examples—see Day 11.
- Revised and updated Connector Architecture examples—see Day 19.

Who Should Read This Book?

This book is intended for experienced Java developers who have been involved with Java development for at least 3 to 6 months. You should be confident writing Java code and familiar with the commonly used Java 2 Standard Edition APIs, such as string handling, JDBC, collections, iterators, and so on.

In addition to a firm grasp of Java, the following knowledge will speed your progress through the book:

- An understanding of how the Web operates, such as the use of a Web browser to retrieve pages of HTML from Web Servers.
- Familiarity with XML syntax to the level of reading small extracts of XML containing elements, attributes, and namespaces.
- An understanding of relational databases and how data is structured in tables. A familiarity with basic SQL to the level of understanding simple queries, inserts, updates, and joins.
- Familiarity with distributed systems, such as n-tier development, client-server programming, and remote procedure calls.

If you are not familiar with one or more of these topics, don't panic! Appendix A provides introductory material on XML. The essential concepts of distributed systems and Web-based development are covered in the book as required.

How This Book Is Structured

This book is intended to be read and absorbed over the course of three weeks. During each week, you read seven chapters that present concepts related to J2EE and the creation of enterprise applications in Java. Care has been taken to try to ensure that concepts and technologies are introduced in an appropriate order, so it is best to read the chapters sequentially if possible.

At the end of each lesson are a set of questions about the subject covered that day. Answers to these questions are provided by the authors. There are also exercises for you to test your newly found skills by creating some related application or service.

The exercises in the book are largely based around a case study that is described in detail at the end of Day 2. The files for the case study and solutions to the exercises can be found on the Web site that accompanies this book. The idea of the case study is that it will help you apply J2EE technologies and techniques in a consistent context and as part of a working application. This should provide you with a deeper understanding of the technology involved and how to apply it than is possible working with standalone examples.

Typographic Conventions

NOTE

> A Note presents interesting, sometimes technical, pieces of information related to the surrounding discussion.

TIP

> A Tip offers advice or suggests an easier way of doing something.

CAUTION

> A Caution advises you of potential problems and helps you avoid causing serious damage.

Text that you type, text that should appear on your screen, and the names of Java classes or methods are presented in `monospace` type.

Source code and updates to this book

All the code and examples in this book are available for download from our Web site, `www.samspublishing.com`, where we also will post updates and corrections as we learn of them.

At the Sams home page, type this book's ISBN number 0672325586 into the "search" window, press return, and you'll be taken to the book's page.

WEEK 1

Introducing J2EE and Enterprise JavaBeans

DAY 1

The Challenge of N-tier Development

The current trend in enterprise program development is to provide n-tier frameworks aimed at delivering applications that are secure, scalable, and available. This market has produced two competing products: Sun Microsystems' Java 2 Enterprise Edition (J2EE) and Microsoft Corporation's .NET Framework. Both products have similar features and capabilities and are designed to provide a software framework that simplifies the development and operation of medium- to large-scale enterprise-wide applications.

A full comparison of J2EE and .NET is beyond the scope of this book but it is useful to examine the different strategies used by the providers of these products. The .NET Framework is a product strategy from Microsoft and, not surprisingly, .NET is only available for Microsoft operating systems. J2EE, on the other hand, is platform-independent and so has advantages in heterogeneous environments.

Vendors such as IBM and BEA, among others, support the J2EE standard and provide commercial-grade J2EE development environments. The J2EE standard is actually an amalgamation of separate APIs and standards that are developed and ratified through an open framework overseen by the Java Community Process (JCP) (see Appendix B "The Java Community Process").

The .NET Framework is under the sole control of Microsoft and lacks some of the integration and legacy features provided by J2EE. J2EE is a single language environment, namely Java. Tools are provided, as part of J2EE, to allow applications written in other languages to interoperate with a J2EE application, but these are primarily for legacy support. The .NET Framework is, in theory, language independent; in reality this means any language supported by Microsoft tools. Due to the omni-presence of Microsoft platforms and the portability and integration advantages of J2EE, it is likely that J2EE and .NET will share the market for Enterprise Application Development.

To understand the enterprise application market, this chapter investigates the principles of multiple tiers, component environments, and standards that underlie the frameworks. One of the objectives will be to give you a clear introduction of concepts and terminology used when discussing such frameworks.

The following are the major topics covered in today's lesson:

- The pitfalls of monolithic software development
- N-tier development as a model for enterprise computing
- Introduction to J2EE, its components and services

Monolithic Development

In the days of the mainframe or the standalone personal computer, when an application was run on a single machine, it was common to find monolithic applications containing all the functionality of the application. All user input, verification, business logic, and data access could be found together. This suited the world of the mainframe and corporate data center because everything was controlled and the systems themselves tended to evolve slowly. However, the high levels of program maintenance required to keep up with today's changing business needs means that applications, written in this way, might have to be updated and recompiled daily. In this world monolithic code is no longer a workable software architecture. Monolithic code is called single or one-tier.

NOTE Even today, if you need a very simple application where, for example, the client application accesses and updates information in a database, locally you need only one tier. However, as you will see, you probably want to use components and/or layers to manage application complexity.

Figure 1.1 shows how this application may look running on a single machine.

FIGURE 1.1

Monolithic code scenario.

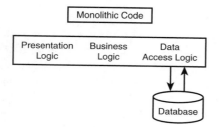

If you are writing a simple utility that does not use network connectivity, the monolithic scenario might suffice. However, any changes required to any part of the functionality may potentially affect other parts. Because the Presentation, Business, and Data Access logic are located within the same piece of application code, recompilation of many parts of the code may be necessary, increasing the overhead of adding or changing functionality. Worse still, changes in part of the code may introduce unintentional bugs in other, seemingly unrelated, parts and the rollout of new versions of the software gets more complicated as more users install and use the application.

The Move into the Second Tier

The move toward 2-tier systems was born from the desire to share data between multiple applications which are installed on different machines. To do this, a separate database server machine is required. Figure 1.2 shows how this is achieved. The application now consists of presentation and business logic. Data is accessible through a remote connection to a database on another machine. Any changes to the Data Access logic should not affect the Presentation or Business logic in the application.

As indicated by Figure 1.2, splitting out Data Access Logic into a second tier keeps the data access independent and can deliver a certain amount of scalability and flexibility within the system.

FIGURE 1.2

2-tier scenario.

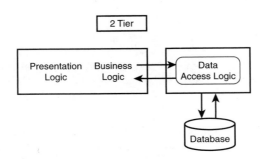

The advantage of having the Data Access Logic split into a separate physical environment means that not only can data be shared, but any changes to the data access logic are localized in that second tier. In fact, the whole of the second tier could be replaced with a different database vendor or implementation as long as the interface between the two tiers remains the same.

This provides an alternative way of looking at the program logic. Each functional component from the monolithic system could be regarded as a separate layer.

The logical division into layers of functionality can be based on the different responsibilities of parts of the code, namely,

- *Presentation Logic*—This dictates how the user interacts with the application and how information is presented.
- *Business Logic*—This houses the core of the application, namely the rules governing the business processes (or any other functionality) embedded in the application.
- *Data Access Logic*—This governs the connection to any data sources used by the application (typically databases) and the provision of data from those data sources to the business logic.

In Figure 1.2 there are two logical layers but the Presentation and Business Logic layers are still lumped together as one piece of potentially monolithic code.

One of the central problems faced by application developers using the type of architecture shown in Figure 1.2 is that the client is full of business code and it still needs to know details about the location of data sources. Because there is such a concentration of functionality on the client, this type of client is generally termed a *thick* client. Thick clients usually need to be updated whenever the application changes.

Because the users of a thick client application have much of the application code installed on their local systems, there is a need to install fresh copies of the updated application when changes are made. This presents a serious manageability issue in terms of roll out and version control and puts constraints on the client systems.

With the advent of the Internet, a standard user interface—the web browser— has become the preferred, and sometimes only, user interface. The ubiquitous acceptance of the web browser as the primary user interface has forced developers to move most of their business logic into the back end application. Because the application logic associated with a client is no longer resident on the user's machine, this type of client is known as a *thin* client. If a 2-tier system is to be adapted for use on the Internet, the thick client part, that contains the business logic and the presentation logic, must be re-written to run on a Web server.

Maintaining separate versions of an application for thick and thin clients leads to larger maintenance and development costs and is best avoided. An alternative strategy is needed, hence the current trend to using three or more tier architectures.

Developing 3-tier Architectures

The decoupling of application logic, as started with the two-tier system shown in Figure 1.2, can be continued with the separation of the Business and Presentation Logic. By housing the separated Business Logic in another tier, the thick client becomes thinner, as Figure 1.3 shows.

FIGURE 1.3

3-tier scenario.

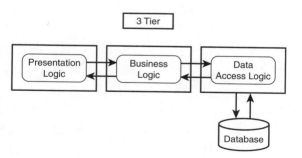

Separating the Presentation Logic into its own tier means that different types of Presentation Logic, such as HTML-based and GUI-based user interface code, can all access the same Business Logic on the middle tier. The separation into more layers makes systems more flexible so that parts can be changed independently. An example of this would be creating a presentation layer specifically targeted at mobile devices. Given the separation of business and presentation functionality, this should not require any changes to the data access logic.

With the logic now separated into different tiers, it is far easier to develop code that is tailored to a particular task. For example, developers who are skilled in the use of Java Web components, such as servlets (see Day 12, "Servlets") and JavaServer Pages (JSPs) (see Day 13, "JavaServer Pages") can write the code for this layer. These developers do not need to know about the technologies used in the business or data access code.

Separation of functionality allows each tier to be written by separate programming teams working to a common interface specification. These teams can work concurrently, potentially reducing project delivery time scales and enabling Rapid Application Development.

Introducing more layers into the software architecture potentially introduces additional complexity in managing the interface boundaries between the layers. Well-designed modular systems reduce this complexity to manageable levels.

Complexity Simplified by Modularity

When designing a system, certain concepts will naturally sit together. By placing these into shared modules, a certain amount of separation can be achieved independently of the layering discussed so far.

Object-oriented (OO) modeling promotes modularity because objects encapsulate their data, or state, and offer functionality through their interfaces. If designed correctly, the dependencies between different objects can be minimized. This reduction in dependency means that the objects are loosely coupled. Loosely coupled systems tend to be easier to maintain and evolve.

Although they are not the whole solution, you have some useful tools for modularizing your applications in Java:

- A Java class improves modularity by housing all state and behavior belonging to an entity into one part of the design.
- A Java package uses modularity to house related classes and interfaces that perform a specific set of functions.

Additionally, you need a way of going beyond simple objects to provide more coarse-grained packages of functionality that can be glued together to create custom applications. To be correctly glued, these packages must conform to certain rules that are defined by a framework. This leads us to components.

Component Technology

A *component* is a unit of functionality that can be used within a particular framework. Component frameworks have evolved to provide support for simplified application development. When using a component framework, a container provides standard services, such as communication, security and persistence. Because standard mechanisms are used for component definition and inter-component communication, it becomes possible to write tools that examine components and display their information to an application writer. A developer can then use the tool to drag and drop these components into his or her application. This can be seen in the typical GUI interface builder environments.

The component principle also applies to non-visual components enabling a complete distributed application to be created from components. One of the benefits of distributed component frameworks is that they can provide language independence. Using Common Object Request Broker Architecture (CORBA), for example, components written in C can communicate with those written in OO languages such as Java and Smalltalk.

In Java, there are several component frameworks from which to choose. The J2EE platform uses components extensively to provide modularity within the layers of an application. As such,

- A Java component is yet another way of using modularity to house all packages required to perform a specific task. In the 3-tier environment, for example, the functionality of the Data Access Logic layer would be split into multiple components.

- A component will publish its interface defining the functionality it offers. This functionality can then be used by the application itself or by other components.

One benefit of modularity is that it enables standard components to be purchased from third parties and easily integrated into an application developed using a standard framework. This approach can reduce the development costs and the time to market.

Another benefit is that the system is more maintainable if identifiable parts are capable of being upgraded and re-implemented with minimal impact on the rest of the system.

Modern N-tier Architectures

If three tiers are better than two tiers, which are better than a monolithic program (generally speaking), then is there any benefit to adding a fourth or fifth layer?

The answer is yes. Additional software layers can be identified from good modular design and separated out onto different physical tiers at suitable boundaries. Deciding what is a suitable boundary is the hard part.

The downside to additional tiers is that extra communication overhead can inflict performance bottlenecks. The upside of multiple tiers is that additional hardware (multiple servers and network bandwidth) can be used to alleviate the bottlenecks and improve reliability using techniques such as server farms and failover clustering.

The modern emphasis on the Internet is driving n-tier architectures and many enterprise service vendors are seeking to exploit this market. Web services are the next generation of n-tier development, allowing applications to be created from components distributed across the Internet. As this model evolves, the distributed Internet *becomes* the computer. This book shows how you can use J2EE technologies to provide Web services (see Day 20, "Using RPC-Style Web Services with J2EE" and Day 21, "Message-Style Web Services and Web Service Registries").

Enterprise applications can be Webcentric, but need not be. To cover Webcentric programming, this book shows how to integrate Servlets (see Day 12) and JavaServer Pages (JSPs) (see Day 13,) into Enterprise applications. Within an organization, or even when creating business-to-business (B2B) links, enterprise applications need not use Servlets or JSPs. In this case, clients may connect directly to business components, in the shape of Enterprise JavaBeans (see Day 4, "Introduction to Enterprise JavaBeans"), over RMI (Remote Method Invocation) or CORBA (see Day 19, "Integrating with External Resources").

As the provision of functionality over the Internet gains importance it becomes important to maintain the integrity of the data in the corporate systems. Transactions and security provide a common mechanism for doing this. Transactions are covered in detail in Day 8, "Transactions and Persistence" and security in Day 15, "Security."

A Model for Enterprise Computing

Given that an n-tier, component-based, Web-friendly environment is needed, what about the detail—what specific functionality is needed to support such applications? The Object Management Group (OMG online at `http://www.omg.org`) has been working with key industry players to produce a component-based software market by hastening the introduction of standardized object software. Many of the OMG's specifications have become a standard part of the Distributed Object Computing landscape, such as the Common Object Request Broker Architecture (CORBA), the Internet Inter-Orb Protocol (IIOP), and the Unified Modeling Language (UML).

By examining some of the key requirements outlined in the OMG's Enterprise Computing Model, it is possible to explore what is required from a modern distributed computing environment.

Lifecycle

One key requirement is that there must be a safe mechanism for creating, copying, moving, and deleting distributed objects. A distributed component environment must provide containers to manage the lifetime of components and assist in their deployment. There are also other lifecycle issues that must be addressed in a distributed environment. For example, distributed garbage collection (getting rid of unused objects) can be handled in different ways according to the operating environment. With Java's Remote Method Invocation (RMI), a distributed leasing mechanism is used. With CORBA, there are lifecycle management services. Microsoft's Distributed COM (DCOM), on the other hand, relies on objects signaling their redundancy.

Persistence

In an enterprise application, you need to be able to store data permanently for later retrieval. Object Database Management Systems (ODBMS) and Relational Database Management Systems (RDBMS) commonly support this requirement. A distributed application environment must provide a way of accessing and updating persistent data in a simple yet flexible way. It is also important to support different types of data persistence (different databases, legacy systems, and so on) and different ways of accessing this data (locally or across a network).

Naming

Distributed applications are formed from components that reside on different machines. The parts of the application that use components on other machines must be able to locate and invoke such components. Therefore, a directory service is needed, in which components or services can register themselves. Any part of the application that wants to use such a service can look up the location of the service and retrieve information about how to contact it.

Common directory services and protocols include the following:

- *CORBA Common Object Services (COS) Naming Service*—This allows you to store object references in a namespace. The COS naming service is widely used in Java-based distributed environments as a way of storing information about the location of remote objects. Further information on COS Naming can be found online at http://www.omg.org.

- *X.500*—This defines an information model for storing hierarchical information and an access protocol called the Directory Access Protocol (DAP). Further information about X.500 can be found online at
http://java.sun.com/products/jndi/tutorial/ldap/models/x500.html.

- *Lightweight Directory Access Protocol (LDAP)*—This is a lightweight version of the X.500 protocol that runs over TCP/IP. Further information on LDAP can be found online at `http://www.openldap.org`.
- *Domain Name System*—This is an Internet protocol that allows translation between host names and Internet addresses. DNS is used by all Internet clients, such as Web browsers. More information on DNS can be found at `http://www.dns.net/dnsrd/rfc/`.
- *Microsoft Active Directory*—The Active Directory service allows organizations to store central information on information and services within an enterprise. Further information on Active Directory can be found online at `http://www.microsoft.com/windows2000/technologies/directory/default.asp`.

Transactions

In a distributed enterprise application, certain business processes will involve multiple steps. For example, a typical exchange of goods or services for payment will need to take payment details, verify those payment details, allocate the goods to be shipped, arrange the shipping, and take the payment. At any stage, the customer might be interrupted or the server could crash, invalidating the entire transaction. If that happens, the enterprise application must be able to retrieve the previous state to continue with the transaction at a later time or to roll back the transaction so that the system is restored to its original state.

Transaction services provide a way of grouping updates to data so that either all of the updates are performed or none of them are performed. A transaction manager will be responsible for ensuring this. Transaction information is persisted so that the state of a transaction can survive a system crash. Transactions can be propagated across distributed method calls and even across message-based systems.

Security

A secure enterprise application environment will typically provide the following:

- *Authentication*—Are you who you say you are?
- *Authorization*—Are you permitted to do the things you are requesting to do?
- *Confidentiality*—Can only you, or other authorized staff access your data?
- *Integrity*—Is the data you see actually the data you stored, and are any changes you make retained (not lost due to system crashes)?

In addition to this, many enterprise application environments will support both programmatic and declarative security. Programmatic security is enforced within the enterprise application itself, while declarative security is enforced by the enterprise application's container.

Java 2 Enterprise Edition (J2EE)

J2EE is an on-going standard for producing secure, scalable, and high availability enterprise applications. The standard defines the services that must be provided by J2EE compliant servers. Services are provided by J2EE containers in which J2EE components will run. Further information on the J2EE specification and components can be found at http://java.sun.com/j2ee.

Although the J2EE specification defines a set of services and component types, it does not contain information on how to arrange the logical architecture into physical machines, environments, or address spaces.

The J2EE platform provides a common environment for building secure, scalable, and platform-independent enterprise applications. Many businesses are now delivering goods and services to customers via the Internet by using such J2EE-based servers. The requirements of such an environment demand open standards on which to build applications, for example,

- Java 2 Platform, Standard Edition (J2SE), a platform independent language
- Components that deliver Web-based user interfaces
- Components to encapsulate business processes
- Access to data in corporate data stores
- Connectivity to other data sources and legacy systems
- Support for XML, the language of B2B e-commerce

Components and Containers

J2EE specifies that a compliant J2EE application server must provide a defined set of containers to house J2EE components. Containers supply a runtime environment for the components. Application Programming Interfaces (APIs) in J2EE are available to provide communication between components, persistence, service discovery, and so on. J2EE application server vendors provide containers for each type of J2EE component:

- Web Container
- Web Services Container
- EJB Container

There are three types of standard components deployed, managed, and executed on a J2EE Server:

- *Web components*—A Web component interacts with a Web-based client, such as a Web browser. There are two kinds of Web components in J2EE—servlet components and JavaServer Page (JSP) components. Both types handle the presentation of data to the user and are described in Days 12, 13 and 14.

- *Web services*—A Web component that exposes servlets and EJB components based on SOAP and HTTP protocols are described in Day 20 and Day 21.

- *EJB components*—There are three kinds of Enterprise JavaBean components— Session beans, Entity beans, and Message-Driven beans. EJBs are described on Day 4, Day 5, "Session EJBs," Day 6, "Entity EJBs," and Day 10, "Message-Driven Beans" respectively, for further information.

Figure 1.4 shows the overall relationships between the different containers and components in the J2EE environment.

FIGURE 1.4

J2EE logical architecture.

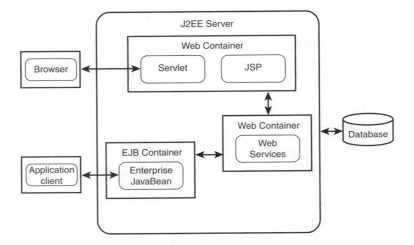

J2EE Standard Services

Containers must provide each type of component with a defined set of services that are covered in detail as you progress through the book. Briefly these services consist of

- *Connectivity*—Containers must support connectivity to other components and to application clients. One form of required connectivity is to distributed objects through both Java Remote Method Invocation (RMI) and CORBA (as implemented by the Java IDL package and RMI over IIOP). Internet connectivity must be provided both through the Hypertext Transport Protocol (HTTP) and its secure form (HTTPS).

- *Directory services*—J2EE servers are required to provide naming services in which components can be registered and discovered. The Java Naming and Directory Interfaces (JNDI) provide a way of accessing these services.

- *Data access and persistence*—Data access is provided through the Java Database Connection API (JDBC). This API enables both the application level to interface with databases and also service providers who build drivers for specific databases.

- *Legacy connectivity*— The Java Connector Architecture (JCA or Connectors) provides J2EE support in integrating Enterprise Information Servers and legacy systems, such as mainframe transaction processing and Enterprise Resource Planning (ERP) systems. This support extends to J2EE service providers who are writing adapters to connect other systems to the J2EE enterprise architecture.

- *Security*—Security is built into the J2EE model. APIs, such as the Java Authentication and Authorization Service (JAAS), assist the J2EE enterprise application in imposing authentication and authorization security checks on users.

- *XML Support*—The JAXP API supports the parsing of XML documents using Document Object Model (DOM), Simple API for XML (SAX), and the XML Stylesheet Language for Transformation (XSLT).

- *Transactions*—A J2EE server must provide transaction services for its components. The boundaries of transactions need to be specified by the container or the application. The container will usually take responsibility for transaction demarcation, although the Java Transaction API (JTA) allows the component to control its own transactions if required.

- *Web Services*—Support for defining and using Web Services supporting the industry standard protocols such as Simple Object Access Protocol (SOAP), Universal Description, Discovery and Integration (UDDI) and Web Service Description Language (WSDL). J2EE containers must support the Java API for XML Messaging (JAXM), Java API for XML-based RPC (JAX-RPC), Java API for XML Registries (JAXR), and SOAP with Attachments API for Java (SAAJ) APIs.

- *Messaging and email*— The Java Message Service (JMS) allows components to send and receive asynchronous messages, typically within an organizational boundary. The JavaMail API enables Internet mail to be sent by components and also provides functionality to retrieve email from mail stores. JavaMail uses the JavaBeans Activation Framework (JAF) to support various MIME types.

Figure 1.5 shows the J2EE architecture updated with the services available to its containers. All of these services are discussed in more detail tomorrow.

FIGURE 1.5

*The J2EE platform
with services
available.*

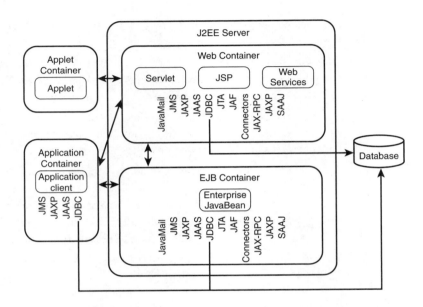

Every J2EE-compliant server must support the services defined in this section. To provide a concrete example of how services should work, the team working on the J2EE Java Specification Request (JSR) is responsible for providing a Reference Implementation (RI) of the J2EE APIs. This RI is freely available from Sun and provides a convenient platform for prototyping applications and testing technologies. The J2EE Reference Implementation (J2EE RI) is described in Day 2, "The J2EE Platform and Roles".

New Features of J2EE 1.4

The main changes introduced for J2EE 1.4 are

- JSP 2.0 Element Language (EL)—covered on Day 13
- JavaServer Pages Standard Tag Library—covered on Day 14
- Web Services—covered on Day 20 and Day 21

Smaller changes were made to incorporate the

- EJB Timer service—covered on Day 5
- EJB QL enhancements—covered on Day 6
- Enhanced JMS API—covered on Day 9 and Day 10

J2EE Blueprints

The J2EE Blueprints are a set of best practices that show how best to implement J2EE applications. The Blueprints provide a concrete implementation of Sun's vision for 3-tier, J2EE-based systems. These can be found online at `http://java.sun.com/j2ee/blueprints`.

Here you will find example online e-commerce application. The best practices covers application design and, in particular, the promotion of the following:

- Code reuse
- Logical functional partitioning
- The separation of areas of high maintenance
- Extensibility
- Modularity
- Security
- Simple and consistent user interface
- Efficient network usage
- Data integrity

The J2EE Blueprints guide you through the design process of J2EE applications, discussing the following topic areas:

- The Client Tier
- The Web Tier
- The Enterprise JavaBeans Tier
- The Enterprise Information Systems Tier
- Design Patterns

In addition, there are discussions on how to package and deploy your enterprise applications.

J2EE Compatibility and Java Verification

To enable Enterprise service providers to test their products against the specification, Sun Microsystems Inc. offers a testing environment. Servers that pass all of the tests can be certified as J2EE compliant. Further details of the Java Application Verification Kit (AVK) can be found online at `http://java.sun.com/j2ee/verified/index.jsp`. A list of certified application vendors' servers can also be obtained from this web site.

The Future of J2EE

Like all Java technologies, J2EE is undergoing continuous improvement and expansion. The best source for information on the latest version of J2EE is the Sun Microsystems' J2EE Web site at http://java.sun.com/j2ee. This book introduces the features and capabilities of the J2EE 1.4 specification.

J2EE changes are initiated and tracked using Java Specification Requests (JSRs) under the auspices of the Java Community Process (JCP). For more details on JCP and current JSRS go to http://www.jcp.org.

Summary

Enterprise application development helps businesses provide Web-enabled, scalable, secure applications quickly. It also enables vendors to produce pluggable tools and services to augment the J2EE standard defined through the Java Community Process. This chapter has shown the journey toward the n-tier environment that underpins the architecture of enterprise application programming. The chapter discussed the basic services that should be available to an n-tier enterprise application.

Q&A

Q I have a monolithic program that I would like to transition into an n-tier application. How do I do this?

A First, you need to identify from the specification what sort of target architecture is required. If your application is to be Web-enabled, you will need to provide Web-oriented functionality in the presentation layer. If you are working with persistent data, you will need data access through a data access layer. You should map out your target architecture based on the services available under the J2EE platform.

Next, you will need to sift through the monolithic code separating out the code belonging to the logical layers. This code might need to be rewritten in such a way as to make it maintainable and extensible. Introduce modularity by adopting object-oriented programming and design classes. Package these classes and design components to have maximum cohesion and loose coupling wherever possible.

To implement and deploy your J2EE application, read the rest of the book and follow the examples.

Q What is the difference between Microsoft's .NET Framework and J2EE?

A You can build enterprise applications with both platforms. Both J2EE and .NET Framework applications can provide good levels of scalability, availability and so forth. The essential difference is largely one of choice. J2EE lets you use any operating system, such as Windows, UNIX, or a mainframe. J2EE's development environment can be chosen to suit developers from a variety of Integrated Development Environment (IDE) and J2EE application server vendors. The .NET Framework is essentially limited to the Windows family of operating systems. This allows it to be more cleanly integrated with the operating system, but reduces the choice of target platforms.

Exercises

To extend your knowledge of n-tier development, try the following exercises:

1. Write a design for a monolithic application to provide a shopkeeper with data concerning stock information.

2. Redesign the application for an n-tier architecture to make it accessible over the Internet.

3. Visit `http://java.sun.com/j2ee` for further details of the J2EE programming tools and utilities.

4. Visit `http://www.microsoft.com` for further details of the .NET framework. Compare and contrast this with the facilities available under J2EE.

The exercises above are designed to make you think about n-tier application design; there are no solutions provided for these exercises.

DAY 2

The J2EE Platform and Roles

Yesterday, you learned about enterprise computing and some of the problems facing developers of enterprise solutions. The day also introduced J2EE, a technology that can help you develop secure, scalable, and platform-independent solutions that meet the needs of today's business.

Today, you will explore the J2EE platform and see what it can offer to help solve your business problems. J2EE is a large framework that boasts a wide-range of components, services, and roles. It is these that you explore today, so that you'll be prepared to start writing code tomorrow. The following are the major topics covered today:

- Understanding how J2EE delivers solutions for today's business
- Introducing the available Web-centric components
- Introducing the use of Enterprise JavaBeans
- Assessing platform roles
- Exploring the packaging and deployment of enterprise applications

Revisiting the J2EE Platform

You learned a lot about enterprise computing yesterday. Specifically you learned about how business needs force the evolution of application architectures; today, most applications are distributed across multiple machines. This n-tier model gives rise to different ways of writing and structuring applications. Units of functionality, or components, provide modularity that allow multiple developers to work on different parts of the application.

Use of a component framework allows developers to apply third-party components to speed development. These loosely coupled components may run as an application on a desktop client, within a Web server, or even on a server that connects to a legacy system.

In addition, data has undergone a revolution. Data sources now go beyond simple relational databases containing tables to encompass databases that contain serialized objects, or plain text files containing XML. Alternatively, data may take the form of user information in an LDAP (Lightweight Directory Access Protocol) naming directory or information in an Enterprise Resource Planning (ERP) system.

J2EE is a framework that supports the requirements of applications developed to support enterprise wide functionality. Although the environment within which J2EE operates might sound daunting, J2EE itself isn't. When you write J2EE applications, you still write Java code, and you still get to use the J2SE classes with which you are familiar.

To successfully use J2EE, you must

- Install and configure your J2EE environment
- Understand J2EE roles
- Appreciate the purpose of containers
- Understand how you can use J2EE components
- Understand the services that containers supply to components
- Learn or explore a new set of APIs

Yesterday's lesson gave an introduction to the first four points in the list. You will explore these in more depth today. After you understand these, you will be ready for tomorrow, when you will start to apply the new APIs and code real applications against them. At the end of today's work you will install Sun Microsystems' J2EE SDK and configure a database for use with the examples and exercises presented in the rest of this book.

Understanding J2EE Components

You saw yesterday that modern software architecture design utilizes an n-tier model where each tier (or layer) implements one aspect of the overall solution. There are many ways to slice and dice the n-tier model, but the following list identifies the most common layers:

- Presentation—The display of information back to the client
- Application—Flow control logic for accessing and using the system
- Business—Encapsulation of business rules
- Data storage—Persistent data storage

Each layer is as loosely coupled as possible from the adjacent layers and should be completely unaware of any other layers. Put simply, a business logic component may have some knowledge of the application and data storage layers but no knowledge at all of the presentation layer.

J2EE provides a number of component technologies that sit within this layered architecture. Each technology is best suited to one or more layers, as follows:

- JavaServer Pages (JSP)—Presentation logic back to the client, typically using HTML
- Servlets—Application logic and business logic
- Enterprise JavaBeans (EJBs)—Application logic, business logic and data storage
- Application Clients—Presentation logic using Swing/AWT based applications
- Applets—Presentation logic using powerful GUI component, typically executing in Web browser

As you can see, there is some overlap between the servlet and EJB technologies, and choosing the best technology for a given problem is not always as easy as it might seem. Sun Microsystems has written a set of J2EE blueprints for guidance on writing J2EE applications. These blueprints incorporate empirical experience as well as abstract theory and can be downloaded from:

```
http://java.sun.com/j2ee/1.4/download.html
```

The rest of today's work will briefly introduce the component J2EE technologies and how they are normally used in an n-tier architecture. The role of the supporting J2EE framework technologies is also discussed. Later lessons in this book will look at these technologies in more detail.

Enterprise JavaBeans

In a typical business application built on the J2EE platform, business logic will be encapsulated in Enterprise JavaBeans (EJBs). It is possible to use other types of component or plain Java objects to implement business logic, but EJBs provide a convenient way of encapsulating and sharing common business logic, as well as benefiting from the services provided by the EJB container.

EJBs are usually described as a distributable component technology. Unlike JavaBeans, which must reside in the same JVM as the client and server, EJBs can reside in different JVMs allowing the client and server to be located on physically separate machines.

The EJB model makes use of two mechanisms found in J2SE--namely Remote Method Invocation (RMI) and the Java Naming and Directory Interface (JNDI)--to facilitate interaction between the EJB and its client. When an EJB is written, the functionality it offers to clients is defined as an RMI remote interface. When an EJB is deployed, its location is registered in the naming service.

A client will then use JNDI to look up the location of the EJB. It will interact with a factory object, which implements the EJB's home interface, to obtain an instance of the EJB. This is equivalent to using new to create an instance of a local object. When the client has a reference to the EJB, it can use the business functionality offered by the EJB. This sequence is shown in Figure 2.1.

FIGURE 2.1

A client uses JNDI and RMI to access an EJB.

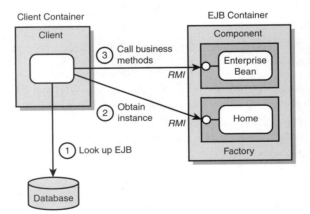

There is a more detailed look at how to use EJBs on Day 4, "Introduction to Enterprise JavaBeans." It is worth mentioning that EJBs can also use local interfaces when the client and server reside in the same J2EE container. Typically this happens when one EJB uses functionality of another EJB. Local interfaces are discussed on Day 6, "Entity EJBs."

Within the required business logic, certain components will be primarily concerned with data and the manipulation of that data, others will focus on the sequencing of business logic and the associated workflow, whereas still others will need to start a large piece of work without waiting for that work to complete. There are three types of EJB covering each of these requirements:

- Session Bean—controlling workflow
- Entity Bean—persistent data
- Message-Driven Bean—asynchronous messages

Session Beans

Session beans are the simplest and probably most common type of EJB. A session bean is primarily intended to encapsulate a set of common business functions.

Session beans offer a synchronous interface through which the client can use the business logic. Session beans are not intended to hold essential business data. The Session bean will either hold no data on an ongoing basis, or the data it does hold will only be relevant to the current user session. If a Session bean wants to obtain data from a database, it can use either JDBC calls or Entity EJBs. Session beans are discussed further on Day 5, "Session EJBs."

Entity Beans

An Entity bean is a representation of some business data and offers a synchronous interface through which the client can access its data and functionality. Entity beans will access underlying data sources (frequently, a database or possibly an ERP system) to collect all the business information they represent. As you will see later, Entity beans are frequently used together with Session beans to provide the business functionality of a system. Entity beans are discussed further on Day 6.

Message-Driven Beans

A Message-Driven Bean (MDB) offers an asynchronous interface to clients. The bean is associated with a particular Java Message Service (JMS) message queue, and any messages arriving on that queue will be delivered to an instance of the Message-Driven bean. As with Session beans, Message-Driven beans are intended to house business logic rather than data, so they will access any data required through JDBC or Entity beans.

To use the services of an MDB, a client will send a message to its associated message queue. Message-Driven Beans and the Java Message Service are discussed further on Day 9, "Java Message Service," and Day 10, "Message-Driven Beans."

Web Applications

To create a Web-based user interface, you need to apply Web-centric components. J2EE provides three types of Web-centric components:

- JavaServer Pages (JSP)
- Servlets
- Web Services

The first two of these components (JSPs and servlets) provide services to clients that use HTTP as a means of communication. For example, JSPs and servlets can interact with the following clients:

- Standard HTML browsers, such as Microsoft Internet Explorer and Netscape Navigator
- Java 2 Micro Edition (J2ME) enabled devices, connecting across a wireless network
- Any Java application using `java.net.URL` objects
- Wireless Markup Language (WML) browsers, such as those found on WAP-enabled mobile phones

Web Services expose application or business logic to a client conforming to industry-defined standard protocols using HTTP and XML as a data exchange medium. Web Services are designed to be technology neutral so that J2EE Web Services can be used by non-Java clients such as Microsoft's .NET. Similarly, J2EE clients can use Web Services provided by non J2EE servers, again with .NET being the obvious alternative.

Servlets

Servlets are Java objects that receive incoming client HTTP requests and generate responses for return to the client (typically a browser). Therefore their primary use is to create dynamic Web pages (pages whose content is dependent on variable data).

Servlets are used to implement application or business logic. Servlets often use supporting EJBS for additional application or business logic. However, servlets can be used without EJBs, in which case the servlet provides the application and business logic and JDBC is used to access the data layer. Servlets are discussed further on Day 12, "Servlets."

Servlets are developed in Java and producing complex HTML documents from within a Java program is a tedious process; JavaServer Pages were introduced to make this much easier while still providing dynamic output.

JavaServer Pages (JSP)

JSPs allow you to dynamically create pages of markup, such as HTML, in response to a client's request. In this respect JSPs are similar to Microsoft's Active Server Pages (ASP).

A JSP consists of a combination of JSP tags, an expression language (EL) and scriplets, which contain the executable code, and static markup, such as HTML. You can think of JSPs as Web pages with embedded Java code. The code contained in the JSP is identified and executed by the server, combined with the static HTML and the resulting page is delivered to the client. This means that the embedded code can generate additional markup dynamically that is delivered to the client alongside the original static markup. The client sees none of this processing, just the resulting HTML.

Servlets and JSPs can both manipulate Java objects and generate HTML pages but each have problems trying to do both jobs. The usual approach for any non-trivial Web Application is to combine servlets and JSPs to take advantage of the strengths of each technology.

Web Application Architecture

Using a single servlet or JSP to process an HTTP request is known as a Model 1 architecture and is shown in Figure 2.2.

FIGURE 2.2

Model 1 Web Application.

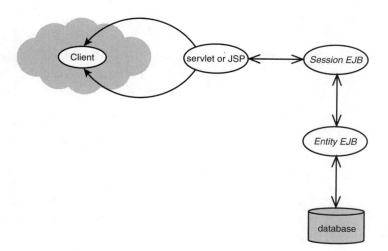

A Model 1 architecture is really only suitable for trivial web applications; it becomes unwieldy when dealing with real world applications.

The Model 2 architecture shown In Figure 2.3 is considered the best approach to developing larger Web Applications.

FIGURE 2.3

*Model 2 Web
Application.*

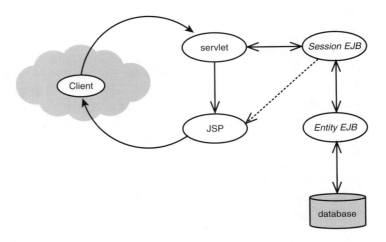

In a Model 2 architecture the incoming HTTP request is handled by a servlet which validates any HTTP request data and updates the database if necessary. Typically Session beans will be used to support the servlet functionality. The Session beans in turn may use Entity beans to encapsulate access to a database. In a simple application, one not making use of EJB technology, simple JavaBean helper classes will be used in place of the EJBs.

Once the servlet has verified the request, and obtained the necessary data to formulate the response, the request is forwarded to a JSP for generating the Web page to return to the client. Typically the JSP will only read data from the Session bean so that the different roles of the servlet as a controller and the JSP as a presentation (or view) component are clearly encapsulated. Experienced developers will recognize this architecture as the Model View Controller (MVC) architecture; the EJBs take the role of the Model component, the JSP is the View and the servlet the Controller.

The Model 2 architecture is so useful that products such as Apache Struts (http://jakarta.apache.org/struts) and Sun Microsystems' JavaServer Faces (JSF from http://java.sun.com/j2ee/javaserverfaces) provide frameworks for building Model 2-based Web applications.

Web interfaces are so pervasive in modern enterprise computing that a new technology called Web Services has come to the fore for providing IT services utilizing the Web (HTTP) technologies.

Web Services

Web Services are XML-based middleware components that applications access over HTTP and Simple Object Access Protocol (SOAP). Web Services enjoy industry-wide support and are not a proprietary solution. In fact, because Web Services use XML and open communication standards, any client that can understand SOAP messages can consume Web Services. J2EE provides a rich framework that facilitates the building, deployment, and consumption of Web Services.

In order to send a message to a remote system, something on that system must be listening for incoming messages. An address to which a client can send a Web Service message is termed a Web Service *endpoint*. The endpoint is described using the Web Service Description Language (WSDL), which tells a client about the location of the endpoint and describes the service that can be found there. The location of a Web Service endpoint is defined as a combination of server name or IP address and a port number on the server at which the Web Service can be found. The description of the Web Service endpoint will define the messages that can be sent to the service, the expected responses, and the protocols over which such messages can be passed (typically SOAP, but other protocol bindings can also be defined).

Web Services are discussed further on Day 20, "Using RPC-Style Web Services with J2EE," and Day 21, "Message-Style Web Services and Web Service Registries."

Application Clients

HTTP clients all use the Web as a means of exchanging data between the client and the server. However, there is still a requirement for non Web-based clients. Such standalone clients will usually be deployed within an organization and will frequently implement the presentation logic using Swing or AWT GUI interfaces, but there is still a role for simple command-line-based interfaces (often when working across simple network connections using Telnet). Application clients are discussed on Day 4.

J2EE Technologies

All J2EE application servers must provide containers to house J2EE components. The role of the container is to provide a component with the resources it needs to operate and a runtime within which to execute. While doing this it must also provide a degree of protection (security) to the application host.

Containers provide a number of services for a component. These services include:

- Lifecycle management
- Threading
- Security
- Transaction management
- Communication with other components

J2EE containers must provide components with certain standard services. Yesterday, you were introduced to some of these services; today, you will explore them in a little more detail and see how they work in conjunction with J2EE components.

Hypertext Transfer Protocol (HTTP)

A WorldWide Web Consortium (W3C) specification defines HTTP 1.1 to support the exchange of data in a widely distributed network. Both JSPs, servlets and Web Services, allow clients to access a J2EE application through the use of HTTP.

HTTP over Secure Sockets Layer (HTTPS)

A Netscape specification defines the Secure Sockets Layer (SSL) 3.0, which is a protocol that manages the secure transfer of data over a network. HTTPS uses SSL as a sub-layer to HTTP to provide secure data transfer over the Internet.

Java Database Connectivity (JDBC)

JDBC is an API that allows you to access any tabular data source including relational databases, spreadsheets, and text files. The API allows you to connect to a database via a driver and then execute Structured Query Language (SQL) statements against that database.

Java Transaction API (JTA)

The JTA API allows you to work with transactions independently of a transaction manager. A transaction is an atomic group of operations (such as the ubiquitous banking application that debits one account and credits another). The transaction is considered complete when all operations are complete. If one operation fails, the other must roll back. A distributed system makes transaction management complex. In such a system, a transaction manager must coordinate transactions across the system.

Java Authentication and Authorization Service (JAAS)

JAAS is a supplement to the Java security framework. It provides both authorization and authentication services in a J2EE environment. (JAAS is similar to the Pluggable Authentication Module (PAM), which provides authentication in a Unix environment.) In common with the Java 2 security framework, JAAS provides access control based on code location and code signers. In addition, JAAS provides access control to a specific user or group of users.

Java API for XML Parsing (JAXP)

The JAXP API allows you to parse XML documents using the Document Object Model (DOM) or the Simple API for XML (SAX). XML is a text-based markup language that describes data. It provides a platform-independent and language-independent method for exchanging data between applications. JAXP also supports the Extensible Stylesheet Language Transformations (XSLT) language for dynamically transforming an XML document into another XML document, HTML, plain text, or some other format.

Java API for XML-based RPC (JAX-RPC)

The JAX-RPC specification defines client APIs for developing Simple Object Access Protocol (SOAP)-based portable Web Services. Developers use JAX-RPC to develop SOAP-based Web Service clients and endpoints. A Web Service endpoint is described using a Web Services Description Language (WSDL) document. JAX-RPC enables clients to invoke Web Services developed across heterogeneous platforms. Also, J2EE components can define Web Service endpoints that can be invoked by heterogeneous clients.

Java API for XML Registries (JAXR)

An XML registry is part of the infrastructure for building, deploying, and discovering Web services. There are several specifications for XML registries, including the ebXML Registry and Repository standard developed by OASIS and U.N./CEFACT (see www.ebxml.org) and the Universal Description, Discovery and Integration (UDDI) specification developed by a large consortium of vendors. JAXR provides an abstract interface to a variety of XML registries.

SOAP with Attachments API for Java (SAAJ)

The SAAJ API is used to manipulate messages conforming to the SOAP specification and SOAP with Attachments note. Originally part of JAXM (Java API for XML Messaging), SAAJ has been separated out to provide support for SOAP without mandating the use of JAXM.

Java Naming and Directory Interface (JNDI)

JNDI provides an API for working with naming and directory services. A naming service simply associates names with objects, for example, the Domain Name System (DNS) used by most Internet services to translate between domain names and IP addresses. A directory service also associates names with objects, but it also provides additional information through attributes using, for example, the Lightweight Directory Access Protocol (LDAP).

Although JNDI provides access to a wide array of naming and directory services, each service must provide a Service Provider. This is similar to JDBC and drivers, but in this instance, it is a naming or directory service and a Service Provider. For example, an LDAP directory must provide an LDAP Service Provider, which JNDI hides from you.

JavaBeans Activation Framework (JAF)

Typically, you use JAF in the context of JavaBeans (that's JavaBeans, not Enterprise JavaBeans!). However, a J2EE product must provide JAF for the JavaMail API to use MIME types. JAF allows you to send emails consisting of different MIME types and attachments.

JavaMail

The JavaMail API provides classes that allow you to work with email. Specifically, it allows you to send and receive emails by using a wide variety of protocols, including POP3, SMTP, and IMAP. Because the API uses JAF, you can create emails that conform to a large number of MIME types. For example, you can create HTML messages that contain embedded graphics or have attachments.

Java Message Service (JMS)

Messaging is the process of communication between applications or components; it does not include application to human communications, such as email. The JMS API allows you to create, send, and receive messages. Message-Driven Beans provide a means for consuming JMS messages within a J2EE environment. Typically Session and Entity beans are message producers but any Java program can produce JMS messages for delivery to an MDB.

Java Interface Definition Language (Java IDL)

Java IDL provides a way for you to access and deploy remote objects that comply with the Common Object Request Broker Architecture (CORBA) defined by the Object Management Group (OMG). IDL provides a language-independent means of defining object interfaces. The OMG provides mappings between various programming languages and IDL. A client written in any language that has an IDL binding can access objects you export using CORBA. For example, a Java client can consume objects written in other languages, such as C++, C, Smalltalk, COBOL, and Ada.

Remote Method Invocation over Internet Inter-Orb Protocol (RMI-IIOP)

RMI is a distributed object system that allows Java objects to interact with other Java objects running in a different virtual machine (usually on a remote host). In practice, you can access these remote objects almost as if they were local; you simply get a reference to the remote object and invoke its methods as if it were running in the same virtual machine.

The actual process of performing a remote method invocation utilizes client-side stubs and server-side skeletons. A client invokes a remote method by making a request on the stub, and this is forwarded to the server where the skeleton converts the request into an actual method call on the remote object. The stub marshals any arguments for the remote method into a serialized form for transfer over the network. The data is un-marshaled by the receiving skeleton, which, in turn, calls the actual service method. Any results from the method call are in turn marshaled up by the skeleton, sent to the stub to be un-marshaled and finally returned to the client.

RMI-IIOP is the transport mechanism used by stubs and skeletons for EJBs. You can also explicitly create RMI-IIOP clients and servers for your own applications by using the RMI compiler (rmic) to generate your RMI-IIOP stubs and skeletons.

You can also use RMI-IIOP as a mechanism for exposing your EJB components to CORBA clients without having to learn IDL. You can specify a flag to the RMI compiler which causes it to generate CORBA IDL on your behalf. After you have the CORBA IDL, this can be used together with an alternative language binding to create a client for the EJB that is written in another language.

Connector Architecture

The J2EE Connector Architecture allows your J2EE application to interact with Enterprise Information Systems (EIS), such as mainframe transaction processing systems, Enterprise Resource Planning (ERP) systems, and legacy non-Java applications. It does this by allowing EIS vendors to produce a resource adapter that product providers can plug into their application servers. The J2EE developer can then obtain connections to these EIS resources in a similar way to obtaining a JDBC connection.

The J2EE Connector Architecture defines a set of contracts that govern the relationship between the EIS and the application server. These contracts determine the interaction between server and EIS in terms of the management of connections, transactions, and security.

J2EE Platform Roles

To create, package, and deploy any J2EE application—other than the simplest—requires the effort of more than one person or organization. For example, in the development arena, a team of developers will write the J2EE components and someone else will assemble the finished application. In the production environment, someone will configure the J2EE environment and deploy the application, and yet another person will monitor the running application and its physical environment. In smaller organizations, there may be no physical distinction between these roles, but they will still be logically separate.

This team, together with Product Providers and Tool Providers, constitute the J2EE platform roles. It is these roles that this section explores.

J2EE Product Provider

A J2EE product must include the component containers and J2EE APIs that conform to the J2EE specification; today's lesson has introduced all of these containers and APIs. Examples of J2EE products include operating systems, database systems, application servers, and Web servers. An organization that supplies a J2EE product is known as the J2EE Product Provider.

The J2EE Product Provider is also responsible for mapping application components to defined network protocols. In addition, the Product Provider must provide deployment tools for the Deployer and management tools for the System Administrator.

The Product Provider is free to provide implementation-specific interfaces that the J2EE specification does not define. Hence, you will occasionally see a warning in a lesson that highlights a vendor-specific piece of functionality.

A list of J2EE compliant vendor offerings is available from `http://java.sun.com/j2ee/compatibility.html`.

Application Component Provider

As you have already seen, a J2EE application consists of components, but it also may consist of other resources, such as HTML pages or XML files. The Application Component Provider creates both these resources and components. Almost all organizations will use several component providers. They may exist in-house, or the organization may outsource component creation or buy in components. Whichever is the case, specialists in the different tiers (presentation, business, and data access) will write the components that relate to that tier. For example, a business tier specialist will write EJBs, whereas a presentation tier expert may write JSPs.

Application Assembler

The Application Assembler's job is to package the application, written by the Application Component Providers, into a J2EE application. The application is packaged into an Enterprise Application Resource (EAR) file (also known as an Enterprise Archive) that must conform to the J2EE specification. Apart from this assembly, the Application Assembler is responsible for providing instructions that state the external dependencies of the application.

Application Deployer

The Application Deployer role is the first that requires knowledge of the production environment. This is because the Application Deployer must deploy the application into that environment. Specifically, the Application Deployer must install, configure, and start the execution of the application.

The installation process is where the Application Deployer moves the application to the server and installs any classes the container requires to perform its duties. During the configuration process, the Application Deployer satisfies any external dependencies that the Application Assembler has stipulated and configures any local security settings (for example, modifies a policy file). The final stage, starting execution, is where the Application Deployer starts the application in readiness to service clients.

Systems Administrator

The Systems Administrator configures and maintains the enterprise network, and monitors and maintains the application once deployed.

Figure 2.4 shows the interactions between each of these roles and their interactions with the J2EE application.

Tool Provider

There are many tools to assist with the creation, packaging, deployment, and maintenance of J2EE applications. Currently, the J2EE specification only defines that the Product Provider must supply deployment and maintenance tools; it does not stipulate what these tools should be. Future releases of the specification are likely to provide further guidelines, so that Tool Providers can supply platform-independent standardized tools sets.

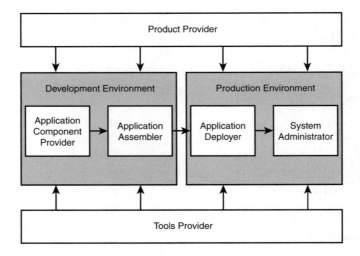

FIGURE 2.4

J2EE roles.

Packaging and Deploying J2EE Applications

The installation of a typical desktop application, such as a word processor, is usually a straightforward affair. The installation program will ask you a few questions about the functionality you require and where it should install its files. It will also examine parts of your desktop machine (such as the Windows registry) to discover whether any components that it relies on are already installed.

The installation of a desktop application is reasonably straightforward because

- The concept of word processing is well understood by most people, so they can make an appropriate judgment on whether they need particular parts of the package or not. There is little in the way of personal tailoring involved.

- All of the installation takes place on a single machine. The installation program knows where to find existing configuration information and where it should install the different parts of the application.

Compared with this, a distributed enterprise application requires a lot more information about the environment in which it is to be installed. This includes, but is not limited to, the following:

- The location of the servers on which the server-side components will be deployed.

- The appropriate level of security that must be enforced for the application. The application must carry with it information about the security roles it expects and the access each role has to the functionality of the application. These security roles must be mapped onto the underlying security principals used in the distributed environment.

- Components that access data and other resources must be configured to use appropriate local data sources.

- The names of components and resources must be checked and potentially changed to avoid clashes with existing applications or to conform to a company-wide naming standard.

- Web components must be configured so that they integrate with any existing Web sites of which they will form a part.

As you can see, this is specialist task, requiring knowledge about the application and the environment in which it is being deployed. The application must carry with it information about the requirements it has of the environment. The Application Assembler defines these requirements when the application is created. The Application Deployer must examine these requirements and map them onto the underlying environment.

J2EE Applications

A J2EE application will consist of zero or more of the following components:

- Web applications packaged as Web Archives (WAR files)
- EJB components packaged as EJB-JAR files
- Client applications packaged as JAR files
- Connectors packaged as Resource Archives (RAR files)

Naturally, there must be at least one component for there to be an application! The components that constitute an application must be packaged together so that they can be transported and then deployed. To this end, all of the components in a J2EE application are stored in a particular type of JAR file called an Enterprise Archive or EAR file.

Given the previous scenario, it should be clear that a J2EE application needs to carry with it information about how its different parts interrelate and the requirements of the environment in which it will be deployed. This information is carried in XML documents called deployment descriptors. There is an overall application deployment descriptor that defines application-level requirements. This application deployment descriptor is also stored in the EAR file.

Each individual component will have its own deployment descriptor that defines its own configuration and requirements. These component deployment descriptors are carried in the individual component archives. Figure 2.5 shows the structure of an EAR file and how the application deployment descriptor, the component archives, and the component deployment descriptors fit within this structure.

FIGURE 2.5

Structure of an Enterprise Archive (EAR).

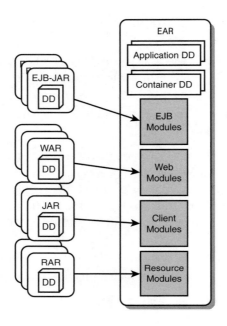

The application deployment descriptor contains application-wide deployment information and can potentially supersede information in individual component deployment descriptors.

NOTE The EAR file can also contain a container-specific deployment descriptor that holds information that is useful to the container but falls outside the scope of the J2EE application deployment descriptor.

The application is split into modules, each of which represents a component. If necessary, a module can contain an additional deployment descriptor to override some or all settings in the deployment descriptor provided in the component archive file.

As you can see from Figure 2.5, components are represented in an EAR file by component archive files. Each module will point to its associated component archive file. Each type of component archive file is a JAR-format file that contains the component's classes and resources together with a component-specific deployment descriptor.

The two most common types of component archive are EJB-JAR files and WAR files.

EJB Components

An EJB-JAR file contains all of the classes that make up an EJB. It also contains any resource files required by the EJB. The properties of the component are described in its associated deployment descriptor, called `ejb-jar.xml`, which is also included in the EJB-JAR file.

The deployment descriptor describes the main class files contained in the EJB-JAR file. The deployment descriptor also specifies which external resources are required by the component and information about the security and transaction settings. This resource and extra information is often referred to as metadata. Figure 2.6 shows a subset of the contents of an EJB deployment descriptor.

2

FIGURE 2.6

An EJB deployment descriptor indicates the main classes in the EJB-JAR file together with the component's metadata.

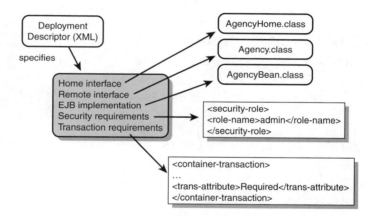

All of the component's metadata can be altered or replaced by the Application Assembler when they bind the component into the application. The Application Deployer can also customize some of the metadata.

NOTE An EJB-JAR file can contain more than one EJB.

EJB-JAR files and their deployment descriptors are discussed in more detail on Days 4 and 5. Other aspects of EJB deployment information, such as security and transactions, are covered later in the book.

Web Components

Servlets and JSPs can also be packaged together into a Web archive resource (WAR) file. The archive file is a JAR-format file that contains the class files, JSP files, and resources required by the Web components (including static HTML files) and a deployment descriptor (called web.xml).

Just as with the EJB deployment descriptor, the WAR deployment descriptor indicates the main classes in the WAR file and the resources required by the components. However, the WAR deployment descriptor also contains Web-specific information, such as the URL mappings for the servlets and JSPs.

WAR files and their deployment descriptors are discussed in more detail on Day 12 and Day 13, "JavaServer Pages."

Application Components

Standalone client applications are packaged into a JAR file containing all the constituent classes and a deployment descriptor called application-client.xml. Application clients are Java applications that directly access EJBs. Application clients are described on Day 4 and Day 5.

Connector Components

Connectors provide resources that can be used by a J2EE component but are not supplied as a standard constituent of the J2EE containers. The connectors you are most likely to come across are connectors to a JMS implementation (see Day 9) and general purpose connectors for accessing external EIS and ERP systems (see Day 19, "Integrating with External Resources").

Summary

Today, you looked in more detail at J2EE and the facilities that it provides. You saw how the different J2EE technologies fit into the n-tier model, and how it provides component frameworks for different types of functionality. You have also seen how Enterprise JavaBeans (EJBs), JavaServer Pages (JSPs) and servlets are the main user-defined components of a J2EE application. You have also seen how supporting J2EE technologies are used to provide cross-component functionality, such as data access, network communication, naming services, transaction management, and security.

You have seen that the separate functions of tool provider, developer, assembler, deployer and administrator work co-operatively to implement and manage the many stages of the lifecycle of a J2EE application. The components of an Enterprise Application are packaged into a single EAR file and this file contains components packaged as JAR files, Web archives (WAR files), or resource archives (RAR files). Each constituent archive file (EAR, WAR, RAR or JAR) includes the required Java class files, and a component-specific deployment descriptor (DD). A deployment descriptor describes not only the component itself, but also the environmental requirements for the container that will host the component.

Q&A

Q Can a J2EE application be written without using any Enterprise JavaBeans?

A Certainly. You can write a Web client application that connects to a servlet in a Web container and have that servlet connect directly to a back-end database. You don't need to add an EJB. An EJB can add value by providing persistent conversational state if that is required. It can also provide transactional security and roll back to a previous state should there be an interruption in the flow of data for any reason.

Q Can a J2EE application be written without using any Web components?

A Certainly. You can write a standalone client application that connects directly to an EJB without the need for a Web-based interface.

Q What type of EJB should I typically use to encapsulate business logic? And which type would I use to contain data and its associated operations?

A For pure business logic, you would typically use a Session bean. If the EJB is to represent underlying application data, you would probably use an Entity bean.

Q How do you package an EJB? What should be in the package?

A An EJB is packaged in an EJB-JAR file. The EJB-JAR file contains the classes for the EJB, any other resources, and a deployment descriptor that contains EJB metadata and describes the external resource requirements of the EJB.

Q What is an EAR file?

A An EAR file houses the application's JAR, WAR, and deployment descriptor files. The Assembler takes on the responsibility of packaging the EAR file, while the Deployer authenticates that the file conforms to the J2EE specification, adds the file to the J2EE server, and deploys the application.

Exercise—Sun Microsystems' J2EE SDK

Before you can start coding real J2EE applications, you need a J2EE implementation and a Java development environment, such as Sun Microsystems JDK or a Java Integrated

Development Environment (IDE). This book refers to and uses the Sun Microsystems' J2EE SDK for all its examples and discussions. The J2EE SDK is a complete reference implementation of J2EE. It includes all the classes, containers, and tools you need to learn J2EE. The J2EE SDK is freely available from http://java.sun.com/j2ee.

To run the example code provided on the Web site accompanying this book, you will also need to install a sample database. Installing the sample database is described at the end of this day's lesson. But first you will install the J2EE SDK 1.4 on your workstation.

NOTE

> The J2EE SDK is free to download, use for learning J2EE, and use as a development tool. Throughout the book the J2EE SDK is also referred to as the J2EE Reference Implementation or J2EE RI.
>
> This book was developed using the J2EE SDK 1.4 and is not backward compatible with J2EE SDK 1.3. While a large part of the Java code is unchanged from J2EE 1.3 to J2EE 1.4 there are significant differences in the way applications are assembled and deployed under J2EE 1.4 SDK.

Downloading Sun Microsystems' J2EE SDK 1.4

At the time of writing this book (January 2004) the J2EE SDK 1.4 was available for a number of platforms including:

- Windows 2000 Professional
- Windows XP Professional
- Sun Solaris SPARC 8, 9
- Redhat Linux 8

For a definitive list of supported platforms you should consult the J2EE SDK release notes at http://java.sun.com/j2ee/1.4/docs/relnotes/releasenotes.html. Obviously you can only use the J2EE SDK 1.4 if your workstation is running a supported operating system.

You should check the release notes to verify the minimal hardware requirements for your platform. The J2EE SDK (like all J2EE servers) requires a significant amount of memory and disk space.

At the time of writing, the J2EE SDK 1.4 depends on J2SE 1.4.2_02. If you are working with an older version of Java, you must upgrade to this version. The J2EE SDK 1.4 optionally includes J2SE 1.4.2_02 as part of the download bundle.

You can download the J2EE SDK 1.4 from `http://java.sun.com/j2ee/`. You will be given a choice of download options including:

- Full package, J2EE SDK 1.4 Application Server, J2SE 1.4.1_02 and samples
- J2EE SDK 1.4 Application Server only
- J2EE SDK 1.4 Samples

If you have already downloaded and installed J2SE 1.4.2_02 (from `http://java.sun.com/j2se`), you can download just the Application Server (the J2EE SDK). This book does not use the J2EE samples but you may want to download them for further study.

At this point you should download the J2EE SDK of your choice. But before you go ahead and and install J2EE SDK following the installation instructions (available from `http://java.sun.com/j2ee/1.4/docs/relnotes/install.html`), read the next section which is a summary of the installation process and includes useful hints for the decisions you will have to make.

CAUTION

For experienced (or just impatient) users the key information for installing the J2EE SDK 1.4 for use with this book is:

- Uninstall any previous J2EE SDK.
- Choose an administrative username of `admin` with a password `password`.
- Set the HTTP server port number to 8000.
- Define the `J2EE_HOME` environment variable.
- Add the `J2EE_HOME/bin` directory to your `PATH` environment variable.

While you are downloading the J2EE SDK you will also find it useful to download additional J2EE documentation from `http://java.sun.com/j2ee/1.4/download.html`. Specifically you will find the following useful:

- J2EE API documentation—This is not included in the J2EE SDK and is essential for any serious J2EE development.
- The J2EE 1.4 Tutorial—Sun Microsystems' official tutorial for developing J2EE applications.
- Java Blueprints for the Enterprise—A Guide to creating robust, scalable, and portable enterprise applications using Java technology.

Installing Sun Microsystems' J2EE SDK 1.4

Before installing the latest J2EE SDK 1.4 you must uninstall any previous 1.4 versions. If you have previously installed J2EE SDK 1.3 you may keep this installation but you must set your development environment to use J2EE SDK 1.4 as described in the section "Configuring Your J2EE SDK 1.4 Development Environment."

If you have already downloaded and installed J2SE 1.4.2_02, you must configure the JAVA_HOME environment variable to point to the J2SE installation directory.

 NOTE
> The J2EE SDK 1.4 requires a Java compiler. You will need a full J2SE SDK and not just the J2SE JRE to run the J2EE SDK even if you do not plan to write and develop the Java code on the same workstation.

To install the SDK follow the supplied installation instructions at `http://java.sun.com/j2ee/1.4/docs/relnotes/install.html`. Your first step will be to execute the installer you have just downloaded:

- Microsoft Windows—Run the `.exe` program.
- Linux/Solaris—Add execute permission to the download and then run it.

After executing the installer you will be guided through the following steps:

1. Read and accept the end user license agreement.
2. Choose an installation directory.
3. If you are installing just the J2EE Application Server you will be prompted with the location of your J2SE 1.4.2_02 SDK. The installation will fail if you do not have a suitable SDK (note that a full SDK is needed, not just a JRE).

   If you are installing the full bundle a suitable J2SE SDK is installed in the same directory as the J2EE SDK.
4. Next, you will provide an administrative username and password. The authors used the name admin and the password password. If you choose different values, you will need to remember to use your values when the administrative usesname and password are referred to in the text.

   At this point you can also save the administrative user details to a user preference file on disk. This will save you having to supply this information every time you administer your server. As a developer you may find it convenient to save this information.

5. As part of the configuration you must choose port numbers for the administration server, HTTP (Web) server and HTTPS (secure Web) server. Unless these conflict with existing services on your system, choose the following values:

   - Admin server—4848
   - HTTP server—8000
   - HTTPS server—1043

   This information is shown in Figure 2.7 which was taken from a Windows XP installation.

NOTE   The authors found that the J2EE SDK 1.4 Nov 2003 installation process selected a random port number for the HTTP port. It is important you select the value 8000 for this port to maintain compatibility with the instructions in this book. If you cannot choose port 8000 because it is already in use, choose a free port and remember that when the instructions in the book use port 8000, you will have to substitute your own port number.

FIGURE 2.7

*Configurable Admin
User and Port Settings
when Installing J2EE
SDK 1.4.*

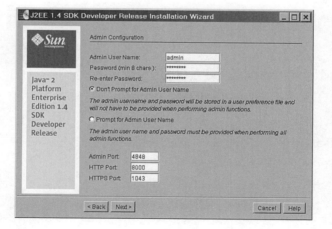

6. Next you choose which parts of the bundle to install. Select the option to Register the Application server and this will install the J2EE SDK 1.4.

7. The last part of the installation process asks you to register your J2EE SDK. You do not need to register the SDK in order to use it.

You have now installed the J2EE SDK and can configure your development environment accordingly.

Configuring Your J2EE SDK 1.4 Development Environment

Having installed the J2EE SDK you should configure your development environment for this SDK. You will need to provide two environment settings:

1. Define the J2EE_HOME environment variable to point to the installation directory where the J2EE SDK was installed.

2. Add the bin sub-directory of the J2EE_HOME directory to your PATH environment variable. This step is optional but is highly recommended otherwise you will have to supply full pathnames for all J2EE SDK commands.

NOTE

> Windows users should note that one of the J2EE SDK utilities is called verifier. Windows already has a verifier utility in the %SystemRoot%\System32 directory included in the PATH settings. To run the J2EE SDK verifier you will either have to place the %J2EE_HOME%\bin directory at the start of the PATH settings or always use the absolute pathname for the J2EE verifier: %J2EE_HOME%\bin\verifier.

You are now ready to startup the J2EE SDK Application Server.

What's in the J2EE SDK

The J2EE SDK contains the following software components:

- A J2EE server
- PointBase, a relational database server
- An HTTP (Web) server
- A Name Service accessed via JNDI
- A Messaging Server service accessed via JMS
- Class files for the J2EE APIs
- Administration, deployment and development utilities

To run the sample code presented in this book, you will need to start the J2EE server and the PointBase database server as discussed in the next section. Starting the J2EE server will also start the JNDI, JMS, and HTTP servers provided with the J2EE SDK.

To develop and deploy your J2EE applications you will need a text editor and Java compiler, and will also use the asant, deploytool and verifier utilities supplied with the J2EE SDK.

To administer the J2EE SDK you will use the asadmin utility or the Web-based Admin Console interface. Generally, administration is kept to a minimum and the case study on the Web site contains asant automated build files for all J2EE SDK administration required by the examples and exercises presented in this book.

The J2EE SDK is a development version of the Sun Microsystems' Java System Application Server (formerly known as Sun ONE Application Server). The Application Server has the concept of multiple domains and the J2EE SDK comes configured with a single domain called domain1.

Figure 2.8 shows a hierarchical view of the directory structure of the J2EE SDK.

FIGURE 2.8

J2EE SDK Directory Structure.

You will find the following directories

- bin – Contains the J2EE SDK utility programs.
- config – J2EE configuration files.
- docs – Documentation for the J2EE SDK. By default this does not contain the J2EE API documentation, which is a separate download (discussed earlier).
- domains/domain1/applications – Installed J2EE applications.
- domains/domain1/config – Domain specific configuration maintained using the Admin Console or asadmin utilities.
- domains/domain1/docroot – Root directory for Web pages.

- `domains/domain1/generated` – Working directory for Java files and classes generated by the J2EE deployment process.
- `domains/domain1/logs` – J2EE SDK log files (in particular `server.log`).

NOTE The main J2EE log file is `domains/domain1/logs/server.log` in the J2EE_HOME directory. Use the Admin Console interface to browse this log file for problems.

In the J2EE SDK bin directory you will find the following utilities that are used at various points in this book:

- `appclient`, a command line utility for running Applicantion Clients
- `asadmin`, a command line admistration interface
- `asant`, a version of Apache Ant for automated building of applications
- `capture-schema`, a utility used to capture database schema for supporting CMP Entity beans (see Day 7, "Container-Managed Persistence and EJB Query Language")
- `deploytool`, GUI-based utility for building EJBs and Web Applications (introduced on Day 4, "Introduction to Enterprise JavaBeans")
- `verifier`, a utility for verifying J2EE compliance of Enterprise Applications containg EJBs and Web components (introduced on Day 4)
- `wscompile`, a utility for compiling Web Services (Introduced on Day 20, "Using RPC-Style Web Services with J2EE")
- `wsdeploy`, a utility for deploying Web Services (Introduced on Day 20)

That's it for a quick tour of the J2EE SDK, you can now start up and verify the J2EE servers as described in the next section.

Starting the J2EE Servers

You will need to start the J2EE server and PointBase database servers in order to work with the examples and case study code examined during the course of the next twenty days.

Starting the J2EE Server

If you are working with Microsoft Windows, the installation process has created entries in your Start menu for all J2EE SDK utilities. Use the Start, programs, Sun Microsystems, J2EE SDK menu to select the commands you require:

- Start Default Domain—Starts the J2EE server
- Start Pointbase—Starts the PointBase database server

If you are working with Solaris and Linux, or want to work from the Microsoft Windows command prompt, you will need to start the servers from the command line. Each server will require its own console window (do not use the Unix shell to start the commands in the background as the servers cannot share the same standard input stream).

The following commands will assume you have included the %J2EE_HOME%\bin (Windows) or $J2EE_HOME/bin (Linux/Solaris) directory in your search path. If you have not done this, prefix each command with %J2EE_HOME%\bin or $J2EE_HOME/bin.

Start the J2EE server with:

```
asadmin start-domain --verbose
```

This will start the default domain (domain1) with the --verbose option so you will be able to see the server log activity in the console window. As a developer you will find this more convenient that using the Admin Console interface to browse the server.log file in the domains log directory.

> **TIP**
>
> Windows users will find it convenient to take a copy of the Start Default Domain shortcut and include the --verbose option in the startup command as follows:
>
> \Sun\AppServer\lib\asadmin-pause.bat start-domain --verbose domain1
>
> With the --verbose option the J2EE server log messages are shown in the console window; without this option the console window contains no useful information.

Verifying J2EE Startup

You can verify that the J2EE Server is up and running by browsing to

```
http://localhost:8000
```

If you chose a different HTTP port at install time you should use this port number rather than 8000 in the previous URL. If you have installed the J2EE SDK correctly you will see the screen shown in Figure 2.9

FIGURE 2.9

*J2EE SDK Web
Interface.*

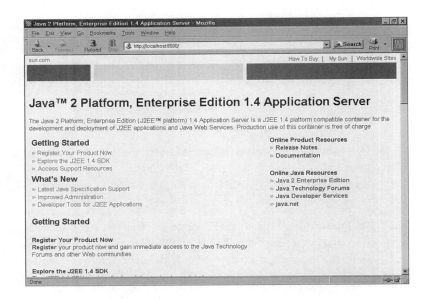

You can also examine the Admin Console Web interface for the J2EE SDK by
browsing to

`http://localhost:4848/asadmin`

Windows users can also use the Start, Programs, Sun Microsystems, J2EE SDK 1.4,
Admin Console menu option.

You will need to supply the admin username and password (admin and password) to
Admin Console. Once you have logged into the Admin Console you will see the administration screen shown in Figure 2.10.

You can use the Admin Console to browse the J2EE server log file by selecting the
Application Server and clicking on the Logging tab.

You have now verified that you have installed the J2EE SDK correctly. You should also
start up the PointBase database server as discussed in the next section.

Starting PointBase Database Server

Start the PointBase server with the Solaris/Linux command:

`$J2EE_HOME/pointbase/tools/serveroption/startserver`

Windows users can use the Start, Programs, Sun Microsystems, J2EE SDK 1.4, Start
PointBase menu option or run the command:

`%J2EE_HOME%\pointbase\tools\serveroption\startserver`

FIGURE 2.10

J2EE SDK Admin Console.

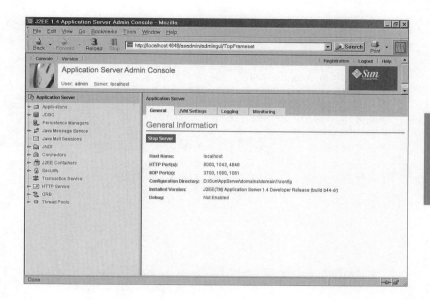

You can start up the database server before or after the J2EE server.

Verifying PointBase Startup

The simplest way to verify the PointBase installation is to run the PointBase Console. To do this run the Linux/Solaris command

```
$J2EE_HOME/pointbase/tools/serveroption/startconsole
```

or the Windows command

```
%J2EE_HOME%\pointbase\tools\serveroption\startconsole
```

You will be prompted to connect to a database. There is only one database provided, `jdbc:pointbase:sample`. You should connect to this database using the username and password of `pbPublic` and `pbPublic`. Enter this information and you will be able to view the database schema for the sample database as shown in Figure 2.11.

When you have finished working with the J2EE SDK you should stop the servers as described in the next section.

Stopping the J2EE Server

To stop the J2EE server you can either:

- Close down the J2EE console window
- Run the J2EE_HOME command `asadmin stop-domain`

- Click on the Stop Server button in the Admin Console Application Server screen (see Figure 2.10)
- Windows users can use the Start, Programs, Sun Microsystems, J2EE SDK 1.4, Stop Default Domain menu option

FIGURE 2.11

PointBase Database Server Console.

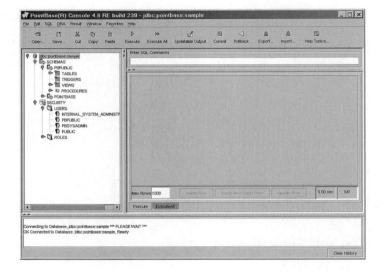

Stopping the PointBase Database Server

To stop the PointBase server you can either:

- Close down the PointBase window.
- Run the J2EE_HOME command `pointbase\tools\serveroption\stopserver`.
- Run the SQL command `shutdown force`.
- Windows users can use the Start, Programs, Sun Microsystems, J2EE SDK 1.4, Stop PointBase menu option.

Troubleshooting J2EE and PointBase

You should have no problems starting up either server. If you do have problems, check the error messages displayed in the relevant window. The most likely problems are discussed in the rest of this section.

Read Only Installation Directory

You will not be able to run J2EE RI and PointBase unless you have installed the J2EE SDK in a writeable directory. If you have installed the J2EE SDK as a privileged user

(Administrator, root, or whomever), make sure that you grant your normal login account read and write permission to the installation directory and all contained files and directories.

Server Port Conflicts

Although the J2EE SDK software uses TCP port numbers that are not normally used by other software, there is always a possibility that there will be a port number conflict.

If a port is used by another software server, a J2EE component will fail to start up. To change the J2EE default port numbers, find the file

```
domains/domain1/config/domain.xml
```

in the J2EE_HOME directory. Take a backup copy of this file, edit with a simple text editor and look for the following line:

```
<config name="server-config">
```

The lines after this define the J2EE servers including the port numbers. Change the numbers that are conflicting with existing software and save your new configuration.

CAUTION

Take care when editing the domain.xml file, as the J2EE server might not start up if this file is corrupt. You should, therefore, always make a backup before editing this file.

You cannot run more than one J2EE RI server on the same workstation.

Optional Software Used in This Book

A Java IDE (JDK) and a J2EE implementation (J2EE SDK) are all you need to learn how to develop J2EE applications. However, areas of this book look at using J2EE applications in a wider context and make use of additional (freely available) software.

So that you are aware of this software, Table 2.1 lists the optional software used in this book. Full instructions for downloading and configuring this software (should you want to do so) are included in the relevant day's instructions. You do not need to download this software at the present time.

TABLE 2.1 Optional Software Used in Daily Lessons

Day	Software	Resource URL
11	Apache James to provide SMTP and POP3 email services	http://james.apache.org/

Exercise—Case Study

To help you understand the role of each of the technologies in the J2EE specification, a single case study will be followed throughout the daily exercises. As you work through the days, a functional implementation of a simple enterprise application will be developed.

The Job Agency

The chosen case study is a simple Job Agency. Jobs are categorized by Location and Skills required for the job. Customers advertise jobs, and Applicants register their location and skills so they can be matched to jobs. Customers and applicants will be notified of job matches by email.

To illustrate the relationships between the different components in the data model for the Agency, a traditional database ERD diagram is shown in Figure 2.12.

Today's exercise, which is described later, will be to create this database and register it as a `javax.sql.DataSource` to the J2EE RI.

The case study has a front office part with the following components:

- Maintaining the location and job lookup tables
- Adding customers and advertising jobs
- Registering job applications

The back office part consists of the following:

- Matching a new job against existing applicants
- Matching a new applicant against existing jobs
- Generating emails

Using the Agency Case Study

Typically, the sample code shown in each day's lesson will use the Customer functionality (jobs and invoices) from the case study. At the end of each day's work, you will then be asked to enhance the case study by adding the Applicant functionality (registering jobs) to the system. A fully-worked solution for the exercises is provided on the Web site included with this book so that you will have a working case study if you choose to omit any day's exercise.

FIGURE 2.12

Case Study ERD.

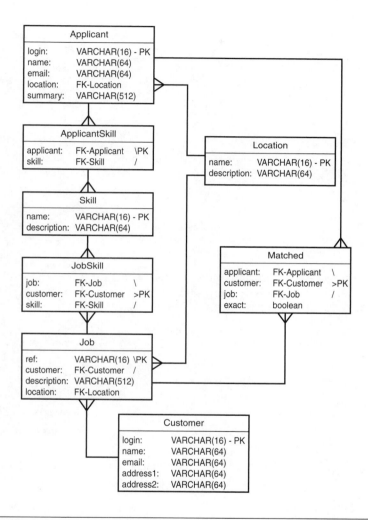

2

Material for some days' exercises, particularly JNDI, JavaMail, JMS and Java Connectors, will primarily use examples and exercises not related to the case study.

Table 2.2 shows roughly what will be covered on each day. Don't worry if some of the terminology is new to you; all will become clear as you work your way through the book.

TABLE 2.2   Daily Workout

Day	Lesson	Exercise
1	Introduce multi-tiered application architectures	No exercise.
2	Introduce the J2EE platform, technologies and roles	Install J2EE RI and case study database.
3	Using JNDI naming and directory services	Write a JNDI namespace browser.
4	Using data sources, environment entries, and EJB references	Build and deploy a simple EJB and client application with J2EE RI.
5	Using Session EJBs to implement business logic	Add a Session bean to register job applicants.
6	Using Entity EJBs to encapsulate access to persistent data	Add Entity beans for the applicant data and refactor the register Session bean.
7	Using Container-Managed Persistence (CMP) and Container-Managed Relationships (CMR) with entity EJBs	Refactor the applicant Entity bean to use CMP and CMR.
8	Adding transaction management to Session and Entity EJBs	Add transaction management to the applicant processing.
9	Using JMS topics and queues	Develop a simple chat room service.
10	Using Message-Driven beans to implement back office functionality	Use Message-Driven Beans to match new or changed applicants to advertised jobs.
11	Adding email capabilities to back office functionality	Use email to send matched jobs to applicants.
12	Developing Web-based applications using servlets	Develop a servlet front end to create a new applicant for the Agency case study.
13	Developing Web-based applications using JavaServer Pages	Use JSPs to register job applicants.
14	Using JSTL and custom Tag Libraries with JSPs	Refactor the register job JSP to use Tag Libraries.
15	Adding security to restrict access to J2EE application functionality and data	Add security to control access to the job skills data.
16	Understanding XML and writing simple XML documents	Develop a utility to generate a Web application deployment descriptor.
17	Using XSL to transform XML documents into different data formats	Transform a TLD document into HTML for viewing in a Web browser.

TABLE 2.2 Continued

Day	Lesson	Exercise
18	Understanding design patterns and recognizing patterns present (and absent) from the case study	Identify which design patterns can be applied to the case study to improve maintainability.
19	Working with legacy systems using the Connector architecture	Identify how the case study could be linked into a legacy invoicing system.
20	Exposing J2EE components as Web Services	Expose Agency case study functionality as a Web Service.
21	Using XML-based registries and asynchronous Web Services	Create a Web Service JobPortal that will take a SOAP message containing new agency customer information and return a generated customer login ID.

By the end of this book, you will have a simple, but functional, job agency enterprise application. The application will have both a GUI-based front end and a Web-based interface and will give you a good grounding in the relative strengths of each J2EE technology and how to apply it. Remember that the case study is an aid to learning and is not intended to be a robust fully functional application.

Practice Makes Perfect

Developing J2EE architectures requires two disciplines:

- Good analysis and design skills
- Practical hands-on experience with the J2EE technologies

The first comes with time and experience, but the lessons in this book will help point you in the right direction to becoming a J2EE designer.

The second discipline comes with practice. If while reading this book you attempt all the exercises, you will learn a lot more than if you just study the sample code shown.

The case study exercises are not complex. They have been designed to take between 30 minutes and 2 hours to complete. The exercises only use information presented and your existing knowledge; you will need to know something about JDBC, Swing, and HTML, but you certainly don't need to be an expert in these technologies. The book *Teach Yourself Java in 21 Days* from Sams Publishing is a good source for improving your knowledge of JDBC and Swing should you require a little refresher course. More importantly, the exercises will give you hands-on coding experience using J2EE.

The Case Study Directory on the Web Site

On the Web site you will find a directory called CaseStudy. In this directory you will find all the code, solutions and build files required for the examples and exercises in this book.

NOTE In order to build, deploy, and run the examples you will need to write additional files into the case study directories. Therefore, you will need to download the CaseStudy directory hierarchy onto your local hard drive in order to build and deploy the code. The instructions in this book refer to the Web site code but assume you have copied this code to your hard drive.

Under CaseStudy, there are 20 sub-directories corresponding to each day's work except yesterday's. Each day will have one or more of the following directories:

- agency—The complete Agency case study so far. This includes code from the examples in the book and the completed exercise if this is based on the Agency case study.
- examples—The code for all the sample programs shown in the book.
- exercise—Any existing code to be used as a starting point for the exercise. Typically, this will be the Agency case study with all the sample code in the book, but excluding the code the reader needs to provide as part of the exercise.
- solution—A solution to the set problem if the exercise does not enhance the Agency case study.

Each day's sub-directory also contains a number of sub-directories used by the automated asant build files supplied with the case study:

- build—A temporary working directory used by the asant build and deploy commands
- classes—Location of the compiled Java class files
- dd—Location of deployment descriptors used for EAR and WAR files
- j2ee-ri—Location of pre-built EAR or WAR files and deployment descriptors for use with deploytool rather than asant build files
- JSP—HTML and JSP files required by Web applications
- src—Java source files

For any given directory there may be additional sub-directories as described in the individual day's instructions.

Using asant Build Files

The case study examples can be built and deployed using `asant` build files provided in each sub-directory. The `asant` utility is a customized version of Apache Ant (see `http://ant.apache.org`) and is included with the J2EE SDK to provide an automated mechanism for building and deploying J2EE components. The case study makes extensive use of `asant` build files to hide the details of the J2EE SDK.

Using the `asant` build files supplied with the case study is simple. Start a command-line window and change directories to the case study code you want to work with (for example, `Day02/exercise`) and enter one of the following commands:

- `asant clean`—Delete all working files ready for a clean rebuild
- `asant compile`—Compile any Java code
- `asant build`—Compile Java code and build any EAR or WAR files required
- `asant deploy`—Deploy the built EAR or WAR file
- `asant verify`—Verify the built EAR file
- `asant verify-web`—Verify the built WAR file
- `asant run`—Run a command line example application
- `asant help`—Provide information about additional `asant` commands you can use

The case study examples will provide additional `asant` commands for use with that day's work. Use the command

```
asant help
```

or just asant to get a list of these additional commands.

You will find `asant` build files (called `build.xml`) in the `CaseStudy` directory and each day's directory. These build files provide `asant` commands for building the examples in all sub-directories and deploying and running the agency case study (if appropriate for the sub-directory). You can do a clean rebuild of every days' exercises and solutions in one go by entering the following command from the `CaseStudy` directory:

```
asant clean build
```

The case study

The case study examples and instructions in the book will also guide you through the use of `deploytool` to assemble and deploy your applications. The `asant` build files support either approach.

Using `deploytool` with the Case Study

Either the `asant` build files or the J2EE SDK `deploytool` utility can be used with the case study examples.

A separate EAR or WAR file is supplied in the `j2ee-ri` directory for use with `deploytool`. The `asant` build files will generate new EAR or WAR files in the build directory and will not modify the files in the `j2ee-ri` directory.

If you use `deploytool` to modify the J2EE application files in the `j2ee-ri` directory, you should make a backup copy before applying your changes.

The `asant` build files support a number of commands for working with the files in the j2ee-ri sub–directory:

- `asant deploy-j2ee-ri`—Deploy the `deploytool` maintained EAR or WAR file
- `asant verify-j2ee-ri`—Verify the `deploytool` EAR file
- `asant run-j2ee-ri`—Run the agency case study client application using the client JAR file in the `deploytool` directory
- `asant tidy`—Will delete the files in `j2ee-ri` and create new ones from the `build` directory (you must run `asant build` first)

The `deploytool` and `asant` build file components are deliberately separated so that you can use either approach for development. The `deploytool` GUI interface is easy to use and instructive, but as you gain experience you may find it a little on the slow side. The `asant` build file approach is noticeably faster than `deploytool`, but assumes you are comfortable hand-crafting the numerous deployment descriptor files required for your applications.

Running Standalone Java Examples

On those days where standalone Java programs are presented as examples, the `asant` build files should be used to run the examples. In most cases the standalone examples require packaging up as a J2EE client application in order to access J2EE functionality such as JNDI and JMS resources.

You can run each standalone example simply by specifying the Java class name (shown in the instructions) as the `asant` parameter. If any of these programs require additional command-line parameters you will be prompted for them.

Installing the Case Study Database

The Job Agency case study requires a small database for storing information about customers, jobs, applicants, and invoices. A Java program to create the database has been provided in the Day 2 exercises on the accompanying Web site. The program uses the PointBase database provided with the J2EE SDK and can easily be adapted to work with any JDBC compatible database.

Find the directory on the Web site called `CaseStudy/Day02/Exercise/src`.

Inside this directory is a Java source file that you should examine:

- `CreateAgency.java`—A program to create the `Agency` database tables

CAUTION

> To create the Agency database, you will need write permission to the J2EE SDK installation directory.

Follow the instructions shown earlier in today's lesson for starting the PointBase and J2EE servers.

To create and install the database, you will need to do the following:

1. Download all the files from the `CaseStudy` directory on the Web site to your local hard disk.

2. Start a command-line prompt window in the `CaseStudy/day02/exercise` directory on your hard drive.

3. Run the command:

   `asant database`

   This will create and populate the tables in the PointBase sample database and create a J2EE datasource resource called jdbc/Agency to access these tables from within a J2EE component. Datasources are discussed in more detail on Day 4.

Check that the `asant` build file displays the BUILD SUCCESSFUL message. You can verify the database was created correctly by looking at the last part of the `asant` output. It should look like:

```
CreateAgency:
     [echo] java -classpath D:\Sun\AppServer\pointbase\lib\pbclient.jar;
➥ D:\Sun\AppServer\pointbase\lib\pbembedded.jar;
➥ D:\Sun\AppServer\pointbase\lib\pbtools.jar CreateAgency
     [java] Loaded driver: com.pointbase.jdbc.jdbcUniversalDriver
     [java] Connected to: jdbc:pointbase:server://localhost/sun-appserv-samples,
new
```

```
[java] Dropping exisiting BMP tables...
[java] Dropped tables
[java] Creating new tables...
[java] Created tables
[java] Inserting table records...
[java] Inserted records
[java] Committed transactions
```

```
database:
```

```
BUILD SUCCESSFUL
Total time: 17 seconds
```

You can start up the Pointbase console as discussed earlier and enter the following database URL to the connection dialog:

```
jdbc:pointbase:server://localhost/sun-appserv-samples
```

Use the username pbPublic and password pbPublic to access the database. In the PointBase console open up SCHEMAS, PBPUBLIC, TABLES and you should see the Agency case study tables (such as Applicant and Customer) as shown in Figure 2.13.

FIGURE 2.13

Agency case study tables viewed from the PointBase console.

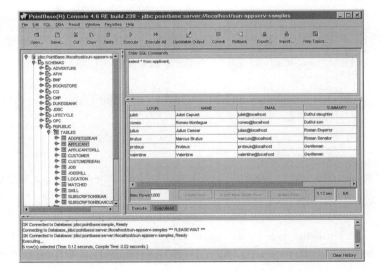

You can examine the data in the tables by executing SQL commands. Figure 2.13 shows the output from the select * from applicant; command.

You can also verify that the jdbc/Agency J2EE datasource resource was created correctly by looking at the asant output for something similar to:

```
asadmin:
    [echo] asadmin.bat create-jdbc-resource --user admin --password password --
connectionpoolid PointBasePool --enabled=true jdbc/Agency
    [exec] Command create-jdbc-resource executed successfully.

set-j2ee:

asadmin:
    [echo] asadmin.bat list-jdbc-resources --user admin --password password
    [exec] jdbc/__TimerPool
    [exec] jdbc/PointBase
    [exec] jdbc/Agency
    [exec] Command list-jdbc-resources executed successfully.
```

You can also use the Web-based Admin Console interface to graphically view the JDBC Resources as shown in Figure 2.14.

FIGURE 2.14

Agency case study jdbc/Agency data-source viewed by J2EE SDK Admin Console.

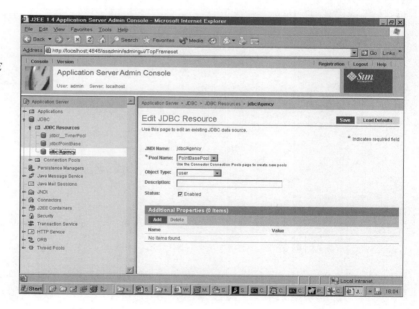

You will need to supply the admin username and password password then open the JDBC, JDBC Resources key to see the jdbc/Agency resource (as shown in Figure 2.14).

That is all you have to do for today. You will actually test the Agency database configuration on Day 4 when you learn how to create and deploy a simple EJB.

DAY 3

Naming and Directory Services

Days 1 and 2 introduced you to enterprise computing concepts and J2EE technologies such as EJBs and Servlets. This chapter will show how the Java Naming and Directory Interface (JNDI) supports the use of many of the J2EE components.

In its simplest form, JNDI is used to find the resources (such as EJBs) that you have registered via the J2EE server. Advanced use of JNDI supports sophisticated storage and retrieval of Java objects and other information.

This day's work will include

- Using Naming and Directory Services
- JNDI and X.500 names
- Obtaining a JNDI Initial Context
- Binding and looking up names
- Name attributes
- Objects and References
- JNDI events and security

Naming and Directory Services

A Naming Service provides a mechanism for giving names to objects so you can retrieve and use those objects without knowing the location of the object. Objects can be located on any machine accessible from your network, not necessarily the local workstation.

A real-world example is a phone directory. It stores telephone numbers against names and addresses. To find people's phone numbers is simply a matter of using their name (and possibly address) to identify an entry in the phone book and obtaining the stored phone number. There are a few complications, such as finding the right phone book to look in, but it is essentially a simple process.

Incidentally, naming services have a similar problem to that of finding the right phone book. This is known as obtaining a context. A name can only be found if you examine the right context (phone book).

A Directory Service also associates names with objects but provides additional information by associating attributes with the objects.

The yellow pages phone directory is a simple form of a directory service. Here, businesses often include advertisements with additional information such as a list of products sold, professional qualifications, affiliated organizations, and even maps to their premises. These attributes add value to the name entry. A directory service will normally provide the ability to find entries that have particular attributes or values for attributes. This is similar to searching the yellow pages for all plumbers running a 24-hour emergency service within a certain area.

Yellow page style phone books also store names under categories—for example, hairdressers or lawyers. Categorizing entries can simplify searching for a particular type of entry. These categorized entries are a form of sub-context within the directory context of the local phone book.

Why Use a Naming or Directory Service?

Naming Services provide an indispensable mechanism for de-coupling the provider of a service from the consumer of the service. Naming services allow a supplier of a service to register their service against a name. Users, or clients, of the service need only know the name of the service to use it.

Think of the phone book once more, and how difficult it would be to find someone's phone number without it. Obtaining your friend's phone number would mean going to their home and asking, or waiting until you meet up with them again—which may be difficult to organize because you can't phone them to arrange the meeting.

At the end of the day, it is very difficult to imagine a world without naming services.

What Is JNDI?

JNDI is a Java API that defines an interface to Naming and Directory Services for Java programs. JNDI is just an API and not, in itself, a Naming and Directory Service. To use JNDI, an implementation of a Naming and Directory service must be available. JNDI provides a service-independent interface to the underlying Service Provider implementation.

Figure 3.1 shows how the JNDI layer interfaces between the Java program and the underlying naming services. Additional naming services can be plugged into the JNDI layer by implementing the Service Provider Interface (SPI) for JNDI.

FIGURE 3.1

JNDI Architecture.

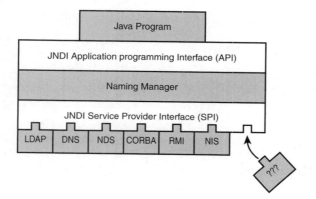

JNDI has been a standard component of J2SE since version 1.3. JNDI is available as a standard Java extension for JDK 1.2 and earlier. JNDI has always been a required component of J2EE.

Common Naming Services

Figure 3.1 shows that JNDI supports plug-in Service Providers for several well-known naming services, including the following:

- Lightweight Directory Access Protocol (LDAP) is the approved standard for an Internet naming service. LDAP is a true directory service and supports attributes as well as names for objects. LDAP is fast becoming the *de facto* directory service for the enterprise.

- Domain Name System (DNS) is the Internet naming service for identifying machines on a network.

- Novell Directory Services (NDS) from Novell provides information about network services, such as files and printers. NDS is found primarily in environments where the main networking software is Novell.
- Network Information Service (NIS) from Sun Microsystems provides system-wide information about machines, files, users, printers, and networks. NIS is primarily found on Solaris systems, but Linux and some other Unix platforms also support it.

JNDI also supports some more specialized naming systems. For example, CORBA for distributed component programming and RMI for distributed Java programming.

Although there is no named Service Provider for Windows Active Directory within JNDI, it is supported. Windows Active Directory supports an LDAP interface, and you can access it via the JNDI LDAP Service Provider Interface.

Naming Conventions

Each naming service has its own mechanism for supplying a name. Perhaps the most familiar naming convention is DNS, where every machine connected to the Internet has a unique name and address. Most readers will recognize the following as a host name used by DNS:

```
www.samspublishing.com
```

In contrast, LDAP names are based on the X.500 standard and use distinguished names that look like the following fictitious example:

```
cn=Martin Bond, ou=Authors, o=SAMS, c=us
```

This format will also be familiar to users of Microsoft's Active Directory service, whose naming system is also based on X.500 but uses a forward slash to separate the various name components:

```
cn=Martin Bond/ou=Authors/o=SAMS/c=us
```

These last two naming conventions have similarities in that they are both hierarchically structured with the more specific names (such as cn=Martin Bond) being qualified by a general name (such as o=SAMS).

JNDI applies minimal interpretation to names specified as String objects. JNDI uses the forward slash character (/) as a name separator to provide a simple name hierarchy called a Composite Name. It is conventional for these composite names to be used to group related names (such as plumbers in the phone book). As an example, JDBC data sources take names of jdbc/XXX and EJBs the form ejb/XXX. While this is only a convention, it does help separate different sorts of named objects within the JNDI name space.

Composite names can span different naming systems. An LDAP name can combine with a file system name to get a composite name:

```
cn=Martin Bond, ou=Authors, o=SAMS, c=us/agency/agency.ldif
```

Here a filename (`agency/agency.ldif`) is appended to an LDAP name. How JNDI interprets this is up to the individual Service Provider.

Incidentally, JNDI calls structured names like the DNS and LDAP names *Compound Names*. JNDI does not interpret compound names, but simply passes them through to the Service Provider.

In addition to forward slash (/), JNDI also treats backslash (\), single quote ('), and double quote (") characters as special. If a compound name or a component of a name contains any of these characters, they must be escaped using the backslash character (\). Remember that backslash and double quotes are also special characters in Java string literals and must be escaped. Therefore to insert a double quote into a JNDI name you must place \\\" into the string literal. For example the following is how to insert the name jdbc/"Agency"—avoid this if you can.

```
"jdbc/\\\"Agency\\\""
```

If the underlying Service Provider uses the forward slash as a name separator (as does the CORBA name service for example), there appears to be a conflict between JNDI and the Service Provider. In practice, this is unlikely to be a problem because JNDI recognizes two sorts of name separation—weak and strong. JNDI always passes the entire name to the Service Provider. A strong name separation implementation (such as LDAP or DNS) simply processes the first part of the composite name and returns the remainder to the JNDI Naming Manager to pass on to other name services. A weak name separation implementation will process the entire composite name. This is not something you need to worry about unless you are writing a Service Provider.

For those programmers who need to do more than use names to look up and bind objects, JNDI provides several classes for manipulating and parsing composite and compound names. The JNDI name support classes in the `javax.naming` package are `Name`, `CompositeName`, and `CompoundName`.

Using JNDI with J2EE RI

As far as this book is concerned the role of JNDI is to support access to the different components of your application. Your J2EE vendor will provide a name service that you can use with each component technology (EJBs, servlets, JSPs and application clients).

This section will concentrate on registering and using named objects within a J2EE application. Later sections will discuss using JNDI as a Java technology outside of a J2EE server.

In simple terms JNDI has two roles within a J2EE server:

1. To bind distributed objects such as EJBs, JDBC datasources, URLs, JMS resources, and so on.

2. To look up and use bound objects.

The following sections provide a simple introduction to these two roles.

Binding J2EE Components

The binding of J2EE components is done by the J2EE container either as part of the process of deploying a component or as a separate operation. You will not normally use the JNDI API to bind any objects.

Tomorrow you will look at the deployment process for registering an EJB against a JNDI name. Today you will consider the Agency case study database you created as part of yesterday's exercise (Day 2, "The J2EE Platform and Roles"). On Day 2 you used a simple Java program to define and populate the database schema. At the same time you also used the J2EE RI `asadmin` command to bind a `javax.sql.DataSource` to a JNDI name for accessing the database from within the applications you will develop in subsequent days of this book. You either used the supplied `asant` build files and entered the command

```
asant create-jdbc
```

or you entered the `asadmin` command yourself. Either way the executed command was:

```
asadmin create-jdbc-resource --connectionpoolid PointBasePool
➥ --enabled=true jdbc/Agency
```

What you did with this command was bind a `DataSource` object against the JNDI name `jdbc/Agency`.

The `asadmin` command is specific to the J2EE RI server but other J2EE servers will have similar utilities for registering JDBC datasources. The J2EE RI also provides a Web-based interface for administration as discussed on Day 2. You can verify that your `jdbc/Agency` object is bound correctly by starting up the J2EE RI server and then browsing to `http://localhost:4848/asadmin/` (MS Windows users can use the Start, Sun Microsystems, J2EE 1.4 SDK, Admin Console menu item). You will need to provide your administrative username and password, which will be `admin` and `password` if you followed the instructions on Day 2.

In the Admin Console Web Application select JDBC Resources and then jdbc/Agency in the left hand window and you will see the view shown in Figure 3.2.

FIGURE 3.2

Case Study
jdbc/Agency
DataSource.

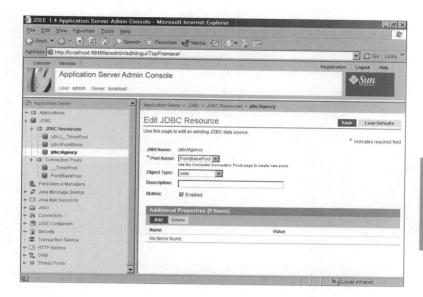

J2EE RI implements a datasource by associating it with a connection pool object, and it is this object that contains the connection information for the database. Other J2EE servers may encode the database connection information with the datasource itself.

In the J2EE RI Admin Console select the jdbc/PointBasePool entry in the left window and scroll the right window down to the Properties section at the bottom of the page as shown in Figure 3.3.

From the Connection Pool properties you can see the Connection URL for the PointBase database used for the case study tables
(jdbc:pointbase:server://localhost:9092/sun-appserv-samples) and the username and password used to access the database (pbPublic in both cases). You don't need to be aware of the details of the database connection information as this is now encapsulated behind a DataSource object.

All you have to do to use the database is know the name the datasource has been registered against, and then look up the DataSource object.

FIGURE 3.3

*J2EE RI Point Base
Pool Connection.*

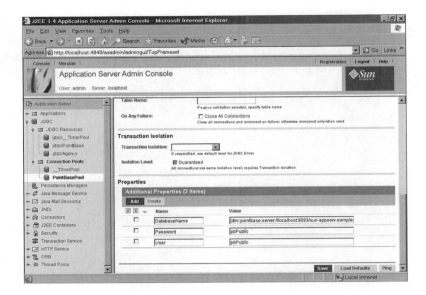

Lookup of J2EE Components

Using JNDI to look up a J2EE component is a simple two-step process:

1. Obtain a JNDI `InitialContext` object.
2. Use this context to look up the required object.

The first step in using the JNDI name service is to get a context in which to add or find names. The context that represents the entire namespace is called the `Initial Context` This `Initial Context` is represented by a class called `javax.naming.InitialContext`, which is a sub-class of the `javax.naming.Context` class.

A `Context` object represents a context that you can use to look up objects or add new objects to the namespace. You can also interrogate the context to get a list of objects bound to that context.

The following code creates a context using the default name service within the J2EE container:

```
Context ctx = new InitialContext();
```

If something goes wrong when creating the context, a `NamingException` is thrown. You are unlikely to come across problems creating the `InitialContext` within a J2EE server (other possible problems are discussed later in the section "Initial Context Naming Exceptions").

Once you have a `Context` object you can use the `lookup()` method to obtain your required component. The following code obtains the `jdbc/Agency` DataSource:

```
DataSource dataSource = (DataSource)ctx.lookup("jdbc/Agency");
```

Note that `lookup()` returns a java.lang.Object and this must be cast into a `javax.sql.DataSource`.

There are two common problems at this stage:

- You mistyped the name, or the object isn't bound to the name service, in which case a `javax.naming.NameNotFound` exception is thrown.

- The object you retrieved was not what you expected and a `ClassCastException` will be thrown.

That's it. You can now use the `DataSource` to access the database. Listing 3.1 shows a simple application that will list the contents of the database tables passed as command line parameters.

LISTING 3.1   Full Text of `AgencyTable.java`

```
import javax.naming.* ;
import java.sql.*;
import javax.sql.*;

public class AgencyTable
{
    public static void main(String args[]) {
        try {
            AgencyTable at = new AgencyTable();
            for (int i=0; i<args.length; i++)
                at.printTable(args[i]);
        }
        catch (NamingException ex) {
            System.out.println ("Error connecting to jdbc/Agency: "+ex);
        }
         catch (SQLException ex) {
            System.out.println ("Error getting table rows: "+ex);
        }
    }

    private DataSource dataSource;

    public AgencyTable () throws NamingException {
        InitialContext ic = new InitialContext();
        dataSource = (DataSource)ic.lookup("jdbc/Agency");
    }
```

3

LISTING 3.1   continued

```java
public void printTable(String table) throws SQLException {
    Connection con = null;
    PreparedStatement stmt = null;
    ResultSet rs = null;
    try {
        con = dataSource.getConnection();
        stmt = con.prepareStatement("SELECT * FROM "+table);

        rs = stmt.executeQuery();
        ResultSetMetaData rsmd = rs.getMetaData();
        int numCols = rsmd.getColumnCount();

        // get column header info
        for (int i=1; i <= numCols; i++) {
            System.out.print (rsmd.getColumnLabel(i));
            if (i > 1)
                System.out.print (',');
        }
        System.out.println ();

        while (rs.next()) {
            for (int i=1; i <= numCols; i++) {
                System.out.print (rs.getString(i));
                if (i > 1)
                    System.out.print (',');
            }
            System.out.println ();
        }
    }
    finally {
        try {rs.close();} catch (Exception ex) {}
        try {stmt.close();} catch (Exception ex) {}
        try {con.close();} catch (Exception ex) {}
    }
}
}
```

Before you can run this example you must have started the J2EE RI default domain and be running the PointBase database server as discussed on Day 2.

Run this application using the supplied asant build files entering the following command from within the Day03/examples directory:

asant AgencyTable

You will be prompted to provide a space-separated list of tables to examine; choose any of the tables shown in yesterdays ERD (such as Applicant, Customer, Location).

NOTE

You must use the supplied asant build files to run today's examples. The name service provided with the J2EE RI must be used by a J2EE component such as a Client Application and cannot be used by a normal command line program. The asant build files wrap up the program as a J2EE Application Client and set up the correct CLASSPATH before running the program. Application Clients are discussed in detail tomorrow and in the section "Using JNDI Functionality" later today.

Hopefully you can see the benefits of using both JNDI and DataSource objects within your enterprise application. Compare the code in Listing 3.1 with the code used to connect to the database in CreateAgency.java program used yesterday (Day02/exercise/src/CreateAgency.java), shown in the following excerpt:

```
Class.forName("com.pointbase.jdbc.jdbcUniversalDriver");
Connection con = DriverManager.getConnection(
                "jdbc:pointbase:server://localhost/sun-appserv-samples,new",
                "pbPublic","pbPublic");
```

In this excerpt the database details are hard coded into the application making it awkward to migrate the application to a new database. If you look at the code for the CreateAgency.java program on the Web site, you will see commented out definitions for the database connection details for the Cloudscape database that was shipped with J2EE RI 1.3. The example in Listing 3.1 has not changed between J2EE RI 1.3 and J2EE RI 1.4 despite the change of database provider.

Other Distributed J2EE Components

Throughout many of the days of this course you will use JNDI to look up many different types of objects:

- EJBs—on most days from 4 through to 14
- The javax.transaction.UserTransaction object on Day 8, "Transactions and Persistence"
- JMS resources on Day 9, "Java Message Service" and Day 10, "Message-Driven Beans"
- Resource Adapters and RMI-IIOP servants on Day 19, "Integrating with External Resources"

For each of these objects, except EJBs, you will use the J2EE RI asadmin command to define the required resources. For EJBs you will use the deploytool application (discussed tomorrow) to define the JNDI name as part of the deployment process for the EJB.

There is one minor twist to using EJBs and RMI-IIOP objects with JNDI and this is the type of object that is stored in the name service.

EJBs use RMI-IIOP and when a JNDI lookup is used to obtain an EJB (or any RMI-IIOP object) you obtain an RMI-IIOP remote object stub and not the actual object you expect. You must downcast the CORBA object into the actual object you require using the `PortableRemoteObject.narrow()` method.

Looking ahead momentarily to tomorrow's work on EJBs, the following code fragment shows how to look up an EJB:

```
InitialContext ctx = new InitialContext();
Object lookup = ctx.lookup("ejb/Agency");
AgencyHome home = (AgencyHome)PortableRemoteObject.narrow(
                      lookup, AgencyHome.class);
```

In this case the EJB is bound against the name `ejb/Agency` and is of type `agency.AgencyHome`. This example has been slightly simplified from the real code which is shown in the next section, "J2EE Java Component Environment."

The `narrow()` method takes as parameters the RMI-IIOP remote stub object and the `Class` object representing the target class for the downcast. This method will throw a `ClassCastException` if the remote stub does not represent the correct class.

J2EE Java Component Environment

One extra issue concerning J2EE components that should be considered now, while you are looking at JNDI within the J2EE server framework, is that of the Java Component Environment.

To explain this concept consider the case where two developers independently design and develop EJBs both of whom use the name `jdbc/Database` as the name of the `DataSource` object used to access the database. An application assembler wants to use both EJBs in a single application but each EJB was designed to use a different database schema. Such a situation may arise if the assembler is "buying in" EJBs developed by external organizations.

The Java Component Environment is designed to resolve the possibility of JNDI resource name conflicts by providing each component with its own private namespace. Every J2EE component has a context within its namespace called `java:comp/env` that is used to store references to resources required by that component. The component's deployment descriptor defines the resources referenced by the component that will need to be defined within the Java Component Environment.

Resources that can be referenced by a J2EE component include:

- Enterprise JavaBeans—discussed primarily on Day 5, "Session EJBs," and Day 6, "Entity EJBs."
- Environment Entries—discussed on Day 5.
- Message Destination References—discussed on Day 10.
- Resource References—discussed today (`DataSource`) and on Day 10 (`ConnectionFactory`).
- Web Service References—discussed on Day 20, "Using RPC-Style Web Services with J2EE."

Returning to the example from the previous section, where the sample code for an EJB lookup was shown without the complication of the Java Component Environment, the actual EJB lookup code is

```
InitialContext ctx = new InitialContext();
Object lookup = ctx.lookup("java:comp/env/ejb/Agency");
AgencyHome home = (AgencyHome)PortableRemoteObject.narrow(
                      lookup, AgencyHome.class);
```

The `ejb/Agency` name is defined as an EJB Reference within the Java Component Environment. As part of the deployment process the EJB Reference will be mapped onto the actual JNDI name used by the EJB (if you are a little lost at this point, don't worry, all will be made clear on Days 4 and 5).

Using JNDI Outside J2EE

JNDI is a required technology for J2SE so you do not need to have a full blown J2EE server in order to use JNDI. In fact if you do any work with RMI-IIOP (CORBA) you will be using JNDI to bind and look up the RMI server objects. This is discussed in detail on Day 19. You may also find yourself using JNDI to access an LDAP service, or Microsoft's Active Directory service through its LDAP interface.

If you are working outside of the J2EE environment there are two obvious questions that need answering:

1. How do I define which type of name service I'm using (CORBA, LDAP, something else)?
2. How do I define the host name and port number of the server on my network?

The supplementary question is then:

- What happens if I don't define the JNDI service correctly?

The following sections discuss the answers to these questions.

3

Defining the JNDI Service

The parameters that you usually need to define for a JNDI service are as follows:

- The Name Service provider classname
- The Name Service host name
- The Name Service port number

A particular server vendor's implementation may require additional parameters.

There are several ways of defining the JNDI service properties for a program, but you only need to use one of them. You can

- Add the properties to the JNDI properties file in the Java runtime home directory
- Provide an application resource file for the program
- Specify command-line parameters to be passed to an application
- Hard-code the parameters into the program

The last option is considered poor practice because it obviously restricts the program to working with one type of JNDI service provider on one specific host.

The first two options are the most suited to production environments. They both require that you distribute simple text configuration files with the program.

JNDI Properties Files

An application resource file called `jndi.properties` defines the JNDI service. The JNDI system automatically reads the application resource files from any location in the program's CLASSPATH and from `lib/jndi.properties` in the Java runtime home directory (this is the `jre` sub-directory of the Java JDK home directory).

The following example shows the `jndi.properties` file for working with the CORBA name service supplied with the J2SE (discussed on Day 19):

```
java.naming.factory.initial=com.sun.jndi.cosnaming.CNCtxFactory
java.naming.provider.url=iiop://localhost:1050
```

Each entry in the property file defines a name value pair. The `InitialContext` object uses these properties to determine the JNDI service provider.

The service provider usually supplies a sample `jndi.properties` file defining the properties that need to be configured with their server. Often the `jndi.properties` file is a component of the JAR files you include in your application's CLASSPATH.

Normally, any given JNDI service will require the following named properties:

```
java.naming.factory.initial
```

You set this property to the classname (including the package) of the Initial Context Factory for the JNDI Service Provider. This value effectively defines which JNDI Service Provider you will use. The classes for the service provider must be included in the CLASSPATH for your application.

```
java.naming.provider.url
```

This defines the URI of the machine running the JNDI service. Often this value omits the protocol prefix and simply defines the hostname and port number. This is the only property that the network administrator needs to customize.

More information on these and other JNDI properties can be found in the API documentation for the Context class and in the JNDI Tutorial from Sun Microsystems.

The simplest way to define the JNDI Service Provider is to configure every client's Java home directory to include the necessary JNDI properties. This approach suits an intranet where all machines are centrally managed.

Another approach is to include a suitable JNDI properties file with the client program and distribute everything as a JAR file (program class files and the jndi.properties file). This suits Web-based intranets or extranets, where applets are used or where you can distribute the client JAR file to users.

Application Properties

Using the -D option, you can supply the JNDI properties on the java command line of an application. This has the disadvantage of requiring long command lines that are hard to remember and easy to mistype. A way around this problem is for you to provide script files to run the application on the target platforms; typically, you might supply Apache Ant build scripts, batch files for Windows, or shell scripts for Linux and Solaris.

The following is an example of a command line that defines the CORBA Name Service factory classes and server:

```
Java -Djava.naming.factory.initial=com.sun.jndi.cosnaming.CNCtxFactory
  ➥ -Djava.naming.provider.url=iiop://localhost:1050 MyClass
```

Providing a jndi.properties file in the application JAR file is a cleaner solution than providing command-line parameters. However, using command-line parameters makes the JNDI properties more apparent when customizing the application for a local site. It is easy to overlook a jndi.properties file in a JAR file.

Hard-Coded Properties

The least desirable way to specify the JNDI properties is via hard-coded values in the program. Hard coding the properties means including the JNDI class names and the server URI in the source code. This is undesirable because should the network architecture change, you must edit, recompile, and redistribute the program. Obviously, you will want to avoid this type of maintenance overhead if you can. The network architecture may change if the JNDI service moves to a different server or you install a new JNDI Service Provider.

The mechanism for defining the service in code is via a hash table of properties passed into the InitialContext constructor:

```
Hashtable env = new Hashtable();
env.put(Context.INITIAL_CONTEXT_FACTORY,
  "com.sun.jndi.cosnaming.CNCtxFactory");
env.put(Context. PROVIDER_URL,  " iiop://localhost:1050");
Context ctx = new InitialContext(env);
```

Notice how the code uses symbolic constants from the Context class rather than using strings representing the properties (such as "java.naming.factory.initial"). This approach makes the code more portable should the property names change in future versions of Java or JNDI.

Having made your decision about how to define the JNDI properties you may still make mistakes, such as not setting the CLASSPATH correctly. The next section takes a quick look at the symptoms of common mistakes made when using JNDI.

Initial Context Naming Exceptions

The exceptions most likely to occur when creating the JNDI InitialContext object are as follows:

```
javax.naming.CommunicationException: Can't find SerialContextProvider
```

This exception usually means the JNDI Server is not running, or possibly the JNDI properties for the server are incorrect.

```
javax.naming.NoInitialContextException:
➡ Need to specify class name in environment or system property,
➡ or as an applet parameter, or in an application resource file:
➡ java.naming.factory.initial
```

This exception occurs when the InitialContext class does not have default properties for the JNDI Service Provider, and the JNDI server properties have not been configured explicitly.

```
javax.naming.NoInitialContextException: Cannot instantiate class: XXX
  [Root exception is java.lang.ClassNotFoundException: XXX]
```

This exception occurs when the class path defined for the JNDI program does not include the JNDI server classes.

```
javax.naming.ServiceUnavailableException:
➡ Connection refused: no further information
[Root exception is java.net.ConnectException:
➡ Connection refused: no further information]
```

This exception occurs when the JNDI properties for the program fail to match the JNDI Service Provider currently in use.

Using JNDI Functionality

You have already seen the most common use of JNDI within the J2EE environment and that is the lookup of objects, usually J2EE components. JNDI can also be used to:

- Bind objects to the name service
- List objects in a context
- Create and delete contexts

These features are briefly discussed in the following sections.

CAUTION

> One word of warning about the security features discussed: Some Name Services (such as LDAP) may use security features to ensure that only authorized programs can change the object bindings or contexts. On a live system, the program must supply valid user credentials when obtaining the initial context (see the "Security" section later in this lesson). If you attempt to modify an existing name or bind a new name without the requisite permissions, a `javax.naming.NoPermissionException` is thrown. The "Security" section of today's lesson covers this in more detail.

Binding and Renaming Objects

Binding an object means adding a name to the Name Service and associating that name with a Java object. The name and object are bound to a context using the `Context.bind()` method. The object to be bound must implement the `Serializable` interface so that the name server can store a copy of the object.

NOTE

> There is a way of binding objects that does not require the class to implement the `Serializable` interface. A class can implement the `javax.naming.Referenceable` interface instead; this is quite specialized and outside the scope of this chapter (this interface is described in the JNDI Tutorial from Sun Microsystems, see `http://java.sun.com/products/jndi/tutorial/`).

The following code fragment taken from Day 19 shows how to bind an RMI-IIOP server (HelloUserImpl) against the name HelloUser:

```
HelloUserImpl hui = new HelloUserImpl();
Context ctx = new InitialContext();
ctx.rbind("HelloUser",hui);
```

If an object is already bound to that name, the Context.bind() method will fail with a NameAlreadyBoundException (which extends NamingException). The method Context.rebind() will unbind any currently bound object before binding the new object.

A Service Provider may not support binding of all types of objects. If the service cannot bind a particular object, it will throw an exception. An exception is also thrown if an invalid name is used. Remember that different Service Providers may have different naming conventions.

An object can be unbound using Context.unbind(), for example:

```
Context ctx = new InitialContext();
ctx.unbind("HelloUser",hui);
```

You can rename objects using Context.rename() by specifying the old name and then the new name as parameters.

```
ic.rename("HelloUser","SayHello");
```

The new name must specify a name in the same context as the old name. An object must be bound to the old name, and the new name must not have a bound object or else a NamingException is thrown.

Changing Contexts

So far you have used the default context returned by the InitalContext constructor. Often you can simplify name look up or improve performance by changing contexts.

J2EE components may find it convenient to change contexts to the Java Component Environment before looking up DataSource objects or EJB references.

Use the Context.lookup() method to look up a sub-context and then use the return Context object for future lookups. For example:

```
Context ic = new InitialContext();
Context ctx = (Context)ic.lookup("java:comp/env");
DataSource ds = (DataSource)ctx.lookup("jdbc/Agency");
```

This is particularly useful if you are doing multiple lookups within one context. The idea is much the same as changing directories in a file system when working within the same directory structure.

Listing Contexts

The namespace represents contexts as names, and you can look these up just like any other name. You can obtain a listing of the names in a context by using `Context.list()`. This method provides a list of name and class bindings as a `javax.naming.NamingEnumeration`, where each element in the enumeration is a `javax.naming.NameClassPair` object. Listing 3.2 shows a simple program to list the names and classes for the example sams sub context.

LISTING 3.2   Full Text of JNDIList.java

```java
import javax.naming.*;

public class JNDIList
{
  public static void main(String[] args)
  {
    try {
      Context ctx = new InitialContext();
      if (args.length == 0) {
        listContext (ctx,"");
      }
      else {
        for (int i=0; i<args.length; i++)
          listContext (ctx,args[i]);
      }
    }
    catch (NamingException ex) {
      ex.printStackTrace();
      System.exit(1);
    }
  }

  public static void listContext (Context ctx, String subctx)
    throws NamingException
  {
    System.out.println("Listing Context: "+subctx);
    NamingEnumeration list = ctx.list(subctx);
    while (list.hasMore())
    {
      NameClassPair item = (NameClassPair)list.next();
      String cl = item.getClassName();
      String name = item.getName();
      System.out.println(cl+" - "+name);
    }
  }
}
```

3

The parameter to the list() method defines the name of the context to list. If this is the empty string, the method lists the current context.

Use the command

```
asant JNDList
```

to run this example program and enter a context, or list of contexts, when prompted. Initially just press return to get a listing of the default context, then try the jdbc context to see the entry for the jdbc/Agency DataSource you used earlier.

The Context.list() method returns the name and the bound object's classname, but not the object itself. It is a lightweight interface designed for browsing the namespace.

A second method, called Context.listBindings(), retrieves the object name, class name, as well as the object itself. This method invokes the extra run time cost of retrieving the object from the name. The listBindings() method also returns a NamingEnumeration, but this time each element is of type javax.naming.Binding. Access methods in the Binding class support retrieval of the information of the bound object.

Listing 3.3 shows a simple recursive tree-walking program that is a useful diagnostic tool for examining JNDI namespaces.

LISTING 3.3 Full Text of JNDITree.java

```java
import javax.naming.*;
public class JNDITree
{
  public static void main(String[] args) {
    Context ctx=null;
    try {
      ctx = new InitialContext();
      listContext (ctx,"");
    }
    catch (NamingException ex) {
      System.err.println (ex);
      System.exit(1);
    }
  }

  private static void listContext (Context ctx, String indent) {
    try {
      NamingEnumeration list = ctx.listBindings("");
      while (list.hasMore()) {
        Binding item = (Binding)list.next();
        String className = item.getClassName();
        String name = item.getName();
```

LISTING 3.3 continued

```
          System.out.println(indent+className+" "+name);
          Object o = item.getObject();
          if (o instanceof javax.naming.Context)
            listContext ((Context)o,indent+" ");
        }
      }
      catch (NamingException ex) {
        System.err.println ("List error: "+ex);
      }
    }
  }
```

Creating and Destroying Contexts

Binding a composite name will automatically create any intermediate sub-contexts required to bind the name. Binding the name such as

```
Day03/examples/jdbc/Agency
```

creates the following sub-contexts if they don't already exist:

```
Day03
Day03/examples
Day03/examples/jdbc
```

you can explicitly create contexts with the `Context.createSubcontext()` method. The single method parameter is the name of the context. If this is a composite name, all intermediate contexts must already exist. The `createSubContext()` method will throw a `NameAlreadyBoundException` if the name already exists.

The `Context.destroySubcontext()` method can destroy contexts. Again, the single method parameter is the name of the context. The context does not have to be empty, because the method will remove from the namespace any bound names and sub-contexts with the destroyed context.

The `destroyContext()` method can throw a `NameNotFoundException` if the name doesn't exist and a `NotContextException` if the bound name is not a context.

Working with Multiple Name Services

You can specify a URL as a parameter to the `Context` `lookup()` and `bind()` methods. For example,

```
Context ic = new InitialContext();
Object obj = ic.lookup("ldap://localhost:389/cn=Winston,dc=my-domain,dc=com");
```

3

This overrides the default context and forces JNDI to perform the lookup against the specified server. You need to take care with this approach, because the CLASSPATH must contain the necessary Service Provider classes, and these must be able to process the request bind or lookup operation. In practice, this means that the URL must use the same Service Provider classes as the initial context.

JNDI Events

JNDI supports an event model similar to the event listeners in the Java AWT and Swing classes. However, the underlying JNDI Service Provider must also provide support for the event model for a client to register event handlers.

The javax.naming.event package supports two types of JNDI event listener (both are sub-classes of NamingListener):

- NamespaceChangeListener reports on changes to the namespace objects that are added, removed, or renamed.
- ObjectChangeListener reports on changes to an object when its binding is replaced (the object has been updated) or attributes are added, removed, or replaced.

Both interfaces define appropriate methods that are called when changes occur in the JNDI namespace. A javax.naming.event.NamingEvent object is passed to the listener method to define:

- The type of event (for example, name added or object changed)
- The name binding before the event occurred
- The name binding after the event occurred

JNDI event handling provides an effective means for monitoring changes to a namespace to maintain up-to-date information about the registered objects.

Directory Services

As discussed at the start of today's work a Directory Service is a Name Service with the ability to categorize names to support complex searches of the name space. The JNDI support for a Directory Service is differentiated from a Name Service by storing attributes as well as an object against a bound name. Typically you will probably use LDAP as your Directory Service, but NDS (Novell Directory Services) is also a Directory Service. The simple name services provided with J2SE (CORBA) and J2EE are not directory services.

An attribute is additional information stored with a name. Storing full name, address, phone number, and email with a person's name is a common use of a directory service.

NDS uses attributes to control access to shared network drives and to configure a user's login environment.

A directory service stores attributes as values against a keyword (LDAP calls them IDs). Directory services usually support searching for names (objects) that have certain attributes defined (or not defined). Searching often supports looking for names with attributes that have a specific value (often wildcard pattern matching is supported). A simple search of a personnel database under an LDAP server might, for example, find all entries with the surname Washington.

LDAP uses a schema system to control which attributes an object must define and those that it may optionally define. Any attributes that you add or delete must not break the schema's requirements. LDAP servers may be able to disable schema checking, but disabling schema checking is usually a bad idea because the schema was created for a purpose.

If you want to see the capabilities of attributes, you must have access to a directory server. The rest of this section shows how to use an LDAP Directory Server.

Using LDAP

Using an LDAP Directory Service requires you to set the JNDI properties to specify the JNDI Service provider from Sun Microsystems and, of course, you must have an LDAP server running.

The J2EE RI does not include an LDAP server, so if you wish to work through this section, and you do not already have an LDAP server, you will have to obtain one from elsewhere. Only certain operating systems provide LDAP servers. Windows NT, 2000, and XP users will have to purchase the enterprise (or server) editions of these operating systems, which are typically significantly more expensive than the usual desktop or professional editions. Sun Microsystems' Solaris 8 Operating Environment includes an LDAP server.

Linux (and Solaris) users can download and install the OpenLDAP implementation, which is an open source server available free of charge for personal use. The Open LDAP server can be downloaded from
`http://www.openldap.org/software/download/`.

Users of Microsoft Windows will have to make other arrangements as OpenLDAP is not available for this platform. If an Active Directory server (which supports an LDAP interface) is accessible on the network or you use the Enterprise (or Server) edition of the Operating System, you are ok. Otherwise, your best solution is to install Linux and OpenLDAP on a spare PC.

To use an LDAP server simply create a `jndi.properties` file with the following entries:

```
java.naming.factory.initial=com.sun.jndi.ldap.LdapCtxFactory
java.naming.provider.url=ldap://localhost:389
```

If the LDAP server is not running on the current machine, replace the name `localhost` with the name or IP address of the actual LDAP server. Port number 389 is the default LDAP port number, and you can omit it if LDAP is running on the default port (or replace it by the actual port number if a non-standard port is being used).

LDAP names conform to the X.500 standard that requires a hierarchical namespace. A Distinguished Name (DN) unambiguously identifies each entry in the directory. The DN consists of the concatenation of the names from the root of the directory tree down to the specific entry.

A sample LDAP DN looks like the following:

```
cn=Martin Bond, ou=Authors, o=SAMS, c=us
```

This will be a familiar structure if you have worked with digital certificates or Active Directory.

Using a Directory Service

Directory Services cannot be accessed through the ordinary `Context` object. Instead, you must use a `javax.naming.directory.DirContext` class. The `DirContext` is a sub-class of `Context`, and you can use it in place of a `Context` when dealing with a Directory Service where you require directory functionality (such as attributes). For example,

```
DirContext ic = new InitialDirContext();
```

The `DirContext` class supports the same `lookup()`, `bind()`, `rebind()`, `list()` and other operations of the `Context` class. Additionally the `DirContext` provides support for attributes.

Attributes are read from the context just like you would look up a name from the context. The `DirContext.getAttributes()` method returns a `NamingEnumeration` that contains a collection of `Attribute` objects. Each `Attribute` has an ID (or key) and a list of values (an attribute can have more than one value for the same key). The following example prints all the attributes for a name specified by `args[0]`:

```
DirContext ctx = new InitialDirContext();
Attributes attrs = ctx.getAttributes(args[0]);
NamingEnumeration ae = attrs.getAll();
while (ae.hasMore()) {
  Attribute attr = (Attribute)ae.next();
  System.out.println(" attribute: " + attr.getID());
```

```
    NamingEnumeration e = attr.getAll();
    while (e.hasMore())
      System.out.println("  value: " + e.next());
}
```

A second form of the getAttributes() method allows you to provide an array of attribute names, and it only returns the values for those attributes. It is not an error to query an attribute that isn't defined; a value is simply not returned for that attribute. The following fragment shows how to find the email and cellphone attributes for a name:

```
String[] IDs = {"email", "cellphone"};
Attributes attrs = ctx.getAttributes("cn=Martin Bond, ou=Authors, o=SAMS, c=us",
                                     IDs);
```

Overloaded versions of the bind() and rebind() methods in the DirContext class take a third Attributes parameter for binding a name. The following example could bind a new entry LDAP entry for cn=Martin Bond (the details of the Person object have been omitted for clarity and the email address has not been defined for privacy):

```
Person martin = …;
Attributes attrs = new BasicAttributes();
attrs.put(new BasicAttribute("email","…"));
attrs.put(new BasicAttribute("description","author"));
ctx.bind("cn=Martin Bond, ou=Authors, o=SAMS, c=us", martin, attrs);
```

As a final point, the DirContext.ModifyAttributes() method supports the addition, modification, and deletion of attributes for a name.

Searching a Directory Service

A powerful and useful feature of attributes is the ability to search for names that have specific attributes or names that have attributes of a particular value.

You use the DirContext.search() method to search for names. There are several over-loaded forms of this method, all of which require a DN to define the context in the name tree where the search should begin. The simplest form of search() takes a second parameter that is an Attributes object that contains a list of attributes to find. Each attribute can be just the name, or the name and a value for that attribute.

The following code excerpt shows how to find all names that have an email attribute and a description attribute with the value author in the o=SAMS name space.

```
DirContext ctx = new InitialDirContext();
Attributes match = new BasicAttributes(true);
match.put(new BasicAttribute("email"));
match.put(new BasicAttribute("description","author"));
```

```
NamingEnumeration enum = ctx.search("o=SAMS", match);
while (enum.hasMore()) {
  SearchResult res = (SearchResult)enum.next();
  System.out.println(res.getName()+", o=SAMS");
}
```

The search() method returns a NamingEnumeration containing objects of class
SearchResult (a sub-class of NameClassPair discussed earlier). The SearchResult
encapsulates information about the names found. The example code excerpt simply
prints out the names (the names in the SearchResult object are relative to the context
that was searched).

The SearchResult class also has a getAttributes() method that returns all the attributes for the found name. A second form of the search() method takes a third parameter
that is an array of String objects specifying the attributes for the method to return. The
following code fragment shows how to search and return just the email and cellphone
name attributes:

```
Attributes match = new BasicAttributes(true);
match.put(new BasicAttribute("email"));
match.put(new BasicAttribute("description","author"));
String[] getAttrs = {"email","cellphone"}
NamingEnumeration enum = ctx.search("o=SAMS", match, getAttrs);
```

Yet another form of the search() method takes a String parameter and a
SearchControls parameter to define a search filter.

The filter String uses a simple prefix notation for combining attributes and values.

You can use the javax.naming.directory.SearchControls argument required by
search() to

- Specify which attributes the method returns (the default is all attributes)
- Define the scope of the search, such as the depth of tree to search down
- Limit the results to a maximum number of names
- Limit the amount of time for the search

The following example searches for a description of author and an email address ending with sams.com with no search controls:

```
String filter ="(|(description=author)(email=*sams.com))";
NamingEnumeration enum = ctx.search("o=SAMS", filter, null);
```

The JNDI API documentation and the JNDI Tutorial from Sun Microsystems provide full
details of the search filter syntax.

JNDI Security

JNDI security depends on the underlying Service Provider. Simple services, such as the transient CORBA name service supplied with J2SE, do not support security. These services allow any client to perform any operation.

In a production environment, security is paramount to ensuring the integrity of the data in the JNDI server. Many organizations will use LDAP to provide a naming service that supports security.

LDAP security is based on three categories:

- Anonymous—No security information is provided.
- Simple—The client provides a clear text name and password.
- Simple Authentication and Security Layer (SASL)—The client and server negotiate an authentication system based on a challenge and response protocol that conforms to RFC2222.

If the client does not supply any security information (as in all the examples shown today), the client is treated as an anonymous client.

The following JNDI properties provide security information:

- `java.naming.security.authentication` is set to a `String` to define the authentication mechanism used (one of `none`, `simple`, or the name of an SASL authentication system supported by the LDAP server).
- `java.naming.security.principal` is set to the fully qualified domain name of the client to authenticate.
- `java.naming.security.credentials` is a password or encrypted data (such as a digital certificate) that the implementation uses to authenticate the client.

If you do not define any of these properties, the implementation uses anonymous (`java.naming.security.authentication=none`) authentication.

It is possible to use a JNDI properties file to supply client authentication information, but more usually you code this information within the client program. Typically, your application will obtain the client authentication dynamically.

If you use SASL (not `simple` or `anonymous`) authentication, the `java.naming.security.authentication` value can consist of a space-separated list of authentication mechanisms. Depending on the LDAP service provider, JNDI can support the following authentication schemes:

- External—Allows JNDI to use any authentication system. The client must define a callback mechanism for JNDI to hook into the client's authentication mechanism.
- GSSAPI (Kerberos v5)—A well-known, token-based security mechanism.
- Digest MD5—Uses the Java Cryptography Extension (JCE) to support client authentication using the MD5 encryption algorithm.

The Day 15, "Security," chapter discuses the topic of J2EE and JNDI security in more detail.

Summary

JNDI provides a uniform API to an underlying naming or directory service. A Naming Service provides a means of storing simple information against a name so the information can be retrieved using the name as a key. A Directory Service stores additional attribute information against a name. Directory Services use attributes to categorize names so that powerful searching of the directory tree structure can be supported.

JNDI supports any naming service provided a Service Provider implementation is available for that service. Standard services supported by JNDI include the following:

- Lightweight Directory Access Protocol (LDAP)
- Novell Directory Services (NDS)
- CORBA
- Active Directory is supported via its LDAP interface

Using JNDI from within a Java program is a simple matter of creating a context and looking up names within that context. The Context class supports naming services, and the DirContext class supports directory services.

After a context has been defined, the lookup() method is used to retrieve the object stored against a name. The bind() and rebind() methods are used to add or changes bound objects, and the unbind() method is used to remove a bound object.

Within J2EE, JNDI is used to advertise components such as the following:

- EJBs
- Datasources (databases)
- Resource adapters
- JMS message queues and topics

Q&A

Q Why is a Name Service so important?

A Without JNDI, it would be a lot harder to provide services such as those implemented using J2EE objects like datasources, message queues, and EJBs. Each vendor would choose their own mechanism for defining how a client program should gain access to the J2EE objects. Some might do this by distributing configuration files, others by using TCP/IP broadcast network packets. Using a Name Service provides a consistent means of providing network services in a portable and platform-independent manner. Not only that, you can move an implementation of a service from one machine to another. In this instance, the server simply updates the Name Service entry to reflect its new location, and the whole process is transparent to the client.

Q Why is JNDI so large? Surely all I need to do is map a name onto a Java object?

A If all you want to do is support J2EE objects, JNDI could be as simple as a name-to-object mapping service. But Sun Microsystems designed JNDI to interoperate with established Directory Services, such as NDS, LDAP, and DNS. By providing Java programming support for these services, the designers of JNDI have ensured it will not be used as a proprietary product with J2EE servers, but as a general interface to fully functional directory services. This design philosophy also provides programmers with a mechanism for developing interfaces to NDS and LDAP in Java rather than some other language, such as C++ or C#.

Exercise

Today the JNDITree.java program in Listing 3.3 has shown you how to display a JNDI namespace. Today's exercise is to write a GUI version of this program using the Swing JTree class. If you already know Swing, you can use JNDITree.java as a guide for your program and go ahead and write your own JNDI browser.

If you do not know Swing, the exercise directory for Day 3 on the accompanying Web site includes a template program called JNDIBrowser.java for you to enhance. The JNDIBrowser program handles all of the Swing initialization, all you have to do is get a list of the names in the JNDI namespace and create a new javax.swing.tree.DefaultMutableTreeNode representing each name and add this to the JTree. When you add a name that is also a context, you need to add all the names in the sub-context.

Comments have been added to the JNDIBrowser.java file to show you where to add your code.

Don't worry if this sounds complex—it isn't. You only have to write about 12 lines of code (most of which you can adapt from JNDITree.java).

Before you rush off and write your first piece of Java code for this book, please review the general discussion of the example code directory structure and Ant build files given on Day 2, "The J2EE Platform and Roles."

You can use the Ant build files supplied in the exercise and solution subdirectories of the Day 3 code on the Web site to compile and run your programs. Enter

```
asant run
```

to compile and run the program.

Optional Exercise—Display Names in Alphabetical Order

If you complete this exercise or simply run the provided solution, you will see that the JNDI names are listed in the order they were added to the context. As a second exercise, change your program to display the names in alphabetical order. The solution called JNDIBrowserSort.java program shows how this can be achieved using the java.util.TreeMap class.

You might find these programs useful for browsing the JNDI namespace while you are developing J2EE applications.

DAY 4

Introduction to Enterprise JavaBeans

J2EE provides different types of components for different purposes. Today, you will start to look at one of the principal types of component in J2EE—Enterprise JavaBeans (EJBs).

The study of EJBs is continued on Day 5, "Session EJBs," Day 6, "Entity EJBs," Day 7, "Container-Managed Persistence and EJB Query Language," Day 8, "Transactions and Persistence," and Day 10, "Message-Driven Beans." As you can see, there is a lot to learn about EJBs, so today serves as a first step on the road to all of this EJB knowledge.

Today, you will

- Examine the different types of EJB available
- See how EJBs are applied
- Explore the structure of one of the EJBs that forms part of the case study to see how the different parts fit together

- Deploy and use some of the EJBs from the case study
- Write a simple client for an EJB

First, you need to understand what EJBs are and why you would use them.

What Is an EJB?

In a typical J2EE application, Enterprise JavaBeans (EJBs) contain the application's business logic and live business data. Although it is possible to use standard Java objects to contain your business logic and business data, using EJBs addresses many of the issues of using simple Java objects, such as scalability, lifecycle management, and state management.

Beans, Clients, Containers, and Servers

An EJB is essentially a managed middleware component that is created, controlled, and destroyed by the J2EE container in which it lives. This control allows the container to manage the number of EJBs currently in existence and the resources they are using, such as memory and database connections.

Each container will maintain a pool of reusable EJB instances that are ready to be assigned to a client. When a client no longer needs an EJB, the EJB instance will be returned to the pool and all of its resources will be released. This pooling and recycling of EJB instances means that a few EJB instances, and the resources they use, can be shared between many clients. This maximizes the scalability of the EJB-based application. The EJB lifecycle is discussed further on Days 5 and 6.

The client that uses the EJB instance does not need to know about all of the work done on its behalf by the container. As far as the client is concerned, it is talking to a remote component that supports defined business methods. How those methods are implemented and any magic performed by the container, such as just-in-time instantiation of that specific component instance, are entirely transparent to the client part of the application.

To benefit from certain services provided by the container, such as automatic security, automatic transactions, lifecycle management, and so on, an EJB is packaged with a deployment descriptor (DD) that indicates the component's requirements for services, such as transaction management and security authorization. The container will then use this information to perform authentication and transaction demarcation on behalf of the component—the component does not contain code to perform these tasks.

Types of EJB

In most texts on this subject you will see pictures of a 3-tier system containing boxes labeled "EJB." It is actually more important to identify what application functionality that should go into an EJB.

At the start of application development, regardless of the precise development process used there is generally some analysis that delivers a model, or set of classes and packages, that represent single or grouped business concepts.

Two types of functionality are generally discovered during analysis—data manipulation and business process flow. The application model will usually contain data-based classes such as Customer or Product. These classes will be manipulated by other classes or roles that represent business processes, such as Purchaser or CustomerManager. There are different types of EJB that can be applied to these different requirements:

- Session EJB—A Session EJB is useful for mapping business process flow (or equivalent application concepts). There are two sub-types of Session EJB—stateless and stateful—that are discussed in more detail on Day 5. Session EJBs commonly represent "pure" functionality and are created as needed.

- Entity EJB—An Entity EJB maps a combination of data (or equivalent application concept) and associated functionality. Entity EJBs are usually based on an underlying data store and will be created on the data within that store.

- Message-Driven EJB—A Message-driven EJB is very similar in concept to a Session EJB, but is only activated when an asynchronous message arrives.

As an application designer, you should choose the most appropriate type of EJB based on the task to be accomplished.

Common Uses of EJBs

So, given all of this, where would you commonly encounter EJBs and in what roles? Well, the following are some examples:

- In a Web-centric application, the EJBs will provide the business logic that sits behind the Web-oriented components, such as servlets and JSPs. If a Web-oriented application requires a high level of scalability or maintainability, use of EJBs can help to deliver this.

- Thick client applications, such as Swing applications, will use EJBs in a similar way to Web-centric applications. To share business logic in a natural way between different types of client applications, EJBs can be used to house that business logic.

4

- Business-to-business (B2B) e-commerce applications can also take advantage of EJBs. Because B2B e-commerce frequently revolves around the integration of business processes, EJBs provide an ideal place to house the business process logic. They can also provide a link between the Web technologies often used to deliver B2B and the business systems behind.

- Enterprise Application Integration (EAI) applications can incorporate EJBs to house processing and mapping between different applications. Again, this is an encapsulation of the business logic that is needed when transferring data between applications (in this case, in-house applications).

These are all high-level views on how EJBs are applied. There are various other EJB-specific patterns and idioms that can be applied when implementing EJB-based solutions. These are discussed more on Day 18, "Patterns."

Why Use EJBs?

Despite the recommendations of the J2EE Blueprints, the use of EJBs is not mandatory. You can build very successful applications using servlets, JSPs or standalone Java applications.

As a general rule of thumb, if an application is small in scope and is not required to be highly scalable, you can use J2EE components, such as servlets, together with direct JDBC connectivity to build it. However, as the application complexity grows or the number of concurrent users increases, the use of EJBs makes it much easier to partition and scale the application. In this case, using EJBs gives you some significant advantages.

The main advantage of using EJBs in your application is the framework provided by the EJB container. The container provides various services for the EJB to relieve the developer from having to implement such services, namely

- Distribution via proxies—The container generates a client-side stub and server-side skeleton for the EJB. The stub and skeleton use RMI over IIOP to communicate.

- Lifecycle management—Bean initialization, state management, and destruction is driven by the container, all the developer has to do is implement the appropriate methods.

- Naming and registration—The EJB container and server provide the EJB with access to naming services. These services are used by local and remote clients to look up the EJB and by the EJB itself to look up resources it may need.

- Transaction management—Declarative transactions provide a means for the developer to easily delegate the creation and control of transactions to the container.

- Security and access control—Again, declarative security provides a means for the developer to easily delegate the enforcement of security to the container.

- Persistence (if required)—Using the Entity EJB's Container-Managed Persistence mechanism (CMP), state can be saved and restored without having to write a single line of code.

All of these container services are covered in more detail as the book progresses.

Now that you know why you would want to use an EJB and how to apply it, you can examine the inner workings of an EJB to understand how all the parts fit together.

What's in an EJB?

So far, you have been presented with a "black box" view of an EJB; it provides business functionality via an RMI remote interface, and it cooperates with its container to perform its duties. To understand, use, and ultimately write EJBs, you will need to know more in concrete terms about the Java programming artifacts that make up an EJB. In other words, what's in one?

There are four components to an EJB:

- The remote interface—Defining the signatures of the business methods for the EJB

- The home interface—Defining the signature of the methods associated with the bean lifecycle (creation, use and destruction)

- The bean itself—A concrete Java class implementing the business and lifecycle method functionality

- The deployment descriptor—Meta data about the EJB, such as component classes, EJB type, transaction demarcation, resource and EJB references, environment entries, and security requirements

The names of the two Java interfaces and the Bean class usually follow a simple convention. For a given remote interface *XXX* the home interface is called *XXX*Home and the bean implementation is *XXX*Bean. (Some users prefer to use *XXX*EJB for the implementation class.) Although this convention is not enforced, it is recommended that you use it when naming your EJB components.

Similarly, as discussed later in the section "The Bean Implementation," there are corresponding rules about the names of methods defined in the interfaces and the names of methods in the bean implementation. Unlike the class names, these rules are part of the EJB specification and must be rigorously applied, otherwise your EJBs will not deploy correctly.

4

The Business Interface

As stated already, the primary purpose of an EJB is to deliver business or application logic. To this end, the bean developer will define or derive the business operations required of the bean and will formalize them in an RMI remote interface. This is referred to as the bean's remote (or business) interface as opposed to the home interface you will look at in a moment.

The actual methods defined on the remote interface will depend on the purpose of the bean, but there are certain general rules concerning the interface:

- As with any RMI-based interface, each method must be declared as throwing `java.rmi.RemoteException` in addition to any business exceptions. This allows the RMI subsystem to signal network-related errors to the client.

- RMI rules apply to parameters and return values, so any types used must either be primitives (`int`, `boolean`, `float`, and the like), or implement the `Serializable` or `Remote` interfaces. Most Java classes, such as `String` and the primitive wrapper classes, implement `Serializable`.

- The interface must declare that it extends the `javax.ejb.EJBObject` interface.

NOTE

Failure to conform to the rules about extending `javax.ejb.EJBObject` and throwing `RemoteException` will cause the interface to be rejected by tools that manipulate EJBs. Additionally, if you use parameter or return types that do not conform to the rules, your bean will compile and even deploy, but will fail with runtime errors.

The issue regarding object parameters and return values is worth considering for a moment. When you pass an object as a parameter into a local method call, a reference to the original object is used within the method. Any changes to the state of the object are seen by all users of that object because they are sharing the same object. Also, there is no need to create a copy of the object—only a reference is passed. This mechanism is known as *pass by reference*.

On the other hand, when using RMI remote methods, only objects that are serializable (that is, implement the `Serializable` interface) are passed. A copy of the object is made and this copy is passed over the remote interface to the method. This has several implications. First, users of a serializable object passed across a remote interface will no longer share the same object. Also, there may now be some performance costs associated with invoking a method through a bean's remote interface. Not only is there the cost of the network call, but also there is the cost of making a copy of the object so that it can be sent across the network. This mechanism is known as *pass by value*.

You can see an example of an EJB remote interface in Listing 4.1—in this case, the one for the Agency EJB used in the case study introduced on Day 2, "The J2EE Platform and Roles."

LISTING 4.1   Remote Interface for the Agency EJB

```
package agency;

import java.rmi.*;
import java.util.*;
import javax.ejb.*;

public interface Agency extends EJBObject
{
    String getAgencyName() throws RemoteException;

    Collection getApplicants()
      throws RemoteException;
    void createApplicant(String login, String name, String email)
      throws RemoteException, DuplicateException, CreateException;
    void deleteApplicant (String login)
      throws RemoteException, NotFoundException;

    Collection getCustomers() throws RemoteException;
    void createCustomer(String login, String name, String email)
      throws RemoteException, DuplicateException, CreateException;
    void deleteCustomer (String login)
      throws RemoteException, NotFoundException;

    Collection getLocations()
      throws RemoteException;
    void addLocation(String name)
      throws RemoteException, DuplicateException;
    void removeLocation(String code)
      throws RemoteException, NotFoundException;

    Collection getSkills()
      throws RemoteException;
    void addSkill(String name)
      throws RemoteException, DuplicateException;
    void removeSkill(String name)
      throws RemoteException, NotFoundException;

    List select(String table)
      throws RemoteException;
}
```

4

The remote interface lives in a package called agency, which will be common to all the classes that comprise the EJB. The definition imports java.rmi.* and javax.ejb.* for RemoteException and EJBObject, respectively. The rest of the interface is much as you would expect from any remote Java interface—in this case, passing Strings and returning serializable Collection objects.

Notice that all the methods must be declared as throwing RemoteException. This means that the client will have to handle potential exceptions that may arise from the underlying distribution mechanism. However, your application will probably want to utilize exceptions itself to indicate application-level errors. These exceptions should be declared as part of the remote interface, as shown by the use of NotFoundException and DuplicateException in the Agency interface.

The Home Interface

To facilitate the creation and discovery of EJBs, each type of EJB provides a home interface. The bean developer will provide an EJB home interface that acts as a factory for that particular EJB. A home interface will extend the javax.ejb.EJBHome interface and will contain the necessary methods identified by the bean developer to allow a client to create, find, or remove EJBs.

There are two ways for a client to get hold of the EJB itself, depending on the type of EJB (Session or Entity) and the way it is intended to be used. The EJB Home interface can contain one or more create() methods to create a new instance of an EJB. So, for example, you can create a new instance of a Session bean before using it. On the other hand, when you interact with Entity EJBs, you will frequently use findXXX() methods to use existing beans. Message-Driven beans do not have a home interface as their lifecycle is more rigidly controlled compared to Session and Entity beans (the Message-driven bean life-cycle is covered in detail on Day 10.

Listing 4.2 shows the home interface for the example Agency EJB.

LISTING 4.2   Home Interface for the Agency Bean

```
package agency;

import java.rmi.*;
import javax.ejb.*;

public interface AgencyHome extends EJBHome
{
    Agency create () throws RemoteException, CreateException;
}
```

The code underlying the home interface will work with the container to create, populate, and destroy EJBs as requested by the client. The effects of the method calls will vary depending on the type of EJB being manipulated. As a result, a request to remove a Session EJB will just result in the EJB being thrown away, while the same request on an Entity EJB may cause underlying data to be removed. The types and effects of different home interface methods are discussed in more detail on Days 5 and 6.

The Bean Implementation

After the interfaces are defined, there is the none-too-trivial task of implementing the business logic behind them. The business logic for an EJB will live in a class referred to as the bean. The bean consists of two parts:

- The business logic itself, including implementations of the methods defined in the remote interface
- A set of methods that allow the container to manage the bean's lifecycle

NOTE
> Although the bean itself must contain these elements, it is possible, indeed common, for non-trivial beans to delegate some or all of their business functionality to other, helper, classes.

4

Drilling down into these areas reveals more about the structure of an EJB.

Implementing the Business Interface

The first thing to note is that the bean itself does not implement the remote interface previously defined. This may seem slightly bizarre at first sight; however, there is a very good reason for this.

In order for the container to apply services, such as access control, on behalf of the EJB the container must have some way of intercepting the method call from the client. When it receives such a method call, the container can then decide if any extra services need to be applied before forwarding the method call on to the bean itself.

The interception is performed by a server-side object called the EJB Object (not to be confused with the interface of the same name). The EJB Object acts as a server-side proxy for the bean itself, and it is the EJB Object that actually implements the EJB's remote interface. Figure 4.1 shows the relationship between the client, the bean, and the EJB Object.

FIGURE 4.1

The EJB Object acts as a server-side proxy for the bean itself.

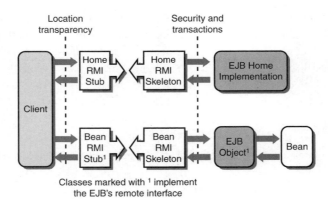

Classes marked with [1] implement the EJB's remote interface

As shown in Figure 4.1, the client calls the business methods on the EJB Object implementation. The EJB Object applies the required extra services and then forwards the method calls to the bean itself.

The J2EE server generates the EJB Object class when you deploy the EJB. The deployment process uses the information you provide in the home and remote interfaces and the DD to generate the required EJB Object class.

Every business method in the remote interface must have a corresponding business method in the bean. The method name, parameters, and return type must be identical and the bean method must throw the same exceptions as the interface method apart from the `RemoteException` required by all remote methods. All business methods must have public visibility.

For example, the remote interface method

`public Collection findAllApplicants() throws RemoteException;` must have the corresponding method in the bean:

`public Collection findAllApplicants();`

If you are using a developer tool that supports the creation of EJBs, it will generally generate empty methods for you to populate. Listing 4.3 shows the outlines of the business methods in the example `AgencyBean` with some of the code removed for clarity.

LISTING 4.3   Business Method Implementation Signatures for the `AgencyBean`

```
package agency;

import java.rmi.*;
import java.util.*;
```

LISTING 4.3   continued

```java
import javax.ejb.*;
// Remaining imports removed for clarity

public class AgencyBean implements SessionBean
{
    public String getAgencyName() { ... }
    public Collection findAllApplicants() { ... }

    public void createApplicant(String login, String name, String email)
      throws DuplicateException, CreateException { ... }

    public void deleteApplicant (String login)
      throws NotFoundException { ... }

    public Collection findAllCustomers() { ... }

    public void createCustomer(String login, String name, String email)
      throws DuplicateException, CreateException { ... }

    public void deleteCustomer (String login) throws NotFoundException { ... }

    public Collection getLocations() { ... }

    public void addLocation(String name) throws DuplicateException { ... }

    public void removeLocation(String code) throws NotFoundException { ... }

    public Collection getSkills() { ... }

    public void addSkill (String name) throws DuplicateException { ... }

    public void removeSkill (String name) throws NotFoundException { ... }

    public List select(String table) { ... }
}
```

An EJB implementation must implement the appropriate javax.ejb class, as described in the section "Implementing the Home Interface." The AgencyBean example is a Session EJB and therefore must extend javax.ejb.SessionBean.

NOTE

Note that your bean methods will only throw business exceptions or standard Java exceptions. They should not throw java.rmi.RemoteException, because this exception should only be generated by the RMI subsystem.

4

Implementing the Home Interface

Remember that the intention of the EJB environment is that you will spend most of your time writing business logic rather than network and database "plumbing." Beyond writing the business logic, the only additional thing the bean writer needs to do is to provide lifecycle "hooks" that allow the container to manage the bean.

Each of the different types of EJBs discussed earlier (Session, Entity, and MDB) has a slightly different lifecycle, but the common parts are as follows:

- Bean creation and initialization
- Bean destruction and removal
- The saving and restoring of the bean's internal state (if applicable)

The details associated with each type of bean lifecycle will be discussed as they are covered. For now, all you need to know is that

- An EJB will implement one or more lifecycle interfaces depending on its type. The interfaces are defined in the `javax.ejb` package.
- Standard lifecycle methods must be provided.
- The lifecycle methods will generally begin with `ejb` so that they can be easily distinguished from the business methods around them, for example, `ejbCreate()`.

Listing 4.4 contains the lifecycle methods in the example `AgencyBean` with most of the implementation code removed for clarity

LISTING 4.4   Lifecycle Methods on the `AgencyBean`

```
package agency;

import java.rmi.*;
import java.util.*;
import javax.ejb.*;
// Remaining imports removed for clarity

public class AgencyBean implements SessionBean
{
    private DataSource dataSource;
    private String name = "";

    public void ejbCreate () throws CreateException {
        try {
            InitialContext ic = new InitialContext();
            dataSource = (DataSource)ic.lookup("java:comp/env/jdbc/Agency");
            name = (String)ic.lookup("java:comp/env/AgencyName");
        }
```

LISTING 4.4   continued

```
        catch (NamingException ex) {
            error("Error connecting to java:comp/env/Agency:",ex);
        }
    }

    public void ejbActivate() { … }

    public void ejbPassivate() { … }

    public void ejbRemove() { … }

    private SessionContext ctx;

    public void setSessionContext(SessionContext ctx) {
        this.ctx = ctx;
    }
}
```

As you can see, the example `AgencyBean` implements the `SessionBean` interface. This means that it must implement the `ejbRemove()`, `ejbActivate()`, `ejbPassivate()`, and `setSessionContext()` methods. The context passed in `setSessionContext()` provides a way for the bean to communicate with the container. It is usual to save the session context object in an instance variable for use by the other bean methods.

In an Entity bean the `ejbCreate()` method takes on the role of constructor in that most of the bean initialization will take place in this method, and corresponds to the `create()` method defined in the home interface. The `ejbCreate()` method is not defined in the `SessionBean` interface, because its signature will vary from one EJB to another (as described tomorrow when Session EJBs are discussed in detail).

The Deployment Descriptor

The final piece of the EJB jigsaw lies in the provision of configuration information, or meta data, for the EJB. This provides a way of communicating the EJB's requirements and structure to the container. If an EJB is to be successfully deployed, the container will have to be provided with extra information, including

- An identifier or name for the EJB that can be used for JNDI lookup to locate the bean.

- The bean type Session, Entity, or Message-Driven.

- The EJB's remote interface class. This interface will typically just be named according to the EJB's functionality, for example, `Agency` or `BankTeller`.

- The EJB's home interface class. The name for an EJB's home interface will typically be derived from its remote interface name.

- The bean class itself. Again, the name for the bean will typically be derived from the associated remote interface name.

- Any name/value pairs to be provided as part of the bean's environment. Effectively, these are variables that can be given values by the assembler or deployer as well as the developer.

- Information about any external resources required by the EJB, such as database connections or other EJBs.

All of this essential information is bundled into a deployment descriptor that accompanies the EJB classes. The deployment descriptor is defined as an XML document, and is discussed in more detail later when examining the packaging of an EJB.

In addition to the essential information, the deployment descriptor can also carry other metadata such as:

- Declarative attributes for security and transactions

- Structural information about bean relationships and dependencies

- Persistence mapping (if applicable)

You will see examples of all of these as you progress through this book.

Verifying an EJB

One of the problems most developers come across when writing EJBs is making sure the bean implementation provides the requisite functionality in the remote and home interfaces. Because your bean does not implement the remote interface (or the home interface), you must manually check that you have defined all the business methods in the bean implementation and that every `create()` method in the home interface has a corresponding `ejbCreate()` method in the implementation.

There are two ways of solving this problem:

- Generate a template bean implementation class from the home and remote interfaces.

- Use a tool that checks the bean implementation against the home and remote interfaces.

The drawback to the first approach is that changes to the home or remote interfaces necessitate regenerating the template class and copying existing functionality into the newly generated template. The process of manually copying existing code into the new template could lead to errors and is best avoided.

Use of a separate verification utility is more common, as this can be used any time changes are made to the interfaces or the implementation. The J2EE RI comes with the `verifier` tool, which validates the contents of an enterprise application and generates a comprehensive list of any errors encountered. The verifier is discussed in more detail in the section "Verifying the Case Study Application."

You are now nearing the conclusion of this whistle-stop tour of the structure of an EJB. After you have examined how an EJB is created and packaged, you will be ready to deploy and use one.

How Do I Create an EJB?

First you have to design and write your EJB classes. After that small task, all that remains is to wrap the class files up as a deployable unit with the deployment descriptor. In reality, not all of the deployment information is defined in the EJB specification. A certain amount of EJB information will, of necessity, be J2EE implementation specific. Consequently there will typically be at least two deployment descriptors in an EJB. Before looking at the deployment descriptors, there are certain caveats you should bear in mind while creating your bean.

Caveats on EJBs

Due to the managed nature of the bean lifecycle, the EJB container imposes certain restrictions on the bean including

- EJBs cannot perform file I/O. If you need to log messages or access files, you must find an alternative mechanism.
- EJBs are not allowed to start threads. The container controls all threading and ensures that the EJB is always multi-thread safe by only allowing a single thread of execution for each EJB.
- EJBs cannot call native methods.
- EJBs cannot use static member variables.
- There is no GUI available to an EJB, so it must not attempt to use AWT or JFC components.
- An EJB cannot act as a network server, listening for inbound connections.
- An EJB should not attempt to create class loaders or change factories for artifacts, such as sockets.

4

- An EJB should not return this from a method. Although not strictly a restriction (the container will not prevent you from doing it), it is identified as being a very bad practice as it would potentially give a client a direct remote reference to the bean rather than the EJB Object. Instead, the bean should query its EJB context for a reference to its associated EJB Object and return that to the caller in place of the this variable.

For a full list of restrictions, see the EJB specification available online at http://java.sun.com/products/ejb/docs.html.

The EJB Deployment Descriptor

The EJB specification defines a standard format for the XML deployment descriptor document that stores EJB meta data. The exact format of a deployment descriptor is usually hidden behind tools (such as the J2EE RI deploytool) that manipulates it on your behalf. However, it is worth examining some of the contents of a deployment descriptor to see how the EJB fits together and how extra information and meta data is provided.

Listing 4.5 shows the deployment descriptor for the example Agency EJB.

LISTING 4.5   Agency Bean EJB Deployment Descriptor

```xml
<?xml version="1.0" encoding="UTF-8"?>
<ejb-jar version="2.1" xmlns="http://java.sun.com/xml/ns/j2ee"
  xmlns:xsi="http://www.w3.org/2001/XMLSchema-instance"
  xsi:schemaLocation="http://java.sun.com/xml/ns/j2ee
  http://java.sun.com/xml/ns/j2ee/ejb-jar_2_1.xsd">
  <display-name>Simple</display-name>
  <enterprise-beans>
    <session>
      <ejb-name>AgencyBean</ejb-name>
      <home>agency.AgencyHome</home>
      <remote>agency.Agency</remote>
      <ejb-class>agency.AgencyBean</ejb-class>
      <session-type>Stateless</session-type>
      <transaction-type>Bean</transaction-type>
      <env-entry>
        <env-entry-name>AgencyName</env-entry-name>
        <env-entry-type>java.lang.String</env-entry-type>
        <env-entry-value>J2EE in 21 Days Job Agency</env-entry-value>
      </env-entry>
      <security-identity>
        <use-caller-identity/>
      </security-identity>
      <resource-ref>
        <res-ref-name>jdbc/Agency</res-ref-name>
        <res-type>javax.sql.DataSource</res-type>
```

LISTING 4.5 continued

```
        <res-auth>Container</res-auth>
        <res-sharing-scope>Shareable</res-sharing-scope>
      </resource-ref>
    </session>
  </enterprise-beans>
</ejb-jar>
```

The essential parts of the deployment descriptor in Listing 4.5 are

- The `<session>` tag delimits the definition of the Agency EJB and indicates that it is a Session EJB.
- The `<ejb-name>` tag defines the name of the EJB, in this case `Agency`.
- The home and remote interface types (as defined by their fully-qualified class file-names) are specified by the `<home>` and `<remote>` tags, respectively. The type of the bean itself is defined by the `<ejb-class>` tag.

In addition, two other parts are of particular note at this point in time:

- An environment entry is defined using the `<env-entry>` tag. This indicates that a `String` property called `AgencyName` should be made available to the bean. The value of the property is `J2EE in 21 Days Job Agency`. The environment defined in the deployment descriptor is made available through JNDI under `java:comp/env`. In this case, the agency name can be retrieved by looking up the name `java:comp/env/AgencyName`. This lookup can be seen in the `ejbCreate()` method of Listing 4.4.
- An external resource is defined using the `<resource-ref>` tag. This defines that a `DataSource` should be made available to this EJB under the name `jdbc/Agency`. As with the environment entry for the agency name, this resource is made available through JNDI under `java:comp/env`, so the EJB can retrieve the `DataSource` by looking up the name `java:comp/env/jdbc/Agency`. Again, this lookup can be seen in the `ejbCreate()` method of Listing 4.4.

The EJB-JAR File

All of the EJB classes and the deployment descriptor should be bundled up in a JAR file. The deployment descriptor is stored in a META-INF directory (the same location as the JAR manifest file) and must be named `ejb-jar.xml`. If there are multiple EJBs packaged in the same JAR file, the deployment descriptor will have multiple EJB definitions in it. The JAR file is then termed an EJB-JAR file to denote its payload. The JAR file itself can be called anything (but obviously a name appropriate to the application makes most sense) and conventionally has a `.jar` file extension.

The EJB-JAR file can also contain any extra resources required by the EJB, such as platform-specific configuration information that does not fit in the standard deployment descriptor.

Typical contents of a platform specific deployment descriptor are

- The JNDI name the EJB must be deployed under
- Mappings between resources referenced in the J2EE components such as EJBs and the actual resources within the J2EE server

An EJB-JAR file can store more than one platform-specific deployment descriptor file, enabling it to be used with different J2EE implementations. Although the EJB-JAR file is now complete, it must form part of an application to serve a useful purpose. J2EE defines that enterprise applications can be built from components (Web, EJB, and Client Application components). Therefore, a second JAR file is used to bundle these J2EE components into a complete J2EE Application, this is called the Enterprise Archive file.

The Enterprise Archive File

The Enterprise Archive (EAR) file contains a number of J2EE components comprising an application and yet another deployment descriptor. This descriptor includes a description of the application, which components it uses, how those components relate to each other, and which specific resources they use. This is the information provided by the Application Assembler and Deployer.

The application deployment descriptor is also an XML document, called application.xml, and it is stored in the META-INF directory of the Enterprise Archive (which although a JAR file the Enterprise Archive typically has a filename extension of .ear not .jar). Listing 4.6 shows the application.xml descriptor for the Agency application.

LISTING 4.6   Agency Bean EJB Deployment Descriptor

```
<?xml version="1.0" encoding="UTF-8"?>
<application version="1.4" xmlns="http://java.sun.com/xml/ns/j2ee"
  xmlns:xsi="http://www.w3.org/2001/XMLSchema-instance"
  xsi:schemaLocation="http://java.sun.com/xml/ns/j2ee
➥ http://java.sun.com/xml/ns/j2ee/application_1_4.xsd">
  <description>Application description</description>
  <display-name>agency</display-name>
  <module>
    <ejb>agency-session-ejb.jar</ejb>
  </module>
  <module>
```

LISTING 4.6   continued

```
    <web>
      <web-uri>webagency.war</web-uri>
      <context-root>/webagency</context-root>
    </web>
  </module>
</application>
```

The `application.xml` file just lists the modules that form the enterprise application, in this case the single Agency EJB contained in `agency-session-ejb.jar`.

An EAR file may also contain one or more platform-specific deployment descriptors for the application enabling it to be used with different J2EE implementations.

How Do I Deploy an EJB?

After an EJB is packaged, it can be deployed in an appropriate J2EE server. This is done using tools supplied by the J2EE Server vendor. Often these will be Java GUI applications, but command-line tools and Web interfaces are also used by some vendors. The typical process is to define the target J2EE server, identify the EAR file to be deployed, supply user credentials (typically administrative username and password) and away you go.

Remember that J2EE defines a separate role for the application Deployer. It may be that, for particular installations the databases or other resource names need to be changed to match the local environment. When configuring the application, the Deployer may need to alter the EJB or enterprise deployment descriptors but will not need to change the Java source code.

When an EJB is deployed into a particular EJB container, the EJB must be plugged into that container. To do this, an EJB Object must be generated based on the EJB's remote interface. This EJB Object will be specific to that EJB container and will contain code that allows the EJB Object to interface with that container to access security and transaction information. The container will examine the deployment descriptors supplied with the EJB to determine what type of security and transaction code is required in the EJB Object.

The container will also generate a class that implements the EJB home interface so that calls to the create, find, and destroy EJB instances are delegated to container-defined methods.

Finally, the container will register the JNDI name for the home interface of the EJB. This allows other application components to create and find this application's EJBs.

After the EJB has been deployed, any subsequent changes to its functionality will mean that the EJB must be redeployed. If the enterprise application or EJB is no longer needed, it should be undeployed from the container.

How Do I Use an EJB?

Given that EJBs are middle-tier business components, they are of little use without a client to drive them. As mentioned earlier, those clients can be Web components, stand-alone Java clients, or other EJBs.

Regardless of the type of client, using an EJB requires the same set of steps—namely, discovery, retrieval, use, and disposal. Listing 4.7 shows a simple client for use with the Agency EJB illustrating these steps. The following three sections cover these steps in more detail.

LISTING 4.7   Simple Agency Client `SimpleClient.java`

```java
package client;

import agency.*;
import javax.ejb.*;
import javax.naming.*;
import java.rmi.*;
import javax.rmi.*;
import java.util.*;

public class SimpleClient
{
    private static String agencyJNDI = "java:comp/env/ejb/Agency";

    public static void main(String[] args) {
        if (args.length == 1)
            agencyJNDI = args[0];
        else if (args.length > 1) {
            System.err.println("Usage: SimpleClient [ AgencyJNDI ]");
            System.exit(1);
        }

        try {
            InitialContext ic = new InitialContext();
            Object lookup = ic.lookup(agencyJNDI);

            AgencyHome home = (AgencyHome)
                PortableRemoteObject.narrow(lookup, AgencyHome.class);
```

LISTING 4.7   continued

```
        Agency agency = home.create();
        System.out.println("Welcome to: "+agency.getAgencyName());
        System.out.println("Customer list: "+agency.getAgencyName());
        Collection customers = agency.findAllCustomers();
        Iterator it = customers.iterator();
        while (it.hasNext())
        {
            String name = (String)it.next();
            System.out.println(name);
        }
        agency.close();
    }
    catch (NamingException ex) {
        System.err.println(ex);
    }
    catch (ClassCastException ex) {
        System.err.println(ex);
    }
    catch (CreateException ex) {
        System.err.println(ex);
    }
    catch (RemoteException ex) {
        System.err.println(ex);
    }
    catch (RemoveException ex) {
        System.err.println(ex);
    }
  }
}
```

Discovery

To create or find an EJB, the client must call the appropriate method on the EJB's home interface. Consequently, the first step for the client is to obtain a remote reference to the home interface. The client obtains the reference by accessing the J2EE server's name service using JNDI.

For this simple process to work, the following three actions must have taken place:

- The developer has defined the EJB reference used in the Java code
- The Deployer has mapped this reference onto the actual JNDI name of the EJB
- The EJB container has registered the home interface using the JNDI name specified as part of the platform specific deployment descriptor

As discussed on Day 3, each J2EE component has its own Java Component Environment space and the JNDI name used in the client code will be prefixed with `java:comp/env`. The object retrieved is a reference to the RMI-IIOP remote stub that must be downcast to the home interface. The following code shows the initial lookup required for the Agency EJB:

```
try
  {
    InitialContext ic = new InitialContext();
    Object lookup = ic.lookup("java:comp/env/ejb/Agency");
    AgencyHome home =
          (AgencyHome)PortableRemoteObject.narrow(lookup, AgencyHome.class);
    ...
  }
  catch (NamingException ex) { /* Handle it */ }
  catch (ClassCastException ex) { /* Handle it */ }
```

Now that you have a reference to the home interface, you can create the EJB.

Retrieval and Use

Once you have a reference to the EJB home interface, you can call the `create()` method you saw defined on the `AgencyHome` interface. The `create()` method returns a remote reference to the newly-created EJB. If there are any problems with the EJB creation or the remote connection, a `CreateException` or `RemoteException` will be thrown. `CreateException` is defined in the `javax.ejb` package, and `RemoteException` is defined in the `java.rmi` package, so remember to import these packages in your client class.

Now that you have a reference to an EJB, you can call its business methods as follows:

```
try
{
  ...
  Agency agency = home.create();
  System.out.println("Welcome to: " + agency.getAgencyName());
  ...
}
catch (RemoteException ex) { /* Handle it */ }
catch (CreateException ex) { /* Handle it */ }
```

The previous code sample shows the `getAgencyName()` method being called on the returned Agency reference. Again, whenever you call a remote method that is defined in an EJB remote interface, you must be prepared to handle a `RemoteException`.

> You will see later that some Entity beans are found rather than created. In this case, all steps are the same except that the `create()` method is replaced by the appropriate finder method and find-related exceptions must be handled. You still end up with a remote reference to an EJB. All of this is covered when Entity beans are discussed on Day 6.

Disposing of the EJB

You have now created and used an EJB. What happens now? Well, if you no longer need the EJB, you should get rid of it by calling its remove method, and set its reference to `null` as follows:

```
// No longer need the agency EJB instance
agency.remove();
agency = null;
```

The `remove()` method can throw `RemoveException`. After calling `remove()` you should obviously not call any business methods on the bean as it has been removed from use. Using an EJB after `remove()` has been called will throw a `RemoteException`.

NOTE

> Normally you would only call the `remove()` method for Session beans. Entity beans (see Day 5) represent data in a persistent data store, and calling `remove()` for an Entity bean would typically remove the data from the data store.

If you do not remove a Session EJB after a default period of inactivity (typically 30 minutes), then the EJB container will remove the bean on your behalf. This is an example of the added value provided by the EJB lifecycle. A lazy or novice developer can forget to remove an EJB and the container will still tidy up and release resources: a bit like your mother tidying your bedroom when you were a young child.

Running the Client

To compile and run the client, you will need the following:

- The J2EE classes.
- Access to the EJB's home and remote interface classes.
- RMI stubs for the home and remote interfaces.
- If the client does not have the JNDI name of the EJB compiled in, you may want to provide this on the command line or through a system property.

4

NOTE

> If your client is a J2EE Web client (such as a servlet or JSP as discussed on Day 12, "Servlets" and Day 13, "JavaServer Pages"), then the client will implicitly have access to the J2EE classes, EJB interfaces, RMI stubs and JNDI name server.

When you deploy the EJB, you can usually ask the container for a client JAR file. This client JAR file will contain all of the classes and interfaces needed to compile the client (as defined in the previous bulleted list). You should add this client JAR file to your CLASSPATH when compiling your client.

Client Applications

Application client programs are simple Java programs with a main() method that run in their own JVM but make use of services provided by the J2EE server. Application clients are usually invoked by a program supplied by the J2EE server vendor. The J2EE RI, for instance, provides a program called appclient for running application clients.

The various J2EE server vendors may handle client applications differently, but the J2EE specification allows for application clients to be packaged into JAR files, together with a deployment descriptor, and deployed to the J2EE server. The J2EE RI uses this approach, and Listing 4.8 shows the application client deployment descriptor file (application-client.xml) for the simple Agency application client shown previously in Listing 4.7.

LISTING 4.8 Application Client Deployment Descriptor application-client.xml

```
<?xml version="1.0" encoding="UTF-8"?>
<application-client version="1.4" xmlns="http://java.sun.com/xml/ns/j2ee"
  xmlns:xsi="http://www.w3.org/2001/XMLSchema-instance"
  xsi:schemaLocation="http://java.sun.com/xml/ns/j2ee
➡ http://java.sun.com/xml/ns/j2ee/application-client_1_4.xsd">
  <display-name>SimpleClient</display-name>
  <ejb-ref>
    <ejb-ref-name>ejb/Agency</ejb-ref-name>
    <ejb-ref-type>Session</ejb-ref-type>
    <home>agency.AgencyHome</home>
    <remote>agency.Agency</remote>
  </ejb-ref>
</application-client>
```

An application client deployment descriptor is used to define J2EE server resources required by the client. In this case, a single EJB reference is needed to define the name of the EJB as used in the code (ejb/Agency) and the type and classes for the EJB.

As with all applications bundled into a JAR file, the class containing the `main()` method entry point is defined by a `Main-class` entry in the JAR Manifest file.

Using the J2EE Reference Implementation

In this section, you will look at how to deploy an EJB in the J2EE Reference Implementation (RI) and how to run the simple application client.

Configuring J2EE RI

On Day 2 you were asked to install and configure the J2EE RI available, free of charge, from Sun Microsystems (at `http://java.sun.com/j2ee`) and build a sample database for the exercises in this book. If you have not already done so go back to Day 2 and follow the instructions for installing the J2EE RI and building the Agency case study database.

As discussed on Day 2, before running any of the tools described in this section, you will need to set the `J2EE_HOME` environment variable to the location on your hard drive where you installed the J2EE reference implementation. You should also add the bin directory below `J2EE_HOME` to your executable search path (`%PATH%` under Windows or `$PATH` under Solaris/Linux) so that you can run J2EE tools and batch files from the command line. You should place the J2EE bin directory at the front of your PATH setting to avoid conflicts with system tools with the same names as the J2EE tools. You should also copy the code in the CaseStudy directory on the accompanying Web site onto your local hard disk, because commands you will run today require write access to the working directory.

4

There are two approaches to building and deploying a J2EE component or application using J2EE RI:

- You can use the `deploytool` provided with the J2EE SDK.
- You can use the `asant` utility supplied with the J2EE SDK (this is a modified version of the popular Apache Ant utility from `http://jakarta.apache.org/ant`). The J2EE tutorial examples for J2EE SDK 1.4 are built and deployed using `asant` build files and `asant` build files are supplied for all the examples used throughout this book.

As a newcomer to J2EE, you will find it informative to use the GUI interface of deploy-tool for building and configuring the EAR and WAR files used to hold your EJBs, applications, and web components. As you gain more experience, you might find the speed of the asant command-line interface to be preferable. You will also find asant build files useful for scripting automated testing procedures.

The disadvantage of using asant is that you will have to write the build files yourself; not to mention hand crafting all the deployment descriptors. Many developers use deploytool once to generate the basic deployment descriptors and then save these descriptors to disk for use with asant build files. That is how most of the examples for this book were developed.

This section will show how to build and deploy J2EE components using deploytool before looking at the asant build files used for the Agency case study example. The directory structure for the book's example code was discussed on Day 2, but as a quick reminder, these are the subdirectories under the exercise directory for Day 4:

- build—A temporary directory used by the asant build files (created when needed)
- classes—The compiled class files
- dd—The deployment descriptor files used by the asant build files
- j2ee-ri—Repository for files manipulated by deploytool
- src—The Java source files
- JSP—The HTML and JavaServer Pages source files

Remember to make sure you are running the J2EE RI server and PointBase database servers and have created the Agency database before starting this exercise.

Opening the Case Study EAR File

Now you are ready to run the deploytool found in the bin directory under the J2EE_HOME directory. Start a command line window in the Day04/exercise directory and enter the command:

```
deploytool
```

You will be presented with a graphic interface for building J2EE components. If you have not set your PATH to include the bin directory under J2EE home you will have to provide the full pathname for deploytool. Windows users can use the Start, Programs, Sun Microsystems, J2EE 1.4 SDK, Deploytool menu or run

```
%J2EE_HOME%\bin\deploytool
```

Solaris and Linux users should enter

`$J2EE_HOME/bin/deploytool`

In `deploytool`, use the File, Open menu to open the supplied agency enterprise archive (EAR) file in `Day04/exercise/j2ee-ri/agency.ear`. The agency application will now be displayed in the list of applications, as shown in Figure 4.2.

FIGURE 4.2

The Agency *application loaded by* `deploytool`.

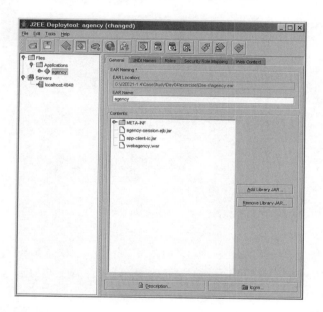

Examining the Case Study Application

You can use `deploytool` to examine and alter deployment descriptor information for the application and, if necessary, for individual components, such as EJBs.

After you open an EAR file, the enterprise application will be selected and deployment information appropriate to the application is available in the tabbed dialog pages in the right pane. In Figure 4.3, clicking on the key icons to the left of each item has exposed the nested structure of the information.

Figure 4.3 shows that the application has three components:

- An Agency JAR file containing a single Agency EJB
- A WebApp WAR file containing a simple Web Application (Web Applications are introduced on Day 12)
- A SimpleClient client application

FIGURE 4.3

The Agency *application loaded by* deploytool.

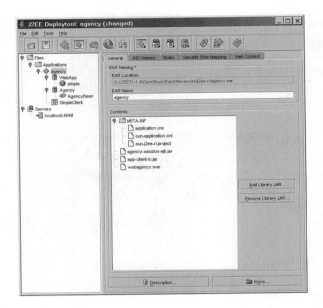

The right `General` pane in Figure 4.3 shows the files comprising the Agency application as follows:

- `META-INF/application.xml`—The application DD as shown in Listing 4.6
- `META-INF/sun-j2ee-ri.project`—A proprietary J2EE RI projects file (you can ignore this)
- `META-INF/sun-j2ee-ri.xml`—A J2EE RI platform-specific DD (discussed in the section "Defining the Platform-Specific Settings")
- `agency-session-ejb.jar`—The JAR file for the Agency EJBs
- `app-client-ic.jar`—The JAR file for the application client
- `webagency.war`—The WAR file for the Web Application

The remaining tabbed dialog-pages in the application pane will be discussed in later days in this book.

With the `agency` application selected in the left pane you can use the Tools, Descriptor Viewer, Descriptor Viewer menu option to examine the `application.xml` deployment descriptor shown in Listing 4.6. You can also use the Tools, Descriptor Viewer, Application Server Descriptor… menu to view the Sun Specific deployment descriptor.

Figure 4.4 shows the EJB JAR specific information with the contents of the JAR file expanded in the right pane.

FIGURE 4.4

Details of the Agency *JAR file.*

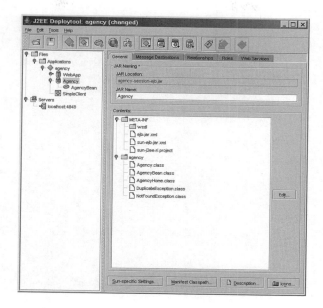

The right General pane in Figure 4.4 shows the files that compose the Agency EJB JAR:

- META-INF/ejb-jar.xml—The EJB DD
- META-INF/sun-ejb-jar.xml—The Sun Specific EJB DD
- META-INF/sun-j2ee-ri.project—A proprietary J2EE RI projects file (you can ignore this)
- agency/Agency.class—The Agency Session bean remote interface (see Listing 4.1)
- agency/AgencyBean.class—The Agency Session bean itself (see Listing 4.3)
- agency/AgencyHome.class—The Agency Session bean home interface (see Listing 4.2)
- agency/DuplicateException.class—Supporting class for the Agency Session
- agency/NotFoundException.class—Supporting class for the Agency Session

With the Agency EJB JAR file selected in the left pane you can use the Tools, Descriptor Viewer, Descriptor Viewer menu option to examine the ejb-jar.xml deployment descriptor shown in Listing 4.5. You can also use the Tools, Descriptor Viewer, Application Server Descriptor... menu to view the Sun Specific EJB deployment descriptor.

Drilling down further into the EJB, Figure 4.5 shows the Agency Session bean itself.

4

FIGURE **4.5**

*Details of the Agency
Session bean.*

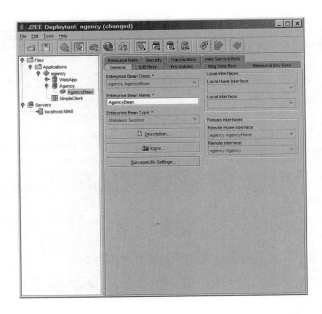

In Figure 4.5 the General tab shows the bean type and component classes for the Agency
Session bean. This information is provided when the bean is created and cannot be
changed thereafter. Creating a Session bean is discussed on Day 5. However, most of the
configuration information for a bean can be changed through the remaining tabbed dialog pages shown in Figure 4.5.

Table 4.1 shows the basic categories of information that can be provided for an EJB.

TABLE 4.1   EJB DD Categories.

Category	Description
Environment Entries	Name value pairs that can be used by the developer but defined by the Deployer/Assembler (see Figure 4.6).
EJB References	References to other EJBs used by this EJB, typically Entity beans referenced by a Session bean, as shown on Day 6.
Resource Environment References	Resource references added to the EJB environment, typically JMS resources, as discussed on Day 10.
Resource References	Resources used by the EJB, such as database connections (see Figure 4.7), JavaMail objects and JMS resources.
Security	Security configuration, as discussed on Day 15, "Security."
Transactions	Transaction requirements, as discussed in detail on Day 8.
Message Destination References	Message-Driven Bean destinations, as discussed on Day 10.

TABLE 4.1 continued

Category	Description
Web Service Endpoints	Web Service endpoints, as discussed on Day 20, "Using RPC-Style Web Services with J2EE," and Day 21, "Message-Style Web Services and Web Service Registries."
Web Service References	References to Web Services, as discussed on Day 21.

The Agency EJB illustrates common requirements for most EJBs. The use of environment references is shown in Figure 4.6, where the displayable Agency name is stored as a String environment reference. The data source definition for the Agency database is shown in Figure 4.7.

FIGURE 4.6

Agency name stored as an environment entry.

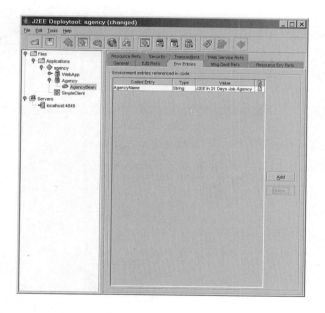

Finally, you can examine the simple application client in the Agency EAR file. In Figure 4.8, the main dialog page for an application client has been selected to show the entry for the Main Class name.

In Figure 4.8, you can see that an application client has similar configuration requirements as an EJB. Most of the tabbed dialog pages available are the same as those for an EJB. Figure 4.9 shows the configuration of the Agency Session EJB reference defined for the simple client.

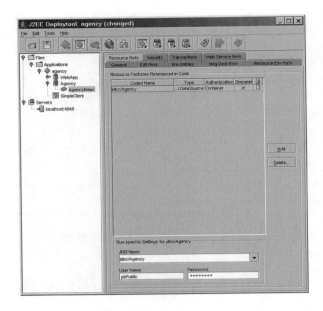

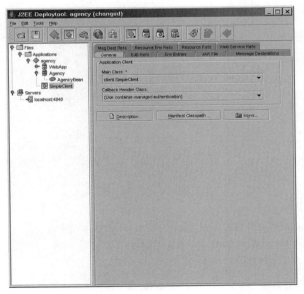

FIGURE **4.9**

Agency Session EJB Reference.

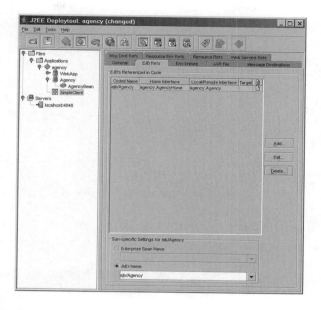

Verifying the Case Study Application

The J2EE RI comes with a `verifier` utility that you can use to validate the contents of an EAR file. The `verifier` can be run from the command line or it can be invoked from the Tools, Verify J2EE Compliance... menu option from within `deploytool`.

NOTE

The authors used J2EE SDK 1.4 released in November 2003 for the development of the code used in this book. Unfortunately they encountered problems when running the `verifier` from within `deploytool`. Specifically running the `verifier` against this simple example incorrectly reported a problem with a missing JNDI name for the `jdbc/Agency` resource reference. Running the command line `verifier` against the same EAR file did not report a problem. You are urged to double check any verification problems reported from `deploytool` by using the command line verifier utility. For the example case study you can do this manually using the command

```
verifier j2ee-ri/agency.ear
```

from within the `Day04/exercise` directory. Alternatively use the supplied `asant` build files (see section "Case Study `asant` Build Files") and enter

```
asant verify-j2ee-ri
```

4

CAUTION

Micosoft Windows users should be aware that there is a standard Windows 2000/XP utility called `verifier`. If you have not put the `%J2EE_HOME%\bin` directory at the start of your PATH environment variable you will have to use the command

`%J2EE_HOME"\bin\verifier`

to run the J2EE SDK verifier. The supplied asant build files for the case study use the fully qualified file name and therefore do not require the PATH to be modified.

You are advised to run `verifier` on all new EAR files or when changes have been made to any of the files composing an EJB. To illustrate the use of the verifier, Figure 4.10 shows the errors produced by a simple mistake in coding the `AgencyBean.java` class; in this case the `ejbCreate()` method was mistakenly defined as `create()`.

FIGURE 4.10

verifer *errors from a missing* `ejbCreate()` *method in* `AgencyBean.java`.

Running the verifier from within `deploytool` produces a list of failed tests or a brief "There were no failed tests" message. Selecting each failed test in turn will supply further information about the test. In Figure 4.10 the message indicates the following:

`[agency.AgencyBean] does not properly declare at least one ejbCreate() method`

A simple mistake can cause the failure of many tests, so do not be alarmed if you see a large number of test failures.

CAUTION

The `verifier` tool works from the on-disk EAR file and not from the in-memory copy created by `deploytool`. Make sure you save your application using the File, Save menu option before running `verifier`.

After you have written, packaged up your application, and verified the application contents, you are ready to deploy.

Deploying the Case Study Application

You can deploy the server-side components of the `agency` application using `deploytool`. To deploy the `agency` application, select the `agency` application item (indicated by a blue diamond under the `Applications` folder in the explorer area in the left-hand panel), and select the Tools, Deploy... menu. This will display the initial deployment screen shown in Figure 4.11.

FIGURE 4.11

Deployment dialog for the Agency case study.

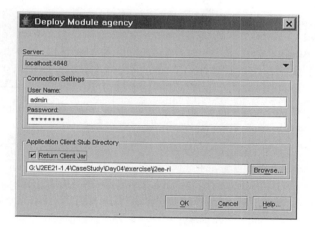

You will need to provide the administrative username and password (`admin` and `password` if you installed the J2EE SDK as described on Day 2). You should also check the Return Client Jar box on the dialogue to ensure your Application Client Jar file is downloaded from the J2EE server. Accept the default location for the client JAR file (this will be the same directory as the EAR file).

Click on OK to proceed with deploying your application and then click Close on the popup window when the deployment completes.

4

NOTE If your J2EE component has already been deployed, the existing version will be undeployed, and then the new version will be deployed. When redeploying an application the J2EE RI will not return a new client JAR file even if asked it to do so. You will either have to do this manually or explicitly undeploy and redeploy your application as described in the section "Managing J2EE RI Applications."

This is the point at which things might go wrong. If you are using the software from the Web site, you should have no trouble, but if you are developing your own example then you might come across problems at this stage. The "Troubleshooting Deployment" section, later on, discusses problems that might occur at deployment. If something does go wrong, study the information in the deployment progress window and also look at the J2EE console window for additional, more detailed information.

Running the Application Client

After you have successfully deployed the server-side components of the application under the J2EE RI, you can run the simple application client to test the application.

To run an application client you must have obtained the client-side JAR file from the deployed application. You did this when you deployed the application by checking the Return Client Jar... box on the deployment popup window. You can also obtain the client JAR file using either deploytool, the Web-based Admin Console, or the command line asadmin utility as described in the following section "Managing J2EE RI Applications."

The client JAR file contains all the client and EJB class files as well as the RMI stub files required to run the application client.

You run a J2EE RI application client using the appclient command (from the J2EE SDK bin directory). The appclient requires the name of the client JAR as its single -client parameter. Assuming you have followed the deployment process described in the previous section, your returned client JAR file will be in the Day02/exercise/ j2ee-ri directory and called agencyClient.jar.

You can run your deployed client as follows (your command entry is shown in bold):

```
appclient -client j2ee-ri/agencyClient.jar
Welcome to: J2EE in 21 Days Job Agency
Customer list: J2EE in 21 Days Job Agency
abraham
alfred
george
winston

Done
```

The client JAR file is always named after the application by appending `Client.jar` to the name of the application.

Congratulations, you have just deployed and run your first J2EE application. If the client fails to run, then look at the errors on the console window or in the `domains/domain1/logs/server.log` file in the J2EE SDK home directory for more information.

If you want to examine the simple Web Application you deployed with the EJB, then browse to the URL `http://lcoalhost:8000/webagency`. You will look at Web Applications in detail on Days 12, 13, and 14.

Managing J2EE RI Applications

You can manage J2EE RI applications using any of the following interfaces:

- `deploytool`
- The `asadmin` command line utility
- The Admin Console web application (`http://localhost:4848/asadmin/`)

Using `deploytool` you can obtain a list of deployed objects by selecting the `localhost:4848` entry under `Servers` in the left pane and a list of deployed components will be displayed, as shown in Figure 4.12.

FIGURE 4.12

Managing J2EE Deployed Objects with deploytool.

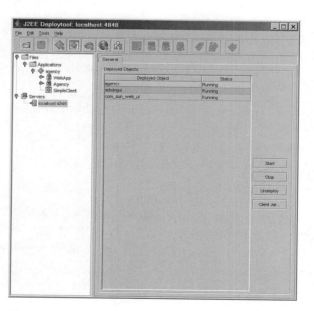

You can start, stop and undeploy an object using the appropriate buttons on this dialog.

Should you need to retrieve a client JAR file from a deployed application you can do this by selecting your application, clicking on the Client Jar... button and specifying a directory location on the popup dialogue window.

If you prefer to work from the command line, then you can use the `asadmin` utility. To deploy an application you use the `asadmin deploy` command. To deploy the example EAR file you have been viewing use the command

```
asadmin deploy --user admin --force j2ee-ri/agency.ear
```

You need to specify the name of your administrative user and the EAR filename; the `--force` option forces a redeployment if the application has already been deployed. You will be prompted for the administrative password unless you have stored this password in a configuration file, or as an environment variable, as described on Day 2 under the installation instructions for the J2EE SDK.

If you want to return the client JAR file when deploying an application use a command such as:

```
asadmin deploy --user admin --force --retrieve j2ee-ri j2ee-ri/agency.ear
```

The `--retrieve` option requires the name of the directory for the client JAR file; the client JAR filename is derived from the application name as described previously.

You can retrieve the client JAR file for a previously deployed application using the `get-client-stubs` command to `asadmin` as follows:

```
asadmin get-client-stubs --user admin --appname agency j2ee-ri
```

This command requires the application name (`--appname` option) and the target directory for the client JAR file.

As discussed on Day 2 `asadmin` will provide useful help messages when an invalid command is entered. And, you can always use the `--help` option to get more information. For example:

```
asadmin -help
asadmin deploy -help
admin get-client-subs --help
```

Finally, you can administer deployed applications using the J2EE RI Admin Console at `http://localhost:4848/asadmin/`. Select the Applications, Enterprise Applications option in the left pane to deploy and undeploy applications as shown in Figure 4.13.

You can only stop, start, deploy and undeploy applications using the Admin Console interface; you cannot return client JAR files.

FIGURE 4.13

Using the J2EE RI Admin Console to Manage J2EE Components.

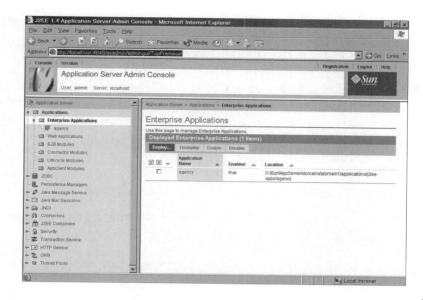

Case Study asant Build Files

As an alternative to using `deploytool` to build and deploy J2EE components, you can use Apache Ant (sometimes called Jakarta Ant) to assemble the EAR or WAR files from the constituent components. Ant is a Java-based, open source, automated build tool that is quickly becoming the *de facto* standard build tool for Java programmers. A version of Apache Ant, called `asant`, is included with the J2EE SDK and example `asant` build files are supplied with the J2EE 1.4 Tutorial examples. A discussion on writing the Ant build files required to assemble a J2EE archive is outside the scope of this book, but the online Ant documentation at `http://ant.apache.org/manual/index.html` gives a good introduction to writing build files. Alternatively you could check out the book *Extreme Programming with Ant* from SAMS Publishing.

On the accompanying Web site, `asant` build files have been provided to compile and package the EAR and WAR files used throughout this book. As described in Day 2, each working directory contains a `build.xml` file that defines the `asant` build targets appropriate for the directory.

The `build.xml` file in the `Day04/exercise` directory will build, deploy, and run the simple client example. In order to help you use `asant` with the case study, each `build.xml` file contains a `help` build target that will tell you which targets you can use for each directory, this is also the default `asant` target. Run the following command from the `Day04/exercise` directory to see what targets are available:

```
asant
```

To remove all the temporary files and then compile and build the case study from scratch, use the command

```
asant clean build
```

The generated agency.ear file is stored in the build subdirectory and is kept separate from the supplied agency.ear file in the j2ee-ri directory. The various deployment descriptors used to build the EAR file are kept in the dd/agency subdirectory.

You can verify the built application using the command

```
asant verify
```

The verification results from this command are stored in the file build/agency.ear.txt.

To deploy the case study from the build directory, use the command

```
asant deploy
```

This will return the client JAR as build/agencyClient.jar. To run the simple client example, use the command

```
asant run
```

You should see the following output:

```
...
appclient:
     [echo] (build) appclient.bat -client agencyClient.jar -name SimpleClient
     [exec] Welcome to: J2EE in 21 Days Job Agency
     [exec] Customer list: J2EE in 21 Days Job Agency
     [exec] abraham
     [exec] alfred
     [exec] george
     [exec] winston

     [exec] Done
```

To undeploy the agency example use

```
asant undeploy
```

If you want to use deploytool to build the EAR file but work at the command line to verify, deploy and run the examples, then you can use the following commands.

Verify the deploytool maintained agency.ear file in the j2ee-ri sub-directory with

```
asant verify-j2ee-ri
```

Deploy and return the j2ee-ri/agencyClient.jar file with

```
asant deploy-j2ee-ri
```

Run the application client (in the `j2ee-ri` sub-directory) using

```
asant run-j2ee-ri
```

To undeploy the agency example you still use

```
asant undeploy
```

Troubleshooting the Case Study Application

If you have encountered difficulties running the case study application, the following may help you in resolving your problems:

- Have you started the J2EE RI?

  If you are not sure, try locating its console window or looking for it in the list of processes or applications on your machine. Try browsing to `http://localhost:4848` to view the Admin Console.

- At J2EE RI install time did you define the HTTP server port to be a different value to 8000?

  Try browsing to `http://localhost:8000` to verify you are using port 8000. If you selected a different HTTP server port number you will have to use your value rather than 8000 as shown in all the examples in this book.

- Have you started the `PointBase` database?

  Try running the initial database test at the end of Day 2 exercise to ensure that the data is present and that the database server is running.

- Have you verified the EJBs?

  Use the `asant` build files to run the command line verifier. Run either

  ```
  asant verify
  ```

  or

  ```
  asant verify-j2ee-ri
  ```

  as discussed in the section "Case Study asant Build Files."

- Have you deployed the EJBs?

  By opening the EAR file, you are simply loading the enterprise application into the `deploytool` environment. You must explicitly deploy the application to the server you are using through the Tools, Deploy menu. Check that you application has been deployed using the Admin Console application at `http://localhost:4848/asadmin`.

4

- Have you retrieved the client JAR file after deploying your application?
  Retrieve your application client using
  `asant deploy-j2ee-ri`
- Does the J2EE RI console window show any exceptions or errors?
- Does the J2EE `server.log` file under the `/domains/domain1/logs` directory in `J2EE_HOME` show errors?

If you still have problems and you suspect there is a problem with the configuration of your J2EE RI, you can re-install, or you could try manually removing the deployed applications. You will find manually removing the applications easier than re-installing.

To manually remove an EJB component, you must perform the following steps, which are described in detail following this list:

1. Stop the J2EE RI server.
2. Remove the application from the J2EE `domains/domain1/applications/j2ee-apps` directory.
3. Remove the application from the J2EE server configuration (`domains/domain1/config/domain.xml`) file.
4. Restart the J2EE server.

You can stop the J2EE server using the command

`asadmin stop-domain`

or simply close down the J2EE RI window.

Once the J2EE RI has stopped you will be able to edit the configuration to manually remove an offending application.

In the J2EE home directory there is a `domains` sub-directory, inside which is a `domain1` directory. Find the `applications/j2ee-apps` directory, and beneath this a subdirectory for each deployed application. Delete the offending application directory. Make sure you do not delete the supplied `MejbApp` and `__ejb_container_timer_app` directories, otherwise you will need to reinstall the J2EE RI.

In the `domains/domain1` directory in the `J2EE_HOME` directory there is a `config` directory and a file called `domain.xml`. For safety, take a backup copy of this file before changing it. Now edit the `domain.xml` file and find the `<applications>` tag element (near the start of the file). Look for a nested `<j2ee-application>` with a `name` attribute matching your application, the entry for the example agency application will look like

```
<j2ee-application enabled="true"
    location="${com.sun.aas.instanceRoot}/applications/j2ee-apps/agency"
    name="agency"
    object-type="user"/>
```

Delete the `<j2ee-application>` element for your application. Make sure you do not delete the `<applications>` element itself or corrupt any other part of this file.

Restart the J2EE server and (hopefully) everything will still work and you can try deploying your application again. If you still have problems, your only option is to remove the J2EE SDK, reinstall and start again.

Summary

Today, you have seen common ways that EJBs are used in applications and why you would want to use them. You have seen that an EJB will have a home interface, a business or remote interface, and an implementation. You have seen how the EJB container will provide much of the underlying code to support the EJB, and that it relies on detailed deployment information that defines the EJB's requirements.

You have also seen that a J2EE application consists of components and deployment information and how the server-side part of such an application can be deployed. You have seen a client that is able to use such server-side components and the code required to write such a client.

Q&A

Q How many Java classes and interfaces must you write to create an EJB?

A The EJB writer must define a remote (or business) interface, a home interface, and the bean implementation itself.

Q Why does an EJB run inside a container?

A The container provides many services to the EJB, including distribution, lifecycle, naming/registration, transaction management, security/authentication, and persistence. If the container did not exist, you would have to write all the code to interact with these services yourself.

Q What issues are there in passing an object as part of a remote method call?

A To be passed as an argument or return type, an object must be either serializable or remote. If it is neither of these, an error will occur at runtime. If an object is defined as serializable, a new copy will be created and passed/returned. This can add to the overhead of making the method call, but it is a very useful tool when trying to cut down the amount of network traffic between clients and EJBs (as you will see later on Day 18).

Q **Most of the deployment descriptor information is straightforward, but what is the difference between a `<resource-ref>` and an `<env-entry>`, and what sort of information is contained in each type of entry?**

A A `<resource-ref>` is part of a deployment descriptor that defines an external resource used by a J2EE component. The `<resource-ref>` will define a name and type for a resource together with other information for the container. To access a resource defined in a `<resource-ref>`, you would use JNDI to look up its name (for example `java:comp/env/jdbc/Agency`).

An `<env-entry>`, on the other hand, contains information that is intended only for the EJB itself. It will define a name, a class type and a value. The contents of `<env-entry>` elements are usually strings. Again, you would use JNDI to look up its name (for example `java:comp/env/AgencyName`).

Exercises

The intention of this day is for you to familiarize yourself with the EJB environment and the use of EJBs. To ensure that you are comfortable with these areas, you should attempt the following tasks.

1. If you have not already done so, follow the steps to deploy the example `Agency` EJB from the `Day04/exercise` directory on the Web site using `deploytool`.

2. Examine the information displayed by `deploytool` and make sure that you can identify where the resource reference for the `Agency` JDBC connection is set, where the environment reference for the agency name is set, and where the JNDI name of the `Agency` EJB itself is set.

3. From within the `Day04/exercise` directory run the command "`asant verify-j2ee-ri`" to verify your application.

4. Use the `appclient` command shown in today's lesson and run the `SimpleClient` example. Make sure that this client runs without errors and successfully lists all the customers in the agency database.

5. Try changing the name under which the EJB is registered in JNDI using `deploytool`. Change the JNDI name used by your client to find the `Agency` EJB and make sure that it still works.

6. Use the `asant` build files instead of `deploytool` to compile, build, verify and deploy the example Agency application.

7. Edit the `dd/agency/sun-j2ee-ri.xml` file (make a backup first of course) and change the JNDI name for the Agency Session EJB. Change the JNDI name used by your client to find the Agency EJB and make sure that it still works.

DAY 5

Session EJBs

On Day 4, "Introduction to Enterprise JavaBeans," you saw that business functionality can be implemented using Session beans, and you deployed a simple Session bean into the EJB container. Today, you learn about

- The uses of Session beans in more detail
- The different Session bean types and how to specify, implement, and deploy both stateless and stateful Session beans
- Common practices and idioms when using Session beans

Overview

As you saw yesterday, Session beans are a key technology within the J2EE platform because they allow business functionality to be developed and then deployed independently of the presentational layer.

For example, you might create an application with a user interface built using Java's Swing API. This application might then provide access to some business functionality for the employees working on the company's internal network. If the underlying business functionality is implemented as Session beans, a different user interface could take its place without having to redevelop the entire application. A Web-based interface would make the application available from the Internet at a single stroke.

There are two types of Session beans: stateful and stateless. Stateful Session beans, as the name suggests, maintain client state and can therefore only be used by a single client. Stateless Session beans maintain no client state and can be shared among many clients. A couple of analogies help explain the differences between them.

At some point, you almost certainly will have used a so-called wizard to guide you through some task--in any modern word-processing program or IDE. A wizard encapsulates a conversation between you the user and the application running on the computer. The steps in that conversation are dictated by the Next and the Back buttons. The wizard remembers the answers from one page, and these sometimes dictate the choices for the next. When you are done, you select the Finish button and the wizard goes away and does its stuff.

The wizard is analogous to a stateful Session bean. The wizard remembers the answers from each page, or put another way, it remembers the state of the conversation. It also provides some service, as characterized by the Finish button. This is precisely what a stateful Session bean does.

On the other hand, you may well have had cause to write or call stored procedures. These are named routines (methods and functions) that are stored in a database. They provide a way to implement business rules on the database.

To invoke a stored procedure, a client-side application needs to know just the name of the stored procedure and the parameters it requires. No knowledge of the underlying database schema is needed.

A stored procedure is analogous to a stateless Session bean. The stored procedure just provides a service and can be invoked by any client.

Session beans provide a service to a client application. In other words, Session beans are an extension of a client's business functionality into the middle tier.

The `javax.ejb` Package for Session beans

Now it is time to add a little more detail. EJBs are written by implementing various interfaces of the `javax.ejb` package. Figure 5.1 shows a UML class diagram of the interfaces in `javax.ejb` that support Session beans.

FIGURE 5.1

The `javax.ejb`
package defines remote
and local interfaces, as
well as an interface for
the Session bean to
implement.

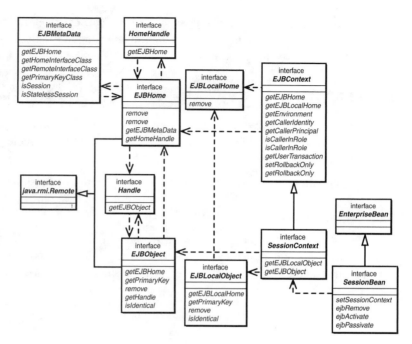

Central to the EJB architecture are the `javax.ejb.EJBHome` and `javax.ejb.EJBObject`
interfaces, common to both Session beans and Entity beans. These both extend the
`java.rmi.Remote` interface, which means that the classes that implement them (not
shown) are available through RMI stubs across the network.

The `javax.ejb.EJBLocalHome` and `javax.ejb.EJBLocalObject` interfaces are local
equivalents, and the classes that implement these are accessible only locally (that is, by
clients that reside within the same EJB container itself). Because local interfaces are
most often used with Entity beans, and also because there's plenty for you to learn today,
there's no major discussion of local interfaces until tomorrow.

The `javax.ejb.EJBContext` interface provides access to the home interfaces and, as you
can see from its method list, also provides security and transaction control. The
`javax.ejb.SessionContext` subclass (only used by Session beans) provides a reference
to the bean's `EJBObject`, that is, its interface for remote clients.

The `javax.ejb.HomeHandle` and `javax.ejb.Handle` interfaces provide a mechanism to
serialize a reference to either a home or a remote interface for use later. This capability is
not often used, so isn't discussed further.

5

The Session bean itself implements the `javax.ejb.SessionBean` interface that defines the bean's lifecycle methods and has an implementation for all of the methods defined in the remote or the home interface.

Specifying a Stateless Session bean

You already know that there are two different types of Session bean—stateful and stateless. You'll see examples of both types today, but the first example you will study is the stateless Agency bean you saw yesterday.

As you will by now have gathered, the responsibilities of Session beans (and indeed, Entity beans) are specified through their remote and home interfaces. These are what the EJB container makes available to the remote clients.

To define a home interface for a stateless Session bean you extend `javax.ejb.EJBHome`; and to define a remote interface you extend `javax.ejb.EJBObject`. Because both `EJBHome` and `EJBObject` extend the `java.rmi.Remote` interface, their methods are restricted as follows:

- All methods must throw `RemoteException`.
- All parameters and return types must either be `Serializable` or `Remote` objects.

The following is the home interface for the `Agency` session bean. If it looks familiar, it should be--you saw this for the first time just yesterday.

```
package agency;

import java.rmi.*;
import javax.ejb.*;
public interface AgencyHome extends EJBHome
{
    Agency create() throws RemoteException, CreateException;
}
```

The `AgencyHome` interface defines a single no-arg method called `create()`. This method returns an `Agency` reference, which is the remote interface for the `Agency` bean.

The EJB specification requires that stateless Session beans must define this single no-arg version of the `create()` method. The bean can perform any initialization it requires there. The `create()` method throws `java.rmi.RemoteException`, as required for remote objects, and can also throw `javax.ejb.CreateException` to indicate that it was unable to initialize itself correctly.

The `create()` method in the home interface requires a corresponding `ejbCreate()` method in the bean class itself. This delegation to a method with an `ejb` prefix is prevalent throughout the EJB specification, so you will become quite familiar with it over the next few days. The corresponding code in the `AgencyBean` class is as follows (this class is discussed in detail in the next section, "Implementing a StatelessSession bean"):

```
package agency;

// some import statements omitted
import java.rmi.*;
import java.util.*;
import javax.ejb.*;

public class AgencyBean implements SessionBean
{
    public void ejbCreate() throws CreateException {
        // implementation omitted
    }

    // code omitted
}
```

Note that the `ejbCreate()` method also takes no arguments because the argument list of this method must match the argument list of the `create()` method in the home interface. The `throws` clause includes `javax.ejb.CreateException`, because that was defined in the home interface, but does not include `java.rmi.RemoteException`. This is because the bean itself is not remote; it is the code generated by the vendor's deployments tools that is remote. The EJB specification requires that `ejbCreate()` method returns `void`.

Listing 5.1 shows the remote interface for the `Agency` Session bean. Again, you saw this yesterday:

5

LISTING 5.1   Remote Interface for the Stateless `Agency` Bean

```
package agency;

import java.rmi.*;
import java.util.*;
import javax.ejb.*;

public interface Agency extends EJBObject
{
    String getAgencyName() throws RemoteException;

    Collection getApplicants() throws RemoteException;
    void createApplicant(String login, String name, String email)
        throws RemoteException, DuplicateException, CreateException;
```

LISTING 5.1   continued

```
        void deleteApplicant (String login)
            throws RemoteException, NotFoundException;

        Collection getCustomers() throws RemoteException;
        void createCustomer(String login, String name, String email)
            throws RemoteException, DuplicateException, CreateException;
        void deleteCustomer(String login)
            throws RemoteException, NotFoundException;

        Collection getLocations() throws RemoteException;
        void addLocation(String name) throws RemoteException, DuplicateException;
        void removeLocation(String code) throws RemoteException, NotFoundException;

        Collection getSkills() throws RemoteException;
        void addSkill(String name) throws RemoteException, DuplicateException;
        void removeSkill(String name) throws RemoteException, NotFoundException;

        List select(String table) throws RemoteException;
}
```

You can see that the Agency Session bean provides functionality, or services, for managing applicants, customers, locations, and skills. These services manipulate data within the database, but there is no underlying state for the bean itself. In each case, the methods throw java.rmi.RemoteException as required and also throw various other exceptions. The DuplicateException and NotFoundException are user-defined exception classes that simply extend java.lang.Exception.

For each of these service methods in the remote interface, there must be a correspondingly named method in the Session bean. As was noted yesterday, this is not because the bean has implemented the remote interface (it hasn't) but because the EJB specification requires it so that the EJBObject proxy (the vendor-generated implementation of the remote interface) can delegate to the bean. The business methods for the AgencyBean have the same signature as those in the remote interface, with the exception that they do not throw java.rmi.RemoteException.

Those are the steps to specifying a stateless Session bean's interface. As you will see later today and tomorrow, specifying the interface of stateful Session beans and of Entity beans follows along very similar lines. In the next section, "Implementing a Stateless Session bean," you will see the implementation of some of these methods.

Implementing a Stateless Session Bean

Implementing a Session bean involves defining a class that implements `javax.ejb.SessionBean` and provides an implementation for the lifecycle methods of the `SessionBean`, implementations of each method in the home interface, and an implementation of each business method in the remote interface. Before looking in detail at how to do all this, you need to be comfortable with the details of the stateless Session bean lifecycle.

Stateless Session Bean Lifecycle

Stateless beans hold no state for any particular client, but they do have a lifecycle—and thus different states—imposed on them by the EJB architecture. Specifically, these are the interactions between the bean and the container in which it has been deployed.

This is a recurrent theme throughout the EJB architecture, so it is important to fully understand it. The methods you define in your bean will be invoked either by the client or by the EJB container itself. Specifically, the methods invoked by the client will be those defined in the remote interface and the `create` methods in the home interface, whereas the methods invoked by the container are those defined by the `javax.ejb.SessionBean` interface.

Figure 5.2 shows the `SessionBean` interface and its super-interfaces.

FIGURE 5.2

The `javax.ejb.`
`SessionBean` *interface
defines certain lifecy-
cle methods that must
be implemented by
Session beans.*

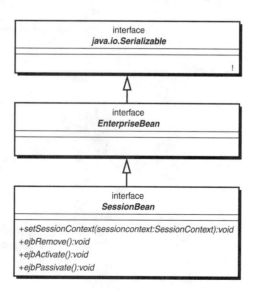

In the case study, the `AgencyBean` class indicates that it is a Session bean by implementing this interface:

```
package agency;

import javax.ejb.*;
// some import statements omitted

public class AgencyBean implements SessionBean
{
    // code omitted
}
```

The lifecycle for Session beans, as perceived by the Session bean and as likely to be enacted by the EJB container, is as shown in the UML state chart diagram in Figure 5.3.

FIGURE 5.3

Stateless Session beans have a lifecycle managed by the EJB container.

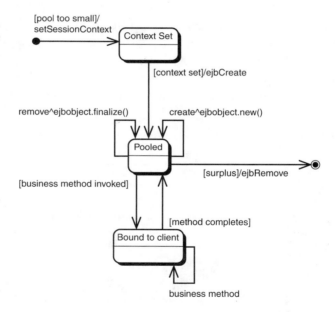

The lifecycle is as follows:

- When the EJB container requires an instance of the stateless Session bean (for example, because the pool of instances is too small), it instantiates the bean and then calls the lifecycle method `setSessionContext()`. This provides the bean with a reference to a `SessionContext` object, providing access to its security and transaction context.

- Immediately after the context has been set, the container will call `ejbCreate()`. This means that the bean is now ready to have methods invoked. Note that the `ejbCreate()` method is not part of the `SessionBean` interface, but nevertheless must be declared in the bean.

- When a client invokes a business method, it is delegated by the bean's `EJBObject` proxy to the bean itself. During this time, the bean is temporarily bound to the client. When the method completes, the bean is available to be called again.

The binding of the bean to the client lasts only as long as the method takes to execute, so it will typically be just a few milliseconds. The EJB specification specifies this approach so that the bean developer does not need to worry about making the bean thread-safe.

To support the case where two (or more) clients need to invoke the service of some stateless Session bean at the same time, most EJB containers hold a pool of Session beans. In general, the pool will never be larger than the maximum number of concurrent clients. If a container decides that the pool is too large or that some Session bean instances are surplus, it will call the bean's `ejbRemove()` method.

If the client calls `create()` or `remove()`, the bean itself is not necessarily affected. However, the client's reference to the bean will be initialized or destroyed. The client is not aware of the complexities of this lifecycle, so the client's perception of a stateless bean is somewhat simpler, as shown in Figure 5.4.

FIGURE 5.4

The client's perception of the bean's lifecycle is simple.

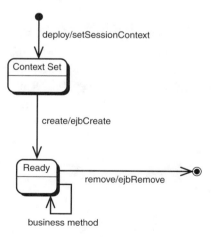

5

From the client's perspective, the bean is simply instantiated when the client calls `create()` on the bean's home interface and is removed when the client calls `remove()` on the bean itself.

Figures 5.3 and 5.4 show how the methods of the SessionBean interface are invoked through the bean's lifecycle. You will have noticed that the ejbActivate() and ejbPassivate() methods are not mentioned; this is because these methods are only called for stateful Session beans, a topic covered later today. However, given that these methods are in the SessionBean interface, they do require an implementation. For stateless Session beans, this implementation will be empty.

Implementing `javax.ejb.SessionBean`

The implementation of the methods of the SessionBean interface is often boilerplate. The setSessionContext() method will typically just save the supplied SessionContext object:

```
private SessionContext ctx;
public void setSessionContext(SessionContext ctx) {
    this.ctx = ctx;
}
```

As already noted, for a stateless Session bean, the ejbActivate() and ejbPassivate() methods should have a null implementation:

```
public void ejbActivate() { }
public void ejbPassivate() { }
```

Although ejbRemove() method is part of the SessionBean interface, you'll learn about its implementation in the next section.

Implementing the Home Interface Methods

The home interface has a single method create(). The ejbCreate() method in the bean corresponds to this method. It makes sense to look up JNDI references in the ejbCreate() method and store them in instance variables. This is shown in Listing 5.2.

LISTING 5.2   AgencyBean.ejbCreate() Method

```
private DataSource dataSource;
private String name = "";
public void ejbCreate () throws CreateException {
    InitialContext ic = null;
    try {
        ic = new InitialContext();
        dataSource = (DataSource)ic.lookup("java:comp/env/jdbc/Agency");
    }
    catch (NamingException ex) {
        error("Error connecting to java:comp/env/jdbc/Agency:",ex);
        return;
    }
```

LISTING 5.2 continued

```
try {
    name = (String)ic.lookup("java:comp/env/AgencyName");
}
catch (NamingException ex) {
    error("Error looking up java:comp/env/AgencyName:",ex);
}
}
```

In this case, the `ejbCreate()` method makes two lookups from JNDI; the first is to obtain a `DataSource` (DataSource objects were covered on Day 3, "Naming and Directory Services"), and the other is to obtain the Agency name environment configuration information.

> **TIP**
>
> Many developers prefer to use the `setSessionContext()` method to initialize a stateless Session bean, as this mirrors the use of the `setEntityContext()` method used for initializing Entity beans (see Day 6, "Entity EJBs").

Incidentally, this is a good place to note that a stateless Session bean does not mean that the bean has no state; just that it has no state that is specific to any given client. In the case of the `Agency` bean, it caches a `DataSource` and its name in instance variables.

The bean's remote interface inherits a `remove()` method from EJBObject and the bean's home interface inherits a `remove()` method from EJBHome. Calls to either of these methods are delegated to the `ejbRemove()` method of the bean. The implementation is usually very simple; it should just reset state:

```
public void ejbRemove(){
    dataSource = null;
    name = null;
}
```

Implementing the Remote Interface Methods

The remaining methods in a Session bean correspond to the business methods defined in the remote interface. The `Agency` Session bean manipulates the data in the `Applicant`, `Customer`, `Location`, and `Skill` tables, providing methods to return all the data in a table, to insert a new item, or to delete an existing item. When deleting rows, dependent rows in other tables are also removed (a cascade delete strategy).

The methods that manipulate the database all require a `java.sql.Connection` to submit SQL to the database. In regular "fat client" applications, the idiom is to create a database connection at application startup and to close the connection only when the user quits the application. This idiom exists because making database connections is expensive in performance terms. When writing EJBs, however, the idiom is the precise opposite. You should obtain the database connection just before it is needed, and close it as soon as your processing is complete. In other words, "acquire late, release early." This is because the EJB container has already made the database connections and holds them in a pool. When your bean obtains its connection, it is simply being "leased" one from the pool for a period of time. When the connection is "closed," in reality it is simply returned back to the pool to be used again.

The `getLocations()` method shows this principle clearly, as shown in Listing 5.3.

LISTING 5.3   `AgencyBean.getLocations()` Method

```
public Collection getLocations() {
    Connection con = null;
    PreparedStatement stmt = null;
    ResultSet rs = null;
    try {
        con = dataSource.getConnection();
        stmt = con.prepareStatement("SELECT name FROM Location");
        rs = stmt.executeQuery();

        Collection col = new TreeSet();
        while (rs.next()) {
            col.add(rs.getString(1));
        }

        return col;
    }
    catch (SQLException e) {
        error("Error getting Location list",e);
    }
    finally {
        closeConnection(con, stmt, rs);
    }
    return null;
}
private void closeConnection (Connection con,
            PreparedStatement stmt, ResultSet rslt) {
    if (rslt != null) {
        try {
            rslt.close();
        }
        catch (SQLException e) {}
    }
    if (stmt != null) {
        try {
```

LISTING 5.3   continued

```
            stmt.close();
        }
        catch (SQLException e) {}
    }
    if (con != null) {
        try {
            con.close();
        }
        catch (SQLException e) {}
    }
}
```

In this method, you can see the DataSource object obtained in the ejbCreate() method in use. The Connection object is obtained from this DataSource object. Another advantage of this approach is that the user and password information does not need to be embedded within the code; rather, it is set up by the deployer who configures the DataSource using vendor-specific tools. As you remember from Day 2, "The J2EE Platform and Roles," in the J2EE RI, the DataSource object is configured using the asadmin command-line tool or the Web-based Admin Console.

The other business methods all access the database in a similar manner and can be examined on the code supplied under the examples directory of Day 5 on the accompanying Web site.

Exceptions

Your bean needs to be able to indicate when it hits a problem. Because the client does not call your bean directly, the EJB specification lays out certain rules as to the types of exceptions your bean can throw. For remote clients, there is also the possibility of network problems.

The EJB specification categorizes exceptions as either application exceptions or system exceptions. These correspond quite closely to the regular Java categories of checked exceptions and runtime exceptions.

Figure 5.5 shows the exceptions in the javax.ejb package, indicating which are application and which are system exceptions.

So, what do these categorizations mean? If a bean throws an application exception, the EJB container will propagate this back to the application client. As you shall see on Day 8, "Transactions and Persistence," any ongoing transaction is not terminated by an application exception. In other words, the semantics of an application exception are pretty similar to a checked exception; generally, the client can recover if desired.

5

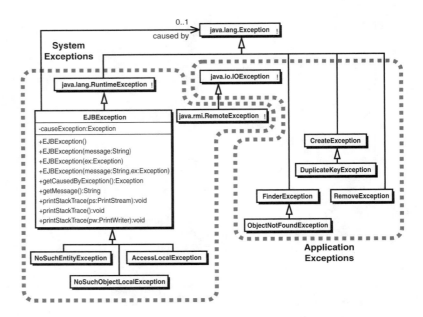

FIGURE 5.5

Exceptions are either system exceptions or application exceptions.

However, if a bean throws a system exception, that indicates a severe problem that will not be recoverable by the client. For example, if the database connection fails, there is very little that the client can do about it. In such a case, the EJB container will take steps to terminate any ongoing transaction because it is unlikely to complete. Moreover, the EJB container will discard the bean instance that threw the exception. In other words, there is no need to code any clean up logic in your bean after a system exception is thrown.

Although all runtime exceptions are classified as EJB system exceptions and the `javax.ejb.EJBException` is a `RuntimeException` provided for your use, this class allows the underlying cause to be wrapped through one of its constructors. The `error()` helper method in `AgencyBean` does precisely this:

```
private void error (String msg, Exception ex) {
    String s = "AgencyBean: "+msg + "\n" + ex;
    System.out.println(s);
    throw new EJBException(s,ex);
}
```

In Figure 5.5, you can see that there is one checked exception, namely `java.rmi.RemoteException`, that is classified as an EJB system exception rather than as an EJB application exception. Your bean code should never throw this exception; instead, it is reserved for the EJB container itself. If your bean has hit a system exception, it should throw an `EJBException` rather than `RemoteException`.

Configuring a Stateless Session bean

With the code compiled, the next step is to deploy the bean onto the EJB container.

As you saw yesterday, EJBs are designed to be portable across EJB containers, and the configuration information that defines the bean's name, interfaces, classes, characteristics, dependencies, and so on, is stored in an XML document called a deployment descriptor. This is provided along with the bean code itself.

As you appreciate from Day 2, there are several EJB roles involved in building a deployment descriptor. The bean provider specifies the information about a given bean ("intra-bean" configuration information, if you like), and the application assembler specifies the information about all the beans in an application ("inter-bean" configuration information). When both the bean provider and application assembler have specified their information, the "portable" deployment descriptor is complete.

However, that's not the end of the story, because the deployment descriptor does not define every piece of configuration information necessary to deploy a bean. In effect, the deployment descriptor defines only the logical relationships and dependencies between the beans. There will also be additional configuration information that maps the logical dependencies of the deployment descriptor to the physical environment. Performing this mapping is the role of the deployer. The two aspects of deployment are captured in two separate deployment descriptor files:

- The portable EJB deployment descriptor defined in the EJB specification (stored as `META-INF/ejb-jar.xml`).

- A vendor-specific deployment settings. The J2EE RI uses an XML descriptor called `META-INF/sun-ejb-jar.xml`, other platforms may use different naming or alternative techniques to capture this information.

Thus, all that is required to port an EJB from one EJB container to another is to create a platform specific deployment descriptor. In other words, the deployer has to redeploy the application, but the bean provider and the application assembler should not have to get involved.

Because manipulating XML documents can be somewhat error prone, most EJB container vendors provide graphical tools to do the work. As you saw yesterday, in the case of the J2EE RI this is the `deploytool` GUI. Unfortunately, many such tools do not distinguish between information that is being saved in the standard deployment descriptor and that which is being saved in the vendor's own auxiliary deployment descriptors. Also, many tools do not explicitly support the EJB architecture's concept of roles, making it possible for a bean provider to start specifying information that might more correctly be

5

decided only by the application assembler or even the deployer. The `deploytool` provided with J2EE RI 1.4 separates out the Sun Specific deployment requirements but still
does not clearly differentiate between developer, assembler and deployer functionality.
Because you may not be using J2EE RI in your own projects, this section presents the
task of deployment by looking at both the J2EE RI `deploytool` and also the underlying
XML deployment descriptor. Understanding the XML deployment descriptor makes the
`deploytool` GUI easier to comprehend. If you choose to use `asant` build files (as discussed on Day 4) you will need to become more familiar with the deployment descriptor
syntax than if you use the `deploytool` GUI interface.

Configuring a Session Bean Using J2EE RI `deploytool`

This section shows how to deploy the Day 5 version of the case study application to the
J2EE RI. You will get the most out of this if you actually perform these steps (but if
you're on a train or plane, just read the text and make do).

As usual, start up the PointBase database server and J2EE RI server before starting
`deploytool` as shown yesterday.

By choosing File, Open, load up the `Day05/examples/j2ee-ri/agency.ear` enterprise
application archive. This defines a single group of Session beans called `Agency`. Their
contents have already been partially configured to contain the appropriate code.
Highlight the Agency application in the explorer on the left side of the `deploytool` GUI
and its contents will be shown on the right side, as shown in Figure 5.6.

The `agency.ear` file you have just opened does not contain the Agency stateless Session
bean.

NOTE

> In the `Day05/examples/j2ee-ri` directory there is an `agency.orig.ear` file.
> This is a copy of the `agency.ear` file. Should you make a mistake in the fol-
> lowing steps you can replace `agency.ear` with this file and start again.

You will now be guided through the process of creating this bean using the `deploytool`
wizard. As each step is performed, you will be shown the component parts of the deployment descriptor that are being created. If you prefer to view the complete application,
you can use the `agency.ear` file in the `Day05/agency/j2ee-ri` directory on the
Web site.

FIGURE 5.6

Partially defined Agency case study EJBs.

Defining a New EJB Session bean

All EJBS must be placed in a JAR file, and an enterprise application (EAR) can contain one or more EJB JAR files. For your own custom applications, it really is up to you whether you choose to use one JAR file or several. In the case study example, many separate JARs have been used. Your first step in adding a new Session bean to the case study is to select the existing Agency JAR file in the right hand pane and then use the File, New, Enterprise Bean… menu option to start the EJB wizard.

You will be presented with an Introduction page describing the steps you are about to perform. You can check the Skip this Screen in Future checkbox on this page if you want to hide it for future EJBs. Click on Next.

The first step in defining the Agency stateless Session bean is to add the required class files to the JAR file. The next screen displayed by the wizard asks you whether to add to an existing JAR or create a new JAR. Select Add to Existing JAR Module, select the Agency JAR. Figure 5.7 shows this dialogue page with the existing JAR file list expanded so you can see the files already included in the JAR file.

Click on the Edit button to add the Agency class files. In the popup dialog, select the following files from the Day05/examples/classes directory:

```
agency/Agency.class
agency/AgencyBean.class
agency/AgencyHome.class
```

FIGURE 5.7

Adding a new EJB.

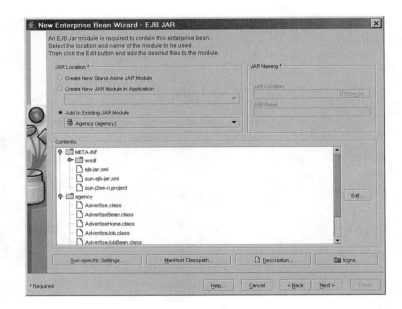

You should have a screen similar to the one shown in Figure 5.8.

FIGURE 5.8

Adding EJB class files to an existing JAR file.

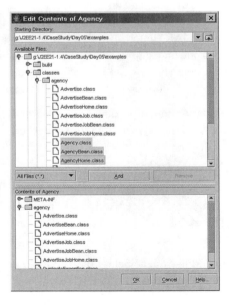

After selecting the Agency Session bean class files in the Edit Contents dialog, click on the Add button to add the files. Now click on OK to return to the wizard dialog and then click on Next to move to the dialog to define the Session bean and its interface classes.

Defining the Session Bean

The wizard General dialog screen shown in Figure 5.9 is used to define the Session bean.

FIGURE 5.9

Defining a stateless Session bean.

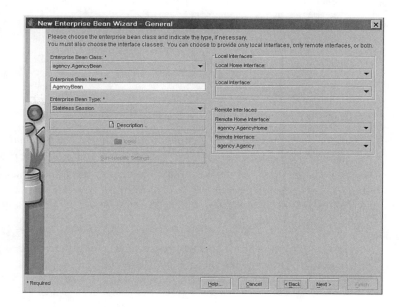

Figure 5.9 shows the Agency EJB configured as a stateless Session bean, the bean class set to agency.AgencyBean, and the Remote and Remote Home interfaces set to agency.Agency and agency.AgencyHome. The interfaces must be configured as Remote interfaces, and the Local interfaces must be left blank. (Local interfaces are discussed tomorrow when Entity beans are described.)

What you are doing using deploytool is building up the JAR file and deployment descriptor for the EJB. The selected class files will be added to the JAR file when you finish the wizard. As you step through each page of the wizard, you will define different parts of the deployment descriptor. To help you understand what information is being added to the deployment descriptor, each dialog step of the process will be related to the generated deployment descriptor.

5

The (fragment of the) underlying deployment descriptor for the Agency bean that is represented in Figure 5.9 is (new entry in bold):

```
<ejb-jar>
  <enterprise-beans>
  …
    <session>
      <ejb-name>AgencyBean</ejb-name>
      <home>agency.AgencyHome</home>
      <remote>agency.Agency</remote>
      <ejb-class>agency.AgencyBean</ejb-class>
      <session-type>Stateless</session-type>
      ...
    </session>
  …
  </enterprise-beans>
…
</ejb-jar>
```

The remaining items of the EJB deployment descriptor are optional and are configured by different pages of the deployment wizard. After you have selected the bean type and required classes, click on the Next button to display the Configuration Options screen. On this screen ensure the Expose Bean as Web Service Endpoint is set to No and click on next. Web service endpoints are discussed on Day 20, "Using RPC-Style Web Services with J2EE."

The last page of the wizard prompts you with common steps needed to complete the EJB configuration. After reading this page you can click on Finish and your partially defined Agency stateless Session bean has been added to the JAR file.

To complete the Agency Session bean configuration you will need to perform the following steps, full details of which are included in subsequent sections:

- Define the Sun Specific JNDI name for the EJB
- Add an Environment Entry for the Job Agency name
- Add a Resource Reference for the Agency database
- Add transaction Management options

To define each of these parameters in deploytool you must select the AgencyBean EJB in the left pane and select an appropriate dialog page in the right pane.

NOTE   With the Agency JAR or any of its EJBs selected in the left pane you can use the View, Descriptor Viewer to study the portable deployment descriptor as you add information through the deploytool GUI interface. Similarly, the View, Descriptor Viewer, Application Server Descriptor can be used to view the Sun-specific deployment descriptor sun-ejb-jar.xml.

Defining the JNDI Name

Select the AgencyBean and the General dialog tab as shown in Figure 5.10.

FIGURE 5.10

EJB General Dialog Page.

Click on the Sun-specific Settings… button and in the popup window change the JNDI name from AgencyBean to ejb/Agency as shown in Figure 5.11.

You do not need to provide values for the other fields because these are server administration settings for the EJB that we are not interested in at the moment. Click on Close to save your new JNDI name. This page has added the following entry to the sun-ejb-jar.xml deployment descriptor file (shown in bold):

```
<sun-ejb-jar>
  <enterprise-beans>
    <name>Agency</name>
...
    <ejb>
      <ejb-name>AgencyBean</ejb-name>
      <jndi-name>ejb/Agency</jndi-name>
    </ejb>
  </enterprise-beans>
</sun-ejb-jar>
```

Remember, you can use the View, Descriptor Viewer, Application Server Descriptor menu option to view the Sun-specific deployment descriptor.

5

FIGURE 5.11

*Defining the Sun-spe-
cific JNDI name for
an EJB.*

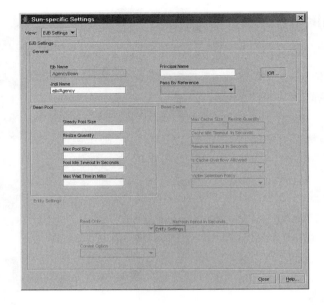

Transaction Management

Continuing with setting the Session bean configuration, select the `AgencyBean` and the
Transactions dialog tab to set the Transaction Management. There are two approaches to
managing transactions:

- Bean-managed, where you code up the transaction start and commit or rollback
  method calls explicitly

- Container-managed, where you add `<container-transaction>` elements to the
  deployment descriptor to define transaction management

Transactions are described in detail on Day 8, but for now you should set your bean to be
container-managed, as shown in Figure 5.12.

When you select container-managed transactions, each method in the interfaces and the
bean must be given a transaction status. The default status is `required` transactions,
meaning that each method will run within a transaction. This is exactly what the Agency
EJB needs, so the default setting for all methods is appropriate. The deployment descriptor entries for transactions will be left until Day 8, when transactions are covered in
detail.

FIGURE 5.12

Defining container managed transactions.

Environment Entries

Now select the AgencyBean and the Env Entries dialog tab to add environment entries that support general EJB configuration information. Environment entries are strongly typed name/value objects.

The Agency bean uses an environment entry to look up its name as a String object. The relevant code is in the ejbCreate() method:

```
InitialContext ic = new InitialContext();
// code omitted
name = (String)ic.lookup("java:comp/env/AgencyName");
```

The EJB specification requires that the EJB container makes the environment entries available under the java component context of java:comp/env. Therefore, this is needed in the JNDI lookup. However, this prefix is not required in the deployment descriptor itself. Click on Add to create an entry for AgencyName as shown in Figure 5.13.

In the underlying deployment descriptor for the Agency bean, the entry shown in Figure 5.13 corresponds to (new entry in bold):

```
<ejb-jar>
  <enterprise-beans>
    <session>
      <ejb-name>AgencyBean</ejb-name>
...
```

5

```
<env-entry>
  <env-entry-name>AgencyName</env-entry-name>
  <env-entry-type>java.lang.String</env-entry-type>
  <env-entry-value>J2EE in 21 Days Job Agency</env-entry-value>
</env-entry>
```
...
```
  </session>
```
...
```
  </enterprise-beans>
</ejb-jar>
```

FIGURE 5.13

*Defining an
Environment Entry.*

To re-emphasize, note that the entry name in the deployment descriptor is `AgencyName`, not `java:comp/env/AgencyName`.

Resource References

Finally, select the `AgencyBean` and the Resource Refs dialog tab to add EJB resource references. These are external entities such as JDBC data sources, email sessions (Day 11, "JavaMail"), URLs, JMS connection factories (Day 10, "Message-Driven Beans"), or general resources as defined by the Connector architecture (Day 19, "Integrating with External Resources").

The `Agency` bean has a dependency on a `DataSource` reference that it refers to as `jdbc/Agency`; this is the database you configured on Day 2. You can see this in the `ejbCreate()` method of the `AgencyBean` code:

```
InitialContext ic = new InitialContext();
dataSource = (DataSource)ic.lookup("java:comp/env/jdbc/Agency");
```

On the Resource Refs page click on Add to create a new resource reference and set the name to be `jdbc/Agency`, type to `javx.sql.DataSource`, `Container` authentication and sharable as shown in Figure 5.14.

FIGURE 5.14

Defining a Resource Reference.

In the deployment descriptor for the `Agency` bean, you have added the following (new entry in bold):

```
<ejb-jar>
  <enterprise-beans>
    <session>
      <ejb-name>AgencyBean</ejb-name>
...
      <resource-ref>
        <res-ref-name>jdbc/Agency</res-ref-name>
        <res-type>javax.sql.DataSource</res-type>
        <res-auth>Container</res-auth>
```

```
        <res-sharing-scope>Shareable</res-sharing-scope>
      </resource-ref>
...
    </session>
...
  </enterprise-beans>
</ejb-jar>
```

As with environment entries the resource reference name you specify to deploytool (and put in the deployment descriptor) does not include the java:comp/env prefix you use in the Java code to do the JNDI lookup.

You will also need to map the resource reference onto an actual resource provided by the J2EE container. In the Sun-specific Settings at the bottom of the Resource Ref dialog page enter the details for the actual datasource to be used. Make sure the entry for jdbc/Agency you have just created is selected and then provide a JNDI name of jdbc/Agency, username of pbPublic and password of pbPublic (as shown in Figure 5.14).

This has updated the Agency EJB entry in the sun-ejb-jar.xml file as follows (new entry in bold):

```
<sun-ejb-jar>
  <enterprise-beans>
    <name> Agency</name>
...
    <ejb>
      <ejb-name>AgencyBean</ejb-name>
      <jndi-name> ejb/Agency</jndi-name>
      <resource-ref>
        <res-ref-name>jdbc/Agency</res-ref-name>
        <jndi-name>jdbc/Agency</jndi-name>
        <default-resource-principal>
          <name>pbPublic</name>
          <password>pbPublic</password>
        </default-resource-principal>
      </resource-ref>
    </ejb>
...
  </enterprise-beans>
</sun-ejb-jar>
```

The Agency EJB configuration is now complete and you can run the verifier to validate the code. Save your changes and then use the Tools, Verify J2EE Compliance… menu option to start up the GUI verifier.

NOTE

The Nov 2003 release of the J2EE RI `deploytool` incorrectly reports errors for the Agency application. You will get three errors referring to a blank JNDI name for the `jdbc/Agency` references in each of the EJBs in the application (`Agency`, `Advertise` and `AdvertiseJob`). You can safely ignore these errors. For your peace of mind you can run the command line verifier on the EAR file you have just updated using the command:

```
asant verify-j2ee-ri
```

Run this command from the `Day05/examples` directory, and don't forget to save the changes you made with `deploytool` first.

At this point, if you were simply deploying EJBs, you could deploy the application, but the case study requires the client application to be updated to reference this new EJB. This is covered later in the section "Configuring J2EE RI Client Applications with `deploytool`."

EJB Deployment Descriptor

Before leaving stateless Session beans, you should be aware that there are several aspects of the deployment descriptor that have not been shown in detail. In Figure 5.10, you saw a set of dialog tabs, only some of which are required for the Agency example. The following configuration options are discussed elsewhere:

- EJB Refs on Day 6, "Entity EJBs"

  EJB references indicate that the bean being deployed uses other EJBs, and the deployer must map the coded EJB name onto the deployed EJB (usually via a JNDI name).

- Message Dest Refs on Day 10, "Message-Driven Beans"

  Message Destination References are Message-Driven Beans that uses this EJB to send messages, and the deployer must link the coded message destination to the actual MDB.

- Resource Env Refs on Day 9, "Java Message Service"

  Resource environment references allow access to so-called "administered objects." In J2EE RI, this includes JMS queues, JMS topics, and connection factories. The deployer must map the coded name onto the actual JNDI used to access the JMS entity.

- Security on Day 15, "Security"

  Security defines authorization requirements for accessing the EJB methods.

5

- Web Service Refs on Day 20, "Using RPC-Style Web Services with J2EE"

  Web Service references refer to Web Services used by this EJB and the deployer must map the coded Web Service URL onto the actual Web Service URL.

You will now consider client applications so you can complete this example. After this, today's lesson will be completed with a look at stateful Session beans.

Client Applications

Yesterday, you saw how a client application uses JNDI to obtain a reference to a Session bean home object and how to obtain a Session bean by calling the appropriate `create()` method. Now that you have a better understanding of how Session beans work, there are a few other points that are worth appreciating.

Design Considerations

First, if your client has a reference to a stateless Session bean, although it should call `remove()` when it is finished with the EJB, this method call doesn't actually do much. In particular, it won't release any bean resources itself. What this will do is allow the EJB container to remove the `EJBObject` proxy for the bean.

Conversely, calling `create()` for a stateless Session bean doesn't necessarily cause `ejbCreate()` to be called on the underlying bean, although the client will have a reference to an `EJBObject` after making this call.

One benefit of stateless beans over stateful beans is that, to the client, they appear to be more resilient. If the client invokes a method on a stateless bean and it throws an exception, the client can still use its reference to try again. The client does not need to discard the reference and obtain a new one from the home interface. This is because, behind the scenes, although the EJB container will have discarded the bean that threw the exception, it can simply select another bean from the pool to service the client's retry attempt.

In contrast, if a stateful Session bean throws an exception, the client must obtain a new Session bean reference and start its conversation over again. This is because the EJB container will have discarded the Session bean that threw the exception, discarding all the client's conversational state in the process.

Exception Handling

Earlier today, you saw the different types of exceptions that a bean can throw. If a bean throws an application exception, the EJB container will propagate it back to the client. If the bean throws an `EJBException` (representing a system exception), the EJB container will, in turn, throw a `java.rmi.RemoteException`.

For the client, any `RemoteException` represents a severe problem. It doesn't really matter to the client if the `RemoteException` has arisen because of a network problem or because of a problem with a bean. Either way, it unlikely to be able to recover.

Table 5.1 lists the system exceptions shown in Figure 5.5 and indicates how each is raised and thrown. As you will see, the majority are raised when the EJB container itself has detected a problem with either transactions or security. You will learn more about transactions on Day 8, and more about security a week later on Day 15.

TABLE 5.1 System Exceptions Are Thrown in a Variety of Situations

What	Event	Client Receives
Any bean	Throws `javax.ejb.EJBException`.	`java.rmi.RemoteException` (or any subclass)
BMP Entity bean	Throws `NoSuchEntityException`.	`java.rmi.NoSuchObject Exception`
Container	The client invokes a method on a reference to a Session bean that no longer exists.	`java.rmi.NoSuchObject Exception`
	The client calls a method without a transaction context.	`javax.transaction.TransactionRequired Exception`
	The client has insufficient security access.	`java.rmi.AccessException`
	A transaction needs to be rolled back.	`javax.transaction.TransactionRolledBack Exception`

If you are wondering what BMP Entity beans are, the phrase is an abbreviation of "Bean-Managed Persistence Entity beans." You'll be learning about those tomorrow.

Configuring J2EE RI Client Applications with `deploytool`

All J2EE RI clients must be added as client applications to an EAR file and deployed in the same manner as EJBs. The example case study simply adds the client applications to the same EAR file as the Session beans.

The Agency case study client application is a Swing GUI client with dialog tabs for customers advertising jobs, applicants registering for jobs, administrators configuring locations and skills and database table debugging. The supplied `agency.ear` example for the Day 5 exercises already includes a partially configured Agency client called `AllClients`.

5

When creating a client application you will need to include all of the classes for the client together with the home and remote interface classes for every EJB used by the client. Continuing the exercise of updating this application to include the Agency EJB you need to add the following files to the AllClients component:

    agency.Agency

    agency.AgencyHome

Add these files using deploytool by selecting the AllClients component in the left pane and the JAR File tab in the right pane. Click on Edit to highlight the two interface classes listed above, and then click on Add to include them in the Agency EJB. Close down the edit dialog box when you have made your additions. You should now have the list of EJB classes shown in Figure 5.15 in your client application.

FIGURE 5.15

Application Client EJB Interface Classes.

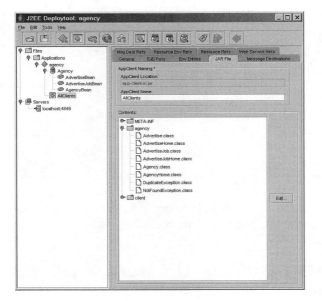

Your final step to complete the addition of the Agency Session bean to the case study is to add the EJB reference for the Agency Session bean to the AllClients component. Select the AllClients component in the left pane and the EJB Refs tab in the right pane. Click on the Add button and in the popup window supply the following information (as shown in Figure 5.16):

- Coded Name—ejb/Agency
- EJB Type—Session
- Interfaces—Remote

- Home Interface—agency.AgencyHome
- Local/Remote Interface—agency.Agency

You will have select lists for all of the values except the coded name. If you do not see the Agency EJB classes in the popup lists you did not include the classes in the client application JAR file as previously described.

FIGURE 5.16

Adding an EJB Reference.

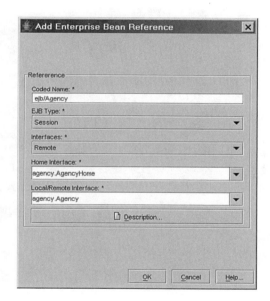

By doing this you have added the following elements to the AllClients entry in the application-client.xml deployment descriptor (shown in bold):

```xml
<?xml version='1.0' encoding='UTF-8'?>
<application-client
     version=" 1.4"
     xmlns=" http://java.sun.com/xml/ns/j2ee"
     xmlns:xsi=" http://www.w3.org/2001/XMLSchema-instance"
     xsi:schemaLocation=" http://java.sun.com/xml/ns/j2ee
     http://java.sun.com/xml/ns/j2ee/application-client_1_4.xsd"
     >
  <display-name> AllClients</display-name>
  <ejb-ref>
    <ejb-ref-name>ejb/Agency</ejb-ref-name>
    <ejb-ref-type>Session</ejb-ref-type>
    <home>agency.AgencyHome</home>
    <remote>agency.Agency</remote>
  </ejb-ref>
...
</application-client>
```

5

Click on OK to add the new EJB reference. You must now provide the platform specific JNDI mapping for the Agency EJB reference. Do this by selecting the Agency EJB row you have just created in the EJB Refs pane, and in the Sun-specific Settings at the bottom of the page select the JNDI Name option and enter `ejb/Agency`. This is shown in Figure 5.17.

FIGURE 5.17

*Defining an EJB
Reference JNDI Name.*

You have now added the following elements to the `AllClients` entry in the `sun-application-client.xml` deployment descriptor (shown in bold):

```
<sun-application-client>
...
    <ejb-ref>
      <ejb-ref-name>ejb/Agency</ejb-ref-name>
      <jndi-name>ejb/Agency</jndi-name>
    </ejb-ref>
...
</sun-application-client>
```

You have now added the Agency Session bean and defined an EJB reference to it in the `AllClients` application. Save your changes and use the Tools, Verify J2EE Compliance... menu option to run verifier to verify the whole application including your newly added EJB reference.

Save your changes and then use the Tools, Verify J2EE Compliance... menu option to start up the GUI verifier.

NOTE

> As previously described the Nov 2003 release of the J2EE RI `deploytool` incorrectly reports errors for the Agency application. The authors suggest you use the command line verifier on the EAR file you have just updated using the command:
>
> ```
> asant verify-j2ee-ri
> ```

Running the Agency Case Study Example

You are now in a position to deploy and run the Agency case study following the steps described yesterday.

If you deployed the Day 4 Agency example a restriction in `deploytool` prevents you from retrieving the client JAR at the same time as you deploy today's example. You can either manually undeploy the previous example or retrieve the client JAR file after redeploying the new example. You can undeploy the existing Agency object by selecting the `localhost:4848` entry in the `deploytool` left pane, choosing `agency` in the right pane and then clicking on `undeploy`.

To deploy the new case study choose the `deploytool` Tools, Deploy menu option, provide your admin username and password, check the Return Client JAR file entry and click on OK. When the deployment completes click on Close to shut down the deployment dialog window.

If you need to you can retrieve the client JAR file after deploying the new example by selecting the `localhost:4848` entry in the `deploytool` left pane, choosing `agency` in the right pane and then clicking on `Client JAR`; save the JAR file to the `Day05/examples/j2ee-ri` directory.

To run the case study open a command line window in the `Day05/examples` directory and enter

```
asant run-j2ee-ri
```

You will be presented with the Agency client with dialog tabs for customers advertising jobs, administrators configuring locations and skills and database table debugging. On the customers tab enter the name `winston` to login and view the jobs advertised by Winston. This is shown in Figure 5.18.

If you prefer to deploy and run from the command line use the command

```
asant deploy-j2ee-ri run-j2ee-ri
```

5

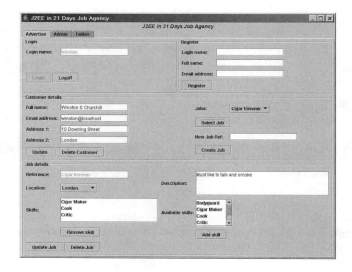

FIGURE 5.18

The Agency Case Study Example.

If you prefer to use the supplied code and deployment descriptors rather than use `deploytool`, then enter the command

```
asant clean build deploy run
```

and then sit back and watch the application deploy and run.

Stateful Session Beans

Now that you have learned how to specify and implement stateless Session beans, it is time to look at stateful Session beans. As you shall see, there are many similarities, but the lifecycle is different and warrants close attention.

Specifying a Stateful Session Bean

Specifying a stateful Session bean is similar to specifying a stateless Session bean. The remote interface defines access to the bean by remote clients, and every method of the remote interface must throw a `RemoteException`. The primary difference (from a specification viewpoint) is that there can be multiple `create()` methods in the home interface of a stateful Session bean.

You will recall that a stateless Session bean allows for only a single no argument `create()` method in the home interface, and this corresponds to the `ejbCreate()` method of the bean itself. For a stateful Session bean, the `create()` method can have arguments and may be overloaded. The arguments to the `create()` method define the initial state of the bean. From the client's viewpoint, this is analogous to invoking a constructor on the bean.

For example, the `Advertise` bean in the case study is stateful. It represents an advertiser of job positions. The home interface for this bean is shown in Listing 5.4.

LISTING 5.4   Stateful Session beanHome Interface—`AdvertiseHome.java`

```
package agency;

import java.rmi.*;
import javax.ejb.*;

public interface AdvertiseHome extends EJBHome
{
    Advertise create (String login) throws RemoteException, CreateException;
}
```

Obviously, the `create()` method has a corresponding `ejbCreate()` method in the `AdvertiseBean` class itself. This `ejbCreate()` method must instantiate the bean with any appropriate state, as shown in Listing 5.5

LISTING 5.5   `AdvertiseBean.ejbCreate()` Method

```
public class AdvertiseBean implements SessionBean
{
    private String login;
    private String name;
    private String email;
    private String[] address;
    private Collection jobs = new TreeSet();

    public void ejbCreate (String login) throws CreateException {
        this.login = login;
        Connection con = null;
        PreparedStatement stmt = null;
        ResultSet rs = null;
        try {
            con = dataSource.getConnection();
            stmt = con.prepareStatement(
    "SELECT name,email,address1,address2 FROM Customer WHERE login = ?");
            stmt.setString(1, login);
            rs = stmt.executeQuery();
            if (rs.next()) {
                name = rs.getString(1);
                email = rs.getString(2);
                address = new String[2];
```

LISTING 5.5   continued

```
                address[0] = rs.getString(3);
                address[1] = rs.getString(4);
            }
            else {
                throw new CreateException (
                    "Create failed to find databse record for "+login);
            }
            loadJobList();
        }
        catch (SQLException e) {
            error("Error creating "+login,e);
        }
        finally {
            closeConnection(con, stmt, rs);
        }
    }
}
```

As an alternative to overloading the create() method, the EJB specification allows for methods named create*XXX*() to be defined in the home interface, with corresponding methods ejbCreate*XXX*() in the bean. These methods can take parameters if required. Whether you choose to use this facility or just use regular overloaded versions of create()/ejbCreate() is up to you.

Other than this one change, being able to pass in state in the create() method, there really is little difference in the specification of a stateful bean compared to that of a stateless Session bean. The remote interface of the stateful Advertise Session bean is shown in Listing 5.6.

LISTING 5.6   The Remote Interface for the Stateful Advertise Bean Advertise.java

```
package agency;

import java.rmi.*;
import javax.ejb.*;

public interface Advertise extends EJBObject
{
    void updateDetails (String name, String email, String[] Address)
        throws RemoteException;
    String getName() throws RemoteException;
    String getEmail() throws RemoteException;
    String[] getAddress() throws RemoteException;
    String[] getJobs() throws RemoteException;
```

LISTING 5.6   continued

```
    void createJob (String ref)
        throws RemoteException, DuplicateException, CreateException;
    void deleteJob (String ref) throws RemoteException, NotFoundException;
}
```

The ejbCreate() method from the home interface supplies the information to the bean so that it can retrieve the data about the advertiser from the database. The remote interface allows this information to be accessed and updated.

Implementing a Stateful Session bean

When implementing a stateful Session bean, there are a number of issues that you must keep in mind. They are discussed in this section.

Stateful Session bean Lifecycle

The client's view of the lifecycle of a stateful Session bean is identical to that of a stateless Session bean and, in truth, more closely matches the actual lifecycle as managed by the container.

From the client's perspective, the bean is simply instantiated when the client calls create() on the bean's home interface, and it is removed when the client calls remove() on the bean itself.

The bean's viewpoint of its lifecycle is as shown in Figure 5.19.

The principle difference between stateful and stateless Session beans is the duration of the time that the bean is bound to the client. With a stateless Session bean, the duration is only as long as the time needed to execute the business method. With a stateful Session bean, however, the bean stays bound until the client releases it. In this way, there is quite a close correspondence between the client's and the bean's perspectives.

When the client calls create() on the home interface, a Session bean instance is obtained. Most EJB containers maintain a pool of unbound Session bean instances, so any unused instance will be chosen. This is then bound to the client. The client can call business methods on the bean, and because the bean will remain bound, these can legitimately save the state pertaining to the client to instance variables. When the client is done with the bean, it calls remove(), which releases the bean back to the pool of unbound instances.

5

FIGURE 5.19

A stateful Session bean's view of its life-cycle includes passivation and timeouts.

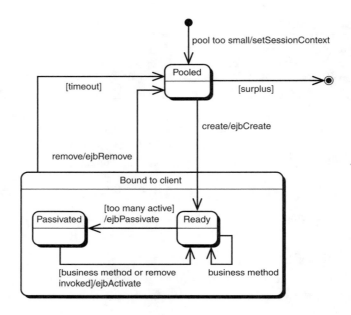

The EJB specification uses the analogy of a shopping cart, and it is easy to see that this is a natural fit. In such a case, the client would obtain a shopping cart bean using `cre-ate()`, call methods such as `addItem()`, `removeItem()`, and `checkout()`, and then release the bean using `remove()`.

If there are many concurrent clients, the amount of memory to manage state for all of the clients can become significant. Moreover, there is nothing to prevent a client from acquiring a bean and then not using it--an abandoned shopping cart in the aisles, if you like. The EJB specification addresses these issues by defining the notions of passivation and of timeouts. Passivation allows the EJB container to release the memory used by a bean, first writing out its internal state to some secondary storage. This is transparent to the bean's client; when the bean is next used, the EJB container first activates the bean. How the EJB container actually implements passivation is not specified, but the specification does require that the Session bean is serializable, so many implementations will take this route and serialize the bean to a file. If a bean is not used for a period of time specified by its timeout, it can be removed and its memory released.

Figure 5.19 showed the bean's viewpoint of its lifecycle but the actual lifecycle, as managed by the EJB container, is likely to be different again. After all, the whole point of passivation is to reduce the number of bean instances; if the bean was merely "put to sleep," that aim would not have been achieved, so Figure 5.20 shows the actual lifecycle used by many EJB container implementations.

- An `ejbCreate()` is required for stateless Session beans. It isn't in the
  `javax.ejb.SessionBean` interface because stateful Session beans won't necessarily have a no-arg `create()` method.

Summary

You've covered a lot of ground today. You've been shown that there are stateless and stateful Session beans, and each has its own lifecycle. You've seen in detail how to specify a Session bean by defining its home and remote interfaces and how to implement a bean by providing corresponding implementations for the methods in the home and remote interfaces. You have also been shown how to implement the lifecycle methods as defined in the `javax.ejb.SessionBean` interface.

You've also read how the deployment descriptor provides configuration information describing the bean's characteristics and dependencies to the EJB container. Additionally, you've seen that those dependencies are logical dependencies that must be mapped by the EJB deployer role to the physical resources defined through vendor-specific auxiliary deployment descriptor.

Q&A

Q What sort of state can stateless Session beans have?

A Somewhat surprisingly, stateless Session beans can store state, but it must be independent of the client. A connection to a database or a reference to another EJB that is not specific to any given client is a typical example of client independent state.

Q What is the prefix that will appear in all JNDI lookups?

A The `java:comp/env` context is guaranteed to exist in a J2EE environment.

Q How are EJB system exceptions different from regular Java exceptions?

A A `RemoteException` can be caused by network problems, which, in the context of distributed J2EE enterprise applications, represent a system-level rather than an application-level exception.

Exercises

The exercise starts where today's example left of. The agency case study already provides a number of beans:

- There is a stateless `Agency` bean that returns lists of all applications, customers, locations and skills in the database.

- There is a stateful `Advertise` bean that allows advertisers (of jobs) to update their name, email, and address, and to manage the jobs they have posted to the job agency.
- There is a stateful `AdvertiseJob` bean that represents an advertised job. This allows the description, location, and required skills to be maintained.

However, it does not define any bean for the potential job applicants at this point. What is required is a `Register` bean that allows applicants to register themselves with the job agency. The exercise is to implement the `RegisterBean`, define this new bean within the supplied `agency.ear` enterprise application, configure the bean, deploy your bean to the J2EE RI, and finally test with either `RegisterClient` or `AllClients` (supplied).

Under the Day 5 exercise directory, you will find the usual subdirectories, including the following:

- `src` The source code for the EJBs and clients
- `classes` Directory to hold the compiled classes; empty
- `build` Working directory for the asant build files to use
- `j2ee-ri` Working directory for using `deploytool` to build and deploy the `agency.ear` application

The `Register` and `RegisterHome` interfaces have been provided for you, under the `src` directory. For example, the `Register` interface is as follows:

```
package agency;

import java.rmi.*;
import javax.ejb.*;

public interface Register extends EJBObject
{
    void updateDetails (
        String name, String email,
        String location, String summary, String[] skills
    ) throws RemoteException;
    String getLogin() throws RemoteException;
    String getName() throws RemoteException;
    String getEmail() throws RemoteException;
    String getLocation() throws RemoteException;
    String getSummary() throws RemoteException;
    String[] getSkills() throws RemoteException;
}
```

Today's exercise is to implement the `RegisterBean`, configure an appropriate deployment descriptor, deploy your bean to the J2EE RI, and then test with the `RegisterClient`. The bean will need to be stateful.

If you need some pointers as to how to go about this, read on.

1. Create a `RegisterBean.java` file and place this in `Day05/exercise/src/agency`.

2. Implement `RegisterBean` to support the `Register` and `RegisterHome` interfaces supplied. Base your implementation on that of `AdvertiseBean`, if you want.

3. Compile the `RegisterBean` code and the other interfaces using the command `asant compile`. (You must be in the `Day05/exercise` directory.)

4. In `deploytool`, open up the existing enterprise application (`Day05/exercise/j2ee-ri/agency.ear`). Then, add the your `Register` bean to the existing Agency `ejb-jar` by using File, New, Enterprise Bean. Specify the contents to include all the required class files.

5. Configure the deployment descriptor for the `RegisterBean` appropriately. The bean will need to be stateful.

7. Map the Register bean onto the Sun-specific JNDI name `ejb/Register`.

8. Define the `ejb/Agency` resource reference to refer to the `ejb/Agency` data source. For the `AllClients` application client, add an EJB reference to the Register Bean, mapping the reference onto the Sun-specific JNDI name `ejb/Register`.

9. Save your application and verify J2EE compliance.

10. Deploy your bean.

11. Use `deploytool` to obtain the client JAR file from the Agency application you have just deployed. Save this as `Day05/exercise/j2ee-ri/agencyClient.jar`.

12. To test out your bean issue the command

    `asant run-j2ee-ri`

13. If you prefer to work from the command line and want to hand edit the deployment descriptors to add the new Register EJB, you can used the command `asant build` to compile the classes and build the EAR file. You can verify using `asant verify`, deploy using `asant deploy` and run using `asant run`

    If you take this approach you will need to update the following deployment descriptor files:

    - `dd/agency/ejb-jar.xml`
    - `dd/agency/sun-ejb-jar.xml`
    - `dd/client/application-client.xml`
    - `dd/client/sun-application-client.xml`

    Follow the example deployment descriptor entries in today's case study for a guide to the deployment descriptor elements you will need to add. However you will

5

need to include the following entry in `ejb-jar.xml` to define the transaction requirements for the Register Session bean:

```
<ejb-jar>
...
  <assembly-descriptor>
...
    <container-transaction>
      <method>
        <ejb-name>RegisterBean</ejb-name>
        <method-intf>Remote</method-intf>
        <method-name>*</method-name>
      </method>
      <trans-attribute>Required</trans-attribute>
    </container-transaction>
  </assembly-descriptor>
</ejb-jar>
```

A solution to the exercise is provided in `Day05/agency`.

Day 6

Entity EJBs

Yesterday, you learned about Session beans, and how they can be used to provide a service to a specific client. Today you will study Entity beans – a completely different type of EJB.

The major topics that you will be covering today are

- How Entity beans represent domain objects, providing services that can be used by all clients

- Specifying, implementing, configuring, and deploying bean-managed persistence (BMP) Entity beans (container-managed persistence (CMP) Entity beans are covered tomorrow)

- How EJBs can provide a local interface in addition to their remote interface

Overview

When building IT systems, the functionality required of the application must be specified and the business objects within the domain must be identified. In "traditional" client/server systems, the application's functionality can be implemented in the front-end application or perhaps using database stored procedures, and the domain objects are usually tables within a database. In building an EJB-based system, the application's functionality corresponds to Session beans, and the business objects correspond to Entity beans.

You saw yesterday that Session beans take on the responsibility of implementing the application's business functionality. There will still be a presentation layer to display the state of those Session beans, but its detail is unimportant in the larger scheme of things.

In the same way, Entity beans take on the responsibility of representing the business domain data. There will still be a persistent data store to manage the data, almost certainly a database, but the Entity beans abstract out and hide the details of the persistence mechanism.

On the very first day you were introduced to n-tier architectures, with the business logic residing in its own tier. With an EJB-based system, both Session and Entity beans are objects, so the business logic could reside in either of them. In practice, the business logic will be split over both, but to make the correct decision, it is worthwhile analyzing what is meant by that phrase "business logic."

Rules and constraints of business logic generally apply across all applications. In other words, it doesn't matter what the business logic is trying to accomplish; it will still need to comply with such rules and constraints. This sort of business logic is best implemented through Entity beans, because Entity beans are business domain objects that can be reused in many different applications.

In the business world, procedures and practices are usually the expression of some sort of application, so Session beans are the best form of EJB to implement this type of business logic.

In other words:

- Session beans should have the business logic specific to an application—application logic. The functionality provided should allow the user to accomplish some goal.
- Entity beans represent business domain objects and should have business logic that is applicable for all applications— domain logic. Usually, this logic will be expressed in terms of rules and constraints on the data.

If there is any doubt as to where the functionality should be placed, it is safer to place it within a Session bean. It can always be moved later if it is found to be truly re-usable across applications.

Figure 6.1 shows a UML component diagram to illustrate that there are at least four logical layers in an EJB-based system. Normally, at least some of these layers will be on the same physical tier.

FIGURE 6.1

EJBs separate out business logic into application and domain logic.

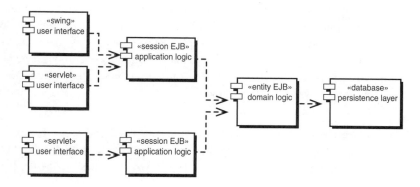

It's natural to compare Entity beans with relational databases, because there is a significant overlap in the objectives of both technologies.

If you like to think in client/server terms, you could think of Session beans as being an extension of the "client," and Entity beans as being an extension of the "server." It's important to realize that many clients can share a given Entity bean instance at the same time, just as many database clients can read the same row from a database table at the same time.

At its simplest, an Entity bean can correspond to nothing more complex than a single row in a database table. But Entity beans may also represent more complex business objects, with data potentially stored in more than one row or table in the database. For example:

- A Customer Entity bean could correspond to a row in a customer table keyed by customer_num. The list of contact phone numbers for that Customer (in a customer_phone_number detail table keyed on (customer_num, phone_num)) may also be part of the Customer Entity bean.

- An Invoice Entity bean might correspond to data in the order and order_detail tables.

- An Employee Entity bean could be persisted in an employee table. The employee's salary history might also be part of the Entity bean.

The entities identified in data modeling are the very same concepts that should be expressed as Entity beans. Entity beans require that a primary key be defined; a primary key cannot be a primitive but can be any serializable java object. The name often given to such primary key classes is something like BeanPK, although it can be anything. You can think of the primary key as some object that identifies the bean.

Even with a solid data model to guide you, selecting Entity beans is not necessarily straightforward. In particular, choosing the granularity of the entities can be problematic. Specifying the interfaces for the Entity beans should help you decide the correct entity model. If an Entity bean interface becomes bloated with lots of methods you should study the purpose of each method and group related methods together. You may find that your single entity is actually two or more separate entities. Conversely, if you have a lot of entities with a couple of methods in each interface, you may find you can amalgamate the small entities in a single business entity.

Once you have identified your entities, creating them as J2EE Entity beans is slightly more complex than creating the Session beans you studied yesterday because you need to supply more information; specifically you have to describe the persistent data.

The `javax.ejb` Package for Entity Beans

Yesterday, you saw the interfaces and classes in the `javax.ejb` package that related to Session beans. Figure 6.2 shows the interfaces and classes relevant to Entity beans.

FIGURE 6.2

The `javax.ejb` *interfaces and classes pertaining to Entity beans.*

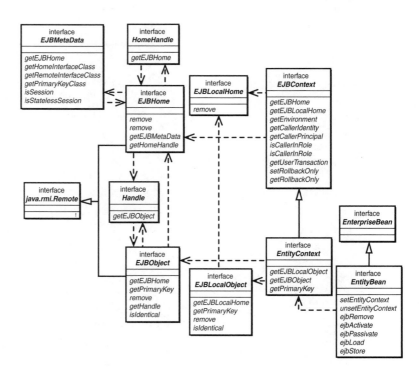

As you can see, many of the supporting classes are common, which is good news because that means there's less to learn. The principle differences are as follows:

- The Entity bean implements `javax.ejb.EntityBean` rather than `javax.ejb.SessionBean`, and there is a different lifecycle.

- The Entity bean is initialized with an `EntityContext` rather than a `SessionContext`. An `EntityContext` exposes a primary key to the Entity bean, a concept not applicable to Session beans.

Other details of the `javax.ejb` interfaces are the same as for Session beans. Briefly, the home and remote interfaces for the Entity bean are defined by extending `EJBHome` and `EJBObject`, respectively, and the local-home and local interfaces by extending `EJBLocalHome` and `EJBLocalObject`. You will be learning more about local interfaces later today, because they are highly relevant to implementing Entity beans.

Entity beans represent persistent data typically stored in a database. The responsibility for persisting the data lies either with the bean itself or with the EJB container. The term for the former approach is bean-managed persistence (BMP), and for the latter it is container-managed persistence (CMP).

Container-managed persistence was part of the EJB 1.1 specification, but attracted much criticism in that release. However, it was radically overhauled in EJB 2.0, and now works in a fundamentally different way. Today, you will concentrate on using BMP and during tomorrow's lesson you will explore CMP.

Remote Versus Local Interfaces

One of the most significant improvements in the EJB 2.0 specification was the inclusion of local interfaces, as well as remote interfaces.

All the beans that you have seen so far have provided only a remote interface. That is, both their home and remote interfaces have extended from `javax.ejb.EJBHome` and `javax.ejbEJBObject`, both of which, in turn, extend the `java.rmi.Remote` interface. For Session beans this ability to invoke methods on a bean without regard for its location is crucial, but is less useful for Entity beans. Very often, a client must deal with many Entity beans to transact some piece of work, and if each of those Entity beans is remote, this will incur substantial network traffic.

A local interface can be specified instead of, or in addition to, the remote interfaces. A local interface does not incur the network overhead of remote interfaces.

To add weight to the need for a local interface for Entity beans, the client of the Entity bean may well be a Session bean (indeed, it is generally considered bad practice to use anything other than a Session bean to interact with Entity beans) and more often than not, this Session bean will be running in the same J2EE container as the Entity. Using remote interfaces, all Session-to-Entity bean calls must be made across the network. Significant performance gains can be made if local, rather than remote, interfaces are used.

As with remote interfaces, local interfaces use the home and proxy concept, with the home interface being extended from `javax.ejb.EJBLocalHome`, and the proxy for the bean extending from `javax.ejb.EJBLocalObject`. Otherwise though, these are regular Java interfaces, and the normal "pass by reference" semantics for objects passed across these interfaces apply.

> **CAUTION**
>
> Local EJB interfaces pass objects by reference, whereas remote interfaces pass objects by value. When writing EJBs that use both interfaces, you should be careful that the bean semantics (behavior) is the same for both interfaces.
>
> Whereas local interfaces do not require the objects passed to be serializable this would create semantic differences between local and remote interfaces – this is not a good design practice.

Local interfaces are not specific to Entity beans; Session beans can also provide local interfaces. Session beans (especially stateless Session beans) can provide a local interface for use by servlets or JSPs running in the same container as well as a remote interface for other clients. In general, it would be expected for the two interfaces to offer similar capabilities, although there is nothing in the EJB specification that enforces this.

Figure 6.3 shows the two sets of interfaces that a bean can provide.

For both interfaces, the EJB home/local-home and proxy objects take responsibility for security (Day 15, "Security") and transactions (Day 8, "Transactions and Persistence"), while home/remote interfaces make the physical location of the bean transparent to the remote client.

To keep things simple, in both the case study and the examples for today and tomorrow the Entity beans have only a local interface.

FIGURE 6.3

EJBs can have local and remote interfaces.

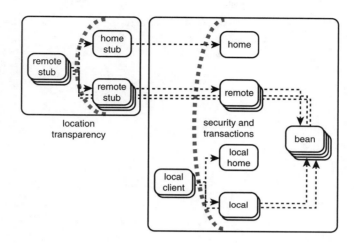

BMP Entity Bean Lifecycle

The lifecycle of both BMP and CMP Entity beans is dictated by the `EntityBean` interface that the bean must implement. This is shown in Figure 6.4.

FIGURE 6.4

The `javax.ejb.EntityBean` *interface defines certain lifecycle methods that must be implemented by Entity beans.*

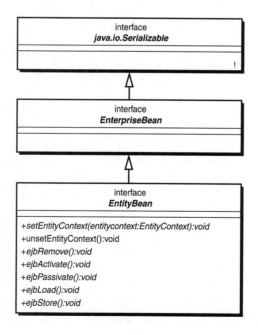

6

To start with, the Entity bean must implement the `javax.ejb.EntityBean` interface, as demonstrated with the `JobBean` class:

```
package data;

// imports omitted
import javax.ejb.*;

public class JobBean implements EntityBean
{
    // implementation omitted
}
```

The lifecycle as perceived by the Entity bean and as managed by the container is as shown in Figure 6.5.

FIGURE 6.5

The `javax.ejb.` `EntityBean` *lifecycle allows Entity beans to be pooled.*

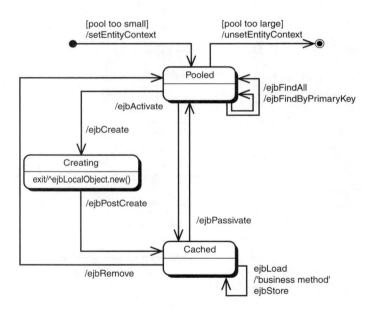

The lifecycle is as follows:

- If the EJB container requires an instance of an Entity bean (for example, if the pool is too small), it will instantiate the bean instance and call its `setEntityContext()` method. The `setEntityContext()` should be used to initialize any state (such as instance variables) required by the Entity bean.

- Pooled instances can service finder methods to locate data within a persistent data store. More on these finder methods shortly.

- A bean can be associated with an `EJBLocalObject` proxy (or `EJBObject` proxy if the remote interface is in use) in one of two ways.

  First, it can be activated by the container via `ejbActivate()` in order to invoke a business method.

  Alternatively, the `ejbCreate()` method can be used to create and initialize a new Entity bean.

- When the bean has been associated with its proxy, business methods can be invoked on it. Before the business method is invoked, the `ejbLoad()` lifecycle method will be called, indicating that the bean should re-load its state from the persistent data store. Immediately after the business method has completed, the `ejbStore()` method is called, indicating that the bean should update the persistent data store with any change in its state.

- Beans can return to the pooled state in one of two ways.

  First, they can be passivated via `ejbPassivate()`. There is usually little to be done in this method, because the bean's state will already have been saved to the persistent data store during the earlier `ejbStore()` method. So passivation will typically simply sever the link from the `EJBLocalObject` proxy to the bean.

  Alternatively, the client may be requesting to remove the bean via `ejbRemove()`. This usually means that the corresponding data in the persistent data store must be deleted.

- Finally, the EJB container can reduce the size of its pool by calling `unsetEntityContext()` on any Entity bean. This bean will then be released for garbage collection.

NOTE

Most commercial EJB containers provide mechanisms to suppress unnecessary `ejbLoad()` and `ejbStore()` calls. None of these mechanisms are in the EJB specification, however.

6

Unlike Session beans, there is no binding of the Entity beans to a specific client; all clients can share Entity beans.

As shown in Figure 6.5 there are two methods called during the creation of a bean. The `ejbCreate()` method is called prior to the `EJBLocalObject` proxy being made available, then the `ejbPostCreate()` method is called after the proxy is available. This is shown in the sequence diagram in Figure 6.6.

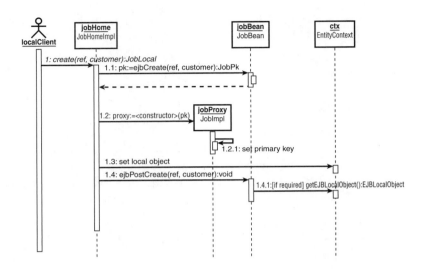

FIGURE 6.6

Both the ejbCreate()
and ejbPostCreate()
*lifecycle methods are
called when an Entity
bean is created.*

Under BMP, the bean has several tasks to perform when its ejbCreate() method is called. It should

- Calculate the value of its primary key (if not passed in as an argument).
- Persist itself to a data store. For a database, this will most likely be in the form of a SQL INSERT statement or statements.
- Save the supplied arguments and its primary key to member variables.
- Return the primary key.

CAUTION

> Because the EJB container is using primary keys for lookups, it means the EJB specification does not allow primary keys to be modified by the application; they must be immutable (read only).

The ejbPostCreate()method allows for additional processing of a new Entity bean after the proxy object has been created but is rarely used. However, an ejbPostCreate() method must be defined for each ejbCreate() method; the parameter list of the ejbCreate() and associated ejbPostCreate() methods must be identical.

The ejbRemove() method is the opposite of the ejbCreate() method; it removes a bean's data from the persistent data store (typically by issuing a SQL DELETE operation). The implementation of ejbCreate() and ejbRemove() is given in the "Implementing javax.ejb.EntityBean" section later today.

That takes care of creating and removing beans, but what about when a bean is queried or updated? The most significant methods of the Entity bean lifecycle are `ejbLoad()` and `ejbStore()`. Together, these methods ensure that the Entity bean is kept in sync with the persistent data store. The `ejbLoad()` method is called immediately prior to any business method (so that a query accesses the most up-to-date data typically using a SQL SELECT statement). The `ejbStore()` is called after the business method completes (so that the bean's state is reflected in the persistent data store typically using a SQL UPDATE statement). Figure 6.7 shows this as a UML sequence diagram.

FIGURE 6.7

The `ejbLoad()` *and* `ejbStore()` *methods keep the bean in sync with the persistent data store.*

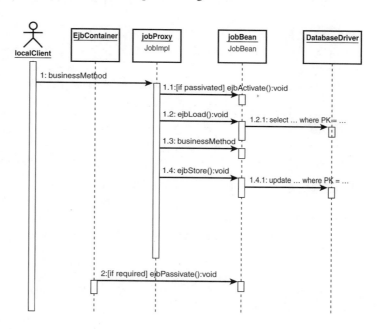

Again, the actual implementation for these methods is given in the "Implementing `javax.ejb.EntityBean`" section later today.

These lifecycle methods allow new beans (and data in the persistent data store) to be created, and existing beans to be removed or updated. But what about actually finding beans that already exist? In other words, in database terms, you have seen the lifecycle methods that correspond to SQL INSERT, DELETE, and UPDATE statements, but what of the SQL SELECT statement?

Existing data is retrieved by finder methods. The EJB specification requires at least one finder method, whose name must be `ejbFindByPrimaryKey()`, and allows other finder methods to be defined by the developer. All finder method names must begin with `ejbFind`. These methods have corresponding `find` methods in the home interface.

6

One obvious question arises, "When the client invokes the finder method on the home interface, which bean actually performs the ejbFindXxx() method?" The answer is perhaps a little unexpected; any unused (that is, pooled) bean will be used by the EJB container. This has implications for the bean lifecycle. Put simply, an ejbFind() method may be called before any other method except setEntityContext(). If an entity bean maintains a connection to a data source, this connection must be initialized in the setEntityContext() method.

Learning the lifecycle methods for both Entity and Session beans can be somewhat overwhelming at first, made all the more complicated because some method names appear for both bean types, but imply different responsibilities. To clarify matters, Table 6.1 compares the two sets of lifecycle methods and identifies those responsibilities.

TABLE 6.1 Responsibilities of Session and Entity Beans Sit in Different Lifecycle Methods

Lifecycle Method	Session Bean	Entity Bean
setXxxContext()	Set context	Set context
unsetXxxContext()	N/A	Unset context
ejbFindByPrimaryKey()	N/A	Acquire reference to proxy
ejbCreate()	Acquire reference to proxy	a) Insert data to persistent data store b) Acquire reference to proxy
ejbPostCreate()	N/A	Access proxy if necessary
ejbActivate()	a) Loaded from (temporary) data store b) Obtain environmental resources	Obtain environmental resources
ejbPassivate()	a) Saved to (temporary) data store b) Release environmental resources	Release environmental resources
ejbLoad()	N/A	Load from (persistent) data store
ejbStore()	N/A	Save to (persistent) data store
ejbRemove()	Release reference to proxy	a) Delete data from persistent data store b) Release reference to proxy

Specifying a BMP Entity Bean

Following the pattern of Session beans, specifying an Entity bean involves defining the local-home and the local interface:

- The local-home interface extends `javax.ejb.EJBLocalHome`.
- The local interface extends `javax.ejb.EJBLocalObject`.

A discussion on each of these interfaces follows.

Local-Home Interface

Listing 6.1 shows the complete `JobLocalHome` interface as an example.

LISTING 6.1   `JobLocalHome` Interface

```
package data;

import java.rmi.*;
import java.util.*;
import javax.ejb.*;

public interface JobLocalHome extends EJBLocalHome
{
   JobLocal create (String ref, String customer) throws CreateException;
   JobLocal findByPrimaryKey(JobPK key) throws FinderException;
   Collection findByCustomer(String customer) throws FinderException;
   Collection findByLocation(String location) throws FinderException;
   void deleteByCustomer(String customer);
}
```

6

Each of these methods has a corresponding method in the bean class itself. Taking the JobBean code as an example, Listing 6.2 shows the template functions for the bean itself:

LISTING 6.2   Job Entity Bean Class Simplified to Show Similarity to JobLocalHome Interface

```
package data;

import java.util.*;
import javax.ejb.*;

public class JobBean implements EntityBean
{
    JobPK ejbCreate (String ref, String customer) throws CreateException {…}
    JobPK ejbFindByPrimaryKey(JobPK key) throws FinderException {…}
    Collection ejbFindByCustomer(String customer) throws FinderException {…}
    Collection ejbFindByLocation(String location) throws FinderException {…}
    void ejbHomeDeleteByCustomer(String customer) {…}
}
```

NOTE   Note that for home methods discussed shortly, the convention is to append `ejbHome`, not just `ejb`, to the bean's method name.

This seems straightforward enough, but note that the return types of the bean's `ejbCreate()` and `ejbFindXxx()` methods are different from the return types of the methods in the local-home interface. Specifically, while the bean returns (to the EJB container) either primary key objects or a `Collection` of primary key objects, the local-home interface methods returns either local proxies (that is, instances of objects that implement the `JobLocal` interface, for the example) or a `Collection` of local proxies.

Create and Remove Methods

The list of exceptions thrown by the local-home methods and the bean's corresponding methods should match in each case. For the `createXXX()` method, the list should be the union of the exceptions thrown by both `ejbCreateXXX()` and `ejbPostCreateXXX()`.

As well as the `create()` method, the local-home interface inherits a `remove(Object o)` method from `javax.ejb.EJBLocalHome`. This corresponds to the `ejbRemove()` lifecycle method of the bean itself.

Finder Methods

Finder methods in the bean return either a single primary key (if a single bean matches the underlying query) or a `java.util.Collection` of primary keys (if there is more than one matching bean). The `ejbFindByPrimaryKey()` method is always required to be one of the bean's methods, although it is not part of the `EntityBean` interface (this is because the argument type and return type will depend on the bean).

> **NOTE**
> It is also possible for finder methods to return a `java.util.Enumeration`. This dates from EJB 1.0 before the Java Collections API was introduced in J2SE 1.2 and should not be used.

Obviously, to specify the `findByPrimaryKey()` method, the primary key of the Entity bean must have been identified. As was noted earlier today, if persisting to a database, identifying the primary key is probably quite easy, because the primary key will correspond to the columns of the primary key of the underlying database table. A custom-developed primary key class is needed when two or more fields identify the bean; otherwise, the type of the single field of the bean that represents the key is used.

> **NOTE**
> If a single field of the bean is used as the primary key, that field must be an `Object` and not a primitive type. Furthermore, the EJB specification does not allow primary keys to change once assigned, so it is best if the class chosen is immutable. The standard `java.lang` classes such as `String`, and the primitive wrapper classes (`Integer`, `Long`, and so on) are all immutable.

Custom Primary Key Classes

As noted earlier, the primary key can be either a field of the bean (in which case, the primary key class is just the class of that field), or it can be a custom-developed class. The latter is required if more than one field is needed to identify the bean.

For the `JobBean`, the primary key is a combination of the customer and the job reference (the `customer` and `ref` fields, respectively). Because the primary key is composite, a custom primary key class is needed; this is the `JobPK` class.

Custom primary key classes are required to follow a number of rules. Specifically,

- The class must implement `java.io.Serializable` or `java.io.Externalizable`.
- The instance variables in the class must all be primitives or be references to objects that are, in turn, serializable.

6

- The `equals()` method and the `hashCode()` methods must be implemented to compare objects using the value of the data in the primary key fields.
- There must be a no-arg constructor (there can also be other constructors that take arguments).

In other words, the class must be what is referred to as a value type (see the discussion of the Value Object pattern on Day 18, "Patterns"). It is usual to define the primary key class to conform to JavaBean semantics by adding getter methods to retrieve the individual fields of the primary key.

NOTE

> At least conceptually, value types are immutable (there should be no setter methods; they cannot be changed). Sadly, the requirement for a no-arg constructor sometimes requires methods to be supplied that will change the primary key fields. However the fields must not be changed once an initial value has been given to the primary key object.

Listing 6.3 shows the JobPK primary key class.

LISTING 6.3   JobPK Class Identifies a Job

```
package data;

import java.io.*;
import javax.ejb.*;

public class JobPK implements Serializable {
    public String ref;
    public String customer;

    public JobPK() {
    }
    public JobPK(String ref, String customer) {
        this.ref = ref;
        this.customer = customer;
    }

    public String getRef() {
        return ref;
    }
    public String getCustomer() {
        return customer;
    }

    public boolean equals(Object obj) {
        if (obj instanceof JobPK) {
```

LISTING 6.3 continued

```
            JobPK pk = (JobPK)obj;
            return (pk.ref.equals(ref) && pk.customer.equals(customer));
        }
        return false;
    }
    public int hashCode() {
        return (ref.hashCode() ^ customer.hashCode());
    }
    public String toString() {
        return "JobPK: ref=\"" + ref + "\", customer=\"" + customer + "\"";
    }
}
```

Note that the ref and customer fields have public visibility. This is a requirement of the EJB 1.1 specification. Each field must correspond—in name and type—to one of the fields of the bean itself. This might seem like a strange requirement, but is needed by the EJB container to manage CMP beans.

Because this is a Value Object, you are required to override the equals() method. To implement the equals() method, test that all fields of the object have the same value as the fields in the provided object. For primitive values, the regular == operator should be used, but for object references, the equals() method must be called.

If you override equals() you must also override hashCode(). To implement the hashCode() method, you must generate an int value that is based entirely and deterministically on the value of the fields, such that

if A.equals(B) then A.hashCode() == B.hashCode().

A simple technique is to obtain the hashCode() values for all of the fields within the bean and XOR these values together (using the ^ operator) to generate the required hash code. This simplistic approach may result in poor distribution of hash codes for primary keys with many fields but is usually sufficient.

6

NOTE

Creating these primary key classes can be somewhat tedious. But remember that if there is a single (non-primitive) field in the bean that identifies that bean, this can be used instead.

Home Methods

In addition to finder, create, and remove methods, it is also possible to define home methods within the local-home interface. These are arbitrary methods that are expected to perform some business-type functionality related to the set of Entity beans rather than an individual bean. In other words, they are an EJB equivalent of static Java class methods.

Some common uses for home methods include

- Defining a batch operation to be performed on all bean instances (such as decreasing the price of all catalogue items for a sale)
- Manipulating the collection of Entity beans rather than individual beans (such as deleting all paid invoices over two years old)

Local Interface

Just as for Session beans with their remote interfaces, the local interface defines the capabilities of the bean. Because an Entity bean represents data, it is usual for many of the local interface methods to be simple getter and setter methods. Listing 6.4 shows the local interface for the Job bean.

LISTING 6.4   JobLocal Interface

```
package data;

import java.rmi.*;
import java.util.*;
import javax.ejb.*;

public interface JobLocal extends EJBLocalObject
{
    String getRef();
    String getCustomer();
    CustomerLocal getCustomerObj(); // derived

    void setDescription(String description);
    String getDescription();

    void setLocation(LocationLocal location);
    LocationLocal getLocation();

    Collection getSkills();
    void setSkills(Collection skills);
}
```

Note that the setLocation() method accepts a LocationLocal reference rather than, say, a String containing the name of a location. In other words, the Job bean is defining its relationships to the Location bean directly, effectively enforcing referential integrity. The client of the Job Entity bean is thus required to supply a valid location or none at all.

Each of these methods has a corresponding method in the bean itself, and must throw the same application exceptions. The implementation is shown in the "Implementing the Local-Interface Methods" section later today.

> **NOTE**
>
> Entity beans can also provide a timer service using the same interface as session beans. EJB timer services were discussed on Day 5.

Implementing a BMP Entity Bean

Implementing an Entity bean involves providing an implementation for the methods of the javax.ejb.EntityBean, and corresponding methods for each method in the local-home and local interfaces.

Implementing `javax.ejb.EntityBean`

The setEntityContext() method is the preferred place to perform JNDI lookups, for example to acquire a JDBC DataSource reference. Listing 6.5 shows how this is done for the JobBean code.

LISTING 6.5 JobBean.setEntityContext() Method

```
package data;

import javax.ejb.*;
import javax.naming.*;
import javax.sql.*;
// imports omitted

public class JobBean implements EntityBean
{
    public void setEntityContext(EntityContext ctx) {
        this.ctx = ctx;
        InitialContext ic = null;
        try {
            ic = new InitialContext();
            dataSource = (DataSource)ic.lookup("java:comp/env/jdbc/Agency");
            skillHome = (SkillLocalHome)
➥ ic.lookup("java:comp/env/ejb/SkillLocal");
```

6

LISTING 6.5   continued

```
            locationHome = (LocationLocalHome)
➥ ic.lookup("java:comp/env/ejb/LocationLocal");
            customerHome = (CustomerLocalHome)
➥ ic.lookup("java:comp/env/ejb/CustomerLocal");
        }
        catch (NamingException ex) {
            error("Error looking up depended EJB or resource",ex);
            return;
        }
    }

    private EntityContext ctx;
    private DataSource dataSource;

    // code omitted
}
```

The unsetEntityContext() method (not shown) usually just sets the member variables to null.

The ejbLoad() and ejbStore() methods are responsible for synchronizing the bean's state with the persistent data store. Listing 6.6 shows these methods for JobBean.

LISTING 6.6   JobBean's ejbLoad() and ejbStore() Methods

```
package data;

import javax.ejb.*;
import java.sql.*;
// imports omitted

public class JobBean implements EntityBean
{
    public void ejbLoad(){
        JobPK key = (JobPK)ctx.getPrimaryKey();
        Connection con = null;
        PreparedStatement stmt = null;
        ResultSet rs = null;
        try {
            con = dataSource.getConnection();
            stmt = con.prepareStatement(
➥ "SELECT description,location FROM JobWHERE ref = ? AND customer = ?");
            stmt.setString(1, key.getRef());
            stmt.setString(2, key.getCustomer());
            rs = stmt.executeQuery();
            if (!rs.next()) {
```

LISTING 6.6   continued

```
                        error("No data found in ejbLoad for " + key, null);
                }
                this.ref = key.getRef();
                this.customer = key.getCustomer();
                this.customerObj = customerHome.findByPrimaryKey(this.customer);
                this.description = rs.getString(1);
                String locationName = rs.getString(2);
                this.location = (locationName != null) ?
➥ locationHome.findByPrimaryKey(locationName) : null;
                // load skills
                stmt = con.prepareStatement(
➥ "SELECT job, customer, skill FROM JobSkill
➥  WHERE job = ? AND customer = ? ORDER BY skill");
                stmt.setString(1, ref);
                stmt.setString(2, customerObj.getLogin());
                rs = stmt.executeQuery();
                List skillNameList = new ArrayList();
                while (rs.next()) {
                    skillNameList.add(rs.getString(3));
                }
                this.skills = skillHome.lookup(skillNameList);
            }
        catch (SQLException e) {
            error("Error in ejbLoad for " + key, e);
        }
        catch (FinderException e) {
            error("Error in ejbLoad (invalid customer or location) for "+
➥ key, e);
        }
        finally {
            closeConnection(con, stmt, null, rs);
        }
    }

    public void ejbStore(){
        Connection con = null;
        PreparedStatement stmt = null;
        try {
            con = dataSource.getConnection();
            stmt = con.prepareStatement(
➥ "UPDATE Job SET description = ?, location = ?
➥  WHERE ref = ? AND customer = ?");
            stmt.setString(1, description);
            if (location != null) {
                stmt.setString(2, location.getName());
            } else {
                stmt.setNull(2, java.sql.Types.VARCHAR);
            }
            stmt.setString(3, ref);
            stmt.setString(4, customerObj.getLogin());
```

6

LISTING 6.6   continued

```
                 stmt.executeUpdate();
                 // delete all skills
                 stmt = con.prepareStatement(
➥ "DELETE FROM JobSkill WHERE job = ? and customer = ?");
                 stmt.setString(1, ref);
                 stmt.setString(2, customerObj.getLogin());
                 stmt.executeUpdate();
                 // add back in all skills
                 for (Iterator iter = getSkills().iterator(); iter.hasNext();){
                     SkillLocal skill = (SkillLocal)iter.next();
                     stmt = con.prepareStatement(
➥ "INSERT INTO JobSkill (job,customer,skill) VALUES (?,?,?)");
                     stmt.setString(1, ref);
                     stmt.setString(2, customerObj.getLogin());
                     stmt.setString(3, skill.getName());
                     stmt.executeUpdate();
                 }
             }
             catch (SQLException e) {
                 error("Error in ejbStore for " + ref + "," + customer, e);
             }
             finally {
                 closeConnection(con, stmt, null, null);
             }
         }
         // code omitted
}
```

In the ejbLoad() method, the JobBean must load its state from both the Job and
JobSkill tables To do this it uses the data in the JobSkill table to populate the skills
field. In the ejbStore() method, the equivalent updates to the Job and JobSkill tables
occur.

Of course, there is the chance that when the bean comes to save itself, the data could
have been removed from the database. There is nothing in the EJB specification to
require that an Entity bean "locks" the underlying data. In such a case, the bean should
throw a javax.ejb.NoSuchEntityException; in turn, this will be returned to the client
as some type of java.rmi.RemoteException.

CAUTION   To keep the case study as small and understandable as possible, the error
handling in JobBean has been simplified. In Listing 6.6, the code will throw
an EJBException (rather than NoSuchEntityException) from ejbLoad() if the
data has been removed. In ejbStore(), it doesn't actually check to see if any
rows were updated, so no exception would be thrown.

More complex beans can perform other processing within the `ejbLoad()` and `ejbStore()` methods. For example, the data might be stored in some de-normalized form in a relational database, perhaps for performance reasons. The `ejbStore()` method would store the data in this de-normalized form, while the `ejbLoad()` methods would effectively be able to re-normalize the data on-the-fly. The client need not be aware of these persistence issues.

Examples of other actions that could be performed in the include `ejbLoad()` and `ejbStore()` methods include:

- Compressing and decompressing text fields to reduce network traffic to a remote database
- Replacing keywords within the text by tokens
- Converting Plain text into XML format, or vice versa
- Expanding addresses from zip (or postal) codes for use by the client

As noted earlier today, there is usually very little to be done when an Entity bean is passivated or activated. Listing 6.7 shows the instance variable references being set to `null` during passivation to aid garbage collection.

LISTING 6.7   JobBean's `ejbActivate()` and `ejbPassivate()` Methods

```
package data;

import javax.ejb.*;
// imports omitted

public class JobBean implements EntityBean
{
    public void ejbPassivate(){
        ref = null;
        customer = null;
        customerObj = null;
        description = null;
        location = null;
    }

    public void ejbActivate(){
    }

    // code omitted
}
```

6

Implementing the Local-Home Interface Methods

The implementation of `ejbCreate()` and `ejbPostCreate()` for the `JobBean` is shown in Listing 6.8.

LISTING 6.8   JobBean's `ejbCreate()` and `ejbPostCreate()` Methods

```
package data;

import javax.ejb.*;
import javax.sql.*;
// imports omitted

public class JobBean implements EntityBean
{
    private String ref;
    private String customer;
    private String description;
    private LocationLocal location;
    private CustomerLocal customerObj; // derived
    private List skills;     // vector field; list of SkillLocal ref's.

    public String ejbCreate (String ref, String customer)
        throws CreateException {
        // validate customer login is valid.
        try {
            customerObj = customerHome.findByPrimaryKey(customer);
        } catch (FinderException ex) {
            error("Invalid customer.", ex);
        }
        JobPK key = new JobPK(ref, customer);
        try {
            ejbFindByPrimaryKey(key);
            throw new CreateException("Duplicate job name: " + key);
        }
        catch (FinderException ex) { }
        Connection con = null;
        PreparedStatement stmt = null;
        try {
            con = dataSource.getConnection();
            stmt = con.prepareStatement(
            "INSERT INTO Job (ref,customer) VALUES (?,?)");
            stmt.setString(1, ref);
            stmt.setString(2, customerObj.getLogin());
            stmt.executeUpdate();
        }
        catch (SQLException e) {
            error("Error creating job " + key, e);
        }
```

LISTING 6.8 continued

```
        finally {
            closeConnection(con, stmt, null, null);
        }
        this.ref = ref;
        this.customer = customer;
        this.description = null;
        this.location = null;
        this.skills = new ArrayList();
        return key;
    }

    public void ejbPostCreate (String ref, String customer) {}
}
```

This particular implementation validates that the customer exists (jobs are identified by the customer and by a unique reference), and that the primary key does not already exist in the database. If the primary key does exist, the bean throws a CreateException; if it doesn't (represented by the ejbFindByPrimaryKey() call throwing a FinderException), the method continues.

An alternative implementation would have been to place a unique index on the Job table within the database and then to catch the SQLException that might be thrown when an attempt is made to insert a duplicate record.

CAUTION

There is a race condition here. It's possible that another user could insert a record between the check for duplicates and the actual SQL INSERT. If the ejbCreate() method is called within a transaction; changing the database isolation level (in a manner specified by the EJB container) would eliminate this risk, although deadlocks could then occur.

Note that the skills field is set to an empty ArrayList. This list will contain SkillLocal references (this being the local interface to the Skill bean), but of course, for a newly created Job bean, this list is empty. The decision for the skills field to hold references to SkillLocal objects rather than, say, just String variables holding the skill names, was taken advisedly. If the skill name had been used (that is, the primary key of a skill), finding information about the skill would require extra steps. Perhaps more compellingly, this is also the approach taken for CMP beans and container-managed relationships, discussed in detail tomorrow.

6

Also noteworthy is the `customerObj` field. The `Job`, when created, is passed just a `String` containing the customer's name. In other words, this is a primary key to a customer. The `customerObj` field contains a reference to the parent customer bean itself by way of its `CustomerLocal` reference.

Both the `skills` and the `customerObj` fields illustrate (for want of a better phrase) bean-managed relationships. For the `skills` field, this is a many-to-many relationship, from `Job` to `Skill`. For the `customerObj` field, this is a many-to-one relationship from `Job` to `Customer`.

The `ejbCreate()` and `ejbPostCreate()` methods both correspond to a single method called `create()` in the bean's local-home interface. The list of arguments to both methods must correspond exactly. It is, however, possible for there to be more than one create method with different sets of arguments using overloaded `createXXX()`, `ejbCreateXXX()` and `ejbPostCreateXXX()` methods.

The `ejbRemove()` method is the opposite of the `ejbCreate()` method; it removes a bean's data from the persistent data store. Its implementation for `JobBean` is shown in Listing 6.9.

LISTING 6.9   JobBean's `ejbRemove()` Method

```
package data;

import javax.ejb.*;
import javax.naming.*;
// imports omitted

public class JobBean implements EntityBean
{
    public void ejbRemove(){
        JobPK key = (JobPK)ctx.getPrimaryKey();
        Connection con = null;
        PreparedStatement stmt1 = null;
        PreparedStatement stmt2 = null;
        try {
            con = dataSource.getConnection();
            stmt1 = con.prepareStatement(
➥ "DELETE FROM JobSkill WHERE job = ? and customer = ?");
            stmt1.setString(1, ref);
            stmt1.setString(2, customerObj.getLogin());
            stmt2 = con.prepareStatement(
➥ "DELETE FROM Job WHERE ref = ? and customer = ?");
            stmt2.setString(1, ref);
            stmt2.setString(2, customerObj.getLogin());
            stmt1.executeUpdate();
```

LISTING 6.9   continued

```
                    stmt2.executeUpdate();
                }
                catch (SQLException e) {
                    error("Error removing job " + key, e);
                }
                finally {
                    closeConnection(con, stmt1, stmt2, null);
                }
                ref = null;
                customer = null;
                customerObj = null;
                description = null;
                location = null;
            }
        // code omitted
    }
```

Each of the finder methods of the local-home interface must have a corresponding method in the bean. By way of example, Listing 6.10 shows two (of the three) finder methods for the JobBean.

LISTING 6.10   JobBean's Finder Methods

```
package data;

import javax.ejb.*;
import java.sql.*;
import java.util.*;
// imports omitted

public class JobBean implements EntityBean
{
    public JobPK ejbFindByPrimaryKey(JobPK key) throws FinderException {
        Connection con = null;
        PreparedStatement stmt = null;
        ResultSet rs = null;
        try {
            con = dataSource.getConnection();
            stmt = con.prepareStatement(
➡  "SELECT ref FROM Job WHERE ref = ? AND customer = ?");
            stmt.setString(1, key.getRef());
            stmt.setString(2, key.getCustomer());
            rs = stmt.executeQuery();
            if (!rs.next()) {
                throw new FinderException("Unknown job: " + key);
            }
```

6

LISTING 6.10   Continued

```
                    return key;
            }
            catch (SQLException e) {
                error("Error in findByPrimaryKey for " + key, e);
            }
            finally {
                closeConnection(con, stmt, null, rs);
            }
            return null;
        }

    public Collection ejbFindByCustomer(String customer)
        throws FinderException {
        Connection con = null;
        PreparedStatement stmt = null;
        ResultSet rs = null;
        try {
            con = dataSource.getConnection();
            stmt = con.prepareStatement(
➥ "SELECT ref, customer FROM Job
➥  WHERE customer = ? ORDER BY ref");
            stmt.setString(1, customer);
            rs = stmt.executeQuery();
            Collection col = new ArrayList();
            while (rs.next()) {
                String nextRef = rs.getString(1);
                String nextCustomer = rs.getString(2);
                // validate customer exists
                CustomerLocal nextCustomerObj =
➥ customerHome.findByPrimaryKey(nextCustomer);
                col.add(new JobPK(nextRef, nextCustomerObj.getLogin()));
            }
            return col;
        }
        catch (SQLException e) {
            error("Error in findByCustomer: " + customer, e);
        }
        catch (FinderException e) {
            error("Error in findByCustomer, invalid customer: " +
➥ customer, e);
        }
        finally {
            closeConnection(con, stmt, null, rs);
        }
        return null;
    }

    // code omitted
}
```

The implementation of the ejbFindByPrimaryKey() method might seem somewhat unusual; it receives a primary key, and then returns it. Of course, what it has also done is validate that an entity exists for the given primary key; if there were none, a javax.ejb.ObjectNotFoundException would be thrown.

The implementation of ejbFindByCustomer() is straightforward; it simply returns a Collection of primary key objects.

The Job bean defines a home method, namely deleteByCustomer(), and the corresponding method in the JobBean class is ejbHomeDeleteByCustomer(), as shown in Listing 6.11.

LISTING 6.11 JobBean.ejbHomeDeleteByCustomer() Home Method

```
package data;

import javax.ejb.*;
import java.sql.*;
import java.util.*;
// imports omitted

public class JobBean implements EntityBean
{
    public void ejbHomeDeleteByCustomer(String customer) {
        Connection con = null;
        PreparedStatement stmt2 = null;
        PreparedStatement stmt1 = null;
        try {
            con = dataSource.getConnection();
            stmt1 = con.prepareStatement(
 ➡ "DELETE FROM JobSkill WHERE customer = ?");
            stmt2 = con.prepareStatement(
 ➡ "DELETE FROM Job WHERE customer = ?");
            stmt1.setString(1, customer);
            stmt2.setString(1, customer);
            stmt1.executeUpdate();
            stmt2.executeUpdate();
        }
        catch (SQLException e) {
            error("Error removing all jobs for " + customer, e);
        }
        finally {
            closeConnection(con, stmt1, stmt2, null);
        }
    }
    // code omitted
}
```

6

Implementing the Local Interface Methods

Each of the methods in the local interface has a corresponding method in the bean itself. The corresponding methods for JobBean are shown in Listing 6.12.

LISTING 6.12   Business Methods of JobBean Correspond to the Methods of the Local Interface

```java
package data;

import java.rmi.*;
import javax.ejb.*;
// imports omitted

public class JobBean implements EntityBean
{
    public String getRef() {
        return ref;
    }
    public String getCustomer() {
        return customer;
    }
    public CustomerLocal getCustomerObj() {
        return customerObj;
    }
    public String getDescription() {
        return description;
    }
    public void setDescription(String description) {
        this.description = description;
    }
    public LocationLocal getLocation() {
        return location;
    }
    public void setLocation(LocationLocal location) {
        this.location = location;
    }
    /** returns (copy of) skills */
    public Collection getSkills() {
        return new ArrayList(skills);
    }
    public void setSkills(Collection skills) {
        // just validate that the collection holds references toSkillLocal's
        for (Iterator iter = getSkills().iterator(); iter.hasNext(); ) {
            SkillLocal skill = (SkillLocal)iter.next();
        }
        // replace the list of skills with that defined.
        this.skills = new ArrayList(skills);
    }
    // code omitted
}
```

LISTING 6.13   continued

```
                    stmt.setString(3, ref);
                    stmt.setString(4, customer);
                    stmt.executeUpdate();
                    stmt = con.prepareStatement(
➡ "DELETE FROM JobSkill WHERE job = ? AND customer = ?");
                    stmt.setString(1, ref);
                    stmt.setString(2, customer);
                    stmt.executeUpdate();
                    stmt = con.prepareStatement(
➡ "INSERT INTO JobSkill (job, customer, skill) VALUES (?, ?, ?)");
                    for (int i = 0; i < skills.length; i++) {
                        stmt.setString(1, ref);
                        stmt.setString(2, customer);
                        stmt.setString(3, skills[i]);
                        stmt.executeUpdate();
                    }
                    this.description = description;
                    this.location = location;
                    this.skills.clear();
                    for (int i = 0; i < skills.length; i++)
                        this.skills.add(skills[i]);
            }
            catch (SQLException e) {
                error("Error updating job " + ref + " for " + customer, e);
            }
            finally {
                closeConnection(con, stmt, null, null);
            }
        }
    }
```

In contrast, Listing 6.14 shows the updated version, which delegates the hard work to the
Job bean:

LISTING 6.14   AdvertiseJobBean.updateDetails() with an Entity Bean Layer

6

```
package agency;

import java.util.*;
import javax.ejb.*;
import data.*;
// imports omitted

public class AdvertiseJobBean extends SessionBean
{
    private JobLocal job;
```

LISTING 6.14   continued

```java
    public void updateDetails(String description, String locationName,
                              String[] skillNames) {
        if (skillNames == null) {
            skillNames = new String[0];
        }
        List skillList;
        try {
            skillList = skillHome.lookup(Arrays.asList(skillNames));
        } catch (FinderException ex) {
            error("Invalid skill", ex); // throws an exception
            return;
        }
        LocationLocal location = null;
        if (locationName != null) {
            try {
                location = locationHome.findByPrimaryKey(locationName);
            } catch (FinderException ex) {
                error("Invalid location", ex); // throws an exception
                return;
            }
        }
        job.setDescription(description);
        job.setLocation(location);
        job.setSkills(skillList);
    }
    // code omitted
}
```

The updated version is much more object-oriented; the knowledge of the database schema has been encapsulated where it rightfully belongs—in the Entity bean layer.

All this means that the AdvertiseJob bean no longer has any dependencies on the jdbc/Agency DataSource object. On the other hand, it does now have dependencies on several of the Entity beans. These are defined using <ejb-local-ref> elements in the deployment descriptor as shown previously when configuring the Job Entity bean.

The revised DD entry for the Agency Session bean looks like this:

```xml
<ejb-jar>

  <enterprise-beans>
    <session>
      <ejb-name>AgencyBean</ejb-name>
      <home>agency.AgencyHome</home>
      <remote>agency.Agency</remote>
      <ejb-class>agency.AgencyBean</ejb-class>
      <session-type>Stateless</session-type>
```

```
    <transaction-type>Container</transaction-type>
    <env-entry>
      <env-entry-name>AgencyName</env-entry-name>
      <env-entry-type>java.lang.String</env-entry-type>
      <env-entry-value>J2EE in 21 Days Job Agency</env-entry-value>
    </env-entry>
    <ejb-local-ref>
      <ejb-ref-name>ejb/JobLocal</ejb-ref-name>
      <ejb-ref-type>Entity</ejb-ref-type>
      <local-home>data.JobLocalHome</local-home>
      <local>data.JobLocal</local>
      <ejb-link>data-entity-ejb.jar#JobBean</ejb-link>
    </ejb-local-ref>
...
  </session>
...
  </enterprise-beans>
...
</ejb-jar>
```

Local EJB references do not need to be added to the platform-specific deployment descriptor because the target bean is defined in the portable ejb-jar.xml deployment descriptor file. The J2EE container can use the JNDI name mapping of the target EJB to create the necessary environment entries for the session bean.

Now that you have seen how to create Entity beans using local interfaces you can review the case example on the Web site. You can build, deploy and run the Agency case study example using the asant build files in the examples directory of Day 6 on the Web site. The application in the examples directory uses only Entity beans for the job advertising functionality, Session beans are still used for registering applicants.

Gotchas

The following is a quick checklist of "gotchas" to help you with your implementation:

- Primary keys must be immutable. In other words, it is not possible to change the value of a primary key for an entity once assigned.

- Sometimes, Entity beans interact with non-data store resources such as a subscription to a JMS topic (covered on Day 9, "Java Message Service," and Day 10, "Message-Driven Beans"). These resources should be acquired in setEntityContext() and released in ejbPassivate() and re-acquired in ejbActivate(). Resources should also be released in unsetEntityContext().

- Finder methods can return a Collection, but they can't currently return a List, Set, or Map object.

6

- If you have two bean references, note that the value of `bean1.equals(bean2)` is unspecified, and that `bean1 == bean2` is also unspecified. Moreover, `hashCode()` may differ for two references to the same underlying EJB. The correct way to compare bean identities is to use `bean.isIdentical()` or to use the `equals()` method on the primary key classes.

- Beware of a reliance on pass-by-reference side-effects when using local interfaces; dependence upon such effects will compromise portability.

Acquire Late, Release Early

In conventional J2SE programs, the idiom is usually to connect to the database at the start of the program when the user logs in, and only disconnect when the user logs out. Holding on to the open database connection while the user logs in substantially improves performance; database connections are relatively expensive to obtain. So, for J2SE programs, the mantra is "Acquire early, release late."

With J2EE programs, things are inverted. The database connection should be obtained just before it is required, and closed immediately after it has been used. In other words, "Acquire late, release early." This is shown in the following `Job` bean code fragment:

```
public void ejbLoad() {
    JobPK key = (JobPK)ctx.getPrimaryKey();
    Connection con = null;
    PreparedStatement stmt = null;
    ResultSet rs = null;
    try {
        con = dataSource.getConnection();
        stmt = con.prepareStatement( … );
        // SQL code omitted

    }
    catch (SQLException e) {
        error("Error in ejbLoad for " + key, e);
    }
    catch (FinderException e) {
        error("Error in ejbLoad (invalid customer or location) for "+ key, e);
    }
    finally {
        closeConnection(con, stmt, null, rs);
    }
}
```

The reason that this works is because the database connection is obtained from a `javax.sql.DataSource` in a J2EE environment, rather than using the `java.sql.DriverManager.getConnection()` method. Obtaining connections from a `DataSource` is not expensive in performance terms because they are logical connections, not physical connections. When such a connection is obtained, it is merely obtained from a connection pool, and when it is "closed," it is simply returned back to the connection pool.

Indeed, using the J2SE idiom of acquire early, release late (for example, by obtaining a connection in `setEntityContext()` and releasing it in `unsetEntityContext()`) can adversely affect performance, because every instantiated bean would have its own database connection. This may well reduce application throughput because the memory resources of both the EJB container and the database server would be increased to handle many open database connections. In comparison, the J2EE idiom means that the number of database connections open is no more than the number of methods concurrently executing.

Summary

Another hard day, but you now have lots of good new material under your belt. You've seen that Entity beans represent persistent domain data with corresponding domain (not application) logic. You've also seen that the constituent parts of Entity beans are pretty much the same as Session beans, though Entity beans also require a primary key class that must be custom-developed if the key is composite.

You've been shown one of the two different ways to implement Entity beans using bean-managed persistence, whereby the persistence code (JDBC, for example) resides within the bean code, container-managed persistence is covered tomorrow.

Finally, you saw that the EJB specification allows local interfaces to be defined for EJBs as well as, or instead of, remote interfaces, and saw several good reasons why Entity beans should always use local interfaces.

Q&A

Q What do Entity beans represent?

A Entity beans represent persistent data that can be accessed and shared by many clients.

Q What are the two types of Entity beans?

A The two types of Entity beans are BMP and CMP.

Q Why are local interfaces preferable to remote interfaces for Entity beans?

A Local interfaces perform better because there is no network traffic when calling a bean through its local interface, and there is also no need to clone serializable objects.

6

Q How does a BMP Entity bean know what its primary key is?

A The primary key can either be passed as an argument of `ejbCreate()`, or it could be generated by the database, or it could be generated by some other bean, or it might be generated as a pseudo-random value using an algorithm that guarantees uniqueness.

Q Which two methods should the primary key class implement?

A The primary key class should implement the `hashCode()` and `equals()` methods.

Exercise

The exercise starts with a version of today's case study that has a complete set of Session beans, but an incomplete set of Entity beans. Where there is no Entity bean, the appropriate Session bean performs direct SQL.

Your task is to both implement an `Applicant` Entity bean and to update the `Agency` and `Register` Session beans to use this new Entity bean.

The `Applicant` bean should map itself to the `Applicant` and `ApplicantSkill` tables and define the following fields:

- `login`   This is the primary key for the `Applicant` Entity bean.
- `name`   of type `String`.
- `email`   of type `String`.
- `summary`   of type `String`.
- `location`   Should be a reference to a `LocationLocal` to ensure referential integrity.
- `skills`   Should be a collection of `SkillLocal` references to ensure referential integrity.

You should find that the structure of your new bean shares many similarities with the `Job` Entity bean. One difference will be the primary key. The `Job` bean required a `JobPK` because it had a composite primary key. For your `Applicant` bean, you do not need to develop a custom primary key class because applicants will be identified simply by their `login`—a simple `String`.

The `ApplicantLocalHome` and `ApplicantLocal` interfaces have already been provided; note their similarity to `JobLocalHome` and `JobLocal`.

The starting point for the `exercise` is in the exercise sub-directory of Day 6 on the Web site. You can use the supplied `asant` build files to compile, build, verify and deploy the example, or you can use `deploytool` and the EAR file in the `j2ee-ri` directory. Refer back to Day 4, "Introduction to Enterprise JavaBeans," and Day 5, "Session EJBs," for further details on how to use the `asant` build files and `deploytool`. Remember to update the different deployment descriptor files in the `dd/agency` directories if you don't use `deploytool`.

Good luck. A working example can be found in the Day 6 `agency` subdirectory on the Web site.

6

DAY **7**

Container-Managed Persistence and EJB Query Language

Yesterday, you saw how to specify, implement, and deploy bean-managed persistence (BMP) Entity beans. Today, you will learn

- How to specify, implement, configure and deploy container-managed persistence (CMP) Entity beans

- How to use the EJB Query Language (EJB QL) to obtain data from a data store

- How to define relationships between CMP Entity beans

Overview of Container-Managed Persistence

The EJB specification provides for two different ways of implementing Entity beans. The first approach, covered yesterday, is for the bean provider to embed the persistence logic within the bean itself—hence the name bean-managed persistence or BMP. The second is for the container vendor to provide that logic, either generated by the EJB container vendor's deployment tools or as part of the EJB container itself. Entity beans built this way are called CMP Entity beans.

NOTE

> CMP Entity beans have always been part of the EJB specification, first in EJB 1.0 and then with some minor refinements in EJB 1.1. There were substantial changes to CMP Entity beans in EJB 2—so substantial, in fact, that CMP 1.1 Entity beans are not forward compatible with EJB 2.
>
> To deal with this, the EJB specification actually provides two different ways to write CMP Entity beans. The first is the legacy 1.1 approach; beans that are written this way indicate it using an entry in their deployment descriptor. The second is using the far more powerful approach introduced in EJB 2.
>
> Today, you will be learning only about the EJB 2 approach.

The "anatomy" of CMP Entity beans is very much the same as BMP Entity beans:

- They both have a local-home (or remote-home) interface that defines the create methods, the finder methods, optional home methods, and a remove method.
- They both have a local (or remote) interface that defines the business methods of the bean.
- Obviously, they both have a bean class itself that implements methods corresponding to the previously mentioned interfaces, and also implements the lifecycle methods inherited from `javax.ejb.EntityBean`.
- Finally, if the primary key is not a standard Java class such as `String` or `Integer`, both BMP and CMP beans have a primary key class.

However, responsibilities of the CMP Entity bean in lifecycle methods are different, because there is no longer any requirement to persist the bean's state; persistence is now the responsibility of the EJB container. There are also changes in the interactions between the container and the bean, as you will see.

Another difference for CMP Entity beans is there is no longer any need to implement the finder methods in the bean. Under BMP, the bean provider writes the appropriate finder methods; under CMP, the container will do this work. However, the bean provider must specify the query to obtain the correct data from the data store using EJB Query

Language (EJB QL). EJB QL shares many similarities with ANSI SQL 92, so if you are familiar with SQL you should not have too many difficulties picking it up.

Entity beans, like tables in relational databases, have relationships. You saw this yesterday with the Job bean, which had relationships with the Skill, Location, and Customer beans. Under BMP, the bean provider must write the code that maintains all of these relationships explicitly. If CMP is used, these relationships can be defined declaratively using container-managed relationships, or CMR.

Relationships between Entity beans are intrinsically fine-grained. Using the Agency case study as an example, a many-to-many relationship between Job and Skill (indicating which skills are needed for which job) would involve many (job, skill) tuples stored in the JobSkill table. Because the performance cost of maintaining a fine-grained relationship across the network would be too severe, the EJB specification requires that container-manager relationships between Entity beans are defined only through local interfaces. Indeed, one of the primary reasons for the introduction of local interfaces in the EJB specification was to make CMR feasible.

N-tier Architecture (Revisited Again) and CMP Fields

CMP has an impact on the n-tier architecture that you have seen on previous days. Figure 7.1 updates a figure that you saw yesterday for CMP Entity beans.

FIGURE 7.1

CMP Entity beans are split into two components.

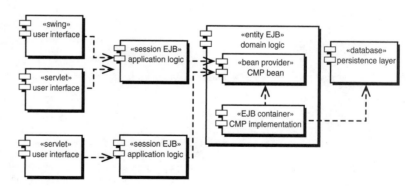

There are still four tiers to the architecture—namely, the interface, application, domain, and persistence layers. However, with CMP, the Entity beans are split into two components. The first component is provided by you, the bean provider, and comprises

- The bean's local-home and local interfaces
- An implementation of the business methods
- Abstract definitions of the accessor methods for the bean's properties (but no implementation, as this is provided by the container)

7

The second component is the concrete implementation of the CMP bean supplied by the EJB container provider from declarative information provided by you. This component has dependencies on both the bean and the persistence layer. The first dependency occurs because the concrete implementation uses the bean provider's abstract bean class as its superclass; in other words, it extends from the CMP bean. The second dependency is because the implementation of the bean performs appropriate data store calls.

You may recognize this design as an instance of the Template design pattern. The abstract CMP bean is a template, defining certain mandatory "hook" methods—specifically, the property accessor methods. As part of the deployment process the EJB container will generate a concrete class implementing the bean property accessor methods using information supplied in the deployment descriptor.

Listing 7.1 shows a CMP version of the Job Entity bean. This bean defines a pair of accessor methods (the getter and setter methods) for each of its properties—ref, customer, description, location, and skills.

LISTING 7.1   The Full Text of CMP Entity Bean JobBean.java

```java
Package data;

import java.rmi.*;
import java.sql.*;
import java.util.*;
import javax.ejb.*;
import javax.naming.*;
import javax.sql.*;

public abstract class JobBean implements EntityBean
{
    // CMP fields
    public abstract String getRef ();
    public abstract void setRef (String ref);
    public abstract String getCustomer ();
    public abstract void setCustomer (String customer);
    public abstract String getDescription ();
    public abstract void setDescription(String description);

    // CMR fields
    public abstract LocationLocal getLocation ();
    public abstract void setLocation(LocationLocal location);
    public abstract Collection getSkills();
    public abstract void setSkills(Collection skills);

    // EJB methods start here

    public void ejbPostCreate (String ref, String customer) {}
```

LISTING 7.1   continued

```
public JobPK ejbCreate (String ref, String customer)
                       throws CreateException {
    setRef(ref);
    setCustomer(customer);
    setDescription("");
    return new JobPK(ref,customer);
}

public void ejbHomeDeleteByCustomer(String customer)
            throws FinderException, RemoveException {
    Collection jobs =
((JobLocalHome)ctx.getEJBLocalHome()).findByCustomer(customer);
    for (Iterator iter = jobs.iterator(); iter.hasNext(); ) {
        JobLocal job = (JobLocal)iter.next();
        iter.remove();
        job.remove();
    }

}

public void ejbLoad() {}
public void ejbStore() {}
public void ejbPassivate() {}
public void ejbActivate() {}
public void ejbRemove() {}

private EntityContext ctx;

public void setEntityContext(EntityContext ctx) {
    this.ctx = ctx;
}

public void unsetEntityContext() {
    this.ctx = null;
}
}
```

Unlike BMP you do not declare the instance variables that correspond to the properties of the Entity bean, so you must use the getter and setter methods for accessing the data. This is reflected in the revised implementation of the `ejbCreate()` method which uses the templated setter methods to store property values for the newly created EJB.

This JavaBean naming scheme means that CMP fields must not start with a capital letter. Thus, customer and even cUSTOMER are valid names, but cUS-TOMER would not be. This is because the methods capitalize the CMP fields, and a capital letter cannot be capitalized!

One immediate advantage of using CMP Entity beans is that it gives the EJB container (through the concrete bean implementation) much more control over populating the bean's state, without compromising good OO principles. For example, it is up to the EJB container whether it chooses to obtain all of the bean's state when the bean is activated or created (eager loading), or whether it chooses to fetch the bean's state from the persistent data store as and when needed (lazy loading).

Another advantage of CMP is that the EJB container only need persist the bean's state to the data store when the bean's state has changed. If a read-only accessor method (a "getter" method) is called, there would be no change in state, and so the concrete implementation does not need to perform an unnecessary update to the data store. Taking this one stage further, when the bean's state is changed, the EJB container only needs to update those fields that have changed and can ignore fields that have not changed. One final advantage worth mentioning is that CMP simplifies the implementation of some value-add services, such as optimistic locking.

You can see from Listing 7.1 that most of the EJB lifecycle methods have nothing to do; this reflects the different lifecycle requirements for CMP Entity beans.

CMP Entity Bean Lifecycle

The actual lifecycle for CMP Entity beans is substantially the same as BMP Entity beans. Compare Figure 7.2 with the lifecycle for BMP Entity beans shown in the previous chapter.

The CMP lifecycle differs from the BMP lifecycle you saw yesterday in that there are no ejbFindXxx() methods for pooled beans. This is not to say that pooled CMP Entity beans do not perform finder methods; they do. However, the EJB container generates the actual code that performs this from EJB QL information provided in the deployment descriptor. There must be a finder method in the bean's local-home interface, but no equivalent ejbFindXxx() method in the bean itself.

FIGURE 7.2

The `javax.ejb.EntityBean` *lifecycle for CMP Entity beans.*

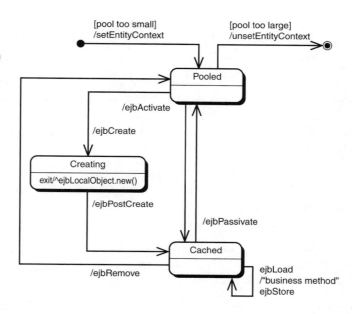

As for BMP Entity beans, the `setEntityContext()` and `unsetEntityContext()` methods must be implemented to look up any required resources (although the resources are likely to be different than those needed for BMP; in particular, the JDBC data source is not needed).

Under BMP, the `ejbCreate()` method was responsible for persisting the newly created bean's state to the persistent data store. Under CMP, the `ejbCreate()` method no longer has to do this, but does still need to set the bean's attributes to the parameters passed in. This can include generating a unique primary key value.

Similarly, the BMP version of `ejbRemove()` was responsible for physically removing the bean's state from the data store, again the CMP version does not need to do this. However, there may be occasions when work does need to be done in the `ejbRemove()` method. For example, the bean might want to prevent the delete from occurring if, for example, removing the bean would violate some referential integrity constraint. In such cases, you need to know that the `ejbRemove()` is called before the container actually removes the data and can throw an `EJBException` to abort the actual database delete.

Next are the `ejbLoad()` and `ejbStore()` methods. As you saw yesterday when using BMP, these methods for the `Job` bean were substantial. This is because they had to maintain the bean's state accessing both the `Job` and `JobSkill` database tables. Under CMP these methods normally have an empty implementation, as all the interactions with the persistent data store are done by the EJB container.

7

However, it may be that the physical schema of the persistent data store (especially if that persistent data store is a relational database) does not correspond exactly with the logical schema of the Entity bean.

For example, in the Agency case study, the `Applicant` table defines two columns—`address1` and `address2`. However, at least conceptually, the `Applicant` Entity bean has a vector field of `address`, of type `String[]`; there could be many lines in the `address` (and it's just that the physical schema of the persistent data store constrains the size of this vector to 2).

Because the `ejbLoad()` method is called after the EJB container has loaded the data, it may renormalize it. In other words, the data in the two CMP fields of `address1` and `address2` can be converted into the `String[]` address field. The bean's clients' view (as presented by the methods of the local interface) is that the `address` field is a vector.

Conversely, the `ejbStore()` method, called just before the EJB container updates the data, can denormalize the data. In other words, the data in the `address` vector field can be "posted" back to the `address1` and `address2` CMP fields.

The `ejbActivate()` and `ejbPassivate()` methods for a CMP Entity bean are pretty much identical to their implementations for a BMP Entity bean; after all, these methods have nothing to do with the persistent data store.

You have now seen the Java code for a CMP Entity bean, but before you can look at writing the EJB QL code for the finder methods you need to understand container-managed relationships. CMR is discussed in the next section.

Container-Managed Relationships

Container-Managed Relationships (CMR) might possibly sound daunting, and certainly from the EJB container vendor's perspective, there could be some fairly complex activity happening behind the scenes. However, from the bean provider's perspective (that is, you), they are fairly straightforward and easy to use.

CMR is defined declaratively through the deployment descriptor, underneath the `<relationships>` element. Therefore, container-managed relationships can only be defined between Entity beans that reside within the same local relationship scope. What this means in practice is that beans that have relationships must be deployed in the same `ejb-jar.xml` file. You will be learning more about declaring CMRs later today, in "Configuring a CMP Entity Bean."

Relationship Types

CMR allows three different types of relationships to be defined between Entity beans:

- One-to-one
- One-to-many
- Many-to-many

The first two relationship types are to be expected, but the last is perhaps more unexpected if you are used to using a relational database. In relational theory, it is not possible to create a many-to-many relationship directly; instead, a link (or association) table is required. An example of an association table is the JobSkill table in the Agency case study database.

NOTE

> Of course, most EJB containers—the J2EE RI included—will persist to a relational database, so will require an association table in the physical schema. If this is the case the association table is defined in the platform specific deployment descriptor for the EJB JAR file.

Relationship Multiplicity

These relationship types actually refer to the minimum and maximum multiplicity (sometimes called cardinality) of the related beans in the relationship. The EJB specification does not define a limit on the maximum multiplicity for a relationship and allows a minimum of zero. Hence, "one-to-many" also allows for none-to-many, one-to-none, and (trivially) none-to-none.

There are sometimes situations when multiplicity must be constrained. For example, it might be the case that a Job must always relate to a Location, but this is not enforced in the case study code. In these cases, it is up to the bean to enforce the constraint. In other words, the Job bean would only define a create() method that accepted a Location bean reference, and if it provided a setLocation() accessor method in its interface, it would ensure that the supplied Location reference was not null.

Related to this is the question, "What happens if a bean is removed?" Suppose that the Job bean relates to a Location, and the Location bean is deleted. The Job bean will be left with a null reference. In relational terms, this is sometimes called a cascade null.

7

Suppose (again) that every Job must always relate to a non-null Location. There are a number of options:

- The first, somewhat radical, option is to remove the related Job beans—in other words, perform a cascade delete. CMR supports this directly (if it is specified through the deployment descriptor) and will remove each Job bean in turn.

- Second, the application can prevent the removal of the foreign key Location bean from occurring. This would be done by implementing an appropriate check in the ejbRemove() lifecycle method.

- Another alternative would be to reassign every impacted Job bean to some new Location. Again, the ejbRemove() method would need to do this work.

The second option is probably the most likely, so you should take care to do this type of minimum multiplicity analysis to make sure that you do not unwittingly end up with beans that have null relationships when the semantics of the problem domain prohibits this from occurring.

Relationship Navigability

In addition to specifying multiplicity of the relationships, CMR also allows the navigability of the relationship to be defined. The navigability is either uni-directional or bi-directional.

Navigability is defined by indicating the name of the field that references the related bean. For example, in a many-to-one relationship between the Job and Location beans, indicating a field of location for the Job bean means that there is navigability from Job to Location. There may not necessarily be navigability in the opposite direction; that would depend on whether the Location bean defines a field called jobs.

CMR Fields

By way of example, the location CMR field for the Job bean has accessor methods of getLocation() and setLocation(), and the skills CMR field has the accessor methods getSkills() and setSkills(). The return type of these methods depends on the multiplicity of the relationship.

The relationship from Job to Location is many-to-one, so the methods that correspond to the location CMR field are as follows:

```
public abstract LocationLocal getLocation();
public abstract void setLocation(LocationLocal location);
```

For single-valued CMR fields, both the return type for the getter and the type for the parameter to the setter is the local interface of the related bean (LocationLocal in this case). The `Job` bean also has a relationship with the `Skill` bean, this time many-to-many. Thus, the `skills` CMR field corresponds to the following methods:

```
public abstract java.util.Collection getSkills();
public abstract void setSkills(java.util.Collection skills);
```

This is a multi-valued CMR field because a collection of values is returned, not just a single value. The collection returned here is a `java.util.Collection` of references to the local interface of the related bean (`SkillLocal` in this case). The EJB specification also allows for return values of `java.util.Set`.

Note that the properties of a bean are either CMP fields, CMR fields, or they are instance variables not managed by the container. Put another way, CMP fields cannot be defined that have references to other beans as their argument or return type; such fields must be defined as CMR fields.

NOTE

> The `Job` Entity bean has a relationship with both the `Location` bean and the `Customer` bean. The `getCustomer()` method returns the name of a customer as a `String`, whereas the `getLocation()` method returns a reference to a `LocationLocal`. You may be wondering why the `customer` field is not enforced using CMR?
>
> The reason is that the `customer` field is part of the primary key for the `Job` bean, and appears in `JobPK`. Every public field in `JobPK` must have a corresponding field in the bean itself. If the `JobPK` class defined its `customer` field to be a reference to a `CustomerLocal`, the `JobPK` class could not be guaranteed to be serializable.

If an Entity bean provides a remote interface, methods corresponding to the CMR field cannot be included in that interface. This is not really surprising because to do so would expose local objects to remote clients breaking the integrity of the EJB container. Table 7.1 compares the use of CMP fields and CMR fields in interfaces.

TABLE 7.1 CMP Fields and CMR Fields and Interfaces

Feature	CMP field	CMR field
Can appear in local interface	Yes	Yes
Can appear in remote interface	Yes, but not recommended; Entity beans should be accessed via local clients.	No
Can accept as parameters and return local references to beans	No. CMP fields deal only with primitives (or Serializable objects).	Yes

7

TABLE 7.1   continued

Feature	CMP field	CMR field
Can accept remote references as parameters and also return them to beans	No. CMP `fields` deal only with primitives (or Serializable objects).	No. Container-managed relationships are defined only through local interfaces of beans.

Now that you have been introduced to CMP Entity beans and have been shown the role of CMR in maintaining inter-bean relationships you can look at the EJB QL language used to define CMP database queries.

EJB QL

EJB Query Language (EJB QL) was introduced in the EJB 2 specification to make CMP Entity beans more portable across EJB containers. Previously, each EJB container vendor created their own proprietary mechanism for specifying the semantics of finder methods. This is no longer the case.

As a language, EJB QL is based on ANSI SQL and bears some similarity with the Object Constraint Language (OCL) that is part of UML.

Syntax and Examples

The EJB Specification formally defines the syntax of EJB QL queries using Bacchus Normal Form (BNF). This can be somewhat heavy to wade through, but is comprehensive. Rather than reproduce the specification (and to keep things simple), this section introduces EJB QL using examples. You should refer to the EJB specification for a full description of the EJB QL syntax.

Like SQL, EJB QL defines a SELECT statement which has a FROM clause and an optional WHERE clause. In SQL, you may recall that the columns listed in the SELECT clause relate to the tables identified in the FROM clause. So in exploring EJB QL, it makes sense to look at the FROM clause before the select statement itself.

FROM Clause

Some simple examples from the case study will show how the EJB QL FROM clause is constructed, assuming that the Job bean has an abstract schema name called Job, that the Customer bean has an abstract schema name called Customer, and so on. The first example is about as simple as it gets:

```
FROM Job AS j
```

This sets up an identification variable called j that refers to the Job schema. The comparison with SQL is obvious, because the syntax is the same, and as with SQL the AS keyword can be omitted. A more complex example using an IN sub-clause is

```
FROM Job AS j, IN (j.skills) AS s
```

This sets up the j identification variable and also a variable called s that refers to each of the skills related to the Job bean.

The IN (j.skills) expression is similar to an OCL expression. Here j refers to the identification variable assigned by the previous AS phrase and skills refers to a CMR field of the j bean. Comparing this to SQL, this most likely would correspond to:

```
FROM       Job AS j
INNER JOIN JobSkill AS s
        ON s.customer = j.customer
       AND s.ref = j.ref
```

Or, if you prefer the old-fashioned way:

```
FROM  Job AS j, JobSkill AS s
WHERE s.customer = j.customer
  AND s.ref = j.ref
```

The following example is a little more complex:

```
FROM Job AS j, IN (j.location.jobs) AS k
```

This sets up j as before and also an identification variable called k that refers to all of the jobs that have the same location as the original job. Note that j.location returns a reference to the Location bean for the Job, so that j.location.jobs returns the Collection of Jobs for that Location. Of course, this Collection will include the original job, but it will include others as well.

Comparing this to SQL, you can see that this is a self-join:

```
FROM       Job AS j
INNER JOIN Job AS k
        ON j.location = k.location
```

or:

```
FROM Job AS j, Job AS k
WHERE j.location = k.location
```

SELECT Clause

The easy case of the SELECT statement is the SELECT OBJECT(o) style where o is an identification variable defined by the FROM clause. This returns all the data from the data store required to instantiate a bean. In SQL terms, you might think of it as an intelligent SELECT * FROM ....

All finder methods must use the SELECT OBJECT(o) style, where the objects returned are of the schema associated with the bean for which the finder is being specified.

In the case study, if the JobLocalHome interface defined a finder method called findAll() to return all jobs, you would provide the following EJB QL query.

```
SELECT OBJECT(j)
FROM Job as j
```

The next example will return back all skills used by any job.

```
SELECT DISTINCT OBJECT(s)
FROM Job as j, IN (j.skills) as s
```

Because some skills will be required by more than one job, the DISTINCT keyword is used to eliminate duplicates.

A second form of a SELECT clause selects a single-value expression which can be a field name in a bean or an aggregate function. A simple single-value SELECT clause is:

```
SELECT DISTINCT j.location.name
FROM Job as j
```

This returns the names of the locations where there are jobs. Comparing this to the following SQL statement, you can see that EJB QL is actually simpler (because of its use of the OCL-like path expressions to navigate between beans):

```
SELECT DISTINCT l.name
FROM Job as j INNER JOIN Location as l ON j.location = l.location
```

However, the following EJB QL SELECT statement is not allowed:

```
SELECT DISTINCT j.skills.name
FROM Job as j
```

This is because the skills CMR field of Job returns a collection of skills, not a single skill. The correct way to phrase this query is as follows:

```
SELECT DISTINCT s.name
FROM Job as j, IN (j.skills) AS s
```

You might like to think of the s identification variable as an iterator over the collection of skills returned by the skills field.

Several aggregate functions were added to the EJB 2.1 specification for use in the SELECT statement. The available functions are: COUNT(), MAX(), MIN(), AVG() and SUM(). These functions have the same behavior as their SQL counterparts. You will not be able to use these functions if you have an EJB 2.0 compliant container that only supports J2EE 1.3.

The following example counts how many locations are in the database:

```
SELECT COUNT(l)
FROM Location as l
```

The following example counts how many locations actually have advertised jobs (as opposed to the total number of locations). Using the DISTINCT qualifier ensures that only different locations are counted.

```
SELECT DISTINCT COUNT(l)
FROM Job as j, IN (j.location) as l
```

Note that, unlike SQL, the SELECT clause in EJB QL can only ever return a single item of information, so the following is not allowed:

```
SELECT DISTINCT j.location.name, j.location.description
FROM Job as j
```

WHERE Clause

The WHERE clause is optional in an EJB QL query, but will be present in the majority of cases. It is used to restrict the objects selected according to some criteria. The following criteria can be used in a WHERE clause:

- Aggregation of conditional expressions using AND, OR.

- Conditional tests involving NOT, =, >, <, >=, <=, and <> operators. These apply variously to numbers, dates, times, strings and booleans. Additionally, Entity beans can be compared using the = and <> operators; you will recall that Entity beans are considered identical if their primary keys are equal.

- Comparisons can involve input parameters, where these correspond to the arguments of the finder methods.

- Arithmetic expressions can use the BETWEEN...AND operator, just as in SQL.

- String expressions can be compared against lists using the IN operator and against patterns using the LIKE operator. Note unlike Java, string literals must appear in single quotes.

- The IS NOT NULL operator exists to determine if an object is null.

There are some more operators to EJB QL and some built-in functions, but first, some examples using these operators.

```
SELECT OBJECT(c)
FROM Customer AS c
WHERE c.name LIKE 'J%'
```

This will find all customers whose name begins with the letter J. Note that the SQL wildcards (% to match none or many characters, _ to match precisely one character) are used.

The following:

```
SELECT OBJECT(j)
FROM Jobs AS j
WHERE j.location IS NULL
```

will find all jobs where the location has not been specified.

```
SELECT l.description
FROM Location AS l
WHERE l.name IN ('London', 'Washington')
```

returns the descriptions of the locations named London and Washington.

Looking ahead to defining your SELECT statements for finder methods in CMP Entity beans, the WHERE clause can also include input parameters. These parameters correspond to the arguments of the finder method, as defined in the local-home interface or bean, respectively.

For example, the Job bean declares the following finder method in the JobLocalHome interface:

```
Collection findByCustomer(String customer);
```

The EJB QL query for this finder method is as follows:

```
SELECT OBJECT(j)
FROM Job AS j
WHERE j.customer = ?1
```

?1 acts as a placeholder, with the 1 indicating that the first argument of the finder method be implicitly bound to this input parameter. Unlike JDBC SQL strings, the number is required. It is also needed in the cases where a single argument is used more than once in the query. For example, consider the following finder method:

```
Collection findLocationsNamedOrNamedShorterThan(String name);
```

This might have an EJB QL query of

```
SELECT OBJECT(l)
FROM Location AS l
WHERE l.name = ?1
OR LENGTH(l.name) < LENGTH(?1)
```

This example uses the built-in function LENGTH that returns the length of a String. In any case, this rather peculiar finder method will find those locations that have the exact name, and will also return any name whose length is strictly shorter than the supplied name. You can see that the ?1 placeholder appears more than once because the name argument needs to be bound to the query in two places.

EJB QL defines just a few more built-in functions. The functions that return a string are CONCAT and SUBSTRING. The functions that return a number are LENGTH, ABS, SQRT, MOD, and LOCATE. This last is effectively the same as the Java method String.indexOf(String str, int fromIndex).

EJB QL defines two final operators—IS [NOT] EMPTY and [NOT] MEMBER OF. Neither of these have any direct equivalents in SQL, but have equivalents in OCL.

The IS [NOT] EMPTY operator is similar to the isEmpty operator of OCL and can be used to determine whether a collection returned by a CMR field is empty. For example,

```
SELECT OBJECT(s)
FROM Skill AS s
WHERE s.jobs IS EMPTY
```

will return all those skills that are not marked as required by any job. This might be the query for a finder method on the SkillLocalHome interface, called something like findNotNeededSkills().

In fact, this type of query can be expressed in SQL, though it does require a sub query:

```
SELECT s.*
FROM Skill AS s
WHERE NOT EXISTS
    (   SELECT *
        FROM JobSkill AS j
        WHERE s.skill = j.skill )
```

The [NOT] MEMBER OF operator is similar to the include operator of OCL. Consider the following finder method:

```
Collection findJobsRequiringSkill(SkillLocal skill);
```

The EJB QL query for this would be

```
SELECT OBJECT(j)
FROM Job AS j
WHERE ?1 MEMBER OF j.skills
```

Again, this can be expressed in SQL using a sub query:

```
SELECT j.*
FROM Job AS j
WHERE EXISTS
    (   SELECT *
        FROM JobSkill AS s
        WHERE j.customer = s.customer
        AND    j.ref     = s.ref
        AND    s.skill   = ?1         )
```

7

ORDER BY Clause

An ORDER BY clause was added to the SELECT statement in the EJB Specification 2.1. If you are working with an EJB 2.0 container that supports J2EE 1.3 you will not be able to use the ORDER BY clause.

The results from a SELECT query can be ordered by any single-value field in the target of the SELECT. To order the agency jobs by reference you would use:

```
SELECT Object(j)
FROM Job AS j
ORDER BY j.ref
```

The ORDER BY clause supports the final qualifier ASC for ascending order (the default) and DESC for descending order. Multiple fields can be specified in the ORDER BY clause. The following example will order the results in descending order of location and ascending order of reference within a location:

```
SELECT Object(j)
FROM Job AS j
ORDER BY j.customer DESC, j.ref
```

Fields in the ORDER BY clause must be simple CMP fields; they cannot be CMR fields. The previous example will not work if j.customer is a CMR field.

So far you have seen EJB QL used to define finder methods. Finder methods perform the same purpose as they did with BMP Entity beans, that of searching for and retrieving one or more Entity beans. Another type of method, called a select method, also uses EJB QL and returns data from a data store, but is needed to support bean functionality as described in the next section.

Select Methods

Entity beans introduce a new set of methods that use EJB QL queries, namely that of select methods. These are like finder methods, in that their purpose is to return data from the persistent data store using container generated functionality.

Select methods are provided to allow bean developers to query the persistent store from within a bean without exposing that query to client code through a finder method. Select methods must be used when a bean needs to query the database for data stored in CMP or CMR fields. Select methods can only be called by the bean itself, so they act as helper methods.

Select methods are defined as abstract methods with the Entity bean implementation and have a name prefix of ejbSelect. The Agency case study does not require select methods but any query that involves CMP or CMR fields can be used. For example, the Job bean could have required a method to count the total number of jobs advertised, but there might have been no need to provide this functionality to clients. This could have been implemented as a select method as follows:

```
public abstract Collection ejbSelectJobCount ();
```

The `ejbSelectJobCount()` EJB QL query string would be simply

```
SELECT DISTINCT COUNT(j)
FROM Jobs AS j
```

The `ejbSelectJobCount()` method would be used just like the abstract getter and setter methods. You now have enough background theory for CMP Entity beans to be able to look at writing and deploying some CMP Entity beans.

Implementing a CMP Entity Bean

Specifying a CMP Entity bean is identical to specifying a BMP Entity bean; it consists of defining the local-home interface, the local interface, and the bean itself. The good news, as you saw in listing 7.1, is that the bean itself is significantly simpler (and quicker to implement).

The Local Interfaces

The requirements of local-home and local interfaces for a CMP Entity bean are the same as for a BMP Entity bean. In fact, if you are converting a BMP Entity bean to CMP you will probably not have to make any changes to the interfaces.

NOTE

> The Agency case study has made changes to the `findByLocation()` methods in the `Job` and `Applicant` Entity beans. In the BMP version, the single parameter was a String. In the CMP version, the parameter must be a `LocationLocal` EJB reference to satisfy the requirement of CMR. The `findByLocation()` methods are used by the Message-Driven Beans to be discussed on Day 10.

For completeness, Listing 7.2 is the local-home interface of the `Job` bean and Listing 7.3 is the local interface.

7

LISTING 7.2   JobLocalHome Interface

```
package data;

import java.rmi.*;
import java.util.*;
import javax.ejb.*;

public interface JobLocalHome extends EJBLocalHome
{
    JobLocal create (String ref, String customer) throws CreateException;
    JobLocal findByPrimaryKey(JobPK key) throws FinderException;
    Collection findByCustomer(String customer) throws FinderException;
    Collection findByLocation(LocationLocal location) throws FinderException;
    void deleteByCustomer(String customer);
}
```

LISTING 7.3   JobLocal Interface

```
package data;

import java.rmi.*;
import javax.ejb.*;
import java.util.*;

public interface JobLocal extends EJBLocalObject
{
    String getRef();
    String getCustomer();

    void setDescription(String description);
    String getDescription();

    void setLocation(LocationLocal location);
    LocationLocal getLocation();

    Collection getSkills();
    void setSkills(Collection skills);
}
```

Just as for BMP Entity beans, implementing a CMP Entity bean involves providing an implementation for the methods of the `javax.ejb.EntityBean` interface, corresponding methods for each method in the home interface, and a business method for each method in the local/remote interface.

Implementing `javax.ejb.EntityBean`

In this section, you will implement the CMP version of the Job Entity bean that was shown previously in Listing 7.1—the same bean was also used on Day 6 when studying BMP Entity beans.

With CMP, the field access and modifier methods must be provided as abstract functions. The EJB container will provide implementations for these methods:

```
// CMP fields
public abstract String getRef ();
public abstract void setRef (String ref);
public abstract String getCustomer ();
public abstract void setCustomer (String customer);
public abstract String getDescription ();
public abstract void setDescription(String description);

// CMR fields
public abstract LocationLocal getLocation ();
public abstract void setLocation(LocationLocal location);
public abstract Collection getSkills();
public abstract void setSkills(Collection skills);
```

The Job bean must define setter methods for the `Ref` and `Customer` properties, even though these are not defined in the local interface. Without these abstract setter definitions, the fields cannot be managed using CMP (as discussed later when describing the `ejbCreate()` method).

Because the bean contains abstract methods, the bean class must also be abstract, as well as extend `javax.ejb.EntityBean`:

```
public abstract class JobBean implements EntityBean {…}
```

A CMP Entity bean will have to provide implementations of any business methods that do not correspond to CMP or CMR fields in the bean. The Job bean has no additional business methods in the local interface.

The Job bean does have a single business method in the home interface—namely the `deleteByCustomer()` method for deleting jobs for a specific customer. An EJB Entity bean (just like a BMP bean) must provide an implementation of this method in `ejbHomeDeleteByCustomer()` as follows:

```
public void ejbHomeDeleteByCustomer(String customer)
            throws FinderException, RemoveException {
    Collection jobs
  ➡ = ((JobLocalHome)ctx.getEJBLocalHome()).findByCustomer(customer);
    for (Iterator iter = jobs.iterator(); iter.hasNext(); ) {
        JobLocal job = (JobLocal)iter.next();
```

7

```
            iter.remove();
            job.remove();
    }
}
```

There is no need to provide implementations of the finder methods in the home interface, as these are defined in the deployment descriptor as described in the section "Deploying a CMP Entity Bean using J2EE RI."

The `ejbCreate()` method simply persists the Entity bean data passed as parameters as follows:

```
public void ejbPostCreate (String ref, String customer) {}

public JobPK ejbCreate (String ref, String customer) throws CreateException {
    JobPK key = new JobPK(ref,customer);
    try {
        ((JobLocalHome)ctx.getEJBLocalHome()).findByPrimaryKey(key);
        throw new CreateException("Duplicate job name: "+key);
    }
    catch (FinderException ex) {}
    setRef(ref);
    setCustomer(customer);
    setDescription("");
    return null;
}
```

Note the use of setter methods to save the bean's state. This contrasts with the BMP equivalent where the fields were written to directly.

The implementation of this method would have been even shorter if the `findByPrimaryKey()` call, checking for duplicates, had been omitted. An alternative approach for the `Job` bean would be to rely on constraints in the underlying database to detect duplicate keys rather than explicitly make the test in the `ejbCreate()` method.

NOTE

> Strictly, the appropriate exception to throw here is a `DuplicateKeyException`, not a `CreateException`. However, the EJB specification does not mandate this.

Under CMP, the bean should return `null` from the `ejbCreate()` method. The reason for this is that the EJB container can access the information that constitutes the primary key anyway, by virtue of the CMP fields.

Removing a bean requires no additional work so the `ejbRemove()` method is trivial:

```
public void ejbRemove() {}
```

CAUTION

> The BMP version of `ejbRemove()` for Job bean resets all the fields to null. When implementing CMP Entity beans, you absolutely must not reset the fields to null. Doing so will cause the EJB container to throw an exception, because the bean's state is required so that the container can remove the correct data from the persistent data store. The `ejbRemove()` method is called before the data is deleted from the store.

Under CMP, the `ejbLoad()` and `ejbStore()` methods have nothing to do unless there is derived data to be maintained. The `JobBean` class has no additional work to do when data is retrieved and stored:

```
public void ejbLoad() {}
public void ejbStore() {}
```

The `ejbLoad()` method is called after the bean's state has been populated, so the bean's state can be read through the accessor methods. The `ejbStore()` method is called prior to saving the data to store.

The `ejbActivate()` and `ejbPassivate()` methods have nothing to do with storing data, so their implementation is unchanged:

```
public void ejbPassivate() {}
public void ejbActivate() {}
```

Under BMP, the `setEntityContext()` method was used to look up various bean home interfaces from JNDI, and also obtain the JDBC `DataSource` called `java:comp/env/jdbc/Agency`. These actions are no longer required as the EJB container maintains the persistent data. The revised `EntityContext` methods for the `JobBean` are:

```
private EntityContext ctx;

public void setEntityContext(EntityContext ctx) {
    this.ctx = ctx;
}

public void unsetEntityContext() {
    this.ctx = null;
}
```

The complete listing for the Job CMP Entity bean was shown in Listing 7.1 at the start of today's discussion.

Now that you have studied how to develop a CMP Entity bean you may be wondering why it is so easy. The answer is that the J2EE server vendor is doing a lot of work on your behalf. But the downside to this is that you will have to provide a lot more information in the deployment descriptors for your EJB. Of necessity, a lot of the extra

7

information is platform-specific. To understand what additional information you need to supply you will now deploy the revised Job entity using the J2EE RI.

Deploying a CMP Entity EJB Using J2EE RI

You should be familiar with deployment by now. The sources for today's examples are in the Day07/examples directory on the accompanying Web site. You can follow the steps for building the EJB example and generate a new EAR file using deploytool, or you can simply build and deploy the completed examples from the command line using the command:

```
asant build deploy
```

If you want to follow today's example to learn how to deploy an EJB using deploytool, start deploytool and open the file Day07/examples/j2ee-ri/agency.ear.

Before you can build a CMP Entity bean with J2EE RI you must capture the database schema as discussed in the next section.

NOTE

> The J2EE RI is a reduced functionality version of the Sun Java System Application Server (http://wwws.sun.com/software/products/appsrvr/ home_appsrvr.html). The deployment process described here is the same as that for the Sun Java System Application Server.
>
> J2EE servers from other vendors will adopt different strategies for defining and deploying CMP Entity beans.

Capturing the Database Schema

In order to map the Entity beans in your application onto a database, the J2EE RI provides a capture-schema utility that will generate an XML file that is used by deploytool for mapping Entity beans onto database tables.

For the Agency case study, you can capture the database schema using the command

```
asant capture-schema
```

This runs the following J2EE RI command:

```
> capture-schema -driver com.pointbase.jdbc.jdbcUniversalDriver
➡ -dburl jdbc:pointbase:server://localhost/sun-appserv-samples
➡ -username pbPublic -password pbpublic
➡ -table APPLICANT -table APPLICANTSKILL -table CUSTOMER
➡ -table LOCATION -table JOB -table JOBSKILL -table SKILL
➡ -out build/agency.dbschema
```

All the capture schema command needs is a database URL, a driver name, and the username and password for accessing the database. You must also supply a list of tables to examine and a file to store the resultant XML schema document. In this example the XML document is saved in the build/agency.dbschema file.

You do not need to be familiar with the details of the schema document; simply treat it as a piece of black box data needed by deploytool to map Entity beans onto tables.

You are now ready to define your CMP Entity beans.

Adding a CMP Entity Bean Using deploytool

With the Day07/examples/j2ee-ri/agency.ear file open in deploytool select the Entity JAR file in the left pane. The EAR file you have opened already contains all the Entity beans for the case study except the Job Entity bean. Figure 7.3 shows the JAR file contents for the Entity beans.

NOTE

This version of the Agency case study includes CMP Entity beans for Skill, Location and Customer but has retained the BMP Entity bean for Applicant. The exercise at the end of today's example is to convert the Applicant bean from BMP to CMP.

FIGURE 7.3

CMP Entity EJB JAR shown in deploytool.

7

In Figure 7.3 it is important to note that the EJB JAR file contents include the `agency.dbschema` file you generated in the previous section. Without this file you will not be able to map the Entity beans onto the database schema.

You can now add the `Job` bean using the File, New, Enterprise Bean... menu option. The Job bean class files are included in the Entity JAR file so you can click Next to step through the Wizard screens until you reach the general page where you define the bean classes. Select the following values:

- Enterprise bean class—`data.JobBean`
- Local Home Interface—`data.JobLocalHome`
- Local Interface—`data.JobLocal`

You do not need to set Bean Type to `Entity` as `deploytool` will detect that your Enterprise Bean class is an Entity bean.

You must explicitly set the bean name to `JobEJB`—it is important that you do not simply accept the default name of `JobBean`, otherwise the table mapping features of `deploytool` will not work correctly. This is shown in Figure 7.4.

FIGURE 7.4

Defining the `JobEJB` *CMP Entity bean classes.*

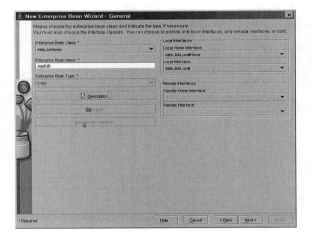

CAUTION

Using the J2EE RI, you must define your CMP Entity bean name with the name of the underlying database table and the suffix EJB. Failure to do this will stop `deploytool` from correctly mapping your bean onto its underlying table. In this example the database table name is `Job`, so the bean name must be `JobEJB`.

Click Next to step forward to the Web Service Endpoint screen, accept the default No option to endpoints and click Next once more.

On the subsequent Entity Settings page you should select Container Managed Persistence (2.0) as the Persistence Management type. You will now see a list of managed fields for the bean; deploytool has generated the managed field names from the setter and getter method names in your bean class. Check the ref, description and customer fields, but leave the CMR fields location and skills unchecked.

In the Abstract Schema Name field (on the right of the window) enter the value Job (don't use the supplied JobEJB schema name).

At the bottom of the screen enter data.JobPK for the primary key class and leave the primary key field name blank. You should now have a screen that looks like Figure 7.5.

NOTE
> The JobEJB Entity bean uses a custom primary key class and does not have a corresponding bean property as the primary key as is derived from the ref and customer CMR fields. If your Entity bean has a CMR field corresponding to the primary key, this field name should be selected from the list supplied in the deploytool Entity dialog page. When you have completed the wizard for adding the JobEJB bean you can look at the other Entity beans in the EAR file, all of which have a named primary key field.

FIGURE 7.5

Defining the JobEJB *CMP fields.*

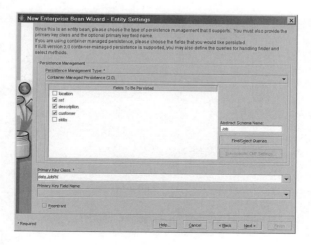

Click Next and then Finish to complete the bean definition.

Your CMP bean will not need a Resource Reference to the jdbc/Agency database as the container manages database access. Nor does the bean require any EJB References.

7

However, you need to specify the bean's transaction requirements (discussed in detail tomorrow). Select the `JobEJB` bean and the Transactions dialog and verify that all the local, local-home and bean methods have `Required` transaction attributes.

You have just added the following entry to the `ejb-jar.xml` deployment descriptor:

```xml
<ejb-jar>
  <display-name>Entity</display-name>
  <enterprise-beans>
...
    <entity>
      <ejb-name>JobEJB</ejb-name>
      <local-home>data.JobLocalHome</local-home>
      <local>data.JobLocal</local>
      <ejb-class>data.JobBean</ejb-class>
      <persistence-type>Container</persistence-type>
      <prim-key-class>data.JobPK</prim-key-class>
      <reentrant>false</reentrant>
      <cmp-version>2.x</cmp-version>
      <abstract-schema-name>Job</abstract-schema-name>
      <cmp-field>
        <description>no description</description>
        <field-name>ref</field-name>
      </cmp-field>
      <cmp-field>
        <description>no description</description>
        <field-name>description</field-name>
      </cmp-field>
      <cmp-field>
        <description>no description</description>
        <field-name>customer</field-name>
      </cmp-field>
...
    </entity>
...
  </enterprise-beans>
  <assembly-descriptor>
    <container-transaction>
      <method>
        <ejb-name>JobEJB</ejb-name>
        <method-name>*</method-name>
      </method>
      <trans-attribute>Required</trans-attribute>
    </container-transaction>
...
  </assembly-descriptor>
</ejb-jar>
```

You need also to define the Entity bean JNDI name by selecting the Job Entity bean in the `deploytool` left pane and the General dialog tab in the right pane. Click on the Sun-specific Settings button and enter `ejb/JobLocal` in the JNDI Name field in the popup window and click Close to return to the main deploytool window. This is the same process as for BMP Entity beans and has added the following entry to the sun-ejb-jar.xml file:

```
<sun-ejb-jar>
  <enterprise-beans>
    <name>Entity</name>
    <ejb>
      <ejb-name>JobEJB</ejb-name>
      <jndi-name>ejb/JobLocal</jndi-name>
    </ejb>
...
  </enterprise-beans>
</sun-ejb-jar>
```

You are now in a position to define the Entity bean finder methods.

Defining Entity Bean Finder Methods

You must provide EJB QL statements for every finder method in your CMP Entity bean. In deploytool select the JobEJB bean and the Entity dialog page and click on the Find/Select Queries button. You will be presented with a popup window listing your finder methods; you will need to select the Finder methods radio button if it is not automatically selected by deploytool. deploytool has generated the list of finder methods from the information in the JobEJB Entity bean's home interface.

You can see that the findByPrimaryKey() method is not included in the deploytool list. The J2EE RI already has sufficient information from the CMP dialog page to be able to generate the EJB QL for this method automatically. However, you will need to supply the EJB QL for the other finder methods.

The findByCustomer() method has the following signature in the home interface:

```
Collection findByCustomer(String customer) throws FinderException;
```

The EJB QL query for this is

```
SELECT OBJECT(j)
FROM Job AS j
WHERE j.customer = ?1
```

In this query the customer name is passed as a parameter to the finder method and is identified by the ?1 parameter in the WHERE clause. Using deploytool, select findByCustomer() from the list of methods and enter the previous EJB QL statement. This is shown in Figure 7.6.

7

FIGURE 7.6

Defining EJB QL for the findByCustomer() *method.*

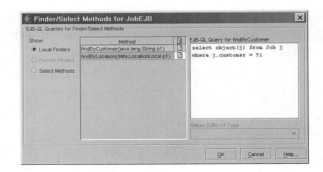

The other finder method is findByLocation():

```
Collection findByLocation(LocationLocal location) throws FinderException;
```

The EJB QL query for this is as follows:

```
SELECT OBJECT(j)
FROM Job AS j
WHERE j.location.name = ?1
```

Add the EJB QL for this query to the deploytool settings and click OK.

You have added the following information to the ejb-jar.xml deployment descriptor:

```
<ejb-jar>
  <display-name>Entity</display-name>
  <enterprise-beans>
...
    <entity>
      <ejb-name>JobEJB</ejb-name>
...
      <query>
        <query-method>
          <method-name>findByCustomer</method-name>
          <method-params>
            <method-param>java.lang.String</method-param>
          </method-params>
        </query-method>
        <ejb-ql>select object(j) from Job j
                where j.customer = ?1</ejb-ql>
      </query>
      <query>
        <query-method>
          <method-name>findByLocation</method-name>
          <method-params>
            <method-param>data.LocationLocal</method-param>
          </method-params>
        </query-method>
```

```
              <ejb-ql>select object(j) from Job j
                    where j.location = ?1</ejb-ql>
          </query>
        </entity>
    …
      </enterprise-beans>
    …
  </ejb-jar>
```

Note that there are no J2EE RI platform-specific deployment descriptor entries for finder methods.

You are now in a position to define the Container-Managed Relationships between the JobEJB Entity bean and other Entity beans in the application.

Defining Entity Bean CMR Fields

As previously discussed relationships can only be defined between beans in the same EJB JAR file. To add your Agency case study relationships you must select the Entity JAR in the left pane and the Relationships dialog in the right pane. Currently, there are no relationships defined in the application because you are still adding the Job bean and the Applicant bean is the old BMP version.

In the relationships dialog, click Add and in the popup window enter the following information to define the relationship between the Job bean and the Location bean; this is a many to one relationship (many jobs per single location):

- Multiplicity—Many to 1 (*:1)
- Enterprise Bean A—JobEJB
- Field Referencing Bean B—location
- Enterprise Bean B—LocationEJB
- Field Referencing Bean A—<none>

The dialog should look like Figure 7.7.

FIGURE 7.7

Defining the CMR fields for Job and Location Entity beans.

7

Click OK. You have now defined the relationship mapping many `Job.location` fields onto the `Location` bean. The `Location` bean does not maintain a list of jobs at that location so this is a uni-directional relationship from `Job` to `Location` (hence no `job` field in the `Location` bean).

A common mistake made at this point is to confuse the database table and column schema with the EJB object relationships. You are currently defining a relationship so do not be tempted to select the `Location.name` field for the Bean B values in the `deploytool` dialog. This would imply that the `name` field of the `Location` bean is a list of jobs at that location, which is not the case. Later, in the section "Mapping Entity Beans to a Database Schema," you will map the underlying database table and columns that represent this relationship.

In `deploytool`, click OK to save this relationship. You have added the following information to the `ejb-jar.xml` deployment descriptor:

```
<ejb-jar>
  <display-name>Entity</display-name>
  <enterprise-beans>
...
  </enterprise-beans>
  </relationships>
    <ejb-relation>
      <ejb-relationship-role>
        <ejb-relationship-role-name>JobEJB</ejb-relationship-role-name>
        <multiplicity>Many</multiplicity>
        <relationship-role-source>
          <ejb-name>JobEJB</ejb-name>
        </relationship-role-source>
        <cmr-field>
          <cmr-field-name>location</cmr-field-name>
        </cmr-field>
      </ejb-relationship-role>
      <ejb-relationship-role>
        <ejb-relationship-role-name>LocationEJB</ejb-relationship-role-name>
        <multiplicity>One</multiplicity>
        <relationship-role-source>
          <ejb-name>LocationEJB</ejb-name>
        </relationship-role-source>
      </ejb-relationship-role>
    </ejb-relation>
  </relationships>
  <assembly-descriptor>
...
  </assembly-descriptor>
</ejb-jar>
```

In deploytool, click Add to define the many-to-many Job to Skills relationship, as shown in Figure 7.8, using the following information:

- Multiplicity—Many to Many (*:*)
- Enterprise Bean A—JobEJB
- Field Referencing Bean B—skills
- Field Type—java.util.Collection
- Enterprise Bean B—SkillEJB
- Field Referencing Bean A—<none>

FIGURE 7.8

Defining the CMR fields for Job and Skill Entity beans.

This time the Job bean has a field for the many sides of the relationship, and so you must specify whether the relationship is represented by a Java Set or a Collection object. As the JobLocal.getSkills() method returns a Collection object you must select java.util.Collection for the field type.

Like the Job and Location relationship this is a uni-directional relationship and so there is no field in the Skill bean representing the jobs with that skill.

Click OK and you have defined this relationship in the ejb-jar.xml deployment descriptor as follows:

```
<ejb-jar>
  <display-name>Entity</display-name>
  <enterprise-beans>
...
  </enterprise-beans>
  </relationships>
    <ejb-relation>
      <ejb-relationship-role>
        <ejb-relationship-role-name>JobEJB</ejb-relationship-role-name>
        <multiplicity>One</multiplicity>
        <relationship-role-source>
          <ejb-name>JobEJB</ejb-name>
        </relationship-role-source>
```

7

```
          </relationship-role-source>
          <cmr-field>
            <cmr-field-name>skills</cmr-field-name>
            <cmr-field-type>java.util.Collection</cmr-field-type>
          </cmr-field>
        </ejb-relationship-role>
        <ejb-relationship-role>
          <ejb-relationship-role-name>SkillEJB</ejb-relationship-role-name>
          <multiplicity>Many</multiplicity>
          <relationship-role-source>
            <ejb-name>SkillEJB</ejb-name>
          </relationship-role-source>
        </ejb-relationship-role>
      </ejb-relation>
  …
  </relationships>
  <assembly-descriptor>
  …
  </assembly-descriptor>
</ejb-jar>
```

You have now defined the portable aspects of your Entity bean, so this is a good time to save your changes.

At this point you should verify your application using the `deploytool` Tools, Verify J2EE Compliance menu option or, after saving your deploytool changes, run the command:

```
asant verify-j2ee-ri
```

If you have any verification failures you should fix them now. Common mistakes are to fail to define Transaction Attributes or to select the wrong CMP field settings on the Entity dialog page.

NOTE

> The authors found the running the Verifier from within `deploytool` generated spurious errors about blank JNDI names for the Entity beans. As long as you defined the `JobEJB` JNDI name as described in the main text you can ignore any errors for blank JNDI names (all of the supplied Entity beans have valid JNDI name settings). This error is not reported by the command-line verifier, which can be run with the command:
>
> ```
> asant verify j2ee-ri
> ```
>
> When running the verifier you may get the following warning:
>
> ```
> INFO: JDO7002: Found unrecognized database generation user policy…
> ```
>
> You can safely ignore this warning.

When you have an application that verifies correctly you can proceed to the next stage to map the Entity bean CMP and CMR fields onto the underlying database schema.

Mapping Entity Beans CMP Fields Using J2EE RI

The J2EE RI platform uses the information in the database schema XML document to map the Entity beans to database tables and columns. You will now generate the platform specific mappings for your Entity beans.

NOTE

The mapping of Entity beans to the database schema is very platform specific. The process described here applies to the J2EE RI 1.4 and Sun Java System Application Server. Other platforms will use different techniques.

The J2EE RI `capture-schema` utility is used to generate a `dbschema` XML document for the database. Information in this XML document is used to map the Entity bean CMP and CMR fields. In particular, the PRIMARY KEY and FOREIGN KEY constraints for all the tables used by CMP entity beans must be defined, otherwise the automatic field mapping will not work. There are also restrictions on table and column names as described in the text.

Before you generate the Entity bean field mapping information, you must have the J2EE RI and PointBase database servers running. If this is not the case, start them as described on Day 2, "The J2EE Platform and Roles," before completing this example.

Furthermore, you must be working with a verified application otherwise the next process will fail. Check that you application verifies correctly before proceeding with this example.

CAUTION

The authors found that the J2EE RI 1.4 Nov 2003 version of `deploytool` consistently locked up and stopped responding to key clicks if the Sun-specific CMP dialog view was shown and the Entity beans had failed to verify correctly. It is imperative that you save your changes to the Agency Application, verify and resolve any errors, before you display the Sun-specific CMP dialog.

In `deploytool`, select the `Entity` JAR in the left pane and the General tab in the right pane and click on the Sun-specific Settings... button. You will be presented with a dialog window for generating the Entity bean to database schema settings.

In the Sun-specific settings dialog window, select CMP from the View list in the top left of the dialog and enter the `jdbc/Agency` CMP Resource JNDI name, as shown in Figure 7.9.

7

FIGURE 7.9

Defining the J2EE RI CMP JNDI Resource.

Next, click on the Create Field Mappings... button. If you have followed the previous steps correctly, and verified your application, you will see the dialog screen in Figure 7.10.

FIGURE 7.10

Mapping the J2EE RI CMP fields using the agency.dbschema XML document.

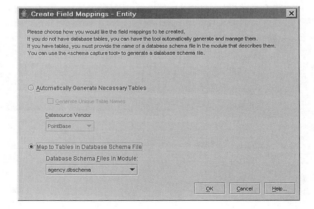

Select the option to Map Tables in Database schema file and select the agency.dbschema file from the list (as shown in Figure 7.10). There are other options for CMP and CMR mappings but today's example will only use the mapping based on the database schema XML document.

Click OK to generate the mappings and when the warning screen advising you that all current CMP mappings will be lost, click OK once more. The mapping will take a few seconds, but when the main Sun-specific CMP dialog screen is displayed select JobEJB in the Enterprise Bean field and you will see the dialog shown in Figure 7.11.

FIGURE 7.11

Mapping the J2EE RI CMP fields for the Job Entity bean.

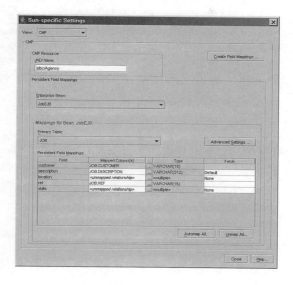

You can see from Figure 7.11 that deploytool has correctly mapped the Job CMP fields to the database schema as shown in Table 7.2.

TABLE 7.2   Job CMP Field to Database Schema Mapping

CMP Field	Table and Column
customer	JOB.CUSTOMER
description	JOB.DESCRIPTION
ref	JOB.REF

deploytool generated these mappings by matching the Entity bean name (JobEJB) to the correct table (JOB) in the database schema file (note the naming convention discussed earlier). Each Entity bean CMP field was matched to a table column with an identical name. You can override the generated mappings for each field by clicking on the ellipsis button (...) between the field name and the column name.

Furthermore, the mapping has identified the Job location and skills fields as CMR fields and tagged them as unmapped relationships (see note).

7

NOTE

> Using the J2EE RI Nov 2003 version of `deploytool` the authors found that the generated mappings incorrectly identified the `location` and `skills` fields as CMP fields rather than CMR fields. This problem is easily resolved.
>
> Close the Sun-specific CMP dialog and select the `JobEJB` and the Entity page. Check and then uncheck the CMP setting for the `location` and then the `skills` fields. Return to the `Entity` JAR dialog page, click on Sun-specific settings and on the CMP dialog screen select the `JobEJB` Enterprise bean. Now the mappings will correctly identify `location` and `skills` as unmapped CMR fields as shown in Figure 7.11.

The Sun J2EE RI uses a separate deployment descriptor called `sun-cmp-mappings.xml` to store the Entity bean CMP and CMR mappings. The CMP mappings for the `Job` bean are represented as

```
<sun-cmp-mappings>
  <sun-cmp-mapping>
    <schema>agency</schema>
    <entity-mapping>
      <ejb-name>JobEJB</ejb-name>
      <table-name>JOB</table-name>
      <cmp-field-mapping>
        <field-name>customer</field-name>
        <column-name>JOB.CUSTOMER</column-name>
      </cmp-field-mapping>
      <cmp-field-mapping>
        <field-name>description</field-name>
        <column-name>JOB.DESCRIPTION</column-name>
      </cmp-field-mapping>
      <cmp-field-mapping>
        <field-name>ref</field-name>
        <column-name>JOB.REF</column-name>
      </cmp-field-mapping>
    </entity-mapping>
    ...
  </sun-cmp-mapping>
</sun-cmp-mappings>
```

You can now finish the Entity bean mappings by defining the two CMR fields in the `Job` bean as described in the next section.

Mapping Entity Beans CMR Fields Using J2EE RI

If you are not already doing so, view the Sun-specific dialog window in `deploytool` by selecting the General dialog tab for the `Entity` JAR of the agency application, and clicking on the Sun-specific settings button.

Select the CMP view and the JobEJB Enterprise bean in the Sun-specific dialog window and you should see the view previously shown in Figure 7.11.

Click on the ellipsis button (...) for the <unmapped relationship> of the location CMR field and you will see the dialog screen in Figure 7.12.

FIGURE 7.12

Mapping the J2EE RI Job bean CMR location field.

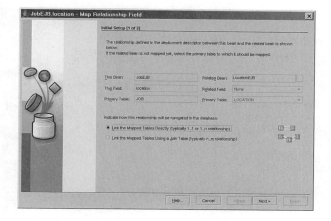

Accept the default Link Mapped Tables option and click Next to get the screen in Figure 7.13.

FIGURE 7.13

Mapping the J2EE RI Job.location CMR field to the JOB. LOCATION and LOCATION.NAME database columns.

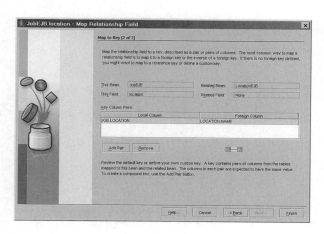

deploytool uses the foreign and primary key information in the database schema XML file to map the CMR columns. The values in Figure 7.13 (JOB.LOCATION and LOCATION.NAME) are correct so click Finish to add the following CMR mapping to the sun-cmp-settings.xml deployment descriptor:

7

```
<sun-cmp-mappings>
  <sun-cmp-mapping>
    <schema>agency</schema>
    <entity-mapping>
      <ejb-name>JobEJB</ejb-name>
...
      <cmr-field-mapping>
        <cmr-field-name>location</cmr-field-name>
        <column-pair>
          <column-name>JOB.LOCATION</column-name>
          <column-name>LOCATION.NAME</column-name>
        </column-pair>
        <fetched-with>
          <none/>
        </fetched-with>
      </cmr-field-mapping>
    </entity-mapping>
...
  </sun-cmp-mapping>
</sun-cmp-mappings>
```

Define the second CMR relationship between `Job` and `Skill` by clicking on the ellipsis
(…) button for the skills field. In the popup dialog window, select the Linked Map
Mapped Tables using a Join Table, as shown in Figure 7.14.

FIGURE 7.14

Mapping the J2EE RI
`Job` *bean CMR* `skills`
field.

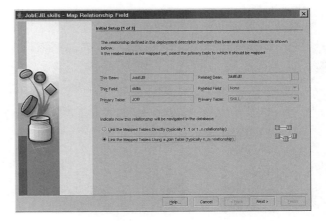

Click Next to map the `Job.skills` field to the `JOBSKILL` table, as shown in Figure 7.15.

Once more, `deploytool` has used the database schema to generate the correct mapping.
The consistent bean and table names, and CMR field and column names together with
the primary and foreign key constraints in the database have simplified the process.

Click Next to map the `JOBSKILL` to `SKILL` table columns, as shown in Figure 7.16.

5. Have the new `ejbCreate()` method check that the applicant name is unique by calling the `ejbFindByPrimaryKey()` method to verify that the login name has not been used previously.

6. All the other EJB lifecycle methods will be no-operation methods.

7. The `setEntityContent()` method does not need to look up any JNDI resources but will need to save the `EntityContext` reference to an instance variable (for use by the `ejbCreate()` method).

8. Use deploytool to delete the existing `ApplicantEJB` bean and add a new CMP version.

9. Specify the `name`, `login`, `email`, and `summary` CMP fields for the new bean. The `java.lang.String login` field is the primary key field.

10. Define the EJB QL statements for the `findAll()` and `findByLocation()` finder methods.

11. Add a one-to-many relationship from `Applicant` to `Location`. Make the relationship bi-directional.

12. Add a many-to-many relationship from `Applicant` to `Skill`. Make the relationship bi-directional.

13. Save the new version and verify the application using the command-line verifier with the command:

```
asant verify-j2ee-ri
```

Remove all verification errors before continuing.

14. Add the Sun-specific JNDI name for the `jdbc/Agency` database and generate the CMP/CMR field mappings.

NOTE

> If deploytool does not correctly identify `location` and `skills` as `<unmapped relationship>` fields for the bean, go to the `ApplicantEJB` Entity dialog and check and uncheck the `location` and `skills` fields in the CMP field list. Return to the Sun-specific CMP settings to define the relationship mappings.

15. Provide relationship mappings for the `location` and `skills` fields.

16. Save your changes and verify the application.

17. Deploy and test the application.

The new application should appear to be no different, as far as the client is concerned, to the one you developed yesterday.

Good luck. A working example can be found in the Day 7 agency directory.

7

WEEK 2

Developing J2EE Applications

DAY **8**

Transactions and Persistence

You have spent the last three days covering EJBs in detail. In particular, you saw yesterday how to specify, implement, configure and deploy container-managed persistence (CMP) Entity beans. Along with BMP Entity beans (Day 6, "Entity EJBs") and Session beans (Day 5, "Session EJBs"), you now have a good appreciation of the EJB technology.

EJBs have been called transactional middle-tier components. Until now, you haven't had to worry too much about transactions in an EJB context because you have been using container-managed transaction demarcation. However, for those cases where you require explicit control, EJB provides two solutions. You can write beans that manage their own transactions—bean managed transaction demarcation—or you can extend the lifecycle of Session beans to give them visibility of the transaction demarcations. You will be learning about both solutions today.

You spent Day 6 and Day 7, "Container-Managed Persistence, Container-Managed Relationships, and EJB Query Language," comparing the two different persistence approaches offered by EJBs in the guise of BMP and CMP Entity beans. The BMP Entity beans were implemented using JDBC, but that is only one of a number of technologies offered by J2EE and Java in general. Today, you will see

- How to manage transactions explicitly in EJBs
- How transactions are managed "behind the scenes" in an EJB environment
- Persistence technologies other than JDBC—specifically, SQLj and JDO

Overview of Transactions

If you've used a relational database before, completed a Computer Studies course, or read any other J2EE book, you've probably read a section like this one already. But read on anyway, if only to be acquainted with some of the J2EE terminology that is used in this arena.

A transaction is an atomic unit of work, where:

- Atomic unit means indivisible—either every step within the transaction completes or none of them do.
- Work here usually means some modification to data within a persistent data store. In database terms, this means one or more INSERT, UPDATE, or DELETE operations. However, strictly speaking, it also applies to reading of data through SELECT statements.

For a persistent data store to support transactions, it must pass the so-called "ACID" test:

- Atomic—The transaction is indivisible; the data store must ensure this is true.
- Consistent—The data store goes from one consistent point to another. Before the transaction, the data store is consistent; afterwards, it is still consistent.

  The age-old example is of transferring money between bank accounts. This will involve two UPDATE operations, one decrementing the balance of account #1 and the other incrementing the balance of account #2. If only one UPDATE occurs, the transaction is not atomic, and the data store is no longer in a consistent state, as money will have been debited from one bank account but not credited to the other (or vice versa).

- Isolation—The data store gives the illusion that the transaction is being performed in isolation. Enterprise applications have many concurrent users who are all performing transactions at the same time, so behind the scenes the data store uses techniques, such as locks, to serialize access to the contended data where necessary.

8

- Durability—If a transaction completes, any changes made to the data as a result of that transaction must be durable. In other words, if the power were to fail immediately after the transaction has completed, the change must still be there when power is reconnected.

  Many data stores use transaction logs to address this requirement. The transaction log holds a journal of changes made to the actual data. When the transaction completes, the log is written to disk, although the actual data need not be.

Many data stores allow transactions to be started explicitly using a statement such as the following:

```
begin transaction t1
```

where t1 is the (optional) transaction name. Transactions are completed using either `commit` (make changes permanent) or `rollback` (undo all changes made in the transaction, and revert all data back to the state before the transaction began). Many data stores will use

```
commit transaction t1
```

and

```
rollback transaction t1
```

NOTE

Some data stores support the concept of nested transactions, whereby (for a single user) one transaction can be started while another transaction is still in progress. In other words, two `begin transaction` statements can be submitted without a `commit` or `rollback` between them.

However, the EJB specification only requires flat transactions, whereby one transaction must be completed before another is begun (see EJB specification, section 17.1.2). Consequently, nested transactions will not be considered further.

To conclude this short introduction, consider the SQL code snippet shown in Listing 8.1. It transfers $50 from account #20457 to account #19834.

LISTING 8.1   Example Fragment of SQL to Transfer Money Between Accounts

```
begin transaction transfer_money

update account
set balance = balance - 50
where account_id = 20457
```

LISTING 8.1   continued

```
update account
set balance = balance + 50
where account_id = 19834

commit transaction transfer_money
```

In effect, there are two different types of commands:

- The first and last statements demarcate the transaction.
- The other statements modify data.

A conventional relational database processes all of the SQL in Listing 8.1, but it is performing two different roles in doing so. To understand and process the transaction demarcation commands, it is acting as a transaction manager. To understand and process the remaining lines, it is acting as a resource manager.

In the EJB specification, these two responsibilities are split. In principle, you can think of the EJB container as acting as the transaction manager, and the persistent data store acting only as the resource manager. The term transaction coordinator is sometimes used instead of transaction manager because there could be more than one resource whose transactions are being coordinated.

Splitting the responsibilities of transaction management and resource management has two consequences. For the bean provider, it means that to start a transaction, the bean must interact both with the EJB container and with the persistent data store. The former interaction is largely implicit because it is configured through the deployment descriptor and the latter interaction is completely implicit if CMP Entity beans are used. The other consequence is that, for the persistent data store, it must defer all transaction control responsibility up to the EJB container. Behind the scenes, there is some quite sophisticated communication going on; you will be shown more about this activity later on today.

Container-Managed Transaction Demarcation

You've spent the last three days writing and deploying EJBs without really having to worry too much about transactions. This isn't to say that there have been no transactions in use; far from it. Every interaction with the database performed in the case study has involved transactions. However, the Session and Entity beans deployed have used container managed transaction demarcation (here referred to as CMTD, though the abbreviation isn't used in the EJB specification). This section discusses the support provided by J2EE for CMTD.

Information in the deployment descriptor indicates when the EJB container should start and commit transactions.

Figure 8.1 shows a diagram that you first saw on Day 6.

FIGURE 8.1

The EJB proxy objects implement transaction (and security) control.

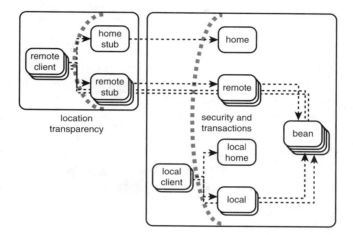

This shows how the EJB proxy objects (those implementing the javax.ejb.EJBObject or javax.ejb.EJBLocalObject interfaces) implement the transaction semantics. This is one of the reasons that a bean must never implement its own remote interface. To do so would mean that it could unwittingly return a reference to itself as a Remote interface, subverting any security and transaction checks performed by its proxy.

Listing 8.2 shows a fragment of the deployment descriptor for the AdvertiseJob Session Bean from Day 5.

LISTING 8.2   Deployment Descriptor for AdvertiseJob Session Bean

```
<ejb-jar>
    <display-name>Agency</display-name>
    <enterprise-beans>
        <session>
            <display-name>AdvertiseJobBean</display-name>
            ...
            <transaction-type>Container</transaction-type>
            ...
        </session>
    </enterprise-beans>
```

LISTING 8.2   continued

```
<assembly-descriptor>
    <container-transaction>
        <method>
            <ejb-name>AdvertiseJobBean</ejb-name>
            <method-name>*</method-name>
        </method>
        <trans-attribute>Required</trans-attribute>
    </container-transaction>
</assembly-descriptor>
</ejb-jar>
```

As you have seen over the last three days, the enterprise-beans element consists of session or entity elements. The session element has a transaction-type sub-element which, under CMTD, should have the value of Container. For entity elements, the transaction-type is not specified because entity beans must always be deployed using CMTD, so it is implicit. You use the transaction-type value of Bean to indicate bean managed transaction demarcation (BMTD) for Session beans.

Each method of the home and remote interfaces must be present in a container-transaction element in the assembly-descriptor section of the DD. Listing 8.2 shows the use of * as a convenient shorthand for defining all interfaces methods as requiring a transaction.

A container-transaction element identifies one or more methods. Each method defines the ejb-name, method-name and the trans-attribute. The trans-attribute element indicates the transactional characteristics to be enforced when the specified method is invoked. A transaction may or may not be in progress; in the terminology of the EJB specification, there may or may not be a current valid transactional context. When a method is invoked, the EJB container needs to know what should occur. For example,

- If there is no transaction in progress, is one needed to execute the method?
- Should a transaction be started automatically if there isn't one?
- Can a transaction be started even if another one is in progress?
- And so on.

There are six possible values; their semantics are shown in Table 8.1.

TABLE 8.1 Different CMTD Semantics Are Indicated by the trans-attribute Element

trans-attribute	Meaning	Notes
NotSupported	Method accesses a resource manager that does not support an external transaction coordinator. Any current transaction context will be suspended for the duration of the method.	The EJB architecture does not specify the transactional semantics of the method.
Required	A transaction context is guaranteed. The current transaction context will be used if present; otherwise, one will be created.	Commonly used.
Supports	Use valid transaction context if available (acts like Required). Otherwise, use unspecified transaction context (acts like NotSupported).	Acts as either Required or NotSupported. This makes the Supports a highly dubious choice. The method must guarantee to work in the same way whether or not there is a transaction context available.
RequiresNew	A new transaction context will be created. Any existing valid transaction context will be suspended for the duration of the method.	Can reduce contention (for example, for a bean that generates unique IDs or for a bean that writes to a log).
Mandatory	A valid transaction context must exist; otherwise an exception will be thrown by the EJB container. The transaction context will be used.	Useful for helper bean methods, designed to be called only from another bean.
Never	There must be no current transaction context. If there is a current transaction context an exception will be thrown by the EJB container. The method invokes with an unspecified transaction context.	Acts as NotSupported.

For Entity beans, only the Required, RequiresNew, and Mandatory values are recommended. The problem with NotSupported, Never, and (if invoked with no current transaction context) Supports is that, in addition to performing the business method, the EJB container must also perform the ejbLoad() and ejbStore() methods. These will be performed with the same transactional context as the business method, which is to say, with no transactional context. What might happen then is somewhat undefined, as the EJB specification is at pains to point out. Indeed, it goes so far as to list four or five different ways in which the EJB container might decide to act.

CAUTION

Never use NotSupported, Never, or Supports as <trans-attribute> values with Entity beans because the ejbLoad() and ejbStore() methods will take place without a transaction context and the EJB specification clearly states that this behavior is undefined.

You are likely to find that the vast majority of your beans' methods will use the Required <trans-attribute> value. Indeed, this is the value that has been used in the case study over the previous days.

The deploytool GUI can be used to configure the transaction information individually for every method, as shown in Figure 8.2.

FIGURE 8.2

deploytool *lets CMT characteristics be defined on a per-method basis.*

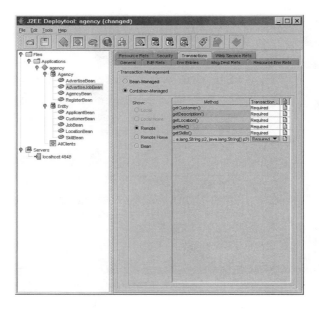

Where you have methods with different transaction requirements, you can supply multiple method elements to the container-transaction, as shown in the following example:

```
<container-transaction>
  <method>
    <ejb-name>AdvertiseJobBean</ejb-name>
    <method-intf>Remote</method-intf>
    <method-name>getRef</method-name>
    <method-params/>
  </method>
  <method>
    <ejb-name>AdvertiseJobBean</ejb-name>
    <method-intf>Remote</method-intf>
    <method-name>updateDetails</method-name>
    <method-params>
      <method-param>java.lang.String</method-param>
      <method-param>java.lang.String</method-param>
      <method-param>java.lang.String[]</method-param>
    </method-params>
  </method>
  ...
  <trans-attribute>Required</trans-attribute>
</container-transaction>
```

The `method` element can identify a method in the home or remote interface; the `method-intf` element is only needed on those rare occasions when there happens to be a method of the same name in both the home and remote interfaces. The `method-name` must be specified. (As discussed previously the value * can be used as a convenient shortcut to indicate all methods.) The `method-params` element is optional and is used to distinguish between overloaded versions of the same method name. If not specified, the `method` element identifies all overloaded versions of the method with the specified name.

TIP

> It is a dubious design practice to have overloaded methods with different transaction requirements. If the transaction requirements are different, the methods perform a different function and should be given different names.

The transaction attribute for a method defined with a specific overloaded signature take precedence over a definition using the unqualified method name. Similarly a transaction attribute for a specifically named method takes precedence over the general wildcard (*) form. Although CMTD means that the EJB container automatically starts, suspends, and completes transactions, this is not to say that the beans themselves cannot influence the transactions. After all, if an Entity bean hits an error condition that means that the transaction should be aborted, it needs some way to indicate this to the EJB container. As an example, consider the often-used example of withdrawing money from a bank account. If the balance would go into the red, (or perhaps more likely, beyond an overdraft limit), the Entity bean that represents the account would want to indicate that the transaction should be aborted.

To do this, the bean uses transaction-related methods provided by its `EJBContext`. In the case of a Session bean, this will be the `javax.ejb.SessionContext` passed in through the `setSessionContext()` method, and for an Entity bean, this will be the `javax.ejb.EntityContext` passed in through `setEntityContext()`. To remind you, Figure 8.3 shows a UML class diagram illustrating the methods provided by these interfaces.

FIGURE 8.3

The `EJBContext` provides access to the current transaction.

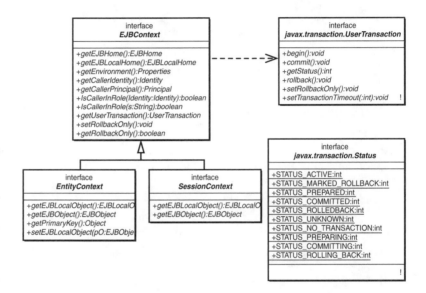

To cause the transaction to be aborted, the CMTD bean can call `setRollbackOnly()`. This instructs the EJB container to prevent the transaction from being committed. The bean cannot rollback the transaction directly, because the transaction itself is "owned" by the EJB container, not the bean.

There is a `getRollBackOnly()` method that can be called to test if a transaction is marked for rollback. This quick test can be used by an EJB to avoid performing a time-consuming operation that will be a waste of time and resources if a transaction is marked for rollback.

The only other transaction-related method in `EJBContext` is `getUserTransaction()`. However, this is intended for use with bean-managed transaction demarcation and cannot be called by a CMTD bean, and any attempt to do so will result in the EJB container throwing a `java.lang.IllegalStateException`.

One last point relating to CMTD beans—they must not make use of any resource manager-specific transaction management methods that would interfere with the EJB container's own management of the transaction context. Consequently, a BMP Entity bean cannot call `commit()`, `setAutoCommit()`, and so on on a `java.sql.Connection` object (an interface that represents a connection to an RDBMS).

If your bean needs more fine-grained control over transactions, the bean must be deployed using bean-managed transaction demarcation. This is discussed next.

Bean-Managed Transaction Demarcation

If an EJB is deployed using bean-managed transaction demarcation (here referred to as BMTD), the EJB container allows the bean to obtain a reference to a `javax.transaction.UserTransaction` object using the `EJBContext` shown in Figure 8.3. Entity beans cannot use BMTD, therefore the following discussion only applies to Session beans and Message-Driven beans. (If you are interested you should read the EJB specification for the design decisions justifying why Entity beans cannot use BMTD.)

Motivation and Restrictions

An EJB might need to be deployed under BMTD if the conditions on which a transaction is started depend on some programmatic condition. It could be that one Session bean method starts the transaction and another Session bean method completes the transaction; in this scenario the Session bean must be stateful, because it is carrying the user transaction state from one method call to another. If you write a BMTD stateless Session bean that does not commit its own transaction, the EJB container will roll back the transaction and throw an exception back to the client (`java.rmi.RemoteException` for remote clients or `javax.ejb.EJBException` for local).

Using the Java Transaction API

When a Session bean is deployed under BMTD, there is an implementation choice as to how it should manage its transactions. If interacting solely with a relational database, the Session bean can manage the transactions directly through the JDBC API. Alternatively, it can use the Java Transaction API (JTA), defined by the classes and interfaces in the `javax.transaction` and the `javax.transaction.xa` packages. The latter approach is preferable because the Java Message Service (see Day 9, "Java Messaging Service"), servlets (see Day 12, "Servlets") and Connector Architecture components (see Day 19, "Integrating with External Resources") also use JTA.

NOTE

> The J2EE specification only discusses transaction interoperability in the context of the JTA API.
>
> If nothing else, the semantics of intermixing JDBC and JTA calls are not exhaustively defined, so this should be avoided to minimize chances of portability problems if moving to a different vendor's EJB container.

For a Session bean to start a transaction, it should first call the getUserTransaction() method of its SessionContext. Obtaining a UserTransaction does not mean that a transaction has been started. Rather, it must be started using the begin() method. The transaction can then be completed using either the commit() or the rollback() method. The current status can also be obtained using getStatus(). This returns an int whose meaning is defined by the constants in the javax.transaction.Status interface. Some of the most common status values are shown in Table 8.2.

TABLE 8.2   Some of the Constants Defined in javax.transaction.Status

Constant	Meaning	Typical actions
STATUS_NO_TRANSACTION	No transaction is active.	tran.begin() to start new transaction.
STATUS_ACTIVE	A transaction is active and can be used.	Use resource manager. tran.commit() to commit tran.rollback() to rollback
STATUS_MARKED_ROLLBACK	A transaction is active, but has been marked for rollback. Any attempt to commit it will result in a javax.transaction. RollbackException being thrown.	tran.rollback()

NOTE

> There are more constants in the Status interface than those listed in Table 8.2. Later today, (in the "Transactions: Behind the Scenes" section), you'll be learning about some of the "under-the-covers" mechanics of transaction management; the full list is presented there.

Listing 8.3 shows a possible implementation for the updateDetails() method of AdvertiseJob bean using BMTD.

LISTING 8.3   BMTD Implementation of `AdvertiseJobBean.updateDetails()`

8

```
package agency;

import javax.ejb.*;
import javax.transaction.*;
// imports omitted

public class AdvertiseJobBean extends SessionBean {
    public void updateDetails (String description,
                               String locationName, String[] skillNames) {

        int initialTranStatus = beginTransactionIfRequired();

        if (skillNames == null) {
            skillNames = new String[0];
        }
        List skillList;
        try {
            skillList = skillHome.lookup(Arrays.asList(skillNames));
        } catch(FinderException ex) {
            error("Invalid skill", ex, initialTranStatus);

            return;
        }

        LocationLocal location=null;
        if (locationName != null) {
            try {
                location = locationHome.findByPrimaryKey(locationName);
            } catch(FinderException ex) {
                error("Invalid location", ex, initialTranStatus);

                return;
            }
        }

        job.setDescription(description);
        job.setLocation(location);
        job.setSkills(skillList);

        completeTransactionIfRequired(initialTranStatus);
    }

    private int beginTransactionIfRequired() {

        UserTransaction tran = this.ctx.getUserTransaction();
        // start a new transaction if needed, else just use existing.
        // (simulates trans-attribute of REQUIRED)
        int initialTranStatus;
        try {
            initialTranStatus = tran.getStatus();
```

LISTING 8.3   Continued

```
            switch(initialTranStatus) {
            case Status.STATUS_ACTIVE:
                // just use
                break;
            case Status.STATUS_NO_TRANSACTION:
                // create
                try {
                    tran.begin();
                } catch(NotSupportedException ex) {
// shouldn't happen (only thrown if asking for nested exception
// and is not supported by the resource manager; not attempting
// to do this here).
                    throw new EJBException("Unable to begin transaction", ex);
                }
                break;

            // code omitted; other Status' covered later

            default:
                throw new EJBException(
                    "Transaction status invalid, status = " +
                    statusAsString(initialTranStatus));
            }
        } catch(SystemException ex) {
            throw new EJBException("Unable to begin transaction", ex);
        }

        return initialTranStatus;
    }

    private void completeTransactionIfRequired(int initialTranStatus) {

        UserTransaction tran = this.ctx.getUserTransaction();

        // if transaction was started, then commit / rollback as needed.
        // (simulates trans-attribute of REQUIRED)
        if (initialTranStatus == Status.STATUS_NO_TRANSACTION) {
            try {
                if (tran.getStatus() == Status.STATUS_MARKED_ROLLBACK) {
                    tran.rollback();
                } else {
                    tran.commit();
                }
            } catch(Exception ex) {
                throw new EJBException("Unable to complete transaction", ex);
            }
        }
    }
}
```

The two helper methods, `beginTransactionIfRequired()` and `completeTransactionIfRequired()`, isolate the actual transaction management code, so it can be reused across different methods.

Deploying a BMTD Bean

Of course, when deploying a bean under BMTD, the deployment descriptor should indicate a `transaction-type` element of `Bean`, and you will not need any container-transaction elements under the `application-assembly` element. Figure 8.4 shows `deploytool` for the `AdvertiseJob` bean, indicating this fact.

FIGURE 8.4

BMTD is indicated through the deployment descriptor, as shown in deploytool.

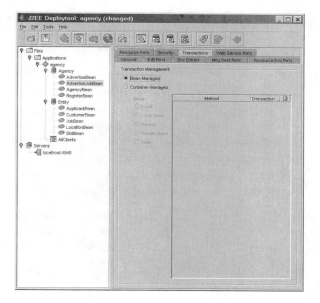

Incidentally, if a BMTD Session bean calls `getRollbackOnly()` or `setRollbackOnly()` on its `SessionContext`, the EJB container will throw a `java.lang.IllegalStateException`. This is reasonable; if a BMTD has access to the `UserTransaction` object, it has no need for these methods. Instead, it can call the `getStatus()` method of `UserTransaction`, and explicitly call `rollback()` if needed.

Client-Demarcated Transactions

In addition to Session beans managing their own transactions, it is also possible for clients to initiate the transaction and have it propagate through to the EJBs. Here, "client" means either an application client written using the Swing GUI (such as you have seen in the case study), or it could equally refer to a Web-based client implemented using servlets and JSPs (as discussed on Day 12, "Servlets," and Day 13, "JavaServer Pages").

For either of these clients, the EJB architecture requires that a `UserTransaction` context be obtained via JNDI and bound under the name of `java:comp/UserTransaction`. So the code fragment shown in Listing 8.4 will do the trick.

LISTING 8.4   Obtaining a `UserTransaction` Object from JNDI

```
// assuming:
// import javax.naming.*;
// import javax.transaction.*;
InitialContext ctx = new InitialContext();
UserTransaction tran =
    (UserTransaction) ctx.lookup("java:comp/UserTransaction");
tran.begin();
// call session and entity beans
tran.commit();
```

That said, if you find yourself needing to use client-demarcated transactions, you should look at your application design and see if you are happy with it. After all, Session beans are meant to represent the business logic of your application, and this should surely include defining the transactional boundaries of changes to persistent data. Application clients should only provide a presentational interface to your application.

If that philosophical argument does not appeal to you, perhaps this might. A rogue client could be coded such that it begins a transaction, interacts with (and therefore ties up) various resources, such as Entity beans, and then not commit. This could seriously impact the performance of your application.

Exceptions Revisited

On Days 5 and 6, you learned the appropriate exceptions for your EJB to throw. In summary,

- To throw an application-level exception (indicating that a possible recoverable condition has arisen), throw any checked exception (excluding `java.rmi.RemoteException`).

- To throw a system-level exception (indicating that a non-recoverable severe condition has arisen), throw any `java.lang.RuntimeException` (usually a subclass of `javax.ejb.EJBException`).

If a bean throws an application-level exception, it is up to that bean whether the current transaction is affected or not. If the bean takes no action other than raising its exception, the current transaction will be unaffected. The exception will simply propagate back to the calling client.

However, CMTD beans may decide to mark the current transaction for rollback, meaning that the "owner" of the transaction (the EJB container or some BMTD bean) will be unable to commit that transaction.

If a BMTD bean hits an error condition, it has a choice. Because it "owns" the transaction, it can simply do a rollback. Alternatively, it might elect to keep the transaction active.

If a bean throws a system-level exception, this will have consequences for any current transaction. If any bean throws a system exception, the EJB container will mark the current transaction for rollback. If that bean happens to be a CMTD bean, and the EJB container started a transaction just before invoking the CMTD method (as a result of a `Required` or `RequiresNew trans-attribute`), the EJB container will rollback that transaction.

To summarize

- An application-level exception may or may not leave the current transaction active; use `getStatus()` or `getRollbackOnly()` to find out.

- A system-level exception will either cause the current transaction to be marked for rollback or actually roll it back.

One last thing on transactions and exceptions. Most of the exceptions in `javax.ejb` (`CreateException`, `RemoveException`, and so on), are application exceptions. The EJB container itself raises some of these exceptions, especially with CMP Entity beans. Rather unhappily, the EJB specification does not mandate whether these application exceptions should mark any current transaction for rollback. Instead, it just indicates that the `UserTransaction.getStatus()` or `EJBContext.getRollbackOnly()` methods should be used to determine the status of the current transaction. In practical terms this means that different EJB containers could have different implementations, compromising portability.

Extended Stateful Session Bean Lifecycle

Occasionally, there is a need for a stateful Session bean to have visibility as to the progress of the underlying transaction. Specifically, a bean might need to know

- Has the transaction started?
- Is the transaction about to complete?
- Did the transaction complete successfully or was it rolled back?

For example, consider the example of a ShoppingCart bean. In its purchase() method, it is likely to modify its internal state. Perhaps it holds its contents in a java.util.List called currentContents. On purchase(), it might move the contents of currentContents to another java.util.List called recentlyBought.

Suppose, then, that the transaction that actually modifies the persistent data store fails to complete. Maybe the shopper doesn't have enough limit left on his or her credit card. Because Session beans are not transactional, the ShoppingCart bean needs to know that it should reset its internal state back to the beginning of the transaction. In other words, it needs to move the contents of the recentlyBought list back over to currentContents.

Obviously, this is no problem for stateful Session beans deployed under BMTD, because they own the transaction anyway and know when the tran.begin() and tran.commit() methods will be invoked. But for CMTD Session beans, this is an issue.

The EJB specification addresses this by extending the lifecycle of the bean. If a stateful Session bean implements the javax.ejb.SessionSynchronization interface, three additional lifecycle methods are defined and will be called at the appropriate points:

- afterBegin()   The transaction has just begun.
- beforeCompletion()   The transaction is about to be committed.
- afterCompletion(boolean)   The transaction has completed. The boolean argument has the value true to indicate that the transaction was committed, or false to indicate that the transaction was rolled back.

Figure 8.5 is a reworking of Figure 5.19 that you saw back on Day 5. It shows the stateful Session bean's view of its lifecycle. (The client's view and the actual lifecycle managed by the EJB container are unchanged.)

One common pattern for using this interface is to use the afterBegin() method to load any data from the data store (perhaps in the form of Entity beans), and then use the beforeCompletion() method to write any cached data that may have changed. One immediate use for this pattern might be with respect to multi-valued container-managed relationship (CMR) fields. You will recall from yesterday that collections returned by the getter method of a CMR field are only valid for the duration of a transaction. The afterBegin() and beforeCompletion() methods scope the duration that such a returned collection can be used.

If the SessionSynchronization interface is implemented by a Session bean, the only allowable values for the trans-attribute element in its deployment descriptor are Required, RequiresNew, or Mandatory. This is because these are the only attributes that can guarantee the presence of a transaction.

FIGURE 8.5

The `SessionSynchronizati` *on interface gives the stateful Session bean visibility to the transactions managed under CMTD.*

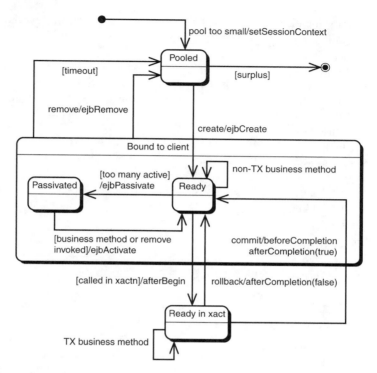

8

Transactions: Behind the Scenes

The EJB specification starts off by listing several goals. One of these reads as follows:

> "The Enterprise JavaBeans architecture will make it easy to write applications: Application developers will not have to understand low-level transaction and state management details, multi-threading, connection pooling, and other complex low-level APIs."

The EJB specification largely succeeds in addressing this goal—as a developer, you really do not need much knowledge about how transactions are managed. The fact that this book only covers transactions today in any detail is testament to that.

Nevertheless, like most technical topics, it can be helpful to have an insight as to what is going on "behind the scenes." But if you want to skip this material and make a shorter day of it, please do so. You can always read it later if you find yourself wanting to know more.

Transaction Managers, Resource Managers, and Two-Phase Commit

You already know about the terms resource manager and transaction manager (or transaction coordinator). In most EJB applications, an RDBMS will take the place of a resource manager, and the EJB container itself will be the transaction manager.

This division of responsibilities is required because in an EJB architecture, the data used by Session beans or represented by Entity beans may reside in more than one persistent data store. For example, one Entity bean might map onto an Oracle database, and another Entity bean may map onto a Sybase database, as shown in Figure 8.6. (The numbers in the diagram will be explained shortly.)

FIGURE 8.6

The J2EE platform separates resources and transaction managers.

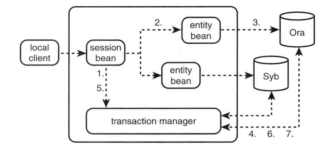

Leaving the transaction management responsibilities with the database is not appropriate. Doing so would mean that each database involved would have its own transaction. If the first transaction succeeded but the second transaction failed, the logical data set represented by the Entity beans would no longer be consistent. The "C" of the ACID test would be broken.

Another case where only a single transaction is required is when interacting with JMS queues or topics. You can imagine that a queue might implement a To Do list. A task on the To Do list might be "invoice customer A for $20," involving an update to a database. If the task is removed from the To Do list as one transaction, and the update to the database performed as another transaction, there is again the possibility that the second transaction can fail. In other words, the task is removed from the To Do list, but no invoice is raised.

The two-phase commit protocol (more commonly called just 2PC) is the mechanism by which the transaction manager (EJB container) interacts with each of the resource managers (RDBMS or JMS queues and topics). In the EJB environment, it works as follows (the numbers correspond to the steps in Figure 8.6):

8

1. The transaction manager within the EJB container creates a new transaction as needed. Generally, this will be when a Session bean's method is invoked.

   If the Session bean has been deployed under CMTD, the bean's proxy will make this request to the transaction manager. If the Session bean is deployed under BMTD, the bean itself will effectively make this request.

2. The Session bean interacts with Entity beans. The current transaction will be propagated through to them (assuming they are deployed with `Required` or `Mandatory` value for their `trans-attribute` element).

3. In turn, the Entity beans interact with the database through an XA-compliant `java.sql.Connection`. "XA-compliant" means it supports a two-phase commit protocol, more on this shortly. If the Entity bean is BMP, the interaction with the RDBMS will be done by the bean itself; if the bean is CMP, the interaction will be by the generated subclass. Either way, it amounts to the same thing.

4. Each of the XA-compliant `Connections` registers itself with the EJB transaction manager. More correctly, a `javax.transaction.xa.XAResource` representing and associated with the `Connection` is registered as part of the current `javax.transaction.Transaction`.

5. When all method calls to the Entity beans have been made, the Session bean indicates to the transaction manager that the transaction should be committed.

6. The transaction manager performs the first "prepare" phase of the commit. It iterates over each of the `XAResources` that constitute the transaction and requests confirmation that they are ready to be committed. In turn, the `XAResource` just delegates this request to its corresponding XA-compliant `java.sql.Connection`. At this stage, any `XAResource` can indicate that it cannot commit the changes and the transaction manager will arrange for every participating `XAResource` to perform a rollback.

7. When all resources have indicated that they are prepared to commit, the transaction manager performs the second "commit" phase. It again iterates over each `XAResource` and requests each one to commit the changes. An `XAResource` is not allowed to reject the second phase commit (that was what the prepare phase was for).

The JTA API

An XA-compliant `java.sql.Connection`, as previously described, is one that provides the ability to return an `XAResource` for registering with the current transaction. The XA protocol is an industry standard, defined by the X/Open group, to allow a transactional resource manager to participate in a global transaction controlled by an external transaction manager. The JTA API is effectively a mapping into Java of this XA protocol.

In fact, the `java.sql.Connection` interface does not mandate XA-compliance, so the previous description was a slight simplification. Instead, XA-compliance is provided by classes and interfaces in the `javax.sql` package, part of the J2EE platform. Some of the more relevant classes of `java.sql`, `javax.sql`, `javax.transaction`, and `javax. transaction.xa` are shown in Figure 8.7.

FIGURE 8.7

The `javax.sql` *and* `javax.transaction` *packages together provide support for 2PC against RDBMSs.*

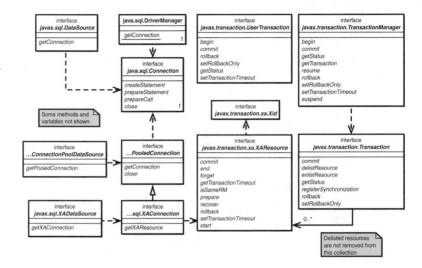

As you know, the `java.sql.Connection` interface represents a connection to a database. Under J2EE, a `javax.sql.DataSource` object is used to obtain a database `Connection` object.

In J2EE enterprise applications, reusing connections through some sort of connection pool is critical to ensuring performance and scalability. Many implementations of `DataSource` provide built-in connection pooling. The connection returned by `DataSource.getConnection()` is effectively a logical connection temporarily associated with an underlying physical connection. When the `close()` method on the logical connection is called, the underlying physical connection is not closed but is, instead, returned to a connection pool.

J2EE also offers another approach for database vendors to provide connection pooling, through the `javax.sql.ConnectionPoolDataSource` interface. This returns `PooledConnection` objects that are physical connections to the database. In turn, these provide a `getConnection()` method that returns a logical connection that wraps them, so the final effect is much the same as before.

TIP

> If you want, you can think of the getConnection() method of
> PooledConnection as leasing the connection from the pool. The close()
> method releases the PooledConnection back into the pool to be used again.

Closely related to ConnectionPoolDataSource is the javax.sql.XADataSource, which
returns javax.sql.XAConnection objects. This is a sub-interface of PooledConnection,
so it works in the same way, providing the getConnection() to return a logical
java.sql.Connection that wraps it. However, it also provides the getXAResource()
method that returns a javax.transaction.xa.XAResource. Consequently, the
XAConnection acts as a bridge between the resource manager's notion of connection and
the transaction manager's notion of resource.

A J2EE-compliant resource manager must be able to support each of these three different
DataSource interfaces (XADataSource, ConnectionPoolDataSource, and DataSource
itself).

What if it Goes Wrong?

You've seen how the 2PC protocol is intended to work. However, the whole point of 2PC
is to ensure transactional consistency, even in the event of an unexpected failure. So,
what happens when it goes wrong?

There are two cases to deal with. First, it could be that a resource manager enlisted into
the transaction may no longer be available when the application (in an EJB context, the
Session bean or its proxy) decides to commit. It could be that the network has failed
since the original interaction with the Entity bean that represents some data residing on
that resource manager.

In the first case, the prepare phase of the 2PC protocol fails. Because the transaction
manager has been unable to get an acknowledgement within its timeout, it will roll back
the transaction. When the resource manager that failed is restarted, it will (as part of its
so-called recovery process) automatically roll back any work done as a part of the transaction.

In the second case, a resource manager becomes unavailable after it has acknowledged
the prepare, but before the commit phase. This rare case causes more problems because
the transaction manager may already have sent the commit message to some other
resource managers. Nevertheless, the transaction manager will continue to send the commit message to all other resource managers.

When the resource manager that failed is restarted, it will detect that it had acknowledged a prepare. It then contacts the transaction manager to determine whether the transaction was actually committed or was rolled back. It then performs the same (commit or rollback) as part of its recovery process.

The prepare phase is more than the transaction manager checking that all resource managers are still available. It is also possible for resource managers to unilaterally decide to abort a transaction for some reason. When this happens, the transaction manager will send a rollback message to all participating resource managers, rather than a commit.

TIP

> If you have done any JavaBean programming, some of this will be starting to sound familiar. The `java.beans.VetoableChangeSupport` class works in a very similar way.

In addition to failures of the prepare or the commit phase of the 2PC, there are also occasional cases when a resource manager may take a so-called heuristic decision that could be in conflict with the semantics of the transaction. For example, a resource manager could have a policy that, once prepared, it will commit if the transaction manager has not confirmed the outcome (commit or rollback) within a certain period. One reason that a resource manager might do this would be to free up resources.

If a heuristic decision is made, it is the responsibility of the resource manager to remember this decision. Put bluntly, this information is required to allow the administrator to correct any issues with the data if the heuristic decision went against the transaction's actual outcome. You might have noted that the `XAResource` interface defines a `forget()` method; this allows the resource manager to finally forget that a heuristic decision was made.

This probably all sounds pretty arcane, but is needed if you want to understand the full set of status values defined by the `javax.transaction.Status` interface. You'll recall that a subset of these was presented in Table 8.2. Table 8.3 shows all of the constants.

TABLE 8.3   All of the Constants Defined in `javax.transaction.Status`

Constant	Meaning	Typical Actions
STATUS_NO_TRANSACTION	No transaction is active.	`tran.begin()` to start new transaction.
STATUS_ACTIVE	A transaction is active and can be used.	Use resource manager. `tran.commit()` to commit. `tran.rollback()` to rollback.

Connecting to a Queue

To send a JMS message, a number of steps must first be performed. You must

1. Obtain a `ConnectionFactory`
2. Establish a `Session`
3. Create a `MessageProducer` object

Although this example is in the point-to-point message domain, the same steps are required for publish/subscribe topics.

The following steps show how to create a queue used later to send a simple text message.

1. Obtain the JNDI initial context.

```
Context context = new InitialContext();
```

2. Contact the JMS provider, obtain a JMS connection from the appropriate `ConnectionFactory`, and create a connection for a queue. The following code uses a connection factory registered against the JNDI name `jms/QueueConnectionFactory`.

```
ConnectionFactory connectionFactory =
➥(ConnectionFactory)context.lookup("jms/QueueConnectionFactory");
Connection connection = connectionFactory.createConnection();
```

The `createConnection()` method throws a `JMSException` if the JMS provider fails to create the queue connection and `lookup()` can throw a `NamingException` if the name is not found.

3. Establish a `Session` for this connection. In this case, the `Session` has transactions set to `false` (transactions are covered later) and `AUTO ACKNOWLEDGE` of receipt of messages. This will throw a `JMSException` if the `Connection` object fails to create a session.

```
Session session = connection.createSession(false,
➥Session.AUTO_ACKNOWLEDGE);
```

NOTE

Although sent messages are not acknowledged, a session can be used to receive messages created by its own connection. This is why an Acknowledge mode must be specified on a session, even if the queue is only used to send messages.

4. Obtain the queue destination using its JNDI name. The `lookup()` method can throw a `NamingException` if the name is not found.

```
Destination destination = (Queue)context.lookup("jms/firstQueue");
```

5. Finally, create a message producer that will be used to send messages. This will throw a `JMSException` if the `Session` fails to create a producer, and an `InvalidDestinationException` if an invalid destination is specified.

```
MessageProducer producer = session.createProducer(destination);
```

Note how the connection factory hides all the implementation details of the connection from the client. It does the hard work of creating resources, handling authentication, and supporting concurrent use.

Now you have a queue that is ready to send messages. But before that, you need to know a little more about JMS messages.

JMS Messages

JMS messages consist of three parts:

- *A header*—Used to identify messages, set priority and expiration, and so on and to route messages.
- *Properties*—Used to add information in addition to the message header.
- *Message body*—There are five message body forms defined in JMS— `BytesMessage`, `MapMessage`, `ObjectMessage`, `StreamMessage`, and `TextMessage`.

Note that only the header is a required component of a message; the other two parts, including the body, are optional.

Message Header Fields

The JMS message header contains a number of fields that are generated by the JMS provider when the message is sent. These include the following:

- `JMSMessageID`   A unique identifier
- `JMSDestination`   Represents the queue or topic to which the message is sent
- `JMSRedelivered`   Set when the message has been resent for some reason

The following three header fields are available for the client to set:

- `JMSType`   A string that can be used to identify the contents of a message
- `JMSCorrelationID`   Used to link one message with another, typically used to link responses to requests
- `JMSReplyTo`   Used to define where responses should be sent

Other header fields may be set by the client but can be overridden by the JMS provider with figures set by an administrator:

The second difference is that this time there is a call to the connection's `start()` method, which starts (or restarts) delivery of incoming messages for this destination. Calling `start()` twice has no detrimental effect. It also has no effect on the connection's ability to send messages. The `start()` method may throw a `JMSException` if an internal error occurs. A consumer can use `Connection.stop()` to temporarily suspend delivery of messages.

The different consumer code is:

```
consumer = session.createConsumer(destination);
connection.start();
```

The message is obtained using the synchronous `receive()` method, as shown next. This may throw a `JMSException`:

```
Message msgBody = consumer.receive();
if (msgBody instanceof TextMessage) {
    String text = ((TextMessage) msgBody).getText();
}
```

If there is no message in the queue, the `receive()` method blocks until a message is available. There are two alternative versions of the `receive()` method:

- `receiveNoWait()`   Retrieves the next message available, or returns `null` if one is not immediately available
- `receive(long timeout)`   Retrieves the next message or returns null if no message is received within the timeout period (milliseconds)

Receive JMS Text Message Example

The code for the entire point-to-point receiver example is shown in Listing 9.2. You will find this code in the `PTPReceiver.java` file in the examples directory for Day 9 on the Web site.

LISTING 9.2   Complete Code for `PTPReceiver.java`

```
import javax.naming.*;
import javax.jms.*;

public class PTPReceiver {

    private Connection connection;
    private Session session;
    private MessageConsumer consumer;

    public static void main(String[] args) {
        PTPReceiver receiver = null;
```

LISTING 9.2   continued

```
        try {
            receiver = new PTPReceiver();
            String textMsg;
            textMsg = receiver.consumeMessage();
            System.out.println ("Received: " + textMsg);
        }
        catch(Exception ex) {
            System.err.println("Exception in PTPReceiver: " + ex);
        }
        finally {
            try {receiver.close();} catch(Exception ex){}
        }
    }

    public PTPReceiver() throws JMSException, NamingException {
        Context context = new InitialContext();
        ConnectionFactory connectionFactory =
➥(ConnectionFactory)context.lookup("jms/QueueConnectionFactory");
        connection = connectionFactory.createConnection();
        session = connection.createSession(false, Session.AUTO_ACKNOWLEDGE);
        Destination destination = (Destination)context.lookup("jms/firstQueue");
        consumer = session.createConsumer(destination);
        connection.start();
    }

    public String consumeMessage () throws JMSException {
        String text = null;
        Message msgBody = consumer.receive();
        if (msgBody instanceof TextMessage) {
            text = ((TextMessage) msgBody).getText();
        }
        else {
          text = msgBody.toString();
        }
        return text;
    }

    public void close() throws JMSException {
        connection.close();
    }
}
```

Run this program using the following asant command:

```
asant PTPReceiver
```

The receiver should print out the single message you sent using the PTPSender example. If you run the receiver again it will block until another message is sent. Try this by running PTPReceiver in one window and then running PTPSender from another window.

Asynchronous Messaging

For many applications, the synchronous mechanism, shown previously, is not suitable and an asynchronous technique is required. To implement this in JMS, you need to register an object that implements the MessageListener interface. The JMS provider invokes this object's onMessage() each time a message is available at the destination.

The consumer example will now be extended to support asynchronous messaging by implementing the MessageListener interface as follows:

```
public class PTPListener implements MessageListener {
```

The message listener is registered with a specific MessageConsumer by using the setMessageListener() method before calling the connection's start() method as follows:

```
consumer.setMessageListener(this);
```

Messages might be missed if you call start() before you register the message listener.

The MessageListener interface defines a single onMessage() method. The JMS provider calls your implementation of this method when it has a message to deliver. The following is an example onMessage() method:

```
public void onMessage(Message message) {
    try {
        if (message instanceof TextMessage) {
            String text = ((TextMessage) message).getText();
            System.out.println("Received: " + text);
        }
    }
    catch(JMSException ex) {
        System.err.println("Exception in OnMessage: " + ex);
    }
}
```

The onMessage() method should handle all exceptions. If onMessage() throws an exception, the signature will be altered and, therefore, not recognized.

An asynchronous receiver must be closed down cleanly. One common technique is to send a special closedown message and this approach is shown in the example in Listing 9.3.

LISTING 9.3   Complete code for `PTPListener.java`

```java
import javax.naming.*;
import javax.jms.*;

public class PTPListener implements MessageListener {

    private Connection connection;
    private Session session;
    private MessageConsumer consumer;

    public static void main(String[] args) {
        System.out.println ("Listener running");
        try {
            PTPListener receiver = new PTPListener();
          }
        catch(Exception ex) {
            System.err.println("Exception in PTPListener: " + ex);
        }
    }

    public PTPListener() throws JMSException, NamingException {
        try {
            Context context = new InitialContext();
            ConnectionFactory connectionFactory =
                (ConnectionFactory)context.lookup("jms/QueueConnectionFactory");
            Destination destination =
                (Destination)context.lookup("jms/firstQueue");
            connection = connectionFactory.createConnection();
            session = connection.createSession(false,
➡Session.CLIENT_ACKNOWLEDGE);
            consumer = session.createConsumer(destination);
            consumer.setMessageListener(this);
            connection.start();
        }
        catch (JMSException ex) {
            try {connection.close();} catch(Exception e){}
            throw ex;
        }
    }

    public void onMessage(Message message) {
        try {
            String text;
            if (message instanceof TextMessage) {
                text = ((TextMessage) message).getText();
            }
            else {
                text = message.toString();
            }
```

LISTING 9.3   continued

```
                System.out.println("Received: " + text);
                message.acknowledge();
                if (text.equals("Quit")) {
                    System.out.println("PTPReceiver closing down");
                    new Thread(new Runnable () {
                        public void run() {
                            try {
                                PTPListener.this.close();
                            }
                            catch(JMSException ex) {
                                System.err.println("Exception in Closer: " + ex);
                            }
                        }
                    }).start();
                }
            }
            catch(JMSException ex) {
                System.err.println("Exception in OnMessage: " + ex);
            }
        }

        public void close() throws JMSException {
            connection.close();
        }
    }
```

The are a number of points to examine in this code:

- The constructor handles any JMS errors and closes down the connection. The exception is then thrown to the caller for processing.

- In the constructor, to illustrate client acknowledgement of messages, the session is created with the CLIENT_ACKNOWLEDGE (rather then the AUTO_ACKNOWLEDGE). In the onMessage() method a call to Message.acknowledge() is now needed to acknowledge receipt of each message.

- In onMessage() a new thread of execution is created to handle the connection closedown. If the Connection.close() method is called directly the listener will deadlock as the close() method cannot complete until the onMessage() method completes, which cannot complete until close() completes, which cannot complete until onMessage() completes and so on.

You can run this example using the command

```
asant PTPListener
```

Use the `PTPSender` example to send messages and then run the command

```
asant PTPQuit
```

to close down the listener. The following code fragment shows the shutdown code for the `PTPQuit` application

```
sender = new PTPSender();
sender.sendMessage("Quit");
```

The Publish/Subscribe Messaging Domain

So far, you have seen how to create a simple point-to-point application with a single sender and receiver. Now you will build a simple bulletin board application to demonstrate the features of the publish/subscribe model.

For this example, a producer will be used that creates messages and publishes them to a bulletin board. Later you will write the subscriber program, which asynchronously listens for messages. The messages are printed to the screen—one at time—in the order they were received.

Remember that, unlike messages in a queue, messages in a topic are immediately distributed to all subscribers. As a result, the timing of the publisher and the subscriber becomes important. Apart from this, the subscriber/publisher code is very similar to the sender/receiver code.

Because subscribers only receive messages when they are active, it would be nice to be able to test for active subscribers before publishing to a topic. Unfortunately, this is not possible.

Publish/Subscribe Messaging Example

Now, you will build a simple bulletin board application. For this example, the bulletin board publisher program will generate 10 simple messages. The subscriber will be a Swing application that will display the messages as they arrive.

The bulletin board uses a topic called `jms/bulletinBoard` created along with the other JMS resources at the start of today's examples.

Bulletin Board Publisher

The same mechanism is used to create a topic as you used to create a queue, so Listing 9.4 should appear very similar to the previous point-to-point sender example.

LISTING 9.4 Bulletin Board Publisher BBPublisher.java

```java
import javax.jms.*;

public class BBPublisher {

    private Connection connection;
    private Session session;
    private MessageProducer producer;

    public static void main(String[] args) {
        BBPublisher publisher = null;
        try {
            publisher = new
➥BBPublisher("jms/TopicConnectionFactory","jms/bulletinBoard");
            System.out.println ("Publisher is up and running");
            for (int i = 0; i < 10; i++) {
                String bulletin = "Bulletin Board Message number: " + i;
                System.out.println (bulletin);
                publisher.sendMessage(bulletin);
            }
        }
        catch(Exception ex) {
            System.err.println("Exception in BulletinBoardPublisher: " + ex);
        }
        finally {
            try {publisher.close();} catch(Exception ex){}
        }
    }

    public BBPublisher(String JNDIconnectionFactory, String JNDItopic)
➥throws JMSException, NamingException {
        Context context = new InitialContext();
        ConnectionFactory connectionFactory =
➥(ConnectionFactory)context.lookup(JNDIconnectionFactory);
        connection = connectionFactory.createConnection();
        session = connection.createSession(false, Session.AUTO_ACKNOWLEDGE);
        Destination bulletinBoard = (Destination)context.lookup(JNDItopic);
        producer = session.createProducer(bulletinBoard);
    }

    public void sendMessage(String msg) throws JMSException {
        TextMessage message = session.createTextMessage();
        message.setText(msg);
        producer.send(message);
    }

    public void close() throws JMSException {
        connection.close();
    }
}
```

In fact if you modify the PTPSender program to use the jms/TopicConnectionFactory and jms/bulletinBoard topic rather than the jms/QueueConnectionFactory and jms/firstQueue resources you can send individual messages. The program BBSender.java on the accompanying Web site is a modified version of PTPSender.

Run the Bulletin Board publisher program using

```
asant BBPublisher
```

This will check that JMS resources are configured correctly and that the program runs okay, but remember that messages published to topics are not persistent. For the subscriber program (which you are about to see) to pick up the messages, you will need to run the publisher program again while the subscriber is running.

Bulletin Board Subscriber

The subscriber is a Swing application that outputs the bulletins as they arrive (see Listing 9.5).

Remember that for this program to receive the bulletins, it must be running when they are published.

LISTING 9.5   Bulletin Board Subscriber BBSubscriber.java

```java
import javax.naming.*;
import javax.jms.*;
import java.io.*;
import javax.swing.*;
import java.awt.*;
import java.awt.event.*;

public class BBSubscriber extends JFrame implements MessageListener {

    private Connection connection;
    private Session session;
    private MessageConsumer consumer;
    private JTextArea textArea = new JTextArea(4,32);

    public static void main(String[] args) {
        BBSubscriber subscriber = null;
        try {
            subscriber = new
➡BBSubscriber("jms/TopicConnectionFactory","jms/bulletinBoard");
        }
        catch(Exception ex) {
            System.err.println("Exception in BulletinBoardSubscriber: " + ex);
            try {subscriber.close();} catch(Exception e){}
        }
```

LISTING 9.5 continued

```java
                show (subscriber);
        }

    private static void show(final BBSubscriber subscriber) {
        subscriber.addWindowListener(new WindowAdapter() {
            public void windowClosing(WindowEvent ev) {
                try {
                    subscriber.close();
                } catch(Exception ex) {
                    System.err.println("Exception in BulletinBoardSubscriber: "
+ ex);
                }
                subscriber.dispose();
                System.exit(0);
            }
        });
        subscriber.setSize(500,400);
        subscriber.setVisible(true);
    }

    public BBSubscriber(String JNDIconnectionFactory, String JNDItopic)
throws JMSException, NamingException {
        super (JNDIconnectionFactory+":"+JNDItopic);
        getContentPane().add(new JScrollPane(textArea));
        Context context = new InitialContext();
        ConnectionFactory connectionFactory =
(ConnectionFactory)context.lookup(JNDIconnectionFactory);
        connection = connectionFactory.createConnection();
        session = connection.createSession(false, Session.AUTO_ACKNOWLEDGE);
        Destination bulletinBoard = (Destination)context.lookup(JNDItopic);
        consumer = session.createConsumer(bulletinBoard);
        consumer.setMessageListener(this);
        connection.start();
    }

    public void onMessage(Message message) {
        System.out.println("Message "+message);
        try {
            if (message instanceof TextMessage) {
                String bulletin = ((TextMessage) message).getText();
                String text = textArea.getText();
                textArea.setText(text+"\n"+bulletin);
            }
        } catch(JMSException ex) {
            System.err.println("Exception in BulletinBoardSubscriber:OnMessage:
" + ex);
        }
    }
```

LISTING 9.5 continued

```
public void close() throws JMSException {
    connection.close();
}
}
```

When you run this program from the command line, a small window will appear. Any messages published to the bulletin board topic while the program is running will appear in this window. You can run this program using the command

```
asant BBSubscriber
```

Creating Durable Subscriptions

When you run the bulletin board example, you will have seen that you need to synchronize the publisher and subscriber and that the subscriber can miss bulletins if it is not running when they are sent. Bulletins are missed because the Session. createConsumer() method creates a non-durable subscriber. A non-durable subscriber can only receive messages that are published while it is active.

To get around this restriction, the JMS API provides a Session. createDurableSubscriber() method. With a durable subscription, the JMS provider stores the messages published to the topic, just as it would store messages sent to a queue.

Figure 9.6 shows diagrammatically how messages are consumed with non-durable and durable subscriptions when the subscriber is inactive during the period when messages are published.

Only messages sent after a subscriber registers a durable subscription are stored. The mechanism for registering a durable subscriber may vary from one implementation of a Message Service to another.

The J2EE RI durable subscribers are created by associating a TopicConnectionFactory with a client ID. The subscription is registered the first time the client connects to a Topic using the durable TopicConnectionFactory and the associated client ID. Effectively, this means that a J2EE RI durable subscriber application must be run once to register the subscriber before any messages will be made durable for that client ID.

FIGURE 9.6

Non-durable and durable subscriptions.

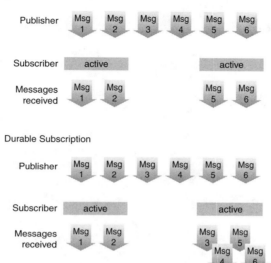

The JMS resources created at the start of these examples included a `TopicConnectionFactory` called `jms/DurableTopicConnectionFactory` associated with the client ID BBS. The example program `BBDurable.java` is a variation of the `BBSubscriber.java` program shown in Listing 9.5. The only changes are in obtaining the connection factory:

```
ConnectionFactory connectionFactory =
    (ConnectionFactory)context.lookup("jms/DurableTopicConnectionFactory");
```

and in creating (and registering) the subscription:

```
Topic bulletinBoard = (Topic)context.lookup("jms/bulletinBoard");
subscriber = session.createDurableSubscriber(bulletinBoard,"BBS");
```

To register the durable subscriber, run the program once and then close down the Swing window:

```
asant BBDurable
```

Now send some messages to the topic using the publisher program from Listing 9.4:

```
asant BBPublish
```

Finally run the subscriber once more to see the messages posted while the subscriber was not connected:

```
asant BBDurable
```

A subscriber can permanently stop receiving messages by unsubscribing a durable subscription with the unsubscribe() method after closing the subscriber.

```
subscriber.close();
session.unsubscribe("BBS");
```

Messages will no longer be stored for this subscription.

Additional JMS Features

The following sections cover some additional features available in JMS. Not all the features of JMS are covered, and you should refer to the JMS API specification for more information.

Message Selectors

The JMS API provides support for filtering received messages. This is accomplished by using a message selector. The createConsumer() and the createDurableSubscriber() methods have variants that allow a message selector to be specified.

The message selector is a string containing an SQL-like conditional expression. Only message header values and properties can be specified in the message selector. It is not possible to filter messages based on the contents of the message body.

```
String highPriority = "JMSPriority = '9' AND topic = 'Java'";
subscriber = session.createConsumer(bulletinBoard, highPriority, false);
```

This selector will ensure that only priority nine messages are received. Note here that topic is a property of the message that has been created and set by the sender.

Notice that for this form of the createConsumer the parameters are as follows:

```
TopicSession.createConsumer(destination, messageSelector, noLocal);
```

You need to set the boolean noLocal parameter to specify whether you want to receive messages created by your own connection. Set noLocal to false to prevent the delivery of messages created by the producer's own connection.

Session Acknowledgement Modes

In most of the examples given so far, auto acknowledgement has been used to send the acknowledgement automatically as soon as the message is received. This has the advantage of removing the burden of acknowledging messages from you, but it has the disadvantage that if your application fails before the message is processed, the message may be lost. After a message is acknowledged, the JMS provider will never redeliver it.

Deferring acknowledgement until after you have processed the message will protect against loss of data. To do this, the session must be created with client acknowledgement.

```
connection.createSession(false, Session.CLIENT_ACKNOWLEDGE);
```

Now when the message is received, no acknowledgement will be sent automatically. It is up to you to ensure that the message is acknowledged at some later point.

```
message = (TextMessage) consumer.receive();
// process the message
message.acknowledge();
```

If you do not acknowledge the message, it may be resent.

A third acknowledgement mode, DUPS_OK_ACKNOWLEDGE, can be used when the delivery of duplicates can be tolerated. This form of AUTO_ACKNOWLEDGE has the advantage of reducing the session overhead spent preventing the delivery of duplicate messages.

Message Persistence

The default JMS delivery mode for a message is PERSISTENT. This ensures that the message will be delivered, even if the JMS provider fails or is shut down.

A second delivery mode, NON_PERSISTENT, can be used where guaranteed delivery is not required. A NON_PERSISTENT message has the lowest overhead because the JMS provider does not need to copy the message to a stable storage medium. JMS still guarantees to deliver a NON_PERSISTENT message at most once (but maybe not at all). Nonpersistent messages should be used when:

- Performance is important and reliability is not
- Messages can be lost with no effect on system functionality

Persistent and non-persistent messages can be delivered to the same destination.

Transactions

Often, acknowledgement of single messages is not enough to ensure the integrity of an application. Think of the classic banking system example where two messages are sent to debit an amount from one account and credit the same amount to another. If only one of the messages is received, there will be a problem. A transaction is required where a number of operations involving many messages forms an atomic piece of work.

In JMS, you can specify that a session is transacted when it is created:

```
createSession(boolean transacted, int acknowledgeMode);
```

In a transacted session, several sends and receives can be grouped together in a single transaction. The JMS API provides `Session.commit()` to acknowledge all the messages in a transaction and `Session.rollback()` to discard all messages. After a rollback, any messages received during the transaction will be redelivered unless they have expired.

To create a transacted session, set the transacted parameter to `true`, as shown in the following:

```
session = connection.createSession(true, 0);
```

For transacted sessions, the `acknowledgeMode` parameter is ignored. The previous code sets this parameter to `0` to make this fact explicit.

There is no explicit transaction start. The contents of a transaction are simply those messages that have been produced and consumed during the current session, either since the session was created or since the last `commit()`. After a `commit()` or `rollback()`, a new transaction is started.

NOTE

> Because the `commit()` and `rollback()` methods are associated with a session, it is not possible to mix messages from queues and topics in the same transaction.

The following example shows a simple transaction involving two messages.

```
Session session = connection.createSession(true, 0);
Destination bank1Queue = (Queue)context.lookup("queue/bank1");
Destination bank2Queue = (Queue)context.lookup("queue/bank2");
MessageProducer bank1Sender = session.createProducer(bank1Queue);
MessageProducer bank2Sender = session.createProducer(bank2Queue);
// .. application processing to create debit and credit messages
try {
    bank1Sender.send(bank1Queue, debitMsg);
    bank2Sender.send(bank2Queue, creditMsg);
    session.commit();
} catch(JMSException ex) {
    System.err.println("Exception in bank transaction:" + ex);
    session.rollback();
}
```

Where a receiver handles atomic actions sent in multiple messages, it should similarly only commit when all the messages have been received and processed.

A JMS provider may provide support for distributed transaction using the X/Open XA resource interface. This is performed by utilizing the Java Transaction API (JTA). JTA was covered on Day 8, "Transactions and Persistence." XA support is optional; refer to your JMS provider documentation to see if XA support is provided.

Multithreading

Not all the objects in JMS support concurrent use. The JMS API only specifies the following objects can be shared across multiple threads

- Connection Factories
- Connections
- Destinations

Many threads in the same client may share these objects, whereas the following:

- Sessions
- Message Producers
- Message Consumers

can only be accessed by one thread at a time. The restriction on single-threaded sessions reduces the complexity required by the JMS provider to support transactions.

Session concurrency can be implemented within a multithreaded client by creating multiple sessions.

Summary

Today, you have had an introduction to JMS messaging, the concept of message producers and consumers, and explored the two supported message domains—point-to-point and publish/subscribe. This has necessarily been an overview of JMS. More information should be obtained from the latest JMS specification and API. Also, refer to the documentation for your JMS provider to determine what features beyond those described here are supported.

Tomorrow, you will utilize your JMS knowledge gained today while examining the third type of EJB—Message-Driven beans.

Q&A

Q What type of JMS message domain should be used to send a message to a single receiver?

A A point-to-point domain is the appropriate choice in this scenario.

Q **What type of JMS message domain should be used to send a message to many receivers at the same time?**

A To send to many receivers, the publish/subscribe message domain is the best choice.

Q **What is the difference between JMSHeader fields and JMSProperty fields?**

A JMS header fields are defined in the JMS API and are mainly set by the JMS provider. JMS property fields are used by clients to add additional header information to a message.

Q **Does JMS guarantee to deliver a message in the point-to-point domain?**

A Messages in the point-to-point domain are PERSISTENT by default and will be delivered unless they have a set timeout that has expired. Point-to-point messages can be set to NON_PERSISTENT, in which case, the message may be lost if a provider fails.

Q **When should I use a durable subscription?**

A Durable subscriptions should be used when a subscriber needs to receive messages from a topic when it is inactive.

Exercise

To extend your knowledge of the subjects covered today, try the following exercise.

1. Create a chat room application. Participants provide their name and can send messages. Participants read messages posted by all other participants.

To assist you in this task, three Java files have been provided in the exercise sub-directory for Day 9 on the accompanying Web site.

The Chat.java and ChatDisplay.java files are complete and need not be edited. These files provide the Swing code to enter and display the chat room messages on the screen.

The TopicServer.java is a starting point for you to further develop the chat server. The initial code simply uses the callback method addMessage to bounce the message back to the screen. The addMessage method uses the interface defined in ChatDisplay.java.

You should edit this file to replace this callback with code to publish the message to a topic. You will then add a subscriber that consumes messages from this topic and displays them on the screen. You add your message to the message box at the top and click Send. The message should then appear in the Bulletin Board window of all Chat programs running.

Add a property called From to the message and set it to the from parameter passed in. This will then be displayed in the chat room window.

A completed TopicServer is included in the solutions sub-directory of Day 9 of the case study. To run the solution, go to the solution directory for Day 9 and type:

```
asant Chat
```

Note that you will need to create the JMS resources using asant create-jms (if you haven't already done so as described in the section "Using JMS with the J2EE RI").

9

DAY **10**

Message-Driven Beans

So far, you have looked at two types of Enterprise JavaBeans (EJB)—the Session bean and the Entity bean. Today you will consider the third and final EJB, the Message-Driven bean. The following topics are covered:

- Similarities and differences with Entity and Session beans
- The life-cycle of a Message-Driven bean
- Writing a Message-Driven bean

Prior to the EJB 2.0 specification, it was not possible to support asynchronous message passing. All EJB method calls had to be synchronous and initiated by the client.

With J2EE 1.3 and later versions, you can use Message-Driven beans to combine the functionality of EJBs with the Java Message Service (JMS) to support asynchronous communication.

Although JMS was covered in detail on Day 9, "Java Message Service," the following is a quick recap of its main features:

- JMS is a Java API that specifies how applications can create, send, receive, and read messages.
- JMS enables communication that is both asynchronous and reliable, while minimizing the amount of knowledge and programming required.
- The implementation of the JMS API is provided by a number of vendors known as Message Service providers.
- Message queues are associated with the point-to-point message domain. Messages in a queue are normally persistent but can only be consumed by one receiver.
- Topics allow a message to be sent to more than one receiver (called a subscriber). Messages are not normally persistent; they are immediately delivered to all existing subscribers.

What Are Message-Driven Beans?

Message-Driven Beans (MDBs) are generally constructed to be message consumers, although they can, like any other EJB, also be used to create and send messages. An MDB lives entirely within the container; it has no security context of its own. When the bean is deployed, it is associated with a particular queue or topic, and is invoked by the container when a message arrives for that queue or topic.

The following are the features of a Message-Driven bean:

- It is anonymous; that is, it has no client visibility. No state is maintained for the client.
- All instances of a particular Message-Driven bean are equivalent.
- The container can pool instances.
- It does not have a local or remote interface.
- It is invoked asynchronously by the container.
- The bean lives entirely within a container; the container manages its lifecycle and environment.

These features are discussed in more detail next.

The Message Producer's View

To the client producing JMS messages, the Message-Driven bean is just an anonymous message consumer. The client need not be aware that the consumer is an MDB. The client simply sends its messages to a destination, either a queue or a topic, and the bean handles the message when it arrives. Therefore, the coding of message producers in an application using MDBs is exactly the same as any JMS application; that is, the message must conform to the JMS specification and the destination must be a Java Naming and Directory Interface (JNDI) registered name. Apart from this, the message does not have to correspond to any particular format.

It is not necessary for the client to be a Java client application or an EJB to take advantage of Message-Driven beans; it can be a Java ServerPages (JSP) component or a non-J2EE application.

Similarities and Differences with Other EJBs

In some respects, an MDB is similar to a stateless Session bean. It is a complete EJB that can encapsulate business logic. An advantage is that the container is responsible for providing functionality for security, concurrency, transactions, and so forth. Like a Session or Entity bean, an MDB has a `bean` class and XML deployment descriptor.

The main difference from the other EJBs is that Message-Driven Beans cannot be called directly by the client. For this reason, they do not have `Home`, `Remote`, or `Local` interfaces, which makes them less prone to misuse by the client.

Unlike Entity and Session beans, MDBs do not have a passive state. Therefore, they do not implement the `ejbActivate()` and `ejbPassivate()` methods.

NOTE

Although a Message-Driven bean is considered to be a stateless object, from the client's view, it can and should retain state in its instance variables. Examples of this are an open database connection and the `Home`, `Local`, and `Remote` interfaces to other EJBs.

Programming Interfaces in a Message-Driven Bean

There are a number of constraints on the contents of a Message-Driven Bean class which must

- Implement the `javax.ejb.MessageDrivenBean` interface
- Implement the `javax.jms.MessageListener` interface
- Have a single constructor, with no arguments

- Have a single public setMessageDrivenContext(MessageDrivenContext ctx) method that returns void
- Have a single public ejbCreate() method with no arguments that returns void
- Have a single public ejbRemove() method with no arguments that returns void
- Have a single public onMessage(Message message) method that returns void
- Not have a finalize() method

The following sections cover these methods in more detail.

Life Cycle of a Message-Driven Bean

The EJB container controls the lifecycle of a Message-Driven bean. The Message-Driven bean instance lifecycle has three states, as shown in Figure 10.1:

- *Does Not Exist*—The Message-Driven bean has not been instantiated yet or is awaiting garbage collection.
- *Method Ready Pool*—A pool of Message-Driven bean instances, similar to the instance pool used for stateless session beans.
- *Processing a message*—The Message-Driven bean has been instantiated and is handling a message.

FIGURE 10.1

The Message-Driven bean life cycle.

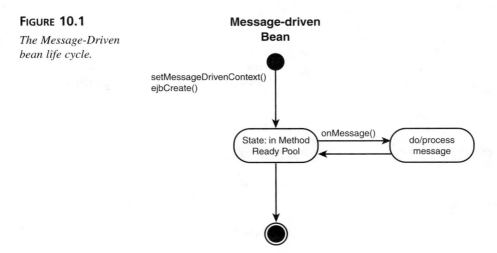

After constructing the new instance of the MDB object, the container invokes the following methods:

- The bean's `setMessageDrivenContext()` method with a reference to its EJB context. The Message-Driven bean should store its `MessageDrivenContext` reference in an instance variable.

- The bean's `ejbCreate()` method. The Message-Driven bean's `ejbCreate()` method takes no arguments and is invoked only once when the bean is first instantiated.

The MDB Context

The `javax.ejb.MessageDrivenContext` interface (see the class diagram in Figure 10.2) provides the MDB with access to its runtime context. This is similar to the `SessionContext` and `EntityContext` interfaces for Session and Entity beans.

FIGURE 10.2

The `MessageDrivenContext` *class diagram.*

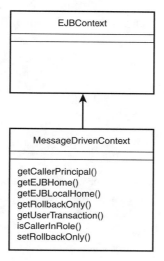

Note that all the `EJBContext` methods are available to an MDB, but because the MDB does not have a local or remote interface, calls to `getEJBHome()` and `getEJBLocalHome()` will throw a `java.lang.IllegalStateException`.

Because MDBs are anonymous and run within the context of the container, and the container does not have a client security identity or role, calls to the `getCallerPrincipal()` and `IsCallerInRole()` methods will also cause an `IllegalStateException`.

Creating an MDB

The `setMessageDrivenContext()` method can throw an `EJBException` if there is a container or system level error of some kind. See the section titled "Handling Exceptions" for more details. What follows is a sample `setMessageDrivenContext()` method that saves its `EJBContext` and JNDI context:

```
private MessageDrivenContext mdbContext;
private Context jndiContext;
public void setMessageDrivenContext (MessageDrivenContext ctx) {
    mdbContext = ctx;
    try { jndiContext = new InitialContext();
    } catch (NamingException nameEx) {
        throw new EJBException(nameEx);
    }
}
```

After calling `setMessageDrivenContext()`, the container calls the bean's `ejbCreate()` method, which takes no parameters. You could use this method to allocate resources, such as a datasource, but in practice, this is usually done in the `setMessageDrivenContext()` method. Therefore, it is normal to find the `ejbCreate()` method empty.

This method is only invoked when the bean instance is first created.

```
public void ejbCreate () throws CreateException
```

After the `ejbCreate()` method has been called, the bean is placed in the method-ready pool.

Method-Ready Pool

The actual point at which MDB instances are created and placed in the method-ready pool is vendor specific. The vendor of an EJB server could design it to only create bean instances when they are required. Alternatively, when the EJB server is started, a number of instances may be placed in the method-ready pool awaiting the first message. Additional instances can be added to the pool when the number of beans is insufficient to handle the number of incoming messages.

MDB instances in the method-ready pool are available to consume incoming messages. Any available instance can be allocated to a message and, while processing the message, this particular bean instance is not available to consume other messages. A container can handle several messages concurrently by using a separate instance of the message bean for each message. Each separate instance obtains its own `MessageDrivenContext` from the container. After the message has been processed, the instance is available to consume other messages. MDBs are always single-threaded objects.

The Demise of an MDB

When the server decides to reduce the total size of the method-ready pool, a bean instance is removed from the pool and becomes available for garbage collection. At this point, the bean's `ejbRemove()` method is called.

You should use this method to close or deallocate resources stored in instance variables and set the instance variable to null.

```
public void ejbRemove()
```

The `EJBException` can be thrown by `ejbRemove()` to indicate a system-level error.

Following `ejbRemove()`, the bean is dereferenced and no longer available to handle messages. It will eventually be garbage collected.

10

NOTE

> The `ejbRemove()` method may not be called if the Message-Driven bean instance throws an exception. This could result in resource leaks.

A Message-Driven bean must not define the finalize method to free up resources; do all the tidying up in `ejbRemove()`.

Consuming Messages

When a message is received, the container finds a Message-Driven bean instance that is registered for that destination and calls the bean's `onMessage()` method.

```
public void onMessage(Message message)
```

This method has a single parameter that contains a single JMS message. The message will have a header, one or more properties (optional), and a message body (consisting of one of the five JMS message body types). JMS messages were covered in some detail on Day 9.

An MDB must provide a single `onMessage()` method. This method should not throw runtime exceptions and it must not have a `throws` clause as part of its method signature. The `onMessage()` holds the business logic of the bean. You can use helper methods and other EJBs to process the message.

Remember, MDB instances are triggered asynchronously; the business logic within the bean must reflect this. You must never presume any ordering to the messages received. Even if the system is implemented within the same JVM, the system vagaries can cause the scheduling of bean instances to be non-deterministic, which means that you cannot be certain when the bean will run.

Handling Exceptions

An MDB can encounter various exceptions or errors that prevent it from successfully completing. The following are examples of such exceptions:

- Failure to obtain a database connection
- A JNDI naming exception
- A RemoteException from invocation of another EJB
- An unexpected RuntimeException

A well-written MDB should never carelessly throw a RuntimeException. If a RuntimeException is not caught in onMessage() or any other bean class method, the container will simply discard the instance (it will transition it to the Does Not Exist state). In this case, the container will not call the ejbRemove() method, so a badly written bean method could cause resource leaks.

Obviously, you need a mechanism to tell the container that you have caught an unrecoverable error and die gracefully. To do this, you use exception layering. You catch the RuntimeException, free up resources, do any other appropriate processing and then throw an EJBException to the container. The container will then log the error, rollback any container-managed transactions, and discard the instance.

Because identical MDB instances are available, from the client perspective, the message bean continues to exist in the method-ready pool to handle further messages. Therefore, a single instance failure may not cause any disruption to the system.

MDB Transactions

The analysis of container-managed versus bean-managed transactions was covered as part of Day 8's material, reread this if you need to recap the benefits of either method of handling transactions. When designing your MDB you must decide whether the bean will demarcate the transactions programmatically (bean managed transactions), or if the transaction management is to be performed by the container. This is done by setting the transaction-type in the deployment descriptor.

```
<transaction-type>Container</transaction-type>
```

Use container-managed transactions unless you have some reason for using bean-managed transactions, such as sending and/or receiving a series of messages that together constitute an atomic processing action. An MDB can only use one of bean-managed or container-managed transactions.

Message Acknowledgment

By default the container handles message acknowledgement for MDBs. If you use container-managed transactions, you cannot change the default, as acknowledgement is handled as part of the transaction.

With bean-managed transactions, you can specify DUPS_OK_ACKNOWLEDGE as an alternative to the default (AUTO_ACKNOWLEDGE). To do this, set the acknowledge-mode element in the deployment descriptor. With DUPS_OK_ACKNOWLEDGE set, you can reduce the session overhead spent preventing delivery of duplicate messages, but only do this if receiving duplicate messages will not cause a problem with the business logic of your bean. MDBs cannot use the CLIENT_ACKNOWLEDGE option and should therefore not call the Message.acknowledge() method.

Using an MDB

MDBs provide an asynchronous interface to the EJB components of your applications. As such they are primarily used to implement so called back office functionality. Typically a session bean delegates functionality to an MDB to allow the client application to continue processing without waiting for a potentially slow operation to complete. A typical example may be a batch update of a database.

As the MDB is not accessible by the client it cannot return information directly to the client. The results of any operations performed by an MDB are typically retrieved by the client using Session beans (or possibly Entity beans). An alternative approach to this client pull model is to implement a client push model where the MDB returns the results of the operation using JMS or JavaMail.

Adding an MDB to the Agency Case Study

To illustrate the use of MDBs you will extend the Agency case study to utilize a Message-Driven bean to match advertised jobs to new applicants as they register with the system or when an applicant updates his or her skills or location.

As each applicant is created, modified, or deleted, a message is sent to the JMS queue jms/applicantQueue. The message includes the applicant's login and a flag to indicate if this is a new applicant or a change to an existing one. An MDB will receive this message and compare the applicant's details with all advertised jobs. The MDB will add an entry to the Matched table in the database if the applicant's location matches a job location and the applicant has at least one of the skills required by the job. If the applicant has all of the skills required for a job, the row added to the Matched table is tagged with an exact match flag.

Deleting an applicant deletes the rows in the Matched table for that applicant.

The steps required to add this functionality to the case study are as follows:

1. Write a helper class called `MessageSender` that creates and sends a message to the `jms/applicantQueue` containing the applicant's login.

2. Amend the `Agency` and `Register` Session beans to call this new method when a new applicant is registered or the applicant's location or skills are changed.

3. Write an MDB called `ApplicantMatch` to

   • Consume a message on the `jms/applicantQueue`

   • Look up the applicant's location and skills information

   • Find all the jobs that match the applicant's location

   • For each of these jobs, find those that require the applicant's skills

   • Determine if the applicant has all or just some of the skills

   • Store applicant and job matches in the `Matched` table

4. Deploy the new EJBs; run and test the application.

Write `MessageSender` Helper Class

This class contains a constructor for the class and two methods—`sendApplicant()` and `close()`.

The constructor takes two parameters, which are strings representing the JNDI names of the JMS connection factory and the JMS queue.

The `sendApplicant()` method is called by the `Agency` Session bean when a new applicant registers with the system and the `Register` Session bean when an existing applicant changes his or her location or job skills. It has two parameters—the applicant's login string and a Boolean denoting if this is a new applicant.

The `close()` method is called before the application is terminated. It sends a message that lets the container know that no more messages will be sent to the queue and frees-up resources.

If you have worked through Day 9, the code for the `MessageSender`, shown in Listing 10.1, should be familiar to you.

LISTING 10.1   `MessageSender` Helper Class

```
import javax.naming.*;
import javax.jms.*;

public class MessageSender {
```

After connecting to the message store, you open a message folder. To do this, create a `javax.mail.Folder` object using the `Store.getFolder()` method specifying the name of the folder as a parameter. Both POP3 and IMAP protocols support the INBOX folder containing messages received by the email server. An IMAP email server supports additional folders but POP3 only supports the single INBOX folder. Open the INBOX using:

```
Folder folder = store.getFolder("INBOX");
```

Now you can open the folder using the `open()` method specifying the mode with which to open the folder. Possible values for the mode are `Folder.READ_ONLY` and `Folder.READ_WRITE`:

```
folder.open(Folder.READ_ONLY);
```

NOTE If you open a folder READ_ONLY, you will not be able to delete the messages from the POP3 mail store after you have read them.

To retrieve the messages from the folder, you can either use the `getMessage()` method to retrieve a message by its message number (its position in the folder) or you can use one of the various `getMessages()` methods to retrieve either all messages or a range of messages. The following example retrieves all messages:

```
Message messages[] = folder.getMessages();
```

The final step in the message retrieval process is to perform some form of user-defined processing on the retrieved messages. In this example, the code simply iterates through the messages printing the subject, sender, time, and then printing the entire message.

```
for (int i=0; i<messages.length; i++) {
  Message msg = messages[i];
  System.out.println(i + ": " + msg.getFrom()[0] + "\t"
          + msg.getSubject() + "\t" + msg.getSentDate() + "\n\n");
  msg.writeTo(System.out);
}
```

As you can see, the `Message` class exposes a number of JavaBean getter methods to access the message attributes. The `writeTo()` method outputs the message content to a specified output stream, which in this example is `System.out`.

That is the message retrieval process completed, but to complete the code you must close the resources used by calling their `close()` methods.

You must pass the `Folder`'s `close()` method a single Boolean parameter indicating whether to delete any messages marked for deletion within the folder on the server. You

11

will learn how to mark messages for deletion in the "Deleting Messages" section of today's lesson.

Closing the Store object disconnects your application from the POP3 server.

Listing 11.8 shows the complete code for this application.

LISTING 11.8   RetrieveMail.java Full Listing

```java
import java.util.Properties;
import javax.mail.*;
import javax.mail.internet.*;
import java.io.*;

public class RetrieveMail {
    public static void main(String[] args) {
        if (args.length!=3) {
        System.out.println("Usage: RetrieveMail POPHost username password");
            System.exit(1);
        }

        String host = args[0];
        String username = args[1];
        String password = args[2];

        try {
            Properties props = new Properties();
            Session session = Session.getDefaultInstance(props, null);

            Store store = session.getStore("pop3");
            store.connect(host, username, password);

            Folder folder = store.getFolder("INBOX");
            folder.open(Folder.READ_ONLY);

            Message messages[] = folder.getMessages();
            for (int i=0; i<messages.length; i++) {
                System.out.println(i + ": " + messages[i].getFrom()[0] + "\t" +
                    messages[i].getSubject() + "\t" +
                    messages[i].getSentDate() + "\n\n");
                messages[i].writeTo(System.out);
            }

            folder.close(false);
            for (int i=0; i<messages.length; i++) {
              Message msg = messages[i];
              System.out.println(i + ": " + msg.getFrom()[0] +
              "\t" + msg.getSubject() +
              "\t" + msg.getSentDate() + "\n\n");
              msg.writeTo(System.out);
            }
```

LISTING 11.8 continued

```
            store.close();
        }
        catch (MessagingException me) {
            System.err.println(me);
        }
        catch (IOException ioe) {
            System.err.println(ioe);
        }
    }
}
```

Run this example using the command:

```
asant RetrieveMail
```

Supply a hostname, username, and password. To read the messages you sent in the previous examples, use the host name localhost, username juliet and password juliet. Any messages stored on your mailHost will now be printed to the screen but will not be deleted from the folder.

Deleting Messages

In the previous example, you retrieved messages from a mail server without deleting them. Of course, in a real-world situation, you could not leave messages on the mail server indefinitely. Normally, you would delete messages after retrieving them.

NOTE

If you are working with an IMAP server you may choose to save the messages in a different folder rather than delete them. Sadly, manipulating and saving messages with an IMAP server is beyond the scope of today's introduction to JavaMail.

To modify the previous example so that messages are deleted after retrieval is a straightforward process. To retrieve and delete messages you must open the folder in READ_WRITE mode. So simply replace the line of code that opened the folder with the following line:

```
folder.open(Folder.READ_WRITE);
```

Deleting messages involves the use of flags. Messages can support a number of flags that indicate the state of a message. The javax.mail.Flags.Flag class supplies predefined

11

flags that are accessible as static fields. See Table 11.3 for a list of flags and their meaning. Note, however, that just because these flags exist doesn't mean that all mail servers support them. In fact, POP3 mail servers typically only support the DELETED flag; IMAP servers normally support more of the flags. To find out exactly which flags your mail server supports, you can call the Folder.getPermanentFlags() method, which returns a Flags object that contains all the supported flags.

TABLE 11.3   Predefined Message Flags

Flag	Description
ANSWERED	The client has replied to the message.
DELETED	The message is marked for deletion.
DRAFT	The message is a draft.
FLAGGED	The client has flagged the message.
RECENT	The message has arrived in the folder since it was last opened.
SEEN	The message has been retrieved by the client.
USER	Indicates that the folder supports user defined flags.

To mark a message for deletion, you use the Message.setFlag() method and supply the flag and a Boolean indicating the flag's value. For example, to mark a message ready for deletion:

```
message.setFlag(Flags.Flag.DELETED, true);
```

For Listing 11.8 you would modify the for loop as follows:

```
for (int i=0; i<messages.length; i++) {
   Message msg = messages[i];
   System.out.println(i + ": " + msg.getFrom()[0] +
    "\t" + msg.getSubject() +
    "\t" + msg.getSentDate() + "\n\n");
   msg.writeTo(System.out);
   msg.setFlag(Flags.Flag.DELETED, true);
}
```

To complete the deletion, you must pass the folder's close() method a Boolean of true. Passing the value of true ensures that any messages marked for deletion are deleted when the folder closes:

```
folder.close(true);
```

That's it. If you want to view the complete modified listing, you will find it in a file called DeleteMail.java on the Web site accompanying this book.

CAUTION	Do not run the DeleteMail example on a live mail store as it will download and then delete all the messages in the inbox.

Once a message has been deleted from a folder, and that folder has been closed, the message no longer exists unless you have kept a local copy. If you change your mind about deleting a message you should mark the message as not deleted using:

```
msg.setFlag(Flags.Flag.DELETED, false);
```

before you close the folder. However if you close the folder with the false parameter

```
folder.close(false);
```

no messages will be deleted and any deleted message flags will be discarded.

Now that you know how to read simple messages, the next step is to read messages with attachments.

Retrieving Email Attachments

Retrieving an attachment from a message is a more involved process than simply reading a normal message. As you saw earlier, an attachment is a part of a multi-part message. When you retrieve a message that has an attachment, you must iterate through the body parts and identify which ones are attachments. After you identify a part as an attachment, you must process it, typically that means writing that part's content to a file.

You cannot simply identify a part as an attachment through its content type, because the sender of the message part may have intended for it to be displayed inline—like the HTML message you created earlier. Fortunately, RFC 2183 defines the Content-Disposition MIME message header. This header allows a message sender to mark body parts as either INLINE (displays within the message text) or ATTACHMENT (the part is an attachment).

The next example simply reads all messages in the mailbox and for any messages with an attachment saves those attachments to a local directory on disk. The first step for handling an attachment is to check each message to see if it is a multi-part message:

```
Message messages[] = folder.getMessages();
for (int i=0; i<messages.length; i++) {
    System.out.println(messages[i].getFrom()[0] + "\t" +
                       messages[i].getSubject());
    Object obj = messages[i].getContent();
    if (obj instanceof Multipart)
        processMessage((Multipart)obj);
}
```

11

For each identified multi-part message the helper method `processMessage()` identifies the message parts that are attachments:

```
private static void processMessage(Multipart multipart)
throws MessagingException, IOException
{
    for (int i=0; i<multipart.getCount(); i++) {
        Part part = multipart.getBodyPart(i);
        String disposition = part.getDisposition();
        if (disposition != null &&
            disposition.equals(Part.ATTACHMENT))
            writeFile(part.getFileName(), part.getInputStream());
    }
}
```

The `processMessage()` uses the `Part.getDisposition()` method to get the part's disposition (how it should be displayed to the user) and checks whether the disposition is of the type `ATTACHMENT`. If the disposition is of the type `ATTACHMENT`, the code gets the attachment filename and an `InputStream` object representing the data and saves the file to disk.

The first task for saving the attachment is to check that the attachment has a valid filename, create one if no filename was given, strip off any filename directory component, and create a `File` object for the attachment (the example stores the file in a local `attach` directory):

```
private static void writeFile(String fileName, InputStream in)
                                throws IOException
{
    if (fileName == null)
        fileName = "attachment.dat";
    File file = new File(fileName);
    file = new File("attach",file.getName());
```

The example code checks to make sure it doesn't overwrite an existing file by generating a unique name (another approach is to prompt the user to confirm overwriting the file):

```
    String rootName = file.getName();
    for (int i=0; file.exists(); i++) {
        file = new File(file.getParent(),""+i+"_"+rootName);
    }
    System.out.println("Saving attachment in: "+ file.getAbsolutePath());
```

The final task is to save the data:

```
    BufferedOutputStream bos =
➡ new BufferedOutputStream(new FileOutputStream(file));
    BufferedInputStream bis = new BufferedInputStream(in);
    byte[] buffer = new byte[2048];
    int n;
```

```
    while ((n=bis.read(buffer,0,buffer.length)) > 0) {
        bos.write(buffer,0,n);
    }
    bos.flush();     bos.close();     bis.close();
}
```

The `InputStream` object for reading the attachment is provided by a `javax.activation.DataHandler` object. This `DataHandler` understands the MIME encoding used in the message and reconstructs the original data for the `InputStream`. The client code is unaware that the attachment is MIME encoded.

Listing 11.9 shows the complete code listing for the `RetrieveAttachment` application.

LISTING 11.9   `RetrieveAttachment.java` Full Listing

```
import java.util.Properties;
import javax.mail.*;
import javax.mail.internet.*;
import java.io.*;

public class RetrieveAttachment {
    public static void main(String[] args)
    {
        if (args.length!=3) {
        System.out.println("Usage: RetrieveAttachment host username password");
            System.exit(1);
        }

        String host = args[0];
        String username = args[1];
        String password = args[2];

        try {
            Properties props = new Properties();
            Session session = Session.getDefaultInstance(props, null);
            Store store = session.getStore("pop3");
            store.connect(host, username, password);
            Folder folder = store.getFolder("INBOX");
            folder.open(Folder.READ_ONLY);
            Message messages[] = folder.getMessages();
            for (int i=0; i<messages.length; i++) {
                System.out.println(messages[i].getFrom()[0] + "\t" +
                    messages[i].getSubject());
                Object obj = messages[i].getContent();
                if (obj instanceof Multipart)
                    processMessage((Multipart)obj);
            }

            folder.close(false);
            store.close();
        }
```

11

LISTING **11.9** continued

```
        catch (MessagingException me) {
            System.err.println(me);
        }
        catch (IOException ioe) {
            System.err.println(ioe);
        }
    }

    private static void processMessage(Multipart multipart)
                                    throws MessagingException, IOException
    {
        for (int i=0; i<multipart.getCount(); i++) {
            Part part = multipart.getBodyPart(i);
            String disposition = part.getDisposition();
            if (disposition != null &&
                disposition.equals(Part.ATTACHMENT))
                writeFile(part.getFileName(), part.getInputStream());
        }
    }

    private static void writeFile(String fileName, InputStream in)
                            throws IOException
    {
        if (fileName == null)
            fileName = "attachment.dat";
        File file = new File(fileName);
        file = new File("attach",file.getName());

        String rootName = file.getName();
        for (int i=0; file.exists(); i++) {
            file = new File(file.getParent(),""+i+"_"+rootName);
        }
        System.out.println("Saving attachment in: "+ file.getAbsolutePath());

        BufferedOutputStream bos =
 new BufferedOutputStream(new FileOutputStream(file));
        BufferedInputStream bis = new BufferedInputStream(in);
        byte[] buffer = new byte[2048];
        int n;
        while ((n=bis.read(buffer,0,buffer.length)) > 0) {
            bos.write(buffer,0,n);
        }
        bos.flush();
        bos.close();
        bis.close();
    }
}
```

Run this example using the command

```
asant RetriveAttachment
```

and supply the hostname, username and password when prompted (localhost, juliet and juliet).

You will of course, need to use the SendAttachmentMail example to first send an email containing an attachment.

Before you look at using JavaMail within the J2EE environment it is worth studying the JavaMail support for authenticated email servers.

Authenticating Users and Security

The JavaMail API javax.mail package provides an Authenticator class that allows access to protected resources, such as a mailbox. You will need to use an Authenticator object if you do not pass the username and password to the Store.connect() method or if you are working with an authenticating SMTP server.

Using an Authenticator object requires you to define your own Authenticator sub-class and then pass an instance of this sub-class to the Session.getDefaultInstance() method as follows:

```
Properties props = new Properties();
props.put("mail.smtp.host","localhost");
props.put("mail.pop3.host","localhost");
Authenticator auth = new MyAuthenticator();
Session session = Session.getDefaultInstance(props, auth);
```

In this example the SMTP host and POP3 host are both defined as properties so that you can see where to supply your own email server host names.

An Authenticator subclass must define the single method getPasswordAuthentication() which returns a PasswordAuthentication object. This object is simply a container for the authentication information and has a constructor that accepts a username and a password. The MyAuthenticator example, shown below, simply prompts the user for his or her username and password:

```
class MyAuthenticator extends Authenticator {
  public PasswordAuthentication getPasswordAuthentication() {
  String username=null;
  String password=null;
  try {
    BufferedReader in =
➡ new BufferedReader(new InputStreamReader(System.in));
    System.out.print("Username? ");
    username=in.readLine();
```

11

```
      System.out.print("Password? ");
      password=in.readLine();
    }
    catch (IOException ioe) {
      System.err.println(ioe);
    }
    return new PasswordAuthentication(username,password);
    }
}
```

If you want to read email using the `Authenticator` use the `Store.Connect()` method with no parameters as follows:

```
Store store = session.getStore("pop3");
store.connect();
```

The full version of this example is supplied in the Day 11 example code on the accompanying Web site as the `AuthenticateRetrieveMail.java` program.

The final task in today's study of JavaMail is to look at extending the Agency case study to use JavaMail.

Using JavaMail Within J2EE Components

The only complication to using JavaMail within a J2EE component is the restriction that EJBs should not do direct file or network I/O. An EJB relies on the J2EE container to provide required I/O services through objects registered with the name service. You have already seen this in practice with the use of `DataSource` objects discussed on Day 4, "Introduction to Enterprise JavaBeans."

To support JavaMail, a J2EE container provides support for resource references to `javax.mail.Session` objects. Figure 11.4 shows the Admin Console screen for the J2EE RI with a Mail Session object called `mail/James` representing James email server running on the local workstation.

FIGURE 11.4

Defining a J2EE RI JavaMail Resource.

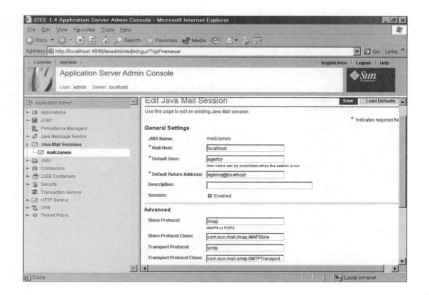

You can create JavaMail resources using the `asadmin` command line interface or the Admin Console. For the Agency case study you can create the JavaMail resources using this `asant` command provided on the Web site:

```
asant create-mail
```

This `asant` target uses asadmin to define the `mail/James` resource.

Using JavaMail requires your EJB code to look up the Session object using JNDI as follows:

```
try {
    javax.mail.Session session = (
➥ javax.mail.Session)ic.lookup("java:comp/env/mail/James"));
}
catch (NamingException ex) { … }
```

Once you have obtained a `Session` object, sending and retrieving email is no different to working with JavaMail from J2SE (as discussed in today's exercise).

The Agency case study in the `Day11/exercise` directory has been augmented to send an email to an applicant whenever an applicant registers with the agency or updates their details. The email includes a list of all matched jobs. To add this extra functionality a new class called `EmailApplicant` has been created to send the email. This new class is shown in Listing 11.10.

11

LISTING **11.10**   EmailApplicant.java Full Listing

```java
package data;

import java.util.*;
import javax.ejb.*;
import java.util.Properties;
import javax.mail.*;
import javax.naming.*;
import javax.mail.internet.*;

public class EmailApplicant  {

    private Set jobs = new HashSet();
    private Session session;

    public EmailApplicant (Session session)  {
        this.session = session;
    }

    public void addJob (JobPK job) {
        jobs.add(job);
    }

    public void newMessage () {
        jobs.clear();
    }

    public void sendMail (String recipient) throws MessagingException {
        System.out.println("emailApplicant: "+recipient+" - "+jobs);
        MimeMessage message = new MimeMessage(session);

        if (jobs.size() == 0)
            message.setText("Sorry, there are no jobs that currently match
➥ your skills and location.\r\n");
        else {
            StringBuffer msg = new StringBuffer();
            msg.append("The following is a list of the jobs that match
➥ your skills and location.\r\n");
            Iterator jobsIter = jobs.iterator();
            while (jobsIter.hasNext()) {
                JobPK job = (JobPK)jobsIter.next();
                msg.append (job.getCustomer() + "/" + job.getRef() + "\r\n");
            }
            message.setText(msg.toString());
        }

        message.setSubject("Email from the Agency Case Study");
        message.setFrom(new InternetAddress("agency@localhost"));
```

LISTING 11.10   continued

```
        message.addRecipient(Message.RecipientType.TO,
➥ new InternetAddress(recipient));

        Transport.send(message);
    }
}
```

The example in Listing 11.10 is given a reference to the Session object when it is constructed and maintains a list of matched jobs for the applicant. When the message is sent the body is simply a list of the matched jobs. The recipient's email address is passed as a parameter to the sendMail() method and the sender's email address is hard coded as agency@localhost.

In Listing 11.10 the sendMail() method throws any JavaMail exceptions back to the caller. This is the correct design approach as it is the responsibility of the caller, rather than EmailApplicant, to handle and possibly recover from exceptions.

The ApplicantMatch MDB has been updated to add jobs to the EmailApplicant object and then call the sendMail() method. The following code shows the changes to ApplicantMatch to send the email:

```
private EmailApplicant emailApplicant;

public void onMessage(Message message) {
...
    try {
...
        emailApplicant.newMessage();
        Collection col = jobHome.findByLocation(location);
        Iterator jobsIter = col.iterator();
        while (jobsIter.hasNext()) {
            JobLocal job = (JobLocal)jobsIter.next();
...
            MatchedPK key = new MatchedPK(login,job.getRef(),job.getCustomer());
            try {
                matchedHome.create(key.getApplicant(),key.getJob(),
➥ key.getCustomer(), exact);
                emailApplicant.addJob(new JobPK(job.getRef(),
➥ job.getCustomer()));
            }
            catch (CreateException ex) {
                System.out.println("ApplicantMatch: failed to create matched
➥ entry: "+key);
            }
        }
        emailApplicant.sendMail(applicant.getEmail());
    catch (javax.mail.MessagingException me) {
```

11

```
            System.err.println("ApplicantMatch: mail error "+me);
        }
    …
    }

    public void setMessageDrivenContext(MessageDrivenContext ctx) {
        this.ctx = ctx;
        InitialContext ic = null;
        try {
            ic = new InitialContext();
    …
        try {
            emailApplicant = new EmailApplicant(
➥ (javax.mail.Session)ic.lookup("java:comp/env/mail/James"));
        }
        catch (NamingException ex) {
            error("Error connecting to java:comp/env/mail/James:",ex);
        }
    }
```

Note that the MessageException object is referenced by its full package name because the javax.mail package is not imported. If the class had imported javax.mail as well as javax.jms there would have been name conflicts for several classes such as Session and Message.

When building the Agency application EAR file the deployment descriptor for the ApplicantMatch class must include a resource reference for the JavaMail Session object. This is shown in the deploytool Resource Refs dialog shown in Figure 11.5.

FIGURE 11.5

Defining a JavaMail Resource Reference.

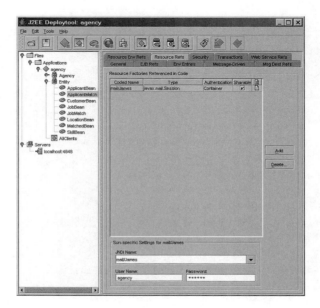

Adding this JavaMail resource adds the following entry to the `ejb-jar.xml` deployment descriptor:

```
<ejb-jar>
  <display-name>Entity</display-name>
  <enterprise-beans>
    <message-driven>
      <ejb-name>ApplicantMatch</ejb-name>
...
      <resource-ref>
        <res-ref-name>mail/James</res-ref-name>
        <res-type>javax.mail.Session</res-type>
        <res-auth>Container</res-auth>
        <res-sharing-scope>Shareable</res-sharing-scope>
      </resource-ref>
    </message-driven>
...
  </enterprise-beans>
...
</ejb-jar>
```

The following Sun-specific entry is added to the `sun-ejb-jar.xml` deployment descriptor to map the resource reference onto the actual resource:

```
<sun-ejb-jar>
  <enterprise-beans>
...
    <ejb>
      <ejb-name>ApplicantMatch</ejb-name>
      <jndi-name>jms/applicantQueue</jndi-name>
      <resource-ref>
        <res-ref-name>mail/James</res-ref-name>
        <jndi-name>mail/James</jndi-name>
        <default-resource-principal>
          <name>agency</name>
          <password>agency</password>
        </default-resource-principal>
      </resource-ref>
...
    </ejb>
  </enterprise-beans>
</sun-ejb-jar>
```

To deploy and run this example enter the following command from within the `Day11/exercise` directory:

```
asant build deploy run
```

Make sure you are running the James email server on the local workstation before running the following test. Remember that matching applicants to jobs requires that the applicant's location match the job's location and there must be at least one skill match.

To test this example, log in as the applicant juliet and add the critic skill; her skills will now partly match the Cigar Maker job advertised by winston (assuming the sample data has not been changed during previous exercises). When you click on the Update button a new message is sent to the ApplicantMatch MDB, which in turn will generate an email to send to juliet.

The Agency case study as it stands is incomplete, as it does not email customers when new applicants match advertised jobs. Adding this functionality is an optional part of today's exercise.

Summary

In today's lesson, you were introduced to common email protocols and the main packages and classes of JavaMail API. Building on this, you saw how to write code that performed a number of day-to-day email tasks, such as sending, retrieving and deleting messages, authenticating users, and sending and retrieving attachments. Finally you studied adding JavaMail resource references to J2EE components for accessing a JavaMail Session object inside the J2EE environment.

Q&A

Q What is the process of receiving email messages and what are the common email retrieval protocols?

A When a mail server receives a message, it places it within the recipient's mailbox. The recipient then connects to the mail server and downloads the message to his or her local machine. The sequence of exchanges between the recipient's machine and the mail server use a retrieval protocol, such as POP3 or IMAP.

Q Why do you need to use the javax.mail.Message class's inner class RecipientType when adding a recipient to a message?

A There are three types of recipient, TO, CC, and BCC, so you must stipulate the type of recipient you want to add to a message. The RecipientType class exposes three static fields that represent the three types of recipients.

Q How do you use the JavaMail API to create an HTML message that includes an embedded image?

A You must create a MimeMultiPart message, with separate MimeBodyPart constituents containing the HTML text and the embedded image.

Q **You have written an application that checks whether messages are flagged as RECENT. If they are, the application retrieves them from the server. Why might the application not retrieve any messages from the POP3 server?**

A The JavaMail API provides a selection of predefined message flags, but there is no guarantee that a mail server will support all these flags. Typically, in the case of a POP3 server, only the DELETED flag is supported, so in this instance, the application will not find any messages marked as RECENT, and thus will not return any messages. Of course, you may not have been sent any new messages!

Exercise

Today's exercise is to add additional email functionality to the Agency case study. In the exercise directory under Day 11 on the accompanying Web site there is a version of the Agency case study that sends emails to applicants whenever they register or change their details. This extra functionality has been added to the JobMatch MDB and is implemented by the EmailApplicant class.

Using the code in the exercise directory as a starting point, your task today is to add functionality to the ApplicantMatch MDB to send email to all customers when a new applicant registers or changes their details. Use the existing code in the JobMatch class as a guide to adding your new functionality. You will find it convenient to either modify the EmailApplicant class to maintain applicant as well as job details, or to simply create a new EmailCustomer class based on the functionality of the EmailApplicant class.

A complete solution can be found in the agency directory under Day 11 on the accompanying Web site. The solution includes a separate EmailCustomer class for managing matched jobs.

The solution provided for the Agency case study is incomplete, as it does not email customers when new applicant details match advertised jobs, nor does it email applicants when new job details match their details. Adding this functionality is left as optional exercise as no solution is provided.

11

DAY **12**

Servlets

On Day 11, "JavaMail," you worked on integrating JavaMail into your applications. This built on the previous chapters that covered the Java Message System and Message-Driven Beans, and you have now completed this book's coverage of asynchronous messaging in J2EE.

Today, you will start to work on the new topic area—providing a Web interface to your application. You will start by using Java servlets with a Web server to handle HTTP requests. These servlets will generate HTML responses to be displayed by using a browser. In today's lesson, you will study

- The power of Java servlets and when to use them
- The supporting technologies, namely HTTP and HTML
- How to create and track HTTP sessions
- How to develop a Web application using servlets, with servlet filtering and event listening

The Purpose and Use of Servlets

A servlet is a server-side component. It can be used to extend the functionality of any Java-enabled server, but most commonly servlets are used to write Web applications in a Web server, as shown in Figure 12.1. They are used to create Web pages where the content is not static. Web pages whose content can change according to input from the user or other variable data are called *dynamic pages*. Servlets are only one way to create dynamic Web pages; you will see another in Day 13, "JavaServer Pages."

FIGURE 12.1

Client/server diagram showing servlets.

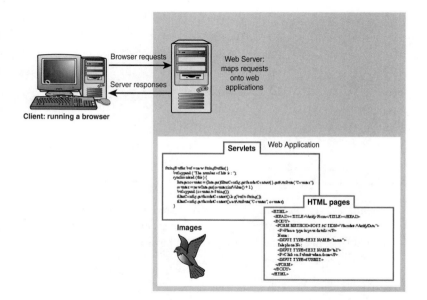

The following are the key features and benefits of Java servlets:

- The servlet API provides an interface that is tailored for Web applications.
- Servlets are server and platform independent. This makes servlets portable and reusable.
- Servlets are efficient and scalable.
- Servlets run within the server, so they can delegate certain functions to be performed by the server on their behalf, such as user authentication.

A servlet is an instance of a class that implements the javax.servlet.Servlet interface. However, most servlets extend one of the implementations of this interface—javax.servlet.GenericServlet or javax.servlet.http.HttpServlet.

The `Servlet` interface declares methods that manage the servlet and its communications with clients. As the servlet developer, you override some or all of these methods to develop your servlet.

Generic servlets have a limited use, so in today's lesson, we will only discuss the more useful `HttpServlet` class. This is an abstract class that is sub-classed to create an HTTP servlet suitable for a Web site. To accomplish this, an HTTP servlet has access to a library of HTTP-specific calls.

Servlets have no client interface. That means they avoid most of the portability issues associated with different display interfaces. An application on the client (typically a browser) takes care of the user interface on behalf of the servlet.

NOTE   Although the browser provides the user interface there may still be portability issues regarding the version of HTML generated by the servlet and which versions are supported by the various browsers. Also, any use of cascading style sheets have portability issues regarding browser support.

After being loaded, a servlet will generally stay resident in the server's memory. In most circumstances, only a single servlet object will be created, and to support concurrent page accesses this servlet is run multithreaded. This avoids the overhead of constructing a new servlet process for every access, saves memory, and makes page access efficient.

For example, if your database server includes sufficient simultaneous connection licenses, a database connection can be shared between threads, thereby reducing the overhead associated with establishing and maintaining the connection.

12

CAUTION   Multithreading aids efficiency and scalability, but the servlet code must be written to be re-entrant. This means that the servlet must handle concurrent access to instance data, and care must be taken to synchronize write access to shared resources.

Because a servlet is tightly integrated with the server, it can utilize capabilities of the server to perform certain actions. It can, for example, use the server's logging capabilities and get the server to authenticate users.

Introduction to HTTP

Before looking at Java servlets in more detail, you will need an understanding of the Web protocol, HTTP (Hypertext Transfer Protocol), and how a browser interprets HTML (Hypertext Markup Language) to display a Web page. If you are comfortable with these topics, feel free to skip to the next section, titled "The Servlet Environment."

HTTP is a protocol standard specified by the Internet Engineering Task force, and its current version is available as RFC 2616 available from `http://www.ietf.org/rfc.html`.

HTTP Request Structure

HTTP is a stateless protocol, and this has the advantage that the server does not have the overhead of tracking client connections. This was completely satisfactory when the primary use of the Web was to transfer static data. Realistically, most dynamic Web applications now require interaction between the client and the server, and information about the client state must be retained between page requests. Later, you will learn how a servlet can overcome the stateless nature of the HTTP protocol by tracking client state using session information stored in the URL, hidden fields or cookies.

HTTP transactions are either a request or a response. Regardless of which type they are, all HTTP transactions have three parts:

- A single request or response line—A client request line consists of an HTTP method (usually `GET` or `POST`) followed by a document address and the HTTP version number being used. For example,

  ```
  GET /contents.html HTTP/1.1
  ```

  uses the HTTP `GET` method to request the document `contents.html` using HTTP version 1.1. The response line contains an HTTP status code that indicates whether the request was successful (understood and satisfied) or if not, why not.

- The HTTP headers—A set of fields used to exchange information between the client and the server. For example, the following tells the server that the client will accept the IOS8859.5 and unicode1.1 character sets:

  ```
  Accept-Charset: iso-8859-5, unicode-1-1
  ```

  The client uses the headers to tell the server about its configuration and the document types it will accept. The server, in turn, uses the header to return information about the requested document, such as its age and location.

- The HTTP body—The HTTP body is optionally used by the client to send any additional information (see `POST` method). The server uses the body to return the requested document.

Listing 12.1 shows a sample GET request. A GET request does not have a body, so this example only contains the request line and headers.

LISTING 12.1   An Example HTTP GET Request

```
GET /some/url.html HTTP/1.1
Accept: image/gif, image/x-xbitmap, image/jpeg,
➥ image/pjpeg,application/vnd.ms-excel, application/msword,
➥ application/vnd.ms-powerpoint, */*
Referer: http://www.somewhere.com/search?sourceid=navclient&q=http+request+
Accept-Language: en-gb
Accept-Encoding: gzip
User-Agent: Mozilla/4.0 (compatible; MSIE 6.0; Windows NT 5.0)
Host: localhost:8000
Connection: Keep-Alive
```

Uniform Resource Identifiers (URIs)

The term Universal Resource Locator (URL) is a well-known term used to identify a resource (such as an electronic document, an image or a mailbox) by its location and the protocol used to access it. A resource could also be accessed by its name and this time a Universal Resource Name (URN) would be used to identify the resource. (In theory, but as yet a method of providing a universal namespace has not been achieved.) Both URLs and URNs are subclasses of Universal Resource Identifiers (URIs).

> **NOTE**   A URL is therefore also a URI and, as URNs are not commonly used, you will often see the two terms used synonymously.

12

Using a simple syntax, URIs make use of a variety of naming schemes and access methods, such as HTTP, FTP, and Internet mail to identify online resources.

The syntax of an HTTP URL is as follows:

```
http_URL = "http://" host [ ":" port] [ path ]
```

where

- host is a legal Internet host domain name or IP address (in dotted-decimal form).
- port is the port number (also known as the socket or service number) to connect to on the host. The default port number for HTTP is 80.
- path is the path to the document on the host.

The term URL is used more often than URI when referring to the HTTP address string and, for this reason, URL is the term that will be used for the rest of today's material.

NOTE   Space characters should be avoided in URL's because they may not be handled correctly on all platforms.

HTTP GET and POST Methods

A Web browser client communicates with the server typically using one of two HTTP methods—GET or POST. Typically, these methods are used as follows:

- GET is used to request information from the server.
- POST is used to send data to the server.

But as with many things, it is not quite that simple. The GET method can also be used to pass information in the form of a query string in the URL, and POST can be used for requests.

The following URL with a query string (the data following the ?) is passed by the GET method and sets a parameter called day to the value 12 (you will learn more about parameters later when you code some real servlets).

```
http://localhost:8000/j2ee?day=12
```

Because the query string is added to the end of the URL, information that is sent as part of a GET request is visible to the client and can be bookmarked and therefore re-run later. You will have seen examples of this many times when browsing the Web, especially when using search engines.

In contrast, the POST method sends its data directly after the HTTP header, in the body of the message, and does not append data to the URL (so even if you bookmark the page the data is not available later). A browser or server is only required to handle GET request lines of 255 characters; therefore, when sending large amounts of information (such as a complex HTML form) the POST request should be used.

In most other respects, the GET and POST methods can be thought of as the same. They both interact with the server and can be used to update or change the current Web page and change server-side properties. As a developer you usually code up your servlets to handle both GET and POST requests.

Other HTTP Methods

The following HTTP methods are used less often, but are covered here for completeness.

- HEAD   This method can be used if the client wants information about a document but does not want the document to be returned. Following a HEAD request, the server responds with the HTTP headers only; no HTTP body is sent.
- PUT   Requests the server to store the body of the request at a specified URL.
- DELETE   Requests the removal of data at a URL.
- OPTIONS   Requests information about the communications options available.
- TRACE   Used for debugging. The HTTP body is simply returned by the server.

HTTP Response Structure

After processing a request an HTTP server sends back an HTTP response to the client. The response has a single response line indicating the status of the response followed by optional header lines and the requested resource. The header will look something like Listing 12.2.

LISTING 12.2   HTTP Response Header

```
HTTP/1.1 200 OK
Date: Tue, 20 Nov 2001 09:23:44 GMT
Server: Netscape-Enterprise/3.5.1G
Last-modified: Mon, 12 Nov 2001 15:31:26 GMT
Content-type: text/html
Content-length: 2048
Page-Completion-Status: Normal
```

12

The server sends back a status code as part of the first line of the response followed by header-fields describing the document. A blank line separates the header from the document itself.

Most of the time, the status code is handled by the browser, but you will be familiar with one or two that are reported to the end user. In particular, you will have no doubt seen the ubiquitous 404 Not Found error that is sent when the server was unable to find the requested URL.

To aid in coding (and debugging) your servlets, it is useful to have a knowledge of the HTTP status codes. Status codes are grouped as shown in Table 12.1.

TABLE 12.1   HTTP Status Code Groups

Code	Description
100-199	Information indicating that the request has been received and is being processed.
200-299	Request was successful.
300-399	Further action is required.
400-499	Request is incomplete.
500-599	Server error has occurred.

The handling of status codes is browser specific, but some status codes you may see include those shown in Table 12.2.

TABLE 12.2   HTTP Status Codes

Code	Error	Description
400	Bad Request	The server detected a syntax error in the request.
401	Unauthorized	The request did not have the correct authorization.
403	Forbidden	The request was denied, reason unknown.
404	Not Found	The document was not found.
500	Internal Server Error	Usually indicates that part of the server (probably your servlet) has crashed.
501	Not Implemented	The server cannot perform the requested action.

As a servlet writer, most of these errors are outside of your control. A 501 error however is generated by the server when a servlet is sent an HTTP request that it does not handle. For example, if you write your servlet to handle only GET requests, but it receives a POST request, a 501 status will be returned.

As part of the response headers, a content type field is used to indicate the format of the data that is being sent in the response. The value for this field is in the Multipurpose Internet Mail Extensions (MIME) type—also used to describe the contents of an email.

NOTE | You can also find out more about MIME by reading RFCs 2045 through to 2049, which you can access at http://www.ietf.org/rfc.html.

Some self-explanatory MIME content types are as follows:

- `text/html`
- `text/plain`
- `image/gif`
- `application/pdf`

The browser can also specify in the request header the MIME types that it will accept.

Introduction to HTML

HTML is the language of the Web. It is used to encode embedded directions (tags) that indicate to a Web browser how to display the contents of a document.

The HTML standard is under the authority of the World Wide Web Consortium. Browser developers have implemented HTML differently, according to their whim, and have added their own proprietary HTML extensions (to the point that different versions of the same browser may handle the same HTML tag differently).

TIP

> In your servlet code, you are advised to restrict the use of HTML to well-established tags and features. All the HTML covered here will work in all the popular browsers.

An HTML document has a well-defined structure consisting of required and optional HTML elements.

An HTML element consists of a tag name followed by an optional list of attributes all enclosed in angle brackets (`<...>`). Tag names and attributes are not case sensitive and cannot contain a space, tab, or return character. Most HTML tags come in pairs—a start tag and an end tag. The end tag is the same as the start tag but has a forward slash character preceding the tag name. For example, an HTML document begins with `<HTML>` and ends with `</HTML>`.

Tags are nested. This means that you must end the most recent tag before ending a preceding one. Apart from this restriction, the actual layout is a completely free format. An indented layout can be used to aid readability but is not required.

Each HTML document has an optional HEAD and a BODY. The HEAD is where you pass information to the browser about the document; text in the header is not displayed as the content of the document. The BODY includes the information (tags and text) that defines

12

the document's content. A well-formed (if a little basic) HTML document is shown in Listing 12.3, the output displayed in Microsoft's Internet Explorer is shown in Figure 12.2.

LISTING 12.3   `SimpleHTMLPage.html` Web Page

```
<HTML>
 <HEAD>
  <TITLE>My Very First HTML Document</TITLE>
 </HEAD>
 <BODY>
  <H1>Here is a H1 header</H1>
  <P>and here is some text - hopefully it looks different from the header</P>
 </BODY>
</HTML>
```

FIGURE 12.2

Screen shot of a simple HTML page.

All tags have a name, and some tags may also have one or more attributes that are used to add extra information. Modern design style is to always enclose attribute values in single or double quotes as this reflects the requirements of XML documents (see Day 16, "Integrating XML with J2EE"). Unlike XML HTML allows simple attribute values (those not containing spaces or other special characters) to be specified unquoted.

A little confusingly, a few common HTML tags do not normally come in pairs because the end tag can be omitted. These include <IMG>, which inserts a graphic image, and <BR>, which causes a line break.

Table 12.3 shows a list of HTML tags and attributes that can be used to format a simple HTML document. Only tags from this list are used in today's lesson. This is not a full list of HTML tags, nor does it show any attributes to the tags. For a definitive list, see the latest HTML specification available from www.w3.org.

TABLE 12.3 Summary of Common HTML Tags

TAG	Description
`<A>`	Create a hyperlink (HREF attribute).
`<BIG>`	Format the text in a bigger typeface.
`<BODY>`	Enclose the body of the HTML document.
` `	Start a new row of text.
`<BUTTON>`	Create a button element within a `<FORM>`
`<FORM>`	Delimit a form. This is used to send user input.
`<Hn>`	Header text, where n is a number between 1 and 6.
`<HEAD>`	Encloses the document head.
`<HTML>`	Used to delimit the entire HTML document.
`<IMG>`	Insert an image.
`<INPUT>`	Create buttons or other elements in a `<FORM>` used to pass information to the server.
`<LINK>`	Used to link an HTML page with a stylesheet.
`<OPTION>`	Define a single option within a `<SELECT>` list, see `<SELECT>`.
`<P>`	Start a new paragraph.
`<SELECT>`	Start the list of `<OPTION>` elements for a multiple-choice menu.
`<TABLE>`	Place text in table format.
`<TD>`	Define the contents of a data cell in a `<TABLE>`.
`<TH>`	Define the contents of a header cell in a `<TABLE>`.
`<TR>`	Define a row of cells within a `<TABLE>`.
`<!-- -->`	Enclose a comment.

12

Listing 12.4 is an HTML document that illustrates the use of some of these tags. It contains an input form with a button and outputs data in the form of a table.

LISTING 12.4 SimpleHTMLForm.html Web Form

```html
<HTML>
  <HEAD>
    <TITLE>Simple HTML Form</TITLE>
    <LINK rel="stylesheet" type="text/css" href="examples.css">
  </HEAD>
  <BODY>
    <H1>Colour Selector</H1>
    <FORM METHOD="GET" ACTION="verifydata">
```

LISTING 12.4 continued

```
<P>Please Type in your name here:</P>
<INPUT TYPE="text" NAME="name">
<P>Now select the color of your choice</P>
<SELECT NAME="color" SIZE="1">
  <OPTION>red<OPTION>green<OPTION>blue</SELECT>
<BR></BR>
<INPUT TYPE="SUBMIT">
<BR></BR>
<TABLE>
  <TR>
    <TH>Color</TH><TH>Description</TH>
  </TR>
  <TR>
    <TD CLASS="red">red</TD><TD>Will bring excitement into your life</TD>
  </TR>
  <TR>
    <TD CLASS="green">green</TD><TD>Will bring you life giving energy</TD>
  </TR>
  <TR>
    <TD CLASS="blue">blue</TD><TD>Will bring peace to your world</TD>
  </TR>
</TABLE>
</FORM>
</BODY>
</HTML>
```

> **NOTE**
>
> Many of the examples in this and subsequent chapters use a `<LINK>` element to associate the Web page with a cascading stylesheet (CSS) to define formatting requirement. In theory different browsers should display Web pages formatted using a stylesheet in the same manner but typically there are minor differences. You do not need to know how stylesheets work in order to understand the basic principles of J2EE Web components, such as servlets, so no detailed discussion of them is included here.

The output of the page in Listing 12.4 from Microsoft's Internet Explorer version 6 is shown in Figure 12.3. The page will look similar, but not necessarily exactly the same, in other browsers.

This completes the brief discussion of HTML; access the latest standard and other documents on the WC3 Web site (`http://www.w3.org`) for more information on the standard.

FIGURE 12.3

Sample HTML page displayed using Microsoft's Internet Explorer version 6.

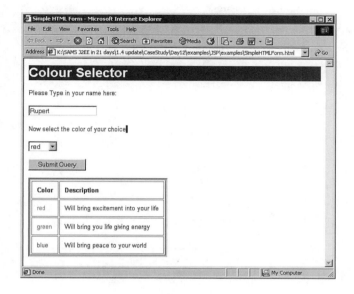

The Servlet Environment

Servlets are Java classes that can be loaded dynamically and run by a Java-enabled Web server. The Web server provides support for servlets with extensions called servlet containers (also known as servlet engines).

Web clients (Web browsers) interact with the servlet using the HTTP request/response protocol that was described earlier.

Servlet Containers

The servlet container provides the following services and functionality:

- The network services over which the requests and responses are sent.
- Registers the servlet against one or more URLs.
- Manages the servlet lifecycle.
- Decodes MIME-based requests.
- Constructs MIME-based responses.
- Supports the HTTP protocol (it can also support other protocols).

A servlet container can also enforce security restrictions on the environment, such as requesting the user to log in to access a Web page.

12

The Servlet Class Hierarchy

The Servlet API specification is produced by Sun Microsystems Inc., and a copy of the latest specification can be downloaded from http://java.sun.com/products/servlet/.

An HTTP servlet extends the javax.servlet.HttpServlet class, which itself extends javax.servlet.GenericServlet, as shown in Figure 12.4.

FIGURE 12.4

Servlet class hierarchy diagram.

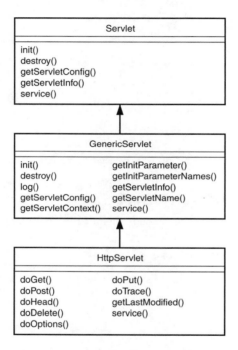

Simple Servlet Example

In Listing 12.5, you will generate a complete HTML page that displays a simple text string. This servlet extends the javax.servlet.http.HttpServlet class and overrides the HttpServlet.doGet() method.

LISTING 12.5 HTMLPage Servlet

```
import java.io.*;
import javax.servlet.*;
import javax.servlet.http.*;

public class HTMLPage extends HttpServlet {
  public void doGet(HttpServletRequest req, HttpServletResponse res)
```

LISTING 12.5   continued

```
    throws IOException {
      res.setContentType ("text/html");  // the content's MIME type
      PrintWriter out = res.getWriter();  // access the output stream
      out.println ("<HTML>");
      out.println ("<HEAD><TITLE>First Servlet</TITLE></HEAD>");
      out.println ("<BODY>");
      out.println ("<H1>My First Servlet Generated HTML Page</H1>");
      out.println ("</BODY>");
      out.println ("</HTML>");
    }
  }
```

When the client browser sends the GET request for this servlet, the server invokes your doGet() method, passing it the HTTP request in the HttpServletRequest object. The response is sent back to the client in the HttpServletResponse object.

The HttpServletRequest interface provides access to information about the request, and its main use is to give access to parameters passed in the URL query string. For this simple example, the request object does not contain any useful information, so it is not accessed in this servlet. You will see how to use the HttpServletRequest object in later examples.

The HttpServletResponse object is used to return data to the client. For this simple example, the data content type is sent as the MIME type text/html. The PrintWriter object encodes the data that is sent to the client.

NOTE

A call to the setContentType() method should always be made before obtaining a PrintWriter object.

12

The out.println statements in Listing 12.5 generate the HTML that the browser will use to display the page.

In order to deploy your simple servlet, you must create a Web Application containing the servlet and store this in a Web Archive (WAR) file ready for deployment to a J2EE server. The following description takes you through the process of creating a Web Application using the deploytool provided with the J2EE RI.

If you do not want to create the Web Application, you can use deploytool to open the example supplied on the accompanying Web site as Day12/examples/j2ee-ri/examples.war and study the HTMLPage Web Component.

After compiling the code, start up the J2EE RI and run deploytool. You will now perform the following steps to deploy the servlet.

1. From the File menu, select New, Web Component. This will bring up the New Web Application Wizard. The first page of the wizard displays simple help information that can be suppressed by the checking the box at the bottom of the page. Click on Next to select the WAR File page.

2. On the WAR File page, select Create New Stand-Alone WAR Module in the WAR Location section. Under WAR Naming, select a location and filename for the WAR file. The location can be anywhere, but the code on the accompanying Web site uses a separate directory called j2ee-ri for storing EAR and WAR files but you must call the WAR file examples.war. Fill in examples as the WAR Name and set the Context root (Sun-specific Setting) to examples.

CAUTION

It is important that you keep the filename of the WAR file and the Web application context root consistent. If you deploy the application using the asadmin command (or the asant deploy-examples-j2ee-ri command), then the J2EE RI uses the name of the WAR file as the context root rather than the value supplied in the deployment descriptor. As long as you keep the WAR filename and context root consistent you will be fine. In this example the context root will be set to examples and the WAR filename to examples.war.

Click the Edit button and add the **HTMLPage** class file from the Day12/ examples/classes directory; deploytool will put the class file in a WEB-INF directory (why is explained later) as shown in Figure 12.5.

3. On the next page, choose Servlet as the Web component type, as shown in Figure 12.6.

4. On the next page, select **HTMLPage** as the Servlet Class (see Figure 12.7). Accept the defaults for the remaining fields on this screen.

5. The next page of the wizard simply reminds you of the common steps needed to complete your Web Component. Select Finish after viewing this page.

6. You will now add a *component alias* for your servlet. Click on your HTMLPage Web component in the left panel of deploytool. Select the Aliases tab in the right panel. Click on Add. Type **/htmlpage**, as shown in Figure 12.8.

FIGURE 12.5

deploytool *adding the class file.*

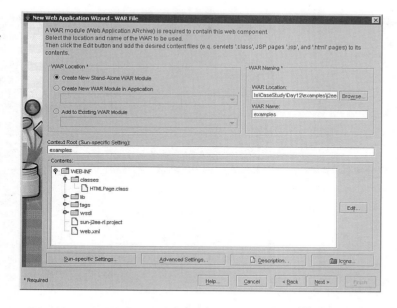

FIGURE 12.6

deploytool *Choose Component Type page.*

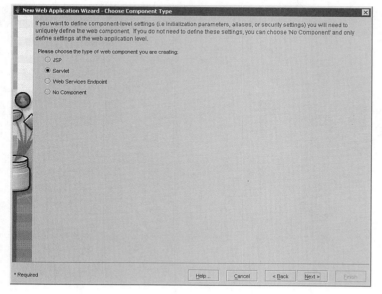

12

FIGURE 12.7

deploytool
*Component General
Properties page.*

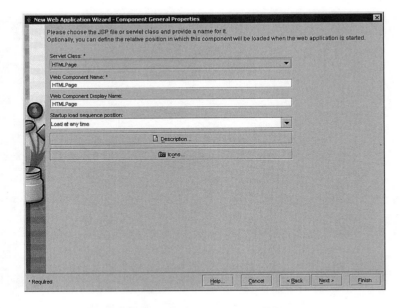

FIGURE 12.8

deploytool *Aliases
page.*

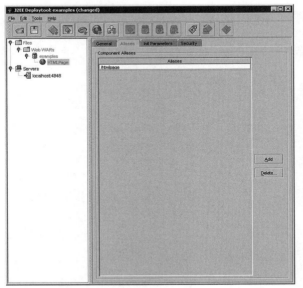

> **NOTE**
>
> The context root and component alias are used in the URL to locate your servlet as follows:
>
> ```
> http://<Web server address>/<Context root>/<Component alias>
> ```
>
> For this example you will browse to `http://localhost:8000/examples/htmlpage`

7. As always, select the Tools, Verify J2EE Compliance menu to check the application; you will need to select the examples WAR file in the left hand pane to enable the Verify menu option. If all is OK, select Tools, Deploy to deploy your Web Application. You will be prompted to provide the administrative username and password before the deployment can proceed.

> **NOTE**
>
> If you are using the asant build files supplied with the case study you can use the command
>
> ```
> asant deploy-examples-j2ee-ri
> ```
>
> to deploy the WAR file you have created in the `j2ee-ri` sub-directory. Alternatively you could use the command
>
> ```
> asant build deploy
> ```
>
> to create and deploy the WAR file from source files. This creates the `examples.war` file in the `build` sub-directory.

Now, start up a Web browser. First, type in the URL for the J2EE Web server (`http://localhost:8000`) and check that the server is up and running (see Figure 12.09).

> **NOTE**
>
> If you installed the J2EE RI with a Web server (HTTP) port other than 8000, then substitute your HTTP port number in this and all other browser URLs. For example, if you configured 1024 as the HTTP port number, then use the URL `http://localhost:1024`.

12

FIGURE 12.9

J2EE 1.4 server page.

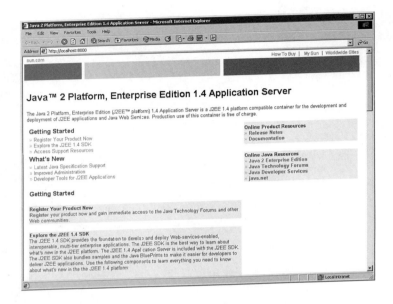

Now access your servlet using the following URL (see Figure 12.10):

`http://localhost:8000/examples/htmlpage`

FIGURE 12.10

HTMLPage *servlet.*

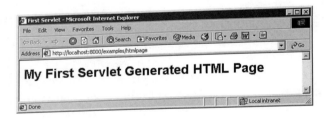

Congratulations, you have just written and deployed your first servlet.

Passing Parameter Data to a Servlet

Your first servlet, although it shows the principle of servlets, was not actually a very good servlet example. As you have probably realized, it could have been written as a static HTML page and you could have avoided all the complication of having to write and compile a servlet. The next example will show the power of servlets.

LISTING 12.7 continued

```
<servlet>
  <servlet-name>VerifyData</servlet-name>
  <servlet-class>VerifyData</servlet-class>
</servlet>
<servlet>
  <servlet-name>HTMLPage</servlet-name>
  <servlet-class>HTMLPage</servlet-class>
</servlet>
<servlet-mapping>
  <servlet-name>VerifyData</servlet-name>
  <url-pattern>/verifydata</url-pattern>
</servlet-mapping>
</servlet-mapping>
<servlet-mapping>
  <servlet-name>HTMLPage</servlet-name>
  <url-pattern>/htmlpage</url-pattern>
</servlet-mapping>
<session-config>
  <session-timeout>30</session-timeout>
</session-config>
<welcome-file-list>
  <welcome-file>index.html</welcome-file>
</welcome-file-list>
<error-page>
  <error-code>404</error-code>
  <location>/error404.html</location>
</error-page>
<jsp-config/>
</Web-app>
```

Table 12.4 contains a short description of the tags used in this deployment descriptor; see the servlet specification for a more complete list.

TABLE 12.4 XML Tags Used in Listing 12.8

XML Tag	Description
Web-app	Root for the deployment descriptor.
display-name	Short name for application, need not be unique.
servlet-name	The official name of the servlet, must be unique.
servlet-class	The servlet's fully-qualified classname.
init-param	Initialization parameters available to the servlet. This is followed by name/value pairs of parameters.
param-name	The name of the parameter.
param-value	The value for the parameter.

12

TABLE 12.4 continued

XML Tag	Description
servlet-mapping	Used to map a servlet to a URL.
url-pattern	Patterns that will map onto this servlet.
session-config	Defines timeout behavior for sessions.
welcome-file-list	Defines a list of files that will be displayed if the user supplied URL denotes a directory rather than an explicit file.
error-page	Used to map an HTTP error status code onto a Web resource, such as an HTML page, that will be displayed instead of the standard browser error pages (see the "Handling Errors" section later in the chapter).

If you use the J2EE RI, the deployment descriptor is created for you. If you are using other Web servers, you may need to manually create the XML for the deployment descriptor.

To be validated, the deployment descriptor requires an XML schema or a Document Type Definition (DTD) file. The XML Schema (or DTD) contains the rules for processing the deployment descriptor and is fully described in the servlet specification.

If you are writing your own deployment descriptor, you will need to follow the XML Schema rules to ensure that it is valid; otherwise, your application will not deploy.

Handling Errors

There are a number of possible error or failure conditions that need to be handled by your servlet. These errors fall into the following two categories:

- HTTP errors
- Servlet exceptions

HTTP Errors

A way of handling HTTP errors in the deployment descriptor has already been briefly mentioned. By using the XML error-page tag, you can ensure that the client is sent an application-specific page when an error occurs. You can use this page to send appropriate information in response to any HTTP error code. The following, for example, replaces the standard HTTP "404 Not found" error page with one that was written for this application:

```
<error-page>
 <error-code>404</error-code>
 <location>/examples/error404.html</location>
</error-page>
```

If the user tries to access a page that is not found on the server, the /examples/ error404.html page will be returned to the client. Using the J2EE RI, this error page redirection can be included in the deployment descriptor by adding an Error Mapping entry to the File Refs tab for your application (see Figure 12.14). Figure 12.14 also shows how to add index.html as a welcome page for your Web application.

FIGURE 12.14

deploytool *File Refs tab.*

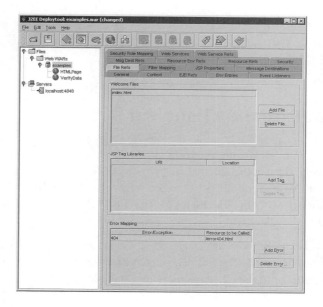

Generating HTTP Status Codes

There may be times when it is useful for the servlet to generate its own HTTP status codes. In an error situation, the servlet can use either of the following methods to set the HTTP status code:

```
public void HttpServletResponse.sendError(int sc)
public void HttpServletResponse.sendError(int sc, String msg)
```

The API defines a set of constants that can be used to refer to HTTP status codes. For example, the error status returned can be set to 404, as in the following:

```
res.sendError(res.SC_NOT_FOUND);
```

This will he handled by the server and browser in exactly the same way as any "404 Not found" error, including using any error-page redirection specified in the deployment descriptor.

Send Redirect

Another useful thing a servlet can do if an error is detected is to redirect the client to another URL. This can also be used in obsolete servlets to redirect the client seamlessly to a new application.

Use `HttpServletResponse.sendRedirect(String location)` to redirect the response to the specified location.

The following will redirect the client to another page called `"/examples/AnotherHTMLPage"`.

```
res.sendRedirect("/examples/AnotherHTMLPage");
```

Servlet Exception Handling

In general, you should take care to catch all servlet-generated exceptions in the servlet and take appropriate action to inform the client what has happened. If you don't, instead of the expected page, the user is likely to see an error page generated by the servlet container. In the case of the J2EE RI the server generated error is a Java exception stack trace. Although you may find the information useful during development, this sort of page sent to the client will leave most users bewildered and worried.

When a fatal exception occurs, there is often nothing to do but tell the client that a serious error has occurred. The following catch block simply returns an HTTP 503 Service Unavailable error to the client, along with a suitable error message:

```
catch (RemoteException ex) {
  res.sendError(res.SC_SERVICE_UNAVAILABLE, "Internal communication error");
}
```

In other situations, it might be appropriate to redirect the user to another URL that has a form that the user can use to report the error:

```
catch (RemoteException ex) {
  res.sendRedirect("/examples/ReportErrorPage");
}
```

A servlet can throw a number of exceptions that will be handled by the server. During initialization or while handling requests, the servlet instance can throw an `UnavailableException` or a `ServletException`. If this happens, the action taken by the server is implementation specific, but it is likely to return a 500 series HTTP response to the client. In this case, you can still use the `error-page` tag in the `Web.xml` file to send the client an appropriate message when the server handles the exception.

Retaining Client and State Information

All but very simple Web applications are likely to require that information of some kind about the client be retained between different page requests. As has been stated, HTTP is stateless and does not provide a mechanism to ascertain that a series of requests have come from the same client.

There are a number of ways of retaining information about clients, such as hidden fields, cookies, and sessions (all described in this section). HTTP sessions are by far the simplest to use and are the recommended approach for Web Applications. Other techniques such as using HTTP cookies or hidden form fields belong to older, non servlet, technologies such as CGI scripts.

Using Session Objects

Sessions identify page requests that originate from the same browser during a specified period of time. Conveniently, a session is shared by all the servlets in an application accessed by an individual client. Servlet containers can implement sessions using one of three techniques:

- Cookies   The server sends a cookie called JSESSIONID with the HTTP response. If the browser disables cookies, then servlet URL Rewriting must be used (see section "URL Rewriting").

- SSL   Secure Sockets Layer has a built-in mechanism allowing multiple requests from a client to be unambiguously identified as being part of a session.

- URL Rewriting   Appends extra information to a URL to identify the session (see section "URL Rewriting").

Regardless of the session tracking technique used, the `javax.servlet.http.` `HttpSession` object identifies a session and is obtained using the `HttpServletRequest.` `getSession()` method. The `HttpSession` object contains the information shown in Table 12.5. This information can be used to identify the session.

TABLE 12.5   Information Accessed Through `HttpSession` Objects

Access Method	Information
`getId()`	Unique session identifier
`getLastAccessedTime()`	The last time the client sent a request associated with this session
`getCreationTime()`	The time when this session was created
`getMaxInactiveInterval()`	The maximum time interval, in seconds, that the servlet container will keep this session open between client accesses

12

TABLE 12.5 continued

Access Method	Information
getAttribute()	Objects bound to this session
setAttribute()	Binds new objects to this session
invalidate()	Invalidates the session allowing the Servlet container to reclaim resources allocated to the session.

Behind the scenes, most Web servers implement session tracking using cookies. Information is stored in the cookie to associate a session identifier with a user. The explicit use of cookies to do the same thing is described later in this section.

Creating a Session

To create a session, the servlet must first get a HttpSession object for a user. The HttpServletRequest.getSession() method returns a user's current session. If there is no current session, it will create one before returning it.

You must call getSession() before any output is written to the response (that is, before accessing the PrintWriter, not just before sending any HTML or other data to the client), otherwise the cookie identifying the session may not be sent back to the client.

You can use HttpSession.isNew() to determine if a session has been created. The following shows the use of getSession() to return an HttpSession object:

```
public void doGet (HttpServletRequest req, HttpServletResponse res)
        throws ServletException, IOException {
  HttpSession session = req.getSession();
  out = res.getWriter();
  if (session.isNew()) {
   /* new session created ok */
  }
}
```

After a session is created, you can start associating objects with the session. The following code could be used in a shopping cart application. It checks to see if the user already has a shopping cart in this session. If no cart exists, one is created.

```
HttpSession session = request.getSession();
ShoppingCart cart = (ShoppingCart)session.getAttribute("candystore.cart");
if (cart == null) {
  cart = new ShoppingCart();
  session.setAttribute("candystore.cart", cart);
}
```

Invalidating a Session

A session can either be manually invalidated or allowed to timeout. The default timeout period is defined in the Web.xml deployment descriptor or through the administrative interface to the Web server. A servlet can control the period of time between client requests, before the servlet container will invalidate this session, with HttpSession.setMaxInactiveInterval(int seconds). Setting a negative time ensures the session will never timeout.

A call to the HttpSession.invalidate() method also invalidates a session and unbinds any objects bound to it. This is a useful thing to do if the user logs out of your application.

Hidden Form Fields

Another way of supporting session tracking is to use hidden form fields. These fields on an HTML page are not seen by the user. To the server, there is no difference between a hidden field and a non-hidden field, but in the browser, hidden fields are not displayed.

The following is an example of a hidden field that could be used to record that the user had read the terms and conditions:

```
<INPUT TYPE="hidden" NAME="terms" VALUE="true">
```

Hidden fields have several disadvantages over HTTP sessions:

- They only work for a sequence of dynamically generated forms.
- They fail if there is an error before the data is permanently stored somewhere.
- They may be modified by rogue users attempting to hack into your application.
- They may expose sensitive or confidential data to other users of the client workstation.

CAUTION

The user can modify the values stored in hidden fields, so they are not secure. Do not use hidden fields to hold data that will cause a problem if it is compromised.

Cookies

The HttpSession interface and hidden fields provide a simple way to track information during a single session, but they both have the drawback that they cannot be used to retain information across multiple browser sessions. To do this, you must create and manage your own data using cookies. You may also need to use cookies if you are writing servlets to interoperate with other Web technologies (such as CGI scripts).

> **CAUTION**
>
> Any use of cookies comes with a major health warning. As you will see, they are easy to forge and, because they are not always handled consistently, they are inherently unreliable.

You need to be aware that, as a security precaution, a browser can be set up to reject cookies. In this case, you will need to use an additional and alternative method (hidden fields or URL rewriting) to track sessions. Also, cookies should not be used when the information is important or sensitive. Cookies are associated with a browser and can be stored as text in the file system on the client's host. Consequently, cookies

- Are not secure because they are easy to edit or replace
- Potentially can be viewed by other users of the same workstation
- Can allow a user to impersonate another user
- Are not available if the user changes his or her workstation or browser

Remember that many users may share some machines, such as Internet café public access terminals.

A cookie has a name and a single value, both of which are strings. It may also have optional attributes, such as a comment, path and domain qualifiers, a maximum age, and a version number. Browsers vary as to how they handle cookie attributes, so use them with caution. The browser may also have a limit on the number of cookies it will handle at any one time and may set a limit on the size of the value for a cookie.

The cookie information is sent as part of the HTTP response header. If the browser accepts cookies, it will store the cookie on the client.

Creating a Cookie

You can use a `javax.servlet.http.Cookie` object to store information that will remain persistent across multiple HTTP connections.

> **CAUTION**
>
> Cookies can be deleted (sometimes automatically by the browser), so your code should never rely on a cookie being available.

The servlet sends cookies to the browser by using the `HttpServletResponse.addCookie (Cookie)` method.

Because the cookie is sent as part of the HTTP response header, you must add the cookie before sending the body of the response. This means a call to `res.addCookie(cookie)` must be made before sending any HTML or other data to the client.

The following code creates a new cookie with a unique identifier (code not shown). In this code fragment, the cookie value is initially left blank and set later using `Cookie.setValue()` to store the URL of the page visited by the user (`getRequestURI()` returns a string containing the URL).

```
String userID = new UniqueID();
Cookie cookie = new Cookie (userID, null);

String cvalue = getRequestURI();
cookie.setValue(cvalue);
res.addCookie(cookie);
```

By default, a cookie lives only as long as the browser session, so you need to use the `cookie.setMaxAge(interval)` method to change the life expectancy of a cookie. A positive interval sets the number of seconds a cookie will live, which enables you to create cookies that will survive beyond the browser session. A negative interval causes the cookie to be destroyed when the browser exits. An interval of zero immediately deletes the cookie.

Retrieving Cookie Data

Creating a cookie was simple. Retrieving one is not quite as straightforward. Unfortunately, there is no way to retrieve a cookie by name. Instead, you must retrieve all the cookies and then find the one that interests you.

To find the value of a cookie, you use the `Cookie.getValue()` method.

The following code can be used to retrieve a cookie with the same name as a `userID` String variable:

```
Cookie cookie = null;
Cookie cookies[] = req.getCookies();
String cvalue = null;
if (cookies != null) {
  int numCookies=cookies.length;
  for(int i = 0; i < numCookies; i++) {
    cookie = cookies[i];
    if (cookie.getName().equals(userID)) {
      cvalue = cookie.getValue();
      break;
    }
  }
}
```

12

URL Rewriting

Not all browsers support cookies, and even those that do can be set up to reject cookies. To get around this problem, your servlet can be set up to use URL rewriting as an alternative way of tracking sessions.

With URL rewriting, the server adds extra information dynamically to the URL. Usually, this information is the session ID (a unique ID associated with a HttpSession object when it is created).

You can use the HttpServletResponse.encodeURL() method to encode the session ID within the response as an added parameter. For example

```
out.println("<FORM action='"+res.encodeURL("/examples/htmlpage")+"'>");
```

adds the session ID to the form's action URL as follows:

```
<FORM action='http://localhost:8000/examples/htmlpage;jsessionid=99484920067B3'>
```

When the client will not accept a cookie, the server to track sessions will use URL rewriting. To ensure that your servlets support servers that use URL rewriting to track sessions, you must pass all URLs used in your servlet through the encodeURL() method.

Servlet Filtering

Filters are a feature that was introduced in version 2.3 of the servlet specification. A filter is a special type of servlet that dynamically intercepts requests and responses and transforms the information contained in them. The main advantage of a filter is that it can be added to existing applications without any need for recompilation.

Filters can have several important uses:

- To encapsulate recurring tasks in reusable units
- To format the data sent back to the client
- To provide authorization and blocking of requests
- To provide logging and auditing

A filter can perform filtering tasks on the request, the response, or both.

Programming Filters

A filter is still a servlet, so it extends HttpServlet but it also implements the javax.servlet.Filter interface.

Instead of doGet() or doPost(), filter tasks are done in a doFilter() method.

So that a filter can access initialization parameters, it is passed a `FilterConfig` object in its `init()` method. A filter can access the `ServletContext` through the `FilterConfig` object and thereby load any resources needed for the filtering tasks.

Filters can be connected together in a `FilterChain`. The servlet container constructs the filter chain in the order the filters appear in the deployment descriptor.

Because filters are added to an application at deploy time, it is possible to map a filter to one or more servlets. This is illustrated in Figure 12.15, where the `AuthenticateUser` filter is applied to all servlets. The `PageCounter` is mapped to `VerifyData` and `HTMLPage`, and the `EncodeResponse` filter only affects requests to the `AgencyTable` servlet.

FIGURE 12.15

Servlet filter chain.

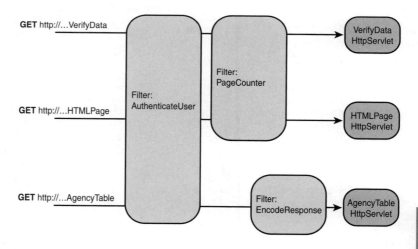

After a filter successfully completes its task, it must then call the `doFilter()` method on the next filter in the chain. The filter chain object is passed to the filter by the server as a parameter to the `doFilter()` method.

```
public void doFilter(ServletRequest req,ServletResponse res,FilterChain chain)
      throws IOException, ServletException {
   .. // filter code
   chain.doFilter(req, res); // call the next filter in the chain
}
```

If it is the last filter in the chain, instead of invoking another filter, the container will invoke the resource at the end of the chain (a normal servlet). If for some reason the filter processing fails, and if it is no longer appropriate to continue servicing the request, there is no need to call `doFilter()` on the next filter in the chain; typically you will forward the request to an error handling page if filter chaining is inappropriate.

In a filter, you must provide an `init(FilterConfig)` method. This `init(FilterConfig)` method is called by the Web server when a filter is being placed into service, and it must complete successfully before the filter can do any filtering work.

The `destroy()` method is called when a filter is being taken out of service, and gives the filter an opportunity to clean up any resources.

The use of these methods will be shown in the following example.

Auditing Filter Example

The filter in Listing 12.8 logs the number of times the application is accessed. A similar technique could be used to intercept requests and authorize the user before calling the servlet to service the request.

LISTING 12.8   Servlet Filter

```
import java.io.*;
import javax.servlet.*;
import javax.servlet.http.*;

public class AuditFilter extends HttpServlet implements Filter {
  private FilterConfig filterConfig = null;

  public void init(FilterConfig filterConfig)
    throws ServletException {
    this.filterConfig = filterConfig;
  }

  public void destroy() {
    this.filterConfig = null;
  }

  public void doFilter(ServletRequest req, ServletResponse res,
➥ FilterChain chain)
        throws IOException, ServletException {
    if (filterConfig == null)
      return;
    StringBuffer buf = new StringBuffer();
    buf.append ("The number of hits is: ");
    ServletContext ctx = filterConfig.getServletContext();
    synchronized (ctx) {
      Integer counter = (Integer)ctx.getAttribute("Counter");
      if (counter == null)
        counter = new Integer(1);
      else
        counter = new Integer(counter.intValue() + 1);
      buf.append (counter.toString());
```

In the `outputTable()` method, it is the `agency.select` bean that actually does the work. It returns a list of all the rows in the table. Note how access to the servlet instance variable must be in a `synchronized` block to make the code multi-thread safe.

```
java.util.List query;  // list of String[], first row = column names
synchronized (agency) {
    query = agency.select(tableName);
}
```

The rows of the table are displayed as an HTML table so the columns line up correctly. The attributes to the HTML TABLE tag set the border and background colors, and the cell padding is increased to improve readability. Rows in a table are separated by `<TR>...</TR>` tags.

```
out.println ("<TABLE BORDER='1' BORDERCOLOR='SILVER' BGCOLOR='IVORY' CELL-
PADDING='5'>");
out.println("<TR>");
```

The first item in the list is an array containing the names of the columns in the table. This is output as HTML table header cells.

```
String[] headerRow = (String[])query.get(0);
for (int i = 0; i < headerRow.length; i++) {
  out.println ("<TH ALIGN='LEFT'>" + headerRow[i] + "</TH>");
}
out.println ("</TR>");
```

The remainder of the rows of the table are output as HTML table data cells.

```
for (int i = 1; i < query.size(); i++) {
  out.println ("<TR>");
  String[] row = (String[])query.get(i);
  for (int r = 0; r < row.length; r++) {
    out.println ("<TD>" + row[r] + "</TD>");
  }
  out.println ("</TR>");
}
out.println ("</TABLE>");
```

Deploying the `AgencyTable` Servlet

Use `deploytool` to create a new WAR file (the example on the accompanying Web site uses the name `webagency.war`), and add the `webagency.AgencyTableServlet` as a Web component. Set the Web context to be `webagency` and the servlet alias to be `AgencyServlet` then the example can be accessed using the URL

```
http://localhost:8000/webagency/AgencyTable
```

You can also use the supplied asant build files to build and deploy the agency example using

```
asant build deploy
```

12

You will need to separately deploy a version of the Agency case study EAR file developed in a previous day's work. You can use the simplest Agency application from Day 5 as your starting point, or any of the Agency applications you may have already deployed from days 6, 8, 10 or 11.

In your new Web Component you will need to add the following class files from the Agency EJB components:

```
agency/Agency.class

agency/AgencyHome.class

agency/DuplicateException.class

agency/NotFoundException.class
```

Add an EJB Reference for the agency EJB by selecting the examples Web Application JAR in the left hand pane and choosing the EJB Refs dialogue page. Figure 12.20 shows the EJB Reference page with the required settings. To add your EJB reference click on the add button and in the popup Add New EJB Reference dialogue box enter the coded Name **ejb/Agency**. Select the session bean and remote interface options and enter agency.AgencyHome and agency.Agency for the home and remote interfaces. When you have added the Agency EJB reference, select this reference and choose the JNDI option at the bottom of the page, then enter ejb/Agency as the EJB JNDI name.

FIGURE 12.20

deploytool *EJB Refs.*

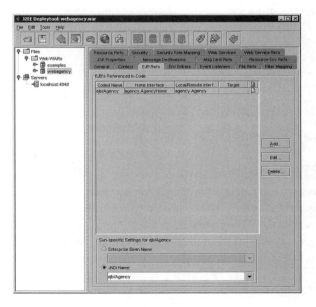

Figure 12.21 shows the output from the servlet example.

FIGURE 12.21

AgencyTable *servlet output.*

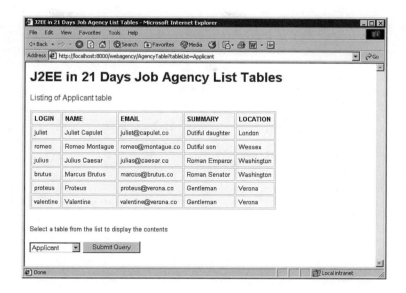

The complete listing of the AgencyTable servlet is provided in Listing 12.12.

LISTING 12.12 AgencyTableServlet.java Servlet Code

```java
import java.io.*;
import javax.servlet.*;
import javax.servlet.http.*;
import agency.*;
import javax.naming.*;
import java.rmi.*;
import javax.rmi.*;
import javax.ejb.*;

public class AgencyTableServlet extends HttpServlet
{
  private final String tables = "<OPTION>Applicant<OPTION>ApplicantSkill
➥ <OPTION>Customer<OPTION>Job<OPTION>JobSkill<OPTION>Location
➥ <OPTION>Matched<OPTION>Skill";
  private Agency agency;
  private ServletContext context;

  public void init(){
    context = getServletContext();
    try {
      InitialContext ic = new InitialContext();
      Object lookup = ic.lookup("java:comp/env/ejb/Agency");
      AgencyHome home =
➥ (AgencyHome)PortableRemoteObject.narrow(lookup, AgencyHome.class);
```

12

LISTING 12.12   continued

```
      agency = home.create();
    }
    catch (NamingException ex) {
      context.log("NamingException in AgencyTableServlet.init", ex);
    }
    catch (ClassCastException ex) {
      context.log("ClassCastException in AgencyTableServlet.init", ex);
    }
    catch (CreateException ex) {
      context.log("CreateException in AgencyTableServlet.init", ex);
    }
    catch (RemoteException ex) {
      context.log("RemoteException in AgencyTableServlet.init", ex);
    }
  }

  public void destroy () {
    context = null;
    agency = null;
  }

  private void outputTable (PrintWriter out, String tableName,
➥ HttpServletResponse res) throws RemoteException{

    java.util.List query;  // first row = column names
    synchronized(agency) {
        query = agency.select(tableName);
    }
    out.println (
➥ "<P><FONT SIZE=+1>Listing of " + tableName +" table</FONT></P>");
    out.println
➥ ("<TABLE BORDER=1 BORDERCOLOR=SILVER BGCOLOR=IVORY CELLPADDING=5>");
    out.println ("<TR>");

    String[] headerRow = (String[])query.get(0);
    for (int i = 0; i < headerRow.length; i++) {
      out.println ("<TH ALIGN=LEFT>" + headerRow[i] + "</TH>");
    }
    out.println ("</TR>");

    for (int i = 1; i < query.size(); i++) {
      out.println ("<TR>");
      String[] row = (String[])query.get(i);
      for (int r = 0; r < row.length; r++) {
        out.println ("<TD>" + row[r] + "</TD>");
      }
      out.println ("</TR>");
    }
```

LISTING 12.12   continued

```
      out.println ("</TABLE>");
    }

  public void doGet(HttpServletRequest req, HttpServletResponse res)
        throws IOException {
    try {
      String agencyName;
      String tableName = null;
      synchronized(agency) {
          agencyName = agency.getAgencyName();
      }
      res.setContentType ("text/html");
      PrintWriter out = res.getWriter();

      // print out form
      out.println ("<HTML>");
      out.println ("<HEAD><TITLE>" + agencyName +" List Tables</TITLE></HEAD>");
      out.println ("<BODY>");
      out.println ("<H1>" + agencyName + " List Tables</H1>");

      tableName = req.getParameter("tableList");
      if (tableName != null) {
        outputTable(out, tableName, res);
      }
      out.println (
        "<P>Select a table from the list to display the contents</P>");
      out.println ("<FORM>");
      out.println (
        "<SELECT NAME=\"tableList\" SIZE=\"1\">" + tables + "</SELECT>");
      out.println ("<INPUT TYPE=\"submit\">");
      out.println ("</FORM>");

      out.println ("</FONT></BODY>");
      out.println ("</HTML>");
    }
    catch (RemoteException ex) {
      context.log ("RemoteException in AgencyTableServlet.doGet", ex);
      res.sendError (res.SC_INTERNAL_SERVER_ERROR);
    }
  }
}
```

Use a browser to access your servlet and check that you can retrieve the data from the database.

Listing 12.12 shows the main drawback to writing servlets: A lot of coding effort is devoted to writing HTML tag information to the response, which can be error prone and make the code logic difficult to follow. Tomorrow you will look at JavaServer Pages which embed Java code inside HTML pages, simplifying the process of writing complex HTML pages.

Summary

Today, you have seen how servlets can be employed in a Web application to add dynamic content to HTML pages. You saw that servlets have no client interface, and the servlet container controls its lifecycle. Because HTTP is a stateless protocol, servlets have to use external means to retain information between client accesses. HTTP session objects are used for tracking servlet sessions but support for cookies is also provided. You have also seen that with event listening and using servlet filters, you can further extend the functionality and reusability of your servlet Web applications.

Servlets generate HTML from within Java code. This works well when the amount of HTML is relatively small, but the coding can become onerous if large amounts of HTML have to be produced. Tomorrow, you will look at another type of servlet called a JavaServer Page (JSP). With JSPs a different approach is taken. With a JSP the servlet Java code is imbedded in the HTML page avoiding the need to have multiple `out.println()` statements.

Q&A

Q What are the two main HTTP methods used to send requests to a Web server? What is the main difference between them? Which should I use to send large amounts of information to the server?

A The two main methods are `GET` and `POST`. `GET` adds any request parameters to the URL query string, whereas `POST` sends its parameters as part of the request body. The size of the URL query string is restricted and it is for this reason that you should use `POST` to send large amounts of information.

Q What are the main uses for a `ServletContext` object?

A The main uses are to set and store attributes, log events, obtain URL references to resources, and get the MIME type of files.

Q What are the names of the methods you must implement to handle HTTP GET and POST requests?

A The methods are `doGet()` and `doPost()`.

Q What are the main uses of a servlet filter?

A Filters can be used to provide auditing and to change the data in or, the format of, the HTTP request or the response.

Exercises

To extend your knowledge of Servlets, try the following exercise.

1. Extend the Agency case study Web interface. Add a servlet that produces a page that can be used to add new customers to the database. The information you will need to collect is the applicant's name, login, and email address. Use the `agency.createCustomer()` method to store this information in the `Customer` table in the database. Check that your servlet works correctly by running your `AgencyTableServlet` to display the contents of the `Customer` table. Remember to ensure that you protect access to shared instance variables (such as references to the Agency and Customer EJBs) inside `synchronized` blocks.

2. Now add a new servlet to delete a customer. The only information you will need to obtain is the login name. Use the `agency.deleteCustomer` method. Again, check that your servlet works correctly by running your `AgencyTableServlet`.

12

DAY 13

JavaServer Pages

Yesterday, you looked at developing Web applications using Java servlets. Servlets have the advantage of being able to generate the HTML Web page dynamically. The disadvantage of servlets is the developer must generate the HTML formatting information from within Java, and this means a lot of `out.println` statements. Servlets can be described as large amounts of boring HTML statements interspersed with small amounts of interesting Java code.

Servlets make it difficult to differentiate the presentation layer from the logic layer of an application. This duality of purpose means that servlets do not allow the roles of HTML designer and Java programmer to be easily separated. Writing servlets requires the members of the development team to be either

- Java programmers who must learn HTML and Web design
- Web designers who must learn Java

In practice, the roles of Web designer and Java programmer are sufficiently different to ensure that there are very few Java programmers who make good Web designers, and similarly few Web designers who make good Java programmers.

Fortunately, there is a solution. JavaServer Pages are another way of providing servlets that are written within the HTML page. Actually, there is a bit more to it than that, but any Java code on a JSP is usually either non-existent or very simple, and can be readily understood by non-Java programmers.

Typically, as discussed on Day 2, "The Java Platform and Roles," servlets and JSPs are both used in a Web Application to take advantage of the strengths of each topic. This subject is discussed in more detail in the section "Web Application Architecture" at the end of today's work.,

First, you need to understand the capabilities of JSPs. In today's lesson, you will

- Examine the differences between a JSP and a normal servlet
- Be introduced to the Element Language (EL) used to add programming elements to a JSP
- Study the JSP lifecycle and what the Web server carries out on your behalf
- Learn how to deploy a JSP
- Learn how to use JavaBeans to hide Java functionality from the JSP
- Learn how to develop a Web application using JSPs

NOTE

The Element Language (EL) was introduced with the early access version of JSTL (see Day 14, "JSP Tag Libraries") and was retrofitted into the emerging JSP 2.0 specification. If you are using a J2EE 1.3 compliant server it will not support EL and you will have to use the alternative syntax shown in examples for today and tomorrow.

Today's work builds directly on the knowledge gained yesterday because many of the mechanisms used in JSPs are the same as servlets.,

What Is a JSP?

A JSP is just another servlet, and like HTTP servlets, a JSP is a server-side Web component that can be used to generate dynamic Web pages. You can think of JSPs as HTML web pages with embedded Java, whereas servlets are Java classes that generate HTML.

To illustrate this difference, Listings 13.1 and 13.2 are the same Web page coded as a servlet and as a JSP, respectively. Each Web page simply reads a parameter called name from the HTTP request and creates an HTML page displaying the value of the name parameter. Listing 13.1 shows the servlet, and Listing 13.2 shows the JSP.

LISTING 13.1 Simple Dynamic Page as a Servlet

```java
import java.io.*;
import javax.servlet.*;
import javax.servlet.http.*;

public class Hello extends HttpServlet {

    public void doGet(HttpServletRequest req, HttpServletResponse res)
                throws ServletException, IOException {
        res.setContentType ("text/html");
        PrintWriter out = res.getWriter();
        String name = req.getParameter("name");
        out.println ("<HTML>");
        out.println ("<HEAD><TITLE>Hello</TITLE></HEAD>");
        out.println ("<BODY>");
        out.println ("<H1>Hello " + name + "</H1>");
        out.println ("</BODY>");
        out.println ("</HTML>");
    }
}
```

LISTING 13.2 Same Dynamic Page as a JSP

```html
<HTML>
  <HEAD><TITLE>Hello</TITLE></HEAD>
  <BODY>
    <H1>Hello ${param.name}</H1>
  </BODY>
</HTML>
```

NOTE

This syntax only works for JSP 2.0 containers (J2EE 1.4 onward). For JSP 1.2 or earlier (J2EE up to 1.3) the following should replace the contents of the <BODY> tag.

```
<H1>Hello <%= request.getParameter("name") %> </H1>
```

13

Here you can see that the JSP not only requires far less typing, but, from the programmer's point of view, a lot of the work is being done for you. How the JSP achieves the same effect with far less code will soon become clear.

Separating Roles

With a servlet, the Java programmer was forced to generate the entire HTML. With a JSP, it is much easier to separate the HTML from the application tasks. With the use of the JavaServer Pages Standard Tag Library (JSTL), JavaBeans, and custom tag libraries, this separation is even more explicit. JSTL and tag libraries are covered in more detail on Day 14.

Using JSPs, the Web designer can concentrate on the design and development of the HTML page. When a dynamic element is needed, the developer can use a pre-written bean or tag library to provide the data. The Java programmer can concentrate on developing a useful set of beans and tag libraries encapsulating the complex Java required to retrieve the data from an EJB, a database, or any other data source.

Translation and Execution

JSPs differ from servlets in one other respect. Before execution, a Web container converts the JSP into a Java servlet. This is done in two stages:

1. The JSP text is translated into Java code.
2. The Java code is compiled into a servlet.

The resulting servlet class processes HTTP requests. This translate and compile process is performed once before the first HTTP request is processed. The JSP lifecycle is covered in more detail later.

JSP Syntax and Structure

Before writing your first JSP, you need to gain an understanding of the syntax and the structure of a JSP.

JSP elements are those parts of the JSP that are translated by the JSP container. Everything else in the JSP is HTML (which is not translated and simply passed to the JSPWriter object); this is often referred to as Template text.

There are two ways of writing a JSP: either using JSP syntax (which resembles but is not XML) or using XML syntax. When a JSP is written using XML syntax it is called a JSP document.

If you are using a JSP 2.0 or later container (available with J2EE 1.4) you can take advantage of an expression language (EL) that makes it much easier to access and manipulate application data within a JSP, without having to write fragments of Java code.

Even if you have a JSP 2.0 container, you are likely to come across the previous syntax (especially if you have to maintain or refactor existing Web applications). This chapter will therefore cover both methods where appropriate.

Like XML tags, JSP tags are case sensitive; an incorrectly specified JSP will be ignored and passed through to the HTML page (like the other HTML tags). Also, like XML, a JSP element with an empty body can combine the start and end tags into a single tag. The following is a JSP element with an empty body:

```
<jsp:useBean id="agency" class="web.AgencyBean">
</jsp:useBean>
```

The following tag is equivalent to the previous example:

```
<jsp:useBean id="agency" class="web.AgencyBean"/>
```

Optionally, a JSP element may have attributes and a body or be nested. You will see examples of all these types during today's lesson. See Appendix A, "An Overview of XML," for more information on XML and the syntax of XML elements.

There are four types of JSP elements that can be placed on a JSP page, which are summarized in Table 13.1.

TABLE 13.1 JSP Elements

Element Type	Description
Actions	JSP-specific tags primarily used to support JavaBeans
Directives	Information used to control the translation of the JSP text into Java code
Expression Language (EL) elements	Provides a simple JavaScript-like syntax for accessing Java objects
Scripting elements	Used to provide the programming logic for the JSP
Comments	Used to document the JSP

The discussion of JSP actions and directives will follow a simple JSP example. In order to understand this example you need to appreciate the basic features of JSP scripting elements and the Expression Language as introduced in the following sub-sections.

Expression Language Elements

EL elements insert the String value of a Java object onto the Web page. EL elements are enclosed in "${" and "}". For example, you have already seen how to output a request parameter with

```
<H1>Hello ${param.name} </H1>
```

EL contains arithmetic and relational operators, as well as implicit objects, that make it easy to access JSP objects. EL can also be used in the attributes of other JSP elements. For more information on EL, see the later section titled "Expression Language."

13

Scripting Elements

Scripting elements on a JSP contain the code logic. The introduction of custom tag libraries, the JSTL, and EL has reduced the need for scripting elements on a JSP page. There are three JSP scripting elements:

- Scriptlets
- Expressions
- Declarations

All scripting elements use a non-XML element syntax that starts with <% and ends with %>. Each type of scripting element is briefly discussed in the following sections.

NOTE

> There is an XML compliant form for each of the scripting elements (such as `<jsp:scriptlet>` ... `</jsp:scriptlet>` for <% ... %> but as the non-XML JSP syntax is more common this will be used in today's lesson. Refer to the JSP specification for more information on JSP documents.

Scriptlets

Scriptlets contain Java statements that are processed when a request is received by the JSP. Scriptlets are processed in the order they appear in the JSP and need not write any information to the Web page. Each Java statement in a scriptlet must be terminated with a semi-colon.

Scriptlets can be used to create local variables, for example:

```
<% int i = 42;%>
<BIG>The answer is <%= i %></BIG>
```

The difference between scriptlet variables and declarations is that scriptlet variables are declared within the `Servlet.service()` method.

Expressions

JSP expressions are single Java expressions that are evaluated, cast into a string and written to the Web page. An expression is introduced with <%= and the Java code must not be terminated with a semi-colon. The following is an expression that will write the current date to the Web page:

```
Today's date is <%= new java.util.Date() %>
```

JSP expressions can be used as values for attributes in HTML and JSP tags. The following example shows how the i element in the items array can be used as the value for a submit button on a form:

```
<INPUT type="submit" value="<%= items[i] %>">
```

Declarations

Declarations are used to introduce one or more variable or method declarations, each one separated by semicolons. A variable must be declared before it is used on a JSP page. Declarations are differentiated from other scripting elements with a <%! start tag. An example declaration that defines two variables is as follows:

```
<%! String color = "blue"; int i = 42; %>
```

You can have as many declarations as you need. Variables and methods defined in declarations are declared as instance variables outside of any methods in the class.

CAUTION

Any instance variables declared in a JSP declaration are inherently not multi-thread safe. These variables must be guarded using synchronized blocks in Java scriptlets and never accessed from within Java expressions.

JSP Comments

There are three types of comments in a JSP page. The first type is called a JSP comment. JSP comments are used to document the JSP page. A JSP comment is completely ignored; it is not included in the generated code. A JSP comment looks like the following:

```
<%-- this is a JSP comment --%>
```

An alternative way to comment a JSP is to use the comment mechanism of the scripting language, as in the following:

```
<% /* this is a java comment */ %>
```

This comment will be placed in the generated Java code.

The third mechanism for adding comments to a JSP is to use HTML comments.

```
<!-- this is an HTML comment -->
```

HTML comments are passed through to the client as part of the response. As a result, this form can be used to document the generated HTML document. Dynamic

13

information can be included in HTML comments using JSP scriptlets and expressions as shown in the following:

```
<!-- comment  <%= expression %> comment  -->
```

First JSP Example

You are now ready to write and deploy your first JSP. The JSP in Listing 13.3 is a very simple JSP that uses EL to provide information about the request. EL is discussed in detail in the section "Element Language."

LISTING 13.3   Full Text of request-info.jsp

```
<HTML>
  <HEAD>
    <TITLE>Request Information</TITLE>
  </HEAD>
  <BODY>
    <P>Server ${header.Host}</P>
    <P>Header Accept-Encoding ${header["Accept-Encoding"]}</P>
    <P>Remote Host ${pageContext.request.remoteHost}</P>
    <P>Request Locale ${pageContext.request.locale}</P>
  </BODY>
</HTML>
```

Start up the J2EE RI and run deploytool and perform the following steps to deploy this JSP:

NOTE | This process is very similar to deploying servlets covered in Day 12. Alternatively you can use deploytool to open the file Day13/examples/ j2ee-ri/examples.war to look at the completed Web Application.

1. From the File menu, select New, Web Component. This will bring up the New Web Application Wizard. Skip over the introductory page if you didn't disable this page when working through the servlet examples yesterday.

2. On the WAR File page, select Create New Stand-Alone WAR File in the WAR Location section. Under WAR Naming, select a location for the WAR file (this can be anywhere, but the code on the accompanying Web site uses the directory Day13/examples/j2ee-ri for storing EAR and WAR files). Call the WAR file examples.war, set the Display Name to examples and set the Context Root

(Sun-specific settings) to examples. Click the Edit button and add the Day13/ examples/JSP/examples/request-info.jsp file.

CAUTION

> It is important that you keep the filename of the WAR file and the web application context root consistent. If you deploy the application using the asadmin command (or the asant deploy-examples-j2ee-ri command), the J2EE RI uses the name of the WAR file as the context root rather than the value supplied in the deployment descriptor. As long as you keep the WAR filename and context root consistent you will be fine. In this example the context root will be set to examples and the WAR filename to examples.war.

3. On the next page, choose JSP as the Web component type and click on Next.

4. On the next page, select /request-info.jsp as the JSP filename (see Figure 13.1). Accept the defaults for the remainder of the parameters on this screen.

FIGURE 13.1

deploytool
*Component General
Properties page.*

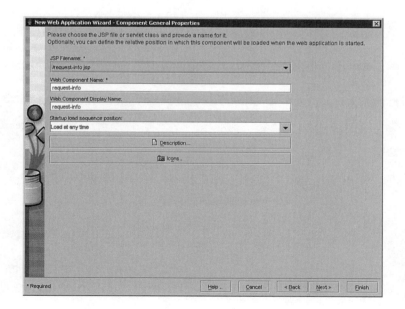

5. Click Next and after viewing the list of next steps, select Finish.

6. You can now add a *component alias* for your JSP (as you did for your servlets yesterday). Click on your request-info Web component in the left panel of deploytool. Select the Aliases tab in the right panel. Click on Add. Type /info.

13

7. Select the Web Application and use the menu Tools, Deploy to deploy it. You will need to supply the name and password of the administrative user defined when you installed the J2EE RI.

Now, start up a Web browser. First, type in the URL for the J2EE Web server (`http://localhost:8000`) and check that the server is up and running.

NOTE

> If, when you installed the J2EE RI, you configured the J2EE HTPP server on an alternate port, replace 8000 with your port number.

As with servlets, the URL to reference the JSP under the J2EE RI is as follows:

`http://<Web server address>/<Context root>/<Component alias>`

Now access your JSP using the following URL (see Figure 13.2):

`http://localhost:8000/examples/info`

As long as you did not make an error copying Listing 13.3, you should see the page shown in Figure 13.2. If you do not see the JSP output but see a stack trace instead, you should read the following sections to understand and fix the problem.

FIGURE 13.2

Browser showing output of request-info.jsp.

You already know that JSPs differ from servlets because they undergo a translation and compilation when first accessed. This means three types of errors can stop the JSP from displaying correctly:

- JSP syntax errors causing the translation to fail
- Java syntax errors causing the compilation to fail
- Java runtime errors throwing an uncaught exception
- HTML errors causing the page to display incorrectly

Finding and correcting these errors can be quite problematic because the information you need to discover the error is not readily available. Before looking at resolving errors, you will need to understand the JSP lifecycle.

JSP Lifecycle

As has already been stated, JSPs go through a translation and compilation phase prior to processing their first request. This is illustrated in Figure 13.3.

FIGURE 13.3

JSP translation and processing phase.

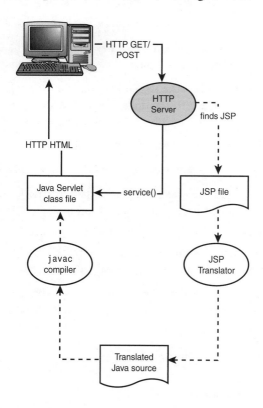

The Web server automatically translates and compiles a JSP; you do not have to manually run any utility to do this. JSP translation and compilation can occur at any time prior to the JSP first being accessed. It is implementation dependent when this translation and compilation occurs but it is usually either

- On deployment
- When the first request for the JSP is received

13

If the latter strategy is used, not only is there a delay in processing the first request, because the page is translated and compiled, but if the compilation fails, the client will be presented with some unintelligible error. If your server uses this strategy, ensure that you always force the translation and compilation of your JSP, either by making the first page request after it has been deployed or by forcing the page to be pre-compiled, as shown below.

With J2EE RI, the translation and compilation only takes place when the page is first accessed. You can find the translated JSP under the J2EE Installation directory in

`domains/domain1/generated/jsp/j2ee-modules/examples/org/apache/jsp`

The generated Java filename will be similar to the original JSP filename. You may find it useful to refer to the translated JSP to understand any compilation errors.

With J2EE RI, you can force the page to be pre-compiled by using your Web browser and appending `?jsp_precompile=true` to the JSP's URL string. To pre-compile the `request-info.jsp` example, you could use the following:

`http://localhost:8000/examples/info?jsp_precompile=true`

Because the compiled servlet is not executed, there are several advantages:

- There is no need to add any request parameters to the URL. So you can simply browse the URL rather than access from a form or another Web page.
- Pages do not have to be compiled in an order determined by the application logic.
- In a large application, less time is wasted traversing already compiled pages to find non-compiled ones, and it is easier to ensure that pages are not missed.

Realistically, you are going to make errors when writing JSPs. These errors can be quite difficult to comprehend because of the way they are detected and reported. There are four categories of error:

- JSP translation
- Servlet compilation
- Servlet runtime exceptions
- HTML presentation

The first three categories of error are detected by the JSP container and reported in an implementation-specific way; the J2EE RI reports the error back to the client using HTML. The last type of error (HTML) is detected by the Web browser.

Correcting each category of error requires a different technique and is discussed in this section.

Translation Errors

If you mistype the JSP tags or fail to use the correct attributes for the tags, you will get a translation error that J2EE RI returns to your browser. With the simple JSP that prints out the date, missing the closing % sign from the JSP expression, as in the following code

```
Today's date is <%= new java.util.Date() >
```

will generate a translation error. Listing 13.4 shows the code for this JSP, and Figure 13.4 shows the browser output reporting the translation error.

LISTING 13.4 `dateError.jsp`

```
<HTML>
<HEAD><TITLE>JSP Date Example</TITLE> </HEAD>
<BODY>
  <BIG>
    Today's date is <%= new java.util.Date () >
  </BIG>
</BODY>
</HTML>
```

FIGURE 13.4

Browser showing JSP translation error.

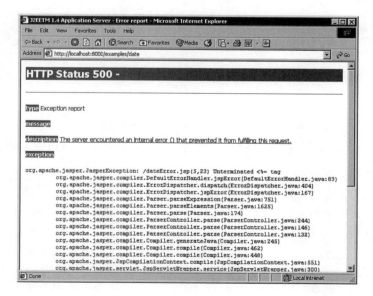

NOTE

> Using the Web browser to report errors is an expedient solution to the problem of reporting errors, but this approach is not used by all J2EE Containers. Some simply write the error to a log file and return an HTTP error to the browser. The JSP specification simply requires the Web server to report the HTTP 500 status code if there is an error on the JSP.

The error in Figure 13.4 shows a parse error defining an unterminated <%= tag on line 5 of the dateError.jsp page. The line that identifies the source of the error is

```
org.apache.jasper.compiler.ParseException: /dateError.jsp(5,23) Unterminated <%=
tag
```

This shows all of the useful information for determining the error. The first part of the line tells you the exception that occurred:

```
org.apache.jasper.compiler.ParseException:
```

In this case, a generic parsing exception reported by the JSP translator. The J2EE RI includes a version of the Apache Tomcat Web server and it is the Jasper container of Tomcat that has reported the error.

The second part of the error identifies the JSP page:

```
/dateError.jsp
```

and the third part specifies the line and column number:

```
(5,23)
```

You know that the error is on line 5 of the dateError.jsp page.

The final part of the error message is a brief description of the problem:

```
Unterminated <%= tag
```

The rest of the error information returned to the Web browser is a stack trace of where the exception occurred in the Jasper translator. This is of no practical use to you and can be ignored.

From the error information you should be able to identify the problem on the original JSP. Depending on the nature of the error, you may need to look at JSP lines prior to the one with the reported error. Sometimes errors are not reported until much later in the JSP. The worst scenario is when the error is reported on the very last line because this means the error could be practically anywhere in the JSP.

Compilation Errors

Compilation errors can occur when you mistype the Java code in a Java scripting element or when you omit necessary page directives, such as import package lists (see the next section). As for JSP translation errors different J2EE containers will report the errors in their own way. Most will simply write the information to a log file and return an HTTP 500 error to the client. All the JSP specification requires is that the container return a 500 series to the client. The J2EE RI also shows the compilation errors on the page returned to the browser, including the line number in error in the generated file and usually a reference back to the line number in the original JSP file.

> **NOTE**
>
> The December 2003 release of the J2EE RI used when writing this book reports a spurious problem running the Java compiler rather than the actual compilation error. You will need to check the server log file to discover the actual error.

A common mistake is to fail to define the package name for a Java class in a scriptlet or expression, for example:

```
Today's date is <%= new Date() %>
```

The following J2EE RI log file extract shows the compilation error that occurs if you make this simple mistake:

```
[#|2003-12-16T13:31:50.498+0000|SEVERE|j2ee-appserver1.4|
➥ org.apache.jasper.compiler.Compiler|_ThreadID=13;|
➥ Error compiling file: /D:/Sun/AppServer/domains/domain1/generated
➥ /jsp/j2ee-modules/examples//org/apache/jsp/dateJavaError_jsp.java
    [javac] Compiling 1 source file
    [javac] D:\Sun\AppServer\domains\domain1\generated\jsp\j2ee-modules\
➥examples\
➥ org\apache\jsp\dateJavaError_jsp.java:45: cannot resolve symbol
    [javac] symbol  : class Date
    [javac] location: class org.apache.jsp.dateJavaError_jsp
    [javac]         out.write(String.valueOf( new Date() ));
    [javac]                                       ^
    [javac] 1 error
```

If you cannot determine the error from the JSP file, you will need to examine the generated Java file specified in the error message.

Listing 13.5 shows the generated code containing the Java error.

13

LISTING 13.5   Fragment of Generated Java Code

```
try {
  _jspxFactory = JspFactory.getDefaultFactory();
  response.setContentType("text/html");
  pageContext = _jspxFactory.getPageContext(this, request, response,
                        null, true, 8192, true);
  application = pageContext.getServletContext();
  config = pageContext.getServletConfig();
  session = pageContext.getSession();
  out = pageContext.getOut();
  jspx_out = out;

  out.write("<HTML>\r\n");
  out.write("<HEAD><TITLE>JSP Date Java Error Example");
  out.write("</TITLE></HEAD>\r\n");
  out.write("<BODY>\r\n  ");
  out.write("<BIG>\r\n    Today's date is ");
  out.write(String.valueOf( new Date() ));
  out.write("\r\n  ");
  out.write("</BIG>\r\n");
  out.write("</BODY>\r\n");
  out.write("</HTML>\r\n");
} catch (Throwable t) {
  if (!(t instanceof javax.servlet.jsp.SkipPageException)){
    out = _jspx_out;
    if (out != null && out.getBufferSize() != 0)
      out.clearBuffer();
    if (pageContext != null) pageContext.handlePageException(t);
  }
} finally {
  if (_jspxFactory != null) _jspxFactory.releasePageContext(pageContext);
}
```

You can use the information provided by the generated code to identify the error in the original JSP. Do not fix the error in the generated file, as this file is replaced when the JSP is next translated.

Java Runtime Exceptions

As part of the code generation process a simple Exception handler is added to the generated code; this can be seen in Listing 13.5. Any exceptions generated by the JSP that are not explicitly caught by try/catch blocks in JSP scriptlets will be reported back to the client as an HTTP 500 error.

In the case of the J2EE RI, a stack trace showing the error is written to the server log file. If the J2EE RI server is running in verbose mode (as discussed on Day 2, "The J2EE Platform and Roles") a copy of the trace is also displayed in the Server console window.

The JSP specification supports the concept of an error page that can be used to catch JSP exceptions, and this is discussed in more detail in the later sections on "The page Directive" and "Error Page Definition." The "Error Page Definition" section later in this chapter shows how to write a simple debugging error page for use during JSP development.

HTML Presentation Errors

The last category of error you can make with a JSP is to incorrectly define the HTML elements. These errors must be solved by looking at the HTML returned to the browser; most browsers have a menu option to let you view the HTML source for the page. After the HTML error is identified, you must relate this back to the original JSP file. Adding HTML comments to the JSP file can help you identify the location of the error if it is not readily apparent.

If no HTML data is returned to the browser, you have a serious problem with the JSP that is causing the generated servlet to fail without writing any data. You will need to examine your Web page very carefully for logic errors in the JSP elements; complex scriptlets are the most likely cause of the problem.

Your first step with a JSP that doesn't return HTML is to remove all of the JSP elements, leaving a plain HTML page, and ensure this is correctly displayed by the browser. Gradually re-introduce JSP elements one at a time until the error reappears. Now you can correct the problem when you have identified where it occurs on the page.

JSP Lifecycle Methods

The JSP equivalent of the servlet init() method is called jspInit() and can be defined to set up the JSP page. If present, jspInit() will be called by the server prior to the first request. Similarly, a method called jspDestroy() can be defined to deallocate resources used in the JSP page. The jspDestroy() method will be called when the page is taken out of service.

These methods must be defined inside a JSP declaration, as shown in the following:

```
<%!
  public void jspInit() {
    …
  }
  public void jspDestroy() {
    …
  }
%>
```

One of the problems with these lifecycle methods is that they are often used to initialize instance variables. Because JSPs are really servlets, the use of instance variables can

13

cause problems with the multi-threading mechanisms used by the Web server for handling multiple page requests. As previously mentioned, access to servlet instance variables should be protected by synchronized blocks.

JSP Directives

Directives are used to define information about your page to the translator; they do not produce any HTML output. All directives have the following syntax:

```
<%@ directive [ attr="value" ] %>
```

where `directive` can be page, include, or taglib. Typically JSP directives are included before the HTML <HEAD> tag of your JSP.

The page and include directives are described here, and the taglib directive is described tomorrow when Tag Libraries are studied in detail.

The include Directive

You use the include directive to insert the contents of another file into the Web page as the page is translated. The included file can contain HTML or JSP tags or both. It is a useful mechanism for including the same page directives in all your JSPs or reusing small pieces of HTML to create common look and feel.

If the include file is itself a JSP, it is standard practice to use .jsf or .jspf, as suggested in the JSP specification, to indicate that the file contains a JSP fragment. These extensions show that the file is to be used in an include directive (and does not create a well-formed HTML page). ".jsp" should be reserved to refer to standalone JSPs.

Listing 13.6 shows a JSP with an include directive to add an HTML banner on the page. The banner is shown in Listing 13.7

LISTING 13.6   Full Text of dateBanner.jsp

```
<HTML>
  <HEAD>
    <TITLE>JSP Date Example with common banner</TITLE>
  </HEAD>
  <BODY>
    <%@ include file="banner.html" %>
    <BIG>
      Today's date is
      <%= new java.util.Date() %>
    </BIG>
  </BODY>
</HTML>
```

LISTING 13.7   Full Text of `banner.html`

```
<P><TABLE border="0" width="600" cellspacing="0" cellpadding="0">
  <TR>
    <TD width="350"><H1>Temporal Information  </H1> </TD>
     <TD align="right" width="250"><IMG src="clock.gif"> </TD>
  </TR>
</TABLE></P>
```

Remember that you must add any `include` files into the Web application as well as the JSP file. In this example, you will need to add `banner.html` and the image file `clock.gif` to the Web Application WAR file.

The page Directive

Page directives are used to define page-dependent properties. You can have more than one page directive in the JSP. A page directive applies to the whole JSP, together with any files incorporated via the `include` directive. Table 13.2 defines a list of the more commonly used page directives.

TABLE 13.2   JSP Page Directives

Directive	Example	Effect
info	`<%@ page info="my first JSP Example" %>`	Defines text string that is placed in the `Servlet.` `getServletInfo()` method in the translated code
import	`<%@ page import="java.math.*" %>`	A comma-separated list of package names to be imported for this JSP. The default import list is `java.lang.*`, `javax.servlet.*`, `javax.servlet.jsp.*`, and `javax.servlet.http.*`.
errorPage	`<%@ page errorPage="/agency/error.jsp" %>`	The server will return the indicated error page to the client should an uncaught exception be thrown by this page.

13

TABLE 13.2 continued

Directive	Example	Effect
isErrorPage	`<%@ page isErrorPage="true" %>` `<%@ page isErrorPage="false" %>`	Indicates whether this page is the target URL for an `errorPage` directive. If `true`, an implicit scripting variable called `exception` is defined and references the exception thrown in the source JSP. The default is `false`.

Using the Agency case study as an example, you can now study a JSP that uses page directives. The program in Listing 13.8 shows an example that displays the name of the Job Agency.

LISTING 13.8   Full Text of `name.jsp`

```
<%@page import="java.util.*, javax.naming.*, agency.*" %>
<%@page errorPage="errorPage.jsp" %>
<%
    InitialContext ic = null;
    ic = new InitialContext();
    AgencyHome agencyHome = (AgencyHome)ic.lookup("java:comp/env/ejb/Agency");
    Agency agency = agencyHome.create();
%>
<HTML>
  <HEAD><TITLE>Agency Name</TITLE></HEAD>
  <BODY>
    <H1><%= agency.getAgencyName() %> </H1>
  </BODY>
</HTML>
```

NOTE   This is not the best way of coding this JSP. You will see in the next section how to use JavaBeans to remove the Java code and simplify this JSP.

Listing 13.8 uses the agency Session bean you developed on Day 5, "Session EJBs," to obtain the name of the agency. Because this JSP uses JNDI and EJB features, it must import the relevant Java packages by using a page directive. This example also uses an error page that is displayed if there is an uncaught exception on the page.

NOTE

The JSP page does not catch the obvious `NamingException` and `EJBException` exceptions that can be thrown by the code in the scriptlet—the JSP error page is used for this purpose.

The error page contains JSP features that you have not yet encountered; these will be explained later.

Deploying this example is a little more complex than the simple `date` example because it must include the additional class files required for the `agency` Session bean.

To deploy the example in Listing 13.8, perform the following steps:

1. Add the Web components to the `examples` WAR file you created earlier or create a new WAR file. Use the New Web Component wizard to define the information shown in step 2.

2. Add the following files for this Web component:
   - `name.jsp`
   - `errorPage.jsp`
   - `agency/Agency.class`
   - `agency/AgencyHome.class`
   - `agency/DuplicateException.class`
   - `agency/NotFoundException.class`

3. Select `name.jsp` as the JSP page.

4. Set the page alias as `/name`.

5. Add an EJB Reference for the agency EJB by selecting the examples Web Application JAR in the left hand pane and choosing the EJB Refs dialogue page. Figure 13.5 shows the EJB Reference page with the required settings. To add your EJB reference click on the Add button and in the popup Add New EJB Reference dialogue enter the coded Name `ejb/Agency`. Select the session bean and remote interface options and enter `agency.AgencyHome` and `agency.Agency` for the home and remote interfaces. When you have added the Agency EJB reference select this reference and choose the JNDI option at the bottom of the page and enter `ejb/Agency` as the EJB JNDI name.

13

Figure 13.5

Adding agency EJB Reference.

The new `name.jsp` Web page can now be deployed and accessed using the URL `http://localhost:8000/examples/name`.

NOTE

You must have previously deployed the agency application; otherwise, the Web interface will not be able to find the agency Session bean. Any version of the agency application will suffice.

Accessing HTTP Servlet Variables

The JSP pages you write are translated into servlets that process the HTTP GET and POST requests. The JSP code can access servlet information using implicit objects defined for each page. These implicit objects are pre-declared variables that you reference from the Java code on your JSP. The most commonly used objects are shown in Table 13.3.

Table 13.3   JSP Implicit Objects

Reference Name	Class	Description
config	javax.servlet.ServletConfig	The servlet configuration information for the page
request	subclass of javax.servlet.ServletRequest	Request information for the current HTTP request

TABLE 13.3 continued

Reference Name	Class	Description
session	javax.servlet.http.HttpSession	The servlet session object for the client
out	javax.servlet.jsp.JspWriter	A subclass of java.io.Writer that is used to output text for inclusion on the Web page
pageContext	javax.servlet.jsp.PageContext	The JSP page context used primarily when implementing custom tags (see Day 14)
application	javax.servlet.ServletContext	The context for all Web components in the same application

The following example rather laboriously writes the value of the name request parameter to the Web page and is another variant of the examples shown in Listings 13.1 and 13.2.

```
<HTML>
  <HEAD><TITLE>Hello</TITLE></HEAD>
  <BODY>
    <H1>Hello <% out.print(request.getParameter("name")); %></H1>
  </BODY>
</HTML>
```

Expression Language (EL)

We now turn our attention to the Expression Language. Although EL is not a general purpose programming language, it does share many characteristics with common languages with which you will be familiar. For example, while it has no flow-control it does have variables and operators.

EL Variables

EL variables are implicit JSP variables, additional EL-specific variables, and any user-defined variables. Today's discussion will focus on using implicit variables and using JavaBeans (see the section "Simplifying JSP pages with JavaBeans"). Setting variables using the JSTL is covered on Day 14.

Implicit Objects

Like JSP, EL defines a number of implicit objects that provide access to request parameters, HTTP headers, cookies, and other container information. However the EL implicit

13

variables and the JSP implicit variables shown in Table 13.3 are different. Table 13.4 lists all the implicit objects available in EL.

TABLE 13.4.   EL Implicit Objects.

Implicit Object	Description	Example of Use
param	A Map of request parameters and their values	`${param.customer}`
paramValues	A Map of String[] containing all the values for each request parameter	`${paramValues.uriList}`
header	A Map of HTTP headers and their values	`${header.Host}`
headerValues	A Map of String[] containing all the values for each HTTP header	`${headerValues.["Accept-Encoding"]}`
cookie	A Map of cookie names and cookie objects	`${cookie["URI-list"]}`
initParam	A Map of context parameters and their values	`${initParam.WebMaster}`
pageContext	A `javax.servlet.jsp.PageContext` object	`${pageContext.request.locale}`

The `pageContext` implicit object provides access to various servlet objects including

- `request`—The HTTP request object
- `response`—The HTTP response object
- `session`—The client session object

For a full list see the API documentation for a description of the classes for the implicit objects.

You have already seen an example of using the `request` object in Listing 13.3 when accessing the remote host submitting a request:

```
<P>Remote Host ${pageContext.request.remoteHost}</P>
```

Looking at this example and the last column in Table 13.4 you may have spotted that there is a general method access mechanism going on here. In JavaBeans, properties of a bean are exposed through getter and setter methods. The EL syntax uses this JavaBean naming mechanism to map identifiers to getter methods.

In the last example, `request` and `remoteHost` are properties of the `PageContext` and `ServletRequest` objects. The Java expression corresponding to the EL expression is

```
pageContext.getRequest().getRemoteHost()
```

Any object that supports JavaBean getter methods can use the EL structured data operators.

You must use the "[ ]" operator instead of the "." operator when the property name is supplied as a runtime expression rather than as a compile-time property name. The following example picks up the value of an HTTP request parameter using the value of another request parameter called paramName.

```
<P>Value of ${param.paramName} is ${param[param.paramName]}</P>
```

It might help to understand this example seeing the equivalent JSP code:

```
<P>Value of <%= request.getParameter("paramName") %>
is <%= request.getParameter(request.getParameter("paramName")}) %> </P>
```

EL Operators

In addition to the "." and "[ ]" structured operators just discussed, EL provides operators commonly found in many programming languages, but does not have assignment or a string concatenation operator. To avoid confusion with special XML characters, some EL operators have alternate forms.

EL provides the following operators:

- Arithmetic—"+", "-", "*", "/" (also "div") "%" (also "mod")
- Relational—"==" or "eq", "!=" or "ne", "<" or "lt", ">" or "gt", "<=" or "le", ">=" or "ge"
- Unary minus—"-"
- Logical—"&&" or "and", "||" or "or", "!" or "not"
- Empty—"empty" (used to test for a null value, an empty string ("") or an empty collection)

Use of most of these operators is the same as for Java. The empty operator is used to test whether a value is empty or not and is discussed in more detail with the JSTL on Day 14.

Apart from its use for accessing object properties, the "[ ]" operator can also be used to access indexed elements in a Java collection. The value inside the "[ ]" operator must be appropriate for the type of collection.

Operator precedence is the same as Java (or C), with "[]" and "." binding most tightly. As with Java, parentheses can be used to change the order of precedence.

13

String concatenation is achieved by using two or more EL expressions within the JSP or element attribute, as in

```
<H2>${pageContext.request.serverName}:${pageContext.request.serverPort}</H2>
```

which will translate to something like

```
<H2>localhost:8000</H2>
```

EL has conversion rules for operands, which help reduce the number of exceptions caused by incorrect data and allow the EL to be written like an untyped language (such as JavaScript or Visual Basic).

The basic conversion rules are as follows:

- `null` is converted to `""`, `0`, `0.0` or `false` as required.
- Numbers are narrowed or widened to match the required data type (for example, `double` to `int` or `int` to `double`).
- Primitives are converted to the appropriate wrapper class (for example `int` to `Integer`).
- `String` objects are converted to numbers using the `valueOf()` method of the appropriate wrapper class.
- All objects are converted to `String` using the `java.lang.toString()` method.

Generally, variables and expressions will be converted as expected.

Simplifying JSP Pages with JavaBeans

One of the problems with writing JSP pages is switching between the Java code and the HTML elements. It is easy to get confused and place syntax errors in the page that can be difficult and time consuming to identify. Using EL, JSTL and JavaBeans on a JSP page can reduce the amount of embedded Java code that has to be written (or indeed remove the need for embedded Java code entirely). JavaBeans and the built-in support in EL for accessing JavaBean properties also help to separate out the presentation and logic components of your application, allowing HTML developers to lay out the Web pages and the Java programmers to develop supporting JavaBeans.

What Is a JavaBean?

A bean is a self-contained, reusable software component. Beans are Java classes that are written to conform to a particular design convention (sometimes called an idiom). The rules for writing a JavaBean are as follows:

- A bean must have a no argument constructor (that is a constructor with no parameters). As long as you do not declare any constructors, the compiler generates a no argument constructor for you as follows:

```
public class NameBean {
  public NameBean () {}
}
```

- Beans can provide properties that allow customization of the bean. For each property, the bean must define getter and setter methods that retrieve or modify the bean property. For example, if a bean has a property called name, the bean class can define the methods getName() and setName().

- The getter method must have no parameters and return an object of the type of the property. The setter method must take a single parameter of the type of the property and return a void. The following example shows a simple bean with a String property called name that can be queried and modified using the defined getter and setter methods.

```
public class NameBean {
  private String name;
  public void setName (String name) {
    this.name = name;
  }
  public String getName () {
    return name;
  }
}
```

> **NOTE**
>
> If a bean property has only a getter method, it is read-only; a write-only method only has a setter method. A property is read/write if it has both getter and setter methods.

Beans can also define business methods to provide additional functionality above and beyond manipulating properties.

Defining a JavaBean

JavaBeans are defined on the JSP using the tag `<jsp:useBean>`. This tag creates an instance of a JavaBean and associates it with a name for use on the JSP.

```
<jsp:useBean id="<bean name>" class="<bean class>" scope="<scope>">
```

The bean name and class are defined by the id and class attributes for the useBean tag.

13

The useBean tag also requires a scope attribute that defines the scope of the bean reference. The possible scope values are as follows:

- page Only available on this page.
- request Available for this HTTP request (this page and any pages the request includes or is forwarded to).
- session The duration of the client session (the bean can be used to pass information from one request to another).
- application The bean is added to the Web context and can be used by any other component in the Web application.

The following code creates an instance of a bean of class NameBean for the current request and associates it with the name myBean.

```
<jsp:useBean id="myBean" class="NameBean" scope="request"/>
```

This bean has been defined using an empty JSP element because the bean is ready to use as soon as it has been defined. However, if the bean must be initialized, an alternate syntax is shown next and described fully in the "Initializing Beans" section later in the chapter.

```
<jsp:useBean id="myBean" class="NameBean" scope="request" >
  <jsp:setProperty name="myBean" property="name" value="winston"/>
</jsp:useBean>
```

Setting Bean Properties

Bean properties are set using the setProperty element. This element requires a bean name (from the ID in the useBean element), a property, and a value attribute, as shown in the following:

```
<jsp:setProperty name="<bean name>"
  property="<property name>" value="<expression>"/>
```

To set the name of the example NameBean to winston, you would use the following:

```
<jsp:setProperty name="myBean" property="name" value="winston"/>
```

As with getProperty, the bean method can be called explicitly from a Java scriptlet:

```
<% myBean.setName("winston"); %>
```

A useful feature of the setProperty tag is that bean properties can also be initialized from the HTTP request parameters. This is accomplished by using a param attribute rather than the value attribute:

```
<jsp:setProperty name="<bean name>" property="<property name>" param="<name>"/>
```

The value of the named parameter is used to set the appropriate bean property. To use a request parameter called name to set the NameBean property of the same name, you could use the following:

```
<jsp:setProperty name="myBean" property="name" param="name"/>
```

In fact, the param attribute can be omitted if the property name is the same as the request parameter name. So the previous example could have been put more succinctly as follows:

```
<jsp:setProperty name="myBean" property="name"/>
```

A last form of the setProperty bean is employed when multiple parameters are used to initialize several bean properties. If the property name is set to *, all of the form request parameters are used to initialize bean properties with the same name:

```
<jsp:setProperty name="myBean" property="*"/>
```

CAUTION The bean must define a property for every parameter in the HTTP request; otherwise, an error occurs.

Initializing Beans

Some beans require properties to be defined to initialize the bean. There is no mechanism for passing in initial values for properties in the jsp:useBean element, so a syntactic convention is used instead.

Conventionally, if a bean must have properties defined before it can be used on the Web page, the jsp:useBean is defined with an element body and the jsp:setProperty tags are defined in the useBean body to initialize the required properties.

For example, assuming that the simple NameBean example requires the name to be initialized, the following useBean syntax would be used:

```
<jsp:useBean id="myBean" class="NameBean" scope="request" >
  <jsp:setProperty name="myBean" property="name" value="winston"/>
</jsp:useBean>
```

Getting Bean Properties

Bean properties are retrieved using an EL variable or the <jsp:getProperty> element. With EL you can use the following to retrieve a property called name from the NameBean bean:

```
${myBean.name}
```

13

Before the introduction of EL the <jsp:getProperty> element was used to access a bean property. This element requires a bean name (from the ID defined in the useBean tag) and property attribute, as shown in the following:

```
<jsp:getProperty name="<bean name>" property="<property name>" />
```

The value of the property is converted to a string and substituted on the Web page.

The following example shows how to retrieve the name property from the NameBean defined earlier and use it as a level 2 heading:

```
<H2><jsp:getProperty name="myBean" property="name"/></H2>
```

An alternative method for accessing a bean property is to use the bean name and get property method inside a JSP scripting element (such as an expression). The following code is an equivalent JSP rendering of the previous examples:

```
<H2><%= myBean.getName() %></H2>
```

NOTE | Both the use of <jsp:getProperty> and scripting elements to access bean properties are likely to fall into disuse with the introduction of EL.

Using a Bean with the Agency Case Study

The next example uses the Agency case study code and refactors the name.jsp Web page shown in Listing 13.8 to use a JavaBean. This time, you will use a bean to hide the complex JNDI lookup and type casting needed to access the agency Session EJB.

The new JSP page is shown in Listing 13.9.

LISTING 13.9   Full Text of agencyName.jsp

```
<HTML>
  <HEAD><TITLE>Agency Name</TITLE></HEAD>
  <BODY>
    <jsp:useBean id="agency" class="web.AgencyBean" scope="request" />
    <H1>${agency.agencyName}</H1>
  </BODY>
</HTML>
```

This is much simpler for a non-Java developer to work with. All of the code required to create the EJB using its JNDI name has been spirited away into a JavaBean of class web.AgencyBean. This bean has properties representing AgencyName, Applicants,

Customers, Locations, and Skills and defines a large number of business methods whose only purpose is to delegate behavior to the underlying agency Session bean.

The full bean code is shown in Listing 13.10.

LISTING 13.10 Full Text of web.AgencyBean.java

```java
package web;

import java.rmi.*;
import java.util.* ;
import javax.ejb.* ;
import javax.naming.* ;

import agency.*;

public class AgencyBean
{
    Agency agency;

    public AgencyBean ()  throws NamingException, RemoteException,
                                 CreateException {
        InitialContext ic = null;
        ic = new InitialContext();
        AgencyHome agencyHome = (AgencyHome)ic.lookup("java:comp/env/ejb/
➥Agency");
        agency = agencyHome.create();
    }

    public String getAgencyName() throws RemoteException {
        return agency.getAgencyName();
    }

    public Collection getApplicants() throws RemoteException {
        return agency.getApplicants();
    }

    public void createApplicant(String login, String name, String email)
                throws RemoteException, DuplicateException,
                       CreateException{
        agency.createApplicant(login,name,email);
    }


    public void deleteApplicant (String login)
                throws RemoteException, NotFoundException{
        agency.deleteApplicant(login);
    }
```

13

LISTING 13.10   continued

```java
public Collection getCustomers() throws RemoteException {
    return agency.getCustomers();
}


public void createCustomer(String login, String name, String email)
            throws RemoteException, DuplicateException,
                    CreateException{
    agency.createCustomer(login,name,email);
}

public void deleteCustomer (String login)
            throws RemoteException, NotFoundException {
    agency.deleteCustomer(login);
}

public Collection getLocations() throws RemoteException {
    return agency.getLocations();
}

public String getLocationDescription(String name)
            throws RemoteException, NotFoundException {
    return agency.getLocationDescription(name);
}

public void updateLocation(String name, String description)
            throws RemoteException, NotFoundException {
    agency.updateLocation(name,description);
}

public void addLocation(String name, String description)
            throws RemoteException, DuplicateException {
    agency.addLocation(name,description);
}

public void removeLocation(String name)
            throws RemoteException, NotFoundException {
    agency.removeLocation(name);
}

public Collection getSkills() throws RemoteException {
    return agency.getSkills();
}

public String getSkillDescription(String name)
            throws RemoteException, NotFoundException {
    return agency.getSkillDescription(name);
}
```

By structuring the Web pages to include a common header file, you can be sure there will be a common look and feel to each page. The header file completes the page <HEAD> section and starts the page <BODY>. This isn't ideal, because the JSP designer has to know that the include file spans two logical components of the HTML page (it would be better to make this two header files, one with the tags to be included in the <HEAD> tag and one with those for the <BODY> tag). But it does serve to show how useful include files can be.

The included header file also defines a bean called agency that can be used on the rest of the page to access the agency Session EJB. The level 1 page heading (<H1>) uses the agency name obtained from the agency bean.

If you haven't encountered HTML style sheets before, the simple one used for the agency is shown in Listing 13.12.

LISTING 13.12   Full Text of agency.css

```
H1, H2, H3 {font-family: sans-serif}
H1 {background-color: navy; color: white }
H2 {color: navy }
H3 {color: blue }
BODY, P, FORM, TABLE, TH, TD {font-family: sans-serif}
```

Without going into detail, all this style sheet does is define font styles and colors for use with the HTML tags on a Web page that links to this style sheet. Older browser support for CSS is erratic, so you may not see all of the desired font changes with your browser if you are not using one of the latest CSS specification compliant browsers.

Returning to the agency portal page, you can use the agency bean defined by the header to access the agency Session EJB functionality. When the user clicks the Show Customer button, the following JSP fragment presents the user with a list of customer names and invokes an advertise.jsp page (via its alias customer/advertise).

```
<FORM action="customer/advertise">
<TABLE>
<TR><TD>Select Customer</TD>
<TD><SELECT name="customer">
<% Iterator customers = agency.getCustomers().iterator(); %>
<% while (customers.hasNext()) {%>
  <OPTION><%=customers.next()%></OPTION>
<% } %>
</SELECT>
</TD></TR>
<TR><TD colspan="2"><input type="submit" value="Show Customer"></TD></TR>
</TABLE>
</FORM>
```

13

The HTML select tag used on this form, and later examples, has been encoded as a scriptlet. On Day 14, you will see how JSTL can be used to achieve the same flow of control.

Listing 13.13 shows all the code of the portal page for the Agency application with support for the customer functionality only.

LISTING 13.13   Full Text of agency.jsp

```
<HTML>
  <HEAD>
  <TITLE>Agency Portal</TITLE>
  <%@include file="header.jsf" %>
  <%@page import="java.util.*" %>
    <H2>Customers</H2>
    <H3>Existing Customer</H3>
    <FORM action="customer/advertise">
      <TABLE>
        <TR><TD>Select Customer</TD>
        <TD><SELECT name="customer">
        <% Iterator customers = agency.getCustomers().iterator(); %>
        <% while (customers.hasNext()) {%>
        <OPTION><%=customers.next()%></OPTION>
        <% } %>
        </SELECT>
        </TD></TR>
        <TR><TD colspan="2"><input type="submit" value="Show
➥Customer"></TD></TR>
      </TABLE>
    </FORM>
    <H3>Create Customer</H3>
    <FORM action="customer/createCustomer">
      <TABLE>
        <TR>
          <TD>Login:</TD>
          <TD><INPUT type="text" name="login"></TD>
        </TR>
        <TR>
          <TD>Name:</TD>
          <TD><INPUT type="text" name="name"></TD>
        </TR>
        <TR>
          <TD>Email:</TD>
          <TD><INPUT type="text" name="email"></TD>
        </TR>
        <TR>
          <TD colspan=2><INPUT type="submit" value="Create Customer"></TD>
        </TR>
      </TABLE>
```

LISTING 13.13 continued

```
    </FORM>
    <H2>Administration</H2>
    <FORM action="admin/admin"><INPUT type="submit" value="Administration Form">
    </FORM>
  </BODY>
</HTML>
```

The exercise for today's lesson will be to add support for registering applicants to this framework.

One last point to raise for the Agency Web pages is that of using a consistent navigation model for each page. JSP `include` files are an ideal method for including consistent hyperlinks in each Web page. The following code fragment shows how a standard footer with a navigation button for returning to the home page is included at the end of each Web page, and Listing 13.14 shows the actual footer page.

```
<%@include file="footer.jsf" %>
</BODY>
</HTML>
```

LISTING 13.14 Full Text of `footer.jsf`

```
<HR></HR>
<FORM>
  <INPUT type="button" value="Return to Agency Menu"
         onClick='location="/agency/agency"'>
</FORM>
```

NOTE

In this case, location is a JavaScript event handler for `Button.onclick` and has nothing to do with the locations for jobs in the case study. Also, the destination (`/agency/agency`) should use URL rewriting to maintain the session ID between page accesses; this is covered on Day 14.

13

If you consider the structure of jobs and applicants in the case study, you will realize that they have two common components:

- A location that will be a value from an HTML select list
- A set of skills (possibly) empty that must also be chosen from a list (in this case, an HTML select list that supports multiple options)

Good Java design practice would be to avoid duplicating the code by putting it in a separate method (or helper class) where the functionality can be reused. With JSP design, you
can factor out the common code into a separate include file. The following code fragment shows how the JSP code for customer's advertised jobs uses include files:

```
<TABLE>
  <TR>
    <TD>Description:</TD>
    <TD><input type="text" name="description" value="${job.description}"></TD>
  </TR>
  <TR>
    <TD>Location:</TD>
    <TD>
      <% String location = job.getLocation(); %><%@include file="location.jsf"%>
    </TD>
  </TR>
  <TR>
    <TD>Skills:</TD>
    <TD>
      <% String[] skills = job.getSkills(); %><%@include file="skills.jsf"%>
    </TD>
  </TR>
</TABLE>
```

Each included file requires a variable to be defined before including the page (location
and skills); this is the equivalent of passing a parameter into a method. This is not an
ideal solution; in tomorrow's exercise, you will revisit this code and use tag libraries to
develop a cleaner solution.

The previous code is part of the advertise.jsp file (see Listing 13.15). This JSP maintains customer details and jobs. It uses two JavaBeans as wrappers around the two
Session EJBs called CustomerBean and JobBean. The JobBean wraps around the
advertiseJob EJB that uses a compound parameter to identify each job (customer login
and job reference). Creating this bean requires careful coding, as shown next. The list of
customer jobs must be processed on the Web page in a loop implemented as a Java
scriptlet, as shown in the following fragment:

```
<% String[] jobs = cust.getJobs(); %>
<jsp:useBean id="job" class="web.JobBean" scope="request">
  <jsp:setProperty name="job" property="customer" param="customer"/>
</jsp:useBean>
<% for (int i=0; i<jobs.length; i++) {%>
  <% job.setRef(jobs[i]); %>
  <H3><jsp:getProperty name="job" property="ref"/></H3>
...
<% } %>
```

Due to the way beans are defined on the page, this code has to be slightly clumsy. The bean is defined once before the Java loop when the customer part of the compound key is defined. Each time round the loop, the bean's setRef() method is called to set the next job reference; this method creates the appropriate advertiseJob Session EJB for use in the body of the loop. An alternative and much better approach is to use a custom tag, as shown on Day 14.

Listing 13.15 shows the entire advertise jobs page. The include files location.jsf and skills.jsf are included on the Web site—not shown here.

LISTING 13.15   Full Text of advertise.jsp

```
<HTML>
  <HEAD><TITLE>Advertise Customer Details</TITLE>
    <%@include file="header.jsf" %>
    <%@page import="java.util.*" %>
    <jsp:useBean id="cust" class="web.CustomerBean" scope="request" >
      <jsp:setProperty name="cust" property="login" param="customer"/>
    </jsp:useBean>
    <H2>Customer details for: <jsp:getProperty name="cust" property="login"/>
    </H2>
    <FORM action="updateCustomer">
      <INPUT type="hidden" name="login" value="<jsp:getProperty
            name="cust" property="login"/>">
      <TABLE>
        <TR><TD>Login:</TD>
          <TD><jsp:getProperty name="cust" property="login"/></TD></TR>
        <TR>
          <TD>Name:</TD>
          <TD><input type="text" name="name" value="<jsp:getProperty
                    name="cust" property="name"/>">
          </TD>
        </TR>
        <TR>
          <TD>Email:</TD>
          <TD><input type="text" name="email" value="<jsp:getProperty
                    name="cust" property="email"/>"></TD>
        </TR>
        <% String[] address = cust.getAddress(); %>
        <TR>
          <TD>Address:</TD>
          <TD><input type="text" name="address" value="<%=address[0]%>"></TD>
        </TR>
        <TR>
          <TD>Address:</TD>
          <TD><input type="text" name="address" value="<%=address[1]%>"></TD>
        </TR>
      </TABLE>
```

13

LISTING 13.15   continued

```
                <INPUT type="submit" value="Update Details">
                <INPUT type="reset">
            </FORM>
            <FORM action="deleteCustomer">
                <input type="hidden" name="customer" value="<%=cust.getName()%>">
                <input type="submit" value="Delete Customer
    <%=cust.getName()%>"></TD></TR>
            </FORM>
            <H2>Jobs</H2>
            <% String[] jobs = cust.getJobs(); %>
            <jsp:useBean id="job" class="web.JobBean" scope="request">
                <jsp:setProperty name="job" property="customer" param="customer"/>
            </jsp:useBean>
            <% for (int i=0; i<jobs.length; i++) {%>
            <% job.setRef(jobs[i]); %>
            <H3><jsp:getProperty name="job" property="ref"/></H3>
            <FORM action="updateJob">
              <TABLE>
                <TR><TD>Description:</TD>
                  <TD><input type="text" name="description" value="<jsp:getProperty
                          name="job" property="description"/>"></TD></TR>
                <TR><TD>Location:</TD>
                  <TD><% String location = job.getLocation(); %>
                      <%@include file="location.jsf"%>
                  </TD>
                </TR>
                <TR><TD>Skills:</TD>
                  <TD><% String[] skills = job.getSkills(); %>
                      <%@include file="skills.jsf"%>
                  </TD>
                </TR>
              </TABLE>
            <INPUT type="hidden" name="customer" value="<jsp:getProperty name="job"
                  property="customer"/>">
            <INPUT type="hidden" name="ref" value="<jsp:getProperty
                  name="job" property="ref"/>">
            <INPUT type="submit" value="Update Job">
            </FORM>
            <FORM action="deleteJob">
              <INPUT type="hidden" name="customer" value="<jsp:getProperty name="job"
                    property="customer"/>">
              <INPUT type="hidden" name="ref" value="<jsp:getProperty name="job"
                    property="ref"/>">
              <INPUT type="submit" value='Delete Job <jsp:getProperty name="job"
                    property="ref"/>'>
            </FORM>
            <% } %>
            <H2>Create New Job</H2>
            <FORM action="createJob">
```

LISTING 13.15 continued

```
        <TABLE>
          <TR>
            <TD>Ref:</TD>
            <TD><INPUT type="text" name="ref"></TD>
          </TR>
          <TR>
            <INPUT type="hidden" name="customer" value="<jsp:getProperty name="cust"
                    property="login"/>">
            <TD colspan=2><INPUT type="submit" value="Create Job"></TD>
          </TR>
        </TABLE>
        </FORM>
        <%@include file="footer.jsf" %>
      </BODY>
    </HTML>
```

To complete the customer functionality, the Web interface requires separate pages for

- Creating a new customer
- Deleting a customer
- Updating a customer
- Creating a new job
- Deleting a job
- Updating a job

Rather than reproduce all of these pages, the page for updating a customer is shown in Listing 13.16 (the others can be examined on the Web site). Each page simply creates the appropriate agency, customer, or job bean using the request parameters, and calls the necessary business method.

LISTING 13.16 Full Text of `updateCustomer.jsp`

```
<HTML>
  <HEAD>
    <TITLE>Update Customer</TITLE>
    <%@include file="header.jsf" %>
    <jsp:useBean id="cust" class="web.CustomerBean" scope="request" >
      <jsp:setProperty name="cust" property="login" param="login"/>
    </jsp:useBean>
    <% cust.updateDetails(request.getParameter("name"),
request.getParameter("email"),request.getParameterValues("address")); %>
    <H3>Updated <jsp:getProperty name="cust" property="login"/> Successfully
```

13

LISTING 13.16   continued

```
      </H3>
      <%@include file="footer.jsf" %>
    </BODY>
</HTML>
```

Error Page Definition

The last file to examine for the case study is the error page file shown in Listing 13.17.

LISTING 13.17   Full Text of `errorPage.jsp`

```jsp
<%@ page isErrorPage="true" %>
<%@page import="java.util.*, java.io.* " %>
<HTML>
  <HEAD>
    <TITLE>Agency Error Page</TITLE>
  </HEAD>
  <BODY>
    <H1>Agency Error Page</H1>
    <H2>There has been an error in processing your request.</H2>
    The following information describes the error:
    <H3>Request Parameters</H3>
    <TABLE border="1">
<%
Enumeration params = request.getParameterNames();
while (params.hasMoreElements()) {
  String name = (String)params.nextElement();
  out.println("<TR><TD>"+name+"</TD>");
  String[] values = request.getParameterValues(name);
  for (int i=0; i<values.length; i++) {
    out.println("<TD>"+values[i]+"</TD>");
  }
  out.println("</TR>");
}
%>
    </TABLE>
    <H3>Request Attributes</H3>
    <TABLE border="1">
<%
Enumeration attrs = request.getAttributeNames();
while (attrs.hasMoreElements()) {
  String name = (String)attrs.nextElement();
  out.println("<TR><TD>"+name+"</TD>");
  out.println("<TD>"+request.getAttribute(name)+"</TD>");
  out.println("</TR>");
}
%>
```

LISTING 13.17 continued

```
    </TABLE>
    <H3>Session Attributes</H3>
    <TABLE border="1">
<%
Enumeration sess = session.getAttributeNames();
while (sess.hasMoreElements()) {
  String name = (String)sess.nextElement();
  out.println("<TR><TD>"+name+"</TD>");
  out.println("<TD>"+session.getAttribute(name)+"</TD>");
  out.println("</TR>");
}
%>
    </TABLE>
    <H3>Exception</H3>
    <%=exception%>
    <H3>Stack Trace</H3>
<%
StringWriter buf = new StringWriter();
PrintWriter sout = new PrintWriter(buf);
exception.printStackTrace(sout);
out.println(buf.toString());
%>
  </BODY>
</HTML>
```

This error page is designed for use during development. When an exception occurs, this page displays information about the exception and various Java variables derived from the request, servlet, and page contexts.

At the top of Listing 13.17 is the line

```
<%@ page isErrorPage="true" %>
```

This tells the translation phase to include a variable called `exception` that refers to the exception that caused the page error. This exception is used to display a stack trace on the error page. The first line of the stack trace will identify

- The name of the generated servlet
- The line number where the exception occurred
- The exception that was thrown
- A brief description of the error

This information can be used to trace back the error to the original JSP file by using the Java code listing for the generated servlet.

13

For a fully-developed and deployed application, it would be better for the error page to display a user-friendly error message and report the error (perhaps via JavaMail) to an administrator.

The Agency case study error pages are designed to illustrate the principles involved in error reporting and are not necessarily an example of best practice.

Deploying the Case Study JSPs

In today's lesson, you have used a large number of files to create the Web interface to the job agency Session beans. You may find it simpler to use the pre-supplied webagency.war file in the Day13/exercise/j2ee-ri directory on the accompanying Web site or you can build the Web application using deploytool.

Finally, if you prefer, you can use the supplied asant build files to build and deploy the Web Agency example using:

```
asant build deploy
```

If you are using deploytool you need to perform the following steps.

1. Start up deploytool and create a new Web component and add it to a new Web Application file called webagency.war. Set the Web Application name to webagency and the Web context to webagency.

2. Add the following JSP files from the src/jsp directory to this war file:

   - admin.jsp
   - advertise.jsp
   - agency.css
   - agency.jsp
   - createCustomer.jsp
   - createJob.jsp
   - createLocation.jsp
   - createSkill.jsp
   - deletCustomer.jsp
   - deleteJob.jsp
   - deleteLocation.jsp
   - deleteSkill.jsp
   - errorPage.jsp
   - footer.jsf

- `header.jsf`
- `location.jsf`
- `modifyLocation.jsp`
- `modifySkill.jsp`
- `skills.jsf`
- `updateCustomer.jsp`
- `updateJob.jsp`
- `updateLocation.jsp`
- `updateSkill.jsp`

3. Add the following class files from the web directory to this WAR file:

- `AgencyBean.class`
- `CustomerBean.class`
- `JobBean.class`

4. Add the following class files from the agency directory to this WAR file:

- `Advertise.class`
- `AdvertiseHome.class`
- `AdvertiseJob.class`
- `AdvertiseJobHome.class`
- `Agency.class`
- `AgencyHome.class`
- `DuplicateException.class`
- `NotFoundException.class`
- `Register.class`
- `RegisterHome.class`

5. Click Next, select JSP for the EJB component, and then click Next.

6. Set the JSP Filename to `agency.jsp` and accept the default Web component name of agency.

7. Click Finish.

8. Highlight the agency Web component in the left-hand panel and select the Aliases tab. Add an alias for the `agency.jsp` of `/agency`.

9. Highlight the web application in the left-hand panel and select the EJB Refs tab. Add the EJB references shown in Table 13.5 (they are all Session beans with a remote interface).

13

TABLE 13.5   Case Study Web Application EJB References

Coded name	Home i/f	Remote i/f	Platform Specific JNDI name
ejb/agency	agency.AgencyHome	agency.Agency	ejb/agency
ejb/advertise	agency.AdvertiseHome	agency.Advertise	ejb/advertise
ejb/advertiseJob	agency.AdvertiseJobHome	agency.AdvertiseJob	ejb/advertiseJob

10. Now you will need to create Web components in the same WAR file for every other JSP. You have added all of the required files, so all you need to do is define each one as a JSP page and give it an alias. Table 13.6 lists all the pages you need to add.

TABLE 13.6   Case Study Web Application JSP Components

JSP Filename	Alias
advertise.jsp	/customer/advertise
admin.jsp	/admin/admin
createCustomer.jsp	/customer/createCustomer
createJob.jsp	/customer/createJob
createLocation.jsp	/admin/createLocation
createSkill.jsp	/admin/createSkill
deletCustomer.jsp	/customer/deleteCustomer
deleteJob.jsp	/customer/deleteJob
deleteLocation.jsp	/admin/deleteLocation
deleteSkill.jsp	/admin/deleteSkill
errorPage.jsp	/errorPage
updateCustomer.jsp	/customer/updateCustomer
updateJob.jsp	/customer/updateJob
updateLocation.jsp	/admin/updateLocation
updateSkill.jsp	/admin/updateSkill

11. Add agency.jsp as a welcome file and errorPage.jsp as an error page using the File Refs tab, as shown in Figure 13.6

12. Use Tools, Deploy to deploy your application.

FIGURE **13.6**

Defining Web Application Welcome and Error pages.

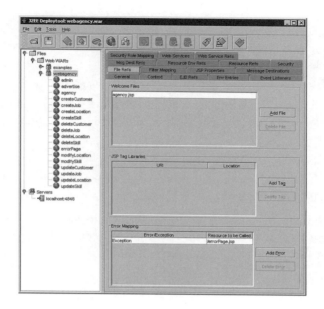

If you have not done so already, you must also deploy the Agency application so that the Web interface can communicate with it.

You can access the case study application, with its new Web front end using `http://localhost:8000/webagency`.

Web Application Architecture

As you have seen JSPs have several advantages over servlets. They

- Are quicker to write and develop
- Focus on the page layout and delegate Java logic to supporting JavaBeans and custom tags (as will be discussed on Day 14)
- Differentiate the Web page presentation (HTML) from the underlying logic (Java)
- Can be written by non-Java–aware developers
- Support a standard error reporting mechanism using the error page directive

13

However, JSPs do have some downsides:

- Error identification and correction is complicated by the translate and compile life-cycle.
- The syntax for manipulating JavaBean objects is clumsy.
- With JSP 1.2 large volumes of embedded Java scriptlets reduce the maintainability of the page. This problem has been alleviated by the introduction of EL and JSTL.

The speed of development and the quick turnaround on look and feel or simple functional changes that is possible with JSPs is a major advantage in modern Web-based applications. Consider using servlets only when the Java code is complex or needs to be "hand crafted" for efficiency.

The current thinking on using servlets and JSPs is to combine the two technologies in what is known as a Model 2 Architecture shown in Figure 13.7. The simpler approach of just using a servlets or a JSP is known as a Model 1 architecture (see Day 2).

FIGURE 13.7

Model 2 Web Application.

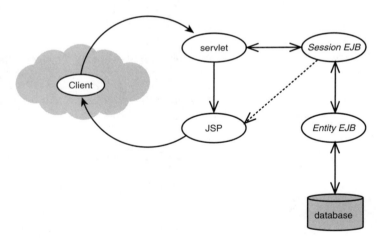

In a Model 2 architecture the incoming HTTP request is handled by a servlet which validates any HTTP request data and updates the database if necessary. Typically, Session beans will be used to support the servlet functionality. The Session beans in turn may use Entity beans to encapsulate access to a database. In a simple application not making use of EJB technology simple JavaBean helper classes will be used in place of the EJBs.

Once the servlet has verified the request and obtained the necessary data to formulate the response, the request is forwarded to a JSP for generating the Web page to return to the client. Typically the JSP will only read data from the Session bean so that the different roles of the servlet as a controller and the JSP as a presentation (or view) component are clearly encapsulated. Experienced developers will recognize this architecture as the Model View Controller (MVC) architecture; the EJBs take the role of the Model component.

The Model 2 architecture is so popular that products such as Apache Struts (http://jakarta.apache.org/struts) and Sun Microsystems' JavaServer Faces (JSF from http://java.sun.com/j2ee/javaserverfaces) provide frameworks for building Model 2-based Web applications.

The Agency case study example uses a model 1 architecture as it is a learning tool. In reality using a model 2 architecture for the Agency case study would show significant benefits in ease of development and maintenance.

An additional advantage of this servlet/JSP approach is that the servlet can use one of several JSPs to present the data according to the type of client making the request. You can define one JSP for HTML clients (PCs) and another for WML clients (mobile phones). In the future, you can add additional clients for, say, XML clients or a presentation language that has not yet been defined. All of these different presentation requirements can be supported by a single servlet. Any future changes to the underlying business rules are only made once in the logic of the servlet, with any necessary changes in the presentation being made in the appropriate JSPs.

Such a variant of the Model 2 architecture is known as a Model View Controller (MVC) architecture. In a J2EE world the Model is implemented using EJBs and JavaBeans, the View components are JSPs and the Controller is a servlet (or multiple servlets).

Summary

Today, you have looked at using JavaServer Pages as a means of developing Web-based J2EE applications. Unlike servlets, JSPs allow you to develop your Web pages in HTML with embedded Java code when dynamic elements are required.

JSP pages are translated into Java servlets and compiled before they are used to service client requests. To the browser, a JSP is no different than any other Web page.

JSP defines elements to supplement the standard HTML tags:

- Directives that are used to pass information to the page translation phase
- Expression Language and JSP expressions to embed dynamic data in the Web page
- JSP scriptlets to provide programming logic
- Actions that define JSP tags used to support JavaBeans

13

JavaBeans are used to encapsulate Java functionality to remove Java code from the Web page. JavaBeans help separate the role of Java developer from that of HTML Web developer. Beans are classes that have a no argument constructor and properties. Bean properties have names, are queried using getter methods, and are updated using setter methods.

In the next lesson, you will look at the JavaServer Pages Tag Library (JSTL) and you will see how to define your own custom tags as part of a tag library. Tag libraries support complex page features, such as the iterative processing of dynamic data (such as a list of customers).

Q&A

Q Why is a JSP a more appropriate way of writing a servlet that is used primarily to display HTML?

A Because the programming logic is embedded in the HTML. This avoids the laborious process of writing large numbers of `out.println()` statements required by normal servlets and makes JSPs easier for non-programmers to produce.

Q What are the four types of errors that can occur on a JSP?

A Translation, compilation, Java runtime and HTML syntax errors.

Q What is the Expression Language?

A It is a language used on a JSP to simplify data access. In conjunction with JavaBeans, JSTL, and custom tag libraries, it enables all the Java code to be removed from the JSP.

Q What are the three JSP actions that support the use of JavaBeans?

A `<jsp:useBean>`, `<jsp:setProperty>`, and `<jsp:getProperty>`.

Q What sort of constructor must a JavaBean have?

A It must have a no argument constructor.

Exercise

Using the JSP code shown in today's lesson, provide the register applicant functionality for the Web interface to the Agency case study. Use the `webagency.war` Web application in the `Day13/examples` directory on the Web site as the starting point for your exercise.

You will need to perform the following steps. Build and deploy your application as you complete each step.

1. Add a createApplicant.jsp page with the alias /applicant/createApplicant to support the create applicant functionality on the agency.jsp page. Model your solution on the createCustomer.jsp page already provided.

2. Using advertise.jsp as a guide, develop a Web page called register.jsp to handle client registration. The links to invoke this page from the agency.jsp home page have already been provided.

3. Add the ability to update the applicant details and code an updateApplicant.jsp page that is accessed from a form on the register.jsp page and has the alias /applicant/updateApplicant.

4. Add functionality to the register.jsp page to delete an applicant and write the deleteApplicant.jsp page (alias /applicant/deleteApplicant).

A solution is provided in Day13/agency on the accompanying Web site.

13

DAY **14**

JSP Tag Libraries

In the previous two days' chapters, you have learned about J2EE Web applications written using servlets and JSPs. You have seen how servlets are most useful when complex Java programming is needed and JSPs are more appropriate to use when the generated Web page requires large amounts of HTML (or JavaScript). So far, to support complex features, you have had to write Java code in JSP in the form of scriptlets. There is another way, however. JSTL (JavaServer Pages Standard Tag Library) and custom tag libraries (TagLibs) provide a natural extension to the JSP tag syntax.

JSTL has been developed to make writing JSPs easier. It has the following advantages:

- Removes the need for JSP writers to manipulate the dynamic data using Java code.
- Supports the JSP Expression Language (EL).
- Provides comprehensive support for common JSP requirements.

JSTL provides many of the features required by JSP authors but does not remove entirely the need for Java code. This is where custom tags come in.

Custom tags are written entirely in Java in separate classes and made available to the JSP through a Tag Library Descriptor (TLD) file.

In today's chapter, you will see how to

- Use JSTL and EL to replace JSP scriptlets
- Deploy the agency case study with the JSTL tag libraries
- Write simple custom tags
- Write a TLD XML deployment descriptor for Tag Libraries

The Role of Tag Libraries

JSPs make it possible for you to develop Web-based applications using Java without being a Java expert. By utilizing well-designed JavaBeans, you can work almost entirely with HTML and JSP tags. However, as you saw in yesterday's work, you will still sometimes need to provide programming constructs in the JSP, and for this you had to use Java scriptlets to realize the full power of JSPs.

JSTL and custom tag libraries extend the JSP philosophy so that it is possible for you to write most, if not all, of your Web pages without using Java code.

This is a big advantage that can be utilized to good effect in development teams. By separating out the Java code into custom tags, a development team can utilize their individual skills more effectively. Java programmers are now used to develop the business logic in custom tags, while HTML/JSP developers can focus on developing the presentation logic and look-and-feel of Web pages. Tag libraries were introduced with JSP 1.1, and the JSTL was incorporated into the J2EE 1.4 specification in 2002. In addition to the JSTL there are a number of other custom tag libraries available; the most extensive collection being the Jakarta Taglibs available from `http://jakarta.apache.org/taglibs/`.

JavaServer Pages Standard Tag Library (JSTL)

The JSTL is a collection of custom JSP tags and a supporting expression language that has been designed to simplify writing JSPs. Full details of the JSTL can be found at `http://java.sun.com/products/jsp/jstl/`. The JSTL is a standard component of J2EE 1.4 but you can also download it for use with J2EE 1.3 compliant servlet containers.

The JSTL specification defines several tag libraries each supporting a particular functional area and having its own JSP namespace and TLD URI. The areas are summarized in Table 14.1.

TABLE 14.1 JavaServer Pages Tag Libraries

Function	Namespace Prefix	TLD URL
Core – conditional, iterators and URL actions	c	http://java.sun.com/jsp/jstl/core
XML processing	x	http://java.sun.com/jsp/jstl/xml
Internationalization and Formatting	fmt	http://java.sun.com/jsp/jstl/fmt
Relational database access and SQL	sql	http://java.sun.com/jsp/jstl/sql
Functions for manipulating strings and collections	fn	http://java.sun.com/jsp/jstl/functions

NOTE

> The prefixes are conventional. You do not have to use these prefixes in your JSP, but unless there are good reasons not to (because of established naming conventions for a development project) it is recommended that you restrict the use of these particular prefixes for JSTL. In this way it is clear that you are using JSTL tags and not other custom tags.

To use a tag library on your web page you will need to include a JSP taglib directive defining the Tag Library Descriptor file in the JSP. A TLD file maps the tag names used in the JSP page onto the Java class that implements the tag. You will look at TLDs in more detail later when you write your own custom tag. For now, you will use the TLDs provided with JSTL.

For most of the examples you will see today, you will use the JSTL core library. The following shows how you would declare this in your JSP:

```
<%@ taglib prefix="c" uri="http://java.sun.com/jsp/jstl/core" %>
```

In the J2EE RI, the JSTL TLDs and libraries are distributed in the archive appserv-jstl.jar in <J2EE_HOME>/lib/. This archive is automatically loaded into your classpath, so you don't need to add it to your Web application.

JSTL Core Library

The JSTL core library provides a number of tags, or actions, that can be grouped according to their use. Table 14.2 shows some of the core library tags.

14

TABLE 14.2   JSTL Core Library Tags.

Action Tag	Description
`<c:out>`	Alternative to using EL expressions.
`<c:set>`	Sets the value of a JSP scoped attribute.
`<c:remove>`	Opposite of `<c:set>`—removes a scoped attribute from the JSP.
`<c:catch>`	Enables you to catch and therefore handle recoverable errors in the JSP.
`<c:forEach>`	Provides a way of iterating over a collection or the equivalent of a `for-loop` construct.
`<c:forTokens>`	Enables iteration over tokens separated by a given delimiter.
`<c:if>`	Provides the equivalent of a programmatic `if` statement.

`<c:choose>`
`<c:when>`
`<c:otherwise>`
	Together these provide a mutually exclusive conditional list similar to the Java `switch` statement.

`<c:url>`	Provides URL rewriting for URL links.

The following sections briefly look at some of these actions.

`<c:out>`

The `<c:out>` action simply evaluates the string value of its value attribute and outputs the result to the Web page. For example,

```
<c:out value="${param.name}" />
```

will output the value of the request parameter called `name`. You saw on Day 13 an easier way to do this with EL. Therefore, the two following statements are equivalent:

```
<H1><c:out value="${param.name}" /></H1>
<H1>${param.name}</H1>
```

The `<c:out>` action provides a useful default value for when the EL expression evaluates to null. For example, the following takes care of the case when the user does not provide a request parameter:

```
<c:out value=${param.name} default="Error name not supplied" />
```

The `<c:out>` action can be used with pre-JSP 2.0 containers that support tag libraries but not the expression language.

`<c:set>`

The `<c:set>` action is used to set a value for a JSP scoped attribute and has a similar role to the `<jsp:useBean>` tag. For example, an attribute called counter could be incremented as follows:

```
<c:set var="counter" value="${counter + 1}" />
```

An attribute is scoped; the scope can be one of the following:

- page
- request
- session
- application

The default is page scope. If you need the attribute to survive beyond the page, you must specify the scope explicitly, as shown here:

```
<c:set var="counter" value="${counter + 1}" scope="session" />
```

NOTE

Attribute names are searched for in each scope in turn. Therefore, a page scope attribute will hide an attribute of the same name in any other scope.

The `<c:set>` action can also set a property of a JavaBean. For example, presuming you have a JavaBean called customer, you can set a property called login to the value of the request parameter of the same name using the target and property attributes, as follows:

```
<jsp:useBean id="customer" class="CustomerBean" scope="request" />
<c:set target="${customer}" property="login" value="${param.login}" />
```

When you use the var attribute, you are setting a scoped variable on the page; when you use a target, this must evaluate to a JavaBean object that has a setter method for the property you want to set.

As you have probably spotted, the `<c:set>` tag used in this way can replace `<jsp:setProperty>` actions. Another very useful feature of the target attribute of `<c:set>` is that you can use it to add elements to a Java Map object. For example, if the CustomerBean example has the following variable declaration:

```
private HashMap info;
```

you can add elements to this map with

```
<c:set target="${customer.info}" property="age" value="22" />
<c:set target="${customer.info}" property="sex" value="male" />
```

14

You can use the `<forEach>` element, described in the following section, to iterate over this map.

`<c:forEach>`

The `<c:forEach>` action provides iteration over any type of Java collection object. This tag is extremely useful and, more than any other JSTL element, is likely to replace scripting elements on a JSP. For example, if the `CustomerBean` has a `jobs` collection containing all the jobs that customer has advertised, you can create a simple list of those jobs using the following:

```
<c:forEach var="job" items=${customer.jobs} >
  <P>${job}</P>
</c:forEach>
```

The body of the element is evaluated repeatedly for every member of the collection specified by the `items` attribute. The `var` attribute provides access to each member object in turn.

Another use of `<c:forEach>` is to access items in a Java `Map`. With a `Map` object, the `key` and `value` properties provide access to the `Map` entries. For example, the following generates a table containing the information you previously saw stored in the `CustomerBean.info` Map:

```
<TABLE>
  <c:forEach var="item" items="${customer.info}" >
    <TR><TD>${item.key}</TD><TD>${item.value}</TD></TR>
  </c:forEach>
</TABLE>
```

`<c:if>`

Not surprisingly, you use `<c:if>` to add a conditional action to a JSP. For example, the following sets a variable in a nested `<c:forEach>` to "true" if the customer job (`custJob`) is found in the collection of agency jobs:

```
<c:forEach var="agencyJob" items="${agency.jobs}" >
  <c:set var="jobFound" value="false"/>
  <c:forEach var="custJob" items="${customer.jobs}" >
    <c:if test="${custJob == agencyJob}" >
      <c:set var="jobFound" value="true"/>
    </c:if>
  </c:forEach>
  <!-- other processing omitted ... -->
</c:forEach>
```

Note that the "==" operator in the test behaves as you would hope: it compares the values of the two variables.

There is no `<c:else>` action, but this functionality can be achieved using the `<c:choose>` action.

`<c:choose>`

The `<c:choose>` action provides a mutually exclusive multi-way conditional statement (like a Java `switch` statement). Each condition is enclosed in a `<c:when>` action; with an `<c:otherwise>` providing a catch-all at the end. You can have a number of `<c:when>` actions, but only the first to have a `test` condition that evaluates to true will have its body processed; all others are ignored. Continuing the customer job example, the `<c:choose>` statement here operates as a if-then-else:

```
<c:forEach var="custJob" items="${customer.jobs}" >
  <c:set var="jobFound" value="false"/>
  <c:forEach var="agencyJob" items="${agency.jobs}" >
    <c:if test="${custJob == agencyJob}" >
      <c:set var="jobFound" value="true"/>
    </c:if>
  </c:forEach>
  <c:choose>
    <c:when test="${jobFound}" >
      ${custJob} is already registered
    </c:when>
    <c:otherwise>
      Registering ${custJob}
      <!-- code ommitted -->
    </c:otherwise>
  </c:choose>
</c:forEach>
```

The `<c:otherwise>` is optional and is only processed if none of the `<c:when>` actions evaluate to true.

`<c:url>`

Maintaining session information when cookies are disabled relies on URL rewriting (this subject was covered on Day 12 "Servlets"). Using the `<c:url>` action, you now have a convenient way of ensuring that your application always uses URL rewriting for any links.

The following example shows how to use the `<c:url>` in the action attribute of an HTML FORM tag:

```
<FORM action='<c:url value="/applicant/register" />'>
```

14

Other JSTL Libraries

The actions in the JSTL core library provide the general purpose and programming constructs required by all JSPs. The other JSTL libraries provide support for more specialized, but still common, requirements.

Internationalization and Formatting Tag Library

Many Web sites need to provide at least some content in different languages, and some require the entire site to be produced in multiple languages. With static content, the solution is to simply provide copies of the pages in each language. The replication is not a big issue (you have to translate the text in any case), but with dynamic pages maintenance of multiple pages providing the same functionality in different languages would be tedious and error prone.

With the use of resource bundles and the JSTL Internationalization and Formatting library, it is now very simple to internationalize your JSP pages. Resource bundles are collections of text strings accessed by a key, as described in the `java.util`. `ResourceBundle` API documentation. You do, of course, have to supply a resource bundle for each language required, each bundle containing equivalent translations of the strings required on the JSP. The resource bundle used is determined by the locale for the JSP. The locale for a Web page is taken from the HTTP request headers supplied by the client but this can be overridden on the JSP page or in the Web Application deployment descriptor. For example the following contrived example sets the locale to `en_US` to ensure the welcome message is printed in U.S. English:

```
<fmt:setBundle basename="messages" />
<fmt:setLocale value="en_US" />
<fmt:message key="welcome" />
```

A number of other actions are provided to format numbers, currencies, and dates according to the client's locale. These actions are also useful for setting consistent formats for data displayed on the JSPs even when internationalization is not required.

SQL Tag Library

As a J2EE exponent, you would probably use a Model View Controller (MVC) architecture for your applications and wrap any database access in an EJB. Nevertheless, for simple Web applications or for testing purposes (checking that your EJB works), the JSTL SQL library provides basic relational database access. As you would expect, the library provides query and update actions as well as transaction control.

Listing 14.1 is a simple HTML form that lists the tables in the Agency database and allows the user to select one.

The JSP that prints out the tables is shown in Listing 14.2. As the name of the table is passed as a request parameter, this JSP can be used to output any table from an SQL database.

LISTING 14.1   tableForm.jsp

```
<%@ taglib prefix="c" uri="http://java.sun.com/jsp/jstl/core" %>
<HTML>
  <HEAD><TITLE>Agency Tables</TITLE></HEAD>
  <BODY>
    <FORM action='<c:url value="/table" />' >
     Select a table to display:
      <SELECT name="table">
        <OPTION>Applicant
        <OPTION>ApplicantSkill
        <OPTION>Customer
        <OPTION>Job
        <OPTION>JobSKill
        <OPTION>Location
        <OPTION>Matched
        <OPTION>Skill
      </SELECT>
      <P><INPUT type="submit"></P>
    </FORM>
  </BODY>
</HTML>
```

LISTING 14.2   table.jsp

```
<%@ taglib prefix="c" uri="http://java.sun.com/jsp/jstl/core" %>
<%@ taglib prefix="sql" uri="http://java.sun.com/jsp/jstl/sql" %>

<HTML>
  <HEAD><TITLE>Agency Table: ${param.table}</TITLE> </HEAD>
  <BODY>
    <H1>Data for table ${param.table}</H1>
    <sql:query var="table" sql="SELECT * FROM ${param.table}" />
    <TABLE border="1">
      <TR>
        <c:forEach var="col" items="${table.columnNames}" >
          <TH>${col}</TH>
        </c:forEach>
      </TR>
      <c:forEach var="row" items="${table.rowsByIndex}" >
        <TR>
          <c:forEach var="col" items="${row}" >
            <TD>${col}</TD>
```

14

LISTING 14.2   continued

```
            </c:forEach>
          </TR>
        </c:forEach>
      </TABLE>
    </BODY>
  </HTML>
```

This code is very simple and almost self-explanatory. You obviously need to include the JSTL sql Taglib and give it the sql prefix. The table name is passed to this JSP in the request parameter called table. The SQL query returns a javax.servlet.jsp.jstl.sql.Result object, which has the following properties:

- rows—An array of java.util.SortedMap with each Map representing a row. The Map key and value properties are used to access the column name and corresponding column value.
- rowsByIndex—An array of Object[]. Differs from rows in that only the column values are available.
- columnNames—An array of String containing the column names.
- rowCount—The number of rows in the result.

Listing 14.2 iterates through all the rows and then through the columns in the row, outputting each row and column value in a table cell.

To view this example, you need to add these two JSPs to a Web application and define a data source called jdbc/Agency for the Agency database. Use the supplied asant build files to build and deploy this example from the Day14/examples directory supplied on the accompanying Web site. To build and deploy use the command:

```
asant build deploy
```

Alternatively, use deploytool to deploy the supplied examples.war file in the Day 14/examples/j2ee-ri directory.

The URL to access the tableForm.jsp is

```
http://localhost:8000/examples/tableForm
```

XML Library

The XML library provides actions for managing XML documents. This library uses the XPath expression language described on Day 17, "Transforming XML Documents," in a similar manner to using EL in the core library.

The XML library has a number of actions providing similar functionality to the core library actions but which take XPath expressions. In addition, you can use the `<x:transform>` action to apply an XSLT stylesheet transformation to an XML document.

Functions Library

Finally, the functions library provides actions for retrieving the length attribute of a collection and manipulating strings. The string manipulation operations provide access to the `java.lang.String` class functions for converting letter case, searching strings, splitting and joining strings and extracting substrings.

Developing a Simple Custom Tag

Unfortunately, using JSTL will not always provide the functionality you need; even when it can, there are circumstances when using your own custom tag might make the JSP simpler to maintain.

A custom tag is made up of two components:

- A Java class file that implements the tag
- An entry in a Tag Library Descriptor (TLD) file that defines the tag's name, its implementing Java class, and additional information necessary to deploy and use the tag

Just as with JSTL, using a custom tag requires a reference to the Tag Library Descriptor (TLD) at the start of the JSP. Multiple Tag Libraries can be used on the same Web page. After the TLD has been referenced, the custom tag from the TLD can be used like any other JSP tag.

Using a Simple Tag

To start writing and using TagLibs, you will implement a very simple custom tag that writes "Hello World" onto your Web page. This isn't a good use of a custom tag, but it will help you understand the principles involved and guide you through the deployment process. After this simple example, you will look at how to use custom tags to remove any remaining Java scriptlets from your JSP applications.

Every custom tag potentially has three parts:

- The starting tag, such as `<demo:hello>`
- The ending tag, such as `</demo:hello>`
- The tag's body, which is the text between the start and end tags

14

A tag that does not have a body is called an empty tag and is usually written as
`<demo:hello/>`.

The example in Listing 14.3 shows an empty tag that inserts `Hello World` on the JSP
page.

LISTING 14.3   Full Text of `helloTag.jsp`

```
<%@ taglib prefix="demo" uri="/demo.tld" %>
<HTML>
  <HEAD><TITLE>Tag Library Hello Demo</TITLE></HEAD>
  <BODY>
    <demo:hello/>
  </BODY>
</HTML>
```

The very first line of the JSP in Listing 14.3 defines the Tag Library and associates the
tags in the library with the demo prefix. Unlike the JSTL tag libraries the custom tag
doesn't use an absolute URI for the library location but defines a tag library name that
will be mapped onto the actual tag library location in the Web Application deployment
descriptor.

The tag itself is used inside the HTML `<BODY>` tag, and its name is `hello`.

Defining Custom Java Tags

You define custom tags by using Java classes that implement one of the
`javax.servlet.jsp.tagext` interfaces shown in Table 14.3.

TABLE 14.3   Interfaces for Custom Tags

Java Interface	Description
Tag	Implement this interface for simple tags that do not need to process the tag body.
IterationTag	Implement this interface for tags that need to process the body text more than once to implement an iterative loop.
BodyTag	Implement this interface for tags that need to process the text in the tag body.

Implementing these interfaces requires that you define several methods to manage the
lifecycle of the custom tag. To simplify custom tag development, two support classes are
provided in the `javax.servlet.jsp.tagext` package. These classes provide default

behavior for each of the required interface methods, and you will simply override the methods you require. Table 14.4 shows the two supporting classes.

TABLE 14.4 Support Classes for Custom Tags

java Class	Description
`TagSupport implements Tag`	Extend this class for tags that do not have a body or do not interact with the tag body.
`BodyTagSupport implements Tag, IterationTag, BodyTag`	Extend this class when the tag body must be processed as part of the tag, such as an iterative tag or a tag that interprets the body in some way.

The `Tag`, `TagIteration`, and `TagSupport` interfaces in the `javax.servlet.jsp.tagext` package define several methods that control the processing of the custom tag. Figure 14.1 summarizes the lifecycle of a Tag Library object.

FIGURE 14.1

The Custom Tag lifecycle.

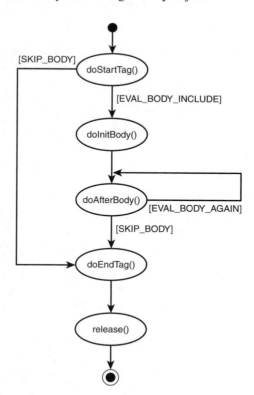

14

The `doStartTag()` Method

The `doStartTag()` method is called once when the start tag is processed. This method must return an int value that tells the JSP how to process the tag body. The returned value must be one of the following:

- `Tag.SKIP_BODY` The tag body must be ignored. The TLD should define the `<body-content>` tag as `empty`.

- `Tag.EVAL_BODY_INCLUDE` The body tag must be evaluated and included in the JSP page. The TLD should define the `<body-content>` tag as `JSP` for tags that extend `TagSupport`, or `JSP` or `tagdependent` for tags that extend `BodyTagSupport`.

The `doEndTag()` Method

The `doEndTag()` method is called once when the end tag is processed. This method must return an int value indicating how the remainder of the JSP page should be processed:

- `Tag.EVAL_PAGE` Evaluate the rest of the page.
- `Tag.SKIP_PAGE` Stop processing the page after this tag.

Where a tag has an empty body, the `doEndTag()` method is still called after the `doStartTag()` method.

The `release()` Method

The `release()` method is called once when the JSP has finished using the tag and is used to allow the tag to release any resources it may have acquired. This method's return type is `void`.

The `doAfterBody()` Method

The `doAfterBody()` method is called after the tag body has been processed and before the `doEndTag()` method is called. This method is only called for classes that implement `IterationTag` or `BodyTag` (those that extend `BodyTagSupport`). It must return one of the following values to the JSP page indicating how the tag body should be processed:

- `IterationTag.EVAL_BODY_AGAIN` This value is used to inform the page that the tag body should be processed once more. The JSP processing will read and process the tag body and call the `doAfterBody()` method once more after the body has been processed again.

  When returning the `EVAL_BODY_AGAIN` result, this method will typically change some value so that when the tag body is processed again, different output is written to the Web page. A simple example would be a tag that executes a database query in the `doStartTag()` method and reads each row of the result set. While there are more rows to process EVAL_BODY_AGAIN is returned. After the last row is processed SKIP_BODY is returned.

- Tag.SKIP_BODY This value marks the end of the processing of the tag body.

The doInitBody() Method

The doInitBody() method is called once after the doStartTag() method but before the tag body is processed. doInitBody() is only used in tags that implement the BodyTag interface (those that extend BodyTagSupport). This method is not called if the doStartTag() method returns SKIP_BODY. The doInitBody() method returns void.

Defining The "Hello World" Custom Tag

If all the lifecycle methods and their return values have left you a little bewildered then a simple example should help to clear things up. The example Hello World tag shown in Listing 14.3 does not have a body, so it need only implement the Tag interface, which is best achieved by extending the TagSupport class and overriding the required methods, as shown in Listing 14.4.

LISTING 14.4   Full Text of HelloTag.java

```java
package examples;

import javax.servlet.jsp.*;
import javax.servlet.jsp.tagext.*;

public class HelloTag extends TagSupport {
    public int doStartTag() throws JspException {
        try {
            pageContext.getOut().print("Hello World");
        } catch (Exception ex) {
            throw new JspTagException("HelloTag: "+ex);
        }
        return SKIP_BODY;
    }

    public int doEndTag() {
        return EVAL_PAGE;
    }

    public void release() {
    }
}
```

14

All the work in this custom tag is done in the `doStartTag()` method. The current output stream is obtained from the page context and used to print the `"Hello World"` string:

```
pageContext.getOut().print("Hello World");
```

The custom tag class is defined as part of the custom tag in the TLD file for the library, as shown next.

The Tag Library Descriptor (TLD)

TLD files map the tag name used in the JSP page onto the Java class that implements the tag. A TLD file is written in XML and an example is given in Listing 14.5, which shows the TLD file for the "Hello World" tag.

LISTING 14.5   Full Text of `demo.tld`

```
<?xml version="1.0" encoding="ISO-8859-1" ?>
<taglib
    xmlns="http://java.sun.com/xml/ns/j2ee"
    xmlns:xsi="http://www.w3.org/2001/XMLSchema-instance"
    xsi:schemaLocation="http://java.sun.com/xml/ns/j2ee/web-
jsptaglibrary_2_0.xsd"
    version="2.0">
  <tlib-version>1.0</tlib-version>
  <jsp-version>2.0</jsp-version>
  <short-name>demo</short-name>
  <tag>
    <name>hello</name>
    <tag-class>demo.HelloTag</tag-class>
    <body-content>empty</body-content>
  </tag>
</taglib>
```

At the present time, the J2EE RI from Sun Microsystems does not include any support for generating this file from within `deploytool`. You will have to write your TLD files by hand and include them in your Web application.

To write a TLD, you will need to be familiar with XML. If you are new to XML, this might be a good time to have a quick look at Appendix A, "An Overview of XML," before continuing to learn how TLD files work. The use of XML in enterprise applications is also discussed on Day 16, "Integrating XML with J2EE."

The start of the TLD file defines the Tag Library and JSP specification conformance for this TLD. After the Tag Library version information is defined, the rest of the TLD is used to specify the custom tags in the library.

In the TLD, a `<tag>` tag defines a custom tag. Several custom tags can be defined in a single library. The minimal requirements for each custom tag are as follows:

- The tag name to be used on the Web page
- The Java class name that implements the tag
- The type of tag body (see Table 14.5)

In the following example, the tag class is `demo.HelloTag`, and the tag name is `hello`:

```
<tag>
  <name>hello</name>
  <tag-class>demo.HelloTag</tag-class>
  <body-content>empty</body-content>
</tag>
```

In this case, the `<body-content>` tag defines the tag to have an empty body. The possible values for the `<body-content>` tag are shown in Table 14.5.

TABLE 14.5 Tag Body Contents

Tag	Description
empty	The tag body must be empty. The page translation will fail if the developer puts any text between the start and end tags.
JSP	The tag contains JSP data and will normally be processed in the same manner as other parts of the page.
tagdependent	The text between the start and end tags will be processed by the Java class and will not be interpreted as JSP tagged content (the JSTL `sql:query` element is an example of this style of tag).

The `<body-content>` type must be compatible with the way the Java code processes the tag.

The TLD file itself is normally included directly in your Web application (as this simplifies distribution). The deployment descriptor `<taglib>` element maps the URI used on the JSP to the location of the TLD in the Web application. It is conventional to include the TLD file in the WEB-INF directory along with the deployment descriptors. The following entry defines the TLD location for the example tag:

```
<jsp-config>
  <taglib>
    <taglib-uri>/demo.tld</taglib-uri>
    <taglib-location>/WEB-INF/demo.tld</taglib-location>
  </taglib>
</jsp-config>
```

14

You will see how to add the `<taglib>` element using `deploytool` in the next section. If you use an absolute URI, as shown in the JSTL examples, you do not need to include a `<taglib>` directive in the DD.

Deploying a Tag Library Web Application

To deploy a Web Application that uses a custom Tag Library, you will follow the same steps as for a Web Application using JSTL. Using `deploytool`, you must add the TLD file and the Tag Library implementation class files when you create the Web component.

Using `deploytool` the mapping of the Tag Library URI to the TLD file location is specified on the File Refs dialogue page for the Web application. Figure 14.2 shows the mapping for the simple `hello` tag example.

FIGURE 14.2

Mapping the Tag Library URI to the TLD.

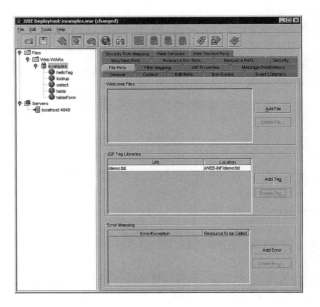

A pre-supplied WAR file is on the accompanying Web site as `Day14/examples/j2ee-ri/examples.war`. You can open the WAR file with `deploytool` and deploy the examples using the File, Deploy menu option.

Alternatively, you can use the `asant` build files supplied on the Web site to build and deploy the example using

```
asant build deploy
```

Use the following URL to view the page

```
http://localhost:8000/examples/helloTag
```

Beyond Simple Tags

You would not normally write tags as simple as the Hello World example. Even so, simple tags like this do serve a purpose. They can be used to retrieve information from the system and display it via the JSP page. The mechanics of accessing the information are hidden inside the custom tag code and are not shown on the JSP page. Hiding complex operations (perhaps a JNDI lookup operation or obtaining data from a database) helps simplify the writing of the Web page.

However, without the ability to pass information into the tag, this functionality has limited use.

Tag Libraries support the following two ways of passing information from the page into the tag:

- Via attributes passed in with the tag
- Via the text in the body of the tag

Using attributes is the most common approach and is discussed in detail in the following section. Use of tag-specific body data is outside the scope of today's exercise.

Tags with Attributes

Attributes are used to pass information into a custom tag to configure the behavior of the tag. Tag attributes are like XML or HTML attributes and are name/value pairs of data. The values must be quoted with single or double quotes.

A simple example might be a tag that lists the rows in a table given a JNDI DataSource and table name as attributes. Listing 14.6 shows how such a tag could be used.

LISTING 14.6   Full Text of lookup.jsp

```
<%@ taglib prefix="demo" uri="/demo.tld" %>
<HTML>
  <HEAD><TITLE>Tag Library Lookup Demo</TITLE></HEAD>
  <BODY>
    <demo:lookup
        dataSource="java:comp/env/jdbc/Agency"
        table="${param.table}"/>
    <H2>Select a table to display:</H2>
    <FORM action='lookup' >
      <SELECT name="table">
        <OPTION>Applicant</OPTION>
        <OPTION>ApplicantSkill</OPTION>
        <OPTION>Customer</OPTION>
```

14

LISTING 14.6   continued

```
          <OPTION>Job</OPTION>
          <OPTION>JobSkill</OPTION>
          <OPTION>Location</OPTION>
          <OPTION>Matched</OPTION>
          <OPTION>Skill</OPTION>
        </SELECT>
        <P><INPUT type="submit"></P>
      </FORM>
    </BODY>
  </HTML>
```

The JSP specification allows attributes to use the Expression Language. In Listing 14.6 the dataSource attribute uses a simple string value whereas the table attribute uses a request time expression.

The TLD description for the tag must define any attributes it uses. Each supported attribute name must be listed together with details of the attribute. Every attribute must have an <attribute> tag with the sub-components shown in Table 14.6.

TABLE 14.6   TLD Tags for Defining Attributes

Tag	Description
attribute	Introduces an attribute definition in the <tag> component of the TLD.
name	Defines the attribute name.
required	Followed by true if the attribute must be provided; otherwise, false.
rtexprvalue	Defines whether the attribute can be specified with a request time expression. Set this element to true to allow EL in the value of the attribute; otherwise, the value must be a string literal.
type	Defines the type of an attribute and defaults to java.lang.String. This element must be defined if the rtexprvalue is true and the attribute value is not a String.

Listing 14.7 shows the complete TLD entry for the lookup tag.

LISTING 14.7   TLD Entry for the lookup Tag

```
<tag>
  <name>lookup</name>
  <tag-class>demo.LookupTag</tag-class>
  <body-content>empty</body-content>
  <attribute>
```

LISTING 14.7 continued

```
    <name>dataSource</name>
    <required>true</required>
    <rtexprvalue>true</rtexprvalue>
  </attribute>
  <attribute>
    <name>table</name>
    <required>true</required>
    <rtexprvalue>true</rtexprvalue>
  </attribute>
</tag>
```

For a tag to support attributes, it must follow the JavaBean idiom of providing get and set methods for manipulating the attributes as shown in Listing 14.8.

LISTING 14.8 Full Text of LookupTag.java

```
package demo;

import java.io.*;
import java.sql.*;
import javax.sql.*;
import javax.naming.*;
import javax.servlet.jsp.*;
import javax.servlet.jsp.tagext.*;

public class LookupTag extends TagSupport {
    private String dataSource;
    private String table;

    public String getDataSource() {
        return dataSource;
    }

    public void setDataSource(String dataSource) {
        this.dataSource = dataSource;
    }

    public String getTable() {
        return table;
    }

    public void setTable(String table) {
        this.table = table;
    }

    public int doStartTag() throws JspException {
        if (dataSource.length()==0 || table.length()==0)
```

14

LISTING 14.8   continued

```
                return SKIP_BODY;
        String msg = null;
        try {
            InitialContext ic = new InitialContext();
            DataSource ds = (DataSource)ic.lookup(dataSource);
            doSelect(pageContext.getOut(), ds, table);
        }
        catch (Exception ex) {
            throw new JspTagException("LookupTag: "+ex);
        }
        return SKIP_BODY;
    }

    private void doSelect (JspWriter out, DataSource ds, String table)
        throws SQLException, IOException
    {
        out.println("<H2>"+table+"</H2>");
        Connection con = null;
        PreparedStatement stmt = null;
        ResultSet rs = null;
        try {
            con = ds.getConnection();
            stmt = con.prepareStatement("select * from "+table);
            rs = stmt.executeQuery();
            out.print("<TABLE border=1>");
            ResultSetMetaData rsmd = rs.getMetaData();
            int numCols = rsmd.getColumnCount();
            out.print("<TR>");
            for (int i=1; i <= numCols; i++) {
                out.print("<TH>");
                out.print(rsmd.getColumnLabel(i));
                out.print("</TH>");
            }
            out.print("</TR>");
            while (rs.next()) {
                out.print("</TR>");
                for (int i=1; i <= numCols; i++) {
                    out.print("<TD>");
                    out.print(rs.getString(i));
                    out.print("</TD>");
                }
                out.print("</TR>");
            }
            out.print("</TABLE>");
        }
        finally {
            try {rs.close();} catch (Exception ex) {}
            try {stmt.close();} catch (Exception ex) {}
```

LISTING 14.8   continued

```
            try {con.close();} catch (Exception ex) {}
        }
    }
}
```

The set method for each attribute specified for the tag is called prior to the doStartTag() method. The doStartTag() and other tag lifecycle methods can use the values of attributes to modify their behavior.

The lookup tag is included the examples.war file on the accompanying Web site and, after deploying the examples, can be viewed using the URL:

```
http://localhost:8000/examples/lookup
```

Note how the JSP and tag combine to suppress the table listing section of the returned Web page if no table name is specified as an HTTP request parameter.

Updating the Agency Case Study

Now that you have seen how to write simple tags, you can use them to clean up complex functionality in your applications. Consider the skills.jsf page you were shown yesterday, which displayed a list of selected skills in an HTML <SELECT> statement as follows:

```
<SELECT name="skills" multiple size="6">
<%
  Iterator allSkills = agency.getSkills().iterator();
  while (allSkills.hasNext()) {
    String s = (String)allSkills.next();
    boolean found = false;
    for (int si=0; !found && si<skills.length; si++)
        found = s.equals(skills[si]);
    if (found)
        out.print("<OPTION selected>");
    else
        out.print("<OPTION>");
    out.print(s);
    out.print("</OPTION>");
  }
%>
</SELECT>
```

Using just the JSTL you can refactor the job list as follows:

```
<SELECT name="skills" multiple size="6">
  <c:forEach var="agencySkill" items="${agency.skills}" >
    <c:set var="skillFound" value="false"/>
```

14

```
    <c:forEach var="jobSkill" items="${job.skills}" >
      <c:if test="${jobSkill == agencySkill}" >
        <c:set var="skillFound" value="true"/>
      </c:if>
    </c:forEach>
    <c:choose>
      <c:when test="${skillFound}" >
        <OPTION selected>${agencySkill}
      </c:when>
      <c:otherwise>
        <OPTION>${agencySkill}</OPTION>
      </c:otherwise>
    </c:choose>
  </c:forEach>
</SELECT>
```

This is not much better than the original JSP version with embedded Java; in fact, you might think that the restricted syntax of JSTL makes this worse than the original. A custom tag can be used to simplify the code, as follows:

```
<SELECT name="skills" multiple size="6">
  <c:forEach var="agencySkill" items="${agency.skills}" >
    <agency:option option="${agencySkill}" selected="${job.skills}"/>
  </c:forEach>
</SELECT>
```

The custom tag here is called <agency:option> and takes two attributes:

- option is the value of the current HTML option tag.
- selected is a list of selected options so that the tag can flag whether the <OPTION> is SELECTED or not.

Emulating the style of the items attribute of the JSTL forEach action, this tag handles collections, arrays, and even scalar Java objects for the selected attribute by accepting a java.lang.Object as the attribute type. This is shown in the following TLD entry for this tag:

```
<tag>
  <name>option</name>
  <tag-class>web.OptionTag</tag-class>
  <body-content>empty</body-content>
  <attribute>
    <name>selected</name>
    <required>true</required>
    <rtexprvalue>true</rtexprvalue>
    <type>java.lang.Object</type>
  </attribute>
  <attribute>
    <name>option</name>
    <required>true</required>
```

```
        <rtexprvalue>true</rtexprvalue>
        <type>java.lang.String</type>
    </attribute>
</tag>
```

Implementing the tag requires a bit of thought on how to handle the different types of parameter that can be given for the selected attribute. Listing 14.9 shows the actual tag.

LISTING 14.9   Full Text of OptionTag.java

```
package webagency;

import java.io.*;
import java.util.*;
import javax.servlet.jsp.*;
import javax.servlet.jsp.tagext.*;

public class OptionTag extends TagSupport {
    private String option = "";
    private Object selected = new String[0];

    public void setOption (String option) {
        this.option = option;
    }

    public String getOption () {
        return option;
    }

    public void setSelected (Object selected) {
        this.selected = selected;
    }

    public Object getSelected () {
        return selected;
    }

    public int doStartTag() throws JspTagException {
        try {
            Iterator it = selectedIterator();
            while (it.hasNext()) {
                String value = it.next().toString();
                if (option.equals(value)) {
                    pageContext.getOut().print("<OPTION
➥selected>"+option+"</OPTION>");
                    return SKIP_BODY;
                }
            }
            pageContext.getOut().print("<OPTION>"+option+"</OPTION>");
        }
```

14

LISTING **14.9**   continued

```
            catch (IOException ex) {
                throw new JspTagException("OptionTag: "+ex);
            }
            return SKIP_BODY;
        }

        private Iterator selectedIterator() {
            if (selected == null)
                return new ArrayIterator (new Object[0]);
            if (selected instanceof Collection)
                return ((Collection)selected).iterator();
            if (selected instanceof Object[])
                return new ArrayIterator ((Object[])selected);
            return new ArrayIterator(new Object[] {selected} );
        }

        private static class ArrayIterator implements Iterator {
            private Object[] arr = null;
            private int i=0;
            public ArrayIterator(final Object[] arr)
                {this.arr = arr;}
            public boolean hasNext ()
                {return i<arr.length;}
            public Object next()
                {return arr[i++];}
            public void remove()
                {throw new UnsupportedOperationException("Remove not supported");}
        }
    }
```

The complexity in the tag shown in Listing 14.9 is in handling the different possible Java objects that can be passed in as the selected attribute. The doStartTag() method uses the helper method selectedIterator() to obtain an iterator for the list of selected options and uses this to determine whether to output <OPTION> or <OPTION SELECTED> before the toString() value of the object. The selectedIterator() method returns the iterator of a collection or creates an object of the nested static class ArrayIterator to create an iterator for an array object.

Writing custom tags like the <agency:option> tag to simplify the HTML tags is such an obvious technique that several tag libraries already do this. Don't rush off and write your own custom tags to replace HTML tags but use those already provided. Both the JavaServer Faces (http://java.sun.com/j2ee/javaserverfaces) and Apache Struts (http://jakarta.apache.org/struts) implementations include custom tags for many of the HTML tags.

There are other simple improvements you can make to the Agency case study if you know how to declare EL variables from within a custom tag, as described in the next section.

Tags that Define EL Variables

An EL variable is an attribute of the JSP page context. A variable can be added using the JSTL `<c:set>` action, or the `setAttribute()` method of the instance variable called `pageContext` that points to the `javax.servlet.jsp.PageContext` object of the Web page. The `setAttribute()` method takes the following parameters:

- The name of the scripting variable. This name is used to refer to the variable on the Web page.
- The object reference to the variable to be added to the page.
- The scope of the variable can be one of the following constants defined in `PageContext`:
    - `PAGE_SCOPE` Available until the current page processing completes (this is the default)
    - `REQUEST_SCOPE` Available until the current request completes allowing the variable to be used by other pages should this page forward the HTTP request
    - `SESSION_SCOPE` Available to all pages in the current session
    - `APPLICATION_SCOPE` Available until the context is reclaimed

The following example adds a `String` variable to the context under the name `"title"` and available to this page and all forwarded pages in this request:

```
String s = "Example Title";
pageContext.setAttribute("title", s, PageContext.REQUEST_SCOPE);
```

The same thing can be achieved using JSTL:

```
<c:set var="title" value="Example Title" scope="request" />
```

To use EL variables in custom tags, you will need to define each variable in the TLD file with a `<variable>` element defining the sub-components shown in Table 14.7.

14

TABLE 14.7   TLD Tags for Defining Variables

Tag	Description
name-given	Defines the name for the scripting variable as a fixed value (cannot be specified if name-from-attribute is defined)
name-from-attribute	Specifies the attribute that is used to define the scripting variable name (cannot be specified if name-given is defined)
variable-class	Specifies the class of the scripting variable
declare	Specifies if the variable is a new object (defaults to true)
scope	Defines the scope of the variable--must be one of NESTED, AT_BEGIN, or AT_END and refers to where in the Web page the variable can be accessed

Using the example `title` variable would require the following entry in the `<tag>` section of the TLD:

```
<variable>
  <name-given>title</name-given>
  <variable-class>java.lang.String</variable-class>
  <declare>true</declare>
  <scope>AT_BEGIN</scope>
</variable>
```

Variable components must be defined before any attribute components for the tag.

You can use scripting variables in the Job Agency case study you developed yesterday to remove one of the perceived weaknesses of defining beans that require initialization parameters.

As a first step, consider the following code fragment from the `advertise.jsp`:

```
<jsp:useBean id="cust" class="web.CustomerBean" scope="request" >
  <jsp:setProperty name="cust" property="login" param="customer"/>
</jsp:useBean>
```

This fragment creates a JavaBean for the customer information. This code looks clumsy. Ideally, you should be able to create the bean and pass in the initialization properties in a single tag. The JSP idiom of setting the bean properties inside the `useBean` start and end tags is a contrived solution forced on you by the way beans are used in the JSP. With custom tags, you can provide a much cleaner solution. The following `useCustomer` tag creates the required bean and adds it to the page context:

```
<agency:useCustomer login="${param.customer}"/>
```

Looking back at the bean (`CustomerBean.java`) used to access the customer details, you will see it is a simple adapter for the `Advertise Session` bean. The `CustomerBean`'s only purpose is to adapt the Session bean interface to the JavaBean semantics required on the Web page. The following code fragment shows part of this Bean class:

```
public CustomerBean () throws NamingException {
    InitialContext ic = new InitialContext();
    advertiseHome = (AdvertiseHome)ic.lookup("java:comp/env/ejb/Advertise");
}
public void setLogin (String login) throws Exception {
    this.login = login;
    advertise = advertiseHome.create(login);
}
public String getName() throws RemoteException    {
    return advertise.getName();
}
```

The key points of the Bean class are

- The bean constructor obtains the home object for the Session bean.
- The setLogin() method creates the bean as a side effect of setting the login attribute.
- All the other methods (such as getName()) simply delegate to the appropriate method in the Session bean.

The Advertise Session EJB was developed to conform to the JavaBean semantics for accessing and setting attributes. Using a custom tag, you can use the Session EJB directly without the need for a bean wrapper class. Listing 14.10 shows the UseCustomerTag.java class that creates the Advertise Session bean for the advertise.jsp page.

LISTING 14.10   Full Text of UseCustomerTag.java

```
package webagency;

import javax.naming.*;
import javax.servlet.jsp.*;
import javax.servlet.jsp.tagext.*;
import agency.*;

public class UseCustomerTag extends TagSupport {
    private String login;

    public String getLogin() {
        return login;
    }

    public void setLogin(String login) {
        this.login = login;
    }
```

14

LISTING **14.10**   continued

```
        public int doStartTag() throws JspException {
            try {
                InitialContext ic = new InitialContext();
                AdvertiseHome advertiseHome =
➥(AdvertiseHome)ic.lookup("java:comp/env/ejb/Advertise");
                Advertise advertise = advertiseHome.create(login);
                pageContext.setAttribute("cust", advertise,
➥PageContext.REQUEST_SCOPE);
            }
            catch (Exception ex) {
                throw new JspTagException("UseCustomerTag: "+ex);
            }
            return SKIP_BODY;
        }

        public int doEndTag() {
            return EVAL_PAGE;
        }
    }
```

The doStartTag() method finds and creates the Advertise Session EJB using the login name passed as an attribute to the tag. The created bean is added to the page context using the name cust, and its scope is set to the current request. Because the session bean uses the same properties as the CustomerBean wrapper class, there are no additional changes required to the JSP code.

Listing 14.11 shows the useCustomer TLD entry with the variable and attribute tags. Note that the login attribute must have an rtexprvalue of true to allow the Web page to pass in the value from the HTTP request parameter.

LISTING **14.11**   getCust Tag Entry in agency.tld

```
<tag>
    <name>useCustomer</name>
    <tag-class>webagency.UseCustomerTag</tag-class>
    <body-content>empty</body-content>
    <variable>
      <name-given>cust</name-given>
      <variable-class>agency.Advertise</variable-class>
      <declare>true</declare>
      <scope>AT_BEGIN</scope>
    </variable>
    <attribute>
      <name>login</name>
```

LISTING **14.11**   continued

```
        <required>true</required>
        <rtexprvalue>true</rtexprvalue>
    </attribute>
</tag>
```

To keep the example code simple, it always stores the bean against the name cust. To be more flexible, you could add an additional parameter (such as beanName) to be used to allow the customer bean variable name to be specified by the JSP developer. In this case, you would set the TLD <variable> information to use this parameter using the <name-from-attribute>beanName<name-from-attribute/> tag.

You can write custom tags for the other Session EJBs (Agency, AdvertiseJob and Register) along the same lines. Doing this will result in the new customer.jsp page shown in Listing 14.12.

LISTING **14.12**   Full Text of advertise.jsp

```
<HTML>
  <%@include file="header.jsf" %>
  <agency:useCustomer login="${param.customer}"/>
  <BODY>
    <H1>${agency.agencyName}</H1>

    <H2>Customer details for: ${cust.login}</H2>
    <FORM action='<c:url value="/customer/updateCustomer"/>'>
      <INPUT type="hidden" name="login" value="${cust.login}">
      <TABLE>
        <TR>
          <TD>Login:</TD>
          <TD>${cust.login}</TD>
        </TR>
        <TR>
          <TD>Name:</TD>
          <TD><input type="text" name="name" value="${cust.name}"></TD>
        </TR>
        <TR>
          <TD>Email:</TD>
          <TD><input type="text" name="email" value="${cust.email}"></TD>
        </TR>
        <TR>
          <TD>Address:</TD>
          <TD><input type="text" name="address" value="${cust.address[0]}"></TD>
        </TR>
        <TR>
          <TD>Address:</TD>
```

14

LISTING 14.12   continued

```
            <TD><input type="text" name="address" value="${cust.address[1]}"></TD>
          </TR>
        </TABLE>
        <INPUT type="submit" value="Update Details">
        <INPUT type="reset">
      </FORM>
      <FORM action='<c:url value="/customer/deleteCustomer"/>'>
        <INPUT type="hidden" name="customer" value="${cust.login}">
        <INPUT type="submit" value="Delete Customer ${cust.login}">
      </FORM>

      <H2>Jobs</H2>
      <c:forEach var="jobRef" items="${cust.jobs}" >
        <agency:useJob customer="${cust.login}" ref="${jobRef}"/>
        <H3>${job.ref}</H3>
        <FORM action='<c:url value="/customer/updateJob"/>'>
          <TABLE>
            <TR>
              <TD>Description:</TD>
              <TD><input type="text" name="description" value="${job.
➥description}"></TD>
            </TR>
            <TR>
              <TD>Location:</TD>
              <TD>
                <SELECT name="location">
                  <c:forEach var="location" items="${agency.locations}" >
                    <agency:option option="${location}" selected="${job.
➥location}"/>
                  </c:forEach>
                </SELECT>
              </TD>
            </TR>
            <TR>
              <TD>Skills:</TD>
              <TD>
                <SELECT name="skills" multiple size="6">
                  <c:forEach var="agencySkill" items="${agency.skills}" >
                    <agency:option option="${agencySkill}"
➥selected="${job.skills}"/>
                  </c:forEach>
                </SELECT>
              </TD>
            </TR>
          </TABLE>
          <INPUT type="hidden" name="customer" value="${job.customer}">
          <INPUT type="hidden" name="ref" value="${job.ref}">
          <INPUT type="submit" value="Update Job">
```

LISTING 14.12 continued

```
      </FORM>
      <FORM action='<c:url value="/customer/deleteJob"/>'>
        <INPUT type="hidden" name="customer" value="${job.customer}">
        <INPUT type="hidden" name="ref" value="${job.ref}">
        <INPUT type="submit" value="Delete Job ${job.ref}">
      </FORM>
    </c:forEach>

    <H2>Create New Job</H2>
    <FORM action='<c:url value="/customer/createJob"/>'>
      <TABLE>
        <TR>
          <TD>Ref:</TD>
          <TD><INPUT type="text" name="ref"></TD>
        </TR>
        <TR>
          <INPUT type="hidden" name="customer" value="${cust.login}">
          <TD colspan="2"><INPUT type="submit" value="Create Job"></TD>
        </TR>
      </TABLE>
    </FORM>
    <%@include file="footer.jsf" %>
  </BODY>
</HTML>
```

You can build and deploy the updated Agency case study from the `Day14/examples` directory using

```
asant build deploy
```

Browse to the URL `http://localhost:8000/webagency` to view the resulting pages. The Agency Web pages won't look any different from yesterday's pages, but you know the underlying implementation is much better.

Iterative Tags

A common requirement for Web pages is to provide a variable number of items in a common format. Although the JSTL core and XML `<forEach>` tags can now be used for iterations, there are occasions when you will need to write your own custom tags to perform iteration.

Iterative custom tags interact with the processing of the start and end tags to ask for the tag body to be processed again, and again, and again....

14

An iterative tag must implement the IterationTag interface. This is most commonly achieved by sub-classing the BodyTagSupport class. The doAfterBody(), method must return IterationTag.EVAL_BODY_AGAIN to process the body again or Tag.SKIP_BODY to stop the iteration. Typically, the doAfterBody() method will change the data for each iteration loop.

The iteration tag has complete control over the body content of the page because it can return values from the page interaction methods, such as doAfterBody() and then tell the JSP processor how to continue processing the page.

The default behavior for the BodyTagSupport class is to buffer the body text of the custom tag and discard it when the end tag is processed. You will have to override this behavior in your custom tag so that it outputs the body text either every time around the iteration loop or once at the end of the tag.

The BodyTagSupport class stores the body content in a BodyTagSupport class instance variable called bodyContent (class javax.servlet.jsp.tagext.BodyContent). The BodyContent class extends the JSPWriter class.

The following code illustrates the normal approach to writing the buffered body content to the Web page:

```
JspWriter out = getPreviousOut();
out.print(bodyContent.getString());
bodyContent.clearBody();
```

The steps required are as follows:

1. Obtain the JSPWriter object that can be used to output the body content text (the getPreviousOut() method).
2. Print the string data buffered in the body content.
3. Clear the body content text after it has been written to the page; otherwise, it will be written more than once.

Typically, the body content is added to the page from within the doAfterBody() method. This keeps the size of the body content down because it is flushed to the page with each iteration and saves on memory usage. If the body content cannot be determined until all of the iterations have completed (or the tag is not an iterative one), you will have to write it to the page in the doEndTag() method.

Cooperating Tags

Cooperating tags are those that share information in some way. JSP information can be shared using the following mechanisms:

- Shared variables
- Hierarchical (or nested) tags

Using Shared Variables

One way wayway of writing cooperating tags is to use EL or scripting variables to pass information between the tags. As previously discussed a tag can create a variable that can be retrieved by an another tag on the current page. Depending on the scope of the variable, it can be passed on to other pages in the same request or to pages in subsequent requests. Variables defined by custom tags have the same scoping rules as other variables defined on the page. Using variables are a very flexible means of passing information between tags.

Hierarchical Tag Structures

An alternative means of passing information between tags is to use a parent/child (or hierarchical) relationship. The parent (outer tag) contains information that is accessed by a child (inner) tag. The parent tag is often an iterative tag, and the child is used to retrieve information for each iteration.

Two static methods are provided in the `javax.servlet.jsp.tagext.TagSupport` class for finding a parent tag from within the child:

- `TagSupport.findAncestorWithClass(from, class)` This method searches through the tag hierarchy until it finds a tag with the same class as the second parameter. The first parameter defines the start point of the search and is typically the `this` object.
- `TagSupport.getParent()` This method finds the immediately enclosing parent tag.

The advantage of this approach over sharing variables is that the information can only be used in the correct context. The scope of the information can be constrained to the Web page between the start and end tags of the parent tag.

Summary

Tag Libraries (TagLibs) define one or more custom tags that can be used to extend the capabilities of JSP. Judicious use of TagLibs can remove most, if not all, of the Java

14

scriptlets from your Web pages. JSTL provides a number of custom tags that will greatly simplify writing JSPs, but they are not the only custom tags available for you to use; the Apache Jakarta Web site contains a large number of taglibs. In addition, you can write your own custom tags.

Encapsulating the Java code in a custom tag will

- Simplify the writing of Web pages
- Reduce development time by removing awkward Java compiler errors from the JSP-generated code
- Integrate business logic constructs more closely into the JSP syntax

JSTL and custom tags can provide programming constructs, such as iteration and selection (`if` statements) for your Web pages. Custom tags can also

- Use attributes to pass information from the Web page to the Java code
- Create scripting variables that can be used on the Web page
- Share information between tags in a hierarchical structure

At times, writing your own tags will be the only option, but where possible, using existing libraries reduces the amount of code you have to develop, and that in turn will reduce the overall development time for your application.

Q&A

Q What are the five constituent libraries of the JSTL.

A JSTL includes a core library, which provides general purpose programming constructs; an SQL library with support for relational database access; an XML library with support for the XPath expression language, with support for managing XML documents; an Internationalization and formatting library, which simplifies writing JSPs for different client locales and a Function library for manipulating strings.

Q What is the name of the Java package that supports the development of custom tags, and what are the two classes that are normally extended by custom tags?

A The custom tag package is `javax.servlet.jsp.tagext`, and the two super classes used for most tags are `TagSupport` and `BodyTagSupport`.

Q What are the five methods you can override when extending `BodyTagSupport`, including parameters and return type? In what order are these methods called when processing the custom tag?

A The `BodyTagSupport` methods in execution order are

1. `int doStartTag()`
2. `void doInitBody()`
3. `int doAfterBody()`
4. `int doEndTag()`
5. `void release()`

Q What does TLD stand for and what is it used for?

A TLD is the Tag Library Descriptor and is used to define the library name and version of the JSP specification to which your tags conform. It also lists every tag in your library.

Q What are the five XML elements that are used in the custom tag `<tag>` entry in the TLD?

A The most common tags used in the `<tag>` entry in a TLD are

1. `<name>` The tag name
2. `<tag-class>` The implementing Java class
3. `<body-content>` How the tag body is defined
4. `<attribute>` Defines an attribute for the tag
5. `<variable>` Defines a scripting variable created by the tag

Exercise

Refactor the `register.jsp` page you developed on Day 13 to use custom tags. Write a `useApplicant` tag that provides support for accessing the `Applicant` Session bean and remove the need for the `webagency.ApplicantBean` class. Model your code on the changes to the `advertise.jsp` page and the new `useCustomer` tag you were shown in today's work. As a starting point for the code for your exercise, use the agency code. The existing `agency.jsp` page includes the code for creating a new applicant and for selecting an existing applicant for update or deletion.

You will need to create the following JSP files to support the register applicant functionality:

- `register.jsp`
- `createApplicant.jsp`
- `deleteApplicant.jsp`
- `updateApplicant.jsp`

14

You can use the versions of these files from Day 13 and modify them to use the tag libraries you developed today for handling locations and skills. In addition, you will need to develop a new custom tag to create an instance of a `Register` Session bean for use on the Web page. Call the new Tag Library class `UseApplicantTag.java`.

Model your implementation and use of this tag on the example `UseCustomerTag` shown in this chapter.

Don't forget to add an entry for the `UseApplicant` tag to the `agency.tld` file.

A solution to this exercise is incorporated in the Agency case study stored in the `agency` sub-directory of Day 14 on the accompanying Web site.

WEEK 3

Integrating J2EE into the Enterprise

DAY 15

Security

So far, you have developed your J2EE application without considering security. Now you will look at how to add security constraints to your system to prevent loss of privacy or to keep unauthorized clients from accessing data and causing accidental or malicious damage.

In today's lesson, you will look at

- How the J2EE specification supports the common requirements for a secure system
- The common terminology used when discussing system security
- Symmetric and asymmetric encryption
- Securing a J2EE application using principals and roles
- Using declarative security for EJBs and Web pages
- Using programmatic security in EJBs and Web pages
- Supplying security credentials to an LDAP naming service provider for JNDI

Security is an essential aspect of most, if not all, enterprise applications. However, defining an application as secure is not as easy as it sounds, because the definition of secure can be interpreted in different ways.

To some users, a Web site is secure if they have to provide a username and password to obtain access to the Web pages. As you will see, just because a site requires a user to log in does not make it secure.

Understanding and applying security requires knowledge of the security terminology and technologies in common use. Before studying J2EE security, the next sections describe basic aspects of IT security. If you are comfortable with basic security principles feel free to skip forward to the "Security in J2EE" section.

Security Terminology

Security has many aspects that can be categorized into the following areas:

- Authentication
- Authorization
- Confidentiality
- Integrity
- Non-repudiation
- Auditing

Each of these categories is discussed in this section.

Authentication

Authentication means identifying a client as a valid user of the system. Identifying a client has two components:

- Initially confirming the client's identity
- Authenticating the client each time it accesses the application

At its simplest level, initial identification requires a user to simply register with an application without any additional identification. More often, a third party, such as the Human Resources department or manager in a company, identifies a user. At its most complex level, usually associated with military systems, identification requires background checks to confirm a user's identity. Identified users are registered with the system and granted access to some or all of the facilities provided by the system (see the "Authorization" later in this chapter).

Registered users of an application must identify themselves each time they use the application. The most common form of authentication is to give each user a unique name (typically an account or login name) and a password associated with that account. Users simply have to provide their account names and passwords to gain access to the application.

The information identifying a client is usually called the user credentials. The most commonly encountered forms of user credentials are as follows:

- Account name and password
- Swipe cards
- Smart cards
- Physical identification systems (biometrics), such as fingerprints and retinal images
- Digital certificates

Authentication is like the entrance gate to a modern theme park. As long as you have a ticket, you are allowed into the park--you have been authenticated. But authentication does not necessarily allow you to use all of the rides and facilities in the park. The means by which you are allowed access to different parts of the theme park is called authorization.

Authorization

Authorization involves controlling access to capabilities of an application according to the authenticated user's identity. Authorization differentiates between different categories or types of users, and grants or denies them access to different parts of the system.

Using the theme park analogy again, you may only be authorized to use certain rides. Rides may have height, weight, or age restrictions that authorize access to some users and deny access to others.

Confidentiality

Another aspect of security relates not to controlling access to functionality but to ensuring that data is only seen by authorized users. In other words, the data remains confidential. Maintaining confidentiality is not just a question of authorizing access to the data but also of ensuring unauthorized access either cannot occur, or if it does, that the data remains "secure." In practical terms, confidentiality is usually achieved by encrypting the data and ensuring that only authorized users can decrypt and access the data.

Integrity

Ensuring data integrity means preventing deliberate or accidental attempts to modify the data in an unauthorized manner. Applying authorization correctly solves most of the data integrity problems concerned with accessing data on a server.

To ensure integrity, data transferred across the network must not be changed or corrupted as it is transferred. The user must be sure that the data they receive is the data that was transmitted. Techniques, such as encryption, checksums, and message digests (see the "Messages Digests and Checksums" section later in today's lesson), help ensure data integrity across networks.

Integrity also means that any changes made to a system are not lost, such as might occur when a server crashes. Good auditing practices (see the "Auditing" section) help prevent the loss of changes to persistent data.

Non-Repudiation

Non-repudiation means being able to prove a user did something, even if the user subsequently denies it. A simple example is to consider a user with online banking facilities. A fraudulent user could transfer money to another bank account and then try to claim this was a spurious transaction and a fault of the banking system. With good accounting processes, the bank can prove this was not the case.

Auditing

Auditing is familiar to database users and has the same meaning in security--providing a record of activity. Good auditing is an adjunct to supporting non-repudiation and integrity. Remember, audit records must themselves be kept secure.

Common Security Technology

Modern software architectures make use of several technologies for supporting system security. This section is a brief look at message digests, Secure Socket Layer (SSL) and digital certificates. To understand these you must first look at data encryption.

Data encryption means converting the data so that it can only be decrypted and read by authorized users. Encrypting data means applying a numerical algorithm that converts the data into another form that can, at a later time, be decrypted to recover the original data. Encryption algorithms typically use a variable component (such as a pass phrase) to "seed" the conversion; this variable component is known as the *key*. Symmetric encryption is so called because it uses the same key to both encrypt and decrypt the data. Asymmetric encryption uses two keys; one key to encrypt the data, and the other to

15

decrypt the data. Asymmetric encryption is commonly known as Public Key Encryption (PKE) because one key can be made public.

Symmetric encryption predates asymmetric encryption, is generally faster and, therefore, is still the most common form of encryption used.

Symmetric Encryption

Symmetric encryption uses one key to both encrypt and decrypt the data.

One of the simplest cryptographic techniques is the Caesar cipher (named because Julius Caesar was reported to have used it). The Caesar cipher simply replaces each letter of the alphabet by another in a mathematically consistent manner (for example, replacing a letter by the one three positions further on, so that A is replaced by D, B by E, and so on, with the last three letters replaced by the first three of the alphabet). Figure 15.1 shows the Caesar cipher.

FIGURE 15.1

The Caesar cipher.

ABCDEFGHIJKLMNOPQRSTUVWXYZ

DEFGHIJKLMNOPQRSTUVWXYZABC

HELLO WORLD ⟶ KHOOR ZRUOG

The Caesar cipher is a specific example of a simple shift substitution cipher when one letter replaces another. A different cipher is obtained by shifting the alphabet by more or less than three letters, as shown in Figure 15.2.

FIGURE 15.2

A Shift cipher.

KEY	
0	ABCDEFGHIJKLMNOPQRSTUVWXYZ
1	BCDEFGHIJKLMNOPQRSTUVWXYZA
2	CDEFGHIJKLMNOPQRSTUVWXYZAB
3	DEFGHIJKLMNOPQRSTUVWXYZABC
25	ZABCDEFGHIJKLMNOPQRSTUVWXY

The number of letters the enciphering alphabet is shifted by is called the cipher key. Given an encrypted message, anyone with the key can decipher the message. Because the same key is used to encrypt and decrypt the message, this is known as a symmetric encryption algorithm.

In programming terms, each letter is represented by a number, and the substitution cipher simply adds the key number to the value of each letter to get the encrypted form. The resultant number must be adjusted to map the last few letters (X, Y, and Z) onto the first few (A, B, and C) letters. This is a very simple algorithm.

In real applications, symmetric algorithms use sophisticated algorithms with number keys of 56 or 128 bits (which for 128 bits means an integer with approximately 40 digits). The algorithms used are usually well known but, due to the size of the keys used, they cannot be easily reversed. In other words, without the key, the original plain text message can only be recovered by applying each possible key in turn. As long as the key is a large one and the encryption algorithm is sufficiently robust, the time taken to crack the cipher with a brute-force method attack, such as applying every possible key, can be hundreds of years.

One of the most widely used symmetric encryption algorithms is called DES (Data Encryption Standard).

Symmetric encryption is used to ensure both data confidentiality and that only the intended recipients, who know the decryption key, can recover the original data.

The big problem with symmetric key encryption is distributing the key to the intended recipients in a secure manner. If a third party intercepts the key when it is distributed, they can also decrypt the message. Asymmetric encryption provides an alternative approach to data encryption that can also solve the problem of secure symmetric key distribution.

Asymmetric Encryption

Asymmetric encryption uses different algorithms to symmetric encryption and requires the use of two keys. One key is used to encrypt the data, and the other is used to decrypt the data. The two keys can be very large numbers, with modern systems using numbers of 1024 bits (an integer with approximately 310 digits). Asymmetric encryption is called public key encryption due to the way the two keys are used.

One of the two keys used in asymmetric encryption is made public, while the other is kept private to the owner. The keys are therefore known, respectively, as the public key and the private key.

15

If data is encrypted with the public key, only the owner of the private key can decrypt it. This approach is used to ensure data confidentiality but is restricted to supporting only one recipient per message. If the private key was known by more than one person, it would undermine the other benefits of using asymmetric encryption such as non-repudiation.

In contrast, using symmetric key encryption allows one message to be distributed to several recipients, as long as each recipient knows the key used to encrypt the message. Distributing the keys used in symmetric encryption is a major problem, because the keys have to be distributed in a secure manner. An attacker obtaining the keys can decrypt the message to recover the original data.

Another use of asymmetric encryption is to support non-repudiation. If a message is encrypted with the private key, it can only have originated from the key owner. Anyone can decrypt the data using the public key with the knowledge that it can only have originated from the owner of the private key. This use of asymmetric encryption is the basis of digital signatures.

Unfortunately, asymmetric encryption is slow compared to symmetric encryption. To improve performance, it may be desirable to use symmetric encryption. The problem here is how to distribute the encryption key to each recipient securely.

A common solution to distributing a symmetric encryption key is to to pass the key with the data. To make this approach secure, the recipient's public key is used to encrypt the symmetric key passed with the encrypted data. The recipient uses the private key to recover the symmetric key and then uses this symmetric key to decrypt the actual data. This technique enables large volumes of data to be encrypted quickly while distributing the encryption key in a secure manner. Secure Sockets uses this technique to encrypt TCP/IP network traffic.

SSL and HTTPS

The Secure Sockets Layer (SSL) is an implementation of public key encryption in TCP/IP networking. TCP/IP communication uses a technology called sockets (sometimes called service or port numbers). All standard TCP/IP services advertise themselves on a fixed socket or port--FTP on 21, Telnet on 23, HTTP on 80, and so on. You have seen socket numbers when using the J2EE RI Web server that runs on port 8000.

```
http://localhost:8000
```

Ordinary socket communication uses plain (unencrypted) data. Any user that can monitor network traffic can read any usernames, passwords, credit card details, bank account information, or anything else passed over the network. This is obviously an unacceptable situation from a security point of view.

One solution to securing confidential data over a network is to encrypt the data within the application. This is an inconsistent solution because some applications will be secure while others are not.

Another solution is to encrypt all network traffic. Because encryption adds an overhead to the network communication, this will affect overall performance and is unnecessary when data does not need to be encrypted.

The workable solution is to seamlessly provide network encryption only for applications that require secure data transmission. Using this approach, any application can encrypt confidential data simply by using the encrypted network communications instead of the usual plain text data transfer. Each application decides if encryption is needed but does not have to implement the encryption algorithms.

SSL is a network encryption layer than can be used by any TCP/IP application. The application has to connect by using a secure socket rather than a plain socket, but otherwise, the application remains unchanged.

Hypertext Transfer Protocol Secure (HTTPS) is the name given to the HTTP protocol when it uses a secure socket. The default port used by an HTTPS is 443. When a URL specifies the HTTPS service, the Web browser connects to an HTTP server but uses SSL to encrypt the data. All the popular Web browsers indicate on the status line when SSL communication is taking place – typically, a closed padlock is used to show that data is encrypted.

Online credit card verification services and banking systems use SSL communication.

Encryption is used primarily to ensure confidentiality of data but sometimes only data integrity is required. The data is not confidential but the data received must be guaranteed to be the data transmitted. Checksums and Message Digests provide a simple and fast mechanism for ensuring data integrity.

Checksums and Message Digests

Data integrity is usually achieved by providing checksums or digests of the data. The data in a message is subjected to a numerical algorithm that calculates one or more validation numbers that are transmitted along with the data. The recipient receives the data and applies the same algorithms to the data. As long as the recipient's calculations yield the same numbers as those transmitted with the data, the recipient is reasonably confident that the data is unchanged.

Checksums use simple algorithms and are primarily intended to detect accidental corruption of data. Message digests use sophisticated algorithms that are designed to prevent deliberate changes to data. The algorithms used in a message digest generate many digits and are chosen so that it is virtually impossible to change the original data without changing at least one digit in the calculated digest.

There are several digest algorithms in use, with Message Digest version 5 (MD5) currently one of the most popular. The MD5 specification can be found at `http://www.ietf.org/rfc.html`.

A common use of digests is found when downloading applications from the Internet, where many of the applications have an associated signature file. A signature file is used to validate the contents of the application file (the one it signs). Signature files usually contain one or more digests of the file they are signing. After downloading the file, a conscientious user can also download the signature file and check the integrity of the download file by calculating the digest of the file and comparing it to the value in the signature file. Programs to calculate digests are widely available on the Internet.

Digital Certificates

Digital certificates are specified by the X.509 international standard and define a format for storing public keys and other information about an entity (it could be a user, a program, a company, or anything that has a public key).

The official specification for the X.500 Directory Service is available from the International Telecommunications Union (ITU) Web site at the following address:

`http://www.itu.int/rec/recommendation.asp?type=folders&lang=e&parent=T-REC-X.509-200003-I`

Digital certificates are often sent with a request for data so that the server can encrypt the data with the recipient's public key.

Digital certificates must be signed by a Certification Authority (CA) to prove their validity. A signed digital certificate contains a message digest of the certificate encrypted using the CA's private key. Any recipient of the certificate can decrypt the digest using the CA's public key and verify that the rest of the certificate has not been corrupted or modified.

Digital certificates can be used to ensure authentication, confidentiality, and non-repudiation.

CAUTION　Valid Digital Certificates have been erroneously issued to individuals spoofing the credentials of trusted companies. A Digital Certificate is only as trustworthy as its Certification Authority.

Security in J2EE

The J2EE specification takes a pragmatic approach to security by focusing primarily on authorization within the J2EE environment and integration with security features that already exist in the enterprise.

You have already seen the J2EE design philosophy of separating roles with the development lifecycle identifying code developers, application assemblers, deployers, and administrators. The J2EE security supports this role-based model by using two forms of security:

- **Declarative security** is defined within the application's deployment descriptor (DD) and authorizes access to J2EE components, such as Web pages, servlets, EJBs, and so on. End user tools, such as the J2EE RI `deploytool`, support declarative security.

- **Programmatic security** is used when declarative security is not sufficient to meet the needs of an application. Security-aware components implement the security requirements by using programming constructs.

The J2EE security specification also requires transparent propagation of security credentials between components. In layman's terms, this means that once clients have logged in to a Web page, they do not need to authenticate themselves again for any EJBs accessed from the Web page. This means the authenticated identity of the user remains the same for all components (Web pages, servlets, client applications, and EJBs).

NOTE

> The J2EE specification requires a J2EE-compliant server to support the Java Authorization Contract for Containers (JACC). JACC defines a contract between a J2EE application server and an authorization policy provider. More information about JACC can be found at `http://jcp.org/jsr/detail/115.jsp`.

The J2EE security domain uses a standard terminology for the specification of the requirements. The terms are principal, role, and role reference, and each is discussed in the following sections.

Principals

Principals represent authenticated entities, such as users. The authentication mechanism is not defined within the J2EE specification, allowing existing authentication schemes to be integrated with a J2EE application.

The downside of not defining how users are authenticated means that some parts of the J2EE security features vary between one manufacturer's implementation and another. As the J2EE specification has evolved, additional security requirements have been incorporated to reduce the variation between implementations.

In a simple implementation, a J2EE principal is a user and the principal's name is the username. However, there is no requirement for a particular implementation to map the real usernames onto unique principal names. In fact, a principal can represent a group of users rather than an individual user. Using principals to implement security requires coordination between the developer and the deployer and can restrict the reusability of a particular J2EE component.

Wherever possible, J2EE security should be based on roles rather than principals because roles are more portable.

Roles

Roles are identified by the developer and represent how components in an application will be used. Typically, a developer will identify roles, such as user, administrator, manager, and so on, and suggest how the functionality in the application will be used by each identified role.

A deployer will map principals (real users and groups of users) onto one or more roles defined in the application. The deployer has total control over how the actual security authentication is mapped onto the J2EE application.

An assembler will combine the roles from many different components to map the security requirements from different components.

To reduce the coupling between the role names used by a developer and the actual role names available to the assembler, the J2EE components uses role references.

Role References

Role references define role names in a J2EE component's deployment descriptor. The developer defines the role reference, and the assembler or deployer maps the references onto an actual role in the target environment.

The relationships between principals, role references, and roles are shown in Figure 15.3.

In order to apply security to the Agency case study you will need to define users in the J2EE RI security domain as described in the next section.

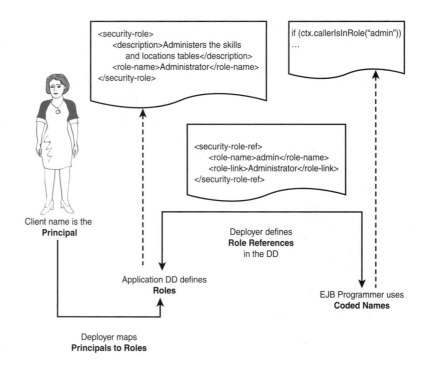

FIGURE 15.3

Mapping J2EE principals and roles.

Working with J2EE RI Security

Before you look at making your J2EE application security aware, you must spend a short time looking at the J2EE RI support for a simple authentication system.

The J2EE RI provides an authentication domain that can be used during application development. The RI security domain supports:

- Realms—A realm defines users that are authenticated using the same mechanism. The J2EE RI defines two realms:
    - file—Consisting of users and passwords stored in an XML file
    - certificate—Consisting of users identified by X.509 digital certificates, (certificates are only used to authenticate Web browser clients)
- Users—Defines a username within the J2EE security domain. In the default realm, the username is the principal name. In the certificate realm, the common name on the certificate is the username.
- Groups—Users in the default realm can be assigned to groups. Groups can be mapped onto role references to simplify security administration.

15

The J2EE RI is not intended to be a commercial server and so the support for administering users is simplistic but sufficient for development purposes. You can administer users using the command line asadmin command or the Web-based Admin Console. Because this book is not a guide to the J2EE RI, no detailed discussion of adding users and groups will be provided. Instead you will use the Day 15 asant build files to create the users required for today's exercise.

For today's examples you will add five users to the file realm using the asant build files supplied in Day15/examples directory. The required sample users are defined in Table 15.1.

TABLE 15.1 Agency Case Study Users

User	Password	Group
agency	agency	Administrator
romeo	romeo	Applicant
juliet	juliet	Applicant
winston	winston	Customer
george	george	Customer

To add these users run the command:

```
asant create-users
```

You do not need to do anything else but if you want to look at the J2EE RI support for users in more detail you can use asadmin to obtain a list of users with the command

```
asadmin list-file-users --user admin
```

Other asadmin commands for working with users are create-file-user, delete-file-user and update-file-user. Use the --help option to any of these commands to obtain details on how to use them.

You can also use the Admin Console Web interface to create and delete users and change an existing user's password. Figure 15.4 shows the Admin Console page displaying the users created for today's examples.

NOTE You must add these users to your J2EE server if you want to use the sample code provided on the accompanying Web site.

FIGURE 15.4

Using Admin Console to View J2EE RI Users.

Security and EJBs

EJB security is determined either by declarative entries added to the deployment descriptor, programmatic constraints coded into the EJBs, or a combination of both.

Ideally, EJB security should only use the declarative approach, but where declarative security cannot represent the application's requirements, security must be encoded in the EJB class. Programmatic security is less portable and may restrict the way an application assembler can combine beans from different sources.

Defining EJB Security

Defining security for an EJB involves

- Defining one or more roles to control access to different areas of your application
- Authorizing access to EJBs and EJB methods according to the client roles
- Mapping roles onto principals in the target server's authentication domain
- Optionally adding programmatic authorization to Session and Entity beans

If you are using the J2EE RI, the security can be defined using `deploytool`. Other J2EE environments may provide GUI tools similar to `deploytool` or, if you are unlucky, you may have to manually edit the deployment descriptor to include the security requirements.

In the rest of this section, you will use `deploytool` to add security to the Agency case study. You will see how extra information is added to the deployment descriptor to define the security requirements.

Defining Roles

There are three distinct roles within the simple Agency application:

- Administrators that can modify the skills and location tables
- Customers that can advertise jobs
- Applicants that can advertise their locations and skills

You may even decide that there are only two roles--administrators and clients (for want of a better term). Clients can register their own skills or advertise jobs for other clients. While this is a perfectly acceptable model, it loses the differentiation between applicants and customers.

Currently, there are no constraints on who can be an applicant and who can be a customer. However, in a real world job agency, it may become necessary to restrict who can be applicants and customers. Perhaps customers will be charged for applicants who match their jobs, so they need to be validated before they can use your system.

Having decided on your roles, you must add them to the deployment descriptor. Roles are associated with JAR files in your application. If several EJBs are defined in the same JAR file, they can share the same roles. EJBs in separate JAR files must define their own roles.

Grouping related EJBs into a single JAR file is a good design practice, not least of all because it allows related beans to share the same security roles.

Applying EJB Authorization

Authorizing access to EJBs involves restricting the methods a given end user can call. When applying authorization to EJBs you must consider where to apply the authorization. You could leave all authorization to the client (Application Client or Web Application), but there are several drawbacks to this approach

- Badly written clients may bypass security constraints.
- The same authorization rules must be applied to all clients duplicating development effort.
- Different clients may apply different authorization rules leading to inconsistent behavior between different components of the same application.

Applying authorization at the EJB level ensures all clients use the same security model. In fact implementing a consistent security model is one of the benefits of using an EJB middleware layer.

Using a combination of Session beans and Entity beans gives you a choice for where to apply authorization. Should it be on the Session beans, the Entity beans or both?

The perceived wisdom is to apply authorization to Session beans. The reasons for not applying security on Entity beans are:

- Entity beans represent persistent data and should only enforce data integrity rules.
- Applying authorization on an Entity bean may unnecessarily restrict the capabilities of a Session bean.
- It reduces the reusability of an Entity bean.
- Entity beans are not normally accessed directly by clients but through a Session bean (as discussed on Day 6, "Entity EJBS.")

Obviously, if you have chosen to expose Entity beans to the client, you should apply security on those beans.

Typically, the authorization in the EJB middleware tier is there to prevent a badly written client from breaking security rules. Normally the Client or Web Application code would ensure that logical flow of control and operations presented to end users would not give them access to unauthorized functionality. Controlling client functionality is discussed later in the sections "Applying Programmatic EJB Security," and "Applying Programmatic Web Security."

The same arguments for not applying security on Entity beans also apply to Message Driven Beans. In fact, because MDBs do not have a client interface they do not have access to security credentials unless they are included in the JMS message itself.

Therefore, the security for the Agency case study EJBs will be applied to the Session beans as discussed in the next section.

Applying EJB Security with J2EE RI

Now you will add security constraints to the Agency case study. If you want to look at the finished results of following the steps described in the rest of this section, you can look at the agency.ear file in the examples/j2ee-ri directory for Day 15 on the accompanying Web site.

If you want to add security to the Agency case study as you have developed it so far, copy the agency.ear file from the Day06/agency/j2ee-ri directory to a working directory and open this copy using deploytool to follow the steps in the rest of this section.

The Agency application has two JAR files--one for the Session beans, and one for the Entity beans. Select the agency Jar file in the left pane and the Roles tab in the right pane. Use the Add button on the Roles page to define the three roles shown in Table 15.2. Figure 15.5 shows the deploytool screen after adding these roles.

TABLE 15.2 Agency Case Study Roles

Role	Description
Administrator	Administers the skills and locations tables
Applicant	Registers details to apply for jobs
Customer	Advertises job details

FIGURE 15.5

Adding security roles.

Roles are defined in the `<assembly-descriptor>` component inside the `<ejb-jar>` tag in the DD. A `<security-role>` tag with `<role-name>` and `<description>` elements defines each role.

The following deployment descriptor fragment shows the entry created for the three roles you have just defined:

```
<ejb-jar>
...
  <assembly-descriptor>
   <security-role>
     <role-name>Administrator</role-name>
   </security-role>
   <security-role>
     <role-name>Applicant</role-name>
```

```
    </security-role>
    <security-role>
      <role-name>Customer</role-name>
    </security-role>
...
  </assembly-descriptor>
</ejb-jar>
```

Defining the Security Identity

After the roles for a JAR file have been defined, you can restrict access to the methods of an EJB. In deploytool, select the AgencyBean EJB and then the Security tab. You will see the screen shown in Figure 15.6.

FIGURE 15.6

Security for EJB methods.

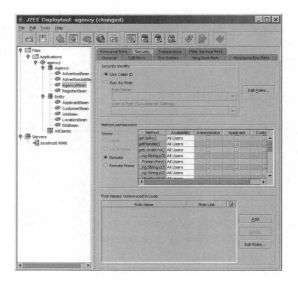

The Security Identity section at the top of this screen shows that authorization is controlled by the caller's identity. There are two options for security identity:

- Use the caller's ID.
- Use a defined role.

In Figure 15.6, Use Caller ID is selected to apply authorization based on the client's identity.

The <security-identity> tag in the deployment descriptor defines how access to an EJB is authorized. The tag is part of the <session> bean definition, and the <use-caller-identity> option is shown in the following extract:

```
<enterprise-beans>
  ...
  <session>
    <display-name>AgencyBean</display-name>
    <ejb-name>AgencyBean</ejb-name>
    <home>agency.AgencyHome</home>
    <remote>agency.Agency</remote>
    <ejb-class>agency.AgencyBean</ejb-class>
    <session-type>Stateless</session-type>
    ...
    <security-identity>
      <use-caller-identity/>
    </security-identity>
    ...
  </session>
  ...
</enterprise-beans>
```

The use of roles for the security identity is discussed in the "Using Roles as the Security Identity" section later in this chapter.

The lower part of the deploytool Security page is the Role References section, and this is discussed in the section "Applying Programmatic EJB Security."

Defining Method Permissions

The Method Permissions section in the middle of the deploytool window shown in Figure 15.6 lists the methods for the interfaces defined for your bean. The radio button selects which interface is displayed. Each bean method is displayed as a row in the table; the columns of this table are the roles defined for the JAR file. By using the cells in this table, you can select which methods can be called by each role.

From Figure 15.6, you can see that the default access (the Availability column) to all methods is All Users which is why, so far, you have been able to access all your application functionality.

In the underlying deployment descriptor, the method permissions are added to the <assembly-descriptor> tag. The <method-permissions> tag associates one or more permissions with one or more methods. A permission is the name of a role specified with the <role-name> tag or the empty tag <unchecked/> to show that access is unchecked (it is callable by all clients). The methods associated with a particular <method-permissions> tag are defined by the <method> tag; this has three variants:

1. Authorize all methods in an EJB using a tag of the following form:

```
<method>
  <ejb-name>EJBname</ejb-name>
  <method-name>*</method-name>
</method>
```

where the * means all methods.

2. Authorize a named method in an EJB using a tag of the following form:

```
<method>
  <ejb-name>EJBname</ejb-name>
  <method-name>MethodName</method-name>
</method>
```

3. Authorize a specific overloaded method in an EJB using a tag of the following form:

```
<method>
  <ejb-name>EJBname</ejb-name>
  <method-name>MethodName</method-name>
  <method-params>
    <method-param>ParameterClass1</method-param>
    ...
    <method-param>ParmeterClassN</method-param>
  </method-params>
</method>
```

TIP

> Using the third form of the `<method>` tag is considered poor design, because there should be no need to differentiate between overloaded functions for security purposes. Overloaded forms of the same method should perform the same function and therefore require the same security permissions. If the security requirements are different, good design would imply using different method names.

The `<method>` tag also allows a `<method-intf>` (method interface) tag for defining the interface name if it is duplicated in the home and remote interfaces. The default deployment descriptor setting for applying method permission to the methods of an EJB is to tag them as `<unchecked/>` in a `<method-permissions>` element as follows:

```
<ejb-jar>
...
  <assembly-descriptor>
...
    <method-permission>
      <unchecked/>
      <method>
        <ejb-name>agency</ejb-name>
```

```
      <method-name>*</method-name>
    </method>
  <method-permission>
...
  </assembly-descriptor>
</ejb-jar>
```

Returning to the `deploytool` screen shown in Figure 15.6, you can see that the default access for all methods (All Users) maps onto the `<unchecked/>` tag in the deployment descriptor. You can examine the deployment descriptor using the Tools, Descriptor Viewer, Descriptor Viewer menu option.

Applying security is now just a matter of deciding which roles can call which methods for every EJB in your application. In the agency bean, you can set the access permissions as shown in Table 15.3.

TABLE 15.3   Agency EJB Authorization

Method	Availability and Roles
removeLocation	Administrator
updateLocation	Administrator
deleteCustomer	Administrator, Customer
getPrimaryKey	All Users
getEJBHome	All Users
getCustomers	All Users
getLocationDescription	All Users
getApllicants	All Users
removeSkill	Administrator
getSkills	All Users
getAgencyName	All Users
getHandle	All Users
select	Administrator
addLocation	Administrator
remove	All Users
updateSkill	Administrator
isIdentical	All Users
addSkill	Administrator
getSkillDescription	All Users
createCustomer	Administrator, Customer

TABLE 15.3   Agency EJB Authorization

Method	Availability and Roles
getLocations	All Users
deleteApplicant	Administrator, Applicant
createApplicant	Administrator, Applicant

TIP

As a general guideline only apply security authorization to business methods; leave all the lifecycle methods accessible to all users. The only proviso to this is if you apply authorization to an Entity bean you will want to restrict access to the ejbCreate() and ejbRemove() methods as these are effectively the business methods for creating and deleting entities.

When you have added the permissions, the security page in deploytool will look similar to that shown in Figure 15.7.

FIGURE 15.7

Security DD for agency EJB.

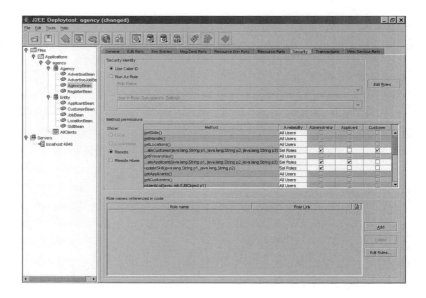

If you haven't already done so, save your agency.ear file at this point.

In this example, authorization is only required for the methods in the remote interface. Some of the methods (such as getSkills()) can be accessed by all users, so the home interface methods (such as create()) must also be available to all users. Consequently, the default authorizations are appropriate for the home interface.

In the deployment descriptor you will have added entries for each role defining the methods accessible to that role. The following extract shows how the `createApplicant()` method is authorized for the `Administrator` and `Applicant` roles:

```
<ejb-jar>
...
  <assembly-descriptor>
...
    <method-permission>
     <role-name>Administrator</role-name>
     <method>
       <ejb-name>agency</ejb-name>
      <method-name>createApplicant</method-name>
     </method>
...
    </method-permission>
    <method-permission>
     <role-name>Applicant</role-name>
     <method>
       <ejb-name>agency</ejb-name>
      <method-name>createApplicant</method-name>
     </method>
...
    </method-permission>
...
  </assembly-descriptor>
</ejb-jar>
```

The remaining three EJBs in the `Agency` application must also have method permissions defined. These are much easier to specify.

The `Advertise` EJB and `AdvertiseJob` EJB must have all the home and remote interface methods accessible to the `Administration` and `Customer` roles only.

At the present time you will not restrict access to the `Register` bean; adding applicant security authorization is the subject of today's exercise.

Make sure you save these changes before completing this example.

After all the method permissions have been defined, the application is now ready for the deployer to map the principals in the target security domain onto the roles you have just defined.

Mapping J2EE RI Principals to Roles

A developer or assembler in the EJB development lifecycle undertakes the process of defining the roles and method permissions. The process of mapping principals to roles is very much a deployer function.

The mapping of roles to the target security domain is outside the scope of the J2EE specification and will vary from one J2EE server to another. The J2EE RI uses `deploytool` to
map roles in the EJB JAR files onto the users and groups defined, or you can use
`asadmin` or the Admin Console.

To map your EJB roles using `deploytool`, select the agency enterprise application (not
the Agency JAR) in the left pane and the Security Role Mapping in the right pane. This
is shown in Figure 15.8.

FIGURE 15.8

*Mapping Roles to
J2EE RI Users and
Groups.*

In Figure 15.8 you can see that `deploytool` has retrieved the role names from all the
JAR files in the application. By selecting a role and clicking the Add User/Group to Role
button, you can map each role onto one or more users or groups in the authentication
domain.

The Agency case study requires the role mappings shown in Table 15.4.

TABLE 15.4   Case study Role Mappings

Role	User	Group
Administrator	agency	
Applicant		applicant
Customer		customer

Figure 15.9 shows the popup window with the list of J2EE RI defined users and groups
ready to be added to the selected roles.

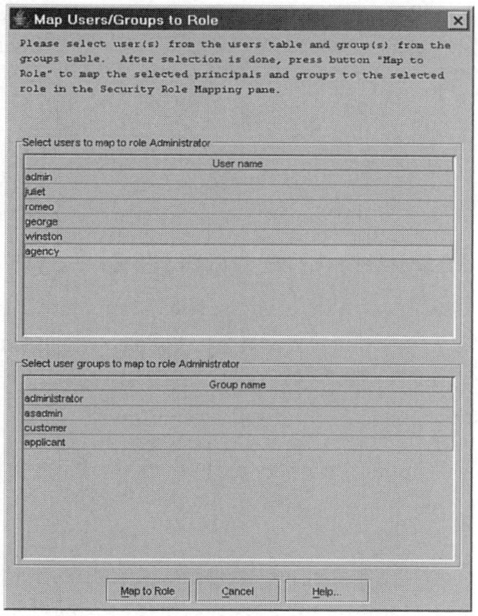

FIGURE 15.9

*Mapping users and
groups to selected
roles.*

If you do not get the popup list shown in Figure 15.9, your deploytool connection to the J2EE RI server has probably been timed out. Close down the
popup window and select the localhost:4848 server in the left deploytool
pane. This will reconnect deploytool to the server. Reselect the agency
application and the Security Role Mapping screen and try again.

You might also come across a problem with deploytool not displaying the
J2EE RI user or group names on the Security Role Mapping screen. Closing
down and restarting deploytool and reconnecting to the J2EE RI server will
usually fix this display problem.

Mapping the roles onto J2EE RI users and groups, as shown in Table 15.4, adds the following entry to the Sun-specific deployment descriptor sun-application.xml:

```
<sun-application>
...
  <security-role-mapping>
    <role-name> Administrator</role-name>
    <principal-name>agency</principal-name>
  </security-role-mapping>
  <security-role-mapping>
```

```
    <role-name>Customer</role-name>
   <group-name>customer</group-name>
  </security-role-mapping>
  <security-role-mapping>
    <role-name>Applicant</role-name>
    <group-name>applicant</group-name>
  </security-role-mapping>
</sun-application>
```

After defining the role mappings for the Agency case study, you can deploy your application.

Deploying and Testing the Secured EJBs

Deploy your application as normal with deploytool using the Tools, Deploy menu option. After deploying the application select the localhost:4848 server in left pane of deploytool, select the agency deployed object in the right pane and click on Client Jar... and save the requested application client to the Day15/examples/j2ee-ri directory.

Alternatively, save your deployool changes and from the Day15/examples directory run the command

```
asant deploy-j2ee-ri
```

You can test the changes to the application using the command

```
asant run-j2ee-ri
```

When you run the command-line client, you will be prompted to supply a username and password.

If you log in as agency, you will have unrestricted access to the application. If you log in as an applicant, such as romeo or juliet, you will only be able to use the applicant registration functionality. Similarly, customers such as winston and george will only be able to access job advertisement functionality.

To verify this, log in as romeo and check that access to the customer and administrative functionality is denied. Figure 15.10 shows the J2EE RI login screen with the username and password entered as romeo. Figure 15.11 shows the exception thrown if romeo attempts to use the unauthorized customer functionality.

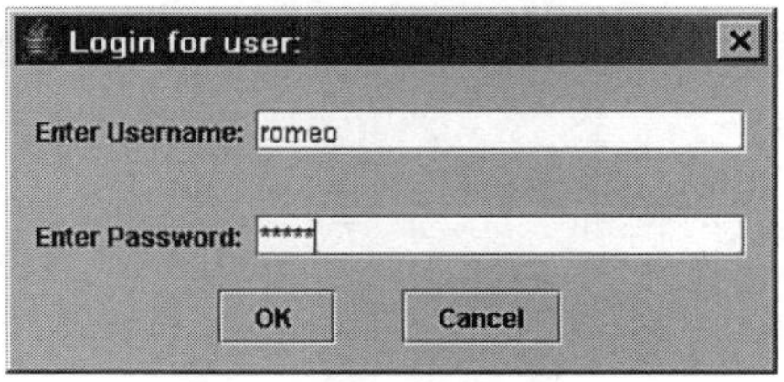

FIGURE 15.10

J2EE RI login prompt.

FIGURE 15.11

J2EE RI exception thrown when attempting unauthorized EJB method call.

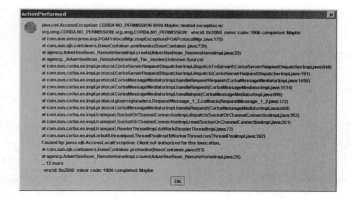

In a real-world application you would catch the security failure exception and display a user-friendly error message. A better design would be to update the client functionality to not present the user with the ability to access unauthorized functionality. To do this you need to understand how to use programmatic security to develop code where the user roles and principal name can be used to configure EJB and client functionality.

Before updating the application client to include programmatic security to make it aware of the underlying security constraints, you will complete your study of EJB authorization by looking at running an EJB as a specified user.

Using Roles as the Security Identity

An alternative to propagating the caller's security identity is to define a bean as using a specific role. This is achieved on an EJB's Security page in `deploytool` by selecting the Run As Role option and selecting the appropriate role from the list of roles displayed. The developer or assembler determines whether to use the caller ID or a specific role for a bean.

The `<run-as>` tag is used to define the role for beans that run with a specified role as follows:

```
<enterprise-beans>
  ...
  <session>
    <display-name>AgencyBean</display-name>
    <ejb-name>AgencyBean</ejb-name>
    <home>agency.AgencyHome</home>
    <remote>agency.Agency</remote>
    <ejb-class>agency.AgencyBean</ejb-class>
    <session-type>Stateless</session-type>
    ...
    <security-identity>
```

```
        <run-as>
          <role-name>Administrator</role-name>
        </run-as>
      </security-identity>
      …
    </session>
    …
</enterprise-beans>
```

Defining the bean to run using a specific role meets the developer's requirements, but the deployer must also map the role onto a principal in the target specific security domain for it to be effective. Defining a bean to run as a specific role is useful when the bean requires special permissions that the client cannot be guaranteed to provide. However, running an EJB in a specified role should be used carefully because it effectively negates the authorization process. Any client with access to the bean automatically gets the appropriate security permissions; therefore, it is imperative that only authorized clients use the bean.

NOTE

When using the `<run-as>` security identity, it is usual to define all bean methods as having `<unchecked/>` access allowing access to all roles. If checked access is applied to the methods, the `<run-as>` role must be defined as the `<role-name>` in the `<method-permission>` tag; otherwise, the method can never be called.

Applying Programmatic EJB Security

If simple declarative security constraints cannot express all of the security policy rules, the developer must resort to adding security into the EJB code.

The `javax.ejb.EJBContext` interface defines two methods for supporting programmatic security:

- `java.security.Principal getCallerPrincipal()` returns an object defining the principal calling the method. The `Principal` class defines a `getName()` method that returns the name of the principal. The `getCallerPrincipal()` method never returns `null`.

- `boolean isCallerInRole(String roleName)` returns `true` if the caller of the method is in the role passed as a parameter.

These two methods allow the developer to use the client's security identity to enable or disable EJB functionality.

Of the two methods, isCallerInRole() is considered portable because the developer doesn't work with actual role names but defines role references (much like EJB references discussed on Day 5, "Session EJBs"). The developer defines the role references used in the code, and the deployer (or assembler) maps this reference onto a real role.

The getCallerPrincipal() method is considered non-portable because the principal name used is dependent on the authentication mechanism used by the target J2EE server. In practice, as long as principal names are not defined as string literals in the Java code, the getCallerPrincipal() method can be used in a portable manner.

Using the Agency case study as an example, you will now augment your system to apply the following client specific constraints and changes in functionality:

- Any client can register as a customer, but the customer name must be the same as the client's principal name.

- Registered applicants or customers can only remove their own details from the system.

- Registered applicants or customers can only access their own data in the system.

- Administrators have unrestricted access to the system.

(You will further restrict applicant functionality as part of today's exercise.) Listing 15.1 shows the ejbCreate() method of the Advertise Session bean that has been modified to prevent clients from accessing data that does not match their principal name. Administrators (role reference admin) are permitted to access data for any client.

LISTING 15.1   The ejbCreate() Method from agency.AdvertiseBean.java

```java
public void ejbCreate (String login) throws CreateException {
  try {
    if (ctx.isCallerInRole("admin") ||
      ctx.getCallerPrincipal().getName().equals(login)) {
        customer = customerHome.findByPrimaryKey(login);
    }
    else
      throw new CreateException("Customer name does not match principal name");
  }
  catch (FinderException ex) {
    error ("Cannot find applicant: "+login,ex);
  }
}
```

The revised ejbCreate() method checks if the caller is not in the admin role and rejects the operation if the customer login name does not match the caller's principal name.

The parameter to the `isCallerInRole()` method is a role reference, and this must be mapped onto a real role by the application deployer. Figure 15.12 shows the `Advertise` bean security page in `deploytool` with the role reference defined.

FIGURE 15.12

Defining a role reference.

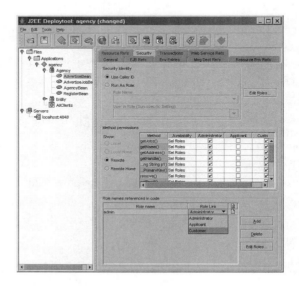

In Figure 15.12, the coded role of `admin` is mapped onto the real role of `Administrator`. The role references for a bean are defined in the bean's entry in the deployment descriptor as follows:

```
<enterprise-beans>
  ...
  <session>
    <display-name>AdvertiseBean</display-name>
    <ejb-name>AdvertiseBean</ejb-name>
    ...
    <security-role-ref>
      <role-name>admin</role-name>
      <role-link>Administrator</role-link>
    </security-role-ref>
    ...
  </session>
  ...
</enterprise-beans>
```

In addition to the change to the `Advertise` EJB, the `Agency` Session bean should also be updated to ensure non-administrator clients can only create or delete customers with a login name equal to the client's principal name (see Listing 15.2).

LISTING 15.2   The Create and Delete Customer Methods from `agency.AgencyBean.java`

```java
public void createCustomer(String login, String name, String email)
    throws DuplicateException, CreateException{
    try {
        if (ctx.isCallerInRole("admin") ||
            ctx.getCallerPrincipal().getName().equals(login)) {
            CustomerLocal customer = customerHome.create(login,name,email);
        }
        else
            throw new IllegalArgumentException(
"Cannot create a customer with a different name to the principal name");
    }
    catch (CreateException e) {
        error("Error adding Customer "+login,e);
    }
}

public void deleteCustomer (String login) throws NotFoundException {
    try {
        if (ctx.isCallerInRole("admin") ||
            ctx.getCallerPrincipal().getName().equals(login)) {
            customerHome.remove(login);
        }
        else
            throw new IllegalArgumentException(
"Cannot delete a customer with a different name to the principal name");
    }
    catch (RemoveException e) {
        error("Error removing customer "+login,e);
    }
}
```

The code uses the `java.lang.IllegalArgumentException` to show the error when the customer login name does not match the principal name.

As with the `agency.AdvertiseBean`, you must also add the `admin` to `administrator` role ref for the Agency session EJB.

The `ejbCreate()` method in `agency.AdvertiseJobBean` should also be updated in a similar manner to the `ejbCreate()` method in `agency.AdvertiseBean`, and the `admin` to `administrator` role ref created for the `AdvertiseJob` session EJB.

The revised application can now be deployed and tested.

Deploying and Testing EJB Programmed Security

Use `deploytool` or the supplied asant build files (remembering to retrieve a new client JAR file). To test the changes, run the client application and log in as `winston`, select the

Customer tab, enter george as the customer name and click the login button. You should now get an exception thrown by the ejbCreate() because the caller principal name does not match the login name supplied as a parameter.

At this point you should revisit the functionality of the client application to improve the user interface. Obvious changes would be

- Suppress display of the customer details page for applicants.
- Use the principal name to automate access to details for a registered customer.
- Suppress display of the applicant details page for customers.
- Use the principal name to automate access to details for a registered applicant.
- Suppress display of the administration pages for non-administrators.

Rather than make these changes in the client application, you will, instead, look at adding security constraints to the Web interface where all these improvements can also be made.

Security in Web Applications and Components

The Web security features of J2EE use the same model as that used for EJB security. Security is implemented using declarations in the deployment descriptor and programming in the Web pages. Authorization is enforced using roles and principals in the same manner as EJB security.

The key concepts for the Web security model are

- Single login--A client is only required to authenticate itself once to access all Web pages in a security realm provided by the Web server.
- Spanning of multiple applications--An authenticated client should be able to use Web pages from different Web applications without having to log in for each application.
- Association with a session--The security credentials must be associated with the servlet session, so that each servlet or JSP can access the credentials when required for programmatic authorization.

The J2EE Web security model specifies requirements for client authentication as well as authorization for Web applications.

Web Authentication

The J2EE servlet specification defines four mechanisms for authenticating users:

- Basic HTTP
- HTTP Digest
- Forms based
- HTTPS Client

These are briefly discussed in the rest of this section.

Basic HTTP Authentication

The HTTP protocol defines a simple authentication system where the Web server can request the client to supply a username and password. The Web client obtains the username and password of the user and returns them to the Web server for authentication. The popular Web browsers display a simple login form for the user to provide authentication information; you do not have to supply your own.

The username and password are returned to the Web server using a simple encoding scheme. Basic HTTP authentication is simple and effective, but it does not provide confidentiality because hackers monitoring network traffic can easily obtain the username and password. In reality, hackers will find it almost impossible to monitor network traffic outside of their own organization. However, malicious company employees with the requisite knowledge and software will be able to monitor internal networks.

To secure usernames and passwords used in basic authentication, it is usual to switch from using HTTP to HTTPS (HTTP with SSL) when browsing secured web pages (see the section "Securing Web Application Login").

HTTP Digest Authentication

HTTP Digest authentication works in a similar manner to Basic HTTP authentication except that the username and password are returned in an encrypted form. The encrypted username and password are more secure against illicit monitoring of network traffic.

The Servlet specification does not require HTTP Digest authentication because it is not widely supported by Web clients at the present time.

Forms-based Authentication

J2EE Web applications can specify their own forms-based authentication. This is similar to basic HTTP authentication, but a form is supplied by the application when a user has to be authenticated. The application can supply an authentication form with the same look and feel as the other Web pages in the application, instead of using the simple form provided by the Web browser. Forms-based authentication sends the username and password in plain text and has the same security weaknesses as basic HTTP authentication.

HTTPS Client Authentication

This is the most secure form of authentication because it requires the client to identify itself using a digital certificate. Client authentication is usually implemented using SSL and is supported by the common Web browsers. This is a large subject area, and there is insufficient space for it to be covered in today's lesson. Using SSL requires web server configuration changes and is specific to each web server vendor. The book *Tomcat Kick Start* from Sams Publishing (ISBN 0-672-32439-3) describes implementing HTTPS client authentication using the open source Apache Tomcat Web server.

After authenticating users, Web applications apply authorization either declaratively, based on a URL, or programmatically within the servlet or JSP code. These two techniques are discussed in the next sections.

Declarative Web Authorization

Authorized access to Web pages is based on the URL of the Web page. By default, all pages are unprotected, but the deployment descriptor for a Web application can define security constraints to force a client to authenticate itself before accessing the protected pages.

Authorization is based on roles and constraints. A Web application defines the roles required to access different functionality within the application. One or more constraints can be defined to authorize access to an individual page or a group of pages based on the roles defined for the application.

As with EJB security roles, the deployer must map the role references used in the deployment descriptor onto principals defined in the target authentication domain.

If declarative security cannot capture your web application security requirements, programmatic security must be used.

Programmatic Web Authorization

Web applications can access the authenticated client's security information using the following methods:

- `boolean HttpServletRequest.isUserInRole(String role)` Returns `true` if the client is in the role passed as a parameter.
- `Principal HttpServletRequest.getUserPrincipal()` Returns a `java.security.Principal` object representing the client's principal. Unlike the

15

EJBContext.getCallerPrincipal() method, this method can return null if the client has not been authenticated.

- String HttpServletRequest.getRemoteUser() Returns the principal name of the client or null if the client has not been authenticated.

These methods are similar to the EJB programmatic security methods discussed previously and are illustrated in the following section.

Applying Web Security using J2EE RI

If you want to examine the agency case study with Web-based security defined, start up deploytool, open the webagency.war file in the Day15/examples/j2ee-ri directory and select the webagency application.

Alternatively, if you want to work through the steps in today's lesson and add security yourself, copy the webagency.war file you developed on Day 14, "JSP Tag Libraries," to a working directory and open it with deploytool.

To illustrate the basic features of J2EE Web security, you will need to configure the Web interface to the Agency case study to authenticate users.

Defining Web Application Roles

Using deploytool select the webagency Web Application and the Security tab. On the security tab select Basic from the list of options in the User Authentication Method section on the form. Use the Settings button to configure additional features for the authentication method. The only configurable property for Basic HTTP authentication is the realm in which to authenticate the user. Enter the value file, as shown in figure 15.13. Click on OK to accept the authentication realm.

FIGURE 15.13

Defining Basic HTTP Web authentication.

Your changes have added a `<login-config>` security constraint to the Web application deployment descriptor as follows:

```
<web-app>
  <display-name>webagency</display-name>
  ...
  <login-config>
    <auth-method>BASIC</auth-method>
    <realm-name>file</realm-name>
  </login-config>
  ...
<web-app>
```

Defining the authentication mechanism does not force any clients to authenticate themselves for pages in the Web application. To force client authentication (login), you will need to add declarative security constraints for the protected Web pages. When the user accesses one of the protected pages, the server will use Basic HTTP authentication to obtain the username and password and validate these credentials against the default security realm

Configuring J2EE RI Declarative Web Security

Still on the Web Application Security page in `deploytool` you can define security constraints for your application. Constraints are based on roles and, to contrast with the example of EJB security that identified applicants and customers as separate roles, the Web application will treat all potential applicants and customers as clients. You will configure two roles for your Web application, as shown in Table 15.5.

TABLE 15.5   Agency Case Study Roles

Role	Description
Administrator	Administers the skills and locations tables
Client	A potential applicant or customer

Before you can define the roles, you must enable the Edit Roles button on the Security page. This is achieved by clicking on the Add Constraints button to create a constraint. Now click on the Edit Roles button and in the popup Authorized Roles for SecurityConstraint window click on Edit Roles. Now you can click on Add to add the roles shown in Table 15.5. Figure 15.14 shows the cascaded windows that you have open.

FIGURE 15.14

Defining Web Application Roles.

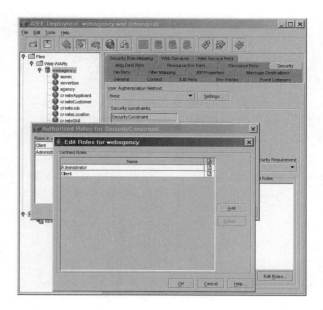

Close down the two popup windows to return to the Security page. Your changes have added the following `<auth-constraint>` elements to the Web Application DD:

```
<web-app>
  <display-name>webagency</display-name>
  ...
    <auth-constraint>
      <role-name>Administrator</role-name>
      <role-name>Client</role-name>
    </auth-constraint>
  ...
</web-app>
```

Before applying these security constraints, it is worth briefly looking at the security transport guarantee.

Using Secure Web Authentication Schemes

Previously you were told that basic HTTP authentication is inherently insecure, as the username and password are not passed using a secure form of encryption. To secure the login process, it is usual to switch to using SSL when accessing protected web pages. This is achieved by applying a constraint on the user data transport mechanism.

The Network Security Requirements option on the Security dialog describes the available options

- NONE—There are no network security requirements.

- `INTEGRAL`—The transfer of the data between server and client must guarantee that the data will not be changed.
- `CONFIDENTIAL`—The transfer of the data between server and client must guarantee that the data cannot be observed.

In practice, choosing an option other than none will ensure that the login process and protected Web pages are accessed using SSL. In a real-world application you would typically set the Network Security option to `CONFIDENTIAL` ensuring the highest level of Web security.

The network requirements are added to the Web application deployment descriptor as defined by the value of the `<transport-guarantee>` in the `<user-data-constraint>` tag.

```
<web-app>
  <display-name>webagency</display-name>
  ...
    <auth-constraint>
      <role-name>Administrator</role-name>
      <role-name>Client</role-name>
    </auth-constraint>
    <user-data-constraint>
      <transport-guarantee>NONE</transport-guarantee>
    </user-data-constraint>
  </security-constraint>
  ...
</web-app>
```

The basic HTTP authentication mechanism is suitable for development and testing, but commercial applications require more "secure" authentication schemes. Because you will never use J2EE RI as a commercial server, learning how to make it completely secure is not a useful exercise; you have many other features of J2EE to learn in the remaining six days.

If understanding and using HTTPS and SSL is necessary for your understanding of J2EE, this is best done with your commercial Web server. Read the documentation and tutorials with your Web server to determine how to secure your applications. The basic understanding of security you have gained from today's work will stand you in good stead if you are implementing certificate-based security.

Now that you have covered the basic requirements for securing a Web Application, it is time to study security constraints.

Applying Web Application Security Constraints

After the application roles and transport guarantee have been defined, you can add one or more security constraints to you application. A security constraint is applied to a Web Application and defines the following:

15

- A list of roles that are authorized by this constraint
- One or more Web resource collections that define the Web pages protected by this constraint
- A list of protected Web pages each defined by a URL pattern and the HTTP request methods GET and POST

Before adding any constraints, you must decide which parts of the agency Web application must be protected. The main portal page (agency.jsp) should be accessible to all users because this page is used to create new customer or applicant details. Existing customers also use this page to access their data.

Functionality for customers, jobs, and applicants should be protected so that only authenticated clients can use those pages. The administration page (admin.jsp), for maintaining skill and location lists, should only be accessible to authenticated clients in the Administration role.

To enforce these restrictions, you will need two separate constraints for your Web application:

- A constraint to allow clients and administrators to access customer, job, and applicant functionality
- A constraint to allow administrators to maintain the skill and location lookup tables

On Day 13, you chose aliases for your Web pages to simplify the definition of the security constraints. All of the customer functionality uses aliases of the form /customer/…; similarly, applicant functionality is /applicant/…. This naming scheme can be used when applying authorization to Web pages.

You have already started to add a security constraint to the agency Web application in order to enable the Edit Roles functionality in deploytool.

The following steps will complete the setup of the first of these constraints:

1. On the Security dialog select the SecurityConstraint you created earlier and change its name to ClientConstraint.
2. In the Authorized Roles section (bottom right of dialog tab), click Edit and add the Client and Administrator roles by using the pop-up window.
3. In the Web Resource Collections section, click Add Collections to add a new resource bundle and rename this Customer.
4. Select the Customer Web Resource Collection section and click Edit Collections to add the protected URL patterns to your constraint. You will need to protect the

individual page names (shown in the next step) and the aliases you defined when deploying the application (shown in step 6).

5. On the popup screen Edit Web Resource Collection page, select the following customer related JSP pages from the list in the top window and click on Add to include these in the collection:

- `advertise.jsp`
- `createCustomer.jsp`
- `createJob.jsp`
- `deleteCustomer.jsp`
- `deleteJob.jsp`
- `updateCustomer.jsp`
- `updateJob.jsp`

6. On the same page, click the Add URL Pattern button and add the pattern /customer/*.

7. At the bottom right of this popup window check the GET and POST HTTP method options. Your window should look like the one in Figure 15.15.

FIGURE **15.15**

*Defining Web
Resource Collections.*

8. Click OK to save your changes.

You have had to protect the real Web page filenames as well as the page aliases because authorization is based on URL patterns and not the physical file location.

15

You may be wondering why you have protected the actual JSP page when the pages themselves always use the page alias. To answer that, you have to remember that the Web is not a secure environment. There are users who will try to break your security by examining HTTP requests and URLs in an attempt to detect logical naming patterns.

Where security is concerned, it is better to err on the side of caution and protect everything rather than leave a loophole for a hacker to exploit.

You must now add a second Resource Collection to the `ClientConstraint` for protecting access to the applicant registration functionality. Create a new Resource Collection (call it `Applicant`) and protect the URL Pattern `/applicant/*` and the following JSP pages for GET and POST HTTP methods:

- register.jsp
- createApplicant.jsp
- deleteApplicant.jsp
- updateApplicant.jsp

The last constraint you need is to protect the administrative functionality on the `admin.jsp` page. Because this requires a different set of roles, you will need to

1. Create a new Security Constraint and call it `AdminConstraint`.
2. Add `Administration` to the Authorized Roles for this constraint.
3. Create a new Web Resource Collection and call it `Administration`.
4. Edit this collection, select the HTTP POST and GET methods and add the URL pattern `/admin/*` and the following pages to this collection:
   - admin.jsp
   - createLocation.jsp
   - createSkill.jsp
   - deleteLocation.jsp
   - deleteSkill.jsp
   - modifyLocation.jsp
   - modifySkill.jsp
   - updateLocation.jsp
   - updateSkill.jsp

After making these changes your Security dialog page will be similar to the one shown in Figure 5.16. Make sure you save your changes.

FIGURE 15.16

*Web Application
Resource Collections.*

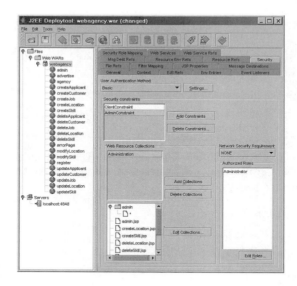

After you have defined all of these changes, the DD will have the `<security-con-straint>` entries, as follows:

```
<web-app>
  <display-name>webagency</display-name>
  ...
  <security-constraint>
      <display-name>AdminConstraint</display-name>
      <web-resource-collection>
          <web-resource-name>Administration</web-resource-name>
          <url-pattern>/admin/*</url-pattern>
          <url-pattern>/deleteLocation.jsp</url-pattern>
          <url-pattern>/updateLocation.jsp</url-pattern>
          <url-pattern>/admin.jsp</url-pattern>
          <url-pattern>/createSkill.jsp</url-pattern>
          <url-pattern>/createLocation.jsp</url-pattern>
          <url-pattern>/modifyLocation.jsp</url-pattern>
          <url-pattern>/deleteSkill.jsp</url-pattern>
          <url-pattern>/modifySkill.jsp</url-pattern>
          <url-pattern>/updateSkill.jsp</url-pattern>
          <http-method>POST</http-method>
          <http-method>GET</http-method>
      </web-resource-collection>
      <auth-constraint>
          <role-name>Administrator</role-name>
      </auth-constraint>
      <user-data-constraint>
          <transport-guarantee>NONE</transport-guarantee>
      </user-data-constraint>
```

```
        </security-constraint>
        <security-constraint>
            <display-name>ClientConstraint</display-name>
            <web-resource-collection>
                <web-resource-name>Applicant</web-resource-name>
                <url-pattern>/customer/*</url-pattern>
                <url-pattern>/register.jsp</url-pattern>
                <url-pattern>/createApplicant.jsp</url-pattern>
                <url-pattern>/updateApplicant.jsp</url-pattern>
                <url-pattern>/deleteApplicant.jsp</url-pattern>
                <http-method>POST</http-method>
                <http-method>GET</http-method>
            </web-resource-collection>
            <web-resource-collection>
                <web-resource-name>Customer</web-resource-name>
                <url-pattern>/customer/*</url-pattern>
                <url-pattern>/createCustomer.jsp</url-pattern>
                <url-pattern>/createJob.jsp</url-pattern>
                <url-pattern>/advertise.jsp</url-pattern>
                <url-pattern>/updateJob.jsp</url-pattern>
                <url-pattern>/updateCustomer.jsp</url-pattern>
                <url-pattern>/deleteCustomer.jsp</url-pattern>
                <url-pattern>/deleteJob.jsp</url-pattern>
                <http-method>POST</http-method>
                <http-method>GET</http-method>
            </web-resource-collection>
            <auth-constraint>
                <role-name>Client</role-name>
                <role-name>Administrator</role-name>
            </auth-constraint>
            <user-data-constraint>
                <transport-guarantee>NONE</transport-guarantee>
            </user-data-constraint>
        </security-constraint>
    ...
</web-app>
```

Finally, before you can deploy your application, you will have to map the Web Application roles onto the J2EE RI users and groups.

Mapping Web Application Platform-Specific Roles

Mapping the Sun-specific user and group names to roles is done using deploytool. Select the webagency application in the left pane and the Security Role Mapping tab in the right pane. You will see the same page as shown in Figure 15.8. You need to add the mappings shown in Table 15.6

TABLE 15.6 Case study Web Role Mappings

Role	User	Group
Administrator	agency	
Client		applicant customer

Figure 15.17 shows the configured Client role mapped onto the `applicant` and `customer` groups.

FIGURE 15.17

*Mapping Web
Application Roles to
J2EE RI Users and
Groups.*

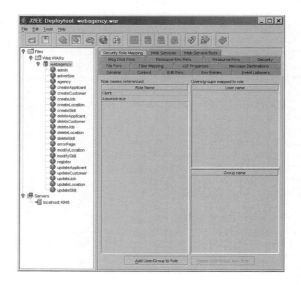

Mapping the roles onto J2EE RI users and groups shown in Table 15.6 adds the following entry to the Sun-specific Web deployment descriptor `sun-web.xml`:

```
<sun-web-app>
  <context-root>/webagency</context-root>
  <security-role-mapping>
    <role-name>Administrator</role-name>
    <principal-name>agency</principal-name>
  </security-role-mapping>
  <security-role-mapping>
    <role-name>Client</role-name>
    <group-name>customer</group-name>
    <group-name>applicant</group-name>
  </security-role-mapping>
  ...
</sun-web-app>
```

15

You can now deploy the secured Web Application using `deploytool` or the supplied asant build files.

Deploying and Testing the Secured Web Interface

You can deploy the Web application using either the Tools, Deploy menu option, or the asant build files. To deploy from the command line, save your `deploytool` changes and run the command

```
asant deploy-j2ee-ri
```

If you want to deploy the supplied example simply enter the command

```
asant build deploy
```

After deploying your application, you can access the main portal page at

```
http://localhost:8000/webagency
```

You will not need to authenticate yourself to this page as it isn't included in any of your resource collections. However, if you select a customer name such as `winston` from the list and access the advertise page, you will be prompted to enter a username and password. This is the basic HTTP security authentication mechanism.

TIP

Typically, once you have logged in to a Web site using your browser, that login will remain valid for that Web site until you close down all browser windows. When testing Web-based security you must make sure you close down all browser windows and not just the current one to reset your login credentials.

Different browser vendors do not share user credentials so you may prefer to use different browsers for different users when developing. You could, for the case study, log in as `agency` using Internet Explorer, log in as `winston` using Netscape, and log in as `romeo` using Mozilla, Opera, or any other browser of your choice.

If, as `winston`, you access the administration pages you will receive an HTTP 403 error (page access is denied or forbidden). You can always add an error page (as discussed on Day 13, "JavaServer Pages" that will map the 403 HTTP response onto a custom error page rather than rely on the browser's error message.

If, still logged in as `winston`, you attempt to access the customer details for a customer other than `winston` you will get the exception thrown by the Advertise EJB due to the programmed authorization that only allows customers to view their own details. You should now redesign the Web interface to take away the ability for a customer to access other customer details by using the remote user's principal name as the key for accessing the customer details. Adding this feature is discussed in the next section on "Applying Programmatic Web Security." Before moving on to add this extra functionality, there is one last test to do.

Close down all browser windows, restart your browser, and browse to the Agency Web page and this time log in as romeo. If you now attempt to access the customer functionality you will see the exception thrown by the Advertise EJB because you are not in the customer EJB role. Unlike the Web Application the EJB model differentiated between applicants and customers. This example illustrates that it is a bad idea to use different security models for EJBs and client components. In a real application you would either make the Web Application differentiate between applicants and customers to match the EJB security model, or have the EJBs recognize clients rather than applicants and customers.

Applying Programmatic Web Security

The Agency case study does not need any programmatic security additions. The component Session beans (advertise and register) ensure that authenticated clients can only access their own details. However, the user interface can be improved by making use of the principal information from the client authentication.

The Agency case study main page (agency.jsp) presents the user with a list of customers and a small form for creating a new customer. There is no need for the user to be given a list of customers if an authentication mechanism is used. The user's login name can be used to obtain the appropriate customer data. Just the customer section of the form is shown in Listing 15.3.

LISTING 15.3   Customer Options in agency.jsp

```
<H1>${agency.agencyName}</H1>
<H2>Customers</H2>
<H3>Existing Customer</H3>
<FORM action='<c:url value="/customer/advertise" />' >
  <P>Existing customer: <input type="submit" value="Login"></P>
</FORM>
<H3>Create Customer</H3>
<FORM action='<c:url value="/customer/createCustomer" />'>
  <TABLE>
    <TR>
      <TD>Login:</TD>
      <TD><INPUT type="text" name="login"></TD>
    </TR>
    <TR>
```

15

LISTING 15.3   continued

```
      <TD>Name:</TD>
      <TD><INPUT type="text" name="name"></TD>
    </TR>
    <TR>
      <TD>Email:</TD>
      <TD><INPUT type="text" name="email"></TD>
    </TR>
    <TR>
      <TD colspan="2"><INPUT type="submit" value="Create Customer"></TD>
    </TR>
  </TABLE>
</FORM>
```

An existing customer simply clicks the Login button and the Web authentication form is displayed for the user to log in. On successful login, the advertise.jsp page is displayed, and this should obtain the current customer from the remote client principal name. To allow an administrator to log in as any user, the webagency.UseCustomerTag class tests the caller's role and, if the authenticated user is an administrator, obtains the customer name from the page parameter. Listing 15.4 shows the new section of code that obtains the customer name.

LISTING 15.4   Customer Name Selection in UseCustomerTag.java

```
  public void setLogin(String login) {
    this.login = login;
  }

  public int doStartTag() throws JspException {
    try {
      InitialContext ic = new InitialContext();
      AdvertiseHome advertiseHome =
        (AdvertiseHome)ic.lookup("java:comp/env/ejb/Advertise");
      String name = login;
      HttpServletRequest request =
        (HttpServletRequest)pageContext.getRequest();
      if (!request.isUserInRole("admin"))
        name = request.getUserPrincipal().getName();

      Advertise advertise = advertiseHome.create(login);
      pageContext.setAttribute("cust", advertise, PageContext.REQUEST_SCOPE);
    }
    catch (Exception ex) {
      throw new JspTagException("UseCustomerTag: "+ex);
    }
    return SKIP_BODY;
  }
```

The `UseCustomerTag` class implements the `<useCustomer>` custom tag used by the `advertise.jsp` web page as follows:

```
<agency:useCustomer login="${param.customer}"/>
```

The login attribute is saved in the custom tag using the `setLogin()` method and the `doStartTag()` method uses this value if the caller is in the admin role, otherwise the user principal name is used.

To support the use of the `isUserInRole()` method in the custom tag, an entry must be added to the deployment descriptor to map the role reference of `admin` onto the real role of `Administrator`. This is done on the Security page of the `advertise` Web component, as shown in Figure 15.18.

FIGURE 15.18

Defining Web role references.

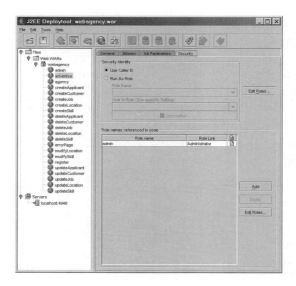

Role references are defined in the `<servlet>` entry in the web application deployment descriptor as follows:

```
<servlet>
  <servlet-name>advertise</servlet-name>
  <display-name>advertise</display-name>
  <jsp-file>/advertise.jsp</jsp-file>
  <security-role-ref>
    <role-name>admin</role-name>
    <role-link>Administrator</role-link>
  </security-role-ref>
</servlet>
```

To complete this example you will also need to define the admin role reference for every JSP that uses the <useCustomer> tag: createJob.jsp, deleteJob.jsp and updateCustomer.jsp.

You can now redeploy the Agency case study and test out the new Web interface.

Deploying and Testing Programmed Web Security

Deploy the revised Web Application and log in and click on the Login button in the customer section of the main agency page. You will now be prompted to log in. Log in as winston and you will automatically see the customer details for this user.

If, as winston, you access the administration pages you will receive an HTTP 403 error (page access is denied or forbidden) as before.

If, as winston, you click on the applicant login button you will see the same stack trace as in the last set of tests you ran. As before, the EJB security is taking precedence over the Web security. You really should rationalize your security models—but that is an exercise for another time.

One more test to do while you are logged on as winston is to enter new customer details; you will have to choose a different login name as duplicate logins are prohibited by the Agency application. When you click on the Create Customer you will once more see a stack trace resulting from the Advertise Session bean rejecting an attempt to access a customer with a login name different to the user principal. If this was a real application you would now refactor the Web interface to remove the ability to register new customers if the user principal has an entry in the Customer table.

At this point you might review the design so that any attempt to access the main agency.jsp page can prompt for the user to log in so that a customized main page is provided based on the user principal details.

A final test requires you to log in as agency (shutdown and restart your browser in order to log in as a different user). As the agency user enter values to create a new customer and click on the Create Customer button. As you are now in the admin role for the EJB you will be able to create and display the customer details without an exception being thrown. To allow an administrator to view any customer details, this functionality has been added to the admin.jsp Web component supplied with today's example on the Web site, but for brevity is not shown here in the book.

That completes the study of EJB and Web security features. Before you attempt today's exercise you will revisit JNDI and study the security implications of using a naming or directory service.

Security and JNDI

Although JNDI is part of J2SE rather than J2EE, name servers are most commonly used with enterprise applications, many of which use J2EE. The underlying Service Provider implements the security for the naming and directory service. In most circumstances, a secure directory service will use LDAP or a service that has an LDAP interface (Active Directory or NDS), and so this section will describe LDAP security requirements.

You may want to check back to Day 3, "Naming and Directory Services," to remind yourself about JNDI before reading the rest of this section.

LDAP security is based on three categories:

- **anonymous**—No security information is provided.
- **simple**—The client provides a clear text name and password.
- **Simple Authentication and Security Layer (SASL)**—The client and server negotiate an authentication system based on a challenge and response protocol that conforms to RFC2222.

If a client does not supply any security information, it is treated as an anonymous client.

Security credentials to JNDI are provided as properties. These can be defined in a jndi.properties file or supplied as a HashTable to the InitialContext constructor.

The following JNDI properties provide security information:

- java.naming.security.authentication is set to a String to define the authentication mechanism used (one of none, simple, or a space-separated list of authentication schemes supported by the LDAP server).
- java.naming.security.principal is set to the fully-qualified domain name of the client to authenticate.
- java.naming.security.credentials is a password or the encrypted data (such as a digital certificate) the authentication mechanism needs in order to authenticate the client.

If values for these properties are defined in code using a HashTable, the string constants defined in the javax.naming.Context class should be used instead. These constants are as follows:

- Context.SECURITY_AUTHENTICATION
- Context.SECURITY_PRINCIPAL
- Context.SECURITY_CREDENTIALS

15

Simple LDAP Authentication

Simple LDAP authentication is easy to use but passes security information, such as the principal name and password, in plain text across the network. Simple authentication is vulnerable to hackers monitoring network traffic to collect usernames and passwords.

To use simple LDAP authentication, the following properties are needed:

- The authentication is set to simple.
- The security principal is the fully-qualified Distinguished Name (DN) of the LDAP user.
- The security credentials are set to the user's plain text password.

The following example shows how to define simple authentication for a fictitious user called Winston with a password of cigar:

```
env.put(Context.SECURITY_AUTHENTICATION, "simple");
env.put(Context.SECURITY_PRINCIPAL, "cn=Winston,ou=Customers,o=Agency,c=us");
env.put(Context.SECURITY_CREDENTIALS, "cigar");

// Create the initial context
DirContext ctx = new InitialDirContext(env);
```

SASL Authentication

If you use SASL authentication, the java.naming.security.authentication value consists of a space-separated list of authentication mechanisms. Depending on the LDAP service provider, JNDI can support the following authentication schemes:

- **External**--Allows JNDI to use any authentication system. The client must define a callback mechanism for JNDI to hook into the client's authentication mechanism.
- **GSSAPI** (Kerberos v5)--A well-known, token-based security mechanism.
- **Digest-MD5**--Uses the Java Cryptography Extension (JCE) to support client authentication using the MD5 encryption algorithm. This is proposed by RFC2829 to be a mandatory default for LDAP v3 servers.

Additional schemes may also be supported.

An LDAP server stores a list of SASL mechanisms against the attribute supportedSASLMechanisms for the root context. Listing 15.5 shows a program that lists out the SASL mechanisms for an LDAP server.

LISTING 15.5 Full Text of `ListSASL.java`

```java
import javax.naming.*;
import javax.naming.directory.*;

public class ListSASL {
    public static void main (String[] args) {
        try {
            // Create initial context
            DirContext ctx = new InitialDirContext();

            // get supported SASL Mechanisms
            Attributes attrs = ctx.getAttributes("supportedSASLMechanisms");
            NamingEnumeration ae = attrs.getAll();
            while (ae.hasMore()) {
                Attribute attr = (Attribute)ae.next();
                System.out.println(" attribute: " + attr.getID());
                NamingEnumeration e = attr.getAll();
                while (e.hasMore())
                    System.out.println("    value: " + e.next());
            }
        }
        catch (NamingException ex) {
            System.out.println ("Naming error: "+ex);
            ex.printStackTrace();
            System.exit(1);
        }
    }
}
```

Remember that the default JNDI server for the J2EE RI is a CORBA name server and does not support a directory naming service so you cannot test this program using the J2EE RI.

The following code fragment shows how the sample user (`Winston`) can define the security credential properties to use Digest MD5:

```java
env.put(Context.SECURITY_AUTHENTICATION, "DIGEST-MD5");
env.put(Context.SECURITY_PRINCIPAL, "cn=Winston,ou=Customers,o=Agency,c=us ");
env.put(Context.SECURITY_CREDENTIALS, "cigar");

// Create the initial context
DirContext ctx = new InitialDirContext(env);
```

To use Digest MD5, the Java Cryptography Extension (JCE) must be installed on your system. JCE is included in JDK 1.4 but must be downloaded from Sun Microsystems' Web site and installed for earlier versions of the JDK.

The subject of JCE and LDAP SASL authentication is a whole day's lesson in its own right, and there isn't time today to do any more work in this area. If you are interested in finding out more about JCE and JNDI security, the JNDI Tutorial on Sun Microsystems' Web site is an excellent starting point.

Summary

Today, you have looked at several aspects of J2EE security. You've studied basic security terminology, including the difference between authentication and authorization.

You have seen how the J2EE specification doesn't specify the authentication schemes that must be used, but relies on a server to provide some form of authentication. The authenticated username is known as a J2EE principal.

J2EE authorization is based on roles defined for each EJB JAR or WAR in the application. Each authenticated principal can be mapped onto one or more roles.

J2EE uses declarative constraints to define authorization based on the roles defined in the application. Each method in an EJB can be authorized for all principals or a specific list of roles. Similarly, individual Web pages can be authorized for specific roles. This declarative programming de-couples the development of the EJB and Web code from the runtime authentication scheme. Declarative security constraints facilitate the separation of the developer role from the assembler and deployer roles.

Programmatic security is used when simple declarative security cannot express the application's authorization requirements. An EJB or Web page becomes security aware by using methods in the J2EE API to obtain the client's principal name or role. This information can be used to change the behavior of an EJB or Web page based on the client's security credentials.

Adding security to a J2EE application is a simple process. Careful design of the functionality in each EJB or Web page enables an assembler to apply consistent security constraints to several J2EE components comprising a complete application.

Q&A

Q What are the six different aspects of security?

A Six aspects of security are

- Authentication
- Authorization
- Confidentiality

- Integrity
- Non-repudiation
- Auditing

Q What are the three participants of the J2EE security domain?

A A Principal represents an entity (typically a user) in the authentication system of the target environment. A Role represents a security role within the application. A Role Reference is used to map a coded role name onto an actual role.

Q What are the two techniques for defining J2EE security?

A Declarative and programmatic.

Q List the two `EJBContext` methods and three `HttpServletRequest` methods used in programmatic security?

A `EJBContext.isCallerInRole()`
`EJBContext.getCallerPrincipal()`

`HttpServletRequest.isUserInRole()`
`HttpServletRequest.getUserPrincipal()`
`HttpServletRequest.getRemoteUser()`

Exercises

Today's exercise comes in two parts:

1. Update the EJB Security Model.

    Using the code in today's lesson for the Advertise EJB as an example, add security for applicant registration functionality in the Register EJB.

    Use declarative security to restrict access to the Register Session bean methods to members of the J2EE RI Applicants group.

    Add programmatic security to the Register EJB to allow administrators to create a Register EJB for any name but restrict customers to only create a Register EJB for their caller principal name.

    Update the Agency bean to restrict the abilities of a non-administrator to create and delete applicants with a login name the same as their principal name. Don't forget to add the role ref mapping admin onto Administrator in the Register session EJB.

    Deploy and test changes before completing part 2.

15

2. Update the Web Application Security Model.

The Web application declarative security was implemented as part of today's sample code.

To add programmatic security to the Web application you need to update the `UseApplicantTag` class to obtain the applicant's name from the security credentials for non-administrators following the sample code in `UseCustomerTag.java` shown in today's lesson. You must add a role reference for the `admin` role to the `register.jsp` and `updateApplicant.jsp` web components.

You also need to update the `agency.jsp` to remove the applicant select list and provide a simple login button for existing applicants (follow the code example for existing customers).

Deploy and test these changes to the Web interface.

Use the files in the Day 15 `examples` directory as a starting point for your exercise. A solution can be found in the Day 15 `agency` directory.

As an optional exercise (no solution provided) you can revisit the EJB and Web security models and use the same model for both parts of the case study to resolve some of the problems identified in the text. You might also want to refactor the Web interface to improve the user's perception of the functionality provided.

DAY **16**

Integrating XML with J2EE

Today, we take a bit of a departure from J2EE and its emphasis on programming elements to look at what is fast becoming the lingua franca of the Internet—the Extensible Markup Language (XML).

Throughout the book so far, you have seen many ways in which XML is used within J2EE applications to describe the structure and layout of the application. Today and tomorrow, you will study XML and its associated APIs and standards to gain a fuller understanding of how XML can be used to exchange data between different components in your applications.

Today, you will learn about

- How XML has evolved from the need for platform-independent data exchange
- The relationship between XML and both Standard Generalized Markup Language (SGML) and Hypertext Markup Language (HTML)
- How to create well-formed and valid XML documents
- The Java API for XML Processing (JAXP)

- How to process XML documents with the Simple API for XML (SAX) and the Document Object Model (DOM)
- How XML is used in the J2EE platform

This book is about J2EE, of which XML is just a component. To learn more about XML, take a look at *Sams Teach Yourself XML in 21 Days*, which covers everything you need to know about XML and related standards.

The Drive to Platform-Independent Data Exchange

Applications essentially consist of two parts—functionality described by the code and the data that is manipulated by the code. The in-memory storage and management of data is a key part of any programming language and environment. Within a single application, the programmer is free to decide how the data is stored and represented. Problems only start when the application must exchange data with another application.

One solution is to use an intermediary storage medium, such as a database, and standard tools, such as SQL and JDBC, to gain access to the data in such databases.

But what if the data is to be exchanged directly between two applications, or the applications cannot access the same database? In this case, the data must be encoded in some particular format as it is produced, so that its structure and contents can be understood when it is consumed. This has often resulted in the creation of application-specific data formats, such as binary data files (.dat files) or text-based configuration files (.ini, .rc, .conf, and so on), in which applications store their information.

Similarly, when exchanging information between applications, purpose-specific formats have arisen to address particular needs. Again, these formats can be text-based, such as HTML for encoding how to display the encapsulated data, or binary, such as those used for sending remote procedure calls. In either case, there tends to be a lack of flexibility in the data representation, causing problems when versions change or when data needs to be exchanged between disparate applications, frequently from different vendors.

XML was developed to address these issues. Because XML is written in plain text, and shares similarities with HTML but uses self-describing elements, XML provides a data encoding format that is

- Generic
- Simple
- Flexible

- Extensible
- Portable
- Human readable
- And perhaps most importantly, license-free

Benefits and Characteristics of XML

XML offers a method of putting structured data in a text file. Structured data is data that conforms to a particular format; examples are spreadsheets, address books, configuration parameters, and financial transactions. While being structured, XML is also readable by humans as well as software; this means that you do not need the originating software to access the data.

Origins of XML

XML was created by the World Wide Web Consortium (W3C) which now promotes and controls the standard. The W3C also promotes and develops a number of other interoperable technologies. The latest XML standard, along with lots of useful information and tools, can be obtained from the WC3 Web site (www.w3.org).

XML is a set of rules for designing text formats that describe the structure of your data. XML is not a programming language, so it is therefore easy for non-programmers to learn and use. In devising XML, the originators had a set of design goals, which were as follows:

- XML should be straightforward to use over the Internet.
- XML should support a wide variety of applications.
- XML should be compatible with the Standard Generalized Markup Language.
- It must be easy to write programs that process XML documents.
- The number of optional features in XML should be kept to the absolute minimum—ideally, zero.
- XML documents should be human-legible and reasonably clear.
- XML documents should be easy to create.
- Terseness in XML was of minimal importance.

XML is based on the Standard Generalized Markup Language (SGML). SGML is a powerful but complex meta-language that is used to describe languages for electronic document exchange, document management, and document publishing. HTML (probably the best known markup language) is an example of an SGML application. SGML provides a rich and powerful syntax, but its complexity has restricted its widespread use and it is used primarily for technical documentation.

XML was conceived as a means of retaining the power and flexibility of SGML while losing most of its complexity. Although a subset of SGML, XML manages to preserve the best parts of SGML and all of its commonly used features while being more regularly structured and easy to use.

XML is still a relatively young technology but it is fast making a significant impact. Already there is an important XML application—XHTML, the successor to HTML, which is now supported by most of the popular Web browsers.

Structure and Syntax of XML

In this section, you will explore the syntax of XML and understand what is meant by a well-formed document.

NOTE

> You will often encounter the terms "well-formed" and "valid" applied to XML documents. These are not the same. A well-formed document is structurally and syntactically correct (the XML conforms to the XML language definition, that is all tags have a correctly nested corresponding end tag, all attributes are quoted, only valid characters have been used, and so on), whereas a valid document is also semantically correct (the XML conforms to some external definition stored in an XML Schema or Document Type Definition). A document can be well-formed but may not be valid.

The best way to become familiar with the syntax of XML is to write an XML document. To check your XML, you will need access to an XML-aware browser or another XML validator. The XML-aware browser or XML validator will allow you to ensure that the XML is well-formed. If the XML references an XML Schema or Document Type Definition (more on these later) the validator can also check that the XML is valid.

An XML browser includes an XML parser. To get the browser to check the syntax and structure of your XML document, simply use the browser to open the XML file. Well-formed XML will be displayed in a structured way (with indentation). If the XML is not well-formed, an appropriate error message will be given.

TIP

> An easy way to validate XML is to use an XML aware browser. The latest versions of most popular browsers are now XML aware. You can download validating XML parsers from Sun Microsystems at www.sun.com/software/xml/developers/multischema/and the Microsoft Developers Network at msdn.microsoft.com/downloads/samples/internet/xml/xml_validator/. There are numerous other XML validators and XML editors vailable from the Internet.

HTML and XML

At first glance, XML looks very similar to HTML. An XML document consists of elements that have a start and end tag, just like HTML. In fact, Listing 16.1 is both well-formed HTML and XML.

LISTING 16.1   Example XML and HTML

```
<html>
 <head><title>Web Page</title></head>
 <body>
  <h1>Teach Yourself J2EE in 21 Days</h1>
  <p>Now you have seen the web page - buy the book</p>
 </body>
</html>
```

An XML document is only well-formed if there are no syntax errors. If you are familiar with HTML, you will be aware that many browsers are lenient with poorly formed HTML documents. Missing end tags and even missing sections will often be ignored and therefore unnoticed until the page is displayed in a more rigorous browser, and fails to display correctly.

XML differs from HTML in that a missing end tag will always cause an error.

We will now look at XML syntax so you can understand what is going on.

Structure of an XML Document

The outermost element in an XML document is called the root element. Each XML document must have one and only one root element, often called the top level element. If there is more than one root element, an error will be generated.

The root element can be preceded by a prolog that contains XML declarations. Comments can be inserted at any point in an XML document. The prolog is optional, but it is good practice to include a prolog with all XML documents giving the XML version being used (all full XML listings in this chapter will include a prolog). A minimal XML document must contain at least one element.

Declarations

There are two types of XML declaration. XML documents may, and should, begin with an XML declaration, which specifies the version of XML being used. The following is an example of an XML declaration:

```
<?xml version ="1.0"?>
```

The XML version element tells the parser that this document conforms to the XML version 1.0 (W3C recommendation 10-February-1998). As with all declarations, the XML declaration, if present, should always be placed in the prolog.

The other type of declaration is called an XML document type declaration and is used to validate the XML. This will be discussed in more detail in the section titled "Creating Valid XML" later in this chapter.

Elements

An element must have a start tag and an end tag enclosed in < and > characters. The end tag is the same as the start tag except that it is preceded with a / character. The tags are case sensitive, and the names used for the start and end tags must be exactly the same, for example the tags <Start>...</start> do not make up an element, whereas <Start>...</Start> do (both tags are letter case consistent).

An element name can only contain letters, digits, underscores _, colons :, periods ., and hyphens -. An element name must begin with a letter or underscore.

An element may also optionally have attributes and a body. All the elements in Listing 16.2 are well-formed XML elements. All attributes must be quoted, both single and double quotes are permitted.

LISTING 16.2   Valid XML Elements

```
<start>this is the beginning</start>
<date day="16th" Month="February">My Birthday</date>
<today yesterday="15th" Month="February"></today>
<box color="red"/>
<head></head>
<end/>
```

Table 16.1 describes each of these elements.

TABLE 16.1 XML Elements

Element Type	XML Element Includes
`<tag>text</tag>`	A start tag, body, and end tag
`<tag attribute="text"> text </tag>`	An attribute and a body
`<tag attribute="text"> </tag>`	An attribute but no body
`<tag attribute="text"/>`	Short form of attribute but no body
`<tag></tag>`	A start tag and end tag but no body
`<tag/>`	Shorthand for the previous tag

16

Although the body of an element may contain nearly all the printable Unicode characters, certain characters are not allowed in certain places. To avoid confusion (to human readers as well as parsers) the characters in Table 16.2 should not be used in tag or attribute values. If these characters are required in the body of an element, the appropriate symbolic string in Table 16.2 can be used to represent them.

TABLE 16.2 Special XML Characters

Character	Name	Symbolic Form
&	Ampersand	`&amp;`
<	Open angle bracket	`&lt;`
>	Close angle bracket	`&gt;`
'	Single quotes	`&apos;`
"	Double quotes	`&quot;`

The elements in an XML document have a tree-like hierarchy, with elements containing other elements and data. Elements must nest—that is, an end tag must close the textually preceding start tag. This means that

`<b><i>bold and italic</i></b>`

is correct, while

`<b><i>bold and italic</b></i>`

is not.

Well-formed XML Documents

An XML document is said to be well-formed if there is exactly one root element, it and every sub-element has delimiting start and end tags that are properly nested within each other and all attributes are quoted.

The following is a simple XML document with an XML declaration followed by a number of elements. The structure represents a list of jobs that could be used in the Agency case study example. In Listing 16.3, the <jobSummary> tag is the root tag followed by a number of jobs.

LISTING 16.3   Example jobSummary XML

```
<?xml version ="1.0"?>
<jobSummary>
 <job>
  <customer>winston</customer>
  <reference>Cigar Trimmer</reference>
  <location>London</location>
  <description>Must like to talk and smoke</description>
  <skill>Cigar maker</skill>
  <skill>Critic</skill>
 </job>
 <job>
  <customer>george</customer>
  <reference>Tree pruner</reference>
  <location>Washington</location>
  <description>Must be honest</description>
  <skill>Tree surgeon</skill>
 </job>
</jobSummary>
```

Attributes

Attributes are name/value pairs that are associated with elements. There can be any number of attributes, and an element's attributes all appear inside the start tag. The names of attributes are case sensitive and are limited to the following characters: letters, digits, underscores _, periods ., and hyphens -. An attribute name must begin with a letter or underscore.

The value of an attribute is a text string delimited by quotes, either single or double quotes may be used. Unlike HTML, all attribute values in an XML document must be enclosed in quotes. Listing 16.4 shows the jobSummary XML document re-written to use attributes to hold some of the data.

LISTING 16.4   JobSummary.xml XML with Attributes

```
<?xml version ="1.0"?>
<jobSummary>
 <job customer="winston" reference="Cigar Trimmer">
  <location>London</location>
```

LISTING 16.4   continued

```
    <description>Must like to talk and smoke</description>
    <skill>Cigar maker</skill>
    <skill>Critic</skill>
  </job>
  <job customer="george" reference="Tree pruner">
   <location>Washington</location>
   <description>Must be honest</description>
   <skill>Tree surgeon</skill>
  </job>
</jobSummary>
```

16

The choice of using nested elements or attributes is a contentious area. There are many schools of thought and it usually ends up being a matter of personal taste or corporate standards. Prior to the introduction of XML Schemas (see section "XML Schemas") there were advantages to using attributes when the values were constrained in some way; such as values that are numbers or specific patterns. XML Schemas also allow element values to be constrained in the same way as attribute values.

Comments

XML comments are introduced by `<!--` and ended with `-->`, for example

```
<!-- this is a comment -->
```

Comments can appear anywhere in a document except within the tags, for example,

```
<item quantity="1lb">Cream cheese <!-- this is a comment --></item>
```

is acceptable, whereas the following is not

```
<item <!-- this is a comment --> quantity="1lb">Cream cheese </item>
```

NOTE _____ | As with commenting code, the comments you add to your XML should be factually correct, useful, and to the point. They should be used to make the XML document easier to read and comprehend.

Any character is allowed in a comment, including those that cannot be used in elements and tags, but to maintain compatibility with SGML, the combination of two hyphens together (`--`) cannot be used within the text of a comment.

Comments should be used to annotate the XML, but you should be aware that the parser might remove the comments, so they may not always be accessible to a receiving application.

Namespaces

When designers define an XML structure for some data, they are free to choose tag names that are appropriate for the data. Consequently, there is nothing to stop two individuals from using the same tag name for different purposes or in different ways. Consider the job agency that deals with two contract companies, each of which uses a different form of job description (such as those in Listings 16.3 and 16.4). How can an application differentiate between these different types of book descriptions?

The answer is to use namespaces. XML provides namespaces that can be used to impose a hierarchical structure on XML tag names in the same way that Java packages provide a naming hierarchy for Java methods. You can define a unique namespace with which you can qualify your tags to avoid them being confused with those from other XML authors.

An attribute called xmlns (XML Namespace) is added to an element tag in a document and is used to define the namespace. For example, the second line in Listing 16.5 indicates that the tags for the whole of this document are scoped within the agency namespace.

LISTING 16.5   XML Document with Namespace

```
<?xml version ="1.0"?>
<jobSummary xmlns="agency">
 <job customer="winston" reference="Cigar Trimmer">
  <location>London</location>
  <description>Must like to talk and smoke</description>
  <skill>Cigar maker</skill>
  <skill>Critic</skill>
 </job>
 <job customer="george" reference="Tree pruner">
  <location>Washington</location>
  <description>Must be honest</description>
  <skill>Tree surgeon</skill>
 </job>
</jobSummary>
```

The xmlns attribute can be added to any element in the document to enable scoping of elements, and multiple namespaces can be defined in the same document using a prefix. For example, Listing 16.6 has two namespaces—ad and be. All the tags have been prefixed with the appropriate namespace, and now two different forms of the job tag (one with attributes and one without) can coexist in the same file.

LISTING 16.6   XML Document with Namespaces

```xml
<?xml version ="1.0"?>
<jobSummary xmlns:ad="ADAgency" xmlns:be="BEAgency">
 <ad:job customer="winston" reference="Cigar Trimmer">
  <ad:location>London</ad:location>
  <ad:description>Must like to talk and smoke</ad:description>
  <ad:skill>Cigar maker</ad:skill>
  <ad:skill>Critic</ad:skill>
 </ad:job>
 <be:job>
  <be:customer>george</be:customer>
  <be:reference>Tree pruner</be:refenence>
  <be:location>Washington</be:location>
  <be:description>Must be honest</be:description>
  <be:skill>Tree surgeon</be:skill>
 </be:job>
</jobSummary>
```

Creating Valid XML

As you have seen, XML validators recognize well-formed XML, and this is very useful for picking up syntax errors in your document. Unfortunately, a well-formed, syntactically-correct XML document may still have semantic errors in it. For example, a job in Listing 16.4 with no location or skills does not make sense, but without these elements, the XML document is still well-formed, but not valid.

What is required is a set of rules or constraints that define a valid structure for an XML document. There are two common methods for specifying XML rules—the Document Type Definition (DTD) and XML Schemas.

Document Type Definitions

A DTD provides a template that defines the occurrence, and arrangement of elements and attributes in an XML document. Using a DTD, you can define

- Element ordering and hierarchy
- Which attributes are associated with an element
- Default values and enumeration values for attributes
- Any entity references used in the document (internal constants, external files, and parameters)

NOTE   Entity references are covered in Appendix A, "An Overview of XML."

DTDs originated with SGML and have some disadvantages when compared with XML Schemas, which were developed explicitly for XML. One of these disadvantages is that a DTD is not written in XML, which means you have to learn another syntax to define a DTD. Another disadvantage is that DTD's are not as comprehensive as XML Schemas and cannot therefore constrain an XML document as tightly as an XML Schema.

DTD rules can be included in the XML document as document type declarations, or they can be stored in an external document. The syntax is the same in both cases.

If a DTD is being used, the XML document must include a DOCTYPE declaration, which is followed by the name of the root element for the XML document. If an external DTD is being used, the declaration also includes the word SYSTEM followed by a system identifier (the URI that identifies the location of the DTD file). For example

```
<!DOCTYPE jobSummary SYSTEM "jobSummary.dtd">
```

specifies that the root element for this XML document is jobSummary and the remainder of the DTD rules are in the file called jobSummary.dtd in the same directory.

An external identifier can also include a public identifier. The public identifier precedes the system identifier and is denoted by the word PUBLIC. An XML processor can use the public identifier to try to generate an alternative URI. If the document is unavailable by this method, the system identifier will be used.

```
<!DOCTYPE web-app
 PUBLIC '-//Sun Microsystems, Inc.//DTD Web Application 2.3//EN'
 'http://java.sun.com/dtd/web-app_2_3.dtd'>
```

NOTE   DOCTYPE, SYSTEM and PUBLIC must appear in capitals to be recognized.

Element Type Declarations

The DTD defines every element in the XML document with element type declarations. Each element type declaration takes the following form:

```
<!ELEMENT name ( content ) >
```

For example, for the jobSummary XML document in Listing 16.4, the jobSummary root element is defined as

```
<!ELEMENT jobSummary ( job* )>
```

The * sign indicates that the jobSummary element may consist of zero or more job elements. There are other symbols used to designate rules for combining elements and these are listed in Table 16.3.

TABLE 16.3   Occurrence Characters Used in DTD Definitions

Character	Meaning
*	Zero or more (not required)
+	One or more (at least one required)
?	Element is optional (if present can only appear once)
|	Alternate elements
()	Group of elements

The following defines an XML job element that must include one location, an optional description, and at least one skill:

```
<!ELEMENT job (location, description?, skill+)>
```

Defining the Element Content

Elements can contain other elements, or content, or have elements and content. The jobSummary element, in Listing 16.4, contains other elements but no text body; whereas the location element has a text body but does not contain any elements.

To define an element that has a text body, use the reference #PCDATA (Parsed Character DATA). For example, the location element in Listing 16.4 is defined by

```
<!ELEMENT location (#PCDATA)>
```

An element can also have no content (the <br> tag in HTML is such an example). This tag would be defined with the EMPTY keyword as

```
<!ELEMENT br EMPTY>
```

You will also see elements defined with contents of ANY. The ANY keyword denotes that the element can contain all possible elements, as well as PCDATA. The use of ANY should be avoided. If your data is so unstructured that it cannot be defined explicitly, there probably is no point in creating a DTD in the first place.

Defining Attributes

In Listing 16.4, the job element has two attributes—customer and reference. Attributes are defined in an ATTLIST that has the following form:

```
<!ATTLIST element attribute type default-value>
```

The *element* is the name of the element and *attribute* is the name of the attribute. The *type* defines the kind of attribute that is expected. A type is either one of the defined constants described in Table 16.4, or it is an enumerated type where the permitted values are given in a bracketed list.

TABLE 16.4   DTD Attribute Types

Type	Attribute Is a...
CDATA	Character string.
NMTOKEN	Valid XML name.
NMTOKENS	Multiple XML names.
ID	Unique identifier.
IDREF	An element found elsewhere in the document. The value for IDREF must match the ID of another element.
ENTITY	External binary data file (such as a gif image).
ENTITIES	Multiple external binary files.
NOTATION	Helper program.

The ATTLIST default-value component defines a value that will be used if one is not supplied. For example

```
<!ATTLIST button visible (true | false) "true").
```

defines that the element button has an attribute called visible that can be either true or false. If the attribute is not supplied, because a default value is supplied, it will be set to be true.

The default-value item can also be used to specify that the attribute is #REQUIRED, #FIXED, or #IMPLIED. The meaning of these values is given in Table 16.5.

TABLE 16.5   DTD Attribute Default Values

Default Value	Meaning
#REQUIRED	Attribute must be provided.
#FIXED	Effectively a constant declaration. The attribute must be set to the given value or the XML is not valid.
#IMPLIED	The attribute is optional and the processing application is allowed to use any appropriate value if required.

Example DTD

Listing 16.7 is the DTD for the jobSummary XML document. Create the DTD in a file called jobSummary.dtd in the same directory as your jobSummary XML document.

LISTING 16.7   DTD for jobSummary XML

```
<!ELEMENT jobSummary (job*)>
<!ELEMENT job (location, description, skill+)>
<!ATTLIST job customer CDATA #REQUIRED>
<!ATTLIST job reference CDATA #REQUIRED>
<!ELEMENT location (#PCDATA)>
<!ELEMENT description (#PCDATA)>
<!ELEMENT skill (#PCDATA)>
```

Don't forget to add the following line to the jobSummary XML at line 2 (following the PI):

```
<!DOCTYPE jobSummary SYSTEM "jobSummary.dtd">
```

View the jobSummary.xml document in your XML browser or other XML validator.

If the browser cannot find the DTD, it will generate an error. Edit jobSummary.xml, remove the customer attribute, and check that your XML validator generates an appropriate error (such as "Required attribute 'customer' is missing").

XML Schemas

As has been already stated, DTDs have some limitations:

- A DTD cannot define type information other than characters.
- DTDs were not designed to support namespaces and, although it is possible to add namespaces to a DTD, how to do so is beyond the scope of this book.
- DTDs are not easily extended.
- You can only have one DTD per document, so you cannot have different definitions of an element in a single document and have them validated with a DTD.
- The syntax for DTDs is not XML. Tools and developers must understand the DTD syntax as well as XML.

To address these issues, the XML Schema structure definition mechanism was developed by the W3C to fulfill the role of DTDs while addressing the previously listed limitations. XML Schemas are XML documents.

16

The XML Schema standard is split into two parts:

- Specifying the structure and constraints on an XML document
- A way of defining data types, including a set of pre-defined types

Because it is a more powerful and flexible mechanism than DTDs, the syntax for defining an XML schema is slightly more involved. An example of an XML schema for the jobSummary XML shown in Listing 16.4 can be seen in Listing 16.8.

> **TIP**
>
> The World Wide Web Consortium Web site provides access to a number of XML schema tools, including XML schema browsers and validators. These tools can be found at `http://www.w3.org/XML/Schema`.

LISTING 16.8   XML Schema for Job Agency JobSummary XML Document

```xml
<?xml version="1.0"?>
 <xsd:schema xmlns:xsd="http://www.w3.org/2001/XMLSchema"
             elementFormDefault="qualified">

  <xsd:element name="jobSummary">
   <xsd:complexType>
    <xsd:sequence>
     <xsd:element name="job" type="jobType"
                  minOccurs="0" maxOccurs="unbounded"/>
    </xsd:sequence>
   </xsd:complexType>
  </xsd:element>

  <xsd:complexType name="jobType">
   <xsd:sequence>
    <xsd:element name="location" type="xsd:string"/>
    <xsd:element name="description" type="xsd:string"/>
    <xsd:element name="skill" type="xsd:string"
                 minOccurs="1" maxOccurs="unbounded"/>
   </xsd:sequence>
   <xsd:attribute name="customer" type="xsd:string" use="required"/>
   <xsd:attribute name="reference" type="xsd:string" use="required"/>
  </xsd:complexType>
 </xsd:schema>
```

The first thing to notice is that this schema exists within a namespace as defined on the second line. The string xsd is used by convention for a schema namespace, but any prefix can be used.

Schema Type Definitions and Element and Attribute Declarations

Elements that have sub-elements and/or attributes are defined as complex types. In addition to complex types, there are a number of built-in simple types. Examples of a few simple types are

- `string` Any combination of characters
- `integer` Whole number
- `float` Floating point number
- `boolean` true/false or 1/0
- `date` yyyy-mm-dd

A complex type element (one with attributes or sub-elements) has to be defined in the schema and will typically contain a set of element declarations, element references, and attribute declarations. Listing 16.8 contains the definition for the `job` tag complex type, which contains three elements (`location`, `description`, and `skill`) and two attributes (`customer` and `reference`).

In a schema, like a DTD, elements can be made optional or required. The `job` element in Listing 16.8 is optional because the value of the `minOccurs` attribute is `0`. In general, an element is required to appear when the value of `minOccurs` is `1` or more. Similarly, the maximum number of times an element can appear is determined by the value of `maxOccurs`. This value can be a positive integer or the term `unbounded` to indicate there is no maximum number of occurrences. The default value for both the `minOccurs` and the `maxOccurs` attributes is `1`. If you do not specify the number of occurrences, the element must be present and must occur only once.

Element attributes can be declared with a `use` attribute to indicate whether the element attribute is `required`, `optional`, or even `prohibited`.

There are more aspects to schemas than it is possible to cover in this book. Visit the WC3 Web site (`www.w3.org`) for more information on XML schemas and all other aspects of XML.

J2EE Support for XML

XML is portable data, and the Java platform is portable code. Add Java APIs for XML that make it easy to use XML and, together, you have the ideal combination:

- Portability of data
- Portability of code
- Ease of use

The J2EE platform bundles all these advantages together.

Enterprises are rapidly discovering the benefits of using J2EE for developing Web Services that use XML for the dissemination and integration of data; particularly because XML eases the sharing of legacy data both internally among departments and with other enterprises.

J2EE includes the Java API for XML Processing (JAXP) that makes it easy to process XML data with applications written in Java. JAXP embraces the parser standards:

- Simple API for XML Parsing (SAX) for parsing XML as a stream.
- Document Object Model (DOM) to build an in-memory tree representation of an XML document.
- XML Stylesheet Language Transformations (XSLT) to control the presentation of the data and convert it to other XML documents or to other formats, such as HTML. XLST is covered on Day 17, "Transforming XML Documents."

JAXP also provides namespace support, allowing you to work with multiple XML documents that might otherwise cause naming conflicts.

NOTE

> Because of the increasing use and importance of XML, JAXP is now incorporated into J2SE 1.4; previously it was available only in J2EE 1.3 or as a separate Java extension.

Parsing XML

So far, you have used Internet Explorer or other third-party tools to parse your XML documents. Now you will look at three APIs that provide a way to access and manipulate the information stored in an XML document so you can build your own XML applications.

The Simple API for XML (SAX) defines parsing methods and Document Object Model (DOM) defines a mechanism for accessing and manipulating well-formed XML. A third API is the Java API for XML Processing (JAXP) that you will use to build a simple SAX and DOM parser. The two parsers you will develop effectively echo the input XML structure. Usually, you will want to parse XML to perform some useful function, but simply echoing the XML is a good way to learn the APIs.

JAXP has the benefit that it provides a common interface for creating and using SAX and DOM in Java.

SAX and DOM define different approaches to parsing and handling an XML document. SAX is an event-based API, whereas DOM is tree-based.

With event-based parsers, the parsing events (such as the start and end tags) are reported directly to the application through callback methods. The application implements these callback methods to handle the different components in the document, much like handling events in a graphical user interface (GUI).

Using the DOM API, you will transform the XML document into a tree structure in memory. The application then navigates the tree to parse the document.

Each method has its advantages and disadvantages. Using DOM

- Simplifies the mapping of the structure of the XML.
- Is a good choice when the document is not too large. If the document is large, it can place a strain on system resources.
- Most, or all, of the document needs to be parsed.
- The document is to be altered or written out in a structure that is very different from the original.

Using SAX is a good choice

- If you are searching through an XML document for a small number of tags
- The document is large
- Processing speed is important
- If the document does not need to be written out in a structure that is different from the original

SAX is a public domain API developed cooperatively by the members of the XML-DEV (XML DEVelopment) Internet discussion group (http://www.xml.org/).

The DOM is a set of interfaces defined by the W3C DOM Working Group. The latest DOM recommendation can be obtained from the W3C Web site (http://www.w3.org).

The JAXP Packages

The JAXP APIs are defined in the J2SDK 1.4 javax.xml.parsers package, which contains two factory classes—SAXParserFactory and DocumentBuilderFactory.

The packages that define the SAX and DOM APIs are

- `javax.xml.parsers`   A common interface for different vendors' SAX and DOM parsers
- `org.w3c.dom`   Defines the DOM and all of the components of a DOM
- `org.xml.sax`   The SAX API

You will now build two applications—one that uses the SAX API and one that uses DOM.

Parsing XML Using SAX

To parse an XML document, you instantiate a `javax.xml.parsers.SAXParseFactory` object to obtain a SAX-based parser. This parser is then used to read the XML document a character at a time. (In the following code fragment the document is obtained from a command-line argument.)

```
SAXParserFactory factory = SAXParserFactory.newInstance();
SAXParser saxParser = factory.newSAXParser();

DefaultHandler handler = new XMLParse();
saxParser.parse( new File(argv[0]), handler );
```

Your SAX parser class must extend the public class `org.xml.sax.helpers.DefaultHandler`. This class defines stub methods that receive notification (callbacks) when XML entities are parsed. By default, these methods do nothing, but they can be overridden to do anything you like. For example, a method called `startElement()` is invoked when the start tag for an element is recognized. This method receives the element's name and its attributes. The element's name can be passed in any one of the first three parameters to `startElement()`, see Table 16.6, depending on whether namespaces are being used.

TABLE 16.6   Parameters to the `startElement()` Method

Parameter	Contents
uri	The namespace URI or the empty string if the element has no namespace URI or if namespace processing is not being performed.
localName	The element name (without namespace prefix) will be a non-empty string when namespaces processing is being performed.
qualifiedName	The element name with namespace prefix.
attributes	The element's attributes.

In the following code example, handling for the qualified name is provided.

```
public void startElement(String uri, String localName,
   String qualifiedName, Attributes attributes)
   throws SAXException {
   System.out.println ("START ELEMENT " + qualifiedName);
   for (int i = 0; i< attributes.getLength(); i++) {
     System.out.println ("ATTRIBUTE " +
       attributes.getQName(i) + " = " + attributes.getValue(i));
   }
}
```

This example prints out a statement indicating that a start tag has been parsed followed by a list of the attribute names and values.

A similar `endElement()` method is invoked when an end tag is encountered.

```
public void endElement(String uri, String localName, String qualifiedName)
    throws SAXException {
   System.out.println ("END ELEMENT " + qualifiedName);
}
```

The full parser is shown in Listing 16.9, but not all of the XML components will be handled. The default action for a parser is for all components to be ignored; only the methods that are overridden in the `DefaultHandler` subclass will be process XML components. For a complete list of the other `DefaultHandler` methods, see Table 16.7 or refer to the J2SDK, v 1.4 API Specification.

LISTING 16.9   Simple SAX Parser

```
import java.io.*;
import org.xml.sax.*;
import org.xml.sax.helpers.DefaultHandler;
import javax.xml.parsers.*;

public class XMLParse extends DefaultHandler {

   public static void main(String argv[]) {
     if (argv.length != 1) {
       System.err.println("Usage: XMLParse filename");
       System.exit(1);
     }
     DefaultHandler handler = new XMLParse();
     SAXParserFactory factory = SAXParserFactory.newInstance();
     try {
       SAXParser saxParser = factory.newSAXParser();
       saxParser.parse( new File(argv[0]), handler );
     }
     catch (ParserConfigurationException ex) {
```

16

LISTING **16.9**   continued

```
          System.err.println ("Failed to create SAX parser:" + ex);
      }
      catch (SAXException ex) {
        System.err.println ("SAX parser exceeption:" + ex);
      }
      catch (IOException ex) {
        System.err.println ("IO exeception:" + ex);
      }
      catch (IllegalArgumentException ex) {
        System.err.println ("Invalid file argument" + ex);
      }
  }
  public void startDocument() throws SAXException {
    System.out.println ("START DOCUMENT");
  }

  public void endDocument() throws SAXException {
    System.out.println ("END DOCUMENT");
  }

  public void startElement(String uri, String localName,
    String qualifiedName, Attributes attributes) throws SAXException {

    System.out.println ("START ELEMENT " + qualifiedName);
    for (int i = 0; i< attributes.getLength(); i++) {
      System.out.println ("ATTRIBUTE " +
        attributes.getQName(i) + " = " + attributes.getValue(i));
    }
  }

  public void endElement(String uri, String localName, String qualifiedName)
        throws SAXException {
    System.out.println ("END ELEMENT " + qualifiedName);
  }

  public void characters(char[] ch, int start, int length)
        throws SAXException {
    if (length > 0) {
      String buf = new String (ch, start, length);
      System.out.println ("CONTENT " + buf);
    }
  }
}
```

The parser first checks for the XML document, the name of which is provided on the command line. After instantiating the SAXParserFactory and constructing the handler, the XML file is parsed—that is all there is to it. This parser reports the occurrence of the start and end of the document—the start and end of elements and the characters that form the element bodies only.

If an entity method is not declared in your parser, the entity is handled by the superclass `DefaultHandler` methods, the default action being to do nothing. Table 16.7 gives a full list of the callback `DefaultHandler` methods that can be implemented.

TABLE 16.7   SAX `DefaultHandler` Methods

Method	Receives Notification of
`characters(char[] ch, int start, int length)`	Character data inside an element.
`startDocument()`	Beginning of the document.
`endDocument()`	End of the document.
`startElement(String uri, String localName, String qName, Attributes attributes)`	Start of an element.
`endElement(String uri, String localName, qName)`	End of an element.
`startPrefixMapping (String prefix, String uri)`	Start of a namespace mapping.
`endPrefixMapping (String prefix)`	End of a namespace mapping.
`error(SAXParseException e)`	A recoverable parser error.
`FatalError (SAXParseException e)`	A fatal XML parsing error.
`Warning (SAXParseException e)`	Parser warning.
`IgnorableWhitespace (char[] ch, int start, int length)`	Whitespace in the element contents.
`notationDecl(String name, String publicId, String systemId)`	Notation declaration.
`processingInstruction (String target, String data)`	A processing instruction.
`resolveEntity(String publicId, String systemId)`	An external entity.
`skippedEntity(String name)`	A skipped entity. Processors may skip entities if they have not seen the declarations. (For example, the entity was declared in an external DTD.)

As this code does not use any J2EE components, you can simply compile and run it from the command line. From the `Day16/examples` directory run the command:

```
> java -classpath classes XMLParse XML/jobSummary.xml
```

Or use the supplied `asant` build files and enter:

```
> asant XMLParse
```

Provide the filename `XML/jobSummary.xml` when prompted:

The output in Figure 16.1 is produced when this SAX parser is used on the `jobSummary` XML in Listing 16.4.

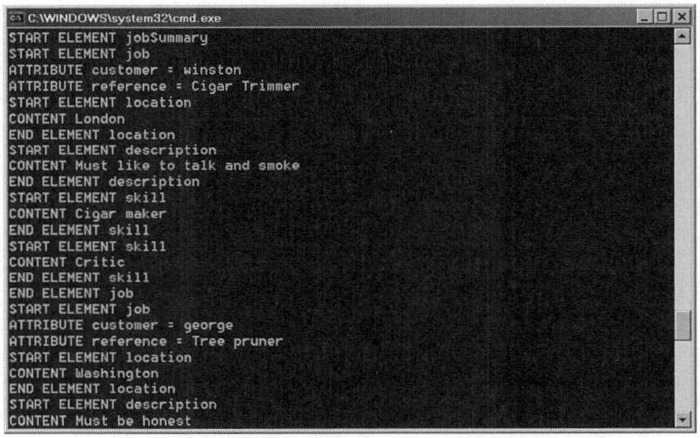

FIGURE 16.1

SAX parser output.

As you can see, the output is not very beautiful. You might like to improve it by adding indentation to the elements or even getting the output to look like the original XML.

In addition to making this parser more robust, the following functionality could be added:

- Scan element contents for the special characters, such shown in a table, and replacing them with the symbolic strings as appropriate
- Improve the handling of fatal parse errors (`SAXParseException`) with appropriate error messages giving error line numbers
- Use the `DefaultHandler` `error()` and `warning()` methods to handle non-fatal parse errors
- Configure the parser to be namespace aware with `javax.xml.parsers.SAXParserFactory.setNamespaceAware(true)`, so that you can detect tags from multiple sources

Having seen a simple SAX parser, you will now build a parser application that uses the DOM API.

Document Object Model (DOM) Parser

When you use the DOM API to parse an XML document, a tree structure representing the XML document is built in memory. You can then analyze the nodes of the tree to discover the XML contents.

Building a DOM Tree

The mechanism for instantiating a DOM parser is very similar to that for a SAX parser. A new instance of a `DocumentBuilderFactory` is obtained that is used to create a new `DocumentBuilder`.

The `parse()` method is called on this `DocumentBuilder` object to return an object that conforms to the public `Document` interface. This object represents the XML document tree. The following code fragment creates a DOM parser and reads the XML document from a file supplied as a command-line argument:

```
DocumentBuilderFactory factory = DocumentBuilderFactory.newInstance();
DocumentBuilder builder = factory.newDocumentBuilder();
Document document = builder.parse(new File(argv[0]));
```

With the `DocumentBuilder.parse()` method, you are not restricted to reading XML only from a file; you can also use a constructed `InputStream` or read from a source defined by a URL.

The Document obtained form the `parse()` method is a subclass of `org.w3c.dom.Node`. To simplify processing of the DOM tree, all of the objects in the tree are either `Node` objects or objects of a sub class of `Node`.

There are a number of methods provided in the `Document` interface to access the nodes in the tree. These are listed in Table 16.8.

The `normalize()` method should always be used to put all text nodes into a form where there are no adjacent text nodes or empty text nodes. In this form, the DOM view better reflects the XML structure.

After parsing an XML document the DOM parser has built an in-memory representation of the document that will look something like Figure 16.2.

The root of the DOM tree is obtained with the `getDocumentElement()` method.

```
Element root = document.getDocumentElement();
```

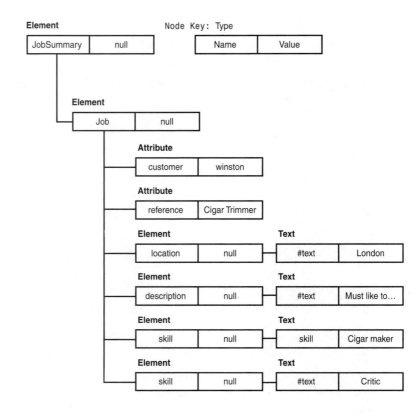

FIGURE 16.2

Diagram of the DOM tree.

This method returns an `Element`, which is simply a subclass of `Node` that may have attributes associated with it. An element can be the parent of other elements.

There are a number of methods provided in the `Document` interface to access the nodes in the tree, some of which are listed in Table 16.8. These methods return either a `Node` or a `NodeList` (ordered collection of nodes).

TABLE 16.8   Document Interface Methods to Traverse a DOM Tree

Method Name	Description
getDocumentElement()	Allows direct access to the root element of the document
getElementsByTagName(String)	Returns a `NodeList` of all the elements with the given tag name in the order in which they are encountered in the tree
getChildNodes()	A `NodeList` that contains all children of this node
getParentNode()	The parent of this node

TABLE 16.8 continued

Method Name	Description
getFirstChild()	The first child of this node
getLastChild()	The last child of this node
getPreviousSibling()	The node immediately preceding this node

In a simple DOM application the getChildNodes() method can be used to recursively traverse the DOM tree. The NodeList.getLength() method can then be used to find out the number of nodes in the NodeList.

```
NodeList children = node.getChildNodes();
int len = (children != null) ? children.getLength() : 0;
```

In addition to the tree traversal methods, the Node interface provides the following methods (among others) to investigate the contents of a node as in Table 16.9.

TABLE 16.9 Document Interface Methods to Inspect DOM Nodes

Method Name	Description
getAttributes()	A NamedNodeMap containing the attributes of a node if it is an Element or null if it is not.
getNodeName()	A string representing the name of this node (the tag).
getNodeType()	A code representing the type of the underlying object. A node can be one of ELEMENT_NODE, ATTRIBUTE_NODE, TEXT_NODE, CDATA_SECTION_NODE, ENTITY_REFERENCE_NODE, ENTITY_NODE, PROCESSING_INSTRUCTION_NODE, COMMENT_NODE, DOCUMENT_NODE, DOCUMENT_TYPE_NODE, DOCUMENT_FRAGMENT_NODE, NOTATION_NODE.
getNodeValue()	A string representing the value of this node. If the node is a text node, the value will be the contents of the text node; for an attribute node, it will be the string assigned to the attribute. For most node types, there is no value and a call to this method will return null.
getNamespaceURI()	The namespace URI of this node.
hasAttributes()	Returns a boolean to indicate whether this node has any attributes.
hasChildNodes()	Returns a boolean to indicate whether this node has any children.

Modifying a DOM Tree

We will now look at using the DOM API—to modify the contents or structure of the XML. Unlike SAX, DOM provides a number of methods that allow nodes to be added, deleted, changed, or replaced in the DOM tree. Table 16.10 summarizes these methods.

TABLE 16.10 Document Interface Methods to Inspect DOM Nodes

Method Name	Description
appendChild(Node newNode)	Adds the new node to the end of the NodeList of children of this node.
cloneNode(boolean deep)	Returns a duplicate of a node. The cloned node has no parent. If deep is true, the whole tree below this node is cloned; if false, only the node itself is cloned.
insertBefore(Node newNode, Node refNode)	Inserts the newNode before the existing refNode.
removeChild(Node oldNode)	Removes the oldNode from the list of children.
replaceChild(Node newNode, Node oldNode)	Replaces the oldNode with newNode in the child NodeList.
setNodeValue(String nodeValue)	Set the value of this node, depending on its type.
setPrefix(java.lang.String prefix)	Set the namespace prefix of this node.

For example, the following code fragment simply creates a new customer element and appends it to the end of the XML document:

```
Node newNode = addXMLNode (document, "Customer", "Columbus");
Element root = document.getDocumentElement();
root.appendChild(newNode);

private static Node addXMLNode (Document document, String name, String text) {
  Element e = document.createElement(name);
  Text t = document.createTextNode(text);
  e.appendChild (t);
  return e;
}
```

The following XML element is added to the XML file that is read in by this example code:

```
<customer>Columbus</customer>
```

Outputting a DOM Tree

Having parsed or created an XML document in memory, a common requirement is to output the DOM tree. The javax.xml.transform class defines a transformer that can be used to output a DOM tree from memory. The following code shows how easy it is to take a DOM tree and output it to the screen:

```
TransformerFactory tf = TransformerFactory.newInstance();
Transformer transformer = tf.newTransformer();
transformer.transform(new DOMSource(root), new StreamResult(System.out));
```

NOTE In Day 17 you will see how to use XML Sylesheets with the `transformer` object to format the transformed output.

A Simple DOM Example

The `WebDDBuilder` example shown in Listing 16.10 is a simple program that creates a new Web Application deployment descriptor and adds a single `<servlet>` and `<servlet-mapping>` element to the tree before writing the updated DD. The Web Application DD was described on Day 12, "Servlets."

16

LISTING 16.10   WebDDBuilder.java

```java
import javax.xml.parsers.*;
import javax.xml.transform.*;
import javax.xml.transform.dom.*;
import javax.xml.transform.stream.*;
import org.xml.sax.*;
import java.io.*;
import org.w3c.dom.*;
import java.util.*;

public class WebDDBuilder {

    public static void main(String argv[]) {
        int argCount = argv.length;
        if (argCount != 2) {
            System.err.println("Usage: WebDDBuilder servlet-class URL-mapping");
            System.exit(1);
        }
        String servletClass = argv[0];
        String URLPattern = argv[1];
        try {
            WebDDBuilder dd = new WebDDBuilder();
            dd.addServlet(servletClass, URLPattern);
            // output document
            dd.print(System.out);
        }
        catch (IllegalArgumentException ex) {
            System.err.println ("Invalid argument" + ex);
            ex.printStackTrace(System.out);
        }
    }

    private static final String SERVLET_VERSION = "2.4";
    private static final String XML_NAMESPACE =
        "http://java.sun.com/xml/ns/j2ee";
```

LISTING **16.10**   continued

```
        private static final String XML_SCHEMA_INST =
            "http://www.w3.org/2001/XMLSchema-instance";
        private static final String XML_SCHEMA_LOC =
            "http://java.sun.com/xml/ns/j2ee
➡    http://java.sun.com/xml/ns/j2ee/web-app_2_4.xsd";

        private static final String SERVLET = "servlet";
        private static final String SERVLET_MAPPING = "servlet-mapping";
        private static final String SERVLET_NAME = "servlet-name";
        private static final String SERVLET_CLASS = "servlet-class";
        private static final String URL_PATTERN = "url-pattern";

        private static final String[] DD_ELEMENTS = {"icon", "display-name",
            "description", "distributable", "context-param", "filter",
            "filter-mapping", "listener", "servlet", "servlet-mapping",
            "session-config", "mimemapping", "welcome-file-list", "error-page",
            "taglib", "resource-env-ref", "resource-ref", "security-constraint",
            "login-config", "security-role", "env-entry",
            "ejb-ref", "ejb-local-ref" };

        private Document document;
        private Element root;
        private HashMap DDElements;

        public WebDDBuilder () {
            DocumentBuilderFactory factory = DocumentBuilderFactory.newInstance();
            try {
                DocumentBuilder builder = factory.newDocumentBuilder();
                document = builder.newDocument();
                root = document.createElement("web-app");
                root.setAttribute("version", SERVLET_VERSION);
                root.setAttribute("xmlns", XML_NAMESPACE);
                root.setAttribute("xmlns:xsi", XML_SCHEMA_INST);
                root.setAttribute("xsi:schemaLocation", XML_SCHEMA_LOC);
                DDElements = createDDMap(DD_ELEMENTS);
            }
            catch (ParserConfigurationException ex) {
                System.err.println ("Failed to create DOM document:" + ex);
            }
        }

        private void addServlet (String servletClass, String URLPattern) {

            //create the servlet name from the servlet class name
            // if fully qualified class name take just last part
            int index = servletClass.lastIndexOf(".");
            String servletName;
            if (index != -1)
```

LISTING 16.10 continued

```
            servletName = servletClass.substring(index+1);
        else
            servletName = servletClass;

        // build the servlet element
        Element servlet_name = document.createElement(SERVLET_NAME);
        servlet_name.appendChild(document.createTextNode(servletName));

        Element servlet_class = document.createElement(SERVLET_CLASS);
        servlet_class.appendChild(document.createTextNode(servletClass));

        Element servlet = document.createElement (SERVLET);
        servlet.appendChild(servlet_name);
        servlet.appendChild(servlet_class);

        // find where in the DOM to insert the new servlet node
        Node refChild = findNode (root, DDElements, SERVLET);
        root.insertBefore(servlet, refChild);

        // build the servlet-mapping element
        Element url_pattern = document.createElement(URL_PATTERN);
        url_pattern.appendChild(document.createTextNode(URLPattern));

        Element servlet_mapping = document.createElement (SERVLET_MAPPING);
        // no need to create servlet name element as we already have one
        // make sure we clone deep so that we get the text node
        servlet_mapping.appendChild(servlet_name.cloneNode(true));
        servlet_mapping.appendChild(url_pattern);

        refChild = findNode (root, DDElements, SERVLET_MAPPING);
        root.insertBefore(servlet_mapping, refChild);
    }

    private void print (PrintStream stream) {
        try {
            TransformerFactory tf = TransformerFactory.newInstance();
            Transformer transformer = tf.newTransformer();
            transformer.setOutputProperty(OutputKeys.INDENT,"yes");
            transformer.transform(new DOMSource(root),
                            new StreamResult(stream));
        }
        catch (TransformerConfigurationException ex) {
            System.err.println ("Failed to create transformer factory:" + ex);
        }
        catch (TransformerException ex) {
            System.err.println ("Failed to transform DOM tree:" + ex);
        }
    }
```

16

LISTING 16.10 continued

```java
private Node findNode (Node treeRoot, HashMap ddSchema, String tagName) {

    // find out index of tagName
    int refKey = getKey (ddSchema, tagName);

    NodeList tags = treeRoot.getChildNodes();
    int tagsLen = (tags != null) ? tags.getLength() : 0;

    // find first tag after tagName in tree
    for (int i = 0; i < tagsLen; i++) {
        Node tag = tags.item(i);
        if (getKey(ddSchema, tag.getNodeName()) > refKey)
            return tag;
    }
    return null;
}

private int getKey (HashMap ddSchema, String tagName) {
    for (int key = 0; key < ddSchema.size(); key++) {
        if (ddSchema.get(new Integer(key)).equals(tagName))
            return key;
    }
    return -1;
}

private HashMap createDDMap(String[] ddSchema) {
    HashMap map = new HashMap();
    for (int i = 0; i < ddSchema.length; i++)
        map.put(new Integer(i), ddSchema[i]);
    return map;
}
```

The WebDDBuilder example in Listing 16.10 starts by creating a new, empty, DOM tree representing an empty Web Application DD. Next the addServlet() method is called to add the servlet name and URL pattern passed as command-line parameters.

The addServlet()method builds two XML DD elements, <servlet> and <servlet-mapping>, using the values supplied as arguments. Each of these elements has a <servlet-name> sub-element, so instead of creating a new element from scratch, addServlet uses the Node.cloneNode() method to create a copy. A deep copy is preformed by passing true as the parameter to cloneNode; this ensures that all the child nodes are also cloned.

Finally, the print() method is called to output the DOM tree using a Transformer object.

As with the SAX example, this code does not use any J2EE components; you can simply compile and run it from the command line. From the Day16/examples directory run the command

```
> java -classpath classes demo.Hello /hello
```

This will create a DD entry for the demo.servlet with URL pattern /hello. Alternatively, use the supplied asant build files and enter

```
> asant WebDDBuilder
```

Provide the servlet name and URL pattern when prompted:

The resultant DD looks like this:

```
<?xml version="1.0" encoding="UTF-8"?>
<web-app version="2.4"
  xmlns="http://java.sun.com/xml/ns/j2ee"
  xmlns:xsi="http://www.w3.org/2001/XMLSchema-instance"
  xsi:schemaLocation="http://java.sun.com/xml/ns/j2ee
➥ http://java.sun.com/xml/ns/j2ee/web-app_2_4.xsd">
  <servlet>
    <servlet-name>Hello</servlet-name>
    <servlet-class>demo.Hello</servlet-class>
  </servlet>
  <servlet-mapping>
    <servlet-name>Hello</servlet-name>
    <url-pattern>/hello</url-pattern>
  </servlet-mapping>
</web-app>
```

Java Architecture for XML Binding

DOM is a useful API allowing you to build and transform XML documents in memory. Unfortunately, DOM is somewhat slow and resource hungry. To address these problems, the Java Architecture for XML Binding (JAXB) has been developed through the Java Community Process (JCP) with an expert group consisting of representatives from many commercial organizations.

JAXB provides a mechanism that simplifies the creation and maintenance of XML-enabled Java applications. It does this by using an XML schema compiler (only DTDs and a subset of XML schemas and namespaces at the time of this writing) that translates XML DTDs into one or more Java classes, thereby removing the burden from the developer to write complex parsing code.

The generated classes handle all the details of XML parsing and formatting, including code to perform error and validity checking of incoming and outgoing XML documents, which ensures that only valid, error-free XML is accepted.

Because the code has been generated for a specific schema, the generated classes are more efficient than those in a generic SAX or DOM parser. Most important, a JAXB parser often requires a much smaller footprint in memory than a generic parser.

Classes created with JAXB do not include tree-manipulation capability, which is one factor that contributes to the small memory footprint of a JAXB object tree. If you want to build an object representation of XML data, but need to get around the memory limitations of DOM, you should use JAXB.

These following two bulleted lists summarize the advantages of JAXB and JAXP so you can decide which one is right for your application.

Use JAXB when you want to

- Access data in memory, but do not need tree manipulation capabilities
- Process only data that is valid
- Convert data to different types
- Generate classes based on a DTD or XML schema
- Build object representations of XML data

Use JAXP when you want to

- Have flexibility with regard to the way you access the data, either serially with SAX or randomly in memory with DOM
- Use your same processing code with documents based on different DTDs
- Parse documents that are not necessarily valid
- Apply XSLT transformations
- Insert or remove components from an in-memory XML tree

Summary

Today, you have had a very quick, and necessarily brief, introduction to XML and the APIs and technologies available in J2EE to parse and generate XML data. You have seen how XML can be used to create flexible structured data that is inherently portable. With DTDs and XML Schemas, you were shown how this data can also be validated. You have been introduced to several different ways of parsing an XML document with SAX, DOM, JAXP, or JAXB, and you should now recognize the advantages and disadvantages of each technique.

Tomorrow, you will extend your XML knowledge to include XML transformations.

Q&A

Q What are the major characteristics of XML?

A XML is a human readable, structured data-encoding format that is generic, simple, flexible, extensible and free to use.

Q What is the difference between well-formed and valid XML.

A Well-formed XML is syntactically and structurally correct. XML is only valid if it complies with the constraints of a DTD or XML schema.

Q What are the J2EE APIs and specifications that support the processing of XML?

A The J2EE APIs and specifications that supports XML processing are JAXP (Java API for XML Processing), SAX (Simple API for XML Parsing), DOM (Document Object Model), and XLST for transforming XML documents

Q What are the main differences between SAX and DOM?

A SAX provides a serial event-driven parser. DOM is more flexible in that it builds an in-memory representation of the document that can be manipulated randomly (that is, nodes can be addressed or processed in any order). SAX is generally more efficient (faster), while DOM can be a heavy user of memory.

Exercise

To practice working with XML, try the following two exercises; the first is relatively simple, but the second requires a little more effort.

1. Extend the `WebDDBuilder` application to optionally read in an existing `web.xml` file and add the new `<servlet>` and `<servlet-mapping>` elements from the servlet class and URL pattern information provided on the command line.

   Hint: Most of the code is already in place. You will need to create another constructor to build the DOM tree from an existing DD whose filename is supplied as the last (optional) parameter on the command line. A simple web.xml file is provided in the `Day16/solution/XML` directory.

TIP

> If your web.xml file has a non-local DTD specified in the DOCTYPE element (this will be the case if you are using a J2EE 1.3 or earlier web.xml file), you will require access to the Web for the parser to validate the XML.

16

2. Enhance your solution to check for duplicate servlet names. The servlet name in a Web Application DD must be unique. Ensure that the program will not add the same servlet class twice by checking for duplicate servlet names before adding the new entry.

A solution is provided in the Day 16 `solution` directory.

DAY **17**

Transforming XML Documents

In Day 16's lesson, "Integrating XML with J2EE," you studied the basic features of the Extensible Markup Language (XML) and the Java for XML Processing API (JAXP). You can now create XML documents using DOM or Java `OutputStream`/`Writer` objects and process existing XML documents using SAX and DOM. As long as you use XML to store information or transfer information between different components in your application, what you already know about XML is probably sufficient.

In Day 16 you also used the `javax.xml.Transform` class to output simple XML documents. But for many applications, you will need to transform your XML documents into other formats, such as HTML, for presentation to a Web client. You may also need to generate a new XML document from an existing one where the new document uses a different XML DTD or schema from the original.

These and other requirements are so ubiquitous among enterprise applications (like those based on J2EE) that tools and standard APIs supporting common capabilities are developing all the time.

In today's work, you will look at

- Techniques for presenting XML data to a Web client
- Applying HTML stylesheets to XML
- The XML Stylesheet Language for Transformation (XSLT) component of the JAXP for transforming XML documents into other formats
- XSLT compilers, such as xsltc

Support for XSLT was incorporated into the J2SE 1.4; the open source Apache Xalan project (http://xml.apache.org/xalan-j) is a popular XSLT implementation for developers working with older versions of J2SE.

Presenting XML to Clients

XML is a useful way of exchanging data between applications and for moving and storing data within an application. However, XML is not very convenient for presenting data to a user because it primarily describes the content of the data and not how this data should be presented to the user.

A user requires that the data be formatted so that it is easy to read. XML defines the data and its metadata, but it does not define how to format the data for presentation. This was in fact one of the design criteria; XML deliberately does define data presentation formats. Because the same data will be presented in different ways to different users, any attempt to include presentation information would turn the XML document into an incoherent mix of data, metadata, and formatting instructions for multiple output devices.

The technique of presenting XML data to a user involves transforming the data from XML to another format. Typical applications are to transform XML into

- HTML for output to a Web browser
- WML for output to a WAP-enabled mobile phone
- PDF for displaying on any graphic client
- Postscript for output to a printer
- RTF or TeX for presentation to a word processor or text formatter
- XML for presentation to another application that requires the data in a different format

The transformation of the XML document can be undertaken either by the server that has access to the document or by the client that controls the display. There are pros and cons for each approach. The more work that is done on the server, the fewer clients it can support. However, relying on the client to perform complex transformations tends to rule out the use of many lightweight (thin) clients.

In practice, most current implementations of XSLT perform the transformations on the server. This means that the server must be aware of all possible client display requirements. In practice, this is not a major problem because most clients support a standard presentation language, such as HTML, WML, and PDF, for visual displays and Postscript for printing.

Presenting XML to Browsers

Web browsers display HTML information. As you saw on Day 16, a well-written HTML page can also be a well-formatted XML document. Given the close relationship between HTML and XML, it is feasible for an HTML browser to be adapted to present XML. Many recent browsers, such as Mozilla, Netscape, Internet Explorer, Opera, and countless others, support presentation of XML documents. However, additional formatting information must be provided with the XML data to enable the browser to format the data. By default, XML documents are rendered in plain text, usually with the XML tags highlighted in color and neatly aligned to highlight the nested tag structure of the document.

Like HTML browsers, there is some variation between the browsers on the market as to how they support presentation of XML. To address this problem, the World Wide Web Consortium (W3C) has defined a standard mechanism called XML Stylesheet Language (XSL) for supplying information on transforming an XML document into different formats. The most common use of XSL, at the present time, is to convert XML into HTML for display by a Web browser, but the technology is much more flexible than this limited use implies.

Early XSL support in popular HTML browsers was based on draft versions of the standard, and some browsers added in their own proprietary extensions. With a fully ratified standard, recent versions of the browsers are now implementing the standard, but at least one manufacturer is maintaining backward compatibility at the expense of standards conformance. You must take into account the variations in client support for XSL when designing your systems. In practice, this means either dictating which client browser is used and targeting your application to that browser, providing multiple XSLT stylesheets for each supported browser, or transforming the XML data into HTML on the server.

XML Stylesheet Language (XSL)

XSL is a family of technologies used to transform XML documents into any other format. The two components of XSL are

- XSLT—XML Stylesheet Language for Transformation (XSLT) is applied to an XML document to transform it to another format.
- XSL-FO—XSL Formatting Objects are used to define formatting semantics in a device independent manner.

XSLT has been widely adopted by the computing industry, and you will look in detail at this technology in the "XML Stylesheet for Transformation" section later in this chapter.

XSL-FO XSL Formatting Objects

Formatting objects define a device-independent grammar for defining how data should be presented. The actual data is intermixed with the formatting objects to define a portable formatted document.

Formatting objects are widely referred to as XSL-FO, but this is not an acronym defined in the W3C standard. You may see XSL-FO written in different forms—XSL:FO, XSLFO, XSL/FO, and others.

Listing 17.1 shows a fragment of an XSL-FO document that defines a table of skills in the Agency case study.

LISTING **17.1**   Fragment of an XSL-FO Document

```
<fo:block font-family="sans-serif" color="blue">
<fo:table border-style="solid">
 <fo:table-body>
  <fo:table-row>
   <fo:table-cell padding="1mm">
    <fo:block>Bodyguard</fo:block>
   </fo:table>
   <fo:table-cell padding="1mm">
    <fo:block>Critic</fo:block>
   </fo:table>
  <fo:table-row>
 <fo:table-body>
<fo:table>
```

As you can see from listing 17.1, XSL-FO is an XML document defining formatting instructions and data. In this example, the formatting objects provide the bulk of the document with a very small amount of data. XSL-FO is quite a verbose format and maintains device independence at the cost of some generalizations; the font name on line 1 is sans-serif instead of a device-specific font name, such as Arial. This helps improve portability of XSL-FO but at the expense of control over the exact rendering of a document on a specific device.

XSL-FO requires two stages for presenting an XML document to a client device.

1. The XML document must be transformed into an XSL-FO document.
2. The XSL-FO document must be transformed into the necessary formatting instructions.

XSLT is used to transform XML into XML-FO. There are several tools around for converting XSL-FO into other formats. One example is the open-source Apache FOP utility that can produce PDF output from an XSL-FO document. FOP can also create a Java Swing application that will display an XSL-FO document using Swing components. More information on FOP can be obtained from `http://xml.apache.org/fop/`.

The main criticism of XSL-FO is that it does not bring anything new to the process of formatting XML documents. HTML and WML already do a very good job of defining the presentation of data for two of the most popular client devices—PCs and mobile phones. Similarly, PDF defines a portable format for online presentation, and Postscript defines a portable format for printing documents. There is no requirement for yet another device independent presentation format.

You can find out more about XSL-FO from online Web resources and the book *Sams Teach Yourself XML in 21 Days* from Sams Publishing.

XML Stylesheet for Transformation (XSLT)

XSLT is a very flexible technique used to transform an XML document into a different format, such as XSL-FO, HTML, WML, PDF, or any format you choose, including an XML document conforming to another DTD or XML schema.

XSLT defines a stylesheet that can be applied to an XML document to transform the XML data into another format. The most common use of XSLT, at the moment, is to transform XML into HTML for display by a Web browser.

An XSLT stylesheet defines rules that will transform the XML data into the new format. The rules are driven by pattern matching XML elements and attributes in the original XML document. A stylesheet transforms any XML document independently from any DTD or schema to which the document may conform. However, the writer of the stylesheet must be aware of the source document's structure to ensure that the stylesheet achieves the desired result.

An XSLT stylesheet is a well-formed XML document in its own right and conforms to a standard defined by the W3C. Listing 17.2 shows the smallest valid stylesheet called `simple.xsl` (conventionally, stylesheets are stored in files with a `.xsl` suffix).

17

LISTING 17.2   Full Text of `simple.xsl`

```
<?xml version="1.0"?>
<xsl:stylesheet version="1.0" xmlns:xsl="http://www.w3.org/1999/XSL/Transform">
</xsl:stylesheet>
```

Although the example stylesheet in Listing 17.2 apparently does nothing, it, in fact, transforms an XML document by removing the XML tags and outputting the remaining text. While this doesn't seem a very useful way of presenting data to a client, it is helpful for understanding the different ways of applying stylesheets to documents.

Applying Stylesheets

There are three ways of applying stylesheets when delivering data to a client such as a Web browser:

- The server uses the stylesheet to transform the XML document into a local file, and the file is sent to the client instead of the original document.
- The stylesheet is sent to the client and then the client transforms the specified XML document for display to the user.
- The server uses the stylesheet to transform the document each time it is requested to a presentation language, such as HTML or WML, and then presents the transformed document to the client.

All three approaches in theory use the same XML data and stylesheet; they differ in where and when the transformation takes place.

Storing Transformed Documents on the Server

Storing the transformed data on the server and presenting this to the client is a good technique when the document changes infrequently and many clients will use the same document. This approach reduces the processing requirements because a new HTML document is only generated when the original data changes.

The downside to this approach is that at least two copies of the data must be retained—the original XML data and the formatted HTML data. There may be several copies of the data formatted for each possible client device. Keeping the formatted documents synchronized with original data can become an administrative nightmare. This increased complexity also introduces additional potential for subtle and hard to identify bugs in the application. This approach is impractical for large enterprise applications.

Presenting XML Documents and Stylesheets to the Client

Sending the stylesheet and the XML document to the client requires an XML/XSLT-aware client. Given that most clients are Web browsers, this means adding XSLT capabilities to the Web browser.

XSLT support is available in many browsers, such as the latest versions of Netscape, Internet Explorer, Mozilla, Opera, and many others. Sadly, not all implementations conform to the W3C standard. If you can ensure that your customers will use a W3C-conformant browser, presenting XML and a stylesheet to the client is a viable approach. Alternatively, you will have to potentially support a different XLST stylesheet for each type of browser. Again this can lead to administrative complications in ensuring each separate XSLT stylesheet is synchronized with the other XSLT stylesheets for a given XML document.

In practice, a web application supporting multiple browsers (especially older, non-XSLT versions) will usually transform the XML documents on the server. The rest of today's work with XSLT will concentrate on applying XSLT transformations on the server.

17

Transforming the XML Document on the Server

A simple approach to transforming XML for presentation by the client is to do the transformation on the server when the client requests the data. The formatted output is sent to the requesting client. Subsequent requests from the same or different clients must reformat the XML source. This approach ensures that the server retains control of the XML data and only presents the client with appropriate data. Because the client is just a simple display device, there is no requirement for the client to support XML or XSLT. The drawback is that the server must devote processing time to transforming the data.

Today's work will concentrate on applying XML transformations from within a Java servlet using the J2SE 1.4 XSLT implementation. If you are using an older version of J2SE, you should download the Java implementation of Apache Xalan from `http://xml.apache.org/xalan-j`. The discussion of the `javax.xml.Transform` classes is the same for both implementations.

Using XSLT in Java Applications

As you saw yesterday, JAXP provides a `javax.xml.transform.Transformer` class that is used to transform XML documents using XSLT. A `javax.xml.transform.TransformerFactory` is used to create a `Transformer` object. A new `TransformerFactory` object is created by the static `newInstance()` method in the factory class.

The following code creates a new `TransformerFactory`:

```
TransformerFactory factory = TransformerFactory.newInstance();
```

A `Transformer` object is created by a `newTransformer()` method in the factory object and optionally takes an XSLT stylesheet as a parameter to the method. The XSLT stylesheet must be accessed using a `javax.xml.transform.stream.Source` object. A `StreamSource` object can be constructed from a `java.io.InputStream` (or a `File` or `Reader` object).

The following code constructs a transformer from the XSLT stylesheet file called `simple.xsl`:

```
Source xsl = new StreamSource(new FileInputStream("simple.xsl"));
Transformer transformer = factory.newTransformer(xsl);
```

A `Transformer` object uses properties to configure information; these properties override properties set in the stylesheet itself. The `Tranformer` class provides suitable default properties but assumes the output document will be another XML document. If you want to change the output document type, you must define the `method` property of the `Transformer` object. Standard values for this property include `html`, `xml`, and `text`, but a particular XSLT implementation might support additional methods (such as `xhtml`). `Transformer` properties are defined in the `javax.xml.transform.OutputKeys` class. The following will configure a Transformer to output HTML rather than XML:

```
transformer.setOutputProperty(OutputKeys.METHOD,"html");
```

The `Transformer.transform()` method is used to transform an XML document using the XSLT stylesheet. The `transform()` method takes two parameters—a `Source` defining the XML document and a `javax.xml.transform.stream.Result` for the output file. A `Result` can be constructed from a `java.io.OutputStream` (or a `File` or `Writer` object).

The following lines will copy the XML document `jobs.xml` (shown in Listing 17.3 and provided on the Web site in the `Day17/examples/JSP/examples` directory) sending the output to the screen.

```
Source xml = new StreamSource(new FileReader("jobs.xml"));
transformer.transform(xml, new StreamResult(System.out));
```

In this case no transformation will take place.

LISTING 17.3   `jobs.xml`

```
<?xml version="1.0"?>
<jobSummary>
 <job customer="winston" reference="Cigar Trimmer">
  <location>London</location>
  <description>Must like to talk and smoke</description>
```

LISTING 17.3 continued

```
  <!-- skills list for winston -->
  <skill>Cigar maker</skill>
  <skill>Critic</skill>
 </job>
 <job customer="george" reference="Tree pruner">
  <location>Washington</location>
  <description>Must be honest</description>
  <!-- skills list for george -->
  <skill>Tree surgeon</skill>
 </job>
</jobSummary>
```

A more useful servlet, which applies a user-selected XSLT stylesheet to a user-selected XML document, is shown in Listing 17.4. This servlet uses `context.getResourceAsStream` to access the XML and XSL files included in the Web Application.

17

LISTING 17.4   Full Text of `ApplyXSLT.java`

```java
import java.util.*;
import javax.xml.transform.*;
import javax.xml.transform.stream.*;

public class ApplyXSLT extends HttpServlet {

  public void doGet (HttpServletRequest request, HttpServletResponse response)
      throws ServletException, IOException, java.net.MalformedURLException
  {
    response.setContentType("text/html");
    PrintWriter out = response.getWriter();
    try {
      if (request.getParameter("show") != null) {
        RequestDispatcher rd =
          getServletContext().getRequestDispatcher("/showXSLT");
        rd.forward(request,response);
      }
      String source = request.getParameter("source");
      int ix = source.lastIndexOf('/');
      String xmlDoc = source.substring(0,ix);
      String xslDoc = source.substring(ix);
      TransformerFactory factory = TransformerFactory.newInstance();

      ServletContext context = getServletContext();
```

LISTING 17.4   continued

```
      Source xsl = new StreamSource(context.getResourceAsStream(xslDoc));
      Transformer transformer = factory.newTransformer(xsl);
      transformer.setOutputProperty(OutputKeys.METHOD,"html");

      out.println("<H2>Transformed Document</H2>");
      Source xml = new StreamSource(context.getResourceAsStream(xmlDoc));
      transformer.transform(xml, new StreamResult(out));

    }
    catch (Exception ex) {
      out.println(ex);
      ex.printStackTrace(out);
    }
    out.close();
  }
}
```

The ApplyXSLT servlet works in conjunction with a ShowXSLT servlet (not shown here but is included with the example code for Day 17 on the Web site accompanying this book). The ApplyXSLT servlet applies the stylesheet while the ShowXSLT servlet simply outputs the original XML document and XSLT stylesheet. To control which servlet is to be used a request parameter called "show" or "apply" is provided with the HTTP request. The first task of either servlet is to forward the request to the other servlet if appropriate using the RequestDispatcher object. A suitable form for use with this servlet is shown in Listing 17.5.

LISTING 17.5   Full Text of xsltForm.jsp

```
<HTML>
<HEAD><TITLE>XLST Transformations</TITLE></HEAD>
<BODY>
  <FORM action="applyXSLT">
    <P>Select an XML document/XSL stylesheet to transform:
    <SELECT name="source">
      <OPTION>/jobs.xml/simple.xsl
      <OPTION>/jobs.xml/basicHTML.xsl
      <OPTION>/jobs.xml/comment.xsl
      <OPTION>/jobs.xml/simpleLine.xsl
      <OPTION>/jobs.xml/simpleStrip.xsl
      <OPTION>/jobs.xml/tableCount.xsl
      <OPTION>/jobs.xml/tableStyle.xsl
      <OPTION>/jobs.xml/textHTML.xsl
      <OPTION>/jobs.xml/table.xsl
      <OPTION>/dd.xml/session.xsl
    </SELECT></P>
```

LISTING 17.5   continued

```
        <P><INPUT type="submit" name="apply" value="Transform Document"></P>
        <P><INPUT type="submit" name="show"
                  value="Show Document/XSLT Stylesheet"></P>
    </FORM>
</BODY>
</HTML>
```

After determining the nature of the HTTP request the `ApplyXSLT` servlet in listing 17.4 reads a request parameter that defines the XML source file and the XSLT stylesheet file, which must be defined in the same Web application as the servlet. To simplify the parameter parsing the two filenames are passed as a single parameter called `source`, each filename being preceded by a forward slash (/). The servlet displays the transformed document.

You will be able to use this form and servlet to examine the example transformations shown today.

To run this demonstration servlet, use the supplied `asant` build files to run the following command from the `Day17/examples` directory:

```
asant build deploy
```

You can access the HTML form as the welcome page for the XLST Web application using the URL

```
http://localhost:8000/examples
```

Select the XML document and XSLT stylesheet pair you want to view and click the "Submit" button. Your screen will look similar to the one shown in Figure 17.1.

FIGURE 17.1

Viewing the simple XML transformation.

So far, you have seen a very simple XLST transformation. You will now look in more detail at XSLT and its capabilities.

If you do not want to use the `ApplyXSLT` servlet, the code on the accompanying Web site includes a simple command line application that accepts a command line of the form

```
Transform stylesheet source [ destination ]
```

from the `Day17/examples` directory you can apply the `simple.xsl` XSLT stylesheet to the sample `jobs.xml` document using the command

```
> java -classpath classes Transform JSP/examples/simple.xsl
➥  JSP/examples/jobs.xml
```

Alternatively, use the supplied `asant` build files and enter

```
> asant Transform
```

and supply the parameters when prompted.

All of the example XSLT stylesheets and XML documents are provided in the `Day17/examples/JSP/examples` sub-directory.

XSLT Stylesheets

In Listing 17.2, you saw a simple XSLT stylesheet that used default transformation rules to remove everything except the text from an XML document. You will now look at how to define your own rules for transforming an XML document.

Rules are based on matching elements in the XML document and transforming the elements into a new document. Text and information from the original XML document can be included or omitted. Components from the XML document are matched using the XPath notation defined by the W3C. You will learn more about XPath in the "Using XPath with XSLT" section later in today's lesson, after you have looked at some simple XSLT templates.

Template Rules

The most common XSLT template rules are those for matching and transforming elements. The following simple example matches the root node of a document and transforms it into an outline for an HTML document.

```
<xsl:template match="/">
 <HTML>
  <HEAD> <TITLE>Job Details</TITLE> </HEAD>
```

```
  <BODY> </BODY>
 </HTML>
</xsl:template>
```

The `<xsl:template>` defines a new template rule and its `match` attribute specifies which parts of the XML document will be matched by this rule. The root of a document is matched by the forward slash (/); other matching patterns are discussed later in the "Using XPath with XSLT" section.

The body of the `<xsl:template>` element is output in place of the matched element in the original document. In this case, the entire document is replaced by a blank HTML document. No other elements in the document will be matched.

If you want to transform other elements in the original document, you must define additional templates and apply those templates to the body of the matched element. The following text adds an `<xsl:apply-templates/>` element to the rule matching the XML document root at the point where additional transformed text should be placed:

```
<xsl:template match="/">
 <HTML>
  <HEAD> <title>Job Details</title> </HEAD>
  <BODY> <xsl:apply-templates/> </BODY>
 </HTML>
</xsl:template>
```

When this rule is applied to the transformed root element, the body of the root element is scanned for further template matches. The output from the other rules is inserted at the point where the `<xsl:apply-templates/>` element occurred.

Listing 17.6 shows an XSLT stylesheet that transforms all of the XML elements into HTML `<STRONG>` elements.

LISTING 17.6   Full Text of `basicHTML.xsl`

```
<?xml version="1.0"?>
<xsl:stylesheet version="1.0" xmlns:xsl="http://www.w3.org/1999/XSL/Transform">
<xsl:template match="/">
  <HTML>
    <HEAD> <TITLE>Job Details</TITLE> </HEAD>
    <BODY>
      <xsl:apply-templates/>
      <P><A HREF='xsltForm.jsp'>Back to xsltForm</A></P>
    </BODY>
  </HTML>
</xsl:template>
<xsl:template match="*">
  <P><STRONG><xsl:apply-templates/></STRONG></P>
</xsl:template>
</xsl:stylesheet>
```

17

In Listing 17.6, the second template rule `match="*"` matches every element in the XML document, replaces it with a `<STRONG>` element, and applies all the templates recursively to the body of the XML element.

CAUTION

> An XSLT stylesheet is an XML document, and you must ensure that the XML remains valid when outputting HTML. In Listing 17.6 the `<STRONG>` text is enclosed inside an HTML paragraph to ensure that the stylesheet remains valid. Many authors of HTML simply insert the paragraph `<P>` tag at the end of the paragraph. This will not work with stylesheets because the un-terminated `<P>` tag is not well-formed XML. Other HTML tags, such as `<BR>` and `<IMG>`, must be treated in a similar manner. You must also quote all HTML attributes as shown in the `<A>` tag in Listing 17.6 in order for the XSLT stylesheet to be valid XML. And, HTML tags must use consistent letter case for both the start and end tags.

Listing 17.7 shows the HTML output from applying the `basicHTML.xsl` stylesheet to the `jobs.xml` file shown in Listing 17.3. (Because the layout includes all the original white-space it is not easy to read. For this reason it may not initially appear to be well-formed HTML, careful inspection will nevertheless show that it is. You will see later how to strip leading and trailing whitespace from the original document.)

LISTING 17.7   Applying `basicHTML.xsl` to `jobs.xml`

```
<HTML>
<HEAD>
<META http-equiv="Content-Type" content="text/html; charset=UTF-8">
<TITLE>Job Details</TITLE>
</HEAD>
<BODY>
<P>
<STRONG>

<P>
<STRONG>

<P>
<STRONG>London</STRONG>
</P>

<P>
<STRONG>Must like to talk and smoke</STRONG>
</P>
```

LISTING 17.7 continued

```
<P>
<STRONG>Cigar maker</STRONG>
</P>

<P>
<STRONG>Critic</STRONG>
</P>

</STRONG>
</P>

<P>
<STRONG>

<P>
<STRONG>Washington</STRONG>
</P>

<P>
<STRONG>Must be honest</STRONG>
</P>


<P>
<STRONG>Tree surgeon</STRONG>
</P>

</STRONG>
</P>

</STRONG>
</P>
    <P><A HREF='xsltForm.jsp'>Back to xsltForm</A></P>
  </BODY>
</HTML>
```

In Listing 17.7, the HTML body starts with two HTML <STRONG> elements correspond-ing to the <jobSummary> root element and the first <job> element. The nested XML ele-ments <location> and <skill> are also output inside <STRONG> tags.

If you studied Listing 17.7 carefully, you will have seen a <META> element inserted into the output in the HTML <HEAD> element. This element was not added by the rules in basicHTML.xsl stylesheet; in this case the XSL processor has identified the output as an HTML document and, on recognizing the HTML <HEAD> element, has inserted the <META> element to identify the contents of the Web page.

Now that you have seen how the templates are applied to the body of a tag, you might be wondering how not to apply the templates but still output the text of an element. You do this by using the `<xsl:value-of select='.'/>` tag. This tag outputs the text of the currently selected XML element without applying any more templates either to this element or any of its descendents.

You will use the `<xsl:value-of>` element when you want to output the text of an XML tag rather than transform it in some way. Listing 17.8 shows a more useful and realistic stylesheet for the `jobs.xml` example file, and Listing 17.9 shows the transformed document.

LISTING 17.8   Full Text of `textHTML.xsl`

```xml
<?xml version="1.0"?>
<xsl:stylesheet version="1.0"
    xmlns:xsl="http://www.w3.org/1999/XSL/Transform">
<xsl:template match="/">
 <HTML>
  <HEAD> <TITLE>Job Details</TITLE> </HEAD>
  <BODY>
    <xsl:apply-templates/>
    <P><A HREF='xsltForm.jsp'>Back to xsltForm</A></P>
  </BODY> </HTML>
</xsl:template>
<xsl:template match="jobSummary">
 <H2>Jobs</H2><xsl:apply-templates/>
</xsl:template>
<xsl:template match="job">
 New Job: <P><xsl:apply-templates/></p>
</xsl:template>
<xsl:template match="description">
 <P>Descriptiom: <xsl:value-of select="."/></P>
</xsl:template>
<xsl:template match="location">
 <P>Location: <xsl:value-of select="."/></P>
</xsl:template>
<xsl:template match="skill">
 <P>Skill: <xsl:value-of select="."/></P>
</xsl:template>
</xsl:stylesheet>
```

In Listing 17.8, the leaf elements of `<description>`, `<location>`, and `<skill>` are output as text rather than expanded using the template rules.

NOTE   Listing 17.8 includes a template for the document root (match="/") and the root element (match="jobSummary"). On Day 16, you learned that the document root is the entire XML document, including the processing instructions and comments outside of the root element.

LISTING 17.9   Applying textHTML.xsl to jobs.xml

```
<HTML>
<HEAD>
<META http-equiv="Content-Type" content="text/html; charset=UTF-8">
<TITLE>Job Details</TITLE>
</HEAD>
<BODY>
<H2>Jobs</H2>

 New Job: <P>

<P>Location: London</P>

<P>Descriptiom: Must like to talk and smoke</P>


<P>Skill: Cigar maker</P>

<P>Skill: Critic</P>

</P>

 New Job: <P>

<P>Location: Washington</P>

<P>Descriptiom: Must be honest</P>


<P>Skill: Tree surgeon</P>

</P>

    <P><A HREF='xsltForm.jsp'>Back to xsltForm</A></P>
  </BODY>
</HTML>
```

Using the `<xsl:value-of>` tag raises two questions:

- What is the text value of an XML element?
- What does the select attribute do?

These questions are answered in the next two sections.

Text Representation of XML Elements

Every XML node has a textual representation that is used when the `<xsl:value-of>` tag is defined within a template rule. Table 17.1 shows how the textual equivalent of each of the seven XML nodes is obtained.

TABLE 17.1   Text Values of XML Elements

Element Type	Description
Document root	The concatenation of all the text in the document
Elements	The concatenation of all the text in the body of the element
Text	The text value of the node, including whitespace
Attributes	The text value of the attribute, including whitespace
Namespaces	The namespace URI that is bound to the namespace prefix associated with the node
Processing Instructions	The text of the processing instruction following the target name and including any whitespace
Comments	The text of the comment between the `<!--` and `-->` delimiters

As you can see from Table 17.1, every node has a textual equivalent. The default rules for an XSLT stylesheet only include the text values for the document root, elements, and all text nodes. By default, the other four nodes (attributes, namespaces, processing instructions, and comments) are not output. Before you can understand the default rules, you will need to study the XPath notation for matching nodes in an XML document.

Using XPath with XSLT

XPath is a means of identifying nodes within an XML document. The W3C identified several aspects of XML that required the ability to identify nodes, for example,

- Pointers from one XML document to another called XPointer (the equivalent of `href` in HTML)
- Template rules for XSLT stylesheets
- Schemas

To ensure that the two requirements for identifying nodes share a common syntax, the XPath notation was defined as a separate standard.

An XPath is a set of patterns that can be used to match nodes within an XML document. There are a large number of patterns that can be used to match any part of an XML document. Rather than reproduce the entire XPath specification in today's lesson, you will just study some examples that will help you understand how to use XPath. Further information about XPath can be obtained from the WC3 Web site.

XPath uses the concept of axes and expressions to define a path in the XML document:

- Axes define different parts of the XML document structure.
- Expressions refer to specific objects within an axis.

Some of the most frequently used axes have special shortcuts to reduce the amount of typing needed. Consider the XSLT stylesheet rule you used to match a `skill` element in the `jobs.xml` file:

```
<xsl:template match="skill">
 Skill: <xsl:value-of select="."/><P></P>
</xsl:template>
```

This matches a child `skill` element using a simple abbreviation. The full XPath notation for this is

```
<xsl:template match="child::skill">
```

The axis is `child` and the expression is an element with the name `skill` (the double colon separates the axis from the expression). The current node from which a path is defined is called the context node.

The `child` axis is used to identify all nodes that are immediate children of the context node. Related axes are

- `self`   The current node
- `parent`   The immediate parent of the context node
- `descendent`   Immediate children of the context node, all the children of those nodes, their children, and so on
- `descendent-or-self`   All descendent nodes and the current context node
- `ancestor`   Any node higher up the node tree that contains a context node

There are other axes defined in the XPath notation not listed here as they will not be discussed in today's lesson.

17

The `match="."` attribute in the example `<xsl:value-of>` element, shown previously, is another example of a shortcut. The full notation is as follows:

```
Skill: <xsl:value-of select="self::node()"/><P></P>
```

The function `node()` refers to the current context node. Additional functions are

- `name()` The name of the context node instead of the body of the node
- `comment()` Selects a comment node
- `text()` Selects a text node
- `processing-instruction()` Selects a processing instruction node

Some simple XPath expressions are as follows:

- `self::comment()` All comments in the current element
- `child::text()` All the text nodes in the immediate child nodes
- `descendent::node()` All the nodes below the context node
- `descendent-or-self::skill` All the nodes named `skill` below the current node, including the current node

Expressions can be more complex and specify a node hierarchy:

- `job/skill` A skill node that is an immediate child of a job node (in full `child::job/child::skill`)

XPath expressions can be arbitrarily long and can contain the following special expressions:

- `..` The immediate parent node defined as `parent::node()`
- `//` The current node or any descendent as `descendent-or-self::node()`
- `*` Any node in the specified axis
- `|` Used to provide alternate patterns

These patterns can be used to identify any node as illustrated by the following examples:

- `jobSummary//skill` Nodes called `skill` defined anywhere below the `jobSummary` node
- `jobSummary/*/skill` `skill` nodes defined as children of children of the `jobSummary` node
- `skill/..` The immediate parent node of a `skill` node
- `location|skill` A `location` or `skill` node

- `parent::comment()|child::text()`   Comment nodes in the immediate parent and text nodes in the immediate child
- `/|*`   The document root and all elements

Attributes can be selected using the `attribute` axis (this can be abbreviated to `@`). For example,

- `attribute::customer`   The attribute called `customer` of any node (not the node itself)
- `job/@reference`   An attribute called `reference` that is associated with a `job` node

In addition to these basic features, XPath supports a powerful matching language supporting variable-like constructs, expressions, and additional functions.

Now that you have a basic understanding of Xpath, you can look at the default rules for a stylesheet.

Default Stylesheet Rules

There are some default stylesheet rules that apply to the whole XML document unless overridden by specific template rules.

The first default rule that ensures all elements are processed is as follows:

```
<xsl:template match="*|/">
 <xsl:apply-templates/>
</xsl:template>
```

A second rule is used to output the text of text nodes and attributes:

```
<xsl:template match="text()|@*">
 <xsl:value-of select="."/>
</xsl:template>
```

A third rule suppresses comments and processing instructions:

```
<xsl:template match="processing-instruction()|comment()"/>
```

If an XML element in the source document matches more than one rule, the most specific rule is applied. Consequently, rules defined in an XSLT stylesheet will override any default rules.

The second default rule specifies that the text value of attributes should be output, but if you use this template on the attributes in `jobs.xml` (Listing 17.3), you will not see the attributes. This is because there is an extra requirement for processing attributes, which is described next.

17

Processing Attributes

Attributes of XML elements are not processed unless a specific rule is defined for those attributes.

An attribute is processed by using the `<xsl:apply-templates>` rule selecting one or more attributes. The third line in the following fragment applies templates to all attributes:

```
<xsl:template match="*">
 <xsl:apply-templates/>
 <xsl:apply-templates select="@*"/>
</xsl:template>
```

This `<xsl:template>` rule matches all elements and applies templates to the child elements and then that element's attributes. It is the second `<xsl:apply-templates>` rule with the `select="@*"` attribute that ensures that all attributes are output, but only because the node itself was matched with the previous `<xsl:apply-templates>` rule. If you only defined the second `<xsl:apply-templates select="@*">` rule, no output would be produced because the node itself would not have been matched and hence no attributes found.

With this extra information, you can now revisit the `jobs.xml` file and define an XSLT stylesheet that will display the job information in an HTML table as shown in Listing 17.10.

LISTING 17.10   Full Text of `table.xsl`

```
<?xml version="1.0"?>
<xsl:stylesheet version="1.0"
    xmlns:xsl="http://www.w3.org/1999/XSL/Transform">
<xsl:template match="/">
  <HTML>
    <HEAD> <TITLE>Job Details</TITLE> </HEAD>
    <BODY>
      <xsl:apply-templates/>
      <P><A HREF='xsltForm.jsp'>Back to xsltForm</A></P>
    </BODY>
  </HTML>
</xsl:template>
<xsl:template match="job">
 <H2>Job ref: <xsl:value-of select="@customer"/>/
➥ <xsl:value-of select="@reference"/></H2>
 <P><xsl:apply-templates select="description"/></P>
 <TABLE border="1">
 <xsl:apply-templates select="skill|location"/>
 </TABLE>
```

LISTING 17.10 continued

```
</xsl:template>
<xsl:template match="description">
 <I><xsl:value-of select="."/></I>
</xsl:template>
<xsl:template match="skill|location">
 <TR>
   <TD><xsl:value-of select="name()"/>:</TD>
           <TD><xsl:value-of select="."/></TD>
 </TR>
</xsl:template>
</xsl:stylesheet>
```

Listing 17.10 brings together several features of XSLT stylesheets that have been described previously. The rule matching a `<job>` element inserts the values of the `customer` and `reference` attributes and the job `description` child element is output in its own paragraph.

Note that the HTML table `border` attribute is enclosed in quotes so that it is valid XML (the same is also true for the `colspan` attribute). Even though HTML does not require these attributes to be quoted, XML does, and this XSLT stylesheet is an XML document.

Figure 17.2 shows the result of applying the `table.xsl` stylesheet from Listing 17.10 to the `jobs.xml` file.

FIGURE 17.2

The XML to HTML table transformation.

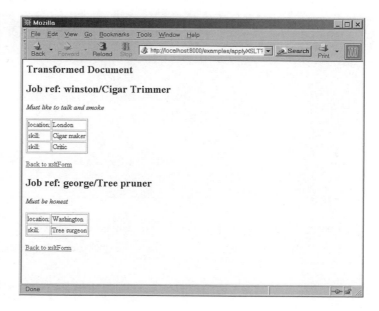

17

XSL supports significantly more complex transformation rules than those shown so far. The next section will provide an overview of some of the additional XSL features.

Using Stylesheet Elements

XSL defines about twenty elements for transforming XML documents. So far, you have seen the `<xsl:template>` element for defining template rules and the `<xsl:apply-templates>` and `<xsl:value-of>` rules for including data in the output document.

Many transformations can be defined just using these three elements. However, some of the more complex requirements require additional support from XSL.

Processing Whitespace and Text

By default, an XSL transformation retains the whitespace in the original document. This may not be required for the following reasons:

- The whitespace is generally ignored when processing the output.
- Users browsing the transformed document may find the whitespace misleading or annoying.
- Some output document formats may be whitespace sensitive, so the transformation must control the way whitespace is written to the output.

The `<xsl:strip-space>` tag can be used to strip leading and trailing whitespace from an element's body. The tag takes an `elements` attribute that defines from which elements to strip the whitespace. Elements are selected using the XPath notation.

Listing 17.11 shows the `simple.xsl` stylesheet shown in Listing 17.2 enhanced to strip whitespace from all elements.

LISTING 17.11   Full Text of `simpleStrip.xsl`

```
<?xml version="1.0"?>
<xsl:stylesheet version="1.0"
    xmlns:xsl="http://www.w3.org/1999/XSL/Transform">
<xsl:strip-space elements="*"/>
</xsl:stylesheet>
```

Applying this stylesheet to the `jobs.xml` document produces the following output:

```
LondonMust like to talk and smokeCigar makerCriticWashingtonMust
➥ be honestTree surgeon
```

No whitespace has been included but, as you can see, this is not particularly readable because the whitespace between the elements has been lost. You could selectively strip whitespace from elements using tags, as shown in the following:

```
<xsl:strip-space elements="jobSummary|job"/>
```

But this will still retain multiple spaces in the non-stripped elements. So what is needed is a way of inserting whitespace into the output stream.

Inserting whitespace into the output stream is best done using the `<xsl:text>` element. Any whitespace inside the `<xsl:text>` element is retained. You could rewrite the default rule for all elements to include a single blank line before each element, as shown in Listing 17.12.

LISTING 17.12 Full Text of `simpleSpace.xsl`

```
<?xml version="1.0"?>
<xsl:stylesheet version="1.0"
    xmlns:xsl="http://www.w3.org/1999/XSL/Transform">
<xsl:strip-space elements="*"/>
<xsl:template match="*">
 <xsl:text>
</xsl:text>
 <xsl:apply-templates/>
</xsl:template>
</xsl:stylesheet>
```

The blank line is inserted by the `<xsl:text>` element. Notice how the closing `</xsl:text>` tag is not indented; otherwise, additional whitespace would have been included. You could not use an empty tag here (`<xsl:text/>`) because you need to insert the end of line into the output document. The output from applying this stylesheet to `jobs.xml` is as follows:

```
<?xml version="1.0" encoding="UTF-8"?>


London
Must like to talk and smoke
Cigar maker
Critic

Washington
Must be honest
Tree surgeon
```

17

Whitespace is automatically stripped from the stylesheet itself, which is why the indented `<xsl:apply-templates/>` tag does not insert any whitespace before the output text.

Adding Comments

You can add a comment to a stylesheet as follows:

```
<xsl:template match="job">
 <!--this is a job definition -->
 <xsl:apply-templates/>
</xsl:template>
```

Using XML comments in this way is treated as an XSLT stylesheet comment and is not inserted into the output stream. To include a comment in the output document, you must use the `<xsl:comment>` element, as shown in the following:

```
<xsl:template match="job">
 <xsl:comment>this is a job definition</xsl:comment>
 <xsl:apply-templates/>
</xsl:template>
```

The following example shows how to insert JavaScript in an HTML page:

```
<xsl:template match="SCRIPT">
 <SCRIPT language="javascript">
  <xsl:text>
   <xsl:comment>
    if (n &lt; 0 &amp;&amp; m &gt; 0) {
     n = m;
    } // </xsl:comment>
  </xsl:text>
 </SCRIPT>
</xsl:template>
```

Another advantage of using `<xsl:comment>` is that the actual comment can be derived from data in the source XML document. The following example inserts the job `customer` and `reference` attributes into a comment:

```
<xsl:template match="job">
 <xsl:comment>Job definition for
  <xsl:value-of select="@customer"/>/<xsl:value-of select="@reference"/>
 </xsl:comment>
 <xsl:apply-templates/>
</xsl:template>
```

Finally, if you want to copy the comments from the original XML document into the transformed document, add the following rule to your stylesheet:

```
<xsl:template match="comment()">
 <xsl:comment><xsl:value-of select="."/></xsl:comment>
</xsl:template>
```

Attribute Values

Some transformations require output element attributes to vary according to the element being processed. As a simple example, think back to Day 16 when you first looked at XML and the simple structure for the job summary, as shown in the following:

```
<?xml version="1.0"?>
<jobSummary>
 <job>
  <customer>winston</customer>
  <reference>Cigar Trimmer</reference>
  <location>London</location>
  <description>Must like to talk and smoke</description>
  <!-- skills list for winston -->
  <skill>Cigar maker</skill>
  <skill>Critic</skill>
 </job>
</jobSummary>
```

This version didn't use attributes to represent the primary key of the job. Imagine that you have to convert this form of document into the new form using attributes. Your first attempt to do this might be as follows:

```
<xsl:template match="job">
 <job
  customer="<xsl:value-of select='./customer'/>"
  job="<xsl:value-of select='./reference'/>"
 />
 <xsl:apply-templates/>
</xsl:template>
```

Unfortunately, this won't work, because XML does not allow you to define elements inside attributes of other elements. You can always insert a < symbol inside an attribute value using < but this would not be interpreted as an element.

To get around the XML restriction of not allowing elements to be defined inside attributes, XSLT lets you insert the value of elements inside attributes by enclosing the XPath name in braces, as shown in the following:

```
<xsl:template match="job">
 <job customer="{./customer}" job="{./reference}" />
 <xsl:apply-templates select='location|description|skill'/>
</xsl:template>
```

To prevent the nested <customer> and <reference> elements from being output by the default template rules, the <apply-templates> element selects the required child elements of the job element. An alternative syntax that excludes the unwanted elements and doesn't need you to explicitly list the required elements uses an XPATH expression notation that has not been discussed today. For completeness, this rule it is:

```
<xsl:apply-templates select="./*[name()!='customer' and name()!='reference']"/>
```

If you want to convert the new style job element (with attributes) back to the one with nested elements, you use the following rule:

```
<xsl:template match="job">
 <job>
  <customer><xsl:value-of select="@customer/></customer>
  <reference><xsl:value-of select="@reference/></reference>
  <xsl:apply-templates/>
 </job>
</xsl:template>
```

Creating and Copying Elements

In the previous section, you saw how to convert one XML document into another by converting nested elements into tags. But what do you do if you want to convert an attribute into an element where the attribute value is the name of the element, or vice versa?

As a simple example, consider an EJB 2.1 Deployment Descriptor (DD) for two Session beans, as shown in Listing 17.13.

LISTING 17.13   Full Text of dd.xml

```
<?xml version="1.0" encoding="UTF-8"?>
<ejb-jar version="2.1"
  xmlns="http://java.sun.com/xml/ns/j2ee"
  xmlns:xsi="http://www.w3.org/2001/XMLSchema-instance"
  xsi:schemaLocation="http://java.sun.com/xml/ns/j2ee
➥ http://java.sun.com/xml/ns/j2ee/ejb-jar_2_1.xsd">
 <display-name>Agency</display-name>
 <enterprise-beans>
  <session>
   <display-name>AgencyBean</display-name>
   <ejb-name>AgencyBean</ejb-name>
   <home>agency.AgencyHome</home>
   <remote>agency.Agency</remote>
   <ejb-class>agency.AgencyBean</ejb-class>
   <session-type>Stateless</session-type>
   <transaction-type>Bean</transaction-type>
  </session>
  <session>
   <display-name>AdvertiseBean</display-name>
   <ejb-name>AdvertiseBean</ejb-name>
   <home>agency.AdvertiseHome</home>
   <remote>agency.Advertise</remote>
```

LISTING 17.13   continued

```
     <ejb-class>agency.AdvertiseBean</ejb-class>
     <session-type>Stateful</session-type>
     <transaction-type>Bean</transaction-type>
    </session>
   </enterprise-beans>
  </ejb-jar>
```

Imagine that a different application (or a future version of J2EE) decided that stateless and stateful Session beans were sufficiently different to warrant using different elements. For example,

```
<stateless>
 <ejb-name>AgencyBean</ejb-name>
 ...
</stateless>
<stateful>
 <ejb-name>AdvertiseBean</ejb-name>
 ...
</stateful>
```

To make this transformation, you need a rule that can generate an element whose name is derived from the original XML document. The XSL element that does this is called `<xsl:element>`, and the transformation shown previously is achieved by the following rule:

```
<xsl:template match="session">
 <xsl:element name="{./session-type}">
  <xsl:apply-templates/>
 </xsl:element>
</xsl:template>
<xsl:template match="session/session-type"/>
```

The name attribute specified in the `<xsl:element>` is the name of the element to define. In this example, the name is the value of the `session-type` child element (remember that braces take the value of a node when defining attributes).

The second rule in the previous example (`<xsl:element name="{./session-type}">`) ensures that the `session-type` child element is not included in the output document.

Sadly, there is one major problem with the previous example. All other elements are output using their text values, the element start and end tags and attributes have been lost from the document. The problem can be overcome using the `<xsl:copy>` element.

The `<xsl:copy>` element is used to copy elements from the XML source to the output document. The following rule is an identity transformation rule (the document is copied without any changes):

17

```
<xsl:template match="*|@*|comment()|processing-instruction()|text()">
 <xsl:copy>
  <xsl:apply-templates
       select="*|@*|comment()|processing-instruction()|text()"/>
 </xsl:copy>
</xsl:template>
```

The template matches all elements and uses the `<xsl:copy>` element to copy the matched element. The body of the `<xsl:copy>` element must apply the template rules to the body of the matched XML node; otherwise, no output will occur.

The full stylesheet for transforming the old style DD into the new style is shown in Listing 17.14. The output from applying this stylesheet is shown in Listing 17.15.

NOTE | Although you can view this example using the ApplyXSLT servlet, it might be easier to use the supplied command-line program called Transform. Run this program using asant Transform and supply the stylesheet name (JSP/examples/session.xsl) and XML filename (JSP/examples/dd.xml); the transformed document will be displayed on the screen.

LISTING 17.14   Full Text of `session.xsl`

```
<?xml version="1.0"?>
<xsl:stylesheet version="1.0"
    xmlns:xsl="http://www.w3.org/1999/XSL/Transform">
<xsl:template match="session">
 <xsl:element name="{./session-type}">
  <xsl:apply-templates/>
 </xsl:element>
</xsl:template>
<xsl:template match="session/session-type"/>
<xsl:template match="*|@*|comment()|processing-instruction()|text()">
 <xsl:copy>
  <xsl:apply-templates
               select="*|@*|comment()|processing-instruction()|text()"/>
 </xsl:copy>
</xsl:template>
</xsl:stylesheet>
```

LISTING 17.15   Applying `session.xsl` to `dd.xml`

```
<?xml version="1.0" encoding="UTF-8"?>
<ejb-jar version="2.1"
  xmlns="http://java.sun.com/xml/ns/j2ee"
```

LISTING 17.15   continued

```
    xmlns:xsi="http://www.w3.org/2001/XMLSchema-instance"
    xsi:schemaLocation="http://java.sun.com/xml/ns/j2ee
➥ http://java.sun.com/xml/ns/j2ee/ejb-jar_2_1.xsd">
 <display-name>Agency</display-name>
 <enterprise-beans>
  <Stateless>
   <display-name>AgencyBean</display-name>
   <ejb-name>AgencyBean</ejb-name>
   <home>agency.AgencyHome</home>
   <remote>agency.Agency</remote>
   <ejb-class>agency.AgencyBean</ejb-class>

   <transaction-type>Bean</transaction-type>
  </Stateless>
  <Stateful>
   <display-name>AdvertiseBean</display-name>
   <ejb-name>AdvertiseBean</ejb-name>
   <home>agency.AdvertiseHome</home>
   <remote>agency.Advertise</remote>
   <ejb-class>agency.AdvertiseBean</ejb-class>

   <transaction-type>Bean</transaction-type>
  </Stateful>
 </enterprise-beans>
</ejb-jar>
```

17

Attributes and Attribute Sets

For the example jobs.xml document in Listing 17.3 and the XSLT stylesheet table.xsl in Listing 17.9, you might like to be able to use a hyperlink to link the customer name to a URL of the form

```
/agency/advertise?customer=<customer_name>
```

Using the sample data from jobs.xml, the output heading for a job for winston would look like the following:

```
<H2>Job ref: <A HREF="/agency/advertise?winston">winston</A>/Cigar Trimmer</H2>
```

Here, the value of the new attribute is derived from the XML source document. This can be achieved by using the <xsl:attribute> element, as shown in the following:

```
<xsl:template match="job">
 <H2>Job ref:
  <A>
   <xsl:attribute name="HREF">
    /agency/advertise?<xsl:value-of select="@customer"/>
```

```
   </xsl:attribute>
   <xsl:value-of select="@customer"/>
  </A>/<xsl:value-of select="@reference"/></H2>
 <TABLE border="1">
 <xsl:apply-templates/>
 </TABLE>
</xsl:template>
```

The `<xsl:attribute>` element defines an attribute for the enclosing element (in this case, `<A>`). More than one attribute can be defined, but all attributes must be defined before any other text or child nodes in the element.

Sometimes, the same attributes must be defined for many different tags. This is a common requirement when applying styles to HTML tables. Consider making every cell in the table contain text with a blue sans-serif font. You could define the style separately for every cell in the table, but this is hard to maintain should the style requirements change. Alternatively, you could use Cascading Style Sheets (CSS), but the most popular browsers still do not support CSS in a consistent manner. An XSL solution is to use an attribute set.

The `<xsl:attribute-set>` element defines the attributes you can apply to multiple elements. An `<xsl:attribute-set>` defining a blue sans-serif font is as follows:

```
<xsl:attribute-set name="rowStyle">
 <xsl:attribute name="face">Arial,sans-serif</xsl:attribute>
 <xsl:attribute name="color">blue</xsl:attribute>
</xsl:attribute-set>
```

An attribute set is applied by using the `xsl:use-attribute-sets` attribute with an element. For example

```
<xsl:template match="skill|location">
 <TR><TD><FONT xsl:use-attribute-sets="rowStyle">
   <xsl:value-of select="name()"/>
 </FONT></TD><TD><FONT xsl:use-attribute-sets="rowStyle">
  <xsl:value-of select="."/>
 </FONT></TD></TR>
</xsl:template>
```

the transformed table definition for the job `skill` and `location` elements is as follows:

```
<TABLE border="1">
 <TR>
  <TD><FONT face="Arial,sans-serif" color="blue">location</FONT></TD>
  <TD><FONT face="Arial,sans-serif" color="blue">London</FONT></TD>
 </TR>
 <TR>
  <TD><FONT face="Arial,sans-serif" color="blue">skill</FONT></TD>
  <TD><FONT face="Arial,sans-serif" color="blue">Cigar maker</FONT></TD>
 </TR>
 <TR>
```

```
       <TD><FONT face="Arial,sans-serif" color="blue">skill</FONT></TD>
       <TD><FONT face="Arial,sans-serif" color="blue">Critic</FONT></TD>
     </TR>
   </TABLE>
```

The complete stylesheet for transforming the jobSummary document into HTML is shown in Listing 17.16.

LISTING 17.16   Full Text of tableStyle.xsl

```
   <?xml version="1.0"?>
   <xsl:stylesheet version="1.0"
       xmlns:xsl="http://www.w3.org/1999/XSL/Transform">
   <xsl:template match="/">
     <HTML>
       <HEAD> <TITLE>Job Details</TITLE> </HEAD>
       <BODY>
         <xsl:apply-templates/>
         <P><A HREF='xsltForm.jsp'>Back to xsltForm</A></P>
       </BODY>
     </HTML>
   </xsl:template>
   <xsl:template match="job">
    <H2>Job ref:
      <A>
      <xsl:attribute name="HREF">
       /agency/advertise?<xsl:value-of select="@customer"/>
      </xsl:attribute>
      <xsl:value-of select="@customer"/>
     </A>/<xsl:value-of select="@reference"/>
    </H2>
    <P><xsl:apply-templates select="description"/></P>
    <TABLE border="1">
    <xsl:apply-templates select="skill|location"/>
    </TABLE>
   </xsl:template>
   <xsl:template match="description">
    <I><xsl:value-of select="."/></I>
   </xsl:template>
   <xsl:attribute-set name="rowStyle">
    <xsl:attribute name="face">Arial,sans-serif</xsl:attribute>
    <xsl:attribute name="color">blue</xsl:attribute>
   </xsl:attribute-set>
   <xsl:template match="skill|location">
    <TR><TD><FONT xsl:use-attribute-sets="rowStyle">
      <xsl:value-of select="name()"/>
    </FONT></TD><TD><FONT xsl:use-attribute-sets="rowStyle">
     <xsl:value-of select="."/>
    </FONT></TD></TR>
   </xsl:template>
   </xsl:stylesheet>
```

17

Additional XSL Elements

XSL supports a number of elements that can provide program language-like capabilities within an XSLT stylesheet. Using these elements requires a good knowledge of the XPath notation. Because you have only seen some of the XPath notation today, you will only look very briefly at the elements that support programming capabilities.

Numbering Elements

A common requirement for many transformations is to insert numeric data into the output document, often to produce numbered lists.

The `<xsl:number>` element is used to insert numbers into the document. By default (that is, without attributes), this element inserts a count of the position of a context node in a list of elements of the same type.

To number the skills defined by a particular job, you could use the following rule:

```
<xsl:template match="skill">
 <TR><TD>
    Skill <xsl:number/>:
 </TD><TD>
  <xsl:value-of select="."/>
 </TD></TR>
</xsl:template>
```

Attributes can be supplied to the `<xsl:number>` element to determine what numeric value is inserted. The `level="any"` attribute is used to count all occurrences of the same type of node, regardless of where the node occurs in the document tree structure. The following example attaches numbers to job definitions:

```
<xsl:template match="job">
 <H2><xsl:number level="any"/>.
    Job ref:

 ...
</xsl:template>
```

Listing 17.17 shows the final stylesheet for transforming the `jobs.xml` document using numbers to count jobs and skills within a job. The resulting Web page is shown in Figure 17.3.

LISTING 17.17   Full Text of `tableCount.xsl`

```
<?xml version="1.0"?>
<xsl:stylesheet version="1.0"
    xmlns:xsl="http://www.w3.org/1999/XSL/Transform">
<xsl:template match="/">
  <HTML>
```

LISTING 17.17 continued

```
      <HEAD> <TITLE>Job Details</TITLE> </HEAD>
      <BODY>
        <xsl:apply-templates/>
        <P><A HREF='xsltForm.jsp'>Back to xsltForm</A></P>
      </BODY>
    </HTML>
  </xsl:template>
<xsl:template match="job">
 <H2><xsl:number level="any"/>.
    Job ref:
    <A>
    <xsl:attribute name="HREF">
     /agency/advertise?<xsl:value-of select="@customer"/>
    </xsl:attribute>
    <xsl:value-of select="@customer"/>
  </A>/<xsl:value-of select="@reference"/>
 </H2>
 <P><xsl:apply-templates select="description"/></P>
 <TABLE border="1">
 <xsl:apply-templates select="skill|location"/>
 </TABLE>
</xsl:template>
<xsl:template match="description">
 <I><xsl:value-of select="."/></I>
</xsl:template>
<xsl:attribute-set name="rowStyle">
 <xsl:attribute name="face">Arial,sans-serif</xsl:attribute>
 <xsl:attribute name="color">blue</xsl:attribute>
</xsl:attribute-set>
<xsl:template match="location">
 <TR><TD><FONT xsl:use-attribute-sets="rowStyle">
    <xsl:value-of select="name()"/>
 </FONT></TD><TD><FONT xsl:use-attribute-sets="rowStyle">
  <xsl:value-of select="."/>
 </FONT></TD></TR>
</xsl:template>
<xsl:template match="skill">
 <TR><TD><FONT xsl:use-attribute-sets="rowStyle">
    Skill <xsl:number/>:
 </FONT></TD><TD><FONT xsl:use-attribute-sets="rowStyle">
  <xsl:value-of select="."/>
 </FONT></TD></TR>
</xsl:template>
</xsl:stylesheet>
```

17

FIGURE 17.3

Applying `tableCount.xsl` *to* `jobs.xml`.

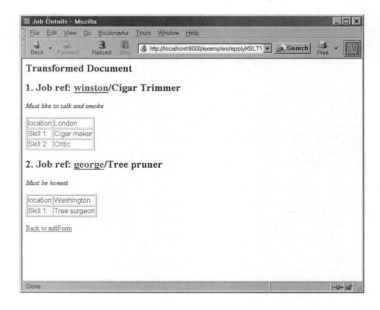

The `<xsl:number>` tag can also be used to

- Insert numeric data obtained from an element or attribute in the XML source document
- Count occurrences of a node
- Count nodes from a given start point
- Use letters or roman numerals instead of decimal integers or insert leading zeroes to make fixed-width numbers

Other Features

XSLT supports the optional inclusion of text in the output document using the following tags:

- `<xsl:if>`   The body of this element is only included if the test defined as an attribute is `true`.
- `<xsl:choose>`   Defines a list of choices, only one of which will be included.
- `<xsl:when>`   Defines a choice for an `<xsl:choose>` element.
- `<xsl:otherwise>`   Defines the default choice for an `<xsl:choose>` element if no `<xsl:when>` element is matched.

> **NOTE**
>
> These tags work in the same way as the JSTL core actions with the same names.

The `<xsl:if>` and `<xsl:when>` elements use a `test` attribute that evaluates an XPath expression and includes the element body if the result of the test evaluates to `true`.

The following example tests if a Session bean from a DD is a stateless bean:

```
<xsl:if test="./session-type='Stateless'">
 …
</xsl:if>
```

The following `<xsl:choose>` example selects different transformations for stateful and stateless Session beans:

```
<xsl:choose>
 <xsl:when test="./session-type='Stateless'">
  …
 </xsl:when>
 <xsl:when test="./session-type='Stateful'">
  …
 </xsl:when>
 <xsl:otherwise>
  …
 </xsl:when>
</xsl:choose>
```

Other XSL elements include the following:

- `<xsl:sort>` Sort elements in alphabetic or numeric order
- `<xsl:include>` and `<xsl:import>` Import rules from other stylesheets
- `<xsl:variable>` Define variables that can be used in other XSL elements
- `<xsl:template>` Define templates that can be inserted in different parts of the transformed output (parameters can be used to customize each instance of a template)

As you can see, XSLT provides a powerful transformation language that really is too large and complex to cover in one lesson. Today's work on XSLT has been designed to give you an overview of what XSLT can do. For more information on XSLT, refer to the specifications on the W3C Web site (`www.w3.org`) or read the book *Sams Teach Yourself XML in 21 Days* from Sams Publishing.

XSLT Compilers

To conclude today's lesson we will take a quick look at XSLT compilers.

One drawback to XLST stylesheets is performance. An XLST processor, such as XALAN, first reads in the XSLT stylesheet and builds an internal structure representing the rules that must be applied. The processor must then read in the XML document, match each element to the defined rules, and generate the required output. All of this takes time.

One way to improve performance is to preprocess the XSLT stylesheet to create a custom program that will transform an XML document in a more efficient manner.

Such a technology is called an XSLT compiler. This is a fast changing area of XSL technology, but the original XSLT compiler, called XSLTC, developed by Sun Microsystems, is now developed and maintained by the Apache project.

Apache provides the XSLTC compiler used to compile an XSL stylesheet into a translet (a set of Java classes). An associated runtime processor is used to apply the compiled translet to an XML document and perform the XML document transformation.

An XSLT translet can be invoked from the command line or included in a developer's application. For more information on XSLTC refer to the Apache XML Project on-line at http://xml.apache.org/xalan-j/xsltc_usage.html.

Summary

Today you have looked at transforming XML documents into other data formats (mostly HTML). The XSLT standard defines an XML stylesheet that specifies how to transform an XML document into a new format. XSLT is commonly used to transform XML data into HTML for presentation by a Web browser.

An XSLT stylesheet defines a set of rules. Each rule

- Is matched against elements in an XML source document
- Defines transformations that are applied to the matched element to create the transformed data
- Can be applied to a selected element or multiple elements including a complete tree hierarchy of elements
- Uses the XPath notation to match XML elements

XSLT compilers are designed to address some of the performance problems of XSLT processors. An XSLT compiler has two components:

- A compiler that generates a translet (a set of Java classes) from an XSLT stylesheet
- A runtime processor that applies a translet to an XML document to perform the transformation

The XSL technology also identifies a portable device independent grammar (XSL-FO) for defining formatting requirements and the document data. XSL-FO is not being widely adopted by the industry at the present time.

You have now finished your excursion into XML and XML transformations. Tomorrow, you will return to Java programming and the J2EE platform to study Java and J2EE design patterns.

17

Q&A

Q What are the two components of XSL?

A XSLT defines a language that is used to write stylesheets that will transform an XML document into a different format.

Formatting objects, or XSL-FO, specifies a device-independent grammar for defining the format of a transformed XML page.

Q What are three techniques for applying an XSLT stylesheet for a Web client?

A • Send the XML document and stylesheet to the client for processing.

- Convert the XML into an HTML file, store the file on the server, and send the file to the client to satisfy future HTTP requests.
- Transform the XML data on the server for every HTPP request for the data.

Q Which XSL element is used to insert the body of a matched XML tag into the output document expanding any nested elements?

A `<xsl:apply-templates/>`

Q What do the ., .., //, and @name XPath shortcuts expand to?

A . expands to `self::node()`

   . expands to `parent::node()`

   // expands to `descendent-or-self::node()`

   @*name* expands to `attribute::name`

Q What are the XSL elements for inserting a comment, inserting an element, inserting an attribute, and copying elements?

A
- `<xsl:comment>`
- `<xsl:element>`
- `<xsl:attribute>`
- `<xsl:copy>`

Exercises

On Day 14, "JSP Tag Libraries," you developed a custom tag library for use with your Web application. Today, you will write an XSLT stylesheet that will transform a Tag Library Descriptor (TLD) document into an HTML page for viewing.

Listing 17.18 shows the `agency.tld` file from Day 14 that you will transform into HTML for display by a Web browser.

LISTING 17.18   Full Text of `agency.tld`

```
<?xml version="1.0" encoding="ISO-8859-1" ?>
<taglib>
  <tlib-version>1.0</tlib-version>
  <jsp-version>2.0</jsp-version>
  <short-name>agency</short-name>
  <tag>
    <name>option</name>
    <tag-class>webagency.OptionTag</tag-class>
    <body-content>empty</body-content>
    <attribute>
      <name>selected</name>
      <required>true</required>
      <rtexprvalue>true</rtexprvalue>
      <type>java.lang.Object</type>
    </attribute>
    <attribute>
      <name>option</name>
      <required>true</required>
      <rtexprvalue>true</rtexprvalue>
      <type>java.lang.String</type>
    </attribute>
  </tag>
  <tag>
    <name>useAgency</name>
    <tag-class>webagency.UseAgencyTag</tag-class>
    <body-content>empty</body-content>
    <variable>
      <name-given>agency</name-given>
```

LISTING 17.18 continued

```
      <variable-class>agency.Agency</variable-class>
      <declare>true</declare>
      <scope>AT_BEGIN</scope>
    </variable>
  </tag>
  <tag>
    <name>useApplicant</name>
    <tag-class>webagency.UseApplicantTag</tag-class>
    <body-content>empty</body-content>
    <variable>
      <name-given>app</name-given>
      <variable-class>agency.Register</variable-class>
      <declare>true</declare>
      <scope>AT_BEGIN</scope>
    </variable>
    <attribute>
      <name>login</name>
      <required>true</required>
      <rtexprvalue>true</rtexprvalue>
    </attribute>
  </tag>
  <tag>
    <name>useCustomer</name>
    <tag-class>webagency.UseCustomerTag</tag-class>
    <body-content>empty</body-content>
    <variable>
      <name-given>cust</name-given>
      <variable-class>agency.Advertise</variable-class>
      <declare>true</declare>
      <scope>AT_BEGIN</scope>
    </variable>
    <attribute>
      <name>login</name>
      <required>true</required>
      <rtexprvalue>true</rtexprvalue>
    </attribute>
  </tag>
  <tag>
    <name>useJob</name>
    <tag-class>webagency.UseJobTag</tag-class>
    <body-content>empty</body-content>
    <variable>
      <name-given>job</name-given>
      <variable-class>agency.AdvertiseJob</variable-class>
      <declare>true</declare>
      <scope>AT_BEGIN</scope>
    </variable>
    <attribute>
      <name>ref</name>
      <required>true</required>
```

17

LISTING 17.18 continued

```
          <rtexprvalue>true</rtexprvalue>
        </attribute>
        <attribute>
          <name>customer</name>
          <required>true</required>
          <rtexprvalue>true</rtexprvalue>
        </attribute>
      </tag>
</taglib>
```

To display this TLD document, you will need to write an XSLT stylesheet that defines rules for the following transformations:

- Put the tag library name in an <H1> element.

- Define a <TABLE border="1"> element to contain all the tags.

- Highlight each tag name using a <STRONG> element.

- Put each tag in a row in the table and put the tag name, body content, a list of the attributes and a list of the variables each in its own cell.

Listing 17.19 shows a suitable HTML page containing one row that meets the previously listed requirements.

LISTING 17.19 Transformed HTML Output

```
<HTML>
  <HEAD>
  <META http-equiv="Content-Type" content="text/html; charset=UTF-8">
  <TITLE>agency TLD</TITLE>
  </HEAD>
  <BODY>
    <H1>Tag Library Name: agency</H1>
    <TABLE border="1">
      <TR align="left" valign="top">
        <TH colspan="4">Tag</TH>
      </TR>
      <TR align="left" valign="top">
        <TH>Name</TH><TH>Body</TH><TH>Attributes</TH><TH>Variables</TH>
      </TR>
      <TR align="left" valign="top">
        <TD><STRONG>option</STRONG></TD><TD>empty</TD><TD>selected<BR>option<BR>
      </TD><TD></TD>
      </TR>
    </TABLE>
  </BODY>
</HTML>
```

To get you started, there is an example TLD (agency.tld) and an empty XSLT stylesheet (tld.xsl) in the Day17/exercise/XML directory on the accompanying Web site. Also included in the exercise/src directory is a simple Java program called Transform that can be used to apply your XSLT stylesheet to an XML document.

To test your XSLT stylesheet run the command

```
> java -classpath classes Transform XML/tld.xsl XML/agency.tld
```

and study the HTML output. You can also use the following command to save the output to a file:

```
> java -classpath classes Transform XML/tld.xsl XML/agency.tld XML/agency.html
```

You can view the file XML/agency.html in your browser.

Alternatively use the supplied asant build files and enter:

```
asant run
```

and browse the output file XML/agency.html as before.

Finally, Figure 17.4 shows a screen snapshot of how your transformed HTML page should appear in a Web browser.

FIGURE 17.4

Applying tld.xsl *to* agency.tld.

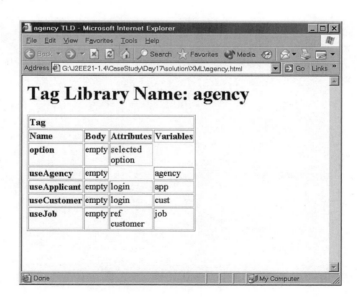

Tag			
Name	**Body**	**Attributes**	**Variables**
option	empty	selected option	
useAgency	empty		agency
useApplicant	empty	login	app
useCustomer	empty	login	cust
useJob	empty	ref customer	job

Tag Library Name: agency

DAY **18**

Patterns

It has often been said that software engineering is more of an art than a science. Small teams, or even individuals, have been able to create sophisticated and powerful solutions using fairly ad-hoc design and development processes. On the other hand, many large projects that have been run on traditional engineering lines have arrived over budget and late, if they arrived at all. One of the main differentiators between successful and unsuccessful projects is the experience of those creating the system architecture and their understanding of the capabilities of the platform on which they are delivering that system.

The patterns movement within software engineering attempts to capture some of the experience of successful architects and designers so that this experience can be applied more widely. The exploration of platform-specific patterns can also help designers apply appropriate patterns in the right place using the right technologies. As the J2EE technology has matured, J2EE-specific patterns have been discovered that should make your life as a J2EE designer and developer easier.

Today, you will

- Explore how the use of patterns can improve the design of systems
- Examine some of the J2EE-specific patterns currently documented
- Discover some of the J2EE patterns that are applied in the case study
- See how other J2EE patterns can be used to improve the design of the case study

Today's intention is to examine the role of J2EE-based patterns and see how such patterns can be applied in the context of the case study.

J2EE Patterns

Being a software designer, developer, or architect is not an easy job. To be truly effective, you must combine an understanding of the features required—the so-called problem domain—with a knowledge of the technologies and products from which the solution will be built. It is difficult for most practitioners to keep abreast of changing technologies in parallel with actually delivering applications to aggressive timescales. What is needed is help to understand the best way to apply technologies and solve common design problems, rather than having to learn from trial and error. Patterns, and specifically in the context of this book, J2EE patterns, can help you do this.

What Are Patterns?

To understand the intent of patterns, it is useful to understand a little bit of their background.

The original inspiration of the software patterns movement came from outside the software industry. It was the work of the architect Christopher Alexander; his considerations of how we design buildings led him to identify and document common features of successful buildings. These common design features were christened patterns, and the documentation of a related set of them is termed a pattern language. Alexander's work can be explored in his writings, such as his book, The Timeless Way of Building.

An architect who designs buildings is constrained only by the qualities of the materials with which the building can be constructed, together with cost constraints and certain physical laws (such as gravity, for example!). This leads architects to experiment with different forms of building, based on new materials and fashions in design. Some of these experiments are successful and turn up whole new ways of living and working. Many more experiments create buildings that are uninhabitable and are torn down in a relatively short time. Most architects need to build useful buildings that form a pleasant environment for those who live and work in them. The intention of Alexander's patterns is to provide a set of proven building blocks on which such architects can base their designs.

Now, consider the preceding paragraph in software terms.

An architect who designs software systems is constrained only by the technologies with which the system can be constructed together with cost constraints and certain physical laws (such as available bandwidth!). This leads architects to experiment with different forms of system, based on new technologies and fashions in design. Some of these experiments are successful and turn up whole new styles of application. Many more experiments create applications that are unusable and are discarded in a relatively short time. Most architects need to build useful applications that create a pleasant experience for those who live and work with them. The intention of software patterns is to provide a set of proven building blocks on which such architects can base their designs.

As you can see from this comparison, the motivations and intentions of architectural and software patterns have much in common.

So, what is a pattern? A short definition of a pattern is "A recurring solution to a problem in a context." (For a general discussion of the definition of patterns, see `http://hillside.net/patterns/definition.html`) Essentially, a pattern is a reusable idea on how to solve a particular problem found in the domain of architecture or design, whether that be physical buildings or software systems. The key aspect of patterns is that they are proven solutions—you discover patterns, you don't invent them!

The concrete form of a pattern is a document describing certain aspects, including the following:

- A statement of the problem that the pattern addresses. This can include a list of conflicting requirements and issues that need to be balanced—known as forces.

- Contexts in which the pattern is known to work.

- A description of the solution, possibly including the detailed workings of the solution as it is applied in one context. For example, a software pattern may include code samples.

A pattern description may also set out different strategies within the pattern. These describe different approaches to solving the problem, possibly using different technologies or techniques, while still applying the same underlying principle.

Although patterns have common central aspects, there is no fixed way of documenting a pattern. Certain groups of patterns and pattern languages will adopt their own style of documentation that suits their needs. The main thing is that it is understandable and accessible.

18

If you want to investigate the general concept of patterns, the philosophy behind them, and the work of Christopher Alexander, try the following locations:

- "Christopher Alexander: An Introduction for Object-Oriented Designers" hosted at `http://g.oswego.edu/dl/ca/ca/ca.html`
- "Some Notes on Christopher Alexander" hosted at `http://www.math.utsa.edu/sphere/salingar/Chris.text.html`

Why Use Patterns?

The intent of patterns, then, is to provide a certain level of what might be termed "distilled wisdom." If people are lucky enough to work alongside a skilled architect or designer when they are learning their trade, they will gain such "wisdom" by osmosis. Patterns help the propagation of such wisdom so that the written pattern becomes a way of gaining some of the wisdom, even if you do not work alongside such a luminary.

The patterns become a tool chest for the designer or architect from which they can select. These tools can help them create an efficient, robust, and flexible solution. As such, the designer or architect must familiarize themselves with the patterns to the extent that they become adept at identifying the type of problem each pattern addresses and the pattern's context. In doing so, they can ensure that they select the right pattern or combination of patterns for the task at hand.

It is important to note that patterns are a guideline for a solution—not a solution themselves. Although some design tools now provide templates for the implementation of common patterns, you cannot just drag-and-drop patterns into an application to form a solution. As a chef will adapt a recipe to suit the ingredients available and the taste of the guests, so a designer may adjust the implementation of a pattern to suit the specific context.

Types of Patterns

Patterns occur in all aspects of life, from spiders' webs to the way a school works. Some patterns are small and specific while others are general and wide-ranging. The same is true of the patterns found in the realm of software. The following are some common types of patterns:

- Architectural patterns define the overall style of the system and frequently include physical partitioning and infrastructure considerations as well as the software itself.
- Design patterns work at the level of software artifacts, such as classes and components, and describe ways in which such artifacts can be built and combined to solve common problems.

- Idioms are ways of solving a particular problem in a given environment, such as a language or platform. Some idioms are the embodiment of a pattern for a particular environment. For example, the Java mechanisms around the `Cloneable` interface and the reflection API are idioms that embody more general creational patterns.

- Process patterns have been identified relating to the actual mechanics of designing and creating the software and systems.

- Analysis patterns list common problems found in a particular business domain and ways in which these problems can be modeled.

The concept of patterns applied in the field of software was popularized mainly by the book Design Patterns—Elements of Reusable Object-Oriented Software written by Gamma, Helm, Johnson, and Vlissides. This is commonly referred to as the "Gang of Four" book, or GoF for short. As its name suggests, this book contains a set of design patterns that are independent of platform and language. Many software patterns, including the J2EE patterns examined later, reference GoF patterns to help the reader understand aspects of the pattern being described.

Because patterns are found at different levels, the design of a system can involve the application of patterns inside patterns. An architectural pattern may define tiers or services from which the system is built. The contents of these tiers and services may be specified in terms of groups of components that conform to design patterns. These components, in turn, may be implemented using language- or platform-level idioms.

Sets of interlocking patterns have been discovered for a particular context or at a particular level. These pattern languages help to promote consistent and coherent use of patterns. One such context is the J2EE platform, and it is a pattern language for this environment that will be explored today.

J2EE Patterns

The term J2EE patterns is used to refer to a set of patterns that have been identified within J2EE-based solutions. These patterns describe how to apply J2EE technologies to address common problems found when creating modern, distributed systems. As such, they fit the criterion stated earlier that they are "a solution to a problem in a context." In the case of J2EE patterns, that context is the J2EE platform and the typical application architectures used when building J2EE applications.

Some patterns come with the territory in that they are found within the J2EE platform itself. However, the term J2EE patterns tends to refer to patterns that can be applied when creating systems on top of the J2EE platform.

18

Some J2EE patterns are simply direct implementations of previously identified patterns using J2EE technologies. An example of this would be the use of publish/subscribe when applying JMS (see Day 9, "Java Message Service"). Other patterns are specific adaptations of known patterns for J2EE-oriented issues. An example of this is the Session Façade pattern, discussed later in the section on "Session Façades and Entity EJBs," that encourages correct use of Entity EJBs.

Given that all J2EE patterns share a common context (namely, J2EE), they form a pattern language within that context. Some J2EE patterns are built on concepts from J2EE patterns or include them as part of a suggested implementation.

NOTE

> The set of J2EE patterns laid out here (and in other places) does not form a closed set from which J2EE applications can be built. An architect or designer can apply generic patterns or architectural patterns as they see fit when creating a J2EE-based solution. The J2EE-specific patterns simply provide a known set of J2EE-oriented solutions.

Pattern Catalogs

Patterns tend to evolve. There is no central body for the approval of patterns. A pattern tends to become accepted over time (or not, as the case may be) by the general audience or designers and architects at which it is targeted. Given this, how do you find patterns that you can apply?

There are various places where you can find information on patterns:

- There are now many general patterns books and repositories. These include the GoF book, the Pattern-Oriented Software Architecture (POSA) book series, the Pattern Languages of Programming (PLoP) book series, and the Hillside online pattern resources hosted at `http://www.hillside.net/`.

- J2EE-specific pattern information is available through the Sun Java Center patterns documented in the Core J2EE Patterns book. The Sun J2EE Blueprints patterns are available at the J2EE Blueprints Web site (`http://java.sun.com/blueprints/ enterprise/`), the proposed J2EE patterns are available at TheServerSide.com (`http://www.theserverside.com/patterns/`), and many patterns with J2EE-related content are available on IBM's DeveloperWorks Web site at `http:// www.ibm.com/developerworks/patterns/`.

- Some products, such as Borland Together (formerly Together/J) at
  `http://www.borland.com/together/`, IBM Rational Software (formerly Rational
  Rose) at `http://www.rational.com`, and Aonix Component Factory at
  `http://www.aonix.com`, provide templates and documentation to help you build
  systems based on common patterns.

In all cases, the patterns are embodied in documentation and examples.

You should note that there is a certain amount of duplication in the world of J2EE patterns. All true patterns are derived from experience and individual designers and architects reflect on their experiences in parallel. As noted, there is no single definitive list of J2EE patterns and there is not even one central forum in which all J2EE designers exchange their thoughts and ideas. Because of this, different people have documented the same patterns in separate pattern catalogs. Sometimes, these patterns have the same name and it is just a matter of there being different descriptions. Don't worry about such overlap and differences in perspective—it can be very useful to have several perspectives on the same concept. However, to keep things simple, we have always referenced a single source in our lists of J2EE patterns.

J2EE-Specific Patterns

18

Now that you understand the rationale and intent of patterns, how can you apply them to your J2EE applications? To do this, you must understand the J2EE design context, and you must also become familiar with the patterns themselves.

Applying Patterns in a Context

Most of the patterns defined for the J2EE platform range between the design and architecture levels. You may be able to apply individual patterns in different styles of architecture, but as a pattern language, the current J2EE patterns are squarely targeted at a 3-tier, Web-based business system. The 3 tiers are usually classified as the presentation or Web tier, the middle or business tier, and the integration or data tier.

As well as consisting of multiple tiers, the target architecture is roughly based on the Model-View-Controller (MVC) principle. MVC is a form of pattern that can be applied at several levels. At the GUI level, it splits the responsibilities for interacting with the user between a data model, a presentation-oriented view, and a controller to govern the interaction. At the architectural level, this translates into Entity EJBs (and various other components) providing a data model, servlets and JSPs providing the view, and Session EJBs providing the controller or business logic. Separating concerns in this way delivers a lot of flexibility. An example of this is that the model and controller (the data and the business logic) can be combined with a variety of views to expose the same functionality to different clients. This is shown in Figure 18.1.

FIGURE 18.1

Multiple views for different types of client within an MVC architecture.

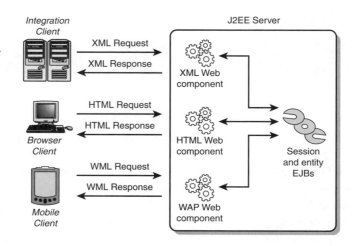

Given this context, and given that an overall application style is in place, why do you need more patterns? Well, the purpose of applying patterns within an n-tier application generally relates to the systemic qualities of the application. Systemic qualities, sometimes called non-functional requirements, refer to qualities such as maintainability, extensibility, scalability, availability, and so on. By applying the patterns outlined today, you should be able to improve at least one of these systemic qualities in your application, if not several. When the case study is examined later, the impact on systemic qualities of the patterns applied is also considered.

If you are designing an application from scratch, it will be second nature to think of applying patterns to the design process. However, many times you will be working within a pre-defined architecture or with an existing application. This does not mean that patterns no longer apply. It is quite possible to apply patterns to existing applications to improve them. It may be that the original design was not well thought out, or that it used the technologies in a naïve way (quite common when technologies are new). A pattern can be retro-fitted to part of the application to improve the systemic qualities of the application and to generally clean it up. This process is called refactoring, and is a key element in many software processes. As part of examining the case study, several potential refactoring scenarios will be considered.

The last thing you need before examining the case study is knowledge of the patterns themselves.

Generic Patterns

Table 18.1 lists some common, generic patterns that are documented in the GoF book.

TABLE 18.1 Common GoF Patterns

Pattern Name	Pattern Description
Proxy	Provides a surrogate for another object or component to control access to it or enable access to it
Decorator	Adds a variable level of functionality dynamically with the ability to plug in or remove components or filters as required (sometimes also known as wrapper or pipes and filters)
Singleton	Provides a single instance of a component and a global point of access to it
Iterator	Provides sequential access to a collection of objects in a way that is independent of the underlying representation
Observer	Defines a relationship between components so that a change in the state of one of them causes a notification of this change to be delivered to the others
Façade	Provides a unified interface for a subsystem, thereby hiding underlying complexity
Command	Encapsulates a request with its data so that it can be presented and executed as a whole, without having to specify many different processing methods

J2EE Presentation-Tier Patterns

Table 18.2 lists patterns that have been identified around the presentation (or Web) tier of an n-tier J2EE application. The origin of each pattern is denoted using initials—SJC (Sun Java Center), BLU (Sun J2EE Blueprints), TSS (TheServerSide.com).

TABLE 18.2 Common J2EE Presentation-Tier Patterns

Pattern Name	Pattern Description
Front Controller (SJC)	A servlet (or JSP) intercepts the request from the user and routes or "adds value" to the request.
Intercepting Filter (SJC)	Provides a Decorator-style (GoF) filter chain as part of a Front Controller.
View Helper (SJC)	Uses a JavaBean or custom JSP tag to encapsulate functionality and separate Java functionality out of a JSP.
Composite View (SJC)	Composes a JSP from several different sub-components to provide a typical, multi-panel Web page view.
Dispatcher View (SJC)	A Front Controller (SJC) intercepts and routes (or dispatches) a request to a JSP (or view). The view or its View Helpers (SJC) retrieve the content and/or data required to populate the view.

18

TABLE 18.2   continued

Pattern Name	Pattern Description
Service to Worker (SJC)	A Front Controller intercepts and routes (or dispatches) a request to a JSP (or view). The Front Controller (SJC) (or its helpers) retrieves the content and/or data required and passes this to the view as JavaBeans.
Service Locator (SJC)	A client-side shared helper object caches frequently used EJB home interfaces and dispenses EJB remote references on request.

J2EE Business-Tier Patterns

Table 18.3 lists patterns that have been identified around the business (or middle) tier of an n-tier J2EE application. The origin of each pattern is denoted using initials—SJC (Sun Java Center), BLU (Sun J2EE Blueprints), TSS (TheServerSide.com).

TABLE 18.3   Common J2EE Business-Tier Patterns

Pattern Name	Pattern Description
Session Façade (SJC)	A Session EJB provides a Façade (GoF) to shield Entity EJBs from direct client access and to obscure the data schema from the client.
Business Delegate (SJC)	A client-side object hides EJB-specific (or JMS-specific) interaction and exposes local business-oriented methods.
Value Object (SJC)	Provides a snapshot of underlying data to be used as a convenient data parcel between client and server to avoid chattiness (excessive network traffic between client and server).
Value Object Builder (SJC)	A constructor of Value Objects (SJC) from disparate server-side data sources. It presents one Value Object-based interface for a set of varied business data.
Composite Entity (SJC)	Creates a coarse-grained business entity from a set of fine-grained data objects, such as Entity EJBs or DAOs.
Value List Handler (SJC)	Has a Session EJB act as a data cache and provide single/multiple data element Iterator (GoF) capability.
Page-by-page Iterator (BLU)	A variant of Value List Handler (SJC).
Fast Lane Reader (BLU)	Retrieves data for reading directly from the database for speed, write data back via Entity EJBs for transactions and consistency.

J2EE Integration-Tier Patterns

Table 18.4 lists patterns that have been identified around the integration (or data) tier of an n-tier J2EE application. The origin of each pattern is denoted using initials—SJC (Sun Java Center), BLU (Sun J2EE Blueprints), TSS (TheServerSide.com).

TABLE 18.4   Common J2EE Integration-Tier Patterns

Pattern Name	Pattern Description
Data Access Object (SJC)	Encapsulates data access behind a common interface that can be implemented in different ways for different data sources. Typically used for data access in servlets and Session EJBs to encapsulate direct database access.
Service Activator (SJC)	Allows an EJB to be called on receipt of an asynchronous message.
EJB Observer (TSS)	An Observer-based (GoF) event pattern providing a strategy using EJBs.

Patterns Within J2EE

As noted previously, certain patterns occur within the J2EE environment itself, including the following:

- The Proxy pattern (GoF) is used widely in J2EE. Examples include RMI stubs as client-side proxies and EJB objects as server-side proxies.
- An EJB home interface acts as a Singleton (GoF) for the creation of EJB instances.
- Servlet filters are a form of the Intercepting Filter pattern (SJC).

There are many other patterns that are applied within the Java and J2EE environments.

Applying Patterns in Context

You now know some of the common patterns that can be applied in J2EE applications. Using this knowledge, you can analyze the case study that has been followed throughout the book to see how they can be applied.

Analyzing the Case Study

Patterns are usually best understood in context. It helps to understand the intention of the design (and its associated code) and what it is trying to achieve so you can understand why a particular pattern helps in that situation. By examining the code for the case study, this section intends to

- Identify some of the places where J2EE patterns have been applied in the case study
- Examine some of those patterns in detail, including how the pattern looks in code
- Consider what other patterns could have been applied in certain places and the changes that would be required to use those patterns
- Understand why other J2EE patterns are not relevant to the design of the case study

The intention is to look at the central patterns that occur (or could occur) within the case study. This section will not contain an exhaustive list of all the patterns used.

When examining any design, it is important to understand the context in which design decisions were made. In this case, it is important to understand that the case study is, in places, intentionally simplistic. There are two reasons for this:

- The case study is essentially a learning tool. Use of production-level code can sometimes obscure (or unnecessarily complicate) the underlying principles or steps required. Hence, various simplifications are made in places that result in sub-optimal design and code.
- The case study follows the same disclosure sequence as the chapters of the book. Every effort is made to ensure that technologies are not used before they are introduced. Because of this, some parts of the design use alternative mechanisms that, again, can be sub-optimal.

The following sections examine different aspects of the case study and the J2EE patterns within it.

Session Façades and Entity EJBs

Probably the most obvious use of a J2EE pattern in the case study are the Session Façades that prevent the clients from accessing the Entity EJBs directly. This applies both for the standalone application clients and the servlets/JSPs. All of the session beans in the Agency (Advertise, AdvertiseJob, Agency, and Register) act in the role of Session Façades because they all manipulate data in Entity EJBs based on requests from the clients.

An example of this relationship is shown in Figure 18.2. This figure shows the class relationships between an AdvertiseClient, its associated AdvertiseBean (the Session Façade), and the CustomerBean that holds the back-end data. The implementation of the

CustomerBean reflects the nature of this relationship because it only has a local home interface. This means that the CustomerBean is only intended for use by other EJBs such as the AdvertiseBean.

FIGURE 18.2

The AdvertiseBean *acts as a Session Façade between the* AdvertiseClient *and the* CustomerBean.

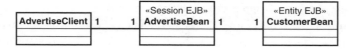

In terms of systemic qualities, the use of a Session Façade has the following impact:

- Maintainability and flexibility—By decoupling the client from the details of the underlying data model, there is a large reduction in dependencies. Fewer dependencies between layers make the system easier to change for maintenance reasons or in the face of changing requirements.

- Security—There is now one point of access for a particular piece of business logic and its associated data.

- Performance—In some ways, a Session Façade will reduce the level of performance because extra code and method calls are introduced. However, designing the Session Façade interface to offer a coarse-grained, business-oriented interface in place of the underlying entity bean's fine-grained, data-oriented interface can frequently offset any reduction in performance because it reduces the number of remote method calls required to perform a task.

Before moving on, consider what you have just seen in terms of the general concept of patterns discussed at the start of this day's material. There are issues surrounding the use of Entity EJBs directly from remote clients. Most designers that have worked with EJBs for some time know of these issues. However, designers who are new to J2EE will not necessarily identify these issues. They may then produce poor quality systems until they learn about such issues by trial and error. By learning from such errors, the designer becomes better at designing J2EE applications. However, this is of little solace to the owner of the poor application on which the designer learned his or her trade.

The designers of the Agency application have used the Session Façade pattern where appropriate. Did they do this because they had learned from personal experience that direct Entity EJB access from distributed clients causes problems, or did they know this from studying J2EE patterns? To all intents and purposes it does not matter how they gained this J2EE design "wisdom," what matters is that the delivered system is of higher quality than it would be without the application of this pattern. By learning and applying the patterns described today, you should be able to improve the quality of the J2EE applications on which you work.

Data Exchange and Value Objects

Within the Agency application, the Session bean data access methods return collections of strings that identify jobs and other domain concepts. The client then uses one of these strings to create another Session bean to retrieve the details associated with that job. An alternative would be to apply the Value Object pattern and use Value Objects to hold the information, such as job details, and to pass collections of these back and forth between the Agency Session bean and the clients.

The question of whether, how, and where to apply Value Objects revolves around the style of the application and the amount of data passed. When using an online catalog, such as those found in e-commerce applications, you will generally present the customer with a list of products. This list will be obtained as the result of some form of query (for example, all the books by Ian Fleming—or even all the products sold that relate to James Bond). The query results will be presented to the customer to make a choice. To make this choice, the customer needs more information about the product than just its name. Additional information could include its type (is it a video of GoldenEye, or a DVD, or a PlayStation game, or a book?), the price, availability, and so on. This means that for every query result, you would want to pass back multiple pieces of information. In this case, encapsulating them in a Value Object would make a lot of sense. You could then return a collection of such Value Objects to the Web-tier client, which would then display them to the customer.

The style of the Agency application is somewhat different from this. Most of the information presented to the user is "top-level" information, such as a list of customers or locations. Information is retrieved and updated as required. Therefore, the application works more on the principle of "browse and drill down," meaning that the "next level" of information (such as the details for a particular customer) is only fetched when required after a selection has been made at the higher level. Passing back collections of Value Objects would be overkill in this situation because only one set of information (applicant or job) is required at any one time.

However, the Value Object pattern can be applied to several of the agency EJB interfaces. Take, as an example, the Advertise interface (shown in Listing 18.1) that is used to update or retrieve information on a particular job advertiser. Because the individual data items, such as the advertiser's name, must be retrieved individually through calls to the Session EJB, the application exhibits excessive chattiness. This means that there are lots of network connections, each one retrieving a small amount of data. This is in contrast to the updateDetails method that takes all of the advertiser's details in a single method call. You can apply the Value Object pattern to convert the repeated method calls into a single method call that returns a single JavaBean. This single JavaBean would contain all of the required information.

To show this pattern-based refactoring in practice, consider two forms of the Advertise interface. The original Advertise interface is shown in Listing 18.1 and has one method for each property defined on the advertiser. The interaction between the client and the Session EJB when loading the advertiser's details is shown in Figure 18.3.

LISTING 18.1   Original Advertise Interface

```
public interface Advertise extends EJBObject
{
  void updateDetails (String name, String email, String[] Address)
                      throws RemoteException;
  String getLogin() throws RemoteException;
  String getName() throws RemoteException;
  String getEmail() throws RemoteException;
  String[] getAddress() throws RemoteException;
  String[] getJobs() throws RemoteException;

  void createJob (String ref)
      throws RemoteException, DuplicateException, CreateException;
  void deleteJob (String ref) throws RemoteException, NotFoundException;
}
```

18

FIGURE 18.3

Interaction between the original AdvertiseClient *and* AdvertiseBean.

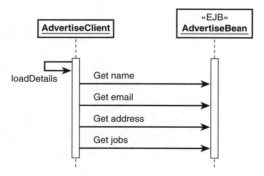

Listing 18.2 shows a refactored interface containing a single query method for the advertiser's details that returns a Value Object of type AdvertiseValueObject. The interaction between the refactored client and Session EJB when loading details is shown in Figure 18.4. As you can see, there are now only two remote method calls made during the load rather than four, thus reducing the chattiness of this part of the application. This change will also reduce the time taken to load the details, because the time taken to make the remote calls will generally dwarf the time spent in local processing.

Note that you can now also use the Value Object as a parameter to `updateDetails` when updating the advertiser's details. Although this change to the update does not improve network performance, it does mean that any changes to the information held per-advertiser need only be made to the Value Object and the code that manipulates Value Objects rather than changing the `Advertise` interface.

LISTING 18.2 A Refactored `Advertise` Interface

```
public interface Advertise extends EJBObject
{
  void updateDetails (AdvertiseValueObject details) throws RemoteException;
  AdvertiseValueObject getDetails() throws RemoteException;

  String[] getJobs() throws RemoteException;

  void createJob (String ref)
      throws RemoteException, DuplicateException, CreateException;
  void deleteJob (String ref) throws RemoteException, NotFoundException;
}
```

FIGURE 18.4

Interaction between the refactored `AdvertiseClient` *and* `AdvertiseBean`.

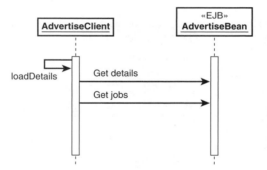

Listing 18.3 shows a possible implementation for the `AdvertiseValueObject`. This is a very simple implementation and it would be quite possible to improve it, such as by providing multiple constructors or allowing smarter addition of address information. However, the code shown is the minimum you would need. Note that the Value Object conforms to the rules for a JavaBean in that it has a no-argument constructor, it uses getter/setter naming, and it is declared as implementing `Serializable`.

LISTING 18.3   AdvertiseValueObject

```java
public class AdvertiseValueObject implements java.io.Serializable
{
 private String _login;
 private String _name;
 private String _email;
 private String[] _address;

 public AdvertiseValueObject() {}

 public String getLogin() { return _login; }
 public void setLogin(String login) { _login = login; }
 public String getName() { return _name; }
 public void setName(String name) { _name = name; }
 public String getEmail() { return _email; }
 public void setEmail(String email) { _email = email; }
 public String[] getAddress() { return _address; }
 public void setAddress(String[] address) { _address = address; }
}
```

Using the AdvertiseValueObject, the code in the client (AdvertiseClient.java) that loads the details would change to that shown in Listing 18.4. The code has changed very little, but the bulk of the data retrieval methods (apart from getDetails and the getJobs method that is used in the loadJobs method) are now local rather than remote.

LISTING 18.4   Refactored loadDetails Method

```java
...
public class AdvertiseClient ...
{
 ...
 private void loadDetails (Advertise advertise) throws RemoteException {
  AdvertiseValueObject details = advertise.getDetails();

  name.setText(details.getName());
  email.setText(details.getEmail());
  String[] address = details.getAddress();

  address1.setText(address[0]);
  address2.setText(address[1]);

  loadJobs(advertise);
 }
}
```

One thing to note is that the list of jobs associated with the advertiser is not included in the Value Object. The client manipulates the jobs separately from the rest of the advertiser details. Therefore, the updating and listing of jobs is kept separate from the manipulation of the advertiser's details.

In terms of systemic qualities, the use of a Value Object has the following impact:

- Performance—There is now one remote method call to retrieve applicant data rather than five.
- Scalability—Fewer calls across the network will reduce the amount of network bandwidth used.
- Maintainability and flexibility—The reduction in dependencies and coupling brought about in the Register interface make subsequent changes to the applicant information easier to manage. Although changes to the contents of the Value Object will require changes in the client and server's internal data and the database schema, there is no need to change the remote interface.

There are also several variations on the Value Object pattern that you may find useful:

- Partial Value Object—If only part of the data held by the server is required by the client, a Value Object can be used that encapsulates precisely the data required.
- XML Value Object—You can extend the Value Object concept by passing an XML document instead of a Java object.

Data Access Without Entity EJBs

When you first started to look at the use of EJBs in the case study, on Day 4, "Introduction to Enterprise JavaBeans," and Day 5, "Session EJBs," Entity EJBs were not yet used to encapsulate the underlying data. Entity EJBs are a fundamental part of the J2EE architecture. They provide an extra level of flexibility by abstracting the underlying data source and, if using CMP, remove the need to write JDBC code. However, you may find that they do not bring any advantage for simpler, read-mostly applications. In this case, you may want to stick with direct database access from Session EJBs.

The Session EJBs from the Day 5 case study use direct database access for all queries and updates. Although direct database access is conceptually simpler than using an Entity EJB, it does mean that the data access code is intermingled with the business logic in the Session bean. This has a negative impact on

- Maintainability—Changes to either the data access code or the business logic will require that you change the Session bean code.
- Flexibility—Should the underlying data source change, such intermingled code is difficult to change.

To overcome these issues, you could apply the Data Access Object (DAO) pattern to the Session EJBs to separate the data access code from the business logic. Using a DAO to house the data access code means that the underlying data source becomes pluggable. The user of the DAO delegates all responsibility for the specifics of data access, such as mechanism, location, and error handling, to the DAO implementation. An example of this pluggability is shown in Figure 18.5.

FIGURE 18.5

A DAO acts as an adapter between the user and the specific data source.

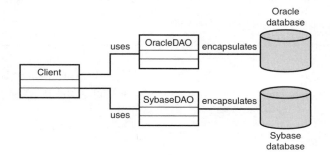

To achieve this level of pluggability, the data and operations associated with the underlying data store must be abstracted. A J2EE DAO will use three mechanisms for this:

- The DAO defines a Java interface that will be implemented by all forms of the DAO. This interface will provide creation, retrieval, update, and deletion (CRUD) methods in much the same way that an EJB home interface does.

- One or more Value Objects represent the data to be used with the CRUD methods. Collections of Value Objects represent returned data. Because the Value Object is an abstraction of the underlying data, this helps to decouple the user of the data from the underlying data access mechanism, such as a JDBC ResultSet.

- Optionally, a factory can be used to determine the type of DAO used. This allows the user of the DAO to leave the implementation selection until runtime.

So, how could you apply a DAO in the pre-entity agency? Well, the first thing would be to decide on the granularity of the DAO or DAOs to be used. You could potentially create one large DAO to represent all of the underlying data in the system, but this would be somewhat unwieldy and difficult to maintain. Probably, the cleanest design would be to create one DAO per table (per type of data) and then see how that worked. Should this cause performance problems, the DAOs could potentially be merged or optimized later.

To illustrate the application of a DAO, consider the two main data types used by the Advertise Session EJB—job and customer. Focusing on the job information, the first thing to do would be to define the interface and Value Object to be used by a potential job-related DAO. Listing 18.5 shows a DAO interface, JobDAO, that could be used for this purpose.

LISTING 18.5   JobDAO, a DAO Interface for Use with Job Information

```
public interface JobDAO
{
 public Collection findByCustomer(String customer) throws Exception;
 public void deleteJob(String ref, String customer) throws Exception;
 public void createJob(String ref, String customer) throws Exception;
}
```

The methods to create and delete jobs are fairly self-explanatory. The findByCustomer method returns a Collection that will contain Value Objects representing all the jobs found that are associated with the given customer. An example of such a Value Object is shown in Listing 18.6. This time, the Value Object has several read-only properties that are set when it is initialized.

LISTING 18.6   JobValueObject, a Value Object for Use with Job Information in a Job DAO

```
public class JobValueObject implements java.io.Serializable
{
 private String _ref;
 private String _customer;
 private String _description;
 private String _location;

 public JobValueObject(String ref, String customer,
            String description, String location) {
  _ref = ref;
  _customer = customer;
  setDescription(description);
  setLocation(location);
 }

 public String getRef() { return _ref; }
 public String getCustomer() { return _customer; }
 public void setDescription(String description) {
  description = description;
 }
 public String getDescription() { return _description; }
 public void setLocation(String location) { _location = location; }
 public String getLocation() { return _location; }
}
```

The DAO interface and Value Object can now be used by an implementation of the DAO DirectJobDAOImpl. The implementation uses the JDBC code previously embedded in the Entity-less AdvertiseBean. Such a DAO is shown in Listing 18.7.

LISTING 18.7   DirectJobDAOImpl, a DAO Implementation That Uses JDBC Calls

```
public class DirectJobDAOImpl extends DirectDAOImpl implements JobDAO
{
 public DirectJobDAOImpl(String jndiName)
  throws SQLException, NamingException {
  super(jndiName);
 }

 public void createJob(String ref, String customer) throws Exception {
  PreparedStatement stmt = null;
  try {
   Connection connection = acquireConnection();
   stmt = connection.prepareStatement(
      "INSERT INTO Job (ref,customer) VALUES (?, ?)");

   stmt.setString(1, ref);
   stmt.setString(2, customer);

   stmt.executeUpdate();
  }
  catch (SQLException e) {
    error("Error creating Job "+ customer +":"+ref, e);
  }
  finally {
   releasePreparedStatement(stmt);
   releaseConnection();
  }
 }

 public void deleteJob (String ref, String customer) throws Exception {
  PreparedStatement stmt = null;
  Connection connection = null;
  try {
   connection = acquireConnection();
   connection.setAutoCommit(false);
   stmt = connection.prepareStatement(
      "DELETE FROM JobSkill WHERE job = ? AND customer = ?");

   stmt.setString(1, ref);
   stmt.setString(2, customer);
   stmt.executeUpdate();
```

18

LISTING 18.7   continued

```
     stmt = connection.prepareStatement(
        "DELETE FROM Job WHERE ref = ? AND customer = ?");

     stmt.setString(1, ref);
     stmt.setString(2, customer);
     stmt.executeUpdate();
     connection.commit();
    }
    catch (SQLException e) {
     try {
      if (connection != null) {
       connection.rollback();
      }
     }
     catch (SQLException ex)
      {}
     error("Error deleting job "+ref+" for "+customer, e);
    }
    finally {
     releasePreparedStatement(stmt);
     releaseConnection();
    }
   }

   public Collection findByCustomer(String customer) throws Exception {
    PreparedStatement stmt = null;
    ResultSet rs = null;
    Collection jobs = new TreeSet();
    try {
     Connection connection = acquireConnection();
     stmt = connection.prepareStatement(
        "SELECT ref FROM Job WHERE customer = ?");

     stmt.setString(1, customer);
     rs = stmt.executeQuery();

     jobs.clear();
     while (rs.next())
     {
      jobs.add(rs.getString(1));
     }
    }
    catch (SQLException e) {
     error("Error loading jobs for "+customer, e);
    }
    finally {
     releasePreparedStatement(stmt);
     releaseResultSet(rs);
```

Listing 18.7 continued

```
    releaseConnection();
  }
  return jobs;
}

private void error (String msg, Exception ex) throws Exception {
  String s = "DirectJobDAOImpl: "+msg + "\n" + ex;
  System.out.println(s);
  throw new Exception(s + ex);
}
}
```

The DAO takes advantage of a programmer-defined superclass that manages the JDBC connection on its behalf. The subclass calls the methods acquireConnection and releaseConnection as required. All the rest of the JDBC manipulation is performed in the DirectJobDAOImpl class. The user of the class simply provides the JNDI string identifying the resource from which the data can be obtained. In this case, the resource will be the data source from which the Agency data can be obtained.

One thing to notice about the DAO implementation shown in Listing 18.7 is that it does not maintain a cache of jobs for the specific customer in the way that the Entity-less AdvertiseBean does. It would be quite possible to create a customer-specific form of the DAO that would cache this information to improve efficiency, if that was found to be beneficial.

Figure 18.6 shows the relationships between the different classes for this job DAO. The AdvertiseBean will instantiate a DirectJobDAOImpl and will call its methods to create, delete, and list jobs. This simplifies the code in the AdvertiseBean enormously and means that the code calls a single, meaningful method rather than containing many lines of JDBC calls and error handling.

The updated createJob method from the Entity-less AdvertiseBean is shown in Listing 18.8. You may notice that this code is now very similar to the code in the version of the AdvertiseBean that uses an Entity EJB. This is not surprising, because the DAO is essentially taking on the role of the Entity EJB in abstracting the data manipulation from the business logic.

18

FIGURE 18.6

Relationships between the classes that make up the job DAO.

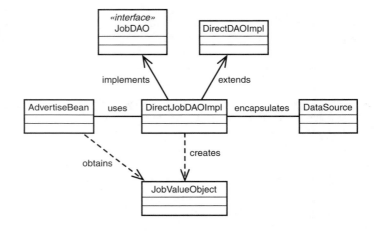

LISTING 18.8 createJob Method from the Entity-less AdvertiseBean Updated to Work with a Job DAO

```
...
public class AdvertiseBean ...
{
 ...
 public void createJob (String ref)
  throws DuplicateException, CreateException {
  try {
   jobDAO.createJob(ref, login);
  }
  catch(Exception ex) {
   error("Could not create job for " + ref, ex);
  }
 }
 ...
```

It is worth noting that in the Sun Java Center definition of Session Façade, the data objects protected from client access can be Entity EJBs, Session EJBs, or DAOs.

In terms of systemic qualities, the use of a Data Access Object has the following impact:

- Maintainability and flexibility—By separating out the data access from the business logic, it is possible to upgrade or replace the data access without affecting the business logic and vice versa.

- Performance—As when adding any extra layer, there will be a certain reduction in performance due to extra object instantiations and method calls. However, these could potentially be offset by optimizations and caching in the DAO layer.

Messages and Asynchronous Activation

On Day 10, "Message-Driven Beans," message-driven beans were added to the Agency to match jobs with applicants and store the results of this matching process for later assessment. The reason for using asynchronous processing was due to the significant amount of time that this may take when the number of jobs or applicants has grown large.

The conversion of a synchronous EJB invocation into a message-driven form is defined by the Service Activator pattern.

In terms of systemic qualities, the use of a Service Activator has the following impact:

- Performance—Because the searching for matching jobs and applicants takes place asynchronously, the level of performance perceived by the client is better (in other words, the server returns immediately rather than "hanging" while the search is performed).

- Scalability—The client updates job or applicant information by calling a method on one of the relevant Session EJBs, such as AdvertiseJobBean. Because each Session EJB will take up server resources (sockets, memory, and so on), the client should use the EJB as quickly as possible. The use of message-driven searching reduces the time that the client uses the Session EJB and so aids scalability.

- Availability—Should the server run out of message-driven beans in the pool (or should the server on which they run become unavailable), the messages can still be queued for delivery. If the service were accessed synchronously, a server outage would cause errors and stop the processing of client requests.

18

Composing an Entity

Although Entity EJBs are often used to represent rows in a database table, this mapping of table to Entity EJB is not necessarily optimal. If an Entity bean is directly based on an underlying database table, and then if the database table changes, so must the Entity EJB and all code that uses that Entity EJB. If there are many related tables, the application code may have to instantiate and use many Entity EJBs to access all of the data it needs. Each additional Entity EJB adds to the complexity of the application code. As more Entity EJBs are required, more RMI calls must be made to access their data, potentially increasing the traffic on the network and slowing down access to the data. Also, the application code may need to contact Entity beans from multiple data stores to retrieve all the data it requires.

To reduce the complexity for the application code and provide a more coherent view of the application's data, a single Entity can be used to represent data stored in multiple places (tables, databases, data stores). This single Entity bean can present a single, coarse-grained interface to the application code (usually a Session EJB).

In J2EE pattern terms, this is termed a Composite Entity. An example of this was seen in the Agency case study on Day 6, "Entity EJBs," when the JobBean was a BMP Entity EJB managing data from both the Job and JobSkill tables. Consequently, the JobBean becomes a coarse-grained entity and any potential JobSkill Entity EJB is removed from the design. You performed the same design refactoring when you implemented the ApplicantBean to access both the Applicant and ApplicantSkill tables.

The JobBean and ApplicantBean BMP Entity EJBs both used JDBC directly to retrieve and update the required data. However, a good case can be made for combining the Composite Entity pattern with the DAO pattern so that the actual JDBC calls are handled in dependent DAO objects.

In terms of systemic qualities, the use of a Composite Entity has the following impact:

- Maintainability and flexibility—By reducing the number of Entity EJBs, the application becomes easier to manage and maintain. Also, the use of one Entity EJB per-table effectively exposes the underlying database schema to the client.
- Performance—Any use of a composite interface as compared to multiple interfaces should reduce the chattiness of the application. However, some of this gain can be offset by a longer load time for the composite. The composite will potentially have to load more data than it needs to serve a simple request. However, there are several strategies, such as lazy loading, that can help address this.

Composing a JSP

JSPs are easy to write and deploy. It is sometimes easy to forget that they are fully-featured and powerful Web components. Poor use of JSP functionality can have as much of an impact on the performance and scalability of your application as poor use of EJBs. J2EE Presentation Tier patterns, such as those listed in the "J2EE Presentation-Tier Patterns" section you saw earlier, can help you improve the quality of your Presentation Tier components and their interactions.

Consider some of the implications of using JSP functionality to deliver Web functionality. One common strategy when developing Web sites is to create one or more templates that define a standard layout for pages displayed to the user. As well as using common colors and styles, each page can display common information (the current location on the site) or functionality (a Home button) in a consistent place. Such templates help to improve the user interface of Web sites and make them easier to navigate. HTML frames have traditionally been used to divide the screen into separate areas to provide this templated look.

When developing JSP-based Web applications, the same principles of usability and navigability still apply. In the case of a JSP, the @include tag can be used to bring in standard functionality in specific parts of a page. The rest of the content in the page is determined by the JSP that is including the templated sections. This style of page composition using JSPs is captured in the J2EE Composite View pattern.

As an example of this, consider the `agency.jsp` from Day 13, "JavaServer Pages," the first few lines of which are shown in Listing 18.9. This JSP uses the `@include` tag to bring in the code from `header.jsf`, as shown in Listing 18.10. This header fragment brings in a set of standard page elements, both functional, such as the error page definition, and visible, such as the style sheet definition. The most visible part of this included fragment is the heading (in the `<H1></H1>` element) showing the agency name that can be seen at the top of Figure 18.7.

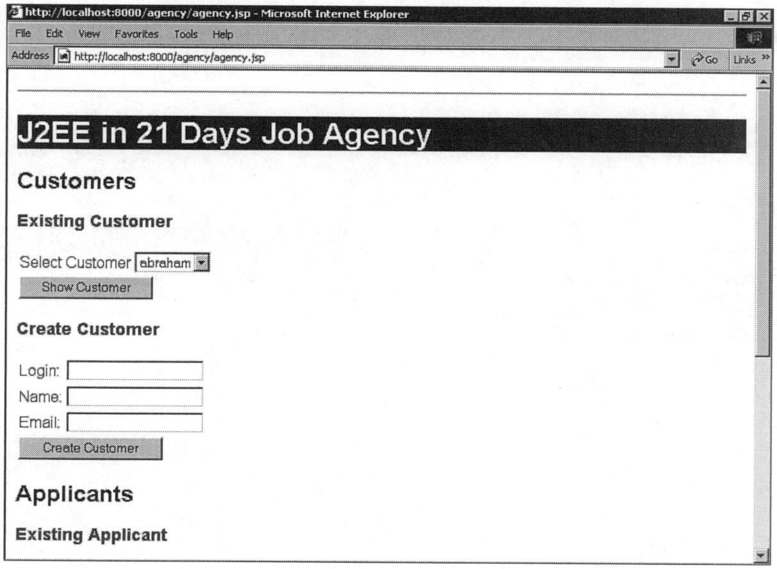

FIGURE 18.7

The heading that shows the name of the Agency *is part of a templated header included in* `agency.jsp`.

LISTING 18.9   Partial Listing of `agency.jsp` from Day 14

```
HTML>
 <%@include file="header.jsf" %>
 <BODY>
  <HR><H1>${agency.agencyName}</H1><P>
  <H2>Customers</H2>
  <H3>Existing Customer</H3>
  <FORM action='<c:url value="/customer/advertise" />' >
   <TABLE>
    <TR>
     <TD>Select Customer</TD>
...
```

LISTING 18.10   header.jsf

```
<%@ taglib prefix="c" uri="/c.tld" %>
<%@page errorPage="/errorPage.jsp" %>
<jsp:useBean id="agency" class="web.AgencyBean" scope="request" />
<HEAD>
 <TITLE>J2EE in 21 Days Agency Web Application</TITLE>
 <LINK rel="stylesheet" type="text/css" href='<c:url value="/agency.css" />' >
</HEAD>
```

The header.jsf fragment is included in all of the JSP pages that are provided for the
Agency's Web interface. All of the other pages (apart from agency.jsp) also include the
footer.jsf fragment at the bottom of the page. The admin.jsp page, shown partially in
Listing 18.11, is an example of this. The footer.jsf fragment, shown in Listing 18.12,
provides a button to take the user back to the main Agency JSP. The resulting admin
page is shown in Figure 18.8.

FIGURE 18.8

admin.jsp *includes
both a header and a
footer to provide
consistent style and a
standard button to
return to the main
screen.*

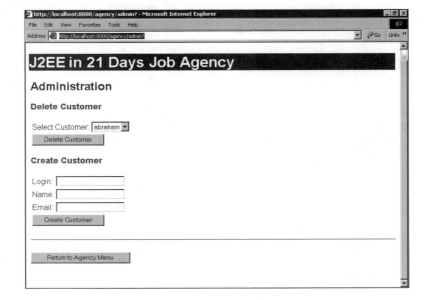

LISTING 18.11   Partial Listing of Day 14 admin.jsp

```
<HTML>
 <%@include file="header.jsf" %>
 <BODY>
  <HR><H1>${agency.agencyName}</H1><P>
```

LISTING 18.11 continued

```
<H2>Administration</H2>
<H3>Modify Existing Location</H3>

...

<%@include file="footer.jsf" %>
</BODY>
</HTML>
```

LISTING 18.12 footer.jsf

```
<HR>
<FORM>
  <INPUT type="button" value="Return to Agency Menu"
         onClick=location='<c:url value="/agency" />' >
</FORM>
```

In terms of systemic qualities, the use of a Composite View has the following impact:

- Maintainability—Because the template used for the pages is modular, particular parts of the template can be re-used throughout the application.

- Manageability—Use of the pattern has benefits in that cleanly separated page fragments make it easier to make changes. However, a plethora of fragments also presents a challenge to manage all of these pieces in a cohesive way.

- Flexibility—The use of a view manager to conditionally include fragments of content makes the application interface very flexible.

- Performance—The runtime generation of a page has a negative impact on performance, particularly when using a view manager. It may be best to have parts of the standard template pre-included when the JSPs are updated and refreshed in the Web application.

JSPs and Separation of Concerns

When designing an application, it is always important to correctly partition the components so that each component, or group of components, performs a specific task or tasks. This separation of concerns leads to fewer dependencies, cleaner code, and a more maintainable and flexible application. The separation of concerns becomes very important when those concerns relate to the skills of the people who must maintain and update parts of the application. In the case of JSPs, there are two distinct skill sets required—user interface design and writing J2EE-level Java code. Because it is rare to find these skills in the same person, these two aspects should be kept apart as much as possible.

Following this principle, the JSPs developed on Day 13 contain a certain amount of Java code to generate dynamic output, but not all of the code required is visible in the JSP pages. The JSPs use three JavaBeans, AgencyBean, JobBean, and CustomerBean, to perform the more involved processing required, such as the interaction with the business-tier EJBs. The J2EE pattern View Helper describes various ways in which encapsulated Java components can be used to hide a lot of the business processing required to create the desired output or view.

To see this in action, consider the AgencyBean, part of which is shown in Listing 18.13. As you can see, the constructor locates an Agency EJB and the rest of the code consists of methods that wrap calls to the EJB. If you look back to Listing 18.10, you can see that an AgencyBean declaration is included in header.jsf so that all pages will have an instance in scope. However, because the bean is scoped by request, the same bean can be shared if requests are forwarded to other JSPs or servlets within the application.

LISTING 18.13   Selected Highlights of AgencyBean.java

```
...

public class AgencyBean
{
 Agency agency;

 public String getAgencyName() throws RemoteException {
  return agency.getAgencyName();
 }

 public Collection findAllApplicants() throws RemoteException {
  return agency.findAllApplicants();
 }

 public void createApplicant(String login, String name, String email)
  throws RemoteException, DuplicateException, CreateException {
  agency.createApplicant(login,name,email);
 }

 public void deleteApplicant (String login)
  throws RemoteException, NotFoundException {
  agency.deleteApplicant(login);
 }

 ...

 public AgencyBean ()
  throws NamingException, RemoteException, CreateException {
  InitialContext ic = null;
```

LISTING 18.13   continued

```
    ic = new InitialContext();
    AgencyHome agencyHome =
            (AgencyHome)ic.lookup("java:comp/env/ejb/Agency");
    agency = agencyHome.create();
  }
}
```

The use of the bean in the page makes it easy to build up JSP content based on the functionality exposed by the bean. The section of JSP code in Listing 18.14 is able to use the
bean without the overhead of including the EJB-specific discovery code. This makes the
page easier to maintain.

LISTING 18.14   Simple Use of the AgencyBean in the Day 14 agency.jsp

```
<FORM action='<c:url value="/customer/advertise" />' >
 <TABLE>
  <TR>
   <TD>Select Customer</TD>
   <TD>
    <SELECT name="customer">
     <c:forEach var="customer" items="${agency.customers}" >
      <OPTION>${customer}
     </c:forEach>
    </SELECT>
   </TD>
  </TR>
  <TR><TD colspan="2"><input type="submit" value="Show Customer"></TD></TR>
 </TABLE>
</FORM>
```

The relationships and interaction between the client, the JSP, and the bean are depicted in
Figures 18.9 and 18.10. Everything to the right of the AgencyBean JavaBean is transparent to the agency JSP.

FIGURE 18.9

*Class relationships for
the AgencyBean View
Helper.*

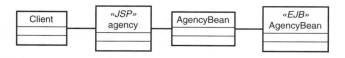

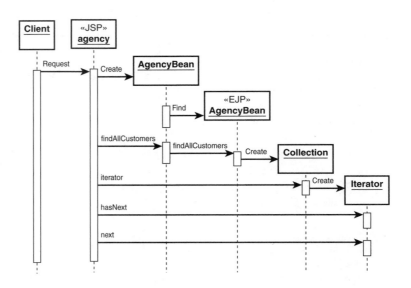

FIGURE 18.10

Sample interaction diagram for the AgencyBean *View Helper.*

As well as using JavaBeans, there are other strategies for delegating code to components outside the JSP. The most powerful strategy is probably the one using a custom tag library. The code fragment in Listing 18.15 shows how even more of the Java code is removed by using the custom agency:useCustomer tag that removes the JNDI name lookup of the Customer EJB from the Web page. This JSP code can now be easily manipulated and interpreted by a Web page designer and the tools used for Web page design.

LISTING 18.15 A Tag Library Used as a View Helper to Remove Code from the Agency JSP

```
<HTML>
 <%@include file="header.jsf" %>
 <agency:useCustomer login="${param.customer}"/>
 <BODY>
  <HR><H1>${agency.agencyName}</H1><P>
   <H2>Customer details for: ${cust.login}</H2>
```

One other strategy for removing code from a JSP is to simply store the code in a JSP fragment and then include the fragment where appropriate. Although this can be effective in some cases, it lacks the encapsulation of the other mechanisms. It is important to note that the importing of these fragments relates more to the View Helper pattern than the Composite View pattern, as it may seem at first glance.

In terms of systemic qualities, the use of View Helpers has the following impact:

- Maintainability—If the code and the HTML of the JSP are separated, it makes it far easier to maintain the two parts. There is much less chance of accidental changes than when code and HTML are mixed.

- Flexibility—If the code behind the helpers changes, for example to use different EJBs or direct database access, there is no need for the JSP to be altered.

- Performance—As with any layering technique, there is the potential for some degradation in performance.

Client-Side Proxies and Delegates

The JavaBeans in the View Helper discussion also act as a shield between the JSP and the business tier functionality. For example, the JSP has no need to know that it is using an EJB when it instantiates an `AgencyBean` JavaBean. The JavaBean encapsulates all of the EJB handling (the custom tag library also does this in later versions). In this role of client-side proxy, the JavaBean provides an implementation of another J2EE pattern, the Business Delegate.

The role of a Business Delegate is to reduce the coupling between the client tier or Web tier code and the business tier implementation. As indicated, encapsulating the implementation of the business logic (as an EJB) reduces coupling. This encapsulation includes not only the lookup of resources but also error handling, retries, and failover, if appropriate. The Business Delegate can also perform caching and mapping of EJB exceptions to application exceptions.

When Business Delegates and Session Façades are used together, there is commonly a 1:1 mapping between them. This occurs in the Day 13 `Agency` code where the `AgencyBean`, `JobBean`, and `CustomerBean` JavaBeans each act as a Business Delegate for the `Agency`, `Job`, and `Customer` Session Façade EJBs, respectively. The primary reason that the Business Delegate does not contain business logic is that such business logic should be factored back into an associated Session Façade.

In terms of systemic qualities, the use of Business Delegates has the following impact:

- Maintainability—The Business Delegate encapsulates the business tier access code. Any changes required to this code can be made in one place.

- Reliability and availability—Retry and failover strategies can be implemented by a Business Delegate to improve the reliability and availability of the access to business tier services.

- Performance—As with any layering technique, there is the potential for some degradation in performance. However, a Business Delegate can also cache information if appropriate, having a positive impact on performance.

18

Locating Services

Because the case study is designed to be simple, it tends to obtain EJB home and remote references on a per-call basis. In a production system, this is one of the areas where caching would be of benefit. The Service Locator pattern describes a way to speed up the retrieval of EJB remote interfaces.

The Service Locator is a derivative of the GoF Singleton pattern. It acts as a central, common service on the presentation or Web tier from which EJB remote references can be obtained. The Service Locator will obtain and cache a reference to the home interfaces of the EJBs it serves. These cached home interfaces are then used to dispense EJB remote interfaces as required. The client code does not need to perform the home interface lookup every time and so becomes more efficient.

In terms of the case study, both the application clients and Web-tier components could use such a service to improve the way they obtain EJB remote references.

In terms of systemic qualities, the use of Service Locator has the following impact:

- Performance—Caching the EJB home interfaces should reduce the time taken to obtain an EJB remote reference. Also, because there are fewer JNDI lookups, there will be less network traffic.
- Reliability and availability—Retry and failover strategies can be implemented by a Service Locator to improve the reliability and availability of the access to business tier services.
- Maintainability—Because all of the EJB lookup (or JMS connection lookup) takes place in one component, there is one place for updates.

Any Other Business

Other J2EE patterns could be applied to the case study if the requirements were different. For example, the case study uses standard J2EE security in a fairly straightforward way. However, if there were more complex security requirements, a Front Controller servlet could be used in the Web tier to enforce such security in a uniform manner without having to place security code in each JSP and servlet. If other functionality, such as logging and audit, were required, the Intercepting Filter pattern could be applied to chain together all of the required common "transparent" functionality (security, logging, and so on) ahead of any access to JSPs and servlets.

Because the data displayed by the Web-based interface is fairly standard, there is no requirement for pre-processing of information in a Front Controller. Nor does any form of routing take place such that the client is shown different pages depending on the context information they submit (for example, a cookie or form field). If such pre-processing and conditional display were to form part of the case study, the patterns Service to Worker and Dispatcher View could be considered when deciding where to place the different responsibilities.

The case study is not an e-commerce system, as many J2EE systems are. Such systems tend to deal with catalogs of products and spend most of their time displaying static information and less time updating information (for example, a customer will browse many pages before placing an order). For e-commerce systems, other patterns in the J2EE catalog, such as Value List Handler and Fast Lane Reader, become relevant.

The different patterns are relevant in different contexts. Some patterns will be irrelevant in some cases, so don't assume that all patterns will be applicable in your system.

Refactoring the Case Study

As you have seen, there are various ways in which the case study can be refactored to improve its systemic qualities. The reason that such refactoring can be performed is down to the context in which the application was written, namely that parts of it were simplified for educational purposes.

As noted earlier, most development work is performed on existing code, so identifying a potential application of a pattern in such code and applying the appropriate refactoring is a useful skill to build. The reason that you would want to apply the refactoring shown is to make the case study a more efficient, maintainable, and scalable application. But why are you doing that? Well, probably because you want to apply that application in the real world to serve real customers. In that case, the context for the application has changed from being an educational J2EE showcase to being a live production application. The change in context alters the requirements and the forces on which the application is based. Such changes will almost inevitably show areas in which changes are required.

As any application is altered, whether that is the addition of new functionality or a change to the systemic quality requirements, certain original design decisions may no longer make as much sense as they did in the original design context. As a result, refactoring of applications and the use of different patterns in different areas over time should become a way of life for software designers and developers. Without suitable maintenance, software will erode over time as the world changes around it.

Directions for J2EE Patterns

There are a number of patterns that have been identified as recurring in J2EE design and development. However, the list of J2EE patterns provided earlier is not a definitive and

18

final one. More J2EE-specific patterns will undoubtedly emerge over time due to various factors:

- Because more applications are developed based on existing J2EE technologies, more patterns may be mined by identifying other common design elements within those applications.
- New patterns will evolve based on newly released technologies that become part of the J2EE platform.
- New applications of all these technologies will lead to new requirements. The solutions to these new requirements will give rise to new patterns of use and, hence, to new J2EE patterns.

Another aspect of the emergence of patterns in environments such as J2EE is that the common patterns become embodied in the environment itself. This was noted earlier where patterns such as Proxy are prevalent in the infrastructure and generated classes of a J2EE application. As J2EE evolves, more patterns will be captured in the underlying platform. An example of this is the introduction of servlet filters in J2EE 1.3, which embodies much of the Intercepting Filter pattern.

Summary

Good design relies on knowledge of the technologies in use and an appreciation of how they best fit together to solve particular problems. Technologies are comparatively straightforward to learn, and there are many sources from which you can obtain information and insight, such as books and training courses. Gaining an appreciation of how best to apply these technologies is more difficult. By studying design patterns, particularly those targeted at a specific platform such as J2EE, you can accelerate your understanding of the design issues in particular environments. Design patterns also provide you with a set of solutions to these issues that can be applied as part of your application design.

Q & A

Q There is much material available on application design and architecture. Why should you use patterns?

A Patterns are mined from concrete examples of design and architectural elements that have been used and proven in delivered systems. A pattern is only a pattern when it has been identified in multiple existing designs or architectures. As such, a pattern is more than just an algorithm or an opinion.

Q **What effect do J2EE patterns have on the systemic qualities of a design, such as scalability and availability?**

A Correctly applied, J2EE patterns will improve one or more of the systemic qualities of a design. As an example, consider the Value Object pattern. The primary purpose of using a Value Object between client and server is to reduce network chattiness, where a client makes repeated calls to a server to obtain a set of related data. By creating a single object to represent such data, only a single method call is required to retrieve the data. This improves the performance and scalability of the system.

Q **Can you only apply J2EE patterns to new designs?**

A No. J2EE patterns can be used to re-shape existing application code to improve its maintainability and other systemic qualities.

Q **Why do J2EE patterns tend to abstract the access to underlying databases?**

A An important part of good design is to reduce the coupling between parts of a system. As an example, consider the use of a Session Façade to hide the underlying structure and relationships of the business data. The Session Façade interface should be business-oriented rather than data-oriented, because the Session Façade provides business services instead of raw data. Obscuring the structure of the data means that this data can be changed at a later date without requiring changes to the client.

Exercises

There are several refactoring exercises that could be performed on the case study. One of the most effective is to use Value Objects between the clients and their associated Session beans. This exercise asks to you perform such a refactoring.

1. Starting with the Agency example under the Day 18 exercise, create a Value Object called `ApplicantValueObject`. This should contain all of the information about an applicant, such as his or her name, email, and so on. The class you create should be a JavaBean, and you must be able to use it as a parameter or return type in an RMI method call.

   Alter the `Register` interface so that it passes `ApplicantValueObjects` between client and server. The interface should only have two methods.

   Alter the `RegisterBean` EJB so that it implements the updated `Register` interface and uses `ApplicantValueObjects`.

Alter the `RegisterClient` application so that it uses the updated `Register` interface and `ApplicantValueObjects`.

Build the updated application and re-deploy it. Make sure that everything still works correctly.

An example solution is available under the agency directory in the Day 18 agency code on the Web site. Examine the sample solution in contrast to your own. How might you improve the sample solution? Areas to consider include the EJB home interfaces, the Value Object constructor, the way the Value Object stores skills, and whether the `Applicant` EJB should create the Value Object.

DAY **19**

Integrating with External Resources

Yesterday, you learned about patterns and how they describe typical application development problems that you might face and how these patterns provide solutions to these problems. One problem that many application developers share is how to integrate a J2EE application with existing non-Java code, applications, or systems. Today's lesson introduces you to some possible solutions to this problem.

The first of these solutions is the J2EE Connector architecture, which allows you to connect to Enterprise Information Systems (EIS), such as Enterprise Resource Planning systems (ERP). Primarily, today's lesson focuses on this architecture, but it also shows you approaches to writing Java code that consume non-Java code libraries (such as legacy C libraries) and non Java remote objects.

Today's lesson covers the following topics:

- Reviewing external resources and legacy systems
- Introducing the Connector architecture

- Introducing Java IDL and CORBA
- Working with RMI over IIOP
- Working with the Java Native Interface
- Reviewing integration technologies

Reviewing External Resources and Legacy Systems

In an ideal world, your entire application might only contain Java components and applications, but it is not an ideal world. Very few architects have the opportunity to design entire Java systems from the ground-up, and very few enterprise developers have the opportunity to solely work on these types of systems. In reality, systems are heterogeneous in nature; that is, they are made up of many different parts. Figure 19.1 shows a complex heterogeneous environment that shows an array of clients attempting to access the services provided by a vast array of non-Java applications and systems.

FIGURE 19.1

A complex heterogeneous environment.

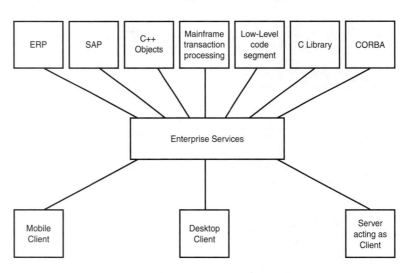

As you can see, the system consists of Enterprise Information Systems, such as ERP, SAP, and mainframe transaction processing systems. In addition, the enterprise services must call on the services provided by legacy code libraries, remote objects written in non-Java programming languages, and code written in lower-level programming languages.

The needs of business and the pressures of the application development cycle means that it is simply not feasible to rewrite all these elements in Java. The only feasible option is that enterprise services provide mechanisms that integrate with these legacy and non-Java elements. Luckily, there are a number of Java technologies that allow you to integrate J2EE applications with these elements. You will explore these technologies in today's lesson.

Introducing Other Connectivity Technologies

There are several Java technologies that allow you to integrate Java applications with non-Java applications. Today's lesson provides an overview of some of these Java technologies:

- Connector Architecture
- CORBA support classes
- RMI over IIOP
- Java Native Interface (JNI)

The J2EE Connector architecture allows J2EE application components to interact with other EIS systems using a standard technology API. The Connector Architecture defines requirements for security and transaction management for use with EIS systems.

The CORBA and RMI over IIOP technologies allow you to create and interface to objects that comply with the Common Object Request Broker Architecture (CORBA). The most important aspect of these Java technologies is that they allow you to write code that interacts with either local or remote objects that might be written in languages other than Java.

In addition, the JNI technology allows you to write Java code that utilizes code libraries written in languages other than Java. For example, you can write code that uses JNI to access C libraries or C++ classes. This means you can call non-Java functions to provide services that are unavailable from Java. The integration that JNI allows works in both directions—both the Java and non-Java sides can create, update, and access Java objects.

19

Connector Architecture

The Java solution to application integration in a heterogeneous environment is the J2EE Connector architecture. The architecture provides a standard way to connect to legacy and non-Java systems. As you will learn, the architecture enables EIS providers to create a single resource that permits any J2EE application server to access the EIS. In addition, the architecture defines a standard API that allows you to program against any supported EIS by using a standard set of API calls.

NOTE | Today's lesson discusses and uses version 1.5 of the Connector architecture.

Overview of the Architecture

The J2EE Connector architecture defines two categories of contract—system and application.

The system contract defines the relationship between a J2EE application server, or a container, and an EIS. The system contract requires the application server and the EIS to collaborate to hide system-level functionality from developers and components. The EIS provider implements its part of the contract through a resource adapter, which plugs into the application server to form a bridge between components and the EIS. Figure 19.2 shows the resource adapter within the J2EE connector architecture.

FIGURE 19.2

The J2EE Connector architecture.

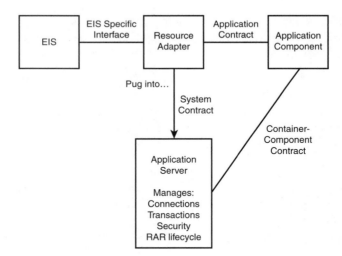

Figure 19.2 also shows how application components, such as an EJB or a JSP, communicate with an EIS through the resource adapter—not through direct communication. The application contract governs this communication through a client API—you will learn more about this contract later in the "Common Client Interface" section of today's lesson.

NOTE

> The `javax.resource.spi` package provides the classes, and interfaces that you require to write a resource adapter for an EIS. The process of writing a resource adapter is outside the scope of today's lesson. If you want to learn more about writing resource adapters, please refer to the J2EE API documentation and the Connector architecture specification at `http://java.sun.com/j2ee/connector/`.

To draw a comparison with other elements of J2EE, you can consider a resource adapter to be similar to a JDBC driver. In both cases, a service provider or a third-party provides a bridge between a non-Java application and Java components. In the case of JDBC, the bridge is a JDBC driver and, in the case of the Connector architecture, the bridge is a system-level software driver known as a resource adapter. In both instances, components communicate to the underlying service via the bridge.

After an EIS provider has written a resource adapter, any J2EE-compliant application server can use that adapter. This means that the EIS provider only has to write one resource adapter to support many application servers. An application server can host several resource adapters—one for each EIS—and, thus, support multiple EISs. To offer you a deeper insight into the relationship between EIS, application server, and application component, the next section of today's lesson looks at the roles and responsibilities defined in the Connector architecture specification.

Roles and Responsibilities

Figure 19.3 shows a simplified representation of the roles, which relate to the process outlined in Figure 19.2.

19

FIGURE 19.3

J2EE Connector architecture roles (simplified).

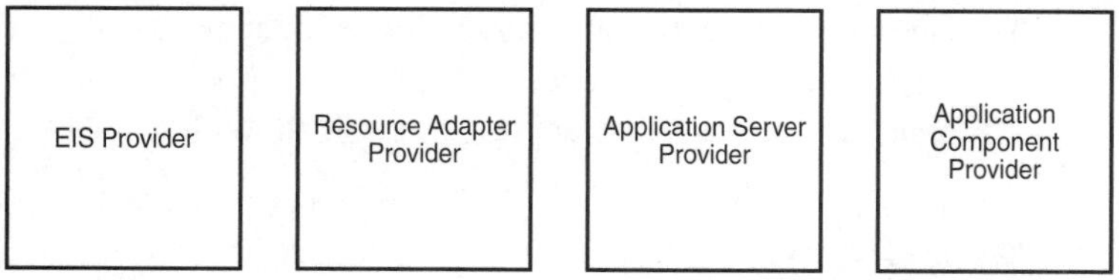

| EIS Provider | Resource Adapter Provider | Application Server Provider | Application Component Provider |

Typically, but not exclusively, the EIS provider and the resource adapter provider are the same person or organization. The resource adapter plugs into the application server, so that the server can provide application components with connectivity to the EIS. The application server manages security, resources, and transactions on behalf of the EIS, so that these system-level functions are transparent to the application component.

In Figure 19.2, you saw how a system contract governs the relationships between an EIS and an application server. The system contract comprises many separate contracts:

- Connection Management contract
- Transaction Management contract
- Security contract
- Lifecycle Management contract
- Work Management contract
- Transaction Inflow contract
- Message Inflow contract

The remainder of this section examines each of these contracts, so that you can gain an understanding of the services available to you as an application developer.

The Connection Management Contract

The connection management contract enables both the application server to pool connections to the EIS, and the application components to connect to the EIS. Typically, when connecting to an EIS, you write code that performs a lookup in the JNDI namespace for a connection factory, which you then use to gain a connection to an underlying EIS. The connection factory, on receiving a request for a connection, delegates responsibility to a connection manager on the application server. The connection manager is then responsible for checking the connection pool for a connection and, together with the application server, providing a connection instance that you can use to access the underlying EIS. Because the application server pools connections, multiple clients can connect to the EIS (and possibly multiple EISs).

The Transaction Management Contract

The transaction management contract allows an application server to manage transactions across multiple EISs if appropriate. Figure 19.4 shows the different types of transactions the Connector architecture recognizes; it also shows how these transactions are managed.

As you can see, the architecture defines two main categories of transaction—external (XA or JTA) transactions and local transactions. The former category includes those transactions that a transaction manager on the application server manages on behalf of the EIS (typically a transaction processing (TP) system). In this scenario, the application server provides all runtime support for transactions, so you do not need to concern yourself with these types of transactions. The latter category, local transactions, includes transactions that the EIS manages itself. In this instance, the server must perform some form of transaction demarcation. The server can perform this demarcation in one of two ways:

- Container managed
- Component managed

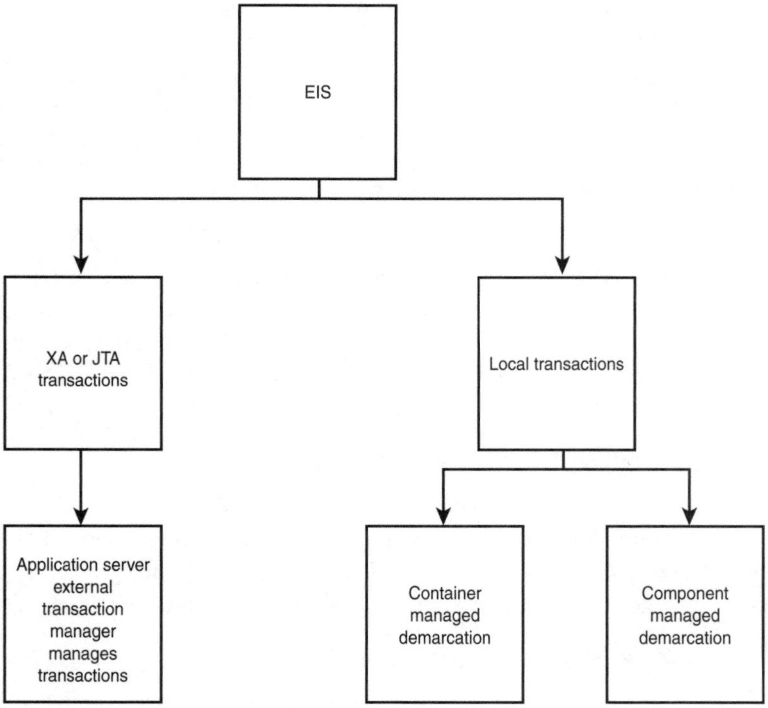

FIGURE 19.4

J2EE Connector architecture transaction management.

Container-managed demarcation is where the component container performs transaction demarcation on behalf of the component, so you do not have to explicitly begin, commit, or rollback transactions.

Unlike container-managed demarcation, component-managed demarcation requires you to manage the demarcation of a transaction. With regard to J2EE application components, containers must support both container- and component-managed transaction demarcation.

NOTE   For a guide to transaction management and how this affects the scalability and performance of your application, refer to Day 8, "Transactions and Persistence."

19

The Security Contract

An EIS will often hold information that might be sensitive (credit card details) or mission critical (prospects details in a call center). It is vitally important for an organization to know that this information is only available to authorized persons. The J2EE Connector architecture security contract stipulates how this security is maintained when J2EE components connect to an EIS. The contract aims to achieve this by extending the J2EE security model to EIS integration through the Connector architecture. One of the key goals of the contract specification is to keep security neutral. That is, the security contract is flexible enough to support a wide-range of security technologies and types of EIS. The two principal ways it achieves this are by not stating

- A mandatory, specific security policy
- A mandatory, specific security technology

The process of signing on to an EIS from an application can occur in two ways. The first is container managed. This is where the application server takes responsibility for signing onto the EIS. Alternatively, the sign on process can be component managed. In this instance, you are responsible for writing the code that provides the authentication and authorization credentials required for sign-on.

Lifecycle Management Contract

The lifecycle management contract provides a mechanism for the application server to start up an instance of a resource adapter when it is deployed or when the application server starts up. The contract also enables the application server to notify the resource adapter to shut down when it is undeployed or the application server is shut down.

Work Management Contract

In a scenario where a resource adapter needs to create threads to perform its tasks, the work management contract allows the application server to execute these threads on behalf of the resource adapter. This has three benefits:

- The resource adapter does not have the overhead of managing thread creation or pooling.
- The application server has more control over its run-time resources and can efficiently pool threads.
- The work management contract allows resource adapters to perform work in cases where they are prevented by the application server from creating their own threads (for security or efficiency reasons).

The work management contract allows the resource adapter to control the security context and transaction context for the threads.

Transaction Inflow Contract

In some situations, the application server might find itself involved in doing work as part of imported transactions from an EIS. In this case, it needs to know how to handle transaction completion (two-phase commits) and crash recovery calls from the EIS. The transaction inflow contract provides this information and also ensures that the ACID (Atomicity, Consistency, Isolation, Durability) properties of the imported transaction are preserved.

Message Inflow Contract

This contract enables the resource adapter to asynchronously deliver messages to Message-Driven beans in the application server in a generic manner that is independent of the messaging mechanism used. This allows a range of message providers, such as Java Message Service (JMS) and Java API for XML Messaging (JAXM), to be plugged into any J2EE-compatible application server via a resource adapter. In addition, J2EE components can access and consume messages from different messaging providers with no change to client code.

Common Client Interface

A resource adapter provides a client API that you can code against. The Connector architecture specification allows a resource adapter to support a client API that is specific to its underlying EIS. For example, an EIS that is a relational database might support the JDBC API. However there are many requirements of a resource adapter that are independent from the underlying EIS. The Connector architecture provides a Common Client Interface (CCI) API to assist a client when performing typical data access operations.

A resource adapter does not have to provide a CCI implementation, but doing so will aid developers who might have worked with the CCI for another EIS resource adapter.

When you code against the CCI, you work with an abstraction of EIS functionality. This means that, like any other standard API, you only have to learn one set of API calls and you will be able to write code that interacts with different EISs.

A CCI resource adapter provides a `ConnectionFactory` that you use to create a `Connection` to the EIS. To locate the `ConnectionFactory`, you must first establish a JNDI `Context` for your current session and then perform a lookup on the JNDI namespace to locate the `ConnectionFactory`. After you locate the `ConnectionFactory`, you can use it to create a `Connection`. As previously mentioned, the `Connection` is an application-level handle that you use to access an EIS instance.

After you have a `Connection`, you create an `Interaction`. An `Interaction` allows you to execute EIS functions. In other words, all the operations you want to perform against

19

the EIS are done through the `Interaction`. Typically, when you execute an EIS function, you also provide the `Interaction` instance with a `Record`. The `Record` holds either the input to, or the output from, an EIS function. For example, you can use a `Record` instance to pass parameters to the EIS function, or you can use a `Record` instance to hold the information the EIS function returns.

As a simple example of how to use the CCI API, the code in Listing 19.1 shows a `countCustomers()` function for the theoretical MyEis resource adapter.

LISTING 19.1   Simple CCI Client `MyEisBean.java`

```java
import java.math.*;
import java.util.*;
import javax.resource.cci.*;
import javax.resource.*;
import javax.naming.*;

public class MyEisBean
{
  public int countCustomers() throws MyEisException {
    Connection con =  null;
    try {
      Context ic = new InitialContext();
      ConnectionFactory cf =
          (ConnectionFactory) ic.lookup("myeis/ConnectionFactory");
      MyEisInteractionSpec iSpec =
          (MyEisInteractionSpec)ic.lookup("myeis/InteractionSpec");
      iSpec.setOperationName("CountCustomers");

      con = cf.getConnection();
      Interaction ix = con.createInteraction();
      RecordFactory rf = cf.getRecordFactory();
      IndexedRecord iRec = rf.createIndexedRecord("InputRecord");
      IndexedRecord rec = (IndexedRecord)ix.execute(iSpec, iRec);

      int count = 0;
      Iterator iterator = rec.iterator();
      if(iterator.hasNext()) {
        Integer result = (Integer)iterator.next();
        count = result.intValue();
      }
      return count;
    }
    catch (NamingException ex) {
      throw new MyEisException(ex.toString());
    }
    catch (ResourceException ex) {
      throw new MyEisException(ex.toString());
```

LISTING 19.1   continued

```
    }
    finally {
      try {con.close();} catch (Exception ex){}
    }
  }
}
```

In Listing 19.1 the code connects to a CCI resource adapter and executes the "CountCustomers" operation to obtain a count of the number of customers in the EIS. The actual EIS implementation is immaterial to this example. All of the complications of connecting to the EIS resource adapter have been hidden behind JNDI objects.

The code starts by using JNDI to look up the CCI resource adapter specific to ConnectionFactory and InteractionSpec objects. InteractionSpec is just an indicator interface and has no methods. A resource adapter must supply its own definition of an InteractionSpec and it is this object that is used to pass information into the resource adapter. In this example the MyEisInteractionSpec class defines a method for setting the operation name to be invoked. Additional methods could be provided in the InteractionSpec object to specify other arguments (not required for this example).

The example code now gets a Connection to the resource adapter from the ConnectionFactory and creates an Interaction object to represent the interaction with the EIS resource. The Interaction.execute() method requires the resource specific InteractionSpec object (created earlier) and an IndexedRecord object to pass parameters into the resource adapter.

The results of the interaction are passed back in another IndexedRecord object. The code obtains an Iterator over the results of the operation and extracts the single Integer result that is a count of the customer records.

Fundamentally that is all there is to using a CCI resource adapter. Obviously this is a very simple example and only shows the basic interaction pattern supported by CCI. A real CCI resource adapter will have a more complex interface and a fully functional implementation of an InteractionSpec class.

You will now see how to install a resource adapter in a J2EE server

Installing a Resource Adapter

A connector architecture resource adapter is conventionally provided as a Resource archive (RAR) file. RAR files, like EAR and WAR files, are JAR files containing all the class files, supporting files and deployment descriptors needed to define the resource adapter.

19

Resource archives are deployed using the same mechanism as Enterprise archives and Web archives. Deploying a RAR file will vary from one J2EE container to another but will typically require running an application (probably web based) and providing the target server details and the location of the RAR file on the local disk.

For the J2EE RI you can use the Admin Console (`http://localhost:4848/asadmin/`) or the command line `asadmin` utility. These applications have already been discussed on Day 4, "Introduction to Enterprise JavaBeans," but as a simple example the local file `myeis.rar` can be deployed using the `asadmin` using the command

```
asadmin deploy --user admin --force myeis.rar
```

Once a resource adapter has been installed you can register resources (such as `ConnectionFactory` objects) against JNDI names. In fact you did this when you created the JMS resources on Day 9, "Java Message Service."

Introducing CORBA

The Object Management Group (OMG) defines the Common Object Request Broker Architecture (CORBA), an architecture that allows you to build distributed objects and services. The architecture is independent of any particular language implementation or system architecture. Thus, you can produce remote objects in one language, say C++, and then consume them from a client object written in another language, such as Java. Because the CORBA standard allows communication between disparate languages, applications, and systems, it is necessarily extensive. However, to understand how CORBA works, there are four main aspects of the architecture that you should appreciate:

- Object Request Broker (ORB)
- The Naming Service
- Inter-ORB communication
- Interface Definition Language (IDL)

NOTE   The OMG has a Web site dedicated to CORBA that you can access at `http://www.corba.org/`.

All communication among objects and clients occurs through the Object Request Broker (ORB). An ORB runs on both the client and the server. Figure 19.5 shows the roles of the ORBs in client-server communication. You can see that a client application makes a request on a stub that exposes the methods of the remote object. The client ORB forwards that request to the remote ORB and, in turn, this ORB forwards the request through the skeleton to the remote object.

FIGURE 19.5

Client interacting with CORBA object.

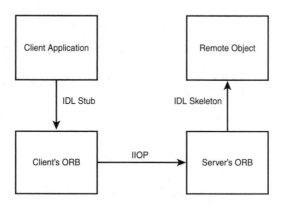

CORBA defines a number of transport protocols that allow distributed ORBs to communicate. The most popular of these is the Internet Inter-ORB Protocol (IIOP), which is based on TCP/IP. Although you will learn more about this protocol later in today's lesson, it is very unlikely that you will have to work with it at a low-level.

The CORBA Naming Service allows you to register an instance of a class, so that a client can look up this instance and gain a reference to it. You will learn more about how this works later in today's lesson in the "Using RMI over IIOP" section.

CORBA IDL

CORBA-compliant remote objects expose interfaces that are defined in Interface Definition Language (IDL). IDL syntax is based on C++ but should be relatively easy to follow by someone familiar with Java.

The following Java interface extract taken from the Agency bean in the case study

```
public interface Agency extends javax.ejb.EJBObject
{
    String getAgencyName() throws java.rmi.RemoteException;

    Collection findAllApplicants() throws java.rmi.RemoteException;
    void createApplicant(String login, String name, String email)
            throws java.rmi.RemoteException, agency.DuplicateException,
                    javax.ejb.CreateException;
    void deleteApplicant (String login) throws java.rmi.RemoteException,
                                        agency.NotFoundException;

    ...
}
```

19

is equivalent to the following IDL module:

```
module agency {
    interface Agency: ::javax::ejb::EJBObject {

        readonly attribute ::CORBA::WStringValue agencyName;
        ::java::util::Collection findAllApplicants( );
        void createApplicant(
            in ::CORBA::WStringValue arg0,
            in ::CORBA::WStringValue arg1,
            in ::CORBA::WStringValue arg2 ) raises (
            ::javax::ejb::CreateEx,
            ::agency::DuplicateEx );
        void deleteApplicant(
            in ::CORBA::WStringValue arg0 ) raises (
            ::agency::NotFoundEx );
    …
};
```

As you can see, there is a strong similarity between the syntax of the two definitions; this similarity has been emphasized by using the full Java class names in the first extract. For example, the Java class `javax.ejb.EJBObject` maps onto the IDL class `javax::ejb::EJBObject`.

After you have an IDL interface, you compile it to produce a client stub and an object skeleton. It is through the stub and skeleton that clients and objects communicate. The OMG provides a number of standard mappings that map CORBA IDL to other programming languages. Examples of these languages include

- Java
- Python
- Smalltalk
- COBOL
- C++

Using the Sun Microsystems' Java IDL tools, you can write, instantiate, and consume distributed objects that comply with CORBA. The J2SE SDK provides tools for mapping between IDL and Java interfaces so you do not have to write or even understand IDL files.

If you want to use CORBA to access a service, the service provider will supply the IDL file for the interface to that service. Once you have an IDL definition of a service, you can use the J2SE supplied `idl2j` utility to generate an equivalent Java interface definition for that service.

With the Java interface for the service, you can write client programs to communicate with the server, as described next in the "RMI over IIOP example" section.

The opposite is also possible. If you have a Java service, you can make this available to non-Java clients by supplying an IDL file for your service's interface. The rmic compiler supplied with the J2SE SDK can be run with the -idl option to generate an IDL file from a Java interface. The rmic compiler is discussed further in the section "Using RMI over IIOP" but as an illustration of its use, the following command

```
rmic -idl agency.Agency
```

was used to generate the previous IDL example.

Using RMI over IIOP

Remote Method Invocation (RMI) is a Java-specific distributed-object system that allows you to create and use remote objects. For example, a Java client program running on one host can obtain a reference to an RMI service running on another host. Once the client program has the remote reference, it can invoke the methods of the remote object as if it were a local object.

As with CORBA applications, you write remote interfaces for an object and generate stubs and skeletons. Also like CORBA, RMI allows a client and a remote object to communicate through client stubs and server skeletons. The stub exposes the methods of the remote object, and the client makes requests against the stub. These requests are forwarded to the server and passed through the server skeleton to the remote object. Unlike CORBA, Java over RMI uses Java interfaces and not IDL files to define and use the remote service.

The original form of RMI used a proprietary protocol, Java Remote Method Protocol (JRMP), to allow objects to communicate. To support interoperability with CORBA, RMI was augmented to use IIOP as well as JRMP; EJB components use RMI-IIOP for client/server communication. The next example application will use RMI over IIOP to show how easy it is to write CORBA-compatible client and server classes.

The RMI over IIOP example allows a remote user to enter a name; the local server prefixes this name with hello and returns the string to the client. At a high-level, the process to achieve this is quite straightforward:

1. Create an interface for the remote object.

2. Write a Java server to implement the interface.

3. Use rmic to generate IIOP stubs and skeletons.

19

4. Use the CORBA naming service to advertise and look up the server.

5. Write a client to look up the service name and call methods on the remote server object.

Listing 19.2 shows the code for the interface for the remote object. As you can see, the interface is quite straightforward, but there are a couple of points to note. The first is that the interface must extend `java.rmi.Remote`. The second is that all methods that the interface declares must throw a `RemoteException`.

LISTING 19.2   `HelloUser.java`

```
import javax.rmi. ProtableRemoteObject;
import java.rmi.Remote;

public interface HelloUser extends Remote {
    public String sayHello(String s) throws RemoteException;
}
```

You must now create the implementation of this interface. Naturally, this implementation class must implement the `HelloUser` interface, but it must also extend `javax.rmi.PortableRemoteObject`. This class provides the server object with much of the basic functionality needed to support CORBA integration. Additionally, all of the class constructors must throw a `RemoteException`. The example server is shown in Listing 19.3.

LISTING 19.3   RMI over IIOP Server HelloUserImpl.java

```
import java.rmi.server.UnicastRemoteObject;
import java.rmi.*;
import javax.naming.*;
import javax.rmi.*;

public class HelloUserImpl extends PortableRemoteObject implements HelloUser {

    // Constructer msut throw RemoteException
    public HelloUserImpl() throws RemoteException {
    }

    public String sayHello(String name) throws RemoteException {
        System.out.println("sayHello "+name);
        return "Hello "+name;
    }
}
```

LISTING 19.3 continued

```
public static void main(String args[]) {
    try {
        HelloUserImpl hui = new HelloUserImpl();

        Context ctx = new InitialContext();
        ctx.rebind("HelloUser",hui);
        System.out.println("Registered");
    }
    catch (Exception e) {
        System.out.println(e.getMessage());
    }
}
}
```

RMI over IIOP uses JNDI (see Day 3,"Naming and Directory Services") to register the service name. The naming service implementation must be a CORBA naming service. A suitable CORBA Object Naming (COSNaming) Service is supplied with the J2SE; you don't need a J2EE server to work with RMI-IIOP as it is part of the JRE.

Before you can run the server example, you must use the rmic compiler supplied with the J2SE SDK to generate the RMI over IIOP skeleton and stub classes. The rmic compiler takes the server class name as a parameter and requires the -iiop switch for generating RMI over IIOP stub files. Following the directory layout scheme of the case study code you will need to enter the following command (from within the Day19/examples directory):

```
rmic -iiop -classpath classes -d classes HelloUserImpl
```

The command creates the class files HelloUserImpl_Tie (the skeleton) used by the server, and HelloUserImpl_Stub (the stub) used by the client. You have now generated all the files you require to run the server.

To run the hello service example, you must start the COSNaming service by entering the command:

```
tnameserv -ORBInitialPort 1050
```

This will tie up the current command line window so you will need to open a second window for the HelloUserImpl server.

The tnameserv application is provided with the JRE and by default runs the name service on port 900. As port 900 is a privileged port it is common practice to supply the command line argument -ORBInitialPort 1050 to run the service on the non-privileged port 1050.

19

As discussed on Day 3 you will need to set the JNDI properties for your `HelloUserImpl` server. The `jndi.properties` file supplied in the Day 19 examples directory contains suitable values for use with the JRE COSNaming service running on port 1050.

NOTE

> If port 1050 on your system is used by another application choose, any free port above 1024 for your service. You will need to update the `jndi.proper-ties` file in the `Day19/examples` directory to reflect the changed port number.

Once the COSNaming service is running, you can start the example `HelloUserImpl` server. Windows users will need to enter

```
java –classpath .;classes HelloUserImpl
```

Solaris/Linux users should enter

```
java –classpath .:classes HelloUserImpl
```

This will tie up the current command line window so you will need to open another window for the `HelloUser` client.

The client code is very simple; it uses JNDI to look up the server object example and then calls the required business methods. A simple client is shown in Listing 19.4.

LISTING 19.4   `HelloUserClient.java`

```java
import java.rmi.*;
import javax.naming.*;
import javax.rmi.*;

public class HelloUserClient {
    public static void main(String args[]) {
        if (args.length>1) {
            System.err.println("Usage: java HelloUserClient");
        }
        try {
            Context ctx = new InitialContext();
            Object obj = ctx.lookup("HelloUser");
            HelloUser hu =
➥ (HelloUser)PortableRemoteObject.narrow(obj,HelloUser.class);
            String reply = hu.sayHello(args.length==1?args[0]:"unknown");
            System.out.println (reply);
        }
        catch (Exception ex) {
```

LISTING 19.4 continued

```
            System.out.println(ex);
        }
    }
}
```

This client is functionally no different from the EJB clients you have seen in examples from previous days in this book. You can now run the client program from the command line.

Windows users should enter

```
java -classpath .;classes HelloUserClient <name>
```

Solaris/Linux users should enter

```
java -classpath .:classes HelloUserClient <name>
```

The RMI-IIOP stub files previously generated using the `rmic` compiler must be in your client's CLASSPATH.

As you run the client you will see a diagnostic message displayed on the server's window as well as the reply message displayed in the client's window.

If you would rather use the supplied `asant` build files to run this example from the `Day19/examples` directory, enter the following `asant` commands to generate the stub files:

```
asant rmic
```

To start the COSNaming service, type

```
asant tnameserv
```

In a separate window start the `HelloUserImpl` server:

```
asant HelloUserImpl
```

In yet another window run the HelloUserClient application:

```
asant HelloUserImpl
```

Finally, to shut down the COSNaming service and your `HelloUserImpl` server, simply type Control-C in the appropriate window, or just close the window.

19

Introducing JNI

The Java Native Interface (JNI) allows you to write Java programs that utilize code written in programming languages other than Java. There are several scenarios where it is preferable or necessary to use non-Java code:

- When you require functionality not supported by the standard Java class library. For example, you may need to access parts of the Win32 API.

- When you want to reuse a library or application already written in another programming language. For example, many organizations possess large legacy C libraries.

- When you want to use features or capabilities of another programming language not readily available in Java.

JNI allows you to write code that supports these scenarios. You can use JNI to declare native methods, and implement the methods bodies in native code, such as C or C++. These native methods can use Java objects and methods in the same way that Java code uses them. Specifically, both native methods and Java methods can create and share Java objects. A native method can also invoke Java methods. For example, Figure 19.6 shows a native method invoking a Java method and passing parameters to it. The Java method performs some processing of the parameters, and returns the result to the native method.

FIGURE 19.6

Native method invoking a Java method.

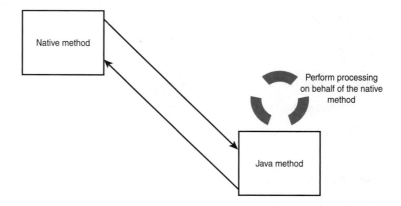

Beyond these interoperability aspects, JNI allows you to perform further tasks including the following:

- Throwing and catching exceptions from a native method to be handled in the Java caller.

- Through the Invocation API, you can embed the JVM into native applications.

- Special JNI functions allow native methods to load Java classes and obtain class information.

- Native methods can use JNI to perform runtime type checking.

A full exploration of JNI is beyond the scope of this book; however, today's lesson aims to provide you with enough information to decide when you might find JNI of use. For further information on the features of JNI, please refer to Sun Microsystems' JNI specification. To complete your introduction to JNI, today's lesson shows you how to write a simple JNI application—namely, Hello World. The example uses a native C function. Although you do not need to know C to understand this example, you will need a C compiler and be able to create a shared library if you want to follow the steps outlined here. Figure 19.7 shows the six steps you will follow to write the application.

NOTE

> The Web site accompanying this book does not include complete asant build file targets for the JNI example because the name and location of the C compiler will vary from one system to another.

FIGURE 19.7

Creating a JNI application.

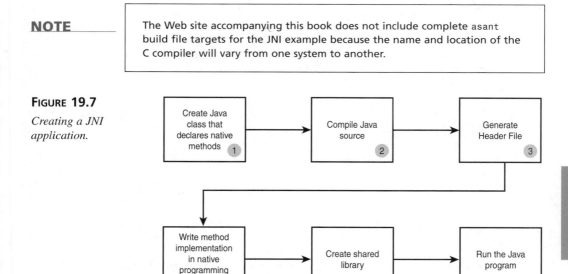

19

As Figure 19.7 shows, the first step is to create a Java class that declares the native method. To do this, declare your class and provide the method signature for the native method. Notice that the code uses the native modifier to indicate to the compiler that the method implementation is a programming language other than Java:

```
class HelloWorld {
    public native void displayHelloWorld();
    ...
}
```

Later, when you write the native code, you will compile it into a shared library. To allow the JVM to load this library into the Java class, you use the loadLibrary() method of the System class in the context of a static initializer. The method takes a single parameter—a string that is the name of the library to load. You only need to pass the root of the library name, because the method modifies the name to suit the current platform. For example, it will use hello.dll on Windows or libhello.so on Solaris/Linux:

```
static {
    System.loadLibrary("hello");
}
```

Finally, you must write the Java main() method in the same way as you would for any other Java class. Listing 19.5 shows the completed code for this class.

LISTING 19.5   HelloWorld.java

```
Package hello;

class HelloWorld {
    public native void displayHelloWorld();
    static {
        System.loadLibrary("hello");
    }

    public static void main (String args[]) {
        HelloWorld hw=new HelloWorld();
        hw.displayHelloWorld();
    }
}
```

For step 2, you compile in the same manner as any other Java class using the javac utility.

Step 3 for creating a JNI application is to generate the header file for the native method using the javah utility with the -jni option. By default, javah creates a C header file for each class listed on the command line and puts the file in the current directory. You can use the -d and -classpath options to javah to specify a CLASSPATH and target directory (just like javac). To generate the header file example, issue the following command (from within the Day19/examples directory):

```
javah -jni -classpath classes -d src hello.HelloWorld
```

The -jni switch instructs javah that it should output a header file for use with JNI. This is now the default behavior in Java 1.2 and later, but earlier versions required the switch. The header file, in this case, is stored in the src directory. You don't need to look at this generated header file, but if you want to open it up in a text editor, the native method signature is as follows:

```
Java_hello_HelloWorld_displayHelloWorld (JNIEnv *, jobject);
```

All generated method signatures follow the same format:

```
Java_packagename_classname_methodname
```

In this application, you will write the native method implementation after writing the Java class file, but in reality you may already have native methods you want to use. In this instance, you must ensure that the native method signature (in the method implementation in native code) matches the method signature in the generated header file.

Now you must write the native implementation of the method. The code in this application is written in C. The code (shown in Listing 19.6) begins by including three header files—jni.h, hello_HelloWorld.h, and stdio.h. All native implementations must include jni.h because this provides information that allows the native language to interact with the Java runtime. You should find this file in the include directory in your JDK. You include hello_HelloWorld.h because this is the header file that you just generated. Finally, you include stdio.h because the printf function (you use this to print Hello world) is contained within this library.

Because this is not a C tutorial, there is only one other thing to note about the code. You can see that the method accepts two parameters of the types JNIEnv and jobject. All native methods must accept these parameters. The first, JNIEnv, is an interface pointer that allows the native code to access any parameters your Java code passes to it. The second parameter, jobject, references the calling object (in other words the this object).

LISTING 19.6 HelloWorld.c

```c
#include <jni.h>
#include "hello_HelloWorld.h"
#include <stdio.h>

JNIEXPORT void JNICALL
Java_hello_HelloWorld_displayHelloWorld (JNIEnv *env, jobject obj)
{
    printf("Hello world\n");
    return;
}
```

Now that you have written the native code, the second-to-last step shown in Figure 19.7 is to compile the header and implementation file into a shared library by using your C

19

compiler. The shared library must have the same name that was used in `loadLibrary()` method in the Java class—namely, `libhello.so` or `hello.dll`. The actually command for this operation depends on the C compiler that you use; the JDK does not provide such a compiler.

To run your application the JVM has to be able to find the shared library. On a Unix system, you must place the `libhello.so` file in a directory included in the `LD_LIBRARY_PATH` environment variable. On a Windows system, place the `hello.dll` in the current directory or in a directory listed in the `PATH` environment variable.

Run the application as you would any other Java application:

```
java hello.HelloWorld
```

When the code executes, the JVM loads the shared library into the Java class. The `main()` method of the Java class invokes the `displayHelloWorld()` method of the native class, which in turn prints Hello world to the standard output.

This example has shown you how to use JNI in a very simple situation. In reality, you may have to integrate large amounts of code using JNI, so standalone command-line applications will certainly be unsuitable for use in the J2EE arena. A viable approach to making legacy code available to J2EE components is to wrap the code using JNI (as you did in the example application). Then, export the code as an RMI remote object, as shown previously. This approach allows J2EE components to interact directly with RMI objects, thus abstracting the underlying legacy code.

NOTE
Enterprise JavaBeans are not permitted to use JNI. The usual approach to accessing native code from an EJB is to wrap an RMI-IIOP service around the native code and use this service from within the EJB.

Summary

In today's lesson, you saw how you can integrate J2EE applications with legacy and non-Java systems. The lesson illustrated the J2EE Connector architecture, including the roles and contracts it defines. Building on this, you learned about the Common Client Interface and then studied an application that utilized it.

The lesson continued by providing you with a high-level introduction to CORBA. You then learned how Java's RMI over IIOP technology allows you to interoperate with CORBA objects.

Finally, you learned how to use the Java Native Interface (JNI) to provide seamless interaction between Java applications and non-Java code, whether it was a lower-level language, a legacy library, or an application written in a non-Java programming language.

There were many aspects to today's lesson, and this breadth meant that it was not possible to provide a complete reference to each of the technologies. However, hopefully it has provided you with enough information on how and why you use these technologies.

Q&A

Q What is the role of a resource adapter in the J2EE Connector architecture?

A A resource adapter is a software driver that acts as a bridge between an EIS and a J2EE container. The J2EE Connector architecture specification defines the relationship between the EIS and an application server through the system contract. The system contract dictates the responsibilities of both parties with regard to connection pooling, transaction management, and security. These operations are transparent to application components, which simply invoke functions on the EIS via an API exposed by the resource adapter.

Q I have a connection to an EIS, but I can't invoke its functions. What am I missing?

A After you establish a connection to an EIS, you must create an `Interaction` object. All EIS functions are invoked through the `Interaction` object.

Q Which Java technologies allow me to consume CORBA objects?

A Two Java technologies allow you to consume CORBA objects—Java IDL and RMI over IIOP. To use Java IDL, you write a remote object's interface in IDL. RMI over IIOP uses the Java-specific RMI technology. Here you write a remote object's interface and then use the RMI compiler to generate stubs and skeletons for use with IIOP, a CORBA transport protocol.

Q I have legacy code written in C that I would like to access remotely. How might I do this?

A You can wrap C code using JNI. After you wrap the code, you can export it as an RMI object, which a client can access remotely.

Exercises

Today's exercise, like that of Day 1, "The Challenge of N-Tier Development," is theoretical rather than practical. Your online sales department is having trouble piecing together

19

all the different elements of the architecture of an e-commerce system. At the heart of the system is a J2EE server. Underlying this there is

- An extensive legacy C library that provides a number of cryptographic functions the system requires
- An ERP that is used for managing customer service

In addition, the application must automatically forward orders to two of the company's suppliers. The first provides a public interface through the use of CORBA objects, and the second through RMI.

Devise a suitable architecture for his e-commerce system. Create a visual representation of the architecture, ensuring that you highlight any J2EE components, the legacy and non-Java elements, and customers and suppliers. Briefly justify your choice of architecture.

DAY 20

Using RPC-Style Web Services with J2EE

As you saw yesterday, there are many ways of integrating existing and third-party applications and components with J2EE applications. However, the plethora of integration mechanisms has long been an issue. It would be better if there were a more consistent way of integrating applications. Additionally, expectations have increased around the capability to integrate applications that span organizations—particularly across the common communication medium of the Internet. Web Services provide a flexible and powerful integration mechanism that can be used to expose existing functionality and components to other organizations or new applications. Today and tomorrow, you will see how you can use Web Service protocols to build bridges between J2EE application components and any other platforms, applications, or components that support those Web Service protocols.

Web Services are seen by many as the next wave of the Internet revolution. The vision is of a Web as rich with functionality as the current Web is with information. The challenge is to expose this functionality in a consistent and usable way.

Today, you learn about

- The concepts underlying Web Services and how Web Services fit with J2EE
- Implementing RPC-style Web Service clients and servers
- Exposing session EJBs as Web Services

First, you need to understand why you would use Web Services.

The aim of the last two days was to describe how to use J2EE technologies to implement and access a Web Service. This chapter will give an overview of how Web Service interactions work and will show how you can use JAX-RPC to generate and consume SOAP messages based on a WSDL interface.

NOTE

> Before proceeding further, please be aware that the subject of Web Services is in itself very large, and there are many books dedicated to this popular topic. Today and tomorrow are intended to give you a start into using Web Services in Java and with J2EE technologies. However, it is not possible to answer every question or pursue every topic. If you would like to find out more about Java and Web Services after you have read through the material in this book, try the following URLs:
>
> - Sun Java Web Services—http://java.sun.com/webservices/
> - IBM DeveloperWorks—http://www-106.ibm.com/developerworks/webservices/
> - Apache XML—http://xml.apache.org/
> - ZapThink—http://www.zapthink.com/
> - Web Services Articles and Information—http://www.webservices.org
> - ebXML home and resources—http://www.ebxml.org

Web Service Overview

This first section provides the underlying information and concepts required to successfully implement Web Services. Before employing Web Services, you should understand which problems they are designed to solve and the motivation behind them. This should ensure that you apply Web Services in appropriate places in your application.

What Is a Web Service?

A *Web Service* is essentially an application component that can be accessed using Web protocols and data encoding mechanisms—primarily HTTP and XML. In some cases, this is a third-party service hosted remotely. A Web Service differs from a traditional component in several ways, not only in the protocols used to access it. Under the component model, a currency conversion component could bring with it a file containing a fixed set of currency conversion rates that must be updated regularly. However, it would be up to you (the component user) to ensure that this information is updated. On the other hand, a Web Service is (or should be) a "living" entity, such that it brings with it any data and "back-end" functionality it requires. Unlike the component, a currency conversion Web Service takes responsibility for any updating of data or functionality. Your application simply uses the conversion service and leaves the details of obtaining the latest data and subsidiary services to those who implement and host the service.

Similarly, a Web Service can represent a courier service or a credit-card processing service. Again, you do not need to concern yourself with how the service is implemented, simply the results of using the service. Many types of Web Services are appearing that provide a sliding scale of functionality from low-level infrastructure to high-level business services.

Applications can be built from services in a similar way to building applications from components. You will combine standard services (such as credit-card authorization) with custom code to create your desired application.

As a software developer, you might write Web Services for others to use. In this case you would

1. Decide what functionality you wish to expose as a service.
2. Implement the service being offered.
3. Describe the service being offered.
4. Publish the description.
5. Inform direct consumers of your Web Service that it is available (or wait for them to discover it).

Alternatively, you may use Web Services as part of your application as follows:

1. Discover an interesting service.
2. Retrieve the description.
3. Plug it into your application.
4. Use the service as the application executes.

This all sounds very easy, but you need a ubiquitous framework for Web Services to stop this from sliding into chaos. The key factor in delivering such a framework is the widespread agreement to use common, Web-based protocols. In the first instance, this comes down to the use of the Simple Object Access Protocol (SOAP), under which XML-encoded messages are sent over some form of transport mechanism—usually HTTP.

20

SOAP is the way in which Web Services communicate. Other protocols are also required to deliver the full framework, and you will encounter these protocols over the course of the next two days.

Why Use Web Services?

Web Services bring similar advantages to the use of components. Using a service allows you to take advantage of another organization's expertise in, say, credit-card processing, without you having to become a specialist in it yourself. The service model enables you to use the most powerful and up-to-date functionality by connecting to a remote running service.

Although a service-based approach to application development is not a new concept, it has traditionally presented difficult challenges:

- Interoperability between different distribution mechanisms, such as CORBA, RMI, and DCOM.
- Application integration, including legacy systems, cross-vendor, and cross-version.
- Web-based business requires cross-organization development and high flexibility to accommodate a rapid rate of change, and safe operation through company firewalls.

Web Services can provide a consistent, cross-organization, cross-vendor framework that will speed up the integration of applications and application components. By selecting existing, widely-used standards, the Web Service framework removes many barriers to integration that existed when using other frameworks. The Web Service model is language- and platform-neutral, so developers anywhere can potentially build and consume Web Services.

Probably the most important factor of all is that all the major application, platform, and technology vendors have adopted the Web Service concept and the associated protocols. This means that Web Services will form a large part of application development over the next few years.

Web Service Technologies and Protocols

The following are some of the more important protocols, technologies, and standards in Web Services:

- **The Simple Object Access Protocol (SOAP)**—Combines XML and Multipurpose Internet Mail Extensions (MIME) to create an extensible packaging format. The SOAP envelope can be used to contain either RPC-style or message-style (document-centric) service invocations. A SOAP message can be carried over many transport mechanisms, including HTTP, SMTP, and traditional messaging transports. Although SOAP began its life outside the World Wide Web Consortium (W3C), ongoing work on SOAP can be found at `http://www.w3.org/2002/ws/`. This includes the latest working drafts of the 1.2 specifications, as well as a link to the version 1.1 specification.

- **The Web Services Description Language (WSDL)**—It is an XML vocabulary used to describe Web Services. It defines operations, data types, and binding information. The WSDL specification can be found at `http://www.w3.org/TR/wsdl`.

- **Universal Description, Discovery, and Integration (UDDI)**—Provides a model for organizing, registering, and accessing information about Web Services. The UDDI specifications can be found at `http://www.uddi.org/`.

- **The Web Service Flow Language (WSFL) and Web Service Collaboration Language (WSCL)**—These are concerned with describing the workflow between services so that their relationships can be encapsulated as part of an application. The description of interactions between Web Services is also described as choreography. More information on WSFL can be found at `http://xml.coverpages.org/wsfl.html`. A W3C working group on choreography has been formed and can be monitored at `http://www.w3.org/2002/ws/chor/`.

- **Electronic Business XML (ebXML)**—Provides a framework for e-commerce that includes the inter-application workflow and the description and discovery of services. It uses SOAP as its transport mechanism but does not directly use WSDL, UDDI, or WSFL. ebXML is a joint initiative between OASIS and the United Nations CEFACT group. The set of ebXML specifications can be found at `http://www.ebXML.org/`.

Web Service Architecture

The idealized interaction between a Web Service–based application and the Web Service itself is shown in Figure 20.1. The overall interaction is very similar to the way that a J2EE client uses an EJB. When a Web Service is created, information about its interface and location are stored in a registry. The Web Service consumer can then retrieve this information and use it to invoke the Web Service.

Some of this consumer/service interaction takes place at design and development time. The interface and service contract information can be registered, regardless of whether the service is active. This information is required by the application builder to create code that uses the Web Service in his application. At runtime, the application can look up the precise location of the Web Service to locate it, very much like a traditional RPC mechanism, such as RMI.

20

FIGURE 20.1

Interaction between Web Service, registry, and service consumer.

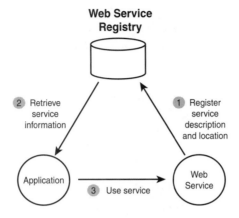

There are several variations on this interaction. A Web Service can be used entirely dynamically in that the service description is discovered and invoked dynamically. Alternatively, the location information discovered at design time as part of the service description can be bound into the client application so that it has no need of the registry at runtime. Indeed, the information about the Web Service might not even be registered in any form of registry. The creator of a Web Service can easily provide service descriptions to potential clients by attaching the necessary WSDL documents to an email message.

Similarly, the way in which an application interacts with a Web Service depends on the service. Some services might provide an RPC-style interface based on request/response operations. In this case, the interface to the Web Service will look like a traditional Remote Procedure Call (RPC) interface as found in Java's RMI. The interaction of an RPC-style Web Service and its clients still uses SOAP messages "under the covers" but it provides a more familiar model for developers to work with. Conversely, other services might work in a message-oriented style by exchanging XML-based documents. In either case, the interaction can be synchronous or asynchronous. There is nothing to stop a Web Service implementation from offering out its services in all four combinations (synchronous RPC-style, asynchronous RPC-style, synchronous message-oriented, and asynchronous message-oriented).

Service developers will define an interface for their services using a description mechanism such as WSDL. This can be based on an existing service implementation, or the service can be developed after the interface is defined.

Application developers will take the service description and write code based on this. In many cases, a client-side proxy will be created for the services and the application will interact with this proxy. However, the precise details of this are left to the client-side developer.

The service implementations will take a variety of forms. On the server-side, an adapter and router will be required to accept inbound SOAP messages and dispatch them to the appropriate service implementation. This performs the role of the Object Request Broker (ORB) in CORBA and RMI or the Service Control Manager (SCM) under DCOM.

The services being invoked can be of varying granularity. You can use Web Service mechanisms to expose fine-grained services, such as currency conversion. However, Web Service protocols are much more suited to exposing coarse-grained services. In some cases these services can represent a whole application, such as an ERP system.

Although much about the Web Service paradigm will seem familiar to you, the use of Web Services, especially third-party Web Services, does bring some extra considerations for developers:

- The fact that the service is hosted elsewhere will impact testing, security, availability, and scalability. Service-Level Agreements (SLAs) will need to be defined for all services used.

- The providers of an external service will have to be paid somehow. There will be associated authentication requirements so that use of the service can be tracked by the providers.

Web Services for J2EE

With the advent of J2EE 1.4, Web Services are now an integral part of J2EE. This section examines at a high level how Web Services fit with the J2EE model and how they can be used with J2EE components.

J2EE Web Service Architecture

J2EE can can be both a provider and consumer of Web Services. Figure 20.2 shows the overall architecture, with business logic being provided by EJBs (although other classes could be used). The functionality offered by the business components will be described by a WSDL document (or similar), and this can then be used to build clients that use this functionality.

SOAP RPC calls will be handled by a router component based around a servlet. This will dispatch calls to the associated EJB or other component. The router that handles document-centric SOAP messages will also be servlet based. In either case, the precise nature of the servlet will depend on the type of underlying transport over which the messages are sent.

20

The J2EE business components may themselves use other Web Services to help them deliver business functionality. In this case, the components will take advantage of the client-side Web Service APIs to call out to these Web Services.

FIGURE 20.2

*Overall J2EE Web
Service architecture.*

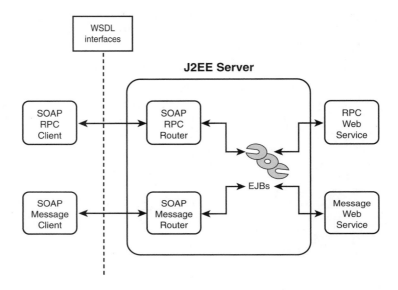

The Web Service runtime will consist of a variety of filters, providers, and helpers that will be used in combination with the routing servlets and basic, low-level APIs. These helpers will deliver additional value on top of the basic APIs, such as ebXML quality of service guarantees.

Tools and Technologies

A number of JSRs in the Java Community Process (JCP) have defined the Web Service APIs and architecture used by J2EE. These include the following:

- **JSR101, the Java APIs for XML-based RPC (JAX-RPC)**—JAX-RPC provides APIs for invoking RPC-based Web Services over SOAP. It defines how interactions should take place and provides the basis for automated tools to produce stubs and skeletons. It also specifies type mapping and marshalling requirements between Java and XML Schema types.

- **JSR067, the Java APIs for XML Messaging (JAXM), and the SOAP with Attachments API for Java (SAAJ)**—These APIs are used to create document-centric SOAP messages that can be exchanged either synchronously or asynchronously. Vendors can provide messaging profiles on top of this that offer value-added services, such as ebXML.

- **JSR093, the Java API for XML Registries (JAXR)**—JAXR defines a two-tier API for accessing registry information stored in XML format. This is targeted at Web Service-related registries, such as UDDI registries and ebXML registry/repositories, as well as other generic XML registries.

- **JSR109, Implementing Enterprise Web Services**—JSR109 does not define any Java APIs. Instead, it defines how J2EE implementations should work with JAX-RPC, SAAJ, JAXM, and JAXR. This includes everything from the schema for XML-based configuration files to the overall programming model envisioned.

All these JSRs have now reached their first release, but work is still ongoing to extend and maintain the capabilities defined in them. The contents and status of these JSRs are available through the JCP Web site at `http://www.jcp.org/`.

The role that each of these APIs plays in the J2EE Web Service architecture is shown in Figure 20.3. All these APIs are included in J2EE 1.4 (as defined in JSR151) and form part of the J2EE Reference Implementation (RI).

FIGURE 20.3

J2EE Web Service APIs.

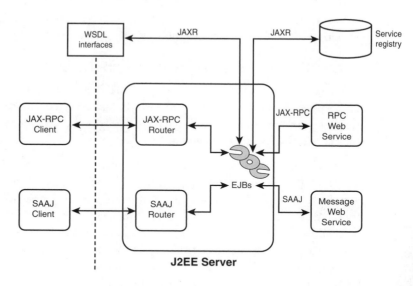

As well as implementations of J2EE 1.4, there are various other sources of Java-based Web Service functionality:

- The Apache Software Foundation provides the Axis toolkit for the creation and use of SOAP-based Web Services that can be deployed in most servlet containers. Axis implements the JAX-RPC and SAAJ APIs and continues to track updates to the associated JSRs as well as the progress of SOAP 1.2. The predecessor to Axis was Apache's SOAP toolkit 2.2. The Axis toolkit can be found at `http://xml.apache.org/axis`.

- For several years, IBM has delivered its its Web Services Toolkit (WSTK) through their Alphaworks developer site. This toolkit has subsequently evolved into the Emerging Technologies Toolkit (ETTK). The ETTK provides a set of tools and APIs on which to build Web Services. The ETTK conforms to the relevant JSRs but also acts as a platform for early delivery of new Web Service APIs such as security and routing. The ETTK integrates with the Apache Tomcat servlet engine and IBM's WebSphere application server. IBM's ETTK and can be found at `http://www.alphaworks.ibm.com/tech/ettk`.

- The reference implementations of the individual APIs are available as part of the Java Web Services Developer Pack (JWSDP), along with other Java APIs for the manipulation of XML. The JWSDP can be found at `http://java.sun.com/webservices`.

If you want to investigate or use Web Service functionality in your applications, the appropriate choice will depend on the style and robustness you require.

Integrating Web Services with J2EE

Most development projects involve using or adapting existing functionality. Projects based on Web Services will be no different. In fact, a project can be specifically focused at exposing existing functionality to clients in the form of Web Services. So, how do you expose existing J2EE functionality as Web Services?

For a traditional J2EE application, business logic is contained in EJBs or plain old Java objects (POJOs). This functionality is usually made available to client applications through servlets and JSPs. If the clients are Web browsers, these Web components will generate and consume HTML. Similarly, if the clients are mobile applications, the Web components may generate and consume Wireless Markup Language (WML). However, these WML Web components share the same business logic—they just provide a different front end or channel for it. Web Service clients are no different in that respect from HTML or WML clients. The SOAP router servlet, together with helper classes, acts as a server-side wrapper for the business logic, delivering it to Web Service clients. This situation is shown in Figure 20.4.

FIGURE 20.4

Web Services are just another channel through which to access business functionality.

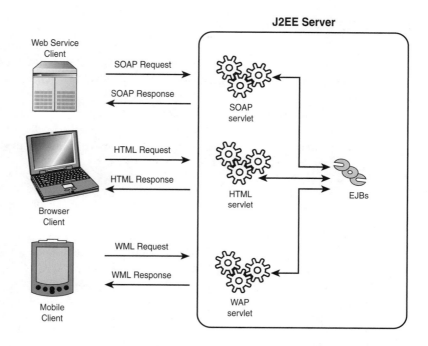

The other type of J2EE component in which application logic can be held is a servlet or JSP. You may ask how you would wrap this functionality for use as a Web Service. Well, the issue here is that many of the Web components in question are already acting as channels to some form of client (as shown in Figure 20.4). Consequently, wrapping them makes no sense. What you should do is create a replacement for such a Web component that is targeted at Web Service clients rather than Web browsers. If your Web components are well designed, you should be able to reuse the JavaBeans, servlet filters, and POJO helper classes as part of your Web Service implementation.

Creating a Web Service with JAX-RPC

As discussed earlier, the JAX-RPC specification defines how Web Service clients written in Java can make RPC-style calls on Web Services and how Web Services can be written in Java to receive such calls. The Implementing Enterprise Web Services specification defined in JSR109 describes how such Web Services and Web Service clients can be used as part of a J2EE application. Although it is possible to use other transport mechanisms and interaction styles, the main focus of JAX-RPC is for making synchronous calls on top of the SOAP transport. Hence, the remainder of today will focus on building clients and servers that take part in this type of exchange.

20

RPC-Oriented Web Services

Remote Procedure Calls (RPCs) made over Web-based protocols are essentially no different from those made over other protocols, such as IIOP, DCOM, or JRMP. The calls are usually synchronous (in other words, the client waits for the method to return before continuing). Zero or more parameters of varying types are passed into the call to provide information to process, and zero or more return values are generated to deliver the outputs of the remote method to the client. The remote method calls are delivered to some form of dispatcher at the remote server that determines which method should be called and arranges for the smooth flow of parameters and return values.

For RPC-style operation, SOAP implementations conform to the preceding description. The difference with SOAP (and other Web-based RPC mechanisms, such as XML-RPC) is that it uses standard, general-purpose transports, such as HTTP, together with a text-based method call description in XML. All the parameters and return values are encoded in XML as part of the SOAP body, while information about the service and method to call are provided in the transport header and possibly the SOAP header. When sent over HTTP, the SOAP header and body are wrapped in another XML document—the SOAP envelope—and this envelope forms the body of an HTTP POST request.

An HTTP-based SOAP message will be delivered to a SOAP router that takes the form of an HTTP servlet (for a Java implementation). The SOAP router will examine the HTTP and SOAP header information and decide how it should forward the message body. This will involve instantiating or calling a particular component or class that will receive the message. The SOAP router, or its helper classes, will also perform the conversion of the XML-based parameters into Java objects and primitives that can be passed as part of the service invocation. Figure 20.5 shows the operation of such a SOAP router. Note that the description of the Web Service is used by both the client and server to help determine the correct mapping between Java and XML for method calls and parameter types.

This is all good, but why go to this effort? Why not use an existing RPC mechanism, such as RMI, or just use HTTP itself?

The justification for not using RMI or CORBA to integrate applications relates to commonality and security. There are at least three different distributed object protocols (CORBA, RMI, and DCOM), each of which has its adherents. The use of HTTP and XML provides a common protocol that is not tied to any vendor. Also, the traditional RPC protocols listed have great difficulty in penetrating most firewalls (not surprising, given their capability to invoke random functionality). However, HTTP (and SMTP) has general right of access through most firewalls, which makes it easier to integrate applications across organizational boundaries (after the security questions are sorted out).

FIGURE 20.5

A Java-based SOAP router.

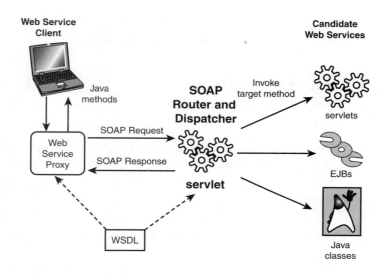

Although raw HTTP is a good transport, it was created to exchange simple HTML messages. This does not provide the sophistication required for a distributed invocation environment. The use of a defined XML message format brings structure to this environment and allows for the interoperability of Web Service clients and servers from different vendors—something that escaped CORBA until comparatively recently.

So, Web Service protocols have some large advantages over traditional RPC protocols. However, you need to be careful about where you apply Web Service protocols. Such protocols are primarily intended for the integration of coarse-grained components or application functionality. As mentioned earlier, this might be exposed at the same system boundary as an HTML interface on the same functionality. Internally, the system might use RMI CORBA or DCOM to distribute functionality across several tiers. This is fine; there is no need to replace all distribution mechanisms with Web Service protocols. Web Service interfaces should usually be exposed only at the system boundary, not within the system itself.

20

Now that you understand the architecture and motivation for RPC-style Web Services, you can create a Java-based Web Service client and server.

The JAX-RPC API

JAX-RPC defines a set of classes, interfaces, principles, and mechanisms for making SOAP-based RPC calls. The main parts are

- **Type conversion between Java types and XML types**—For simple types, such as strings and primitive types, very little work is required. More effort is required from either the tools or the developer when mapping more complex types between Java and XML.
- **Mapping between SOAP operations defined in WSDL and Java remote method calls**—Essentially, WSDL interfaces are represented in Java by Remote interfaces.
- **The server environment and how calls are received and directed**—The receiving Java class has access to particular information about the SOAP call provided through a service context. The lifecycle of a servlet-based service is defined.
- **A client- and server-side SOAP message handler mechanism similar in concept to servlet filters.**
- **Client programming model describing the relationship between interfaces and stubs, and how these are obtained in different environments such as J2SE and J2EE.**

The essential principle is that JAX-RPC tries to make the development of SOAP-based clients and servers fairly simple and intuitive for Java developers. To start your journey through Web Services, the first example is a simple, servlet-based JAX-RPC service and a standalone client for it.

Creating a Simple Service

NOTE

All the examples in the rest of this chapter refer to the J2EE Reference Implementation. However, the information required and the techniques used are common across all implementations of JAX-RPC. Basically, the tools might change but the artifacts and information you have to provide as a developer don't.

The initial service is servlet-based and will just pass strings back and forth to exchange greetings. After you are comfortable with this simple service, we will move on to look at how to provide a Web Service front-end for a session EJB.

Files and Tools

In common with other J2EE components, a J2EE-based Web Service implementation consists of multiple parts:

- A reference to the implementation of the functionality to be exposed by the Web Service, which can point to simple Java classes bundled with the component or which can refer to one or more EJBs
- Code that maps between the exposed functionality and the container—for example, skeletons (or ties) and serializers
- A WSDL definition of the interface implemented by the service
- Configuration files that tell the J2EE implementation more about how the service should be deployed and the services it requires from its container

A Web Service client has similar code and configuration files but does not carry an interface definition or service implementation information.

All the configuration files are encoded in XML. Some of them are reasonably simple and can easily be created by hand. Other files, such as the WSDL interface definition, are far more complex and will typically be generated by tools. The stubs and skeletons required will also be automatically generated. To generate the stubs, skeletons, and WSDL interface definition, we will use the wscompile tool provided as part of the J2EE Reference Implementation.

Defining the Interface and Implementation

As with RMI, a remote interface definition is central to the use of JAX-RPC. This interface is either written by a developer and then used to generate a WSDL file, or the Java interface is generated from a pre-provided WSDL file. In the examples we look at today, the WSDL file is generated from the Java interface definition. The Java interface definition must extend java.rmi.Remote and all methods must be declared as throwing java.rmi.RemoteException. The simple Web Service is based around a simple Java Remote interface, Greeting, containing a single method called sayHelloTo(). The sayHelloTo() method takes a single String parameter—the name of the person to greet—and returns the resultant greeting. The Greeting interface is shown in Listing 20.1.

20

LISTING 20.1   Interface for the Greeting Service (`Greeting.java`)

```
package wsexamples;

import java.rmi.Remote;
import java.rmi.RemoteException;

public interface Greeting extends Remote
{
    public String sayHelloTo(String name) throws RemoteException;
}
```

The `sayHelloTo()` method is the Web Service equivalent of the "Hello World!" program used as a first step in learning programming languages such as C and Java. In Web Service terms, the method is simple because it takes a single parameter and returns a single value. These values are both strings, and strings are easily marshaled between the on-the-wire XML representation used by SOAP and the internal `java.lang.String` type.

The `Greeting` interface is implemented by the `GreetingImplementation` class. The `sayHelloTo()` method simply appends the name passed in onto a suitable greeting and passes back the resultant string. The GreetingImplementation class is shown in Listing 20.2.

LISTING 20.2   Implementation of the Greeting Service (`GreetingImplementation.java`)

```
package wsexamples;

public class GreetingImplementation implements Greeting
{
    public String sayHelloTo(String name)
    {
        return "Hi there " + name;
    }
}
```

As you can see, there is nothing special about the `GreetingImplementation` class. If you did not know that `Greeting` was a `Remote` interface, the rest of the class gives you no indication. As stated earlier, this first example will be a servlet-based Web Service. However, there is no servlet definition in the interface or implementation. As the creation of a servlet to implement a given interface is something of a predictable task, all this can be automated. Think of the implementation class as being like the bean class in an EJB—it will get surrounded by "scaffolding" as it is deployed and configured. This "scaffolding" consists of the fixed infrastructure provided by J2EE, such as the SOAP routing servlet discussed earlier, and some files specifically generated for your service, such as the Web Service stub and skeleton files.

Web Service Compiler Configuration File

When you created EJBs earlier, you had to include various configuration files to tell the container about the EJB and its requirements. The same principle applies for a JAX-RPC Web Service. Somehow, a variety of artifacts must be created that describe the service for potential clients and help to integrate the service with its container. In the J2EE Reference Implementation, the main tool for this is wscompile. The wscompile tool can generate WSDL, server-side scaffolding, and client-side scaffolding. For the time being, you will concentrate on the WSDL and server-side scaffolding.

wscompile requires a variety of information about the artifacts you need to create. You define this information in an XML-encoded configuration file. The root element is configuration and its sole attribute indicates that the file conforms to the RI's JAX-RPC schema:

```
<configuration xmlns="http://java.sun.com/xml/ns/jax-rpc/ri/config">
```

Within this root element you will typically define one of two child elements:

- service—Contains information to help generate a WSDL file based on a Remote interface
- wsdl—Defines information about a Web Service definition from which a Remote interface is to be generated

The element you require will depend on whether you are starting from a Java interface definition or starting from WSDL. In this case, you will start from the code and generate the WSDL. Although this is convenient as a learning exercise, it is not the best practice to follow when creating industrial-strength Web Services. Some of the reasons for this are discussed in the section "Starting from WSDL" later today.

In this case, because you are generating a WSDL file from a Remote interface, you need a service element within the root. The attributes of this element define the following:

- The name of the service (name) that is to be defined in the WSDL description.
- The target namespace (targetNamespace) within which the service's messages and message parts are to be defined.
- The namespace (typeNamespace) within which the service's data types are to be defined.
- The package into which generated Java artifacts are to be placed (packageName). Because you are only defining a WSDL document at the moment, this is not used, but it must still be provided; otherwise, wscompile will fail.

20

The resultant element will look something like this:

```
<service name="GreetingService"
        targetNamespace="urn:J2EE21Examples"
        typeNamespace="urn:J2EE21ExamplesTypes"
        packageName="wsexamples"
>
```

Each service element can contain one or more interface elements. The interface element describes a Web Service endpoint that is exposed as part of the service. The name attribute defines the name of the Java interface that implements the methods to be exposed. This should be set to the fully qualified name of the interface you created earlier (you can also specify the name of the implementation, or servant, class using the servantName attribute although this does not affect the generation of the WSDL):

```
<interface name="wsexamples.Greeting"
servantName="wsexamples.GreetingImplementation"/>
```

Listing 20.3 shows a full wscompile configuration file that will generate the WSDL for the simple Greeting interface shown earlier.

LISTING 20.3   wscompile Web Service Configuration File (config-service.xml)

```
<?xml version="1.0" encoding="UTF-8"?>
<configuration
  xmlns="http://java.sun.com/xml/ns/jax-rpc/ri/config">
  <service
      name="GreetingService"
      targetNamespace="urn:J2EE21Examples"
      typeNamespace="urn:J2EE21ExamplesTypes"
      packageName="wsexamples">
      <interface name="wsexamples.Greeting"
servantName="wsexamples.GreetingImplementation"/>
  </service>
</configuration>
```

You define which artifacts you want wscompile to generate using command-line options. Once you have created the configuration file shown in Listing 20.3, you can use wscompile to generate the WSDL description and mapping file for the Greeting service.

Under Microsoft Windows:

```
wscompile -define -classpath %CLASSPATH%;classes -nd ws\generated -mapping
ws\generated\mapping.xml ws\config-service.xml
```

Under Unix:

```
wscompile -define -classpath $CLASSPATH:classes -nd ws/generated -mapping
ws/generated/mapping.xml ws/config-service.xml
```

The line shown assumes that the compiled classes for Greeting and GreetingImplementation reside in the classes subdirectory and that the configuration file is in the ws subdirectory. The -define flag indicates that you want just the service definition at the moment (no server or client artifacts), the -nd flag indicates that the resultant WSDL file should be placed in the ws/generated subdirectory, and the -mapping flag indicates where the generated mapping file is to be saved.

The code for all of today's examples is on the Web site that accompanies this book. You will find them in the examples directory for Day 20. With the code supplied on the accompanying Web site, you can use the following Ant command to build the supplied Greeting service, which includes the creation of the WSDL and the mapping file:

```
asant build
```

The WSDL File

The WSDL file generated by wscompile is shown in Listing 20.4. It is worth taking a few moments to study this information because it provides a good insight into the way that Web Services work.

LISTING 20.4   Generated GreetingService WSDL (GreetingService.wsdl)

```xml
<?xml version="1.0" encoding="UTF-8"?>

<definitions name="GreetingService"
             targetNamespace="urn:J2EE21Examples"
             xmlns:tns="urn:J2EE21Examples"
             xmlns="http://schemas.xmlsoap.org/wsdl/"
             xmlns:xsd="http://www.w3.org/2001/XMLSchema"
             xmlns:soap="http://schemas.xmlsoap.org/wsdl/soap/">
    <types/>
    <message name="Greeting_sayHelloTo">
        <part name="String_1" type="xsd:string"/>
    </message>
    <message name="Greeting_sayHelloToResponse">
        <part name="result" type="xsd:string"/>
    </message>
    <portType name="Greeting">
        <operation name="sayHelloTo" parameterOrder="String_1">
            <input message="tns:Greeting_sayHelloTo"/>
            <output message="tns:Greeting_sayHelloToResponse"/>
        </operation>
    </portType>
    <binding name="GreetingBinding" type="tns:Greeting">
        <soap:binding transport="http://schemas.xmlsoap.org/soap/http"
➥style="rpc"/>
            <operation name="sayHelloTo">
```

20

LISTING 20.4   continued

```
                <soap:operation soapAction=""/>
                <input>
                    <soap:body encodingStyle="http://schemas.xmlsoap.org/soap/
➡encoding/"
                               use="encoded"
                               namespace="urn:J2EE21Examples"/>
                </input>
                <output>
                    <soap:body encodingStyle="http://schemas.xmlsoap.org/soap/
➡encoding/"
                               use="encoded"
                               namespace="urn:J2EE21Examples"/>
                </output>
            </operation>
        </binding>
        <service name="GreetingService">
            <port name="GreetingPort" binding="tns:GreetingBinding">
                <soap:address location="REPLACE_WITH_ACTUAL_URL"/>
            </port>
        </service>
</definitions>
```

The document consists of the following sections:

- **The XML prolog (<?xml ...?>) and root element(definitions)**—The namespace declarations on the root element show that the operations defined here
  belong in the namespace urn:J2EE21Examples and that this namespace is also represented by the tns prefix. The default namespace declaration indicates that all
  unqualified elements and attributes come from the W3C's WSDL definitions. The
  xsd prefix denotes types from the W3C XML Schema definition, whereas the soap
  prefix denotes types from the SOAP schema.

- **The types section**—There are no complex types in the Greeting interface, so all
  the type definitions required come from the XML Schema. Hence, the types element is empty.

- **WSDL message definitions**—These define two matched messages: a request and a
  response. The request (Greeting_sayHelloTo) takes a single string parameter, and
  the response (Greeting_sayHelloToResponse) also returns a single string.

- **WSDL portType definitions**—A portType is the equivalent of an interface definition. It contains one or more operation definitions, which in turn are built from
  the message definitions in the document. In this case, there is a single operation
  defined in the Greeting called sayHelloTo. This consists of the two messages,
  Greeting_sayHelloToRequest and Greeting_sayHelloToResponse, seen earlier.

- **The `binding` element**—Called `GreetingBinding`, it indicates that clients can access the `Greeting` port type through the SOAP protocol. Now that you have an interface (`portType`), you can define the protocols over which that interface can be accessed. The WSDL `operation` is mapped to a SOAP `operation` with input and output `soap:body` elements defined to map the request and response.

  Within this WSDL binding, a SOAP binding (`soap:binding`) is defined— Because SOAP can work with a variety of underlying transports and it can work in an RPC-centric or document-centric way, the attributes on the `soap:binding` indicate that it is an RPC-style binding that uses HTTP.

- **Finally, an instance of the service is defined in the WSDL `service` element**—A WSDL `service` contains a list of WSDL `port` elements. Each `port` element defines a specific instance of a server that conforms to one of the WSDL `binding` elements defined earlier.

  Again, in the case of the simple `Greeting` service, the `service` element (named `GreetingService`) contains a single WSDL port called `GreetingPort`. This specifies that a server conforming to the `GreetingBinding` can be found at the SOAP `address` defined by the `location` attribute.

This is a very simple WSDL document defining a very simple service. WSDL documents are typically far longer and more complex. Because of this, WSDL is largely intended for manipulation by tools and applications.

By examining the WSDL document, you can see how the information defined in the `wscompile` configuration file forms part of the WSDL. The `targetNamespace` and `tns` prefix in the WSDL are associated with the `targetNamespace` defined in the configuration file. The name of the WSDL `service` comes from the `name` attribute of the `service` element in the configuration file. The WSDL `port` is formed by appending the string "Port" to the name of the `interface` defined as a child of the `service` element in the configuration file.

One thing to note about the generated WSDL is that it is not complete. All the relevant type definitions are there (none in this case, but you will see more later), as are the definitions of the operations and their parameters and the protocol bindings. However, in the SOAP `address` associated with the `port` element, there is no endpoint address (the `location` is set to "REPLACE WITH ACTUAL URL"). This is not surprising because this WSDL has been generated from a class on the disk and `wscompile` has no way of knowing where this service will be deployed. Part of the deployment process will involve filling out this WSDL endpoint information so that the WSDL can be employed by a Web Service client.

20

The Mapping File

The mapping file—mapping.xml—provides a link between information in the WSDL document and the Java code supplied to support the service defined. There is a 1-1 relationship between mapping files and WSDL documents, and there are other constraints on the WSDL to assist the mapping, such as there being only one service description in a WSDL file. A full list of these restrictions and a detailed description of the mapping file (termed the "JAX-RPC Mapping Deployment Descriptor") can be found in section 7.3 of the document Web Services for J2EE document that was produced by JSR109.

Thankfully, the mapping file for our simple Greeting service is itself simple. It starts with a standard prolog and the root element java-wsdl-mapping:

```
<?xml version="1.0" encoding="UTF-8"?>
<java-wsdl-mapping version="1.1"
                   xmlns="http://java.sun.com/xml/ns/j2ee"
                   xmlns: "xsi=http://www.w3.org/2001/XMLSchema-instance"
                   xsi:schemaLocation="http://java.sun.com/xml/ns/j2ee
                       http://www.ibm.com/webservices/xsd/j2ee_jaxrpc_
➥mapping_1_1.xsd">
```

Within the root, you define package-mapping elements that map the namespaces using the WSDL to Java packages in which you define your classes. For the simple service, you just need to indicate that the service defined in the WSDL document under the target namespace of urn:J2EE21Examples is associated with the code defined in the Java package wsexamples:

```
<package-mapping>
    <package-type>wsexamples</package-type>
    <namespaceURI>urn:J2EE21Examples</namespaceURI>
</package-mapping>
```

The remainder of the mapping file defines how the WSDL service, port and binding relate to the parts of the Java Greeting interface defined earlier. The full mapping file is shown in Listing 20.5.

LISTING 20.5 Mapping File for the Simple Greeting Service (mapping.xml)

```
<java-wsdl-mapping version="1.1"
                   xmlns="http://java.sun.com/xml/ns/j2ee"
                   xmlns:xsi="http://www.w3.org/2001/XMLSchema-instance"
                   xsi:schemaLocation="http://java.sun.com/xml/ns/j2ee
                       http://www.ibm.com/webservices/xsd/j2ee_jaxrpc_
➥mapping_1_1.xsd">
  <package-mapping>
    <package-type>wsexamples</package-type>
    <namespaceURI>urn:J2EE21ExamplesTypes</namespaceURI>
```

LISTING 20.5   continued

```
    </package-mapping>
    <package-mapping>
      <package-type>wsexamples</package-type>
      <namespaceURI>urn:J2EE21Examples</namespaceURI>
    </package-mapping>
    <service-interface-mapping>
      <service-interface>wsexamples.GreetingService</service-interface>
      <wsdl-service-name xmlns:serviceNS="urn:J2EE21Examples">
➥serviceNS:GreetingService</wsdl-service-name>
      <port-mapping>
        <port-name>GreetingPort</port-name>
        <java-port-name>GreetingPort</java-port-name>
      </port-mapping>
    </service-interface-mapping>
    <service-endpoint-interface-mapping>
      <service-endpoint-interface>wsexamples.Greeting</service-endpoint-interface>
      <wsdl-port-type xmlns:portTypeNS="urn:J2EE21Examples">portTypeNS:Greeting
➥</wsdl-port-type>
      <wsdl-binding xmlns:bindingNS="urn:J2EE21Examples">bindingNS:GreetingBinding
➥</wsdl-binding>
      <service-endpoint-method-mapping>
        <java-method-name>sayHelloTo</java-method-name>
        <wsdl-operation>sayHelloTo</wsdl-operation>
        <method-param-parts-mapping>
          <param-position>0</param-position>
          <param-type>java.lang.String</param-type>
          <wsdl-message-mapping>
            <wsdl-message xmlns:wsdlMsgNS="urn:J2EE21Examples">wsdlMsgNS:
➥Greeting_sayHelloTo</wsdl-message>
            <wsdl-message-part-name>String_1</wsdl-message-part-name>
            <parameter-mode>IN</parameter-mode>
          </wsdl-message-mapping>
        </method-param-parts-mapping>
        <wsdl-return-value-mapping>
          <method-return-value>java.lang.String</method-return-value>
          <wsdl-message xmlns:wsdlMsgNS="urn:J2EE21Examples">wsdlMsgNS:
➥Greeting_sayHelloToResponse</wsdl-message>
          <wsdl-message-part-name>result</wsdl-message-part-name>
        </wsdl-return-value-mapping>
      </service-endpoint-method-mapping>
    </service-endpoint-interface-mapping>
</java-wsdl-mapping>
```

20

Packaging and Deploying the Simple Web Service Using J2EE RI `deploytool`

This section shows how to deploy the simple Web Service to the J2EE RI. You will get the most out of this if you actually perform these steps (but if you're on a train or plane, just read the text and make do).

As usual, start up the PointBase database server and J2EE RI server before starting `deploytool`.

Creating the Web Service WAR

You will package up the Web Service in a WAR file, so choose File, New, Web Component to create a new one. Click Next to skip the introduction screen and move onto the WAR file creation screen. You will be creating a New Stand-Alone WAR Module so ensure that this option is selected. Next, under WAR Naming, browse to a location in which you wish to save your WAR file and provide "wsgreeting" as the File Name.

Now you can populate your WAR with the files you saw earlier. Under the Contents section, click the `Edit` button to display the Edit Contents of wsgreeting screen. Browse to find the class files (`Greeting.class` and `GreetingImplementation.class`), the WSDL file (`GreetingService.wsdl` – created in folder build/generated), and the mapping file (`mapping.xml` – created in folder build/generated). Add each of these files to the contents as shown in Figure 20.6 and click OK.

Your WAR file settings should look similar to those in Figure 20.7.

Click Next to move on to the Choose Component Type screen and select Web Services Endpoint. Click Next to move onto the Choose Service screen. Under the Service Definition, the WSDL File drop-down list should offer you the `GreetingService.wsdl` file and the Mapping File drop-down list should offer you the `mapping.xml` file. Select these two files so that your screen looks like that in Figure 20.8. You will see that the service name has been picked up from the WSDL file.

Now click Next to move onto the Component General Properties window. Select wsexamples.GreetingImplementation as your Service Endpoint Implementation (this will be offered from the drop-down list). Again, the fields will be populated based on the information in the file.

Click Next to move on to the Web Service Endpoint screen. Select wsexamples.Greeting as your Service Endpoint Interface. In the WSDL Port section, set the Namespace to be `urn:J2EE21Examples` and ensure that the `Local Part` becomes `GreetingPort` as shown in Figure 20.9.

FIGURE 20.6

Populating the Web Service WAR with class and configuration files.

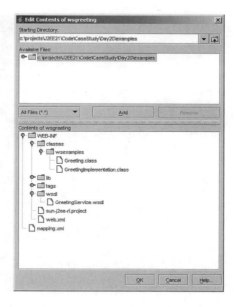

FIGURE 20.7

The settings for the Web Service WAR file.

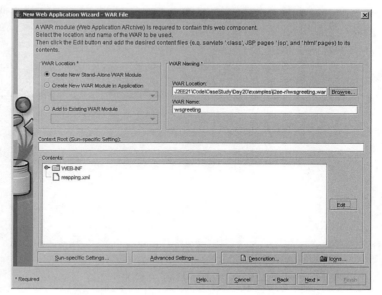

20

FIGURE 20.8

*Selecting the WSDL
and mapping files.*

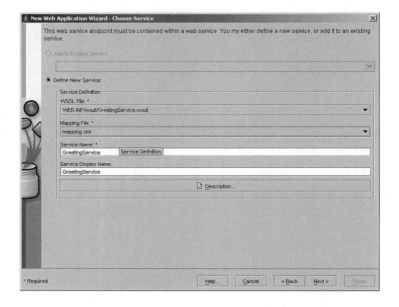

FIGURE 20.9

*Configuring the Web
Service Endpoint.*

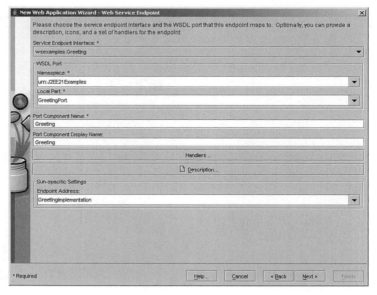

That completes the initial configuration, so click Next followed by Finish. You should be
presented with a deploytool screen that looks like Figure 20.10.

FIGURE 20.10

Web Service WAR in `deploytool`.

Configuring the WAR and Component

There are three final bits of Sun-specific configuration that are needed to complete the Web Service WAR. First, select the General tab of the `wsgreeting` WAR file (as shown in Figure 20.10). Set the `Context Root` field to `/wsgreeting`.

Now select the `GreetingImplementation` component in the left-hand pane. Select the `Aliases` tab and `Add` an alias of `/GreetingService` as shown in Figure 20.11.

Finally, select the `Endpoint` tab and change the `Endpoint Address` at the bottom of the tab to be `GreetingService`. You should now save your WAR file and you are ready to deploy your service.

During this process, `deploytool` has generated several new files for you:

- **The `web.xml` file**—This contains the servlet definition for your Web Service. One part of this defines a servlet and indicates that `wsexamples.GreetingImplementation` is the servlet class. Obviously, the `GreetingImplementation` class you saw earlier is not a servlet, but this is indicative of more Web Service scaffolding. As the Web component is marked as a Web Service, the container to which it is deployed will hook it up to a SOAP router servlet during deployment. The other part of the file is the alias you added mapping `/GreetingService` to the `GreetingImplementation` servlet:

20

```
<servlet>
    <display-name>GreetingImplementation</display-name>
    <servlet-name>GreetingImplementation</servlet-name>
    <servlet-class>wsexamples.GreetingImplementation</servlet-class>
</servlet>
<servlet-mapping>
    <servlet-name>GreetingImplementation</servlet-name>
    <url-pattern>/GreetingService</url-pattern>
</servlet-mapping>
```

- **The `sun-web.xml` file**—This contains the sun-specific configuration performed toward the end of the configuration. This includes the setting of the context root and the mapping of the Web Service endpoint information (the names of the service and port) to the servlet used to implement the service:

```
<sun-web-app>
  <context-root>/wsgreeting</context-root>
  <servlet>
    <servlet-name>GreetingImplementation</servlet-name>
    <webservice-endpoint>
      <port-component-name>Greeting</port-component-name>
      <endpoint-address-uri>GreetingService</endpoint-address-uri>
    </webservice-endpoint>
  </servlet>
</sun-web-app>
```

- **The `webservices.xml` file**— This file is described in the JSR109 document as the "Web Services Deployment Descriptor" and is described in the next section.

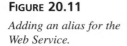

FIGURE 20.11

Adding an alias for the Web Service.

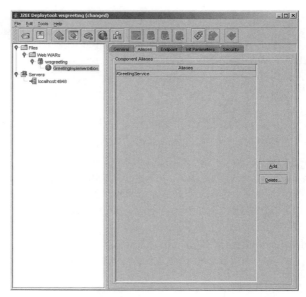

The Web Services Deployment Descriptor

The Web Services Deployment Descriptor contains a list of the Web Services being deployed and the ports each one of them contains. The root element is `webservices`, which contains one or more `webservice-description` elements. Within the `webservice-description` element there is some information about the overall service, such as the name of the service, the associated WSDL file, and which mapping deployment descriptor should be used for this particular Web Service:

```
<webservice-description-name>GreetingService</webservice-description-name>
<wsdl-file>WEB-INF/wsdl/GreetingService.wsdl</wsdl-file>
<jaxrpc-mapping-file>mapping.xml</jaxrpc-mapping-file>
```

Each `webservice-description` element contains one `port-component` element for each port in the service. For your simple `Greeting` service, there is just a single port you can call `GreetingPort`. This suggested name is intentionally different from the name used in the WSDL document to help you differentiate it:

```
<port-component>
    <display-name>Greeting</display-name>
    <port-component-name>Greeting</port-component-name>
    ...
</port-component>
```

The `wsdl-port` element below the `port-component` element defines the associated port name from the WSDL you generated earlier—`GreetingPort`—and the namespace in which it is defined—`urn:J2EE21Examples`:

```
<wsdl-port xmlns:wsdl-port_ns__="urn:J2EE21Examples">wsdl-
port_ns__:GreetingPort</wsdl-port>
```

The `service-endpoint-interface` element within the `port-component` defines the Java interface associated with this port. In your case, this is the fully qualified name of the interface you are supplying in the WAR file:

```
<service-endpoint-interface>wsexamples.Greeting</service-endpoint-interface>
```

The other useful bit of information in the `port-component` is the link to the implementation. The `service-impl-bean` in this case defines a link to the `GreetingImplementation` defined in the `web.xml` file:

```
<service-impl-bean>
    <servlet-link>GreetingImplementation</servlet-link>
</service-impl-bean>
```

Deploying the Service

Now you can deploy the service. Select the `wsgreeting` WAR in the left-hand pane of `deploytool` and then select Tools, Deploy from the menus. Provide your administrator

20

user name and password if prompted and ensure that the message "Operation Completed Successfully" is displayed on the Distribute Module screen.

During this deployment, all of the server-side scaffolding, such as the server-side skeletons, will be generated by the container into which you are deploying. Note that there is no need in this case to ask for a client JAR file because you will contact the service over SOAP. The only thing needed to create the artifacts used by the client is the WSDL description (after all, the Greeting Web Service could be implemented in Microsoft .NET if it was developed by someone else).

You can now access the simple Web Service at the URL `http://localhost/wsgreeting/GreetingService`. Putting this URL directly into a browser will not have much effect as browsers issue HTTP GET commands while Web Services generally use HTTP POST. However, you can test that your service is there by asking it for its WSDL description. To do this, add "?WSDL" onto the end of the URL and type it into your browser:

`http://localhost/wsgreeting/GreetingService?WSDL`

This will return the deployed WSDL file as shown in Figure 20.12.

FIGURE 20.12

Querying the Web Service for its WSDL.

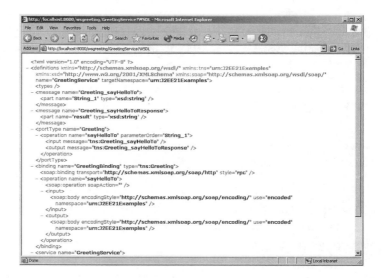

The WSDL document is identical to the one in the Web Service WAR, but it now contains the location information for the deployed service (remember that the original WSDL had its location set to `REPLACE WITH ACTUAL URL`):

```
...
<service name="GreetingService">
  <port name="GreetingPort" binding="tns:GreetingBinding">
    <soap:address xmlns:wsdl=http://schemas.xmlsoap.org/wsdl/
                  location="http://localhost:8000/wsgreeting/GreetingService"/>
  </port>
</service>
...
```

In the next section, you will use this WSDL file to generate stubs through which a client application can contact the Web Service.

Consuming the Simple Greeting Service

To use your Web Service you need a client. For the purposes of this exercise, this client will be a standard Java class with a main method. However, it could also be a J2EE component such as a JSP or EJB. The differences with such clients are discussed later.

To call the Web Service from a client, you could use low-level APIs to create and send SOAP messages. However, one of the main intentions of JAX-RPC is to provide the developer with a familiar development model. Hence, you will again use the tools to create a stub (or proxy) that represents the service for the client. The stub exposes Java methods that match the SOAP operations supported by the server. The client application can simply call these Java methods to invoke the functionality of the service. The J2EE RI tool used is again wscompile. You can use wscompile to take the WSDL description of the deployed service and create client-side stubs through which to invoke the service.

In this case the configuration file needs client-focused information provided in a wscompile configuration file similar to the one used earlier to generate the WSDL in the section "Web Service Compiler Configuration File." The file still has a root element of configuration, but in place of the service element you use a wsdl element. The packageName attribute of the wsdl element indicates that the generated Java classes and interfaces should reside in the package client. The location attribute specifies that the WSDL file to use should be retrieved from the deployed service. This means that it contains the correct endpoint location information for the service you deployed. The client configuration file is shown in Listing 20.6.

LISTING 20.6   wscompile Client Configuration File (config-client.xml)

```
<?xml version="1.0" encoding="UTF-8"?>
<configuration xmlns="http://java.sun.com/xml/ns/jax-rpc/ri/config">
    <wsdl location="http://localhost:8000/wsgreeting/GreetingService?WSDL"
➡packageName="client"/>
</configuration>
```

20

NOTE

> Do not use the original WSDL file without the location information when
> creating your client. Stubs generated from WSDL that do not contain a valid
> endpoint will fail at runtime unless one is set programmatically. This is a
> more flexible mechanism, but it makes them more complicated to use.
> Dynamic endpoint allocation is fine later, but for the time being we will be
> working with the endpoint URL encoded in the WSDL.

When you call wscompile, you should ask it to generate the client scaffolding you need
(-gen:client). If you are working in a development environment that does not provide
code completion based on introspection, you should also specify the –keep option so that
the .java files are still around for inspection:

```
wscompile –gen:client -d classes –keep –s build/generatedproxy
➥ws/config-client.xml
```

The client-side scaffolding shares many files with the server-side scaffolding, including
any complex types, serializers, and a serializer registry to map types to serializers.
However, the following client-specific artifacts are also generated:

- **Greeting interface**—This is generated from the WSDL port description. It is
  almost identical to the remote Java Greeting interface from which the WSDL was
  generated.
- **GreetingService interface**—This defines a single method getGreetingPort()
  that returns a client-side proxy for the service implementing the Greeting inter-
  face.
- **GreetingService_Impl class**—This is a factory class that represents the Web
  Service as a whole. You can obtain client-side proxies from instances of this class.
  For your simple service, this will just serve client-side proxies that implement the
  Greeting interface.
- **Greeting_Stub class**—This is the client-side proxy itself that implements the
  client-side Java Greeting interface generated from the WSDL.

You can build a Web Service client using these generated classes. To use these classes,
you should either import the namespace in which they were generated (client derived
from the client configuration file as shown in Listing 20.6) or place your client class in
the same namespace:

```
package client;
```

You can create your client code in a simple main() method. Don't forget that all these
method calls can generate RemoteExceptions, so be sure to place them all inside a

try/catch block. The first thing to do is instantiate the factory that represents the Web Service:

```
GreetingService serviceProxy = new GreetingService_Impl();
```

From this service proxy, you can then obtain an interface proxy:

```
Greeting interfaceProxy = serviceProxy.getGreetingPort();
```

As the interface proxy implements the client-side Greeting interface, you can call the sayHelloTo() method on this, passing the name of the person to greet:

```
String response = interfaceProxy.sayHelloTo("Fred");
```

This call will trigger a SOAP request to the simple Greeting Web Service. The service will prepend the message you defined in your implementation and return the result. The full code for a sample simple Web Service client is shown in Listing 20.7.

LISTING 20.7   Client for Simple Web Service (GreetingClient.java)

```
package client;

public class GreetingClient
{
    public static void main(String[] args)
    {
        try
        {
            GreetingService serviceProxy = new GreetingService_Impl();

            Greeting interfaceProxy = serviceProxy.getGreetingPort();

            String response = interfaceProxy.sayHelloTo("Fred");
            System.out.println("Response from greeting service was: " +
➥response);
        }
        catch (Exception ex)
        {
            ex.printStackTrace();
        }
    }
}
```

20

You compile and run your client as you would any other Java application, but ensure that the generated client-side classes are on your classpath. To generate the client-side scaffolding, compile the pre-provided client class and run it, use the following Ant directive:

```
asant run
```

This will communicate with the web service you deployed earlier. You should see the following message:

```
Response from greeting service was: Hi there Fred
```

So, now you have created, deployed, and invoked a simple Web Service under J2EE using JAX-RPC.

One final question before moving on from here is how to re-target this Web Service client at a different endpoint. By default, the stub uses the endpoint URL encoded into the WSDL document. As you move from development into test, staging, and live environments, the URL of the endpoint will probably change. However, you do not necessarily want to regenerate your proxies at every stage. Instead, you can set the endpoint for the stub to use as follows (in this example "ELEPHANT" is the name of the host on which the service is deployed):

```
javax.xml.rpc.Stub stub = (javax.xml.rpc.Stub)interfaceProxy;
stub._setProperty(ENDPOINT_ADDRESS_PROPERTY,
              "http://ELEPHANT:8000/wsgreeting/DIFFERENT_NAME");
```

You can then define the endpoint address as a property that can be picked up by the running program.

CAUTION

When re-targeting a proxy at a different endpoint, you should ensure that the endpoint supports the same port type—even down to the name of each part of each message. Some services may be forgiving on this (that is, the names could differ and it will still accept the operation invocation), but others are not.

Building More Robust Web Services

The service you have created so far is fairly simplistic. When you come to create real Web Services, you will need to consider additional issues such as lifecycle and scalability. You will also approach certain tasks in a different way.

Starting from WSDL

When a system is designed, the designers will create UML diagrams (or the like) to represent the system entities and interactions between them. Tools can then generate programming artifacts, such as Java classes and interfaces based on this information. If the system will be based on Web Services, such artifacts will include WSDL descriptions of the required services. You, as a Java developer, will then be presented with a WSDL description that requires a Java implementation. The creation of WSDL independently from code is generally a better approach than starting from code and generating WSDL for reasons discussed in the sidebar "Always Start from the WSDL."

Always Start from the WSDL

One of the reasons for the popularity of WSDL and SOAP as mechanisms for defining and implementing Web Services is that they are relatively simple. A benefit of this simplicity is that they provide a low barrier to entry for any platform or programming language that wants to join the Web Service party. However, despite their simplicity, WSDL and SOAP documents are not very friendly for humans. The sheer volume of information contained in a nontrivial interface definition and the amount of prior protocol knowledge required to fully grasp the meaning of some of the elements and attributes mean that you would not want to use WSDL documents or SOAP packets as bedtime reading.

It is good practice in any partitioned application to clearly define the interfaces between components. This is especially true of distributed applications. For this reason, most distribution mechanisms encourage developers to start by defining their distributed interface. In the case of RMI, this interface is defined in Java, whereas in other environments, such as CORBA and DCOM, the interface is defined in a language-neutral Interface Definition Language (IDL). This makes sense as RMI is mostly concerned with Java-to-Java communication, whereas CORBA and DCOM are both independent of any particular programming language. The use of IDL enables cross-language interoperation, which can be somewhat trickier if you start with RMI.

WSDL is largely another form of IDL. It allows you to define your interfaces, their protocol bindings, and the location at which the service is deployed. However, WSDL documents, like IDL documents, are somewhat inaccessible for the average developer. There is a lot of detail to learn, and it is tricky to edit raw WSDL. Because of this, most Web Service toolkits and products (including Apache Axis, Microsoft Visual Studio .NET, and the J2EE RI) provide the capability of generating a WSDL document from a language artifact, such as a Java interface definition or an ASP.NET ASMX page. The principle here is that you can just write things in the language with which you are familiar and have them exposed as a Web Service. You do not have to write any WSDL to allow a Web Service client to consume your Web Service implementation. This has many similarities to the way that a CORBA client can consume an RMI interface using a CORBA IDL interface generated with the `-idl` option to `rmic`.

Although interface generation makes an otherwise potentially awkward task a lot easier, there is a fundamental flaw in this approach, which is this:

WSDL, like IDL, was never intended to represent rich object-oriented interfaces.

The implication of this will become clear later, as you define a rich remote interface with parameters and return values consisting of encapsulated objects and collections of objects. When such an interface is translated into WSDL, the result is a far simpler description containing structures and arrays. This means that a lot of information about the behavior that you have associated with your data is lost at the Web Service interface.

20

When you have a rich environment at each end of the conversation, rich artifacts, such as instances of developer-defined classes, can be passed with little, if any, effort. However, if you do not know what environment is at the far end, you lose the ability to do this. If your Web Service client is a Perl application, how would it deal with your complex objects? Hence, WSDL and SOAP must cater to the lowest-common-denominator in order to provide a low barrier of entry for platforms and languages.

When a WSDL generation tool attempts to convert a developer-defined Java class into WSDL, it must cut some corners to make it fit in the data-centric typing system used by WSDL. This means that data becomes "raw"—effectively just data structures and arrays of data structures. The structure and relationships of such a description in many ways reflects quirks of the language from which it was generated. This can make it quite unwieldy when imported into a different language. The alternative is to define a pair of custom serializers and deserializers that will map your language artifact into a richer on-the-wire representation. However, this means that the sender or receiver at the other end must also know about your format and have a matching serializer/deserializer pair for their platform. Neither of these scenarios is particularly helpful.

In summary, the best approach is to start by defining the interface—in this case in WSDL. You can then use the Web Service toolkits to generate language artifacts from the WSDL. This will always provide a fairly "clean" structure as you are going from a simpler type system (data only) into a more complex one (data + behavior). If you then choose to provide custom serialization to turn the simple types into complex types, you are quite at liberty to do so. However, it is very much your own decision and does not force an unwieldy description on the other end of the conversation. It is well worth investigating tools that simplify the creation of WSDL documents—for example xmlspy—(see http://www.xmlspy.com) as these will take away the pain associated with writing WSDL by hand.

Rather than having to work out manually what sort of Java class would match that WSDL description, the J2EE RI (in common with other J2EE implementations) provides a tool to perform the mapping of the SOAP operations and XML Schema types in the WSDL document into Java artifacts. The wscompile tool can produce server-side skeletons from the WSDL document in the same way that it creates client-side stubs. One of these server-side artifacts will be a Java Remote interface that reflects the definitions from the WSDL file. You can then implement this interface (as you did previously) and package your service for deployment. The implementation still implements the Remote interface; the only difference is that this is the generated one. The build sequence is also slightly different in that you will need to run wscompile before building your Web Service implementation class rather than afterward as you did before. The rest of the configuration files would be almost identical to those for the basic greeting service.

Exposing EJBs Through Web Service Protocols

The types of application functionality exposed through Web Service protocols will be many and varied. The variety of such applications will match, if not exceed, the variety of browser-based applications found on the Web. This means that Web Service applications will have a variety of requirements for such systemic qualities as scalability, availability, performance, and so on. Essentially, Web Service applications are just like any other application. Because of their requirements for scalability and availability, the functionality behind many Java-based Web Services will be implemented using EJBs. What is needed then is a simple way to expose this functionality while keeping overhead to the minimum.

EJBs as Web Service Facades

On Day 18, the role of the facade pattern was discussed as a way of reducing network traffic and creating a simpler, coarse-grained interface from a set of fine-grained interfaces. The use of a Session Facade providing coarse-grained access to entity EJBs has been particularly successful.

As Web Services are intended to be a coarse-grained interface to underlying functionality, the Facade pattern also applies at a Web Service boundary. Indeed, an overarching Session Facade may contain the coarse-grained representation of the business logic implemented by combinations of entity and session EJBs in the application. This overarching Session Facade is ideal to be exposed using Web Service protocols—indeed it may have been created for just such a purpose.

You will now examine an example that uses a stateless session EJB as a Façade for some of the agency functionality from the case study. The façade will provide a list of jobs available at a given location. The stateless session bean will call on underlying entity beans to retrieve the required data. The client will be a standalone Java client just as for the servlet-based Web Service implementation.

Defining the Interface and Implementation

JAX-RPC allows you to expose a stateless session bean so that it can be accessed through Web Service protocols. In developer terms, the main difference between an EJB exposed through JAX-RPC and one exposed through RMI is that you do not provide the same interface files. For an RMI-based EJB, you will provide a home interface and an EJB business interface that extends `javax.ejb.EJBObject` or `javax.ejb.EJBLocalObject`. An EJB developed to be exposed as a Web Service does not have a home interface. The relationship between the client and server is

20

different and the client delegates all lookup of services to the proxy as you saw in the `GreetingClient` class earlier. Similarly, the business interface is defined slightly differently to reflect the different relationship. While the interface for a Web Service EJB is still a `Remote` interface, it must directly extend `java.rmi.Remote` rather than one of the `EJBObject` variants.

NOTE

> As it stands, you cannot use the same interface definition for the EJB Remote interface and the Web Service using the tools provided with the J2EE RI (wscompile will generate an error if your Web Service interface extends `javax.ejb.EJBObject` rather than `java.rmi.Remote`). This can be seen as a good thing, as it might tempt people to always specify the EJB remote interface as a Web Service interface for the associated EJB. You should not just automatically expose all stateless session EJBs as Web Services. However, if you have a well-crafted, coarse-grained facade implemented as a stateless session EJB, there is no reason you should not expose this as a Web Service.

Listing 20.8 shows an interface that can be used to expose an EJB method that lists the job vacancies registered with the job agency at a particular location. You can see that the interface extends `Remote` and the `findJobsAtLocation()` method is labeled as throwing `RemoteException`. The interface defines a single method that takes a location as a string and returns a string array of job information. Nothing much indicates that this interface is part of an EJB.

LISTING 20.8   A Web Service Interface for Agency Functionality (`Service.java`)

```java
package agency;

import java.rmi.*;

public interface Service extends Remote
{
    public String[] findJobsAtLocation(String location) throws RemoteException;
}
```

The implementation, on the other hand, looks like a typical session EJB as shown in listing 20.9. Examination of the code reveals that it has the usual lifecycle methods for a stateless session bean and retrieves the local resources it needs in its `setSessionContext()` method. The only resource it uses is a reference to the home interface of the entity Job EJB.

The bean implements the single business method—findJobsAtLocation()—defined on the Service interface. The implementation of this method uses the findByLocation method on the JobHome interface which returns a list of the jobs at the given location. The method creates a Job EJB instance for each job in the list and calls the getCustomer() and getRef() methods on its JobLocal interface. The strings created from the job information are stored in an array to be returned to the caller.

LISTING 20.9 An Enterprise Bean to Underpin a Web Service (ServiceBean.java)

```java
package agency;

import java.util.*;
import java.rmi.*;
import javax.ejb.*;
import javax.naming.* ;

import data.*;

public class ServiceBean implements SessionBean
{
    private JobLocalHome jobHome;

    public String[] findJobsAtLocation(String location)
    {
        String[] jobs = null;
        try
        {
            Collection col = jobHome.findByLocation(location);
            jobs = new String[col.size()];
            Iterator it=col.iterator();
            for (int i=0; i < jobs.length; ++i)
            {
                    JobLocal job = (JobLocal)it.next();
                    jobs[i] = job.getCustomer() + "/" + job.getRef();
            }
        }
        catch (Exception ex)
        {
            // In response to any error just return null
            jobs = null;
        }
        return jobs;
    }

    // EJB methods start here


    public void ejbCreate () throws CreateException {}
```

20

LISTING 20.9   continued

```java
public void ejbActivate(){}

public void ejbPassivate(){}

public void ejbRemove(){}

private SessionContext ctx;

public void setSessionContext(SessionContext ctx)
{
    this.ctx = ctx;
    InitialContext ic = null;
    try
    {
        ic = new InitialContext();
        jobHome = (JobLocalHome)ic.lookup("java:comp/env/ejb/JobLocal");
    }
    catch (NamingException ex)
    {
        error("Error looking up java:comp/env/ejb/JobLocal",ex);
        return;
    }
}

private void error (String msg, Exception ex)
{
    String s = "ServiceBean: "+msg + "\n" + ex;
    System.out.println(s);
    throw new EJBException(s,ex);
}
}
```

The only real difference between this bean implementation and any other stateless session bean is that exceptions are treated differently. When it is exposed through a native RMI interface, the bean implementor can assume that the caller has some way of dealing with any exceptions thrown by the bean, so any errors can be raised as exceptions. However, in Web Service terms, you are less certain how an exception will appear to a client and so it is safer to adopt a less Java-specific stance. In this case, an error is indicated by a null return value. The handling of errors and exceptions in Web Services is discussed later in the section "Web Service Errors and Exceptions."

Web Service Compiler Configuration File

As with the servlet-based Web Service, you will need to provide additional information in addition to the standard J2EE deployment descriptor for this type of component. In the

J2EE Reference Implementation, you again use wscompile to generate this information. The configuration file used to generate the artifacts for the agency Service bean, shown in listing 20.10, is almost identical to that for the servlet-based Web Service, as shown in Listing 20.3 (only the names have changed).

LISTING 20.10   wscompile Web Service Configuration File (config-service.xml)

```xml
<?xml version="1.0" encoding="UTF-8"?>
<configuration
  xmlns="http://java.sun.com/xml/ns/jax-rpc/ri/config">
  <service
      name="AgencyService"
      targetNamespace="urn:J2EE21Agency"
      typeNamespace="urn:J2EE21AgencyTypes"
      packageName="agency">
      <interface name="agency.Service"/>
  </service>
</configuration>
```

The wscompile command line is identical to that for the servlet-based Web Service, and the same files will be produced, namely the WSDL description and the mapping.xml file.

As before, the sample code is on the Web site that accompanies this book. As it forms the basis of the exercise, you will find this example in the exercise directory for Day 20. With the code supplied on the accompanying Web site, you can use the following Ant command to build the supplied agency Web Service, which includes the creation of the WSDL and the mapping file:

```
asant build
```

The WSDL File

As the interface is different from the greeting service defined earlier, the WSDL generated will also be different. As the findJobsAtLocation() method returns something other than a simple type, a complex type is defined in the types section of the WSDL description:

```xml
<types>
    <schema targetNamespace="urn:J2EE21AgencyTypes"
            xmlns:tns="urn:J2EE21AgencyTypes"
            xmlns:soap11-enc="http://schemas.xmlsoap.org/soap/encoding/"
            xmlns:xsi="http://www.w3.org/2001/XMLSchema-instance"
            xmlns:wsdl="http://schemas.xmlsoap.org/wsdl/"
            xmlns="http://www.w3.org/2001/XMLSchema">
        <import namespace="http://schemas.xmlsoap.org/soap/encoding/"/>
        <complexType name="ArrayOfstring">
```

20

```
                <complexContent>
                    <restriction base="soap11-enc:Array">
                        <attribute ref="soap11-enc:arrayType"
➥wsdl:arrayType="string[]"/>
                    </restriction>
                </complexContent>
            </complexType>
        </schema>
</types>
```

Without going into too much detail, the new type—ArrayOfString— is defined to be an unbounded array of the simple string type. This new type is defined in the scope of the urn:J2EE21Agency namespace specified for types in the wscompile configuration file. This ArrayOfString type can then be used later in the WSDL document to define the return type of the findJobsAtLocation operation:

```
<message name="Service_findJobsAtLocationResponse">
    <part name="result" type="ns2:ArrayOfstring"/>
</message>
```

As you can see, the findJobsAtLocation response is defined to contain an ArrayOfString, which is scoped to namespace ns2 (ns2 is defined to be urn:J2EE21Types in the overall definitions element). Other than this, the WSDL document is very similar to the greeting service WSDL described earlier.

The Mapping File

As you would expect, the mapping file is also very similar to that for the greeting service. It contains nothing specific to the service being implemented by an EJB and simply reflects the changes in the interface, such as the use of the array of strings as a return type:

```
<java-wsdl-mapping version="1.1" ...>
    <service-endpoint-interface-mapping>
    ...
        <service-endpoint-method-mapping>
        ...
            <wsdl-return-value-mapping>
                <method-return-value>java.lang.String[]</method-return-value>
                <wsdl-message xmlns:wsdlMsgNS="urn:J2EE21Agency">
                    wsdlMsgNS:Service_findJobsAtLocationResponse
                </wsdl-message>
                <wsdl-message-part-name>result</wsdl-message-part-name>
            </wsdl-return-value-mapping>
        </service-endpoint-interface-mapping>
    ...
    </service-endpoint-method-mapping>
    ...
</java-wsdl-mapping>
```

Packaging and Deploying the Agency Web Service Using J2EE RI `deploytool`

This section shows how to deploy the simple Web Service to the J2EE RI. As noted before, you will need to start up the PointBase database server and J2EE RI server before starting `deploytool`.

Creating the Agency EAR

By choosing `File`, `Open`, load up the `Day20/exercise/j2ee-ri/agency.ear` enterprise application archive. This defines a single group of Entity beans called `Entity` which will be used by the Web Service session bean. Highlight the Agency application in the explorer on the left side of the `deploytool` GUI and its contents will be shown on the right side, as shown in Figure 20.13.

FIGURE 20.13

Partially built Agency case study EAR.

You will package up the Web Service in an EJB-JAR file, so choose File, New, Enterprise Bean to create a new one. Click Next to skip the introduction screen and move onto the EJB-JAR file screen. You will be creating your New JAR Module in the Application called agency, so ensure that this option is selected. Next, under JAR Naming, enter "agency-session-ejb" as the File Name.

20

Now you can populate your EJB-JAR with the files you saw earlier. Under the Contents section, click the Edit button to display the Edit Contents of agency-session-ejb screen. Browse to find the class files (Service.class and ServiceBean.class), the WSDL file (AgencyService.wsdl), and the mapping file (mapping.xml). You will also need to add the interface definitions for the entity beans used that can be found under the folder Day20\exercise\classes\data. Add each of these files to the contents as shown in Figure 20.14 and click OK.

FIGURE 20.14

Adding class and con-figuration files to EJB-based Web Service.

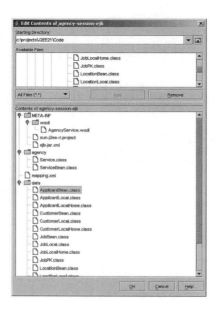

Now click Next to move onto the General screen. Select agency.ServiceBean as your Enterprise Bean Class (this will be offered from the drop-down list). Ensure that the Enterprise Bean Type is set to Stateless Session. There is no need to define home, local or remote interfaces for this Web Service bean. So click Next to move to the Configuration Options screen.

Ensure that Expose Bean as Web Service Endpoint is selected and click Next.

On the Choose Service screen in the Service Definition section, select AgencyService.wsdl as your WSDL File and mapping.xml as your mapping file (these will be offered from the drop-down lists). The other fields will be populated based on the information in the files as shown in Figure 20.15.

FIGURE 20.15

Service definition for EJB-based Web Service.

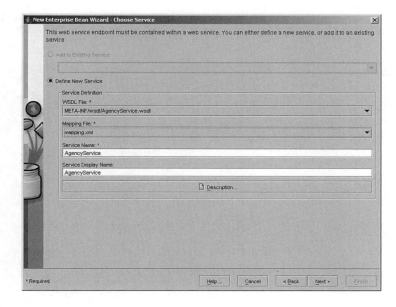

Click Next to move on to the Web Service Endpoint screen. Select agency.Service as your Service Endpoint Interface. In the WSDL Port section, set the Namespace to be urn:J2EE21Agency and ensure that the Local Part becomes ServicePort. In the Sun-specific Settings section, set the Endpoint Address to be jaxrpc/ServiceBean as shown in Figure 20.16.

FIGURE 20.16

Endpoint configuration for EJB-based Web Service.

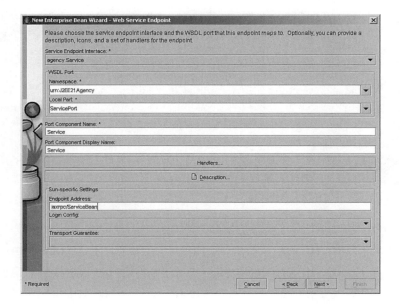

20

That completes the initial configuration, so click Next followed by Finish. You should be presented with a deploytool screen that looks like Figure 20.17.

FIGURE 20.17

EJB-based Web Service viewed in deploytool.

Configuring the EJB Component

To complete the Web Service configuration, highlight the agency-session-ejb in the left-hand pane and select its Web Services tab. Select the AgencyService in the list and in the Sun-specific Setting section, set the WSDL Publish Location to be jaxrpc/ServiceBean?WSDL as shown in Figure 20.18.

To complete the EJB configuration, highlight the ServiceBean itself in the left-hand pane and select the EJB Refs tab. Click Add and add a reference to the JobBean setting the name to ejb/JobLocal, type to Entity, interfaces to Local, and the home and local interface names to data.JobLocalHome and data.JobLocal respectively. This is shown in Figure 20.19. Once this is added, select the reference and change the Sun-specific settings for ejb/JobLocal to data-entity-ejb.jar#JobBean.

FIGURE 20.18

WSDL location configuration.

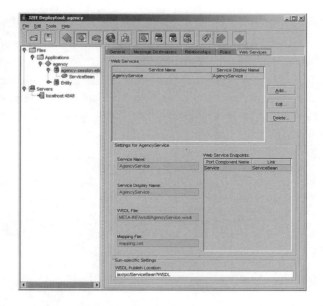

FIGURE 20.19

Adding entity references to the EJB-based Web Service.

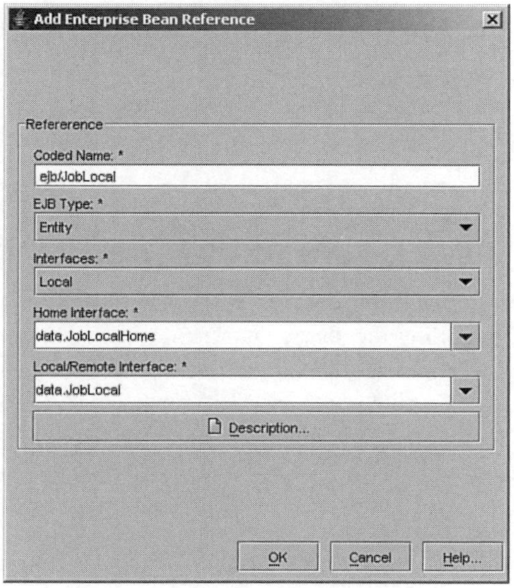

20

During this process, `deploytool` has generated several new files for you:

- **The `ejb-jar.xml` file**—This contains the EJB definition for your Web Service and looks like a standard stateless session bean deployment descriptor.

- **The `sun-ejb-jar.xml` file**—This contains the Sun-specific configuration performed during the bean configuration. This includes the setting of the endpoint URI and the location from which the WSDL description can be recovered:

```
<sun-ejb-jar>
    <enterprise-beans>
        ...
        <ejb>
            <ejb-name>ServiceBean</ejb-name>
            <jndi-name>ServiceBean</jndi-name>
            <webservice-endpoint>
                <port-component-name>Service</port-component-name>
                <endpoint-address-uri>jaxrpc/ServiceBean</endpoint-address-
➥uri>
            </webservice-endpoint>
        </ejb>
        <webservice-description>
            <webservice-description-name>AgencyService</webservice-
➥description-name>
            <wsdl-publish-location>jaxrpc/ServiceBean?WSDL</wsdl-publish-
➥location>
        </webservice-description>
    </enterprise-beans>
</sun-ejb-jar>
```

- **The `webservices.xml` file**— This is described in the next section.

The Web Services Deployment Descriptor

The Web Services Deployment Descriptor for the EJB is similar to that for the servlet-based Web Service, containing the service description and pointers to the WSDL and mapping files. The principal difference is that the port-component points to an EJB rather than a servlet:

```
<webservices ...>
    <webservice-description>
    ...
        <port-component>
            <service-impl-bean>
                <ejb-link>ServiceBean</ejb-link>
            </service-impl-bean>
        </port-component>
    </webservice-description>
</webservices>
```

Deploying the Service

Now you can deploy the service. Select the Agency EAR in the left-hand pane of deploytool and then select Tools, Deploy from the menus. Provide your administrator user name and password if prompted and ensure that the message "Operation Complete Successfully" is displayed on the Distribute Module screen.

As with the servlet-based Web Service, all of the server-side scaffolding required for the Web Service is generated during deployment. There is no client JAR file because you will contact the service over SOAP so the only thing needed to create the artifacts used by the client is the WSDL description.

You can now access the simple Web Service at the URL http://localhost/jaxrpc/ ServiceBean and its WSDL is available at http://localhost/jaxrpc/ ServiceBean?WSDL.

The WSDL document is identical to the one in the EJB-JAR file, but it now contains the location information for the deployed service:

```
...
<service name="AgencyService">
  <port name="ServicePort" binding="tns:ServiceBinding">
    <soap:address xmlns:wsdl=http://schemas.xmlsoap.org/wsdl/
                  location="http://localhost:8000/jaxrpc/ServiceBean"/>
  </port>
</service>
...
```

In the next section, you will use this WSDL file to generate stubs through which a client application can contact the Web Service.

Consuming the Simple Greeting Service

As you might expect, the client for a Web Service based on an EJB is very similar to one for a Web Service based on a servlet. The client will need to obtain a stub that represents the PortType of the deployed service. This can be generated by running wscompile against the WSDL file retrieved from the deployed Web Service. The wscompile configuration file (client-config.xml) is almost identical except that it points to a different URL:

```
<wsdl location="http://localhost:8000/jaxrpc/ServiceBean?WSDL"
➥packageName="client"/>
```

The wscompile command line is identical to the one used for the servlet-based Web Service you saw earlier. After you have generated the stubs and factories, you can use them in your client. The client will be similar to the servlet-based Web Service client shown in Listing 20.7, but obviously the types and methods implemented by them will be different. The following client-specific artifacts are generated that can be used in the client:

- **Service interface**—This is generated from the WSDL port description. It is almost identical to the remote Java Service interface from which the WSDL was generated.

- **AgencyService interface**—This defines a single method getServicePort() that returns a client-side proxy for the Web Service implementing the Service interface.

- **AgencyService_Impl class**—This is a factory class that represents the Web Service as a whole. You can obtain client-side proxies from instances of this class. For your simple service, this will just serve client-side proxies that implement the Service interface.

- **Service_Stub class**—This is the client-side proxy itself that implements the client-side Java Service interface generated from the WSDL.

A client for the Web Service ServiceBean is shown in Listing 20.11. Again, this shares the namespace of the proxies (client) and catches RemoteExceptions. The client calls the findJobsAtLocation passing in the location string provided on the command line. It then prints out the job information returned from the Web Service.

LISTING 20.11   Web Service Client for the ServiceBean

```
package client;

public class AgencyServiceClient
{
    private static String location = "%";

    public static void main(String[] args)
    {
        if (args.length == 1)
        {
            location = args[0];
        }
        else if (args.length > 1)
        {
            System.err.println("Usage: AgencyServiceClient [ location ]");
            System.exit(1);
        }
```

LISTING 20.11   continued

```
        try
        {
            AgencyService serviceProxy = new AgencyService_Impl();

            Service interfaceProxy = serviceProxy.getServicePort();

            System.out.println("Using Location: "+location);

            System.out.println("Job list: ");
            String[] jobs = interfaceProxy.findJobsAtLocation(location);
            for(int i=0; i<jobs.length; ++i)
            {
                System.out.println(jobs[i]);
            }
            System.out.println("\nDone\n");
        }
        catch (Exception ex)
        {
            ex.printStackTrace();
        }
    }
}
```

You compile and run your client as you would any other Java application, but ensure that the generated client-side classes are on your classpath. To generate the client-side scaffolding, compile the pre-provided client class and run it, using the following Ant directive:

```
asant AgencyServiceClient
```

This will communicate with the EJB-based web service you deployed earlier. If you enter the location "London," you should see the following message:

```
[java] Using Location: London
[java] Job list:
[java] winston/Cigar trimmer
```

So, now you have created, deployed, and invoked an EJB-based Web Service under J2EE using JAX-RPC.

Other Considerations for Web Services

So far, the Web Services you have seen have used simple parameters, such as strings and integers and have been free from errors. However, in the real world, most systems will need to pass complex types such as arrays, classes, and data structures and will need to

20

cope with issues such as error handling. During the rest of today, you will look at such issues.

Web Service Errors and Exceptions

The use of Web Service protocols implies that your application is making calls across network boundaries. As such, you must be prepared to handle any network-related errors that occur. As the Web Service interface is based around a Java remote interface, any client code must catch and handle `java.rmi.RemoteException`. A `RemoteException` will be generated in response to any unhandled runtime exceptions that occur. Such exceptions are mapped to SOAP fault elements that are included in the body of the response from the server.

You can define domain exceptions—for example, `InvalidProductCodeException`—on your Web Service remote interfaces. These exceptions are defined in the service WSDL as `fault` elements. Such `fault` elements are marshaled back to the client in the SOAP message that forms the response from the server. For a Java client, the exception will be regenerated in its original form and rethrown. The handling of fault elements by non-Java clients will depend on the support for WSDL-defined `fault` elements in that environment. A Java exception is a complex type, so the JAX-RPC runtime must be able to marshal and unmarshal at least some of its contents (such as its message). Therefore, exceptions must conform to certain rules to be successfully passed. These rules are similar to those for JavaBeans and are defined in section 5 of the JAX-RPC specification (JSR101).

Context and Lifecycle of JAX-RPC Web Services

The servers created so far have been very simple. However, real-world applications require more sophistication. It is important to know about and control the lifetime of your service instances. The service might need to initialize itself when it is created and release resources when it is destroyed. Similarly, it might need to obtain information relating to this call, such as the identity of the caller or message header settings.

The lifecycle and state management of your Web Service implementation will depend on the type of component that underlies it. If you have built a Web Service based on a stateless session EJB, a new bean will be instantiated for each call and it will follow the stateless session EJB lifecycle. If you are using a servlet-based implementation, there is no guarantee that successive calls will use the same instance. In both cases, JSR109 explicitly states that there should be no reliance on state shared across calls. This means that, although JAX-RPC programming looks like traditional RPC programming in which you communicate with a specific object, it does not behave this way. It has much in common with the design and use of stateless session EJBs in that no assumptions about users or their states can be made.

In some Web Service implementations, you can use HTTP cookies to maintain an ongoing conversation between client and server (as used by servlet and JSP session state). However, this is not very helpful because it ties the service implementation to the HTTP protocol. If you want to maintain any form of state in a Web Service, you should explicitly persist that state—probably in a database. You will then need to issue the client with some form of identifier for this state as a return value from the method. Although this can seem clunkier than the use of HTTP-based session state, this "exposed state" is more suited to Web Service interaction. Think of a service that allows you to place and track orders. When placing the order, you will be issued with some form of order identifier. If you need to track the progress of the order, you will submit the order identifier as part of the tracking request. This is the level of granularity at which you should think about Web Service state. It may be hours, or even days, between the placing of the order and the tracking request. You should not expect to keep a session open across this time period, and you should not expect all requests to be made across a particular protocol (HTTP). If this does not sit easily with your design, you are probably not using Web Services at the right level of component granularity and you may be better off using another protocol such as RMI for your client/server communication.

The lifecycle of a stateless session EJB is well documented. It has methods that tell it when it is being readied for use (setSessionContext/ejbCreate) and when it is being discarded (ejbRemove). If you are using a servlet-based Web Service implementation, your class can optionally implement the javax.xml.rpc.server.ServiceLifeCycle interface to receive the same information. This interface defines an init method that passes a context object and a destroy method that perform the same roles as setSessionContext/ejbCreate and ejbRemove, respectively.

The context passed into the ServiceLifeCycle.init method is an implementation of the javax.xml.rpc.server.ServletEndpointContext interface. The primary purpose of this interface is to provide access to the javax.xml.rpc.handler.MessageContext implementation for the current Web Service invocation. The basis of the message context for a SOAP message is extra information contained in the SOAP headers. You can also cast the MessageContext to a javax.xml.rpc.handler.soap.SOAPMessageContext to retrieve the SOAPMessage and the SOAP actor information. The following code fragment shows how you would obtain information from the MessageContext in a servlet-based Web Service:

```
public void init(Object context)
{
  ServletEndpointContext endpointContext = (ServletEndpointContext)context;

  MessageContext messageContext = endpointContext.getMessageContext();
```

20

```
// Examine Web Service call headers
String correlationId = (String)(messageContext.getProperty("CorrelationId"));
...
}
```

The `MessageContext` is made available to an enterprise bean through the `getMessageContext` method that has been added to the `javax.ejb.SessionContext` interface.

In some cases, you need to perform common processing of incoming messages, maybe message inspection and rejection, or some form of transformation of the message content. If your application design calls for a Front Controller or Intercepting Filter (see Day 18 for details), you would typically use a mechanism such as servlet filters to implement this functionality. The JAX-RPC specification provides a similar message pre- and post-processing mechanism that is independent of the container type called handlers. An in-depth discussion of handlers is beyond the scope of this chapter, but basically you can set up a chain of one or more handlers that will pre-process incoming messages or post-process message responses. The handlers have access to the message itself and the `MessageContext`, so they can communicate with the Web Service implementation by setting or altering values in the `MessageContext`.

Mapping Between Java and SOAP/WSDL Types

For simple types, SOAP and WSDL use the representations defined in "XML Schema Part 2: Datatypes" that is part of the W3C XML Schema standard. There is a straight mapping for all Java primitive types except for `char`. There is also a straight mapping for the Java `String` class.

If you defined a Web Service with the following (unlikely) method:

```
public void test(byte byteArg, short shortArg, int intArg, long longArg,
                 float floatArg, double doubleArg,
                 boolean boolArg, String stringArg)
```

this would map into WSDL as follows:

```
<definitions name="GreetingService" targetNamespace="urn:J2EE21Examples"
             xmlns:tns="urn:J2EE21Examples"
             xmlns="http://schemas.xmlsoap.org/wsdl/"
             xmlns:xsd="http://www.w3.org/2001/XMLSchema"
             xmlns:soap="http://schemas.xmlsoap.org/wsdl/soap/">
  <types/>
  <message name="Greeting_test">
    <part name="byte_1" type="xsd:byte"/>
    <part name="short_2" type="xsd:short"/>
    <part name="int_3" type="xsd:int"/>
    <part name="long_4" type="xsd:long"/>
    <part name="float_5" type="xsd:float"/>
```

```
        <part name="double_6" type="xsd:double"/>
        <part name="boolean_7" type="xsd:boolean"/>
        <part name="String_8" type="xsd:string"/>
    </message>
    <message name="Greeting_testResponse"/>
    ...
</definitions>
```

Note that all the arguments are mapped to a type using the xsd prefix, which refers to the http://www.w3.org/2001/XMLSchema namespace. All these mappings are performed without any extra effort on your part, as are String, Date, Calendar, BigInteger, and BigDecimal. Arrays of these built-in types are also supported automatically. Sections 4 and 5 of the JAX-RPC specification (JSR101) define standard mappings between Java and XML types for an implementation of JAX-RPC.

NOTE
You may notice that the Java type char is missing. This is because there is no direct mapping between a Java char and an XML Schema type. Hence, it is not one of the Java types that is automatically marshaled.

When you start to work with other complex Java types, and arrays of those types, more effort must be put into the representation of these mappings. Consider what is done by RMI when you pass Java objects between a client and server:

- RMI uses the Java serialization mechanism to convert the contents of the object into a byte stream that can be sent across the network.

- Both client and server must have a definition for the type being passed (or must be able to get hold of one).

- The remote interface definition uses standard Java syntax to indicate where objects are used as parameters or return values.

When using complex Java types as part of a Web Service, you must address the same issues. However, there is the added complication that you must do this in a platform- and language-independent way. Therefore, the following is needed to pass complex parameters as part of a Web Service method:

- Provide a mechanism to marshal and unmarshal the contents of a complex Java type into an XML format that can be used as part of a SOAP message

- Deliver the marshalling and unmarshalling mechanism on both the client and the server

- Indicate in the WSDL definition that certain parameters or return values are complex types, and provide a mapping between the complex types and their associated marshalling/unmarshalling code

20

Consider also the situation where you are provided with WSDL that has been generated from a non-Java Web Service, such as a Web Service implemented using Microsoft .NET components. This may also contain definitions for complex types that must be mapped into Java types to use that Web Service from Java.

Somebody has to do this mapping, and it is not necessarily straightforward. Sometimes it can be done using automated tools, while at other times it may require custom code.

Marshaling Complex Types

A certain amount of complex type mapping is done for you. If your complex types are fairly straightforward, they can be defined according to JavaBeans principles (default constructor, getters and setters, serializable). Such types can be automatically marshaled into and out of XML by a JAX-RPC implementation, so in this case you will not be required to write any additional code to get these types across a Web Service interface.

Web Service design is heavily influenced by two aspects: statelessness and data-only passing. As discussed in the sidebar "Always Start from the WSDL," a WSDL description defines data that is passed back and forth between clients and servers. There is no way of specifying functionality, so all the on-the-wire types are defined only in terms of their data. This fits well with coarse-grained component design principles where you should not really be handing out combinations of data and functionality but designing your interfaces so that functionality is encapsulated in the component and data is passed in and out. Complex data structures that cross the component boundary then become Data Transfer Objects (DTOs) as discussed on Day 18. In Java terms, a Data Transfer Object should be implemented as a JavaBean.

In some cases, a simple JavaBean style class is not enough to represent the data being manipulated. If you need more control over what is included in the XML messages being exchanged, you can define custom serializers and deserializers to be included as part of your Web Service. You briefly saw some of the automatically generated serializers and deserializers when looking at the structure of the deployed WAR file in the section "Deploying the Service." A type registry is defined to associate the XML data structures in the message with particular Java types. The appropriate serializer or deserializer is called to marshal data between the two formats.

A complete discussion of complex type mapping is beyond the scope of this book; however, if you are interested, this is covered in sections 15 and 19 of the JAX-RPC specification (JSR101).

Summary

Today, you have seen how Web Service protocols and application styles provide a future route for many application integration projects. Web Services provide a framework for the integration of internal or external applications using HTTP and XML. You have seen that Web Service protocols provide a better solution when exposing functionality for integration than existing RPC or Web mechanisms, and you have explored the Web Service functionality offered in J2EE.

You deployed a servlet-based JAX-RPC Web Service and then called this Web Service through a proxy generated from its WSDL. You deployed an EJB-based JAX-RPC Web Service and used the WSDL generated from it to create a Web Service client. You examined how state and lifecycle are handled for Web Service implementations, and you looked at issues around complex type mapping when marshaling between Java objects and XML data types.

Q&A

Q SOAP uses HTTP as a transport, so does this mean that it is restricted to synchronous interaction?

A Any transport can be used for a SOAP message as long as someone creates a binding for it. SOAP bindings have been defined for SMTP, and such bindings can be created for any other transport mechanism, such as FTP or MQSeries, regardless of whether such mechanisms are synchronous or asynchronous.

Also, although HTTP is inherently synchronous, you can use it to pass XML documents that consist of business "messages" and that form part of a workflow. If the sender of the message is also capable of receiving such messages, it may receive a response of some form at some future point in time. This uses two synchronous interactions to create asynchronous behavior.

Q Can I use JAX-RPC to send an XML document rather than performing an XML-based RPC call?

A Although it is possible to send an XML document as a parameter to an RPC call using JAX-RPC, document-centric interactions are intended to be serviced by the SOAP with Attachments API for Java (SAAJ) and the Java API for XML Messaging (JAXM). You will encounter SAAJ and JAXM in more detail tomorrow.

Q What sort of information is contained in a WSDL document?

A A WSDL document contains two basic types of information. It contains the interface for the Web Service that consists of type information, message definitions (parameters and return types), operation definitions (methods that can be called), port types (groupings of methods), and bindings that define how port types are

20

carried over different transports. A WSDL file also contains specific location information for a Web Service in the form of ports that provide a specific location for an instance of a port type and service descriptions that define groups of ports.

Q Why can I only expose stateless session EJBs as Web Services under JAX-RPC and not other types?

A Although JAX-RPC provides an RPC-style interface to a Web Service, the whole ethos of Web Services is based around a stateless model of operation. The maintenance of state in traditional RPC terms relies on either an ongoing connection or a protocol-specific token being passed. Neither of these suits the style and granularity of Web Service interaction. All Web Service implementations under JAX-RPC for J2EE are required to be stateless, so only stateless session EJBs match this requirement.

Exercises

Today's exercise is to extend the JAX-RPC front end for the Agency case study so that a client can find all the applicants at a specific location. In the exercise directory under Day 20 on the accompanying Web site there is a version of the Agency case you have seen in this chapter. Your task is to add to the Service EJB a method that takes the name of a location and returns an array of strings representing the applicants registered at that location.

The provided files consist of the stateless session bean discussed in this chapter (Service) that allows you to list all the jobs at a particular location.

If you need a few pointers, you should:

1. Update the Service.java and ServiceImplementation.java files in day20/ exercise/src/agency. You can get a list of applications for a location using the findByLocation method on the ApplicantHome interface.

2. Build the classes using asant build-service.

3. Open the ear file created in the build folder and add to the Service EJB an ejb reference for the applicant home interface.

4. Verify and deploy your EAR to your J2EE RI application server (using deploytool or asant deploy-service).

5. Update the AgencyServiceClient.java file in day20/exercise/src/client to call your new method.

6. Build the client using asant build-client and then run it with asant run-client.

A complete solution can be found in the agency folder on the Day 20 folder on the accompanying Web site.

WEEK 3

DAY 21

Message-Style Web Services and Web Service Registries

Yesterday, you learned about Web Service architecture and you created your own RPC-style Web Services. Although RPC-style interaction is a common style of distributed interaction, many applications also use message-oriented mechanisms to decouple parts of the system. Today, you will use the same Web Service protocols to perform a message-style interaction.

The final part of your exploration of Java Web Services will examine the use of XML-based registries. Part of the Web Service architecture involves the lookup of Web Service information in a registry, but the Web Service information you used was not obtained that way. Today, you will see how such registration and retrieval can be simplified using a standard Java API.

Today, you will

- Look at how message-style Web Service interactions differ from RPC-style interactions
- Send and receive SOAP messages using the SOAP with Attachments API for Java (SAAJ)
- Examine the role of Web Service registries
- Walk through code based on the Java API for XML Registries (JAXR) that registers and retrieves information using a UDDI registry

Today's intention is to use message-based Web Services (as opposed to RPC-based ones) and to interact with a Web Service registry.

Message-based SOAP Services

So far, you have examined Web Services largely from an RPC-oriented perspective. For the first part of today, you will examine how message-based Web Services can be used under J2EE.

Message-Style Versus RPC-Style

To a large degree, there is little difference between the mechanics of message-style and RPC-style Web Services. Essentially, a message-style Web Service uses a single operation with a single parameter. This single parameter is an XML document to be processed. There is no reason why you could not define an RPC-style interface that takes a single parameter that is an XML document. Under the covers, in SOAP-land, these interfaces would look largely the same. However, there are some differences in application style:

- RPC services offer a related group of operations. There may be some implication of retained state between operations on the same interface.
- Message services tend to work on document-centric interactions, such as a workflow in which each service accepts the document, changes or processes part of it, and then passes it on.

There are pros and cons to both RPC-style services and message-style services. The choice between them will largely depend on how your application works. This choice is the same as between RMI interfaces and JMS messages in non-Web Service J2EE. As with RMI and JMS in J2EE applications, you can mix and match RPC-style and message-style Web Services as required. RPC-style Web Services can be used to build applications that require synchronous interaction to deliver functionality directly to users, whereas message-style Web Services are used to create more loosely-coupled applications such as order processing and workflow.

Creating a Client

A messaging client must do two things:

- Create a message to send to the service
- Obtain a connection to the service, or some proxy for it, over which the message can be sent

In terms of a SOAP messaging client, it will send an XML document, possibly with some non-XML attachments. As a developer, if you know the SOAP specifications well, you can use the standard Java HTTP support and XML APIs, such as DOM, to create your own SOAP messages. However, it is far preferable to use a standard API to help you create and populate a SOAP message. A SOAP message has a fixed format, as shown in Figure 21.1, so the API will need to reflect this.

As you can see, the overall message is packaged using MIME to delineate the XML part of the message from the attachments. The XML part of the message is encapsulated in a SOAP envelope. Within the SOAP envelope, there is a SOAP header that contains information relating primarily to the transportation of the message and a SOAP body that holds the principal payload of the message. Both the header and the body consist of XML elements with content, attributes, and namespace information. Your chosen API must allow you to access and populate the contents of a SOAP envelope.

To send the message, you could create a direct connection to the target service. Otherwise, you could pass it to an intermediary that will route the message to its eventual destination. In both cases, you will need an address for the target service.

You will frequently require some form of reply to your message. The way this is sent depends on the style of interaction. If you send directly to the service, the response could be returned from the call. Otherwise, if the response is to arrive later, you will have to supply your own endpoint information to the service for it to use as the return address for the message. You will also need some mechanism to handle this response when it arrives.

Creating a Service

A message-based service has a single entry point to which messages are delivered. This follows the same principle you have seen for JMS servers and Message-Driven beans. Messages will be received by the service and processed according to their purpose. A synchronous service will generate a response or acknowledgement during the processing and then return this to the sender. An asynchronous service will delegate the message processing to another thread of execution and then return from the call, allowing the sender to proceed. An asynchronous service can send a response to the original sender at a later time as long as it has a return address of some form.

21

FIGURE 21.1

The contents of a SOAP message.

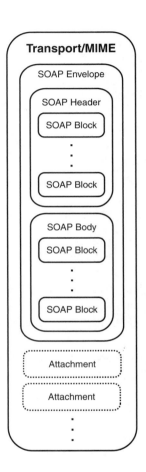

To receive messages, a service must listen on a named endpoint. In the case of direct, synchronous services, the client will use this endpoint information to send a message directly to the service. For routed services, the routing system must deliver the message to the target service when it arrives at its destination.

A service can potentially process a single type of message or it could process multiple types. In the latter case, there must be some way for it to determine which type of message has been received to process it correctly. One option is to apply a form of the Command pattern where the message contains information about how it should be processed. It is possible to put such information in the SOAP header, SOAP body, or in an attachment. However, embedding the command in the SOAP body is generally the best way.

Sending and Receiving SOAP Messages with SAAJ

The SOAP with Attachments API for Java (SAAJ) provides an API for the creation, manipulation, and exchange of SOAP messages. Figure 21.2 shows how an SAAJ client and server interact. As you can see, the client simply populates a SOAP envelope with an XML message and then sends this directly to the server. An SAAJ client can interact with any Web Service that complies with the SOAP 1.1 standard, and a service based on SAAJ can interact with any Web Service client that complies with that standard. To guarantee such interoperability, Sun delayed the release of J2EE 1.4 so that there was time to ensure it met the requirements of the Web Service Interoperability (WS-I) Basic Profile 1.0.

FIGURE 21.2

SAAJ client and server.

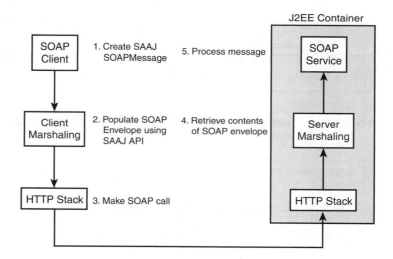

Implementing an SAAJ-based Web Service

To see SAAJ in action, you will now examine a service example that interacts with the agency EJBs you saw earlier in the case study to list the jobs available at a particular location. The server consists of a servlet that uses SAAJ to receive and unpack the SOAP messages containing the location name and the request type. In response, the server will retrieve the job information and package it up as an XML response for the client.

Processing a SOAP Message Using SAAJ

The implementation for an SAAJ-based Web Service takes the form of an ordinary Java servlet. The servlet runs inside a servlet container and processes the SOAP message

21

using the SAAJ API. HTTP-based SOAP messages are delivered to the doPost method of a servlet. For the service example, this method will need to

- Retrieve the MIME headers from the HTTP request. These are needed to help generate the SAAJ representation of the SOAP message.
- Extract the SOAP message from the HTTP request.
- Convert the XML-encoded request type and location into a Java representation.
- Locate the jobs through the agency EJBs.
- Convert the Java representation of the jobs into XML.
- Send the XML-encoded job list back top the caller.

There are two main parts to this process—manipulating the message and its contents and marshaling in to and out of XML. The service example contains two classes split along these lines. The LocationInformationService class is the servlet-based service class that manipulates the message while the ServerMarshaler takes care of converting between the Java and XML representations of the data passed between client and server.

Receiving and Accessing a SOAP Message Using SAAJ

To process a SOAP message containing a location at which to look for jobs, your servlet must first override the doPost method:

```
public class LocationInformationService extends HttpServlet
{
    public void doPost(HttpServletRequest request, HttpServletResponse response)
                                               throws ServletException,
➥IOException
    {
        ...
    }
    ...
}
```

The servlet request contains the SOAP message from the client. However, you don't want to have to process it all yourself, so at this point you can start to use the SAAJ APIs. The first thing to do is to obtain information about the MIME format of the request. This information allows SAAJ to determine the different segments of the message shown previously in Figure 21.2 and to handle any attachments that may form part of the message. To retrieve this information, you create an instance of javax.xml.soap.MimeHeaders from the HTTP headers contained in the HttpServletRequest object by retrieving the headers from the request and adding them to the MimeHeaders. Listing 21.1 shows a helper method—getMimeHeaders—that does this.

LISTING 21.1   Retrieving the MIME Headers

```
public class LocationInformationService extends HttpServlet
{
    public void doPost(HttpServletRequest request, HttpServletResponse response)
                                            throws ServletException,
➥IOException
    {
        MimeHeaders mimeHeaders = getMimeHeaders(request);
        ...
    }
    ...

    private MimeHeaders getMimeHeaders(HttpServletRequest request)
    {
        Enumeration httpHeaders = request.getHeaderNames();
        MimeHeaders mimeHeaders = new MimeHeaders();

        while (httpHeaders.hasMoreElements())
        {
            String httpHeaderName = (String)httpHeaders.nextElement();
            String httpHeaderValue = request.getHeader(httpHeaderName);

            StringTokenizer httpHeaderValues =
➥new StringTokenizer(httpHeaderValue, ",");
            while (httpHeaderValues.hasMoreTokens())
            {
                String headerValue = httpHeaderValues.nextToken().trim();
                mimeHeaders.addHeader(httpHeaderName, headerValue);
            }
        }

        return mimeHeaders;
    }
}
```

The MIME header information can be used by an instance of javax.xml.soap.
MessageFactory to extract the SOAP message from the requests input stream. You pass
the input stream from the request, together with the MIME headers, to the
createMessage method on the MessageFactory instance. This method processes the
stream and creates an instance of SOAPMessage. Listing 21.2 shows another helper
method for your servlet—extractSoapMessage—that retrieves the SOAPMessage from
the request.

21

LISTING 21.2   Retrieving the SOAP Message Sent by the Client

```
public class LocationInformationService extends HttpServlet
{
    public void doPost(HttpServletRequest request, HttpServletResponse response)
                                                throws ServletException,
➥IOException
    {
        ...
        SOAPMessage soapRequest = extractSoapMessage(mimeHeaders, request);
        ...
    }
    ...
    private SOAPMessage extractSoapMessage(MimeHeaders mimeHeaders,
➥HttpServletRequest request)
                                                                throws
➥SOAPException, IOException
    {
        InputStream inStream = request.getInputStream();

        MessageFactory factory = MessageFactory.newInstance();
        SOAPMessage message = factory.createMessage(mimeHeaders, inStream);

        return message;
    }
}
```

After you have the SOAPMessage containing the request, you need to unmarshal the
XML-encoded request type and location. The ServerMarshaler that forms the other part
of the Web Service defines methods to perform this manipulation. Listing 21.3 shows
how the ServerMarshaler is used to retrieve the information which is subsequently
checked before being passed to an agency EJB.

LISTING 21.3   Retrieving the Request Type and Location

```
public class LocationInformationService extends HttpServlet
{
    public void doPost(HttpServletRequest request, HttpServletResponse response)
                                                throws ServletException,
➥IOException
    {
        ...
        String requestType =
        ServerMarshaler.getRequestTypeFromMessage(soapRequest);
        String location = ServerMarshaler.getLocationFromMessage(soapRequest);

        if (requestType == null || requestType.length() == 0)
        {
```

LISTING 21.3 continued

```
            log("LocationInformationService: no request type provided");
            return;
        }

        if (location == null || location.length() == 0)
        {
            log("LocationInformationService: no location provided");
            return;
        }
        ...
    }
    ...
}
```

Now that you have the request type and the location, the next step is to generate the response. The response will need to be passed back to the client in another SOAPMessage, so before generating the response you should obtain a message to hold it. Listing 21.4 shows this.

LISTING 21.4 Creating a SOAPMessage to Send Back to the Client

```
public class LocationInformationService extends HttpServlet
{
    public void doPost(HttpServletRequest request, HttpServletResponse response)
                                                throws ServletException,
➡IOException
    {
        ...
        MessageFactory factory = MessageFactory.newInstance();
        SOAPMessage soapResponse = factory.createMessage();
        ...
    }
    ...
}
```

As with many other factories under J2EE, the way you obtain a factory depends on your relationship with a container. If you are running outside of a container, you can simply create a new instance of the factory:

```
MessageFactory messageFactory = MessageFactory.newInstance();
```

Alternatively, if such a factory is registered with the container, it can be obtained through JNDI. As with all such resources, if your client is long-running, you should close and release the connection when you are no longer using it.

21

This SOAPMessage can then be filled with the list of jobs. This involves calling the findByLocation() method of the Job entity EJB which takes the name of a location and returns a collection containing the jobs at that location. The ServerMarshaler also takes responsibility for converting the list of jobs into XML-encoded format through its addJobsToMessage() method. The creation of the response message is shown in Listing 21.5.

LISTING 21.5   Populating the SOAPMessage with Jobs

```
public class LocationInformationService extends HttpServlet
{
    static final String jobJNDI = "java:comp/env/ejb/JobLocal";

    public void doPost(HttpServletRequest request, HttpServletResponse response)
                                                    throws ServletException,
➥IOException
    {
        ...
        InitialContext ic = new InitialContext();

        if (requestType.equalsIgnoreCase("jobsAtLocation"))
        {
            String[] jobs = null;

            Object lookup = ic.lookup(jobJNDI);

            JobLocalHome jobHome =
➥(JobLocalHome)PortableRemoteObject.narrow(lookup, JobLocalHome.class);

            Collection col = jobHome.findByLocation(location);
            Iterator it = col.iterator();

            jobs = new String[col.size()];
            for (int i = 0; i < col.size(); ++i)
            {
                JobLocal job = (JobLocal)it.next();
                jobs[i] = job.getCustomer() + "/" + job.getRef();
            }

            ServerMarshaler.addJobsToMessage(jobs, soapResponse);
        }
        ...
    }
    ...
}
```

After you have the SOAPMessage containing the receipt, you then need to send it back to the caller using the HttpServletResponse. Before sending any data, you must set the status of the call to `HttpServletResponse.SC_OK` and set the `"content-type"` HTTP header to be `'text/xml; charset="utf-8"'` to indicate that the message contains XML. You can then get the output stream from the response and write the message contents using the `writeTo` method on the `SOAPMessage`. Flush the output stream after sending the message to ensure that it is fully sent to the client. This final set of message processing steps is shown in Listing 21.6.

LISTING 21.6 Returning the SOAPMessage to the Client

```
public class LocationInformationService extends HttpServlet
{
    public void doPost(HttpServletRequest request, HttpServletResponse response)
                                                   throws ServletException,
➥IOException
    {
        ...
        response.setStatus(HttpServletResponse.SC_OK);

        response.setHeader("content-type", "text/xml; charset=\"utf-8\"");

        OutputStream outStream = response.getOutputStream();
        soapMessage.writeTo(outStream);

        outStream.flush();
        ...
    }
    ...
}
```

With the addition of suitable exception handling and import statements, this concludes the code for the message handling. This service depends on the use of the `ServerMarshaler`, so you will examine this next.

Server-side Marshaling Between Java and XML

When using JAX-RPC, the tools generate marshaling classes that marshal data between Java and XML. There is the same need when creating SAAJ messages, but there is no strict framework as there is with JAX-RPC. The SAAJ API provides methods for you to manipulate the contents of the SOAP envelope so that you can add your own XML documents to the SOAP body. However, you are faced with some choices:

- SAAJ provides a custom API for populating `SOAPMessages` and accessing their contents. Although this is slightly quirky, it ensures that the contents of the message are correctly scoped to the appropriate namespaces.

21

- You can build your message using the standard XML DOM API as the message contents can be treated as DOM Nodes. If you are more familiar with DOM you may find this more straightforward, but there is more scope for errors in namespace manipulation.

- Another alternative would be to use the Java Architecture for XML Binding to provide automated marshaling between Java and XML. However, JAXB is not included in J2EE 1.4 so, again, this is something that could be used at a subsequent release (or you could use the implementation in the Java Web Services Developer Pack).

For this example, you will use the SAAJ API to create an XML document within the SOAP envelope. This is what the ServerMarshaler class does. The SAAJ API provides access to the different parts of the SOAP envelope, as shown in Figure 21.3. A SOAP message consists of a SOAP part and a set of optional attachments. To populate or process a SOAP message, you need to retrieve the SOAP part represented by the javax.xml.soap.SOAPPart class. You can retrieve the SOAP part through the getSOAPPart method on the SOAPMessage. You can then retrieve the SOAP envelope, represented by the javax.xml.soap.SOAPEnvelope class, from within the SOAP part using the getEnvelope method:

```
SOAPEnvelope soapEnvelope = soapMessage.getSOAPPart().getEnvelope();
```

FIGURE 21.3

The parts of a SOAP message accessible through SAAJ.

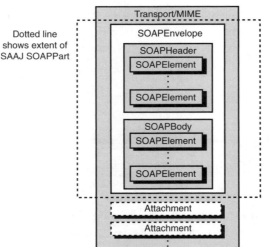

From within the SOAPEnvelope, you can retrieve representations of the SOAP header (javax.xml.soap.SOAPHeader) and the SOAP body (javax.xml.soap.SOAPBody). Here's an example:

```
SOAPBody soapBody = soapEnvelope.getBody();
```

The next steps depend on whether you are processing a SOAPMessage you have been sent or creating a new one. The first thing the server needs to do is extract information from the SOAPMessage sent by the client. Listing 21.7 shows an example of the message contents sent by a client. The message body contains two elements—one for the request type and another for the location.

LISTING 21.7   Request Message Contents

```
<agency:request xmlns:agency="http://J2EE21/agency">
    <agency:type>jobsAtLocation</agency:type>
    <agency:location>London</agency:location>
</agency:request>
```

To process this message, you will have to obtain a child of the body element named <request> and then retrieve specific children of that <request> node called <type> and <agency>. However, the SAAJ API provides only the SOAPElement.getChildElements() method that returns an Iterator for the collection of child elements matching the given name. To extract the single element you expect, you simply iterate onto the first element and cast this to be a SOAPElement. The ServerMarshaler class contains a helper method, getChildElementByName(), to perform this common set of steps for you as shown in Listing 21.8.

LISTING 21.8   getChildElementByName Method from ServerMarshaler Class

```
private static SOAPElement getChildElementByName(Name name, SOAPElement element)
                          throws SOAPException
{
  Iterator childIterator = element.getChildElements(name);

  if (childIterator.hasNext())
  {
    SOAPElement childElement = (SOAPElement)childIterator.next();

    return childElement;
  }
  else
  {
```

21

LISTING 21.8   continued

```
      throw new SOAPException("element " + name.getQualifiedName() + "
➥is missing");
  }
}
```

You may have noticed the use of the `javax.xml.soap.Name` type as a parameter to the `getChildElementByName()` method. The SAAJ API uses these specifically qualified name constructs rather than strings to enforce correct namespace usage. Any time an element is created within the `SOAPEnvelope`, a `Name` is required. The names for your messages `Name` need to be defined within a specific namespace, such as `"http://J2EE21/agency"`.

Armed with the `getChildElementByName()` method and the SAAJ methods you have seen so far, you can now retrieve the request type from the message. The `ServerMarshaler` method that does this, `getRequestTypeFromMessage()`, is shown in listing 21.9. This method takes the `SOAPMessage` retrieved from the message factory and extracts the request type (in this case 'jobsAtLocation'). A `Name` is first created representing the `<request>` element using the `SOAPEnvelope`'s `createName()` method. This name is passed to the `getChildElementByName()` method along with the `SOAPBody`. This works since `SOAPBody` is a subclass of `SOAPElement` and so it can be processed by `getChildElementByName()`. This is then repeated to obtain the `<type>` child element from under the `<request>`. The text contents of the `<type>` element can then be retrieved using the `SOAPElement.getValue()` method. The code to retrieve the `<location>` is almost identical.

LISTING 21.9   getRequestTypeFromMessage() Method from ServerMarshaler Class

```
    ...
    static final String nsAgency = "http://J2EE21/agency";
    static final String prefixAgency = "agency";

    public static String getRequestTypeFromMessage(SOAPMessage soapMessage)
➥throws SOAPException
    {
      SOAPEnvelope soapEnvelope = soapMessage.getSOAPPart().getEnvelope();
      SOAPBody soapBody = soapEnvelope.getBody();

      // Retrieve the request element from under the body
      Name requestName = soapEnvelope.createName("request", prefixAgency,
➥nsAgency);
      SOAPElement soapRequest = getChildElementByName(requestName, soapBody);
```

LISTING 21.9 **LISTING 21.9** continued

```
    // Retrieve the type element from under the request
    Name typeName = soapEnvelope.createName("type", prefixAgency, nsAgency);
    SOAPElement soapType = getChildElementByName(typeName, soapRequest);
    String type = soapType.getValue();

    return type;
  }
  ...
```

The other marshaling required on the server is to convert the array of job strings into XML. Recall from the application code in Listing 21.5 that the addJobsToMessage() method is passed a SOAP message to populate. The code for this method is shown in Listing 21.10. You can retrieve the SOAPEnvelope from the message passed and subsequently the SOAPBody. You can then add a new SOAPBodyElement using the addBodyElement method to represent the top level XML <response> element. You must pass an appropriate Name for the newly created element. This must be obtained from the SOAPEnvelope of the message that will contain the element. The return value from addBodyElement() is a SOAPElement representing the new node.

LISTING 21.10 addJobsToMessage() Method from ServerMarshaler Class

```
    ...
    static final String nsAgency = "http://J2EE21/agency";
    static final String prefixAgency = "agency";

    public static void addJobsToMessage(String[] jobs, SOAPMessage soapMessage)
    ➥throws SOAPException
    {
      SOAPEnvelope soapEnvelope = soapMessage.getSOAPPart().getEnvelope();
      SOAPBody soapBody = soapEnvelope.getBody();

      // Create a response element under the body
      Name responseName = soapEnvelope.createName("response", prefixAgency,
    ➥nsAgency);
      SOAPBodyElement soapResponse = soapBody.addBodyElement(responseName);

      // Indicate how many job elements there are in the response
      Name numJobsName = soapEnvelope.createName("numJobs", prefixAgency,
    ➥nsAgency);
      SOAPElement soapNumJobs = soapResponse.addChildElement(numJobsName);
      soapNumJobs.addTextNode("" + jobs.length);
```

21

LISTING 21.10   continued

```
      // Create a set of job elements under the response
      Name jobsName = soapEnvelope.createName("jobs", prefixAgency, nsAgency);
      SOAPElement soapJobs = soapResponse.addChildElement(jobsName);

      Name jobName = soapEnvelope.createName("job", prefixAgency, nsAgency);

      for (int i = 0; i < jobs.length; i++)
      {
        SOAPElement soapJob= soapJobs.addChildElement(jobName);
        soapJob.addTextNode(jobs[i]);
      }
   }
   ...
```

You create elements to represent the list of jobs (<jobs>) and the number of jobs in that list (<numjobs>) below the <response> element by using the SOAPBodyElement's addChildElement method. These new elements are of type SOAPElement. As you iterate through the list of jobs, you add one <job> element for each job below <jobs>. You add the text for the <numJobs> and <job> elements using the addTextNode method on SOAPElement. Once again, the created elements must be associated with the correct XML namespace by creating a Name for them.

Note that during all of this, javax.xml.soap.SOAPExceptions might be thrown by the various methods and constructors used. Please refer to the SAAJ API documentation for specific details.

Packaging and Deploying the Simple Web Service Using J2EE RI deploytool

This section shows how to deploy the simple Web Service to the J2EE RI. The packaging and deployment of this SAAJ servlet is similar to any other J2EE servlet.

As usual, start up the PointBase database server and J2EE RI server before starting deploytool.

By choosing File, Open, load up the Day21/examples/j2ee-ri/agency.ear enterprise application archive. This defines a single group of Entity beans called Entity. The contents of the enterprise archive have already been partially configured to contain the appropriate code and configuration for the entity beans. Highlight the Agency application in the explorer on the left side of the deploytool GUI and its contents will be shown on the right side, as shown in Figure 21.4.

Figure 21.4

Partially defined Agency case study enterprise archive.

The agency.ear file you have just opened does not contain the Web archive for the SAAJ location information servlet.

NOTE

In the Day21/examples/j2ee-ri directory there is an agency.orig.ear file. This is a copy of the agency.ear file. Should you make a mistake in the following steps you can replace agency.ear with this file and start again.

You will now be guided through the process of creating the SAAJ Web Service using the deploytool wizard. If you prefer to view the complete application, you can use the agency.ear file in the Day21/agency/j2ee-ri directory on the Web site.

Creating the Web Service WAR

You will package up the SAAJ Web Service in a WAR file, so choose File, New, Web Component to create a new one. Click Next to skip the introduction screen and move onto the WAR file creation screen. You will be creating a New WAR Module in Application agency, so ensure that this option is selected. Next, under WAR Naming provide "wsagency" as the WAR Name.

Now you can populate your WAR with the files you saw earlier. Under the Contents section, click the Edit button to display the Edit Contents of wsagency screen.

21

Browse to the Day21/examples/classes directory to find the SAAJ servlet class files (LocationInformationService.class and ServerMarshaler.class), the entity bean interface definitions (all classes in the Day21/examples/classes/data directory), add them to the contents as shown in Figure 21.5 and click OK.

FIGURE 21.5

Adding class files to the WAR.

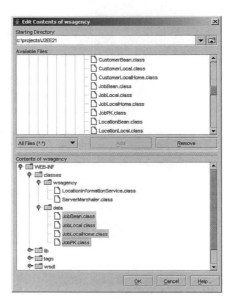

Back at the WAR file screen, click Next to move onto the Choose Component Type screen and select Servlet. Now click Next to move onto the Component General Properties screen. Select wsagency.LocationInformationService as your Servlet Class (this will be offered from the drop-down list). The other fields will be populated based on the servlet name as shown in Figure 21.6. Click Next and then Finish to create the WAR file.

During this process, deploytool has created the web.xml and sun-web.xml files discussed on Day 12. There are no entries in these files that specifically indicate that this servlet forms part of a Web Service.

Configuring the WAR and Component

To complete the Web Service WAR configuration, you will need to define its context root, alias and EJB references for the Entity beans. First, select the General tab of the agency WAR file (as shown in Figure 21.7). Set the Context Root field to /wsagency.

FIGURE 21.6

Configuring the servlet properties.

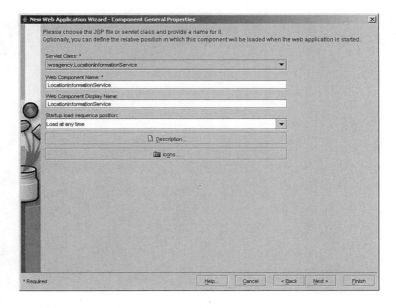

FIGURE 21.7

Setting the Web Service context root.

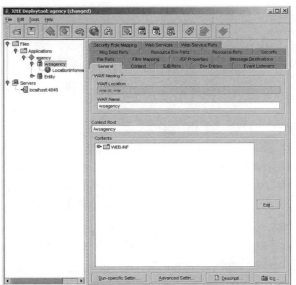

Now select the LocationInformationService component in the left-hand pane. Select the Aliases tab and Add an alias of /LocationServices as shown in Figure 21.8.

21

FIGURE 21.8

Configuring an alias for the Web Service servlet.

To complete the EJB configuration, highlight the wsagency JAR in the left-hand pane and select the EJB Refs tab. Click Add and add a reference to the JobBean setting the name to ejb/JobLocal, type to Entity, interfaces to Local, and the home and local interface names to data.JobLocalHome and data.JobLocal, respectively. This is shown in Figure 21.9. Once this is added, select the reference and change the Sun-specific settings for ejb/JobLocal to data-entity-ejb.jar#JobBean.

Deploying the Service

Now you can deploy the service. Select the Agency EAR in the left-hand pane of deploytool and then select Tools, Deploy from the menus. Provide your administrator user name and password if prompted and ensure that the message "Operation Completed Successfully" is displayed on the Distribute Module screen.

You can now access the SAAJ Web Service at the URL http://localhost:8000/ wsagency/LocationServices. The HTTP GET handler for the servlet should give you a message as shown in Figure 21.10.

In the next section, you will run a standalone client application that exercises the SAAJ Web Service.

FIGURE 21.9

*Adding entity refer-
ences for the Web
Service servlet.*

FIGURE 21.10

*Successful deployment
message from the Web
Service servlet.*

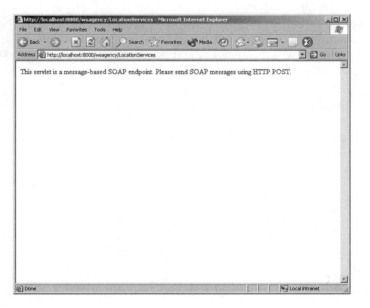

21

Consuming the SAAJ Web Service

To use your Web Service you need a client. For the purposes of this exercise, this client will be a standard Java class with a main method. However, it could also be a J2EE component such as a JSP or EJB or a non-Java client. The client will create a SOAP message containing a given location, send the service a request for a list of jobs at that location and print out the list when it returns.

Sending a Basic SOAP Message

The SAAJ API provides a simple way to send a straightforward SOAP message. An SAAJ client will create a SOAP message using the SAAJ API and send that message to a SOAP server at a specified URL.

The first thing to do is create the SOAP message. To do this, you need an instance of the MessageFactory class that you saw earlier. From this you obtain a SOAPMessage to populate with your request. This is identical to the way you created the response SOAPMessage in the servlet earlier.

You now have an empty SOAP envelope you can populate. The message to be sent in this case is a request for a list of jobs. You have the same marshaling issues as on the server-side and these are discussed shortly from the client perspective. The client class, SAAJAgencyClient, uses a ClientMarshaler helper class to marshal between Java and XML. The method addRequestToMessage() takes the message type ("jobsAtLocation") together with the location itself and creates a request document in the given SOAPMessage. Listing 21.11 shows the client creating a SOAPMessage and populating it.

LISTING 21.11   Creating the SOAP Message

```
public class SAAJAgencyClient
{
    private static String location = "%";

    public static void main(String[] args)
    {
        // Obtain location from command line arguments
        ...

        MessageFactory messageFactory = MessageFactory.newInstance();

        // Populate message with request type of "jobsAtLocation"
        // and location
        SOAPMessage soapRequest = messageFactory.createMessage();
```

LISTING 21.11 continued

```
        ClientMarshaler.addRequestToMessage("jobsAtLocation", location,
➥soapRequest);

        ...
    }
}
```

Now that the message is ready, the client needs a `javax.xml.soap.SOAPConnection` to send the message. This is created from a `javax.xml.soap.SOAPConnectionFactory`. As with the `MessageFactory`, the `SOAPConnectionFactory` can be instantiated directly using the `newInstance()` method or can be obtained through JNDI if one is registered with the J2EE container in which the component is running. The `createConnection()` method of the `SOAPConnectionFactory` returns a `SOAPConnection`.

As SAAJ is used to make direct SOAP calls to servers, you must specify the address (or endpoint) of the target server using a `java.net.URL`. In this case, the target URL is that of the server you deployed earlier, namely `http://localhost:8000/wsagency/` `LocationServices`.

The SOAP server happens to be implemented using Java and SAAJ but this is not essential. The server could equally well be implemented in Perl or as an ASP.NET components written in C#. Note that the URL for the Web Service looks just like any other servlet address and contains no special indications that it is a Web Service rather than an HTML interface.

You now have the two things you need—a message and somewhere to send it—so you can now send the message using the `SOAPConnection`'s `call()` method. The `call()` method takes as parameters the message itself and the target endpoint to which it should be delivered. The sequence of obtaining the connection and making the call is shown in Listing 21.12.

LISTING 21.12 Sending the SOAP Message

```
public class SAAJAgencyClient
{
    ...
    public static void main(String[] args)
    {
        ...

        SOAPConnectionFactory connectionFactory = SOAPConnectionFactory.
➥newInstance();
```

21

LISTING 21.12   continued

```
        SOAPConnection connection = connectionFactory.createConnection();
        URL endpoint = new URL("http://localhost:8000/wsagency/
➥LocationServices");

        // Send request
        soapResponse = connection.call(soapRequest, endpoint);

        ...

    }
}
```

Because the service you are calling is a synchronous, request/response service, you will receive a SOAP message as a response. In application terms, this message contains an XML document listing the jobs at the location you provided. To process this list, you need to retrieve the XML document from the SOAP message. This XML document will be contained in the SOAP envelope. Once again, the ClientMarshaler class encapsulates the conversion from XML to Java and provides a getJobsFromMessage() method that creates an array of Java Strings. These strings can then be printed out as shown in Listing 21.13.

LISTING 21.13   Printing Out the List of Jobs

```
public class SAAJAgencyClient
{
    ...
    public static void main(String[] args)
    {
        ...

        // Retrieve job list from response
        System.out.println("Job list: ");
        String[] jobs = ClientMarshaler.getJobsFromMessage(soapResponse);
        for(int i = 0; i < jobs.length; i++)
        {
            System.out.println(jobs[i]);
        }

        System.out.println("\nDone\n");

        ...

    }
}
```

Client-side Marshaling Between Java and XML

The client-side marshaling is very similar to the server-side marshaling except that it performs the actions in reverse. The `addRequestToMessage()` and `getJobsFromMessage()` methods create instances of the `Name` class and manipulate instances of `SOAPEnvlope`, `SOAPBody` and `SOAPEnvelope`. The `ClientMarshaler` is shown in Listing 21.14.

LISTING 21.14 The ClientMarshaler

```java
package client;

import java.util.Iterator;

import javax.xml.soap.Name;
import javax.xml.soap.SOAPBody;
import javax.xml.soap.SOAPBodyElement;
import javax.xml.soap.SOAPElement;
import javax.xml.soap.SOAPEnvelope;
import javax.xml.soap.SOAPException;
import javax.xml.soap.SOAPMessage;

public class ClientMarshaler
{
  static final String nsAgency = "http://J2EE21/agency";
  static final String prefixAgency = "agency";

  public static void addRequestToMessage(String type, String location,
➥SOAPMessage soapMessage) throws SOAPException
  {
    SOAPEnvelope soapEnvelope = soapMessage.getSOAPPart().getEnvelope();
    SOAPBody soapBody = soapEnvelope.getBody();

    // Create a request element under the body
    Name requestName = soapEnvelope.createName("request", prefixAgency,
➥nsAgency);
    SOAPBodyElement soapRequest = soapBody.addBodyElement(requestName);

    // Create a type element under the agencyRequest
    Name typeName = soapEnvelope.createName("type", prefixAgency, nsAgency);
    SOAPElement soapType = soapRequest.addChildElement(typeName);
    soapType.addTextNode(type);

    // Create a location element under the agencyRequest
    Name locationName = soapEnvelope.createName("location", prefixAgency,
➥nsAgency);
    SOAPElement soapLocation = soapRequest.addChildElement(locationName);
    soapLocation.addTextNode(location);
  }
```

21

LISTING 21.14 continued

```java
public static String[] getJobsFromMessage(SOAPMessage soapMessage) throws
➥SOAPException
  {
    SOAPEnvelope soapEnvelope = soapMessage.getSOAPPart().getEnvelope();
    SOAPBody soapBody = soapEnvelope.getBody();

    // Retrieve the response element from under the body
    Name responseName = soapEnvelope.createName("response", prefixAgency,
➥nsAgency);
    SOAPElement soapResponse = getChildElementByName(responseName, soapBody);

    // Retrieve the numJobs element from under the response
    Name numJobsName = soapEnvelope.createName("numJobs", prefixAgency,
➥nsAgency);
    SOAPElement soapNumJobs = getChildElementByName(numJobsName, soapResponse);

    int numJobs = Integer.parseInt(soapNumJobs.getValue());
    String[] jobs = new String[numJobs];

    // Retrieve the jobs element from under the response
    Name jobsName = soapEnvelope.createName("jobs", prefixAgency, nsAgency);
    SOAPElement soapJobs = getChildElementByName(jobsName, soapResponse);

    // Retrieve the jobs and put them in an array
    Iterator jobIterator = soapJobs.getChildElements();

    for (int i = 0; i < numJobs && jobIterator.hasNext(); i++)
    {
      SOAPElement jobElement = (SOAPElement)jobIterator.next();
      jobs[i] = jobElement.getValue();
    }

    return jobs;
  }

  private static SOAPElement getChildElementByName(Name name, SOAPElement
➥element)
                                                    throws SOAPException
  {
    Iterator childIterator = element.getChildElements(name);

    if (childIterator.hasNext())
    {
      SOAPElement childElement = (SOAPElement)childIterator.next();

      return childElement;
    }
    else
```

LISTING 21.14   continued

```
    {
      throw new SOAPException("element " + name.getQualifiedName()
➥+ " is missing");
    }
  }
}
```

As with the server-side marshaling, SOAPExceptions might be thrown by the various methods and constructors used. Please refer to the SAAJ API documentation for specific details.

Running the Simple Client

You compile and run your client as you would any other Java application. The client is built as part of the following Ant directive:

```
asant build
```

You can run the client program using

```
asant run
```

This will prompt you for a location and then send a SOAP message to the SAAJ web service you deployed earlier. Provide the location "London" and you should see the following message printed out (depending on how many jobs you have registered for London):

```
[java] Using Location: London
[java] Job list:
[java] winston/Cigar trimmer

[java] Done
```

So, now you have created, deployed, and invoked a simple Web Service under J2EE using SAAJ.

More Complex Message Exchange

So far you have looked at simple message exchange. This section examines other issues when exchanging SOAP messages.

Headers and Attachments

As well as XML information in the SOAP body, SAAJ allows you to add and retrieve header information and attachments.

21

The SOAPHeader can be obtained from the SOAPEnvelope with the getHeader method. If you are creating a message, you can populate the header using the addHeaderElement method that returns a SOAPHeaderElement. You can then add text or attributes to this header element, as shown in the following:

```
Name txName = envelope.createName("TransactionId", "acme",
                                  "http://acme.com/transactions");
SOAPHeaderElement headerElement = header.addHeaderElement(txName);
headerElement.addTextNode("78d2892ea8af625323c7");
```

There are also specific methods for associating a particular SOAP actor or the SOAP mustUnderstand attribute to a header element.

When receiving a message, an Iterator can be retrieved with the examineHeaderElements method. This Iterator can be used to search through the header elements.

Additionally, you may want to add attachments to your SOAP messages containing non-XML data or additional XML documents. To do this, first create an instance of javax.xml.soap.AttachmentPart to attach to a message by using one of the createAttachmentPart methods on the SOAPMessage class. You can provide the data for your attachment directly (as a String or javax.xml.transform.Source) or through a content handler (part of the JavaBeans Activation Framework [JAF]). These attachments can be any form of data, so the key thing is to set the appropriate MIME type. If providing the data directly, you must specify the MIME type when creating the attachment. When using a content handler, this can supply the correct MIME type to the AttachmentPart object.

After you have created an AttachmentPart object, you attach it to the SOAP message using the addAttachmentPart method on the SOAPMessage class. The code required to create an attachment from an image at a given URL is shown in the following code:

```
SOAPMessage message = ...
...
URL url = new URL("http://acme.com/acme_logo.jpg");
AttachmentPart attachment = message.createAttachmentPart(new DataHandler(url));
message.addAttachmentPart(attachment);
```

Registries for Web Services

As you saw on Day 3, "Naming and Directory Services," naming and directory services are an important part of any distributed environment. J2EE uses JNDI as a way of accessing information about application resources and the location of remote services, such as EJBs and databases.

Because Web Services also operate in a distributed environment, Web Service-oriented naming and directory services are required. In fact, the scope of such services is broader under the Web Services model than under J2EE, because the service will hold organizational and business information as well as Web Service metadata and location information. In Web Service terms, the place to find this information is called a registry or repository.

What Is a Web Service Registry?

As discussed yesterday, a Web Service client can retrieve information about the Web Service it wants to use from a registry. The registry contains information about the service being offered (from currency conversion to the supply of 10-ton trucks). This information includes details about the organization offering the service, the technical access information for the service (interface and transport), and where to find the service.

Tools can be built to browse and search this Web Service registry information. The information retrieved can then be plugged into client applications so that they can integrate with the supplier of the service. This integration can range from fully manual, where a human selects the interface and writes client code to invoke it, to fully automatic, where the selection and invocation are performed by the client application itself.

Why Do I Need One?

To cooperate, applications need information about what services exist and where to find them. You can do this manually by exchanging service definition files, such as WSDL documents. This procedure is reasonably okay when interacting with known business partners. However, manual exchange does have some drawbacks because it does not allow you to find new suppliers of services, and your information must be updated whenever a service location changes.

One alternative is to exchange service information in a partially dynamic way with your business partners by obtaining service definition information from the server on which the service itself is located. Such a mechanism is described in the Web Service Inspection Language (WSIL or WS-Inspection) specification. Again, this method of interaction is reasonably okay if you already know where the server is.

To engage in fully dynamic Web Service use, what you really need to do is search for companies or services that match a specific profile (type of business, type of service, location of business, and so on). From this list, you can choose an appropriate service, and then retrieve its technical information with the minimum of fuss. At runtime, it is possible to check the service information again in case the service location has changed.

21

How Do They Work?

There are two basic ways of finding information in a registry. One way is to drill-down, starting at a known location. Under this model, you can iterate through the registry entries below the current location and potentially recurse down through their children or follow links from them to find the information you require. The alternative mechanism is to globally search the registry for the information you require. In this case, you would search based on a particular piece of information about the service you require, such as the organization's name, its line of business, or the interface definition of the service for which you are looking. The use of these three types of search criteria (frequently called white, yellow, and green pages, respectively) provide you with a lot of flexibility for locating the Web Service you need.

What will usually happen is that you will use some form of search to locate an initial registry entry, such as the top-level registry entry describing an organization's business, and then drill down from there to examine the services available.

One issue here is that for searches to be effective, people must agree on ways of describing and categorizing information. This gives rise to classification systems or taxonomies. There are various common taxonomies set up by industry standards bodies to classify information in their particular areas. Such taxonomies can be used as part of the classification of a Web Service in a registry to help clients find the right form of service. Some examples of useful taxonomies include the North American Industry Classification System (NAICS) and the United Nations Standard Products and Code System (UNSPSC).

Types of Registry

Web Service registries come in a variety of forms:

- Global registries are publicly available and open to all types of business—This is similar in concept to the global Domain Name System (DNS) that lets you find anyone's Internet Protocol (IP) assigned to the hostname that forms part of their Uniform Resource Locator (URL).

- Private registries can be set up behind organizational firewalls—These will facilitate the location of Web Services on a company's intranet.

- Site-specific registries will list all of the services offered at the site associated with the registry—For example, `acme.com` could host a registry service that helped you to locate all Web Services provided by `acme.com`.

- Marketplace registries are set up and maintained by a market maker (a third party or industry consortium)—Such registries may or may not be publicly available, but will provide some form of selection or quality check on the providers of services before including them in the registry.

There is a good whitepaper about Web Service registry styles on the Web Services part of IBM's DeveloperWorks site at `http://www-106.ibm.com/developerworks/webservices/library/ws-rpu1.html`.

Just before leaving the general topic of Web Service registries, it is worth considering how your application—and your business—will actually use Web Services. If you are looking to use Web Services provided by suppliers as part of a supply chain, you may want to use some of the dynamic capabilities of a Web Service registry to locate suppliers and services. However, not all of the information you require will be found dynamically. In real life business terms, you will not necessarily change your supplier of ball bearings from minute to minute. There are other criteria by which you choose your business partners (quality, timeliness, trust, and so on). Therefore, for most applications, the selection of suppliers will usually take place at human speeds and involve humans in the selection. After the selection is made, dynamic lookups can be performed to discover and use the technical service interface and location information.

Marketplaces can also help here. A marketplace can provide a qualitative judgement of potential suppliers, making the selection of previously unknown suppliers less risky. This type of qualitative judgement already takes place in various areas of business, such as organizations that provide credit ratings for businesses. Employing such a service helps you to manage your risk when selecting potential business partners. Given such a rating ability, if a marketplace can offer five trustworthy and high-quality suppliers, you can potentially spread the load across these equal suppliers. Even so, this type of dynamic interaction is more likely in information-based areas, such as financial data and transactions, than in the realms of 10-ton truck purchase.

ebXML Registry and Repository

One of the principal types of Web Service registry is the ebXML Registry and Repository (R&R). The ebXML R&R plays a central role in the ebXML model of e-commerce, as shown in Figure 21.11.

The ebXML R&R acts as a storage area for the central business document definitions, or Core Components, that are used in ebXML business messages. An organization (Company A) that wants to advertise its services in an ebXML R&R will base its service descriptions on these Core Components and will then implement the service (shown as steps 1 and 2). Company A and its services will then be registered in the ebXML R&R (step 3), including a Collaboration Partner Profile (CPP) that describes the different bindings for each service and the roles and workflows associated with it.

21

FIGURE 21.11

*Discovery and negotia-
tion based around an
ebXML registry and
repository.*

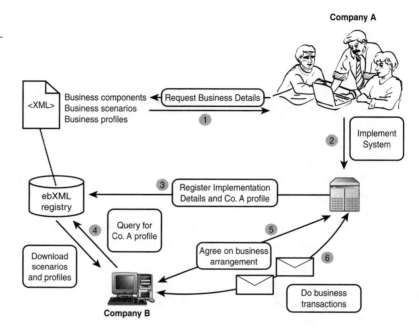

When Company B searches the registry for a service, it can select Company A's offering
and download the service information (step 4). Company B can then use the information
in Company A's CPP to determine how it should interact with Company A's services. It
can then contact Company A with a suggested Collaboration Partner Agreement (CPA)
that details the bindings and service interactions required (step 5). This CPA forms the
basis of the contact between the two companies. When a CPA has been agreed on by the
two companies, business transactions can begin between the two new partners according
to the terms set out in the CPA (step 6). Messages sent between the partners will reference a CPA identifier (CPAid) to indicate of which interaction they are a part.

UDDI Overview

UDDI defines an information model for a registry of Web Service information and a set
of SOAP messages for accessing that information. The information contained can be
split into two parts:

- Business information—This provides the name and contact information for the
  business. It also provides a list of the categories (based on the taxonomies mentioned earlier) under which the business should be "registered" to help a user find
  the business.

- Service information—This gives information about which Web Services are
  offered by the business, their interfaces, and location(s).

At the lowest level, you have the description of a specific Web Service. As you have seen from WSDL, this will contain a description of the service interface and endpoint information telling the user where to find the service. UDDI splits this information between two structures:

- A structure called a `tModel` is used to describe the Web Service's interface, such as the operations, parameters, and data types it uses. Separating such interface information from the service location information means that `tModels` can be stored independently and shared by multiple different services from different businesses. This greatly aids the discovery of compatible service offerings. Although commonly conceptualised as a Web Service description, the information in a `tModel` can describe any mechanism for accessing a service, including email, phone, or fax.

  If you are building a `tModel` from a WSDL interface, you would include the WSDL messages, parameters, return values, complex types, `PortTypes`, and `Bindings`.

- The UDDI `bindingTemplate` structure uses `tModels` to define which particular service is being offered and also provides the location of the service. The location information defines specific endpoints at which the service can be found.

  Again, in WSDL terms, the extra information in the `bindingTemplate` correlates to the WSDL `port` and `service` information.

At a higher level, a `businessService` is used for the logical grouping of services, as defined in `bindingTemplates`. At the top level is a UDDI `businessEntity` that contains the business information. Each `businessEntity` contains one or more `businessServices`.

The UDDI API provides a set of SOAP operations to search for information within this model and to retrieve the relevant parts.

Accessing Information in a UDDI Registry

In this section, you will examine how information in a UDDI registry can be accessed from Java.

NOTE   The subject of accessing, updating, and searching UDDI-based registries would fill a book in itself. This section is intended to give you a head start in using a UDDI-based registry rather than showing you all the nuts and bolts required.

21

As a Java developer, you do not really want to have to build SOAP messages to communicate with a UDDI registry. What you want is a Java-based API that hides away the SOAP manipulation. There are various alternatives, including

- UDDI4J and UDDI4J-WSDL—IBM's Java implementation of the UDDI API
- JAXR—The Java API for XML Registries developed through the JCP

Because this is a book about J2EE and JAXR is included in J2EE, the rest of this chapter concentrates on the use of JAXR.

Choosing a Registry to Query

Before you start manipulating data in a registry, you must choose which registry you will use:

- A public production registry—This is a "live" business registry, such as those hosted by IBM and Microsoft. You should only manipulate "real" business data in these registries. You can search such a registry freely, but if you want to publish data, you will be required to obtain a login and password.
- A public test registry—This is a generally available resource for testing the registration and discovery of Web Services. As with production registries, public test registries are hosted by IBM and Microsoft. If you want to publish data about your test services, you will be required to obtain a login and password.
- A locally hosted registry—There are several UDDI registries available that you can configure in your own environment (IBM's downloadable UDDI registry and jUDDI are two examples). These registries can be used internally within your company for Web Service discovery and testing.

Using JAXR for Registry Access

The Java API for XML Registries (JAXR) is an attempt to provide a unified model of access to XML-based information stored in registries and repositories. The intent is that this will provide a standard API for such access to ease the development of applications that depend on this information.

A Generic Approach

Some registry APIs, such as IBM's UDDI4J, are specifically targeted at UDDI access. As you know, UDDI is not the only XML-based Web Service registry; the ebXML Registry and Repository also fills this role. In addition, there are various other XML-based registries that are used in different e-commerce frameworks. JAXR provides a set of generic

APIs that work on a generic registry information model. Existing registries can then be mapped onto this generic framework, giving developers the ability to access information in different registries using the same API. This should bring the level of consistency to XML-based registry access that JNDI and JDBC have brought to directory services and databases, respectively.

The overall JAXR architecture is shown in Figure 21.6. The client interacts with the JAXR Pluggable Provider layer that acts as a standard interface and rendezvous point. Underneath the Pluggable Provider, a particular registry-specific provider will be used to obtain information from a particular type of registry. This style of architecture has much in common with those of JDBC and JNDI. In fact, it is anticipated that many JAXR providers will, at least initially, be developed as bridges to existing registry providers, in a similar style to the JDBC-ODBC bridge.

FIGURE 21.12

JAXR architecture.

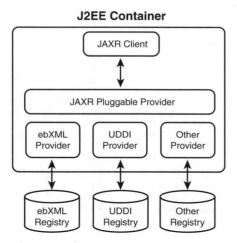

JAXR defines its own information model onto which other information models (such as UDDI or ebXML) can be mapped. The JAXR information model (defined in the package `javax.xml.registry.infomodel`) contains interfaces for some concepts which you encountered earlier, including the following:

- `Organization`—Similar to a UDDI `businessEntity`
- `Service`—Similar to the UDDI `businessService` and `tModel`, containing interface and category information for a service
- `ServiceBinding`—Similar to the UDDI `bindingTemplate`, containing location information for a service instance
- `Concept`—Similar to UDDI categories, used for classifying organizations and services

21

Collections of such interfaces are passed to and returned from JAXR query and manipulation methods.

The class `javax.xml.registry.RegistryService` represents the registry service. After the client has obtained a `RegistryService` reference, it can discover the capabilities of the registry service. Capabilities can be generic or business related. The capabilities are defined in levels, and there are currently two levels—0 and 1. Every JAXR Provider must implement the level 0 capabilities. More advanced providers will also implement the level 1 capabilities. The capability interfaces are

- The `BusinessLifeCycleManager` interface—Enables you to create, update, and delete `organizations`, `services`, `ServiceBindings`, and `concepts`. Each method returns a `BulkResponse` that contains a collection either of keys identifying individual registry entries or of exceptions indicating that a save or delete operation failed. This is a level 0 capability.
- The `GenericLifeCycleManager`—Enables you to save or delete any form of registry entry. This is a level 1 capability.
- The `BusinessQueryManager`—Enables you to find organizations, services, or concepts based on names, concepts, and binding information. This is a level 0 capability.
- The `SQLQueryManager`—Enables you to submit a SQL query that is executed against the registry data. This treats interface types (for example, `Organization`) as if they were database table names. This is a level 1 capability.

Because the principal registries for Web Services are the ebXML Registry and Repository and the UDDI Registry, the JAXR specification defines bindings for UDDI and ebXML. These bindings detail the mappings between the different registry information models.

Contacting a Registry Using JAXR

To begin working with a registry using JAXR, you first need a connection to the registry. This connection is represented by an implementation of the `javax.xml.registry. Connection` interface. As a first step toward obtaining a connection, you need an instance of `javax.xml.registry.ConnectionFactory`:

```
Context context = new InitialContext();
ConnectionFactory factory = (ConnectionFactory)context.lookup("eis/JAXR");
```

You then need to tell the factory the location of your preferred registry server. This is done through properties:

```
Properties riRegistryProperties = new Properties();

riRegistryProperties.setProperty("javax.xml.registry.queryManagerURL",
          "http://uddi.ibm.com/testregistry/inquiryapi");

riRegistryProperties.setProperty("javax.xml.registry.lifeCycleManagerURL",
          "http://uddi.ibm.com/testregistry/publishapi");

factory.setProperties(riRegistryProperties);
```

Now that the factory is targeted at a particular registry, you can use it to create a connection to that registry:

```
Connection connection = factory.createConnection();
```

Authentication credentials must also be supplied before the registry service is used. Credentials will almost certainly be required to update information in the registry and may even be required for access to information. The credentials are contained in an instance of java.net.PasswordAuthentication:

```
String user = ...
String password = ...

char[] passwordArray = password.toCharArray();

PasswordAuthentication pwdAuthentication =
                       new PasswordAuthentication(user, passwordArray);
```

These credentials are then stored in a java.util.HashSet (there may be more than one set of credentials) and associated with the connection:

```
Set credentials = new HashSet();
credentials.add(pwdAuthentication);

connection.setCredentials(credentials);
```

At this point you are ready to interact with the registry. You can either store or retrieve information through this connection.

Storing Information in a Registry Using JAXR

As a simple example of what you can do through JAXR, the following code adds a simple entry into a registry. To update the contents of a registry, you must interact with the business lifecycle manager. The Java representation of this, an instance of javax.xml.registry.BusinessLifecycleManager is obtained from the RegistryService instance, which is itself obtained from the connection:

21

```
RegistryService registryService = connection.getRegistryService();

BusinessLifecycleManager lifecycleManager =
                registryService.getBusinessLifeCycleManager();
```

You can then use the lifecycle manager to create entities within the registry. If you are adding a new organization, you use the `createOrganization()` method:

```
Organization regOrganization =
            lifecycleManager.createOrganization(organizationName);
```

You will also want to provide a description for the organization as part of the entry. If the registry is public, it can be accessed by people from many countries. The registry you are using might be able to deliver its contents in a variety of languages based on user location and local information. However, this implies that the information itself must be available in various languages. To provide for this, descriptions are supplied as an instance of `javax.xml.registry.infomodel.InternationalString`, which is capable of representing multiple, localized versions of the same string. You can add localized descriptions to the `InternationalString` or remove unwanted ones:

```
InternationalString regDescription =
            lifecycleManager.createInternationalString(organizationDescription);

regOrganization.setDescription(regDescription);
```

You might want to define a contact person for your organization. In which case, you must obtain an instance of `javax.xml.registry.infomodel.User` from the lifecycle manager:

```
User regPrimaryContact = lifecycleManager.createUser();
```

You can then define the contact's name as a `javax.xml.registry.infomodel.PersonName` and associate this with the `User`:

```
PersonName regContactName = lifecycleManager.createPersonName(contactName);
regPrimaryContact.setPersonName(regContactName);
```

The contact person might have one or more telephone numbers by which they can be contacted. You can create one or more `javax.xml.registry.infomodel.TelephoneNumber` instances through the lifecycle manager:

```
TelephoneNumber regContactNumber = lifecycleManager.createTelephoneNumber();
```

These telephone numbers can then be associated with the contact person:

```
regContactNumber.setNumber(contactNumber);
Collection numbers = new ArrayList();
numbers.add(regContactNumber);
regPrimaryContact.setTelephoneNumbers(numbers);
```

You can also do the same for email addresses using the `createEmailAddress` method to obtain instances of `EmailAddress` and associate them with the contact person:

```
EmailAddress emailAddress = lifecycleManager.createEmailAddress(contactEmail);
Collection addresses = new ArrayList();
addresses.add(emailAddress);
regPrimaryContact.setEmailAddresses(addresses);
```

Finally, this person can be defined as the primary contact for your organization:

```
regOrganization.setPrimaryContact(regPrimaryContact);
```

You are now ready to commit this information back to the registry. You do this by creating a collection to hold the updated information. Each type of information should be contained in a separate collection:

```
Collection organizations = new ArrayList();
organizations.add(regOrganization);
```

This collection is then passed to the appropriate saveXXX method on the lifecycle manager instance:

```
BulkResponse bulkResponse = lifecycleManager.saveOrganizations(organizations);
```

Any errors that occurred during the update can be retrieved through the `getExceptions` method on the `BulkResponse` returned from the save operation:

```
Collection exceptions = bulkResponse.getExceptions();

if (exceptions == null)
{
  System.out.println("Saved organizations");
  pending.clear();
  return true;
}
else
{
  System.err.println("Got exceptions when trying to save organizations");
  return false;
}
```

If your saving operations were successful, you can call the `BulkResponse.getCollection` that returns a collection of `RegistryObject` instances. In this case, this will be a single copy of the `Organization` you saved. The `Organization` will now have its unique registry key set (accessible through the `getKey` method). This unique key can be used to update and delete the entry.

21

> During all of this, `javax.xml.registry.JAXRExceptions` can be thrown by
> the various methods and constructors used. Please refer to the JAXR API
> documentation for specific details.

You can now write some code to list out the entry you have added.

Retrieving Information from a Registry Using JAXR

An application that retrieves information from a registry uses the same connection initialization and information model as one that updates a registry. However, instead of dealing with the lifecycle manager, it deals with the query manager:

```
BusinessQueryManager queryManager = registryService.getBusinessQueryManager();
```

There are various things that you can supply to the query manager that affect the information it returns. The most obvious thing is a pattern defining some or all of a name:

```
Collection namePatterns = new ArrayList();
namePatterns.add("Wid");
```

In this case, the collection will be passed to the `findOrganizations` method on the query manager as a set of name patterns to match. By default, the pattern is the start of the name to match. You can also supply find qualifiers that affect, among other things, how the information is returned:

```
Collection findQualifiers = new ArrayList();
findQualifiers.add(FindQualifier.SORT_BY_NAME_DESC);
```

You can then pass these two pieces of information to the `findOrganizations` method on the query manager:

```
BulkResponse bulkResponse = queryManager.findOrganizations(findQualifiers,
                                    namePatterns,
                                    null,
                                    null,
                                    null,
                                    null);
Collection organizations = bulkResponse.getCollection();
```

Again, the `BulkResponse` returned can be queried for exceptions or instances of `RegistryObject` that match the query criteria. You can iterate through the collection of `Organizations` and report the information you find there:

```
System.out.println("There are " + organizations.size() + "
➥organizations that begin with " + queryString);

Iterator iterator = organizations.iterator();
while (iterator.hasNext())
{
  Organization organization = (Organization)iterator.next();

  System.out.println("Organization name:\t\t" +
➥organization.getName().getValue());
  System.out.println("Organization description:\t" +
➥organization.getDescription().getValue());
  ...
}
```

Some of the attributes of the organization are themselves collections, such as the contact person's email addresses:

```
Collection emailAddresses = primaryContact.getEmailAddresses();
Iterator emailIterator = emailAddresses.iterator();
if (emailIterator.hasNext())
{
  EmailAddress address = (EmailAddress)emailIterator.next();
  System.out.println("Primary contact email:\t" + address.getAddress());
  ...
}
```

You can assemble this code into a registry lister that lists the entry added previously.

Summary

Today, you sent SOAP messages between an SAAJ client and server. You used the SAAJ API to populate and process the XML message contents. You then examined how this simple exchange could be improved by using headers and attachments or by progressing to JAXM for value-added services.

You have seen how registries play a vital role in allowing Web Service clients to locate and use Web Services. UDDI and ebXML both provide SOAP-based interfaces for such interactions. You examined JAXR code that created a simple entry in a registry and then queried the registry for that entry.

Q&A

Q Can an EJB be an SAAJ server?

A There is no explicit binding to allow an EJB to be bound to an SAAJ endpoint. However, there is no reason why an SAAJ servlet cannot act as an adapter, invoking methods on an EJB in response to SOAP messages received.

21

Q **What is the difference between SAAJ and JAXM?**

A SAAJ provides a fairly low-level API for the manipulation of SOAP messages. All SAAJ messages are sent synchronously and point-to-point. JAXM has the same low-level API for access to message contents but allows you to send messages through a JAXM Provider that can add a higher level of service in terms of reliability and routing.

Q **Why are different categories of information required in a UDDI registry?**

A When you come to search for Web Services, you may know only certain things about them, such as the name of the company that offers the service or the type of interface you expect from the service. By providing business (white pages), category (yellow pages), and technical (green pages) information, UDDI provides a lot of flexibility in the way that you can search for Web Services.

Q **Why does JAXR have its own information model?**

A JAXR defines its own information model so that it can remain independent of the actual registry implementation. If JAXR were to use an existing model, such as UDDI or ebXML, this would compromise its ability to provide support for a wide range of Web Service registries and repositories.

Exercises

Today's exercise is to extend the SAAJ servlet for the Agency case study so that a client can find all the applicants at a specific location. In the exercise directory under Day 21 on the accompanying Web site there is a version of the Agency case you have seen in this chapter. Your task is to add support to the servlet for another message that contains the name of a location and returns an array of strings representing the applicants registered at that location.

The provided files consist of the SAAJ servlet discussed in this chapter (`LocationInformationService`) that allows you to list all the jobs at a particular location.

If you need a few pointers, you should:

Update the `LocationInformationService.java` and `ServerMarshaler.java` files in `day21/exercise/src/agency` to take a new message called "applicantsAtLocation." You can get a list of applications for a location using the `findByLocation` method on the `ApplicantHome` interface.

Build the classes using `asant build`.

Open the EAR file created in the build folder and add to the Service EJB an ejb reference for the applicant home interface.

Verify and deploy your EAR to your J2EE RI application server (using `deploytool` or `asant deploy-service`).

Update the `SAAJAgencyClient.java` file in `day21/exercise/src/client` to call your new method.

Build the client using `asant build` and then run it with `asant run`.

A complete solution can be found in the agency folder on the Day 21 folder on the accompanying Web site.

21

Appendixes

APPENDIX **A**

An Overview of XML

Throughout the book, there are many examples of how XML can be used within J2EE applications. Day 16, "Integrating XML with J2EE," and Day 17, "Transforming XML Documents," cover the topic of XML in some detail. This appendix is here to provide a quick reference that should enable you to comprehend XML examples used in this book.

XML is often described as portable data that co-exists alongside Java's portable code. Many new initiatives in Java use XML in a central role, so it is rapidly becoming a standard part of the Java developer's toolkit.

This appendix examines:

- The syntax and structure of an XML document
- Ways of defining XML structure, such as DTD and XML schema
- How different XML dialects can be identified

What Is XML?

XML has arisen from the need for a portable data format.

Essentially, XML is a standard for representing data in a text document. XML provides a framework for representing almost any kind of data, which is one of the reasons why it has attracted so much interest.

An XML document consists of text-based tags used to provide the document structure (similar to those used in HTML) together with the data itself. All XML documents consist of elements and optional declarations and comments.

Elements

An element has the following form:

```
<start_tag attributes>body<end_tag>
```

For example,

```
<book title="Teach Yourself J2EE in 21 Days">A very useful book</book>
```

In XML, unlike HTML, the tags are not predefined. As the author of an XML document, you are free to invent whatever tags are appropriate for the data you are describing.

When defining an XML tag, you may include attributes that further describe the tag. In the previous example, the title of the book is supplied as an attribute to the book tag.

The body of an element is all the text, including any nested tags, enclosed by the start and end tags.

An element need not have any attributes or even a body.

Tag names and attribute names must start with a letter or underscore and can contain any number of letters, numbers, hyphens, periods, or underscores, but they cannot include spaces. Names are letter case sensitive. Unlike HTML all XML attributes must be quoted (both single and double quotes are accepted).

The following are alternative forms for an element:

```
<tag>text</tag>
<tag attribute="text">text</tag>
<tag attribute="text"></tag>
<tag></tag>
<tag attribute="text"/>
<tag/>
```

The last two in this list show examples where the start and end tag have been combined. This is done simply to reduce clutter in the document.

Tags must nest. That is, an end tag must close the textually preceding start tag. For example,

```
<B><I>bold and italic</I></B>
```

The following is not well-formed XML:

```
<B><I>bold and italic</B></I>
```

To be well-formed XML, the </I> end tag must precede the </B> so the tags nest correctly.

The tags provide

- Information about the meaning of the data
- The relationships between different parts of the data

There must be exactly one top-level element in an XML document, called the root element, which must enclose all the other elements in the document.

The following is a well-formed XML document:

```
<jobSummary>
  <job customer="winston" reference="Cigar Trimmer">
    <location>London</location>
    <description>Must like to talk and smoke</description>
    <skill>Cigar maker</skill>
    <skill>Critic</skill>
  </job>
</jobSummary>
```

The root element is <jobSummary>...</jobSummary>. The <job> element has two attributes and encloses further elements.

Declarations

Declarations are used to provide information to the XML parser. They are of two forms. The first is a Processing Instruction and is enclosed in <? ... ?>.

The following example tells the parser that the document has been written using XML version 1.0 and the UTF-8 character encoding:

```
<?xml version ="1.0" encoding="UTF-8"?>
```

The second form of declaration is an XML Document Type Declaration and is enclosed in <! ... >:

```
<!DOCTYPE jobSummary SYSTEM "jobSummary.dtd">
```

<table>
<tr><td>CAUTION</td><td>Do not confuse a Document Type Declaration, which is the XML element containing declarations indicating the grammar that should be applied to validate an XML document, with the grammar itself, which is defined by a Document Type Definition (DTD) or XML Schema. DTDs and Schemas are explained later in this appendix.</td></tr>
</table>

Document Type Declarations are used to inform the parser of the correct structure of the XML document and to validate the XML. There is more information on the different types of document type declarations in section "Document Type Definition" later in this appendix. The DOCTYPE type declaration will become less common as the newer XML Schema approach is used to define an XML document structure.

If declarations appear in an XML document, they must precede the root element. This section is usually referred to as the prolog.

Comments

As well as elements and declarations, an XML document can contain comments that help to clarify the document content for human readers. Comments can be used anywhere within an XML document that a tag could appear. An example is as follows:

```
<!-- This is a really good book -->
```

Special Characters

The characters in Table A.1 have a special meaning in XML and, if required in the contents of an element, they must be replaced with the symbolic form.

TABLE A.1   Special XML Characters

Character	Name	Symbolic Form
&	(ampersand)	&amp;
<	(open angle bracket)	&lt;
>	(close angle bracket)	&gt;
'	(single quotes)	&apos;
"	(double quotes)	&quot;

Other special characters, such as non-printing characters, that may cause problems during processing, should be replaced by entities that give their decimal value. For example, ^A becomes &#01;.

If you are familiar with HTML, you will recognize the technique of replacing certain characters or including characters not found in standard character sets (such as ©) with a character entity that is either &name; or &#nnn; (where nnn is a numeric representing the character). As an HTML user, you are also probably aware that browsers can interpret character entities differently. This means the character encoding you are familiar with may not conform to the standard. Refer to the W3C Web site to find a list of the character entities for the ISO-8859-1 (Unicode 2.0) character set. Only those character entities defined in the standard should be used in XML.

For data containing large amounts of special characters, you can use a CDATA section. This begins with the string <![CDATA[and ends with]]>. Any characters between the start and end of a CDATA section are not processed by the parser and are just treated as a text string.

Namespaces

Namespaces are used to scope tags within a document. The use of multiple namespaces allows different tags to have the same name but different meanings in a single XML document.

An attribute called xmlns (XML Name Space) is added to an element tag in a document and is used to define a namespace for the body of the element.

The following is a document with two namespaces:

```
<?xml version ="1.0"?>
<jobSummary xmlns:ad="ADAgency" xmlns:be="BEAgency">
  <ad:job customer="winston" reference="Cigar Trimmer">
    <ad:location>London</ad:location>
    <ad:description>Must like to talk and smoke</ad:description>
    <ad:skill>Cigar maker</ad:skill>
    <ad:skill>Critic</ad:skill>
  </ad:job>
  <be:job>
    a completely different form of the job element
  </be:job>
</jobSummary>
```

Enforcing XML Document Structure

If XML is used to transfer information between applications, there needs to be a mechanism for ensuring that the XML is not only syntactically correct but also is structurally correct. In fact, there are two common mechanisms for this:

- Document Type Definitions
- XML Schemas

DTDs were the original form of validation but could not be manipulated by the same tools (such as JAXP, which is discussed on Day 16) as the XML documents they described. This was seen as a disadvantage of DTDs, and XML Schemas were defined as XML documents that define the structure of other XML documents. And before you ask, yes there is an XML Schema that defines the XML Schema structure (see http://www.w3.org/2001/XMLSchema.xsd); there is even a DTD for XML Schemas (see http://www.w3.org/2001/XMLSchema.dtd).

Document Type Definition (DTD)

A Document Type Definition (DTD) is a way of defining the structure of an XML document. DTD elements can be included in the XML document itself or in a separate external document. The syntax used to define a DTD is different from XML itself.

The following is a sample DTD that describes the jobSummary XML:

```
<!DOCTYPE jobSummary>
<!ELEMENT jobSummary (job*)>
<!ELEMENT job (location, description?, skill*)>
<!ATTLIST job customer CDATA #REQUIRED>
<!ATTLIST job reference CDATA #REQUIRED>
<!ELEMENT location (#PCDATA)>
<!ELEMENT description (#PCDATA)>
<!ELEMENT skill (#PCDATA)>
```

The !DOCTYPE element must include the name of the root element. If the remainder of the document type definitions are stored in an external file, it will have the following form:

```
<!DOCTYPE root_element SYSTEM "external_filename">
```

If the definitions are included in the XML document itself, the !DOCTYPE element must appear in the document prolog before the actual document data begins. In this case, the !DOCTYPE element must include all the DTD elements with the following syntax:

```
<!DOCTYPE jobSummary [
  <!ELEMENT jobSummary (job*)>
  <!ELEMENT job (location, description?, skill*)>
  <!ATTLIST job customer CDATA #REQUIRED>
  <!ATTLIST job reference CDATA #REQUIRED>
  <!ELEMENT location (#PCDATA)>
  <!ELEMENT description (#PCDATA)>
  <!ELEMENT skill (#PCDATA)>
]>
```

The other elements (!ELEMENT and !ATTLIST) are described in this section.

Elements

Element declarations take the following form:

```
<!ELEMENT element_name (content)>
```

where `element_name` is the XML tag and `content` is one or more of the values shown in Table A.2.

TABLE A.2 DTD Content Specifications for Elements

Content Type	Syntax	Element contains
Element	`<!ELEMENT tag (sub1)>`	Sub-element only
#PCDATA	`<!ELEMENT tag (#PCDATA)>`	Text only
EMPTY	`<!ELEMENT tag (EMPTY)>`	Nothing
ANY	`<!ELEMENT tag (ANY)>`	anything (text or elements)

NOTE

#PCDATA limits the content of the element to character data only; nested elements are not allowed. Do no confuse with CDATA sections in XML that are used to present large areas of un-interpreted text.

The characters in Table A.3 can be used to combine multiple element content types to define more complex elements.

TABLE A.3 Content Characters Used in DTD Definitions

Character	Meaning
,	Sequence operator, separates a list of required elements
*	Zero or more (not required)
+	One or more (at least one required)
?	Element is optional
|	Alternate elements
()	Group of elements

The following is a declaration for the `job` element:

```
<!ELEMENT job (location, description?, skill*)>
```

The `job` element consists of, in order, one location, an optional `description`, and an optional list of `skill` elements.

Attributes

Attribute declarations take the following form:

```
<!ATTLIST element_name attribute_1_name (type) default-value
                       attribute_2_name (type) default-value>
```

An attribute type can be any one of the types shown in Table A.4, though CDATA (text) is the most common.

TABLE A.4   DTD Attribute Types

Type	Attribute is a...
CDATA	Character string.
NMTOKEN	Valid XML name.
NMTOKENS	Multiple XML names.
ID	Unique identifier.
IDREF	An element found elsewhere in the document. The value for IDREF must match the ID of another element.
ENTITY	External binary data file (such as a GIF image).
ENTITIES	Multiple external binary files.
NOTATION	Helper program.

The default-value item can also be used to specify that the attribute is #REQUIRED, #FIXED, or #IMPLIED. The meanings of these values are presented in Table A.5.

TABLE A.5   DTD Attribute Default Values

Default Value	Meaning
#REQUIRED	Attribute must be provided.
#FIXED	Effectively a constant declaration. The attribute must be set to the given value or the XML is not valid.
#IMPLIED	The attribute is optional and the processing application is allowed to use any appropriate value if required.

Entity References

Another DTD element not mentioned so far is an entity reference. An entity reference has more than one form. The first, called a general entity reference, provides shorthand for often-used text. An entity reference has the following format:

```
<!ENTITY name "replacement text">
```

NOTE

This is, in fact, how the special characters are handled. The character entity & is defined as <!ENTITY & "&">.

The entity reference called name can be referred to in the XML document using &name;, as shown in the following:

```
<!DOCTYPE book [
...
<!ENTITY copyright "Copyright 2002 by Sams Publishing">
]>

<book title="J2EE in 21 Days">A very useful book &copyright;</book>
```

The second form, called an external entity reference, provides a mechanism to include data from external sources into the document's contents. This has the following format:

```
<!ENTITY name SYSTEM "URI">
```

For example, if the file Copy.xml that can be retrieved from the Sams Web site contains the following XML fragment:

```
<copyright>
  <date>2002</date>
  <publisher>Sams Publishing</publisher>
</copyright>
```

this can be referenced in any XML document as follows:

```
<!DOCTYPE [
...
<!ENITITY copyright http://www.samspublishing.com/xml/Copy.xml>
]>
<book>
  <title>J2EE in 21 Days>
  ...
  &copyright;
  <synopsis>All you need to know about J2EE</synopsis>
</book>
```

XML Schema

Like DTDs, an XML Schema can be used to specify the structure of an XML document. In addition, it has many advantages over DTDs:

- Schemas have a way of defining data types and includes a set of pre-defined types.

- A schema is namespace aware.

- It is possible to precisely specify the number of occurrences of an element (as opposed to a DTD's imprecise use of ?, *, and +) with the minOccurs and maxOccurs attributes.

- The ability to restrict the values that can be assigned to predefined types.

- A schema is written in XML.

The following is a schema to define the jobSummary XML:

```
<?xml version="1.0"?>
<xsd:schema xmlns:xsd="http://www.w3.org/2001/XMLSchema"
➥ elementFormDefault="qualified">

  <xsd:element name="jobSummary">
    <xsd:complexType>
      <xsd:sequence>
<xsd:element name="job" type="jobType" minOccurs="0"
➥ maxOccurs="unbounded"/>
      </xsd:sequence>
      </xsd:complexType>
    </xsd:element>

  <xsd:complexType name="jobType">
    <xsd:sequence>
      <xsd:element name="location" type="xsd:string"/>
       <xsd:element name="description" type="xsd:string"/>
<xsd:element name="skill" type="xsd:string" minOccurs="1"
                          maxOccurs="unbounded"/>
    </xsd:sequence>
      <xsd:attribute name="customer" type="xsd:string" use="required"/>
      <xsd:attribute name="reference" type="xsd:string" use="required"/>
  </xsd:complexType>
</xsd:schema>
```

In schemas, elements can have a type attribute that can be one of the following:

- string—Any combination of characters
- integer—An integral number
- float—A floating-point number
- boolean—true/false or 1/0
- date—yyyy-mm-dd

There are considerably more predefined simple data types. A full list can be obtained from the W3C Web site.

An element can also be a complex type, which is a combination of elements or elements and text.

The number of times an element can appear is controlled by two attributes:

- minOccurs
- maxOccurs

For example, the following `skill` element must appear at least once and can occur any number of times:

```
<xsd:element name="skill"    type="xsd:string"
              minOccurs="1"  maxOccurs="unbounded"/>
```

Elements can be made optional by setting the value of the `minOccurs` attribute to `0`.

Element attributes can be declared with a `use` attribute to indicate whether the element attribute is `required`, `optional`, or even `prohibited`.

A declaration of a complex type generally includes one of the following that specifies how the elements appear in the document:

- `all`—All the named elements must appear, however they may be in any order.
- `choice`—One, and only one, of the elements listed must appear.
- `sequence`—All the named elements must appear in the sequence listed.

Where to Find More Information

More information on XML standards can be found at various Web sites, the most important being the W3C Web site, which is found at `http://www.w3.org`.

Day 16 covers in more detail the subject of creating and validating XML. It introduces the Java API for XML Processing (JAXP) that allows you to use J2EE to parse and create XML.

Other related XML subjects, such as XSLT, Xpath, and XPointer, are covered on Day 17. A brief introduction to these subjects follows:

- XSL is a stylesheet language for XML. XSL specifies the styling of an XML document by using XSL Transformations to describe how the document is transformed into another XML document.
- XSLT is a language for transforming XML documents into other XML documents. A transformation expressed in XSLT is called a stylesheet.
- XPointer provides a mechanism to "point" to particular information in an XML document.
- XPath is a language for identifying parts of an XML document; it has been designed to be used by both XSLT and XPointer. XPath gets its name from its use of a compact path notation for navigating through the hierarchical structure of an XML document.

With the XPath notation, it is, for example, possible to refer to the third element in the fifth Job node in a XML document.

XPath is also designed so that it can be used for matching (testing whether or not a node matches a pattern). The form of XPath used is XSLT.

Everything in this appendix and a lot more is also covered in some detail in the *Sams Teach Yourself XML in 21 Days*, Shepherd, ISBN 0-672-32093-2. This book covers everything you need to know about XML to "hit the ground running."

APPENDIX **B**

The Java Community Process

Many of the lessons in this book have referred to JSRs (Java Specification Request). If you are not familiar with the Java Community Process (JCP), you may wonder exactly what a JSR is and how it affects J2EE technologies. This appendix provides you with an introduction to both JSRs and the JCP, and explains why they affect J2EE and you as a developer.

Introducing the JCP

The Java platform is developed within an open framework, unlike some other technologies. The JCP is the framework within which this open development occurs. It involves a number of interested parties, potentially including yourself, who develop or modify:

- Java technology specifications
- Technology Compatibility Kits (TCK)
- Reference Implementations (RI)

The JCP revolves around JSRs, which are the formalized requests that JCP members make when they want to either develop a new Java technology specification or modify an existing specification. Before you discover what is involved in the process of converting a JSR to a finalized specification, you will learn who is involved in the JCP.

Getting Involved

There are five main groups involved with the JCP. Each group plays a defined role that ensures that the JCP delivers Java technology specifications that meet the needs of developers and organizations, and ensure the continued stability and cross-platform compatibility of Java technologies.

JCP Members

Any individual or organization can become a member of the JCP. To become a member, you must sign the Java Specification Agreement (JSPA) and pay a fee, which, at the time of writing, is $5,000 per year for commercial entities and $2,000 per year for all other entities.

JCP members are responsible for the submission of JSRs that are then further developed by Expert Groups. These groups consist of experts that JCP members may nominate either themselves or other members for. One JCP member will lead each Expert Group and is responsible for forming the group and adding experts to that group. JCP members also have the right to vote on Executive Committee ballots; you will learn about these a little later.

Expert Groups

Each expert group is responsible for forming a specification and its RI and TCK from a JSR. In addition, once they form the specification, they are responsible for the maintenance of that specification.

When JCP members make nominations for Expert Group members, they ensure that the group will consist of individuals who are experts in the technology to which the specification relates. In addition, they ensure that the Expert Group includes enough depth and breadth of knowledge to enable the final specification to be of real use to developers and organizations.

The Public

Any member of the public can become involved with the JCP without having to become a full member of the JCP or pay a fee. The main ways that members of the public can become involved are by reviewing and commenting on

- Any specification JCP members develop
- Any new or revised JSR
- Proposed error corrections and modifications to existing specifications

Process Management Office (PMO)

The PMO is a group within Sun Microsystems that manages the day-to-day running of the JCP. The group does not involve itself with actual formation of JSRs or the final specifications.

Executive Committees

There are two Executive Committees, each overseeing different elements of the Java platform. One committee looks after the Standard Edition and Enterprise Edition, and the other looks after the Micro Edition. It is the responsibility of an Executive Committee to oversee the work of the Expert Groups to ensure that specifications do not overlap or conflict with each other. The Executive Committee is not involved with the JCP on a day-to-day process, but instead, reviews the work of Expert Groups at defined points of the JCP. Specifically, an Executive Committee selects JSRs for development, provides guidance for the PMO, and approves

- Draft specifications
- Final specifications
- Maintenance revisions of a specification
- The transfer of maintenance responsibilities between JCP members

Each Executive Committee consists of sixteen seats. Of these, only one is permanent--held by Sun Microsystems. Of the remaining seats, ten are ratified and five are elected. Each of these seats is held for three years, and its holder is determined on a rolling basis; thus, five seats are either ratified or held open for election each year.

Understanding the JSR Process

There are several stages to transforming an initial JSR to a final specification, and each involves different entities concerned with the JCP. However, the process consists of three main stages, which are shown by Figure B.1.

FIGURE B.1

The JCP process.

Initiation → Community Draft → Public Review and Specification Finalization

As you can see, the process consists of three main sections. The first, Initiation, is where a JCP member submits a JSR. This JSR is open for review by JCP members and the public. Once reviewed, the Executive Committee decides whether to approve the request. If the request is approved, the process moves into the Community Draft stage.

This stage is where the Expert Group is formed. The Expert Group then writes the first draft of the specification and makes the draft available for Community Review by JCP members. The Expert Group may update the draft at this point, or they may pass the draft immediately to the Executive Committee for approval. If the draft is approved, the process moves into the final stage--Public Review and Specification Finalization.

This final stage commences with the group posting the draft on the Internet so that the public can review and comment on it. After the public review is complete, the Expert Group may modify the draft to include feedback from the public. At this point, the group prepares the proposed final draft and ensures that the RI and TCK are complete. After the proposed final draft is complete, the group passes it to the Executive Committee for final approval. If the specification is approved, it is then released.

After the Expert Group releases the final specification, the specification is not simply abandoned. Instead, it is subject to an ongoing process of review and modification. Within this process, there might be requests for revisions or enhancements to the specification, or a need for further clarification and interpretation of the specification. The Executive Committee is responsible for reviewing each proposed change, and will decide on a suitable course of action to implement the change.

Taking the Next Step

This appendix has provided you with a brief overview of the Java Community Process, the roles you can play within in it, and the lifecycle of a Java Specification Request. If you want to find out more or get involved, you can do so by visiting http://www.jcp.org.

If you simply want to browse the JSR archive, you can do so by visiting http://www.jcp.org/jsr/overview/index.jsp.

GLOSSARY

This appendix lists new or uncommon terms used throughout this book and provides a brief definition.

3-Tier The 3-tier model for enterprise applications, as used by J2EE, that splits the application functionality into three parts: presentation, business, and integration. Components that deliver these three types of functionality will typically live on their own tier of servers, so that the three types of functionality are physically, as well as logically, separated. See also n-tier.

Active Directory Active Directory is Microsoft's directory service, first delivered as part of Microsoft Windows 2000.

ANSI The American National Standards Institute is a private, non-profit organization that administers and coordinates the U.S. voluntary standardization and conformity assessment system.

ANSI SQL ANSI SQL represents a standard for SQL programming that is independent of any one specific implementation. The first ANSI SQL standard was published in 1989, but most vendors now support the update published in 1992. See also ANSI SQL 92.

ANSI SQL 92 ANSI SQL 92 refers to the version of the SQL specification published by ANSI in 1992. This forms the basis of most current SQL implementations by major vendors. See also SQL.

Ant (or Apache Ant)　An automated build tool included in the J2EE RI (see also Apache Software Foundation) under the name `asant` (Application Server Ant).

Apache Software Foundation (or just Apache)　The Apache Software Foundation is an umbrella organization that supports a range of open-source projects being pursued under the Apache banner. Notable among these projects are the Jakarta Project, which delivers the Tomcat servlet and JSP implementation, Ant build tool, and James email server. Together with the XML Project, which oversees the development of the Crimson and Xerces parsers, the Jakarta Project also delivers the Xalan XSLT processor and the Axis SOAP engine. See also Axis, Jakarta.

Application Client　A J2EE application client is a client-side J2EE component that has access to a subset of the J2EE APIs provided by the J2EE client container. A J2EE application client must be invoked within the context of a J2EE client container, such as the `runclient` container provided by the J2EE RI.

Application Layer　The application layer is a term used to refer to the logical layer containing the interaction with the user of the application. This can include not only Web-based interaction using servlets and JSPs with a Web browser, but also application clients.

Application Server　An application server is a server-side container for components of an n-tier application. In Java terms, a typical application server will provide all of the J2EE APIs and container types. Application servers can also provide additional functionality, such as CORBA, COM, or Web Service support. Common application servers include BEA WebLogic, IBM WebSphere, Sun ONE Application Server, JBoss and OpenEJB.

Asymmetric Key Encryption　Encryption that uses two keys to encrypt and decrypt the data. One key is made public and is used by senders to encrypt messages for the recipient. Only the recipient can decrypt the key as the other key is kept private and held only by the recipient. Asymmetric encryption is usually known as Public Key Encryption (PKE). The most widely known algorithm used today is RSA.

AVK (Java Application Verification Kit)　The AVK (formerly the Compatibility Test Suite) is a testing environment from Sun Microsystems for validating J2EE compliant application servers.

Axis　The Apache Axis project is part of the Apache XML project. Axis is a Java-based SOAP toolkit that allows you to build and invoke Web Services from Java components. See also Apache.

Bean　See JavaBean.

Bean-Managed Persistence (BMP) See BMP.

Bean-Managed Transaction Demarcation (BMTD) See BMTD.

BMP (Bean-Managed Persistence) An Entity EJB can take responsibility for persisting and retrieving its own internal state when prompted by its container. This is commonly done by including JDBC code in the appropriate lifecycle methods. This style of Entity EJB persistence is termed Bean-Managed Persistence. See also CMP.

BMTD (Bean-Managed Transaction Demarcation) An EJB can take control of its own transactions by making API calls to start and end transactions. This is termed Bean-Managed Transaction Demarcation. See also CMTD.

Business Tier The set of machines on which the business components execute in an n-tier or 3-tier application. See also n-tier, 3-tier.

CA(Certification Authority) A trusted organization that verifies the authenticity of a digital certificate of another organization. See Digital Certificates.

Certification Authority (CA) See CA.

Client Tier See Presentation Tier.

CMP (Container-Managed Persistence) An Entity EJB can delegate responsibility for persisting and retrieving its internal state to its container. This is termed Container-Managed Persistence. See also BMP.

CMR (Container-Managed Relationships) Under EJB 2.0 and later (and J2EE 1.3 and later), it is possible to specify relationships between Entity EJBs in such a way that the container will automatically manage the lifecycle of the whole interconnected web of entities according to those relationships. This means that entities that are referenced by other entities will automatically be instantiated and populated when required, with no need for code in either the client or the containing Entity. Such relationships are termed Container-Managed Relationships.

CMTD (Container-Managed Transaction Demarcation) An EJB can delegate control of its transactions to its container, which will start and end transactions on behalf of the EJB. This is termed Container-Managed Transaction Demarcation. See also BMTD.

Collaboration Protocol Agreement (CPA) See CPA.

Collaboration Protocol Profile (CPP) See CPP.

Compatibility Test Suite (CTS) See AVK.

Component A component is a grouping of functionality that forms a coherent unit. This unit can be deployed in a component container independent of other components. Applications can then be built by calling on the functionality of multiple, specialist components. J2EE applications are built from various types of components, such as Web Components and EJBs. See also Container.

Connector See JCA (Java Connector Architecture).

Container A container provides services for a component. These services can include lifecycle management, security, connectivity, transactions, and persistence. Each type of J2EE component is deployed into its own type of J2EE container, such as a Web Container or an EJB Container. See also Component.

Container-Managed Persistence (CMP) See CMP.

Container-Managed Relationships (CMR) See CMR.

Container-Managed Transaction Demarcation (CMTD) See CMTD.

Cookie A cookie is a short text string sent as part of an HTTP request and response. Because HTTP is a stateless protocol, cookies provide a way of identifying the same client across multiple HTTP requests. Any cookie sent by a server is stored by the client and then submitted whenever another request is made to the same server or domain. Cookies form the basis of most Web-based session management.

CORBA (Common Object Request Broker Architecture) CORBA, from the Object Management Group (OMG), defines a distributed environment consisting of client-server connectivity integrated with a set of distributed services. CORBA clients and servers connect to a local Object Request Broker (ORB) for connectivity and can register and discover each other in the Common Object Services Naming Service (COS Naming). There are many other CORBA services defined, including security, transaction, and persistence.

CPA (Collaboration Protocol Agreement) A CPA is an XML document that defines an agreement between two parties who are using ebXML to conduct e-business. The CPA defines an intersection of the two parties' CPPs, specifying which protocols and mechanisms they will use to exchange information and services. See also CPP.

CPP (Collaboration Protocol Profile) A CPP is an XML document that defines the services and capabilities offered by an organization that provides e-business services using ebXML. See also CPA.

Crimson The Crimson XML parser from Apache is used to provide the XML parsing functionality of the Sun JAXP reference implementation. See also Apache, Xerces.

CTS (Compatibility Test Suite)   See AVK.

Custom Tag Library   See Tag Library.

Data Encryption Standard (DES)   See Symmetric Data Encryption.

Data Tier   See Integration Tier.

Declarative attributes   Declarative attributes provide a way for a component to specify requirements to its container by means of attributes defined in the deployment descriptor. These requirements can include when to start and stop transactions and the level of security required by different parts of the component. Delegating control of such functionality to the container and defining them in the deployment descriptor rather than using code means that they are more easily changed when configuring an application.

Deployment Descriptor   A deployment descriptor defines metadata for the component or application with which it is associated. J2EE deployment descriptors are XML documents that convey the requirements that a component or application has of its container (such as security requirements). The deployment descriptor can also define the relationships between different classes in the component, naming information, persistence requirements, and so on.

DES (Data Encryption Standard)   See Symmetric Data Encryption.

Design pattern   See Pattern.

Digital certificate   A digital certificate provides a way of signing digital data in such a way that it authoritatively proves the identity of the sender. Certificates are usually issued by trusted third parties called Certification Authorities. See Asymmetric Key Encryption and Certification Authorities.

DNS (Domain Name System)   DNS is the mechanism whereby Internet applications can resolve host names (such as java.sun.com) to IP addresses (such as 192.18.97.71), acting as a basic directory service. It also provides reverse resolution and information on the location of email servers.

Document Object Model (DOM)   See DOM.

Document Type Definition (DTD)   See DTD.

DOM (Document Object Model)   The document object model is an API defined by the W3C for manipulating and traversing an XML document. The API is defined in language-neutral (CORBA) IDL, and Java-based XML parsers provide a Java-language mapping of it. DOM is one of the two main parsing APIs provided by JAXP (the other is the simple API for XML). See also JAXP, SAX, and W3C.

Domain Layer   The term domain layer is sometimes used to denote the group of logical components that provide the data model for an application. These components are manipulated by other components in the business layer to perform business-oriented functionality.

Domain Name System (DNS)   See DNS.

DTD (Document Type Definition)   The structure of an XML document can be defined using a DTD. The DTD syntax forms part of the XML specification, but is somewhat limited in its descriptive capabilities. For this reason, it is being superseded by XML Schema. See also XML Schema.

EAI (Enterprise Application Integration)   Many existing enterprise applications reside on systems, such as mainframes. Providing connectivity and interoperability with such systems for an n-tier application is commonly termed Enterprise Application Integration. Some n-tier reference models will refer to an integration tier, which is a combination of components that connect to databases and EAI components, sometimes called enterprise information systems. See also EIS.

EAR (Enterprise Archive)   An EAR file contains the components and deployment descriptors that make up an enterprise application. An EAR is the unit of deployment for a J2EE server (that is, how the J2EE server expects applications to be packaged).

ebXML (Electronic Business XML)   The ebXML initiative has produced a set of e-business standards that range from data transportation to the choreography of business processes. These standards provide a platform for e-business and a set of value-added services when sending e-business messages. See also CPA, CPP, JAXM.

Electronic Business XML (ebXML)   See ebXML.

EIS (Enterprise Information Systems)   An enterprise information system is any source of enterprise data, such as a database or mainframe. EIS systems will be accessed through an integration tier. See also EAI.

EJB (Enterprise JavaBean)   An EJB is a J2EE business component that lives within a J2EE EJB container. EJBs can be Session beans, Entity beans, or Message-driven beans. An EJB consists of home and remote interface definitions, the bean functionality, and the metadata required for the container to correctly interact with the bean.

EJB Container   An EJB container provides services for the EJBs deployed within it. It will control access to the EJB instances and will call the lifecycle methods on each EJB at the appropriate time. The container also provides the persistence and relationship mechanisms used by Entity EJBs.

ejb-jar   An `ejb-jar` file contains one or more EJBs together with the deployment descriptor and resources needed by them. The `ejb-jar` is a unit of deployment for EJB business components. See also EJB.

EJB QL (EJB Query Language)   EJBs that use CMP must specify the results expected from the various finder methods defined on their home interface. EJB QL provides a container-independent way of doing this by allowing the developer to associate EJB-based queries with the different finder methods.

EJB Query Language   See EJB QL.

EL (Expression Language)   A simple scripting language originally defined as part of JSTL but incorporated into JSP 2.0 (J2EE 1.4) to provide a weakly typed grammar for accessing JSP variables.

Enterprise Application   An enterprise application consists of one or more J2EE components packaged in an EAR archive. An enterprise application is the end result of a J2EE development.

Enterprise Application Integration (EAI)   See EAI.

Enterprise Archive (EAR)   See EAR.

Enterprise Information Systems (EIS)   See EIS.

Enterprise JavaBean (EJB)   See EJB.

Enterprise Resource Planning (ERP)   See ERP.

Entity EJB (or Entity Bean)   An Entity EJB is a data component used in a J2EE application. Entities frequently map onto domain Entities discovered during analysis and design.

ERP (Enterprise Resource Planning)   ERP packages provide pre-packaged, configurable components that provide core enterprise functions, such as personnel management and operations. Such systems are core to enterprise operations, so they must be integrated with other enterprise applications, such as those developed using J2EE. Information from such systems can be retrieved and manipulated through J2EE Connectors or Web Services. See also JCA.

Expression Language   See EL.

eXtensible Markup Language (XML)   See XML.

eXtensible Stylesheet Language (XSL)   See XSL.

eXtensible Stylesheet Language Formatting Objects (XSL-FO)   See XSL-FO.

eXtensible Stylesheet Language Transformations (XSLT)   See XSLT.

Home Interface   The home interface of an EJB is a remote factory interface that is registered using JNDI. Clients will discover this interface and use its methods to create, remove, or find one or more EJBs. See also EJB.

HTML (Hypertext Markup Language)   HTML is the language used to define Web pages that display in a Web browser, such as Netscape Navigator or Microsoft Internet Explorer. See also HTTP.

HTTP (Hypertext Transfer Protocol)   HTTP is the standard transport mechanism used between Web clients and servers. It is used to fetch HTML documents, and also as the underlying transport for Web Services. HTTP servers can be set up on any TCP endpoint, but are usually found on port 80 or common alternatives (8000, 8080, 8888, and so on). See also HTML, HTTPS, and Web Service.

HTTPS (Secure Hypertext Transfer Protocol)   HTTPS uses SSL to encrypt HTTP traffic between a client and a server and to authenticate the server to the client (and possibly vice versa). HTTPS uses a different endpoint (443) from standard HTTP. See also HTTP.

HyperText Markup Language (HTML)   See HTML.

HyperText Transfer Protocol (HTTP)   See HTTP.

IMAP (Internet Message Access Protocol)   IMAP is a flexible way of dealing with Internet-based email. Using IMAP, messages stay in a user's mailbox on the server while the client retrieves metadata about them (such as the size, sender, and so on). The client can then selectively download messages, rather than having to download all emails in one go. See also POP.

Initial Context   A JNDI initial context is the starting point for JNDI interaction. J2EE components will obtain an initial context to discover resources, properties, and other J2EE components.

Integration Tier   The set of machines on which the data access components execute in an n-tier or 3-tier application. See also n-tier, 3-tier.

Internet Message Access Protocol (IMAP)   See IMAP.

J2EE   Java 2 Enterprise Edition.

J2EE application   See Enterprise Application.

J2EE Component   A J2EE component is the basic unit of a J2EE application. Different components will serve different purposes, such as presentation of data, provision of business logic, or access to underlying data. See also Web Component.

J2EE Container A J2EE container provides the services and environment required by a particular type of J2EE component. See also Web Container.

J2EE Pattern A J2EE Pattern is a pattern that is implemented using J2EE technologies. J2EE Patterns can help improve the quality of the J2EE applications within which they are applied. See also Pattern.

J2EE Reference Implementation (RI) See J2EE RI.

J2EE RI (J2EE Reference Implementation) The J2EE RI (or the Java 2 SDK Enterprise Edition) serves as a proof-of-concept for the technologies defined in the J2EE specification. The team that produces the JSR for each version of J2EE is responsible for delivering a reference implementation for it. The J2EE RI is freely downloadable and provides a useful test environment for J2EE developers.

J2EE Server A J2EE server is the underlying J2EE platform that provides the services required by J2EE containers. J2EE servers are typically delivered in the form of application servers. See also J2EE Container.

Jakarta Project The Jakarta Project is the overarching project for Java-oriented development at the Apache Foundation. This includes the Tomcat servlet and JSP engine. See also Apache.

JAF (JavaBeans Activation Framework) JAF provides a way of associating a particular MIME type with an application or component that knows how to process data of that MIME type. JAF is used in various parts of J2EE including JavaMail and Web Services.

James An open source SMTP and POP3 mail server provided through the Jakarta Project. See also Apache.

JAR (Java Archive) JAR files are a compressed archive format in which Java classes and associated resources are typically stored. All of the various archives used by J2EE are delivered in JAR files. See also EAR, ejb-jar, WAR.

Java API for XML Messaging (JAXM) See JAXM.

Java API for XML Parsing (JAXP) See JAXP.

Java API for XML Registries (JAXR) See JAXR.

Java API for XML-based RPC (JAX-RPC) See JAX-RPC.

Java Architecture for XML Binding (JAXB) See JAXB.

Java Archive (JAR) See JAR.

JavaBean   A JavaBean is a Java class that conforms to certain rules on method naming, construction, and serialization. JavaBeans are used within J2EE to contain Java functionality and data in Web components or as data carriers between layers. Note that JavaBeans and Enterprise JavaBeans (EJBs) are totally different technologies. See also EJB.

JavaBeans Activation Framework (JAF)   See JAF.

Java Application Verification Kit (AVK)   See AVK.

Java Connector Architecture (JCA, Connectors)   See JCA.

Java Community Process (JCP)   See JCP.

Java Database Connectivity (JDBC)   See JDBC.

Java Data Objects (JDO)   See JDO.

Java IDL   Java IDL is the delivery mechanism for CORBA IDL support under Java. The Java IDL compiler allows you to compile CORBA IDL into Java stubs and skeletons that can be used to communicate with remote CORBA objects. See also CORBA.

JavaMail   JavaMail is part of the J2EE platform that allows you to send and receive email messages.

Java Message Service (JMS)   See JMS.

Java Naming and Directory Interface (JNDI)   See JNDI.

JavaServer Faces (JSF)   see JSF.

JavaServer Pages (JSP)   See JSP.

JavaServer Pages Standard Tag Library (JSTL)   See JSTL.

Java Transaction API (JTA)   See JTA.

Java Transaction Service (JTS)   See JTS.

Java Web Service (JWS) file   See JWS.

Java Web Services Developer Pack (Java WSDP)   See Java WSDP.

Java WSDP (Java Web Services Developer Pack)   The Java WSDP provides an integrated toolkit containing standard implementations of Web services standards, such as WSDL and SOAP, as well as implementations for Web application development, such as (JavaServer Pages) and all of the technologies included in the Java XML Pack (JAX Pack). It enables the building of web services, web applications and XML applications. See JAX Pack.

JAXB (Java Architecture for XML Binding) JAXB defines an architecture for marshalling data between Java and XML formats. It provides tools to convert XML DTDs and Schemas into Java classes.

JAXM (Java API for XML Messaging) JAXM defines how J2EE components send and receive XML-based messages over SOAP. See also SOAP.

JAXP (Java API for XML Processing) JAXP defines the interfaces and programming model for the parsing, manipulation, and transformation of XML in Java.

JAX Pack (or Java XML Pack) The JAX Pack provides an interim delivery mechanism for the various XML-related APIs currently under development. The Java Web Services Developer Pack (Java WSDP) incorporates all the technologies included in JAX Pack. See also Java WSDP, JAXM, JAXP, JAXR, JAX-RPC.

JAXR (Java API for XML Registries) JAXR defines how a J2EE component will access and manipulate XML data held in XML-oriented registries, such as UDDI and the ebXML registry and repository.

JAX-RPC (Java API for XML-based RPC) JAX-RPC defines how J2EE components make and receive XML-based RPC calls over SOAP. It specifies the relationship between the definition of an interface in WSDL and the Java binding for that interface. See also SOAP, UDDI.

JCA (Java Connector Architecture) The JCA defines how external data sources, such as ERP systems, should be made available to J2EE components. The JCA mechanism is very similar to the JDBC standard extension that allows components to discover and use data sources defined by the container.

JCP (Java Community Process) The JCP is the process under which vendors and individuals in the Java community work together to create and formalize the APIs and technologies used in the Java platform. Standardization efforts under the JCP are referred to as Java Specification Requests (JSRs). See also JSR.

JDBC (Java Database Connectivity) JDBC provides data access for Java applications and components.

JDO (Java Data Objects) JDO specifies a lightweight persistence mechanism for Java objects. Its functionality lies somewhere between Java Serialization and entity EJBs.

JMS (Java Message Service) JMS specifies how a J2EE component can produce or consume messages by sending them to, or retrieving them from, a queue or a topic. JMS supports both the point-to-point model and the publish/subscribe model of message passing.

JNDI (Java Naming and Directory Interface)   JNDI provides a generic API for access to information contained in underlying naming services, such as the CORBA CoS Naming service. JNDI is used by J2EE components to discover resources, configuration information, and other J2EE components.

JSF (JavaServer Faces)   JSF provides a framework for developing user interfaces in Web Applications. JSF is an emerging technology and is included, the Java Web Services Developer Pack from Sun Microsystems.

JSP (JavaServer Pages)   JSPs provide a model for mixing static tagged content, such as HTML or XML, with content dynamically generated using Java code. Such code can be embedded in the page itself or, more usually, encapsulated in a JavaBean or tag library. See also JavaBean, Tag Library.

JSP Directive   Directives are messages to the JSP container that are embedded in a JSP page. They appear as tags delimited by `<%@ %>`. Directives include `page`, `taglib`, and `include`. A common example would be a page directive that defines the error page for this JSP. See also JSP, JSP Error Page.

JSP Error Page   An error page can be defined for each JSP page to handle any errors occurring on that page. Any unhandled exceptions will cause the error page to be displayed. The same error page can be shared between multiple JSP pages. An error page is basically a JSP page that has access to error-specific information, such as the exception that caused the error. See also JSP.

JSP Expression   A JSP expression is a Java statement that is executed, and the result of this statement is coerced into a string and output at the current location in the page. Expressions are delimited by `<%= %>`. A typical example would use a Java statement to evaluate the current date or time to be inserted at the current location. See also JSP.

JSP Scriptlet   A JSP scriptlet is a section of Java code embedded in a JSP page and delimited by `<% %>`.

JSR (Java Specification Request)   A JSR is a project under the auspices of the JCP that defines a new standard for a Java API or technology. JSRs are run by groups of experts drawn from vendors and the broader Java community. See also JCP.

JSTL (JavaServer Pages Standard Tag Library)   A standard JSP tag library for common functionality, such as conditional evaluation and looping. See also Tag Library.

JTA (Java Transaction API)   The JTA defines an API that allows J2EE components to interact with transactions. This includes starting transactions and completing or aborting them. The JTA uses the underlying services of the JTS. See also JTS.

JTS (Java Transaction Service)   The JTS is a low-level, Java-based mapping of the CORBA Object Transaction Service. Transaction managers that conform to JTS can be used as part of a J2EE environment to control and propagate transactions on behalf of J2EE components. J2EE components will not use JTS directly, it is used on their behalf by their container or through the JTA. See also JTA.

JWS (Java Web Service file)   A JWS file is a Java class file with a .jws extension. When placed under the appropriate part of the Apache Axis hierarchy, this Java class will automatically be exported as a Web Service. See also Axis.

Kerberos   Kerberos is a strong, distributed security mechanism that uses encryption and signed "tickets" to allow clients and servers to interoperate in a secure manner.

LDAP (Lightweight Directory Access Protocol)   LDAP is a standard protocol for accessing data in a directory service. Common directory services such as Microsoft's Active Directory and Novell's NDS support LDAP. JNDI can be used to deliver LDAP requests using the LDAP service provider. See also Active Directory, JNDI, NDS.

Lightweight Directory Access Protocol (LDAP)   See LDAP.

Local Home Interface   A local home interface is an EJB factory interface that returns EJB local interfaces. The local home interface is for use by clients that run in the same server and reduces the overhead associated with remote RMI calls. See also Home Interface, Local Interface.

Local Interface   A local interface is a business- or data-access interface defined by an EJB that is intended to be used by clients running in the same server. Using a local interface reduces the overhead associated with remote RMI methods. Local interfaces form the foundation for container-managed relationships used by Entity EJBs. See also CMR, Local Home Interface, Remote Interface.

MD5 (Message Digest version 5)   See Message Digest.

MDB (Message-Driven EJB)—A Message-Driven bean is an EJB that processes JMS messages. The bean implements an onMessage method, just like a JMS message consumer. Messages delivered to the associated queue will be passed to the MDB's onMessage method, so the MDB will be invoked asynchronously (the client could be long gone).

Message-Driven EJB (or Message-Driven Bean, MDB)   See MDB.

Message Digest   A security mechanism whereby the data in a message is subjected to a numerical algorithm that calculates one or more validation numbers that are transmitted along with the data. The recipient can perform the same calculation on the data and as long as the digest numbers match the recipient be reasonably confident the message has not been corrupted in some way. Checksums are a very simple form of digest.

Microsoft SQL Server   Microsoft SQL Server is Microsoft's flagship enterprise database. SQL Server is now part of Microsoft's .NET server range. J2EE components can access data in a SQL Server database through standard data access mechanisms, such as JDBC. See also JDBC.

MIME (Multipurpose Internet Mail Extensions)   MIME provides a way of defining a multi-part message in which each part contains a different type of data. Within the message, each part has its own MIME header defining the content type of that part and delimiting that part from the other parts. Common uses of MIME include Internet email and SOAP.

Multipurpose Internet Mail Extensions (MIME)   See MIME.

N-Tier   Modern distributed applications are defined in terms of multiple tiers. A 3-tier application has three physical tiers containing presentation, business, and data access components. In reality, applications can have many more physical tiers, each of which can be some specialization of the three tiers listed, or as a representation of ultimate clients and data sources. As such, these applications are referred to as n-tier to indicate that there are a variable number of tiers (3 or more). See also 3-tier.

NDS (Novell Directory Services)   NDS is Novell's popular directory service, originating from its NetWare family of products.

Novell Directory Services (NDS)   See NDS.

OASIS (Organization for the Advancement of Structured Information Standards)   OASIS is a non-profit, international consortium that creates interoperable industry specifications based on public standards, such as XML and SGML. OASIS is one of the sponsors of ebXML. See also ebXML.

Object-Oriented Database Management System (OODBMS)   See OODBMS.

Object Relational Database Management System (ORDBMS)   See ORDBMS.

OODBMS (Object-Oriented Database Management System)   An OODBMS provides persistent storage that supports the OO paradigm so that data definition can be done in terms of classes, inheritance, and methods. Data retrieval can be performed in terms of object instances in contrast to record sets. See also ORDBMS.

Oracle   Oracle produces several J2EE-related products. The Oracle database can be used as an enterprise-class data store as part of a J2EE application. The Oracle application server is itself a J2EE application server that can host a J2EE-compliant application. As you would expect, this gives performance and functionality benefits when combined with Oracle's database.

ORDBMS (Object Relational Database Management System)   An ORDBMS provides an OO mapping on top of a traditional relational database. This means that the developer can work in terms of objects and classes, and the ORDBMS takes the responsibility for mapping these classes and objects to the underlying database tables. See also OODBMS.

Organization for the Advancement of Structured Information Standards (OASIS)   See OASIS.

Pattern   A pattern is a solution to a problem in a given context. Patterns commonly occur in software design and architecture. By using patterns, designers and architects can improve the quality of the software and systems they produce.

PKE (Public Key Encryption)   see Asymmetric Key Encryption.

Platform Specific Deployment Descriptor   The deployment descriptors provided with J2EE components and applications provide standard information about the properties and configuration of those components and applications. The auxiliary deployment descriptor defines additional, non-standard information about the J2EE application or component that is used by a specific J2EE container or application server. Hence, the contents of the auxiliary deployment descriptor are specific to that environment. See also Deployment Descriptor.

Post Office Protocol (POP/POP3)   See POP.

POP/POP3 (Post Office Protocol)   POP defines a way for an email client, such as Eudora, to retrieve messages from a mailbox maintained by an email server. All messages must be downloaded before they can be examined or read. See also IMAP, SMTP.

Presentation Layer   The presentation layer is a term used to refer to the logical layer containing the interaction with the user of the application. For a Web-based application, this typically means the generation of HTML or XML by servlets and/or JSPs. For an application client, the presentation is typically done through a Swing GUI.

Presentation Tier   The set of machines on which the presentation components execute in an n-tier or 3-tier application. See also 3-tier, N-tier.

Public Key Encryption (PKE)   see Asymmetric Key Encryption.

Reference Implementation   See J2EE RI.

Remote Interface   The business or data access methods exposed by an EJB are referred to as its remote interface. The interface extends the RMI `Remote` interface, indicating that it is to be used outside of the current virtual machine. Each EJB has one remote interface, and this is the type returned by finder and creator methods on the EJB's home interface.

Remote Method Invocation (RMI)   See RMI.

Remote Procedure Call (RPC)   See RPC.

Remote Reference   A remote reference is an object reference that refers to a remote object. The method calls made through the remote reference will be propagated to the remote object using RMI. In J2EE terms, a remote reference will usually refer to an EJB or its home interface and will be retrieved from a finder/creation method or through JNDI, respectively. See also RMI.

RI   See J2EE RI.

Rivest Shamir Adleman (RSA)   see Asymmetric Key Encryption.

RMI (Remote Method Invocation)   RMI is a Java-based, object-oriented RPC mechanism. All communication with EJBs in a J2EE application is done via RMI (except for Message-driven beans). RMI defines a syntax and mechanism for accessing remote Java objects and also for passing serialized Java objects between client and server. See also RMI-IIOP.

RMI-IIOP   RMI-IIOP defines a way that RMI RPC calls can be carried over the CORBA IIOP transport. This allows for interoperability between different J2EE application servers as well as between RMI clients and servers and CORBA clients and servers. See also CORBA, RMI.

RPC (Remote Procedure Call)   An RPC is a method call that spans processes, frequently across a network. A client-side stub (or proxy) and a server-side skeleton (or stub) will make the issuing of RPCs look similar to a local method call. See also CORBA, RMI.

RSA (Rivest Shamir Adleman)   See Asymmetric Key Encryption.

SAAJ (SOAP with Attachments API for Java)   Provides a mechanism for producing and consuming SOAP messages. See also SOAP.

SAX (Simple API for XML)   SAX was defined by members of the XML-DEV email list (and formalized by David Megginson) as a way of processing XML in Java. The

SAX API is event-driven, notifying the Java program as XML elements and content are encountered. SAX is generally regarded as lighter-weight than the DOM API and is delivered as part of JAXP. See also DOM, JAXP.

Scriptlet   See JSP Scriptlet.

Secure HyperText Transfer Protocol (HTTPS)   See HTTPS.

Secure Sockets Library (SSL)   See SSL.

Servlet   A servlet is a Web component that is written entirely in Java. Servlets have a defined lifecycle and allow Web developers to consume (most commonly) HTTP requests and generate responses. Responses can be in the form of HTML, XML, or any text or binary format. See also JSP, Web Component.

Session EJB (or Session Bean)   Session EJBs are intended to house business logic and processing in a typical J2EE application. Session EJBs will provide business services to the presentation tier and will use Entity EJBs, connectors, or direct database access to retrieve business data.

Session EJBs can be either stateful (they retain state between invocations) or stateless (state is not retained between invocations).

SGML (Standard Generalized Markup Language)   SGML is a forerunner of both HTML and XML. It is a very flexible general purpose markup language that, like XML, can be used to mark up any form of data. However, its flexibility leads to it being somewhat unwieldy. The originators of XML intended to keep much of the flexibility of SGML while deriving a simpler syntax. See also XML.

Simple API for XML (SAX)   See SAX.

Simple Mail Transfer Protocol (SMTP)   See SMTP.

Simple Object Access Protocol (SOAP)   See SOAP.

SMTP (Simple Mail Transfer Protocol)   The SMTP standard defines how email servers send messages to each other. SMTP forms the backbone of the Internet email delivery system. See also IMAP, POP.

SOAP (Simple Object Access Protocol)   SOAP is an XML-based, de-facto standard for the encoding of XML-based messages. The messages can be intended as method names and parameters for a remote procedure call, or as an XML-encoded message to be processed and potentially passed on. SOAP is used as the underlying transport for all Web Services. SOAP is being formalized under the auspices of the W3C. See also JAX-RPC, JAXM, SOAP-RP, Web Service.

SOAP Routing Protocol   See SOAP-RP.

SOAP-RP (SOAP Routing Protocol)   SOAP-RP is an evolving standard that adds the ability to route SOAP messages. The original SOAP specification only dealt with SOAP messages sent between two parties. A fully-functional messaging system should be able to support multi-hop messages. This is the intention of SOAP-RP. See also SOAP.

SQL (Structured Query Language)   SQL is a language used to create, update, retrieve, delete, and manage data in a relational database. SQL statements are defined from simple selection of data to the invocation of parameterized stored procedures. Although the core SQL statements are standardized, some vendors provide their own extensions. See also ANSI SQL, ANSI SQL 92.

SQL 92   See ANSI SQL 92.

SQLJ   SQLJ defines a way of embedding SQL statements in Java code and, as such, is an alternative to the use of JDBC. SQLJ also defines how Java code can be used to create stored procedures. SQLJ is a vendor-independent initiative. More information can be found online at `http://www.sqlj.org`.

SSL (Secure Sockets Layer)   SSL defines a standard way of using Asymmetric Encryption across a sockets connection. This includes authentication of the server (and optionally the client) using digital certificates, and the exchange of encryption keys. SSL is commonly used as the basis for transporting secure versions of higher-level protocols, such as secure HTTP (HTTPS). See also HTTPS and RSA.

Standard Generalized Markup Language (SGML)   See SGML.

Stateful Session EJB (or Stateful Session Bean)   See Session EJB.

Stateless Session EJB (or Stateless Session Bean)   See Session EJB.

Structured Query Language (SQL)   See SQL.

Sybase   Sybase is one of the major database server vendors. Their products include the Adaptive Server database and the EAServer application server.

Symmetric Key Encryption   Encryption that uses the same key to encrypt and decrypt the data. The most widely used algorithm today is DES or one of its variants.

Tag Library   A tag library defines a set of XML-compliant tags that can be used as part of a JSP. Each tag is associated with a particular piece of Java code. When the JSP processor encounters one of these tags, it will invoke the associated Java code. The Java code may generate new content, or it may perform other tasks such as looping or access to J2EE resources. See also JSP.

Taglib   See Tag Library.

Tag Library Descriptor   See TLD.

TCK (Technology Compatibility Kits)   A kit comprising a suite of tests, tools and documentation provided by the Java Community Process. The TCK should be used to verify that a product complies with a particular Java technology specification. See also JCP.

Technology Compatibility Kits   See TCK.

TLD   The Tag Library Descriptor file contains entries that map the tag names used in a JSP page onto the Java class files that implement that tag.

Tomcat   The Tomcat servlet engine is an open-source Java implementation delivered by the Apache Foundation. Tomcat (and the associated Jasper JSP engine that is delivered with it) have formed the reference implementation for servlets and JSPs. Tomcat can run as a standalone server, or it can be plugged into most Web servers, including the Apache Web Server. See also Jakarta Project.

UDDI (Universal Description, Discovery and Integration)   UDDI is one of the main technologies used for registration and discovery of Web Services. UDDI defines a set of SOAP messages that can be used to access XML-based data in a registry. It also defines a registry information model to structure the data stored and make it easier to search and navigate.

UDDI4J   UDDI4J is a Java-based API from IBM that provides Java wrappers for the UDDI SOAP messages. This API fills the same role as JAXR. See also JAXR, UDDI.

UML (Unified Modeling Language)   UML defines a largely diagrammatic language for capturing system requirements and expressing system design in object-oriented terms. UML diagrams are commonly used to illustrate class relationships and object interactions. UML was created from a merger of previous OO methodologies, including Booch, Jacobsen, and Object Modeling Technique (OMT).

UML Class Diagram   A UML class diagram represents a domain entity of some form that has usually been discovered by analysis. This entity can represent information, functionality, or both. An example would be a `Customer` class that had attributes and functionality associated with the role of a customer. Class diagrams can also be used to represent the relationships between different classes in a system. See also UML.

UML Collaboration Diagram   A UML collaboration diagram is a way of showing interactions between objects at the same time as showing the relationships between the objects. It combines some of the features of a class diagram with some of the features of a sequence diagram. See also UML.

UML Component Diagram   A UML component diagram shows the components in a system and their dependencies. See also UML.

UML Interaction Diagram   The term "UML interaction diagram" refers to any one of several forms of UML object-based diagrams that show the interactions between objects, such as sequence diagrams. See also UML Sequence Diagram.

UML Sequence Diagram   A UML sequence diagram shows the interactions between two or more objects over time. Each object is represented by a "swim lane" down the page, and messages are shown passing to and fro. See also UML.

Unified Modeling Language (UML)   See UML.

Uniform Resource Identifier (URI)   See URI.

Uniform Resource Locator (URL)   See URL.

Universal Description, Discovery and Integration (UDDI)   See UDDI.

URI (Uniform Resource Identifier)   A URI is a string-based name for an abstract or physical resource. The URI specification defines how specific resource identifiers, such as URLs, should be formatted. If you like, a URI is the "abstract base class" of other resource identifiers, such as URLs. See also URL.

URL (Uniform Resource Locator)   A URL is a string-based name for identifying a resource available across the Internet. An absolute URL begins with the protocol (http), then a colon (:), and then the specific address using that protocol. This usually contains a hostname, a relative path, and possibly other components. An example of a URL is `http://java.sun.com`. See also URI.

Validation   See XML validation.

W3C (World Wide Web Consortium)   The W3C is a vendor-neutral body created in 1994 by Tim Berners-Lee to lead the development of common Web protocols. The W3C has more than 500 Member organizations from around the world.

WAP (Wireless Access Protocol)   WAP is a standard protocol for transporting data between a mobile device and a server. Most WAP servers take the form of gateways that provide onward access to Internet resources. The WAP protocol layers take the place of TCP/IP, and are designed to allow for the unpredictability of mobile connectivity. See also WML.

WAR (Web Archive)   A WAR file is the unit of deployment for one or more Web components. A WAR file is a JAR-format file that contains servlets and/or JSPs together with deployment information and additional resources required by the component. See also EAR, JAR.

Web Application   A Web application provides functionality accessible over the Web, usually from a Web browser. A Web application can be delivered in a WAR file and deployed under a compliant Web container. See also Enterprise Application, WAR.

Web Archive (WAR)   See WAR.

Web Component   A Web component is a unit of functionality that forms part of a Web application or Enterprise application. A Web component consists of one or more JSPs and/or servlets together with deployment information and additional resources required by the component. A Web component is deployed into a Web container that controls its access to resources and its lifecycle. See also Enterprise Application, WAR, Web Application, Web Container.

Web Container   A Web container provides services, such as access control, resource access, and lifecycle management for one or more Web components. See also Web Component.

Web Service   A Web Service is a programmatic interface for functionality accessible using Web protocols. Web Services are accessed over SOAP and may be registered in Web Service registries, such as UDDI. The functionality of a Web Service is usually defined in terms of WSDL. See also ebXML, SOAP, UDDI, WSDL.

Web Service Registry   A Web Service registry is an XML-based repository for information about Web Services. Service providers will register their services in such a repository and clients will search for required services there. Examples of Web Service Registry standards include UDDI and the ebXML Registry and Repository standard. See also ebXML, UDDI.

Web Services Description Language (WSDL)   See WSDL.

Web Services Developer Pack (WSDP)   See WSDP.

Web Tier   See Presentation Tier.

Well-formed (of an XML document)   An XML document is said to be well-formed if it obeys certain rules regarding structure laid down in the XML standard. XML documents that are not well-formed cannot be manipulated by XML tools, such as parsers, and will generate errors when processed. See also XML, XML Validation.

Wireless Access Protocol (WAP)   See WAP.

Wireless Markup Language (WML)   See WML.

WML (Wireless Markup Language) WML is a markup language, similar to HTML, that is targeted at mobile devices. Due to the limited nature of most mobile displays, WML is far less feature-rich than HTML. WML documents are delivered to mobile devices over WAP. See also WAP.

World Wide Web Consortium (W3C) See W3C.

WSDL (Web Services Description Language) WSDL is an XML syntax for describing a Web Service interface, the protocols through which that interface can be reached, and the location of one or more servers that implement the interface. See also Web Service.

WSDP (Web Services Developer Pack) WSDP is a development environment from Sun Microsystems for developing Web Services. The pack includes a servlet and JSP engine (Tomcat) and support for JAXB, JAXM, JAXP, JAXR, SAAJ, JSF and JSTL.

WSDL4J WSDL4J is a Java-based API for WSDL manipulation defined by IBM. See also WSDL.

Xalan Xalan is an open-source XSLT processor from the Apache Foundation that is written in Java and is accessible from Java. Xalan supports the TrAX API for Java-based XML transformations. Xalan is used by the JAXP reference implementation as the basis for its XSLT transformation support. See also Apache.

Xerces Xerces is an open-source XML parser from the Apache Foundation that is written in Java and accessible from Java. Xerces supports the SAX and DOM APIs and is very popular in the Java community. It is likely that Xerces will soon be merged with Crimson to create a single Apache XML processor. See also Apache, Crimson.

XML (eXtensible Markup Language) XML is a tag-based syntax for adding information into text documents. XML does not define any specific tags, rather it defines the structure and conventions to be used by custom tags created for a variety of purposes. XML documents consist of a set of elements (delimited by opening and closing tags) and optional attributes on those elements. The XML specification is defined and maintained by the W3C. See also W3C.

XML Schema The XML Schema standard defines an XML grammar that can be used to define the contents of an XML document. An XML schema can define the data types expected, sequencing of XML elements, the presence and values of attributes, and so on. XML schemas are associated with XML documents using namespaces. XML Schemas are replacing Document Type Definitions (DTDs) for describing XML documents. See also XML, DTD.

XML validation   A valid XML document is a well-formed XML document that conforms to a particular DTD or XML Schema. A parser can be asked to validate an XML document against a DTD or schema and will generate errors if the structure checking fails. See also DTD, Well-formed, XML Schema.

XPath   The W3C XPath standard describes a syntax for selecting parts of an XML document. XPath is used by XSLT to identify which parts of the source document are to be transformed by a particular rule. See also XSLT.

XPointer   The W3C XPointer standard describes how a fragment of an XML document can be identified using a URI combined with XPath syntax. This is similar in concept to an HTML-based URL that includes an anchor (for example `http://www.tempuri.org/usefulfacts.html#WEBSERVICES`) to locate a specific part of the document. See also XPath.

XSL (eXtensible Stylesheet Language)   The W3C XSL standard covers both XSLT and XSL-FO. Originally, there was intended to be a single XML-oriented style sheet language (such as is the case with the Cascading Style Sheet Language for HTML), but two distinct elements of functionality were identified (transformation and rendering), so two separate standards were spawned. See also XSL-FO, XSLT.

XSL-FO (eXtensible Stylesheet Language Formatting Objects)   XSL-FO defines a set of XML-based formatting objects that can be used to render a document. XSL-FO is a more generic rendering format than, for example, HTML, and can be used on a wider variety of devices and applications. See also XSL.

XSLT (eXtensible Stylesheet Language Transformations)   XSLT is a declarative language and processing model used to convert one dialect of XML into another dialect of XML (or some other text-based format). XSLT is frequently used when importing or exporting business documents in XML format. See also XSL.

INDEX

Symbols

ejbLoad( ) method, 199-201, 210, 249, 265

EJBLocalHome interface, 147, 196

    BMP Entity EJBs

        custom primary key classes, 205-207

        defining, 203

        exceptions, 204

        finder methods, 205

        home methods, 208

EJBLocalObject interface, 147

EJBObject interface, 106, 109, 147

ejbPassivate( ) method, 154, 183, 199, 250, 265

ejbPostCreate( ) method, 199-200, 214-215

ejbRemove( ) method, 153, 200, 249, 375, 381-382

EJBs (Enterprise JavaBeans), 20, 30, 81-82.

    See also **entity beans; session beans**

    access controls, 105

    agency application

        asant build files, 139-141

        deploying, 135-136

        testing, 136-137

        troubleshooting, 141-143

    Agency remote interface source code, 107

    application development modeling, 103

    ApplicationMatch example

        code listing, 384-387

        ejbCreate( ) method, 382

        ejbRemove( ) method, 382

        findByLocation( ) method, 383

        getLocation( ) method, 383

        InitialContext interface, 382

        onMessage( ) method, 382

        skillMatch counter, 383

    authorization, applying, 601-602

    bean-managed transaction demarcation, 305

        deployment, 309

        restrictions, 305

        Session EJBs, 305-309

    BMP Entity, defining interfaces, 203-209

    business interface, 106

        implementing, 109-111

        methods, 106

business logic overview, 109

client-demarcated transactions, 310

clients

    applications, 124-125

    executing, 123-124

    SimpleClient.java, 120-121

CMP (container-managed persistence) fields, mapping, 277-280

CMP Entity

    abstract accessor methods, 246-248

    abstract classes, 245

    CMR (container-managed relationships), 250

    cmr-fields, 252

    defining finder methods, 271-273

    defining LocalHome interface, 261-262

    deploying using J2EE RI, 266-271

    JobBean.java code listing, 246-247

    lifecycle management, 248-249

    overview, 244-245

    relationship types, 251-252

    usage guidelines, 288

CMR (container-managed relationships)

    fields, 273-276

    mapping, 280-285

common uses, 103-104

components, 105

configuration information, 113-115

container-managed transaction demarcation, 298-305

containers

    performance tuning, 225-226

    services, 102-105

creation cycle, 115

creation restrictions, 115

declarative security

    deploying, 612-613

    method permissions, 605-609

    role mappings, 609-612

    roles, 601-603

CORBA (Common Object Request Broker Architecture), 772-773
  IDL (Interface Definition Language), 773-775
  IIOP (Internet Inter-ORB Protocol), 773
  Naming Service, 773
  ORB (Object Request Broker), 772
JNI (Java Native Interface), 780-784
  HelloWorld.java example, 782
  HelloWorldImp.c example, 783-784
RMI (Remote Method Invocation) over IIOP, 775-779

F

Facade pattern, 731, 823
Fast Lane Reader pattern, 732
FatalError( ) method, 665
fields
  CMP Entity Beans, mapping fields, 277-285
  hidden form fields, 471
  JMS (Java Message Service) headers, 346-347
files
  EARs (Enterprise Application Archives), 43
  EJB-JAR, 45
    CMR (container-managed relationships), 250
    deployment descriptors, 117
  jndi.properties, 84-85
  request-info.jsp, 500-502
  ser, 325
  transaction logs, 297
  WAR (Web Archive) files, 46
filters, 474
  AuditFilter example
    code listing, 476-477
    doFilter( ) method, 481-482
  deploying, 477-478

  filter chains, 475
  Java servlets, 474-476
  JNDI (Java Naming and Directory Interface), 96
  methods, 474-476
findAncestorWithClass( ) method, 581
findByLocation( ) method, 383
findByPrimaryKey( ) method, 205
finder methods
  BMP Entity EJBs, LocalHome interface, 205
  CMP Entity Beans, defining, 271-273
  EJB QL, compared to select methods, 260-261
  Entity EJBs, 201, 217-219, 244, 248
    dangers, 223-224
finding
  objects, 96
    JNDIFilter.java application, 96
    JNDISearch.java application, 96
    search( ) method, 96-97
  services with Service Locator pattern, 756
FIXED value (DTD attributes), 656, 898
FLAGGED flag (email), 423-424
flat transactions, 297
float type (XML Schema), 659
footer.jsf file, 751
<FORM> tag (HTML), 449
formatting
  library tags (JSTL), 554
  XML documents
    applying stylesheets, 684
    browser support, 685
    on servers, 685
    XSL-FO, 682-683
    XSLT, 683-684, 690-696
forms
  hidden fields in Java servlets, 471
  HTML (Hypertext Markup Language), 449-450
forms-based authentication, 619
forward slash (/), name separator, 74-75

hasAttributes( ) method, 669

hasChildNodes( ) method, 669

hashCode( ) method, 207

HEAD method, 445

<HEAD> tag (HTML), 449

header.jsf file, 750

headers

    Agency Web site, 528-529

    HTTP (Hypertext Transfer Protocol), 446-447

    JMS (Java Message Service), 346-347

    SOAP messages, 871-872

headers (HTTP), 442

Hello service (MyHelloService.wsdl), 851-857

hello tag (XML), 557, 561-562

HelloWorld application (JNI), creating, 781-784

HelloWorld.java file, 782

HelloWorldImp.c file, 783-784

hidden form fields in Java servlets, 471

hierarchical tag structures

    findAncestorWithClass( ) method, 581

    getParent( ) method, 581

    JSP, 581

Hillside.net Web site, 725, 728

home interfaces

    EJBs, 108-109

        discovery step, 121

    methods, implementing, 154-155

    stateless Session EJBs, defining, 148

home methods

    Entity EJBs, 208

    implementing with select methods, 260

<home> tag, 117

HTML (Hypertext Markup Language), 447

    compared to XML, 647

    documents

        HTML form example, 449-450

        simple HTML page example, 448

    email, 409-410

        absolute URLs, 411

        HTMLSource.html code listing, 412

        multi-part messages, 415

        sending, 411

    presentation errors (JSPs), 509

    tags

        <A>, 449

        <BIG>, 449

        <BODY>, 449

, 449

        <BUTTON>, 449

        <FORM>, 449

        <HEAD>, 449

        <HTML>, 449

        <IMG>, 449

        <INPUT>, 449

        nesting, 447

        <OPTION>, 449

        <P>, 449

        <SELECT>, 449

        syntax, 447

        <TABLE>, 449

        <TD>, 449

        <TH>, 449

        <TR>, 449

    XML documents, displaying in Web browsers, 681

<HTML> tag (HTML), 449

HTTP (Hypertext Transfer Protocol), 36, 442

    Basic authentication, 619-622

    Digest authentication, 619

    error handling, 466-468

    HTTPS (HTTP over SSL), 36

    methods

        DELETE, 445

        GET, 444

        HEAD, 445

        OPTIONS, 445

        POST, 444

L

unsetEntityContext( ), 210, 239, 249
unsubscribe( ), 362
updateDetails( ), 234
Warning( ), 665
Microsoft Active Directory, 18
Microsoft Developers Network Web site, 647
Microsoft Web site, Active Directory
resources, 18
MIME (Multipurpose Internet Mail
Extensions), 401, 446
Content-Disposition header, 425
email attachments, sending, 412-413
specifications, viewing, 401
MimeMessage object, 406
MimeMessage( ) method, 406
Model 1 Web architecture, 542
Model 2 Web architecture, 542-543
Model-View-Controller (MVC)
Model 2 Web architecture, 543
patterns, 729-730
modeling in application development (EJBs),
103
modes, session acknowledgement modes, 363
ModifyAttributes( ) method, 95
modifying
attributes, ModifyAttributes( ) method, 95
DOM trees, 669-670
modularity of applications
role of classes, 14
role of components, 15
role of packages, 14
monolithic development
disadvantages, 11
structure, 10-11
transitioning to n-tier, 24
multi-part messages
BodyPart objects, 414
sending, 415
multimedia email, 409-410
absolute URLs, 411
embedded images, creating, 414-417
multi-part messages

BodyPart objects, 414
sending, 415
sending, 411
multiplicity in relationships, 251-252
Multipurpose Internet Mail Extensions
(MIME), 401, 446
multithreading, 365, 441
MyHelloService.wsdl file, 851-857

N

n-tier development, 9-10, 28
advantages, 15-16
business tier
EJBs (Enterprise JavaBeans), 30,
192-193, 245-248
entity beans, 31
Message-driven beans, 31
session beans, 31
client tier, 35
Enterprise Computing Model, 16
lifecycle, 17
naming, 17-18
persistence, 17
security, 18
transactions, 18
presentation tier
JSPs (JavaServer Pages), 33
Web-centric components, 32
transitioning to, 24
name( ) function (XPath), 698
name-from-attribute tag (XML), 574
name-given tag (XML), 574
name.jsp page, 512
names. *See also* **naming services**
composite names, 75
compound names, 75
URLs (Uniform Resource Locators), 92
X.500, 94

How can we make this index more useful? Email us at indexes@samspublishing.com

Q - R

queries
EJB QL syntax, 254
JDO, 330
querying Entity EJBs, 201
question mark (?), DTDs (Document Type Definitions), 897
QueueReceiver object
createReceiver( ) method, 351
PTPReceiver example, 351
receive( ) method, 351
receiveNoWait( ) method, 351
start( ) method, 351
queues
creating, 345-346
defined, 336, 339
quotation marks
name separators, 75
XML (Extensible Markup Language) symbolic form, 894

read-only installation directory, 58
reading attributes, getAttributes( ) method, 95
realms, 598
receive( ) method, 351
receiveNoWait( ) method, 351
receivers, synchronous
createReceiver( ) method, 351
PTPReceiver example, 351
receive( ) method, 351
receiveNoWait( ) method, 351
start( ) method, 351
RECENT flag (email), 424
redirecting clients, 468
refactoring, 757
patterns, 730
Reference Implementation. *See* **RI**
references
Entity EJBs, obtaining, 232-234
role references, 597

RegisterBean bean, 379-381
registration (EJB services), 104
registries (Web Services), 845-846, 872
advantages of, 873
defined, 873
ebXML R&R (Registry and Repository), 875-876
global registries, 874
JAXR (Java APIs for XML Registries), 795
marketplace registries, 874-875
private registries, 874
searching, 874
site-specific registries, 874
UDDI (Universal Description, Discovery, and Integration), 876
accessing with JAXR (Java API for XML Registries), 878-880
bindingTemplate structure, 877
locally hosted registries, 878
public production registries, 878
public test registries, 878
tModel structure, 877
relationships
cascade null, 251
CMP Entity EJBs, 245
cmr-fields, 252-254, 273
navigability, 252
types, 251-252
composite primary keys, 253
multiplicity, 251-252
release( ) method, 560
remote interfaces. *See also* **business interface (EJB)**
compared to local interfaces, 195-196
methods, implementing, 155-157
stateless Session EJBs, defining, 148
transactions, 300
Remote Method Invocation. *See* **RMI**
Remote Method Invocation. *See* **RMI over IIOP**
<remote> tag, 117
RemoteException exception, 108, 158

Warning( ) method, 665

Web applications

deployment descriptors, 464-466

directory structure, 463-464

EJBs, 103

security, 618

Basic HTTP authentication, 619-622

declarative authorization, 620, 623-627

Digest HTTP authentication, 619

forms-based authentication, 619

HTTPS client authentication, 620

programmatic authorization, 620-621,
632-635

secure authentication schemes, 624

Web Archive (WAR) files, 46

simple Web Service

configuring, 813-814

creating, 810-812

Web authentication, 619

Basic HTTP authentication, 619-622

Digest HTTP authentication, 619

forms-based authentication, 619

HTTPS client authentication, 620

secure authentication schemes, 624

Web authorization

declarative authorization, 620

network security requirements, 623-624

roles, 622

security constraints, 624-631

programmatic authorization, 620

Agency case study, 632-635

getRemoteUser( ) method, 621

getUserPrincipal( ) method, 620

isUserInRole( ) method, 620

Web browsers

XML data presentation, 681

XSLT support, 685

Web components, 20

Web Container, 19

Web interface (Agency case study)

advertise.jsp, 533-535

agency.jsp, 530-531

deploying, 538-541

EJB references, 539

errorPage.jsp, 536-538

look and feel, 528

agency.css style sheet, 529-530

footers, 531-532

headers, 528-529

portal page, 527-528

structure and navigation, 526-528

updateCustomer.jsp, 535-536

**Web interfaces, adding (Agency case study),
525-526**

**Web Service Client for ServiceBean listing,
836**

Web Service Description Language. *See*
WSDL

Web Service Flow Language (WSFL), 791

Web Services, 35, 788

advantages of, 790

Apache XML Web site resources, 788

architecture, 791-793

customer/service interaction, 792

service implementations, 793

complex type mapping, marshaling, 842

components, 20

Container, 19

context, 838-840

ebXML Web site resources, 788

EJB facades, 823

errors, 838

exceptions, 838

function of, 788-790

IBM DeveloperWorks Web site resources,
788

J2EE Web Services

architecture, 793-794

integrating with existing components,
796-797

JSRs (Java Specification Requests), 796

toolkits, 795-796

lifecycle management, 838-840

X - Y - Z

Your Guide to Computer Technology

www.informit.com

Other Related Titles

J2EE Developer's Handbook
Paul Perrone, et al
0-672-32348-6
$59.99 USA/$86.99 CAN

JavaServer Pages Developer's Handbook
Nick Todd and Mark Szolkowski
0-672-32438-5
$49.99 USA/$71.99 CAN

Sams Teach Yourself XML in 21 Days
Steven Holzner
0-672-32576-4
$39.99 USA/$57.99 CAN

Building Web Services with Java, 2e
Steve Graham, et al
0-672-32641-8
$49.99 USA/$71.99 CAN

Securing Web Services with WS-Security
Jothy Rosenberg and David Remy
0-672-32651-5
$39.99 USA/$57.99 CAN

BEA WebLogic Workshop 8.1 Kick Start
Al Saganich, et al
0-672-32622-1
$34.99 USA/$49.99 CAN

Extreme Programming with Ant
Jeremy Poteet and Glenn Niemeyer
0-672-32562-4
$34.99 USA/$49.99 CAN

Covert Java
Alex Kalinovsky
0-672-32638-8
$34.99 USA/$49.99 CAN

Struts Kick Start
James Turner and Kevin Bedell
0-672-32472-5
$34.99 USA/$49.99 CAN

BEA WebLogic Server 8.1 Unleashed
Mark Artiges, et al
0-672-32487-3
$59.99 USA/$86.99 CAN

SAMS

t Master
entmaster.com

...ne of the world's leading ...ng and consultancy ...working with key software ...rovide leading-edge content to ...udiences. This content, combined ...business knowledge helps enable ...ss decision makers, developers and ...rofessionals to keep abreast of new ...itiatives, helping them build innovative enterprise solutions.

We also offer educational and content consultancy, identifying the most effective strategies for the development and deployment of materials. Our unique approach encompasses technical, business and educational requirements. This ensures that developed content not only offers the right level of specialist knowledge but that it addresses commercial requirements and is structured in the most effective way. This covers a range of media, including web, print and CD.

Other Content Master books:

Tomcat Kick Start
ISBN: 0-672-32439-3
JavaServer Pages Developer's Handbook
ISBN: 0-672-32438-5

Content Master

Tortworth House
Tortworth
Wotton-under-Edge
Gloucestershire
GL12 8HQ
http://www.contentmaster.com
Call +44 1454 269222

Content Master has worked with customers to develop strategies to address:

- Internal and external web sites
- Internal systems and business documentation
- Internal and external training materials
- Content development strategies
- Training business strategies

Our other core products and skills include the following;

- Books for publication: Working with the major publishing houses, we author books aimed at the technical and business decision maker audiences
- Content creation:
  - White papers
  - Case studies
  - Blueprints
  - Website Content
  - Deployment guides
  - Software development kits
  - Best practice documentation
  - Business Decision Maker seminars
  - Sales and marketing collateral
- Courseware: we write classroom based and multi-media training courses for leading software companies, usually under the brand of the commissioning vendor
- Resource: we regularly provide the following to our partners:
  - Program managers
  - Technical writers
  - Subject matter experts
  - Testing facilities and resource
  - Editors
  - Instructional designers
  - Consultants